LIBYAN STUDIES

Select Papers of the late
R. G. GOODCHILD

R. G. Goodchild

LIBYAN STUDIES

Select Papers of the late
R. G. GOODCHILD

Edited by
JOYCE REYNOLDS

PAUL ELEK
London

Published 1976 by Elek Books Ltd
54–8 Caledonian Road London N1 9RN

© Goodchild Memorial Committee 1976

ISBN 0 236 17680 3

Made and Printed in Great Britain by
The Garden City Press Limited
Letchworth, Hertfordshire SG6 1JS

TABLE OF CONTENTS

Preface and Acknowledgments   vii

List of subscribers to the Richard Goodchild Memorial Fund   ix

Richard Goodchild: a biographical note   xiii

Bibliography of R. G. Goodchild   xvii

Key to bibliographical abbreviations   xxi

TRIPOLITANIA   1

1. Roman Tripolitania: Reconnaissance in the Desert Frontier Zone
   GJ cxv (June 1950), 161–78   3

2. The *Limes Tripolitanus* in the light of Recent Discoveries
   JRS xxxix (1949), 81–95   17

3. The *Limes Tripolitanus* II
   JRS xl (1950), 30–8   35

4. Oasis Forts of *Legio III Augusta* on the Routes to the Fezzan
   PBSR xxii (1954), 56–68   46

5. The Romano–Libyan Cemetery at Bir ed-Dreder
   QAL iii (1954), 91–107   59

6. Roman Sites on the Tarhuna Plateau of Tripolitania
   PBSR xix (1951), 43–77   72

7. Inscriptions from Western Tarhuna   107

8. Hoards of Late Roman coins in the Market of Lepcis Magna   114

9. The unfinished "Imperial" baths of Lepcis Magna
   LibAnt ii (1965), 15–27   118

10. Medina Sultan (Charax—Iscina—Sort)
    LibAnt i (1964), 99–106   133

CYRENAICA   143

11. Mapping Roman Libya
    GJ cxviii (1952), 142–52   145

12. Arae Philaenorum and Automalax
    PBSR xx (1952), 94–110   155

13. "Libyan" Forts in South-west Cyrenaica
    Antiquity xxv (1951), 131–44   173

14. Boreum of Cyrenaica
    JRS xli (1951), 11–16   187

15. The Roman and Byzantine *Limes* in Cyrenaica
    JRS xliii (1953), 65–76   195

16. The Forum of Ptolemais (Cyrenaica)
    QAL v (1967), 47–51   210

17. The Decline of Cyrene and Rise of Ptolemais: Two New Inscriptions
    QAL iv (1961), 83–95   216

18. A coin-hoard from "Balagrae" (El-Beida), and the earthquake of
    A.D. 365
    LibAnt iii–iv (1966–7), 203–11   229

19. Synesius of Cyrene: Bishop of Ptolemais   239

20. Byzantines, Berbers and Arabs in seventh-century Libya
    Antiquity xli (1967), 115–24   255

A HOLE IN THE HEAVENS   269

Index   343

PREFACE AND ACKNOWLEDGMENTS

When Richard Goodchild died in 1968 his friends and colleagues wished to establish some memorial to him. After consultation as widespread as possible it seemed that the overwhelming majority were in favour of a volume of papers collected from his writing on Libyan subjects; a project which had the added advantage of providing for publication of some unpublished material found among his papers and kindly made available by his mother, Mrs. Dora Goodchild. In selecting from his published articles I have tried to maintain a reasonably coherent theme while illustrating as many as possible of Goodchild's interests and skills, including something of his writing in lighter vein.

In a collection of this sort there is inevitably some overlapping of material from article to article, but to remove the repetitions would seem an unjustified editorial intervention and it is hoped that readers will accept them without irritation. They are also asked to remember the date at which each of these articles was written (it is printed at the head of each), for it has seemed equally unjustifiable to "bring them up to date" in any serious way; their interest is in no way diminished by the very few details in which they may be held to require modification and their importance to scholarship lies in part in what they said at the date of writing. A few notes have been added to provide readers with basic later bibliography and to alert them to points of recent controversy, a small number of obvious printing errors has been corrected, some attempt has been made to introduce a degree of consistency in spelling and bibliographical citation; but all additions and any changes of wording that result are printed in square brackets. The maps have been redrawn by Mrs. Maureen Verity in order to achieve reasonable consistency in presentation; otherwise the original illustration has been reproduced wherever possible. Where blocks have been lost we have had to offer substitutes though this has not always been possible either.

The Memorial Committee wishes to express its warmest gratitude for permission to reprint published articles as follows:
to the Editor of *Antiquity* for articles from *Antiquity* for 1951 and 1967; to L'Erma di Bretschneider for articles from *Quaderni di Archeologia della Libia* for 1954, 1961, 1967; to The Faculty of Archaeology of the British School at Rome for articles from *The Papers of the British School at Rome* for 1951, 1952, 1954; to The Council of the Roman Society for articles from *The Journal of Roman Studies* for 1949, 1950, 1951, 1953; to the Royal Geographical Society for articles from *The Geographical Journal* 1950, 1952; to the late Mr. Awad Sadawiya,

Director of Antiquities for Libya, for articles from *Libya Antiqua* 1964, 1965 and 1966–7.

They are also grateful for help of various kinds in the preparation of the volume to Mr. Breyek Atiyah, Mr. Michael Ballance, Mr. Sebastian Brock, Lady Brogan, Professor Donald Bullough, Mrs. Janet Chapman, Mr. Michael Crawford, Sir Duncan Cumming, Mr. Charles Daniels, Miss Shelagh Gibson, Mrs. Dora Goodchild, Professor Philip Grierson, Mr. Mark Hassall, Mr. Hassan Hassouna, Mr. Denys Haynes, Mr. G. S. Holland, Professor Barri Jones, Mr. Awad Sadawiya, Mr. David Smith, Professor Donald Strong and Mrs. Maureen Verity. They are also well aware of their debt to the kindness and helpfulness of the publisher.

June 1974   Joyce Reynolds

The publishers and the Goodchild Memorial Committee wish to acknowledge permission to reproduce photographs as follows:

Superintendency of Antiquities, Tripolitania, 15, 24, 31, 32, 34, 35, 36, 37, 40, 89, 92
R. G. Goodchild, 16, 17, 18, 19, 20, 29, 30, 56, 57, 66, 67, 68, 69, 70, 71, 72, 73, 74, 75, 76
M. H. Ballance, 21, 33, 62, 63
Royal Air Force, 22, 23, 53, 64 and 65 (Flying Officer McGillivary)
14/20 King's Hussars, 26, 27, 28
J. B. Ward Perkins, 39
David J. Smith, 54, 55
Aerofilms Ltd, 84
Kelsey Museum, Michigan, 90, 91

LIST OF SUBSCRIBERS TO THE RICHARD GOODCHILD MEMORIAL FUND

This volume is published with the help of subscriptions made to the Richard Goodchild Memorial Fund by the following subscribers.

A † marks the names of those who have died.

Abdussaid, Abdul Hamid, c/o Department of Antiquities, Cyrene (Shahat), Cyrenaica.

Abdussalam, Fadullah, c/o Department of Antiquities, Cyrene (Shahat), Cyrenaica.

Alderson, Barbara (Mrs.), 1 Pear Tree, Itchenor, Nr. Chichester, Sussex.

Anderson, John, Cotton Hall House, Eton College, Bucks.

Arthur, Christopher, Bellevue House, Low Fell, Gateshead, Co. Durham.

Ashmole, Bernard (Prof.), The Mill House, Iffley, Oxford.

Atiyah, Breyek, c/o Department of Antiquities, Cyrene (Shahat), Cyrenaica.

Balsdon, J. P. V. D., Exeter College, Oxford.

Barr, F. T., c/o Oasis Oil Co., P.O. Box 395, Libya.

Bazama, Abdussalam, c/o Department of Antiquities, Tolmeita, Cyrenaica.

†Beard, H. R., Gorse Cottage, Little Eversden, Cambridgeshire.

Black, Duncan, 6 St. Vincent Street, Edinburgh 3.

Boardman, John, Ashmolean Museum, Oxford.

Boase, T. S. R., 6 Atherton Drive, London S.W.19.

Boyd, M. J. (Prof.), Department of Latin, University of Belfast, Belfast.

Bradfield, Maitland, Yarnton Manor, Yarnton, Oxon.

Brogan, Olwen (Lady), 1 Hedgerley Close, Cambridge.

Brunt, P. A. (Prof.), Brasenose College, Oxford.

Buckmaster, Martin (Hon.), 8 Redcliffe Square, London S.W.10.

Bullough, D. A. (Prof.), 21 Park Valley, The Park, Nottingham.

Buttrey, T. V. (Prof.), Department of Classical Studies, University of Michigan, Ann Arbor, Mich. 48104.

Cassels, J. S., 10 Beverley Road, London S.W.13.

Chapman, H. P. A., Guildhall Museum, 55 Basinghall Street, London E.C.2.

Chittick, H. N., c/o British Institute of History & Archaeology in E. Africa, The Mansion House, Choromo, P.O. Box 47680, Nairobi.

Clark, Anthony J., 19 The Crossways, Onslow Village, Guildford, Surrey.

Clarke, Joan (Mrs.), Gunney Vale, 64 Bellevue Road, Wivenhoe, Colchester, Essex.

Clauson, B. J. H., 28 Kensington Court Gardens, London W.8.

Cook, R. M. (Prof. & Mrs.), Museum of Classical Archaeology, Little St. Mary's Lane, Cambridge.

Corbett, P. E. (Prof.), Department of Archaeology, University College, Gower Street, London WC1E 6BT.

Corke, Shirley (Mrs.), Eversheds, Abinger Hammer, Surrey.

Cotton, M. Aylwin (Dr.), British School at Rome, Via Gramsci, 61, Rome 00197.

Dallas, W. T., Toat House, Pulborough, Sussex.

Daniels, C. M., University of Newcastle-upon-Tyne, Newcastle-upon-Tyne NE1 7RU.

D'Arms, J. H., University of Michigan, Ann Arbor, Mich. 48105.

Dean, Arthur (Sir), 66 The Avenue, Worcester Park, Surrey.

Dimbleby, G. W. (Prof.), Institute of Archaeology, 31–34 Gordon Square, London W.C.1.

Douglas-Watt, Ian, Department of Geography, University of Hull, Hull.

†Dunlop, A. I. (Mrs.), Torwood, 73 London Road, Kilmarnock, Ayrshire.

Farrar, Raymond A. H., Royal Commission on Historical Monuments (England), Fielden House, 10 Great College Street, London S.W.1

Foyer, Theodore B., Jr., P.O. Box 693, Tripoli.

Frend, W. H. C. (Prof.), The University, Glasgow W.2.

Frere, Sheppard S. (Prof.), Netherfield House, Marcham, Abingdon, Berks.

Frost, Weldon G., P.O. Box 404, Tripoli.

Graham, Johnny A. N., c/o Foreign & Commonwealth Office, London S.W.1.

Greaves, Audrey (Miss), 1 Pear Tree, Itchenor, Nr. Chichester, Sussex.

Grierson, P. (Prof.), Gonville & Caius College, Cambridge.

†Hamilton Browne, L., 15 Farley Court, Melbury Road, London W.14.

Hanson, J. C. (Miss), 67 Valley Road, Ipswich.

Hanworth, (The Viscountess), Folly Hill, Ewhurst, Cranleigh, Surrey.

Harden, Donald (Dr.), London Museum, Kensington, London W.8.

Harrison, Martin (Prof.), University of Newcastle-upon-Tyne, Newcastle-upon-Tyne NE1 7RU.

Haseldon, Sidney, 1 Pear Tree, Itchenor, Nr. Chichester, Sussex.

Hassall, Mark, Institute of Archaeology, 31–34 Gordon Square, London W.C.1.

Haynes, D. E. L., Department of Greek and Roman Antiquities, The British Museum, London.

Hey, R. W. (Dr.), Churchill College, Cambridge.

Hodson, Roy (Dr.), Institute of Archaeology, 31–34 Gordon Square, London W.C.1.

Hopkins, Clark, 7 Harvard Place, Ann Arbor, Mich. 48104.

Husseini, Salem, c/o Department of Antiquities, Cyrene (Shahat), Cyrenaica.

Isserlin, B. S. J., Department of Semitic Languages & Literatures, University of Leeds, Leeds 2.

Jerrom, Michael, 40 Tyrone Road, Thorpe Bay, Essex.

Johnston, C. H., Hill House, Encamp, Andorra.

†Jones, A. H. M. (Prof.), Jesus College, Cambridge.

Kenyon, Kathleen (Dr.), St. Hugh's College, Oxford.

MacCarthy-Morrogh, E. T. (Mrs.), 1 Pear Tree, Itchenor, Nr. Chichester, Sussex.

Mangin, Paul (Major), Red Co. Desert Regiment, Sultans Armed Forces, B.F.P.O. 63a.

Margary, J. D., Yew Lodge, East Grinstead, Sussex.

Marquardt, Donald E., P.O. Box 690, Tripoli.

Maxim, Beryl (Miss), 1 Pear Tree, Itchenor, Nr. Chichester, Sussex.

McBurney, C. B. M. (Dr.), 5 Grange Road, Cambridge.

McDonald, A. D. (Dr.), Clare College, Cambridge.

Megaw, A. H. S., c/o British School of Archaeology, 52 Odos Souedias, Athens.

Oxford University Archaeological Society, c/o Pitt Rivers Museum, Parks Road, Oxford.

Owen, M. M. (Mrs.), 12 Gunter Grove, London S.W.10.

Parker, John, Department of History, University of York, Heslington, York YO1 5DD.

Parr, Peter J., Institute of Archaeology, 31–34 Gordon Square, London W.C.I.

Pedley, John G. (Prof.), University of Michigan, Ann Arbor, Mich. 48105.

Perowne, Stewart, 44 Arminger Road, London W 12.

Phillips, C. W., 103 Ditton Road, Surbiton, Surrey.

Ralegh Radford, C. A., Culmcott, Uffculme, Devon.

Reynolds, Joyce (Miss), Newnham College, Cambridge.

Riley, D. N., 3 High Ray Close, Sheffield 11.

Rivet, A. L. F., University of Keele, Keele, Staffs.

Salem, Ali, c/o Department of Antiquities, Benghazi, Cyrenaica.

Seton Watson, C., Oriel College, Oxford.

Smallwood, Mary E. (Dr.), Latin Department, Queen's University, Belfast 7.

RICHARD GOODCHILD

a biographical note

Richard George Goodchild was born on 18 July, 1918 at Crossmead, Exeter, the son of George and Dora Goodchild. From his parents he inherited talents which influenced his later career—notably a good and fluent style of writing from his novelist father and with it, no doubt, something of the detective instinct which was one element in his archaeological work; a keenly observant eye from his artist mother. He was brought up in Exeter and was always proud of his Devonian connections (indeed in his moments of excitement one could sometimes hear a Devon lilt in his speech) and his first enthusiasm for archaeology was aroused by the Roman remains there. He was educated at Cranleigh School and was already digging as a schoolboy, receiving at this stage much help from S. E. Winbolt. From Cranleigh he went to Oriel College, Oxford, to read Modern History and the fruitful effects of this discipline on his interests and thinking are apparent from his bibliography; they counterbalanced a lack of Classical training, despite the fact that he eventually found himself working very largely on Classical sites. It should be said, however, that he was too good a scholar not to supplement his history by wide reading in Classical authors; he had in fact taught himself far more Greek than many of his colleagues realised, while his Latin—as he took pleasure in recalling—was firmly based on the drilling given at his preparatory school by "an elderly school-mistress of the old type".

At Oxford, as in his later years at school, he was constantly involved in excavation, and very particularly in the notable dig undertaken by the Oxford Archaeological Society at Frilford, where he collaborated with R. C. Atkinson and J. S. P. Bradford; he also collected the results of his work at Exeter to form a thesis presented for part of the examination for his first degree in 1939.

Then came war service in the Royal Artillery (the regiment in which his father had served in the First World War). It was an interruption of his career which, however, also provided new experiences that he turned to profit. His "first command" was a coast defence battery in Sussex, within the Saxon Shore area of Roman Britain. In a moment of boredom, so he said, he found himself driven to the Army Regulations for reading matter—and soon became something of an expert in them. The result was, at the time, to make him a very useful and popular "Prisoner's Friend" at Courts Martial, since he had come to know those regulations as few of his fellow-officers did, and, in the long run, to arouse his historian's curiosity for military affairs, including soldiers' psychology. Hence grew a special interest in the Roman army which informed much of his work in

Libya, as it did in Britain; indeed he once started a book on the later Roman army, though unfortunately very little of the manuscript survives. But the major effect of his war service was to introduce him to the Mediterranean world which came to be the home of his choice for many years. He was at one time or another in Iraq, Syria, Lebanon, North Africa, Italy and, after fighting in Europe ended, in Syria again—and by that time able to spend all his leave studying Roman remains.

After demobilisation he returned to Oxford as a research student, but was restless for the sun and in 1946 took up an appointment as Antiquities Officer under the British Military Administration in Libya. This involved care, maintenance and further study of the coastal cities excavated by Italian archaeologists between the wars as well as of the scattered and hitherto somewhat neglected monuments of the Tripolitanian hinterland which became the main focus of his own research. His pioneer surveys, which produced first the outline of the Roman road system and then the two sheets of the Map of Roman Libya, together with his observations on a number of inland sites, are fundamental to our knowledge of Roman Libya; and whatever details have been modified in the light of later discoveries they continue to be required reading for all students of Libyan history, and of Roman frontier studies in Africa.

In 1948 he moved to Italy to be Librarian of the British School at Rome. During three years spent in Rome he continued his surveys in Libya, extending them now increasingly into Cyrenaica; but he also strengthened existing and established new, cordial and lasting relationships with many Italian scholars, acquired an enviable command of the Italian language, and developed a remarkable knowledge and a very real understanding of the Italian people and their history. His affection for Italy was a deep one and his Italian friends meant very much to him. It was one expression of this feeling that throughout his career he worked in close and friendly co-operation with the Italian archaeologists appointed to office in Tripoli (Professors Giacomo Caputo, Ernesto Vergara-Caffarelli and Antonino Di Vita) and the members of the Italian Archaeological Mission to Cyrenaica (headed by Professor Sandro Stucchi).

In 1953, when a vacancy occurred for a Controller of Antiquities in Cyrenaica under the newly-independent government of Libya, he took it and held the post with distinction until 1966, excepting only the year 1961 which he spent in Dar es Salaam, helping to establish the British Institute of Archaeology in East Africa. During the eleven years of his Controllership he was based in Cyrenaica, and for most of the time lived in Cyrene or Apollonia—virtually "in the field". He excavated, or organised excavation, on the major city sites of Cyrene, Apollonia, Ptolemais and Tauchira and on a number of country sites, notably the Asklepieion of Balagrae (Beida) and the village at Lamluda; but at the same time he continued surveys of the remoter areas and kept a vigilant eye on all antiquities especially in districts threatened with development. He also made great efforts to encourage foreign scholars to undertake compilation of catalogues of unpublished material in museums and on sites, as well as new excavations. Above all he gave much time and thought to creating an efficient local antiquities service—not simply an organisation, but one staffed by Libyans. The strong feeling he felt for Libya and the understanding of her problems, the sense of humour with which he could accept difficulties, frustrations and even failures, his care for archaeology and archaeological monuments, all contributed to his remarkable success. He had a good eye for promise in the members of his staff, however few the advantages they had previously had, and spared no pains to further the education and provide all possible help to anyone showing potential who was at all responsive.

Obviously enough he was working at full stretch throughout the period and his responsibilities in the field, together with the difficulty of obtaining all the books he needed, inevitably limited his achievement in publication of what he found, though that achievement was not in fact a small one. He varied his academic work from time to time with some pseudonymous journalism—mainly for the weekly English-language newspaper, *The Sunday Ghibli,* published in Tripoli. On at least one occasion he edited this paper while its owner/editor (C. H. Johnston) was on leave; and he was delighted when some of his readers commented on the decidedly nineteenth-century tone of his issues. He was also responsible for a number of serious, though not academic, articles in it (he was particularly good on the story of Tripoli Castle and on the fate of a cargo of gold sovereigns lost in the sea off Susa during the war); and in addition (though few knew it) he was the author of the Christmas Ghost Stories, which were one of its popular features.

In 1966 he decided to leave Libya, spent a happy year in the Kelsey Museum of Archaeology at Ann Arbor, Michigan, and returned to Europe in the summer of 1967 to take up his appointment as Professor of the Archaeology of the Roman Provinces at the London Institute of Archaeology. His year in Michigan was spent partly in working over the results of his recent excavation at Apollonia for the volume on the city to be published by the University of Michigan, partly in the completion of an up-to-date description of the site of Cyrene, which appeared, in a German language version, in 1971, and partly in re-examining the evidence concerning the murder of Herbert de Cou, epigraphist with the Norton Expedition to Cyrenaica in 1911—a problem which attracted the detective, the archaeologist and the modern historian in him, as well as the devotee of Cyrene. During the autumn of 1967 he worked at the London Institute and had already made his mark there; but in January 1968, shortly after delivering a lecture on Apollonia to the Society for the Promotion of Roman Studies, he was taken ill. He died on 18 February, 1968, having worked in hospital until the end.

His devotion to his work, which was completely without self-interest, commanded respect everywhere. Mildly eccentric and often an isolate, he was nevertheless full of humanity—so that those who visit Libya now will constantly hear him praised with affection both for his archaeological achievement and for the generous but unobtrusive help of many kinds that he gave to his colleagues and neighbours. His dry wit was another important facet of his personality enabling him to light up a conversation with a flash that was often shrewdly illuminating as well as very amusing.

BIBLIOGRAPHY OF R. G. GOODCHILD

1937

"The Roman brickworks at Wykehurst Farm in the Parish of Cranleigh", (with a note on a Roman tile-kiln at Horton, Epsom). *Surrey Arch. Colls.* xlv (1937), 74–96.
(with S. E. Winbolt) "A Roman Villa at Lickfold, Wiggonholt." *Sussex Arch. Colls.* lxxviii (1937), 13–36.
"The Roman Coins from Exeter." *NC* xvii (1937), 139–41.
(with J. G. Milne) "The Greek Coins from Exeter." *NC* xvii (1937), 124–8.

1938

"Martin Tupper and Farley Heath." *Surrey Arch. Colls.* xlvi (1938), 10–25.
"A Priest's Sceptre from the Romano-Celtic Temple at Farley Heath, Surrey." *AntJ* xviii (1938), 391–6.

1939

(with J. S. P. Bradford) "The Excavations at Frilford, Berks., 1937–8." *Oxoniensia* iv (1939), 1–70.

1940

(with A. Shaw Mellor) "The Roman Villa at Atworth." *Wiltshire Archaeological Magazine* xlix (1940), 46–95.

1941

"Romano-British Disc-Brooches derived from Hadrianic Coin-types." *AntJ* xxi (1941), 1–8.

1943

(with A. W. G. Lowther) "Excavations at Farley Heath, Albury, during 1939." *Surrey Arch. Colls.* xlviii (1943), 31–40.
"T-shaped corn-drying ovens in Roman Britain." *AntJ* xxiii (1943), 148–53.

1946

Roman Exeter (Exeter, 1946).
"The Origins of the Romano-British Forum." *Antiquity* xx (1946), 70–7.

1948

Roman Roads and Milestones in Tripolitania. (*Discoveries and Research in 1947*). Reports and Monographs of the Department of Antiquities in Tripoli I (1948).

1949

(with J. B. Ward Perkins) "The *Limes Tripolitanus* in the light of recent discoveries." *JRS* xxxix (1949), 81–95.

"The coast road of Phoenicia and its Roman Milestones." *Berytus* ix (1949), 91–127.

(with M. V. Taylor) "Discussion of K. M. Kenyon, *Excavations at the Jewry Wall Site, Leicester.*" *JRS* xxxix (1949), 142–5.

"The 'Roman Road' on Winterfold Common, Albury." *Surrey Arch. Colls* 1 (1949), 147–9.

"Some Inscriptions from Tripolitania." Reports and Monographs of the Department of Antiquities in Tripoli II (1949), 29–35.

1950

"Roman Milestones in Cyrenaica." *PBSR* xviii (1950), 83–91.

"The *Limes Tripolitanus* II." *JRS* xl (1950), 30–8.

"Roman Tripolitania: Reconnaissance in the Desert Frontier Zone." *GJ* cxv (June 1950), 161–78.

"Two Monumental Inscriptions of Lepcis Magna." *PBSR* xviii (1950), 72–82.

"The Latino-Libyan Inscriptions of Tripolitania." *AntJ* xxx (July-Oct., 1950), 135–44.

1951

"Boreum of Cyrenaica." *JRS* xli (1951), 11–16.

" 'Libyan' Forts in South-West Cyrenaica." *Antiquity* xxv (1951), 131–44.

"Roman Sites on the Tarhuna Plateau of Tripolitania." *PBSR* xix (1951), 43–77.

1952

"Mapping Roman Libya." *GJ* cxviii (1952), 142–52.

"The Ravenscar Inscription." *AntJ* xxxii (1952), 185–8.

"Farming in Roman Libya." *Geog. Mag.* xxv (1952), 70–80.

"The Decline of Libyan Agriculture." *Geog. Mag.* xxv No. 3, July (1952), 147–56.

"Arae Philaenorum and Automalax." *PBSR* xx (1952), 94–110.

(with J. B. Ward Perkins) "L'aggere di Lepcis—una risposta." *ArchClass* iv (1952) (fasc. 2), 284–7.

"Euesperides—a devastated site." *Antiquity* xxvi (1952), 208–12.

1953

(with J. B. Ward Perkins) "The Roman and Byzantine Defences of Lepcis Magna." *PBSR* xxi (1953), 42–73.

(with J. B. Ward Perkins) "The Christian Antiquities of Tripolitania." *Archaeologia* xcv (1953), 1–84.

"The Roman and Byzantine Limes in Cyrenaica." *JRS* xliii (1953), 65–76.

"Leicester City Wall in Sanvey Gate: Excavations in 1952." *Trans. Leicestershire Archaeolog. Soc.* xxix (1953), 15–29.

1954

(with J. R. Kirk) "The Romano-Celtic Temple at Woodeaton." *Oxoniensia* xix (1954), 15–37.

Tabula Imperii Romani: Sheet H.I. 33 Lepcis Magna (Society of Antiquaries, London, 1954).

Tabula Imperii Romani: Sheet H.I. 34 Cyrene (Society of Antiquaries, London, 1954).

"Oasis Forts of *Legio III Augusta* on the Routes to the Fezzan." *PBSR* xxii (1954), 56–68.

Benghazi—The Story of a City. Government Press, Benghazi (1954). See also 1962.

"La Necropoli Romano-Libica di Bir Ed-Dreder." *QAL* iii (1954), 91–107.

1955

(with G. Caputo) "Diocletian's Price Edict at Ptolemais (Cyrenaica)." *JRS* xlv (1955), 106–15.

1956

(with R. J. Forbes) "Roads and Land Travel" *apud* C. Singer, E. G. Holmyard, A. R. Hall and T. I. Williams (eds.). *A History of Technology* II, 493–533 (Clarendon Press, Oxford).

1957

"The Mosaic of Qasr el Lebia." *I.L.N.* 14 Dec., 1957, No. 6184, vol. 231, 1035–8.

1958

(with J. M. Reynolds and C. J. Herington) "The Temple of Zeus at Cyrene." *PBSR* xxvi (1958), 30–62.

1959

Cyrene and Apollonia—An historical guide. Libya, 1959.

1960

"A Byzantine Palace at Apollonia (Cyrenaica)." *Antiquity* xxxiv (1960), 246–58.

(with W. Widrig) "The West Church at Apollonia in Cyrenaica." *PBSR* xxviii (1960), 70–90.

1961

"The Decline of Cyrene and Rise of Ptolemais: Two New Inscriptions." *QAL* iv (1961), 83–95.

"Helios on the Pharos." *AntJ* xli (1961), 218–23.

1962

(with J. M. Reynolds) "Some Military Inscriptions from Cyrenaica." *PBSR* xxx (1962), 37–46.

(with C. H. Kraeling) "The 'Odeon' and Related Structures." *apud* C. H. Kraeling Ptolemais, 89–96.

Benghazi—The Story of a City. Benghazi (1962), 2nd edition.

1963

Cyrene and Apollonia: An Historical Guide. Department of Antiquities (Eastern Region), United Kingdom of Libya. 2nd edition (1963).

1964

"Medina Sultan (Charax—Iscina—Sort)." *LibAnt* i (1964), 99–106.
"The Fountain of the Maenads at Ptolemais." *LibAnt* i (1964), 121–6.
"Archaeological News (Cyrenaica)." *LibAnt* i (1964), 143–5.

1965

(with J. M. Reynolds) "The City lands of Apollonia in Cyrenaica." *LibAnt* ii, (1965), 103–8.
"The Unfinished 'Imperial' baths of Lepcis Magna." *LibAnt* ii (1965), 15–28.
"Archaeological News 1963–1964 (Cyrenaica)." *LibAnt* ii (1965), 137–9.

1966

"Chiese e Battisteri Bizantini della Cirenaica." *CCAB* (Ravenna, 1966), 205–23.
"Fortificazioni e Palazzi Bizantini in Tripolitania e Cirenaica." *CCAB* (Ravenna, 1966), 225–50.

1967

"Byzantines, Berbers and Arabs in seventh century Libya." *Antiquity* xli (1967), 115–24.
"The Forum of Ptolemais (Cyrenaica)." *QAL* v (1967), 47–51.

1968

(with J. G. Pedley and D. White) "Recent discoveries of archaic sculpture at Cyrene. A preliminary report." *LibAnt* iii/iv (1966/7), 179–98.
"A coin-hoard from 'Balagrae' (El Beida), and the earthquake of A.D. 365." *LibAnt* iii/iv (1966/7), 203–12.
"Review of: P. Mingazzini, *L'insula di Giasone Magno a Cirene*." *LibAnt* iii/iv (1966/7), 257–9.

POSTHUMOUS PUBLICATIONS

"Death of an Epigrapher: the killing of Herbert De Cou." *The Michigan Quarterly Review* viii. 3 (1969), 149–54.
"The Roman Roads of Libya and their Milestones." *Libya in History, Acts of a conference held at Benghazi in 1968* (Benghazi, 1970).
Kyrene und Apollonia. (Zürich, 1971), to be published also, it is hoped, in the English version.

KEY TO BIBLIOGRAPHICAL ABBREVIATIONS

Titles of journals are normally abbreviated according to the practice of L'Année Philologique.

Titles of books and articles cited once only are given in full in the footnotes; those cited more than once are abbreviated according to the list below; those cited more than once by the authors' names with reference to the list of works below.

Baradez, J., *Vue aerienne de l'organisation romaine dans le Sud-Algerien. Fossatum Africae* (Paris, 1949).

Barth, H., (1) *Wanderungen durch die Küstenländer des Mittelmeeres* (Berlin, 1849); (2) *Travels and Discoveries in North and Central Africa, 1849–55* (London, 1857).

Bates, O., *The Eastern Libyans* (London, 1914).

Bauer, G., "Notizie sulla regione di Orfella", *Bollettino Geografico* iii (Ufficio Studi, Governo di Tripolitania) (1932).

Beechey, F. W. and H. W., *Proceedings of the Expedition to Explore the Northern Coast of Africa* (London, 1828).

Beguinot, F., "Di Alcune iscrizioni in caratteri Latini e in lingua sconosciuta, trovate in Tripolitania", *Rivista degli Studi Orientali* xxiv (1949).

Belardinelli, A., *La Ghibla* (Tripoli, 1935).

Butler, A. J., *The Arab Conquest of Egypt* (Oxford, 1902).

Caetani, L., *Annali dell'Islam* (Milan, 1911).

Cagnat, R., *L'Armée romaine de l'Afrique* (Paris, 1913).

Cagnat, R. and Merlin, A., *Inscriptions Latines d'Afrique* (Paris, 1923).

Caputo, G., "La protezione dei monumenti di Tolemaide negli anni 1935–42", *QAL* iii (1954).

Cary, M., *The Geographic Background of Greek and Roman History* (Oxford, 1949).

Cerratta, L., *Sirtis* (Avellino, 1933).

Chabot, J. B., *Receuil des inscriptions libyques* (Paris, 1940).

Comparetti, D., "Iscrizione cristiana di Cirene", *ASAA* i (1914).

Cowper, H .S., *The Hill of the Graces* (London, 1897).

Cuntz, O. (ed.), *Itineraria Romana I: Itineraria Antonini* (Lipsiae, 1929).

Della Cella, P., *Viaggio da Tripoli di Barberia alle frontiere occidentali dell' Egitto* (Genoa, 1819).

De Ruggiero, E., *Dizionario Epigrafico di Antichità Romane.*

Di Vita, A., "Il 'limes' romano di Tripolitania nella sua concretezza archaologica e nella sua realtà storica", *Lib Ant* i (1964).

Druon, H., *Etudes sur la vie et les oeuvres de Synésius, évêque de Ptolemais dans la Cyrénaique au commencement du Ve siècle* (Paris, 1859).

Edrisi (ed. Dozy and De Goeje), *Description de l'Afrique et de l'Espagne* (Leyde, 1866).

El Bekri (ed. De Slane), *Description de l'Afrique septentrionale* (Algier, 1913).

Ferri, S., "Firme di legionari della Siria nella Gran Sirte", *Rivista della Tripolitania* ii (1926).

Fitzgerald, A. (ed.), (1) *The letters of Synesius of Cyrene* (London, 1926); (2) *Essays and Hymns of Synesius of Cyrene* (two volumes, London, 1930).

Freund, G. A., "Viaggio lungo la Gran Sirte", *Pioneri Italiani in Libia* (Milan, 1912).

Guey, J., "Note sur le limes Romain de Numidie et le Sahara au IVe siècle", *Mél. d'Arch. et d'Hist.* lvi (1939).

Hamilton, J., *Wanderings in North Africa* (London, 1856).

Haynes, D. E. L., *The Antiquities of Tripolitania* (Libya, 1959).

Honigmann, J., *Le Synekdemos d'Hierocles et Georges de Chypre* (Brussels, 1939).

Jones, A. H. M., *Cities of the Eastern Roman Provinces* (Oxford, 1971).

Kraeling, C. H., *Ptolemais, City of the Libyan Pentapolis* (Chicago, 1962).

Lacombrade, P., *Synésios de Cyrène, Hellène et Chrétien* (Paris, 1951).

Levi Della Vida, "Le Iscrizioni Neopuniche della Tripolitania", *Libya (già Rivista della Tripolitania)* iii (1927).

Lyon, G. F., *A Narrative of Travels in Northern Africa in the years 1818, 19 and 20* (London, 1821).

Maspero, J., *Organisation Militaire de l'Egypte Byzantine* (Paris, 1912).

de Mathuisieulx, M., "Rapport sur une mission scientifique en Tripolitaine", *Nouvelles Archives des Missions scientifiques* x (1902), xii (1904), xiii (1906).

Mezzetti, O., *Guerra in Libia* (Rome, 1933).

Miller, K. (ed.), *Itineraria Romana* (Stuttgart, 1916).

Müller, K., *Geographi Graeci Minores* (Paris, 1855).

Pacho, J. R., *Relation d'un voyage dans la Marmarique et la Cyrenaique* (Paris, 1827).

Pando, J. C., *The Life and Times of Synesius of Cyrene* (Washington, 1940).

Reynolds, J. M. and Ward Perkins, J. B. (eds.), *Inscriptions of Roman Tripolitania (IRT)*, (Rome, 1952).

Rohlfs, G. F., (1) *Von Tripolis nach Alexandrien* (Bremen, 1871); (2) *Kufra* (Leipzig, 1881).

Romanelli, P., (1) "Tre iscrizoni tripolitane di interesse storico", *Epigraphica* i (1939); (2) Il limes romano in Africa *Quaderni dell'Impero: Il limes romano* x (Rome, 1939); (3) *La Cirenaica Romana* (Verbania, 1943).

Schlumberger, D., "Bornes frontières de la Palmyrène", *Syria* xx (1939).

Smith, R. M. and Porcher, E. A., *History of the recent discoveries at Cyrene* (London, 1864).

Smyth, W. H., *The Mediterranean, a memoir physical, historical and nautical* (London, 1854).

Stein, E., *Histoire du Bas Empire II* (Paris, 1949).

Stucchi, S., *L'Agorà di Cirene I: I lati nord ed est della Platea inferiore* (Rome, 1965).

Vergara-Caffarelli, E., *Fasti Archaeologici* xii (1959).

Vischer, H., *Across the Sahara from Tripoli to Bornu* (London, 1910).

Ward Perkins, J. B., "Gasr es-Suq el-Oti: a desert settlement in Central Tripolitania", *Archaeology* iii (1950).

TRIPOLITANIA

Goodchild's work in Tripolitania is here represented by ten papers of which seven embody his major discoveries and conclusions on the *Limes Tripolitanus*. Subsequent work has supplemented these in some details but they remain fundamental to study of the subject, as is apparent from a recent paper of Antonino di Vita which surveyed the present state of knowledge (*Il "limes" romano di Tripolitania nella sua concretezza archeologica e nella sua realtà storica* in *Libya Antiqua* i (1964) 65–98). One minor point of linguistic controversy should be noted here: the use of the word *limitanei* in these papers to describe the natives who were settled as farmers in the frontier zones and called upon by the Romans to act as a local militia was strongly contested by Professor A. H. M. Jones (*Later Roman Empire* II (Oxford, 1964) 653); by the end of his life Goodchild inclined to accept Jones's view that they were better described as *gentiles* (see *Fortificazioni* 226, "Il termine *limitanei* che è convenientemente applicato a questi agricoltori non è forse del tutto esatto, e probabilmente è più esatto designarli come '*gentiles*' "). But "*gentiles*" is not perfectly satisfactory either and "*limitanei*" has been left to stand. The foundation date of Gheria el Gharbia, and consequent deductions, have been altered in accordance with the discovery of a new inscription (see p. 58, n.26).

ROMAN TRIPOLITANIA: RECONNAISSANCE IN THE DESERT FRONTIER ZONE

[From *The Geographical Journal* cxv (1950)]
Plates 1–7, 16, 19 and 38

In the years 1946–9 during the greater part of which period I had the privilege of serving as Antiquities Officer with the British Military Administrations in Libya, I visited a considerable number of ancient sites in the central sector of the frontier zone (*limes*) of Tripolitania between the Gebel escarpment and the line of the Wadi Zemzem. The *limes Tripolitanus* was the easternmost of a series of frontier zones protecting the Roman provinces of Africa. It ran for some 1,000 km. from Turris Tamalleni (the modern Telmine, on the edge of the Chott el Djerid) to its eastern terminus at Arae Philaenorum [Ras el-Aáli], near "Marble Arch" [see below, p. 155 f.]), on the borders of ancient (Cyrenaica. Of this total length, the eastern 300 km. from the great salt marsh of Sebcha Tauorga to Arae Philaenorum, have still to be explored. Most important however, historically and geographically, is the central sector between the Tunisian frontier and Sebcha Tauorga. This protected the prosperous coastal cities of Sabratha, Oea and Lepcis against the Numidian tribes of the interior and, at the same time, embraced an area of great agricultural importance, the olive-bearing zone of the Tripolitanian Gebel.

PREVIOUS EXPLORATION

The archaeology of the interior of northern Tripolitania has not received, during the last half-century, the attention that it clearly merits. This is the more surprising when one recalls how many of the great African explorers of the early nineteenth century found time to examine and record the ancient remains which they met with on their way to the Fezzan and Central Africa. Commander (later Rear-Admiral) W. H. Smyth was the first European to penetrate deep into the Roman frontier zone. He visited the important remains of Ghirza in the Wadi Zemzem; and although his journey, made in 1817, seemed to him a disappointment, that was largely because of his failure to appreciate the significance of what he saw there.[1] Seven years later Major Dixon Denham, returning from the Fezzan, visited the same site and made important records of the Roman reliefs and inscriptions. It was in 1818 that Captain G. F. Lyon, on his way to Murzuch, discovered the Roman fortress at Bu Ngem, and made a drawing of one of its gateways, subsequently demolished by the Turks to provide materials for a fort of their own. Unfortunately the great expedition of the Beechey brothers in

1821–2, from Tripoli to Cyrenaica, did not pass through the Tripolitanian hinterland, but many small defensive towers, of a type characteristic of the Roman frontiers in Libya, were seen by these travellers along the shores of the Syrtis, and carefully described in their Report.[2]

In 1851 the German explorer Barth, travelling to Lake Chad on behalf of the British government, encountered in the Tripolitanian Gebel and between Mizda and Tabunia various Roman structures which he has described. It was this same explorer who illustrated the Roman mausoleum at Germa, the southernmost monument of Romano-Libyan architecture in Africa. Rohlfs, bound for Kufra ten years later noted numerous ancient watchtowers in the Orfella region of inner Tripolitania, and justly remarked that many of them were of early Islamic date.[3]

The contribution of these early travellers to our archaeological knowledge of the Tripolitanian *limes* was a very substantial one. But they were all intent on reaching distant destinations, and could spare little time to examine in detail the zones through which they passed. Not until 1895–6, when H. S. Cowper made an admirable archaeological survey of the Tarhuna plateau, was any part of the hinterland studied as a region; and it was only in 1901–4 that an attempt was made, by the French explorer Méhier de Mathuisieulx, to follow all the main routes of northern Tripolitania and obtain a general picture of the geography, geology, and archaeology of the whole territory.[4]

As had been expected, the years of Italian occupation (1911–42) opened up the interior of Tripolitania to widespread European penetration, and to the exploratory activities of this period we owe most of what we know of the geography of the area. Italian officials and soldiers stationed in remote outposts often took a deep interest in local topography and history, as is shown by two useful monographs on the Ghibla and Orfella regions.[5] The existing cartography of Tripolitania is based almost entirely on Italian work (see Appendix). Archaeological research, too, was particularly intense in pre-war Tripolitania, but it was mainly concentrated in the coastal regions; and although Professors R. Bartoccini and G. Caputo carried out important excavations in the areas of Asabaa and Tarhuna respectively, the *limes* area south of the Gebel never came fully within the orbit of Italian archaeological activity. This was because, in the first place, the colonial antiquities service, understaffed in trained archaeologists, had major excavations in progress on the coastal sites, and could not take on new commitments; and secondly because the scientific missions which arrived from Italy after 1930 were not unnaturally eager to get to grips with the then newly-conquered Fezzan.[6] The *limes* area, north of the Wadi Zemzem, remained as it had been throughout the nineteenth century, eclipsed by the greater fascination of the regions further to the south. Historians concerned with the problem of Rome's desert frontier could only draw on the important, but often misleading, reports written by Mathuisieulx. The erroneous conception of the *limes Tripolitanus* as a linear frontier drawn along the crest of the Gebel, and not—as we now know it to be—a deep defensive zone, largely springs from this source.

THE ARCHAEOLOGICAL REMAINS

The archaeology of inner Tripolitania, which is, monumentally, almost exclusively Romano-Libyan, is closely linked with its geography. As one goes inland, one leaves behind the purely Mediterranean civilisation of the Roman cities on the coast, and enters a zone where Mediterranean and Saharan elements are mixed. It is significant that the city—the most characteristic feature of the Roman Empire—is entirely absent in the interior of Tripolitania, and that the only known Roman villages are those which sprang up along the Roman road which passed along the crest of the Gebel. We have identified two of these villages during the last three years, one at Ain Wif (the ancient Thenadassa) which Mr. Ward Perkins and the writer examined in 1948, the other at Medina Doga (the ancient Mesphe) identified by the writer in 1947 and surveyed last summer.[7] The survey of the latter site was greatly facilitated by the geometrical precision with which Italian farmers have planted a "grid" of olive-trees, 20 m. apart, on top of the ancient ruins. It is not often that the field archaeologist finds his site already "pegged out" in this manner!

Apart from these two sites, and others still to be identified on the same Roman road, the archaeological remains of the interior are normally Roman farmhouses, standing either alone or in groups of two or more,[8] the mausolea which very frequently accompany these farms, and the extensive series of terrace-walls which occupy many of the wadi-beds. Roman dams are occasionally found in the Gebel region (as, for example, the remarkable—and still unexplained—series in the Wadi Dauùn near Tarhuna),[9] but further to the south the remains of hydraulic installations suggest that the aim was not so much to impound rain water in open reservoirs (the high rate of evaporation would have made this a profitless task) as to stem its flow by means of catchment barriers, and to divert it either into covered cisterns or, by means of irrigation channels, over the surface of cultivated ground.

The plain of the Gefara, singularly destitute of ancient remains, marks a broad barrier between the coastal and interior cultures of the Roman period; and it is only in the region of Lepcis Magna, where the Gebel meets the sea, that the transition is sudden. The Gebel itself—and by the term Gebel is normally meant the fertile northern edge of the Tripolitanian plateau—was, in ancient times, the main olive-growing region of Tripolitania. As early as the middle of the first century B.C., the inhabitants of Lepcis Magna were able to draw on the produce of hundreds of thousands of olive-trees, and the planted areas probably increased during the Roman period. Throughout the Gebel area the traveller encounters the massive uprights of Roman olive-presses, at one time suspected of being "megalithic" monuments of prehistoric origin. In a fortified olive-farm at Msufiin, near Garian, the writer excavated last summer numerous fragments of Christian inscriptions of the fourth century A.D., in which the "opulence", "abundance", and "prosperity" of God were praised, a reflection no doubt on the general economic prosperity of the countryside during that period.[10]

A comparison between the olive plantations of the Roman period, and the Italian plantations of today springs readily—perhaps too readily—to mind. Examination of these two periods of agricultural development reveals more points of contrast than of comparison. In the first place, the development of the Gebel in the Roman period was the result, not of any sudden phase of "colonisation", but of many years of gradual plantation. Secondly, the Roman olive-farms were occupied in the main by more or less romanised members of the indigenous population and not by immigrant settlers. Third, and most important of all, the archaeological evidence leaves little doubt that the ancient olive-farms were

scattered, almost haphazard, over the countryside and not laid out mathematic-
ally, in chess-board design, oblivious of contours and natural obstacles. To obtain
a visual impression of the Gebel countryside in Roman times, it is better to leave
the areas of recent colonisation, and to study instead the surviving zones of indigenous plantation at Cussabat or Garian. Our air photograph of the hill-top
village of Msufiin, near Garian, shows clearly the careful terracing of the hillsides carried out not merely to increase the cultivable area, but to protect the
adjacent olives from the ever-present danger of soil-erosion. Undoubtedly the
olive trees were denser in the Roman period, but the general pattern of land-use
was much the same. The mound of Henscir Taglissi, in which were found the
Christian inscriptions previously referred to, lies in the centre of the photograph.

Our recent researches have however been concerned both with the military
and the economic aspects of Roman settlement in this frontier zone. An earlier
generation of archaeologists believed that a series of large Roman forts ran
along the crest of the Gebel, forming a linear frontier. We found no confirmatory
evidence of any such defensive system. On the contrary, the normal unit of
defence in the Gebel—as in the area further to the south—seems to have been
the fortified farm, a tower-like structure originally two or three storeys high, and
usually surrounded by a broad ditch. These buildings must have resembled the
signal-towers shown on Trajan's column and often discovered in the frontier
regions of Britain and Germany; but their function was more comprehensive, for
they were clearly the homes of the farmers who cultivated the surrounding
countryside. Inscriptions testify that these towers, which often have olive-presses
built into, or adjoining them, were classed as *centenaria*, and their owners were
in many cases *centenarii*, a *centenarius* being the territorial army rank equivalent
to the centurion of the Roman regular army.

The southern limits of the main area of ancient olive cultivation can be determined with some accuracy by the distribution of Roman olive-presses, and
these limits coincide almost exactly with the edge of the "high plain" climatic
zone, and the beginning of the "steppe". The present rainfall isohyet of this line
of demarcation is approximately 200 mm. per annum. South of this line the
rainfall diminishes rapidly, Beni Ulid enjoying a modest 60–70 mm., and Mizda
often suffering several successive years with no rainfall at all.[11] Yet the steppe
and desert areas south of the Gebel were, in the Roman period, capable of supporting a considerable sedentary population, as is shown by the extensive remains
of fortified farmhouses as far south as the Wadi Zemzem. This was probably
due, partly to a slightly higher rainfall during the Roman period, but mainly to
the existence of numerous wadis running south-eastwards from the Gebel water-
shed, the beds of which retained sufficient moisture to make possible the cultivation of cereals, dates and even vines. After exceptionally heavy rainfall some
of the more favoured wadis, such as the Wadi Beni Ulid, are flooded even today;
but it would be rash to assume that such winter flooding was normal during the
Roman period, and that it was the basis of the agricultural system.[12] The region
south of the Gebel must always have been a marginal one, and its successful
agricultural exploitation was largely due to the skilful way in which the Romano-
Libyan farmers terraced the beds of the wadis, and built catchment walls along
their sides to prevent the rain-water which poured off the surface of the plateau
from washing away the precious soil. These catchment walls consist of a double
line of flat stones, the intermediate space having originally been filled with clay:

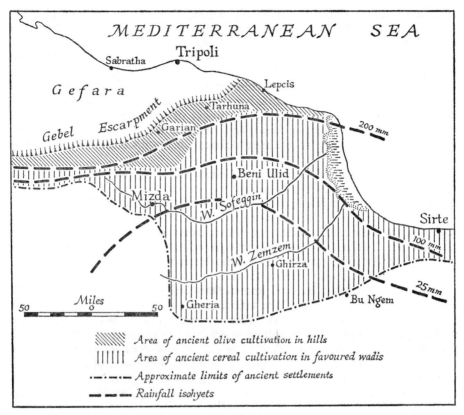

MEDITERRANEAN SEA
Tripoli
Sabratha
Gefara
Lepcis
Gebel Escarpment
Tarhuna
Garian
200 mm
Beni Ulid
Mizda
W. Sofeggin
Sirte
W. Zemzem
Ghirza
100 mm
25 mm
Miles
50   0   50
Gheria
Bu Ngem

⫶⫶⫶⫶ Area of ancient olive cultivation in hills
||||| Area of ancient cereal cultivation in favoured wadis
·—·—·— Approximate limits of ancient settlements
▬ ▬ ▬ Rainfall isohyets

Fig. 1

the stones broke the force of the winter torrents, the clay prevented the water from seeping through the barriers. Nowadays however the clay filling has largely disappeared and the double lines of flat stones give the misleading impression of having formerly been aqueducts—an interpretation completely refuted by their levels. The terrace-walls, across the full width of the wadi-beds, were dry-built of rough stones: they have survived the centuries remarkably well.

In this southern desert region the Roman fortified farms have much the same character as those of the Gebel; but they invariably stand on the sides of the wadis, and their state of preservation is very much better, due to the drier climate. Whereas in the Gebel the upper storeys have usually collapsed, forming flat-topped mounds, in the Ghibla and Orfella regions these structures are still standing two or three storeys high and even have the butt-ends of their original floor-beams visible in their walls. Their plans are essentially Saharan: the outer walls are pierced only by a single doorway, light being admitted to the living rooms from the open courtyard, or light shaft, around which they stand. To students of provincial Roman archaeology, accustomed to a sharp distinction between the "villa" and the "fort", these African structures come as a surprise.

More impressive than the simple, if robust, fortified farms, are the funerary monuments which almost invariably accompany them. These are built of finely-cut ashlar throughout, and have in many cases a wealth of ornamental detail in characteristic Romano-Libyan style, of the type which so disgusted W. H. Smyth in 1817. That traveller, a great geographer but a disappointing archaeologist, described the tombs of Ghirza as "of a mixed style and in very indifferent taste, ornamented with ill-proportioned columns and clumsy capitals ... loaded with absurd representations of warriors, hunters, camels, horses and other animals". He thought that this site might be the origin of the legend of Ras Sem, the "petrified city" of the Libyan desert, and lamented the fact that the propagators of this fable should be "so glaringly deficient in the discernment bestowed by education".[13]

Italian soldiers viewed the ruins of Ghirza with very different emotions. To them these funerary monuments seemed to represent an oasis of Italic culture in the heart of barren and inhospitable land. One officer wrote, after his first glimpse of Ghirza, "one sees ... these age-old monuments, majestic and full of grace in their delicate colonnades, contrasting indescribably with the surrounding squalor, abandon and loneliness, resisting the ravages of time and remaining to attest the boundless power and greatness of Rome the dominator".[14]

Neither viewpoint does justice to these remarkable monuments, or to the numerous similar ruins, less well known than Ghirza, scattered throughout the Sofeggin and Zemzem basins. The artistic merits or failings of these structures are of relatively minor importance: their interest lies in the fact that they represent a hybrid Romano-Libyan culture which brought prosperity to deserts which previously and subsequently knew no settled human occupation. The "absurd representations" of men and animals are valuable documents of the life of the countryside during the period of its greatest recorded prosperity. From these reliefs and especially from those at Ghirza, we can obtain an impressive picture of the daily life of the people of the frontier zone; horses and camels ploughing the wadis, corn and vines being harvested, date cultivation, hunting scenes and, more rarely, scenes of frontier strife with the desert peoples.

The great agricultural exploitation of the Tripolitanian interior during the Roman period was not in fact, as later colonisers wished to believe, an experiment in European colonisation in a backward area. It was rather an attempt at settling an indigenous and semi-nomadic people as static farmers to act as a human barrier against invasion by more dangerous nomads. Inscriptions, whether in Latin or Libyan, show clearly that the occupants of the fortified farms and the constructors of the tombs were Libyans, and probably belonged to the ethnic group known as the *Arzuges* in later Latin literature. The strong influence of Punic on their language suggests that these people came from the stock of those *Libo-phoenices* to whom Strabo refers.

THE HISTORY OF ANCIENT SETTLEMENT IN THE INTERIOR

Our existing evidence is still inadequate to throw much light on the detailed history of settlement in the *limes* zone of Tripolitania. The only building of "fortified farmhouse" type which can be rigidly dated belongs to the years A.D. 244–6; many others appear to belong to the fourth century A.D., and there are a large number which are clearly early Islamic in date.[15] The main period of settlement south of the Gebel seems indeed to fall within the margins A.D. 200–900, and thus to have continued long after the Roman frontier had ceased to exist. For the earlier period we have information from documentary sources, including that remarkable Roman "Army List", the *Notitia Dignitatum*, which shows how the Tripolitanian frontier was divided up into zones under zone commanders (*praepositi limitis*). For the later period history is almost silent, although Corippus, the epic poet of the Byzantine wars in Libya, gives some interesting, if vague, glimpses of the times when the people of the former frontier zone had become the enemies of the Eastern Roman Empire. How soon after the first Arab invasions the Libyan population of the *limes* zone abandoned Christianity or paganism in favour of Islam is unrecorded, but the continued occupation of Romano-Libyan farmhouses in the early Islamic period, and the conversion of a church into a mosque by the addition of a *mihrab*, alike suggest a gradual and tranquil transition.[16] It was only during the second wave of Arab invasions that settled life, either for the climatic reasons referred to above, or because of insecurity, gradually became impossible in the majority of the wadis and the reduced and impoverished population became nomadic, or settled in centres such as Mizda and Beni Ulid. The Wadi Beni Ulid preserves, even today, all the characteristics of the landscape in Roman times. Its terraced and culti-vated bed, fringed on either side by the rocky wastes of the plateau, represents the original appearance of those wadis in the *limes* area which are now com-pletely desiccated and abandoned. The unit of human habitation is however no longer the fortified farmhouse; the population, now highly concentrated in this area, occupies a series of small villages clustered along both sides of the wadi. The change from the isolated life of the farm to the communal life of the village must have hastened the process of "arabisation".

GENERAL CONCLUSIONS

The routes followed by the writer during the last three years are marked on the accompanying map together with other routes in the hinterland of Misurata, between Bir Dufan and Sebcha Tauorga, which my colleague Mr. Michael de Lisle examined last summer when I was temporarily incapacitated. It will be evident from the map how many important areas remain to be covered, especially in the western Gebel between Zintan and the Tunisian border, and also between Mizda and the oases of the Gheriat. For these two latter areas we have the records made by Corò and Barth respectively, and it is clear that the archaeo-logical remains are of the general category already described. It seems probable however that the general limits of Roman settlement, as shown on our map, are substantially correct, even if isolated monuments, such as the mausoleum of Germa, lie outside them.

It need hardly be pointed out that many of the conclusions which have been reached as a result of these initial reconnaissances will require supplementing and modifying in the light of future research. In particular, our chronological deductions, based on a very few inscriptions, and on a comparative study of the architecture of the fortified buildings, require confirmation from more sub-stantial evidence. In this problem one of the best methods of approach is the study of a single area as a geographical and archaeological unit, with a detailed

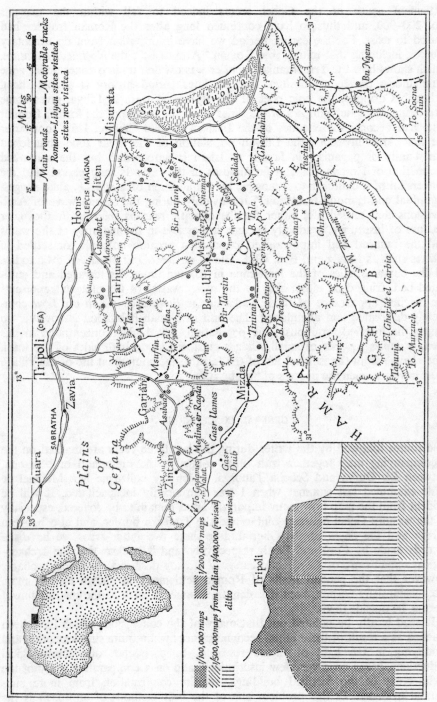

Fig. 2 Modern routes and ancient sites in Tripolitania

* *

examination of its ancient remains. Work of this type is being carried out in the Cussabat–Marconi area by Mr. E. D. M. Oates, Rome Scholar in archaeology at the British School at Rome, and will undoubtedly have important results.[17] It must be remembered that excavation—the only ultimate arbiter in problems of archaeological chronology—is far more difficult on these African sites than it is, for example, in Great Britain. Huge quantities of fallen rubble will have to be removed from the fortified farms before their floor-level can be reached; and those buildings which are best preserved and stand highest are often the most dangerous ones in which to work, owing to the inclination of their ruinous walls. Those planning campaigns of excavation will have to bear these factors in mind, as well as the difficulty of recruiting digging gangs in the more remote areas.

Air survey and photography, which we used for the first time last summer, will undoubtedly have their value in the prosecution of research, but it would be unwise to anticipate such remarkable results as Poidebard and Baradez have obtained in Syria and Numidia. The Roman frontiers of Libya were always of minor importance, and their military installations appear to have been on a correspondingly small scale.[18] Tripolitanian fortified farmhouses, rarely more than 30 m. square, are not so photogenic as the large fortresses of the major frontiers. No signs have yet been observed either on the ground or from the air of those linear *fossata* which are such an important feature of Baradez's discoveries. The greatest value of air photography in the interior of Libya will probably be found to lie in its revelation of extensive cultivation and irrigation systems.

We have not so far been able to investigate that section of the Tripolitanian *limes* which lay along the coastal regions of the Greater Syrtis. The classic work of the Beechey brothers and preliminary observations made more recently suggest that we shall find there, as in the Sofeggin and Zemzem basins, that the fortified farmhouse was the main unit of defence.[19] The same may well prove to be the case in the hinterland of Cyrenaica which I hope to examine during the current year.

These archaeological reconnaissances were made possible by the helpful attitude of the Administration in Tripolitania and, in particular, of its Chief Administrator, Mr. T. R. Blackley, C.B.E., and Chief Secretary, Mr. H. Mercer, M.C., D.F.C., who, in the midst of more urgent problems, have given the greatest encouragement and support to such studies. Among the numerous officers of the Administration who have given assistance at various times, I must particularly mention Lieut.-Colonel P. J. Sandison, Sudan Defence Force (then Deputy Chief Secretary in Tripolitania) and Captain C. C. Tower, Coldstream Guards (then Civil Affairs Officer for the Desert Areas). Doctor Cesare Chiesa, Director of the Museo Libico in Tripoli, accompanied me on many occasions, and to Professor Giacomo Caputo, Superintendent of Monuments in Tripolitania, I am indebted for constant help and advice. The help given by the British armed forces in Tripolitania has been indispensable, and the results obtained during the summer of 1949, when air survey and photography were first applied to this *limes* problem, were largely due to the co-operation both of the First Infantry Division and of the Royal Air Force station at Castel Benito. In concluding these acknowledgments, I need hardly say how great has been my debt to Mr. J. B. Ward Perkins, Director of the British School at Rome, who accompanied me on several tours and with whom I am collaborating in the publication of some of their results. The post-war revival of archaeological research in Tripolitania has been largely the result of his own inspiration and example.

APPENDIX

THE CARTOGRAPHY OF THE REGION

Existing large-scale maps of the Tripolitanian *limes* area are of varied quality. Two Italian bodies were concerned with map-making in Libya before the war. The first, the *Ufficio Studi* of the Tripolitanian (later Libyan) colonial government, directed for many years by the eminent geographer E. De Agostini, undertook the preparation of a series of 1/400,000 maps covering the whole country. From these, the British G.S.G.S. series of 1/500,000 maps have been compiled. The first sheets published by the *Ufficio Studi* were purely "schizzi dimostrativi", compiled from a small number of astronomical observations and from the verbal reports of travellers. A complete revision, based on ground observations and closed traverses, was in progress before the war, but certain sheets (including the areas of Mizda and Beni Ulid, of extreme interest to the archaeologist) were never fully revised.[20] Moreover, the hurried reduction of these maps to a 1/500,000 scale for use in the Libyan campaigns of the last war hardly improved their quality, and, in contrast with Cyrenaica, the amount of air photographic cover available for war-time revision was extremely small. That many complaints were made by war-time users of these maps is hardly surprising.[21]

The second Italian body concerned with map-making in Tripolitania was the *Istituto Geografico Militare*, which prepared a series of excellent 1/100,000 maps, originally intended to extend as far south as the thirtieth parallel. Had this aim been achieved the archaeologist would be excellently served. But the increasing pre-occupation with military matters which followed the Ethiopian War resulted in the diversion of survey parties from the centre of the territory to the Tunisian and Egyptian frontiers, where maps of undoubted military, but scant topographical or archaeological interest, were compiled. Nonetheless these 1/100,000 sheets are, despite the limited area they cover, of the greatest accuracy and use, and it is only unfortunate that the copies now generally available in Tripolitania are war-time editions produced hastily by mobile map units. Although these sheets have the advantage of a metrical "grid", the standard of printing is much below that of the originals.

The traveller in inner Tripolitania, whether geographer or archaeologist, has at his disposal therefore a very mixed series of maps. For the Gebel areas of Tarhuna and Garian he can obtain reliable, if badly printed, 1/100,000 maps, on which ancient sites can be plotted with reasonable accuracy. For the *limes* areas further to the south, he is normally dependent on extremely poor 1/500,000 maps, or on enlargements of them on the 1/200,000 scale. Moreover, the army draughtsmen who re-drew these sheets from the Italian originals appear to have had much difficulty with the place-names, which are quite frequently mis-spelt.[22]

[New maps were issued for the Libyan government in 1963 by the American Army Map Service (AM) Corps of Engineers. They include Series P761 (1/50,000) which covers the coastal and Gebel areas and Series P502 (1/250,000) which includes the Beni Ulid and Mizda zones.]

EXISTING MOTOR-ROUTES

The itinerant archaeologist, with limited time at his disposal, is necessarily dependent on motor-transport and, although this method of movement is ideal in open country of Western Desert type, there are few parts of the Tripolitanian *limes* zone which can accurately be described as open desert. Apart from the great bowl of the upper Sofeggin between Zintan and Mizda, and the lowest reaches of the main *wadis* near their junction with the Sebcha Tauorga, the country everywhere presents the appearance of a rocky plateau intersected by innumerable *wadis*, often steep-sided. In most areas the traveller has to decide whether to keep to the surface of the plateau and ruin his tyres, or attempt to follow the sandy and boulder-strewn beds of the *wadis*. The latter solution would normally be the best were it not that the *wadis* of greatest interest to the archaeologist have, almost invariably, long series of ancient terrace walls across their full widths, over which any vehicle must bump for miles, to the detriment of its springs. It is imperative, in these conditions, to make the fullest use of the existing roads and tracks whether they be the pre-war Italian routes, the war-time tracks beaten down by convoys of military vehicles, or the numerous roads recently constructed and maintained for the sole purpose of exporting esparto-grass from the collecting and baling centres which have been established throughout the Gebel zone. Many of the minor routes do not appear on the existing maps, being of recent construction; and many routes which do appear on the maps have either long been washed out or, since their original purpose was purely military, no longer justify the expense of upkeep.

It may be useful, for the benefit of future travellers, to list some of the routes which have been followed. For the detailed topography of most of them the reader is referred to the excellent guide *Libya* published by the Italian Touring Club in 1937, and to a comparatively rare series of itineraries published in 1914 under the title *Manuale Itinerario della Tripolitania*, with later supplements. The Italian forms of place names have been retained throughout the present paper, since these forms appear on all the existing maps, and the advantages of concordance between bibliography and cartography outweigh the minor irritation of finding, for example, Shemek transcribed as Scemech.

There are four main routes of penetration into the interior, of which the best known is the western route from Tripoli to Gadames via Nalut, followed by many tourists and journalists in the pre-war days when luxury buses and "pseudo-Saharan" hotels offered African glamour with a minimum of discomfort.[23] Times have since changed: Gadames is now under French administration, and tourists from Tripoli rarely go as far as Nalut. As the writer's reconnaissances have not yet extended into the area between Zintan and the Tunisian frontier, the Gadames route has not been used. The remaining three routes of penetration are Tripoli–Garian–Mizda, Tripoli–Tarhuna–Beni Ulid and Misurata–Gheddahia–Bu Ngem, all of which are of importance to the archaeologist, and have been followed recently. The Garian–Mizda and Tarhuna–Beni Ulid roads are regularly maintained and in tolerably good condition today, but the Gheddahia–Bu Ngem road, severely "corrugated" by heavy war-time use, is a tedious one. From Mizda a road in poor condition goes southwards to the oases of Gheriat, and from Beni Ulid a rough track, adequate for robust vehicles, goes south-eastward via Bir Tala and Ghirza to join the Gheddahia–Hun road at Bu Ngem. The sector of this road between Bir Tala and Ghirza is, curiously enough, omitted on the military "Going Overprint" (November 1942) of the appropriate 1/500,000 map sheet, in which the area in question is marked as "generally impassable"; and the information on these "Going Overprints" is, in general, to be treated with extreme caution. Also from Beni Ulid, reasonably good roads go southwards to Scemech in the Wadi Sofeggin and north-eastward, via Mselleten and Bir Dufan, to meet the coast at Zliten and Misurata.

Apart from the bitumenised Gebel road linking Nalut with Garian, and Tarhuna with Homs (the centre section between Garian and Tarhuna was never constructed, and a rough military road between these two places has since been interrupted), there is an important lateral route, running mainly in desert terrain, which follows the line of the upper and middle Sofeggin basins. Leaving the Gebel road at Zintan one can, with suitable vehicles, motor south-eastwards to Mizda, passing important *limes* outposts at Gasr Duib and Gasr Uames, and following the approximate line of a Roman road, the course of which is marked out by milestones.[24] From Mizda one can continue eastwards, still following the Sofeggin, to Bir Scedeua and thence by Gasr Tininai to Scemech and Bir Tala. Mizda itself was undoubtedly a Roman outpost of strategic importance, as two Roman roads meet there, but its Roman fort must be buried beneath one of the two Berber villages which now occupy the small oasis. East of Mizda the Sofeggin narrows to become a deep gorge and the level of its bed drops 200 metres in its passage to Scemech.

This sector of the Sofeggin has many ancient sites, but the road through the Wadi is badly blocked by wind-blown sand, and a faster route (passing only one major ancient site, at Bir Dreder[25]) can be used by following the Gheriat road as far as the Wadi Gellali and then branching eastwards across open country to Bir Dreder and Bir Scedeua. The area of Bir Scedeua offers to the archaeologist a remarkable series of Romano–Libyan fortified farmhouses with adjoining mausolea, as well as a curious natural phenomenon, Ain el-Mizragh, a deep cleft in the surface of the rocky plateau which is the favourite haunt of pigeons. A nearby landing-ground, no longer usable, enabled Marshal Balbo, that prince of "*cacciatori*", to indulge his favourite sport without a tiring desert ride. Rues et-Tabel, a group of low hills on the opposite side of the Sofeggin to Bir Scedeua boasts the only inhabited house between Mizda and Beni Ulid, built recently by Hassan Shebani, official distributor of government rations to the nomadic Ulad Bu Seif.[26] A little further to the east, and visible for many miles, is Senam Tininai, a small Romano–Libyan temple, the only known pagan shrine in the whole Sofeggin basin.

The minor routes followed by the writer are too numerous to list here in detail, but reference must be made to a road of considerable geographical interest which goes eastwards from Garian, crosses the summit of the Garian massif near the highest mountain in northern Libya (El Glaa, 968 metres) and then descends southwards to terminate at Bir Tarsin. On this route one can observe clearly the gradual transition from "high plateau" vegetation to "steppe" and eventually to rocky desert. Bir Tarsin itself, marked by an abandoned Italian fort and a war-memorial, is a group of some twenty wells of the greatest importance to local nomads who bring their camels and goats to water here. The surrounding plateau is bleak to a savage degree, and one does not envy the Italian garrisons who occupied this post. According to many Italian maps Bir Tarsin is linked with Mizda by a good motor-road, but no such road actually exists, and the intermediate country is almost impassable to vehicles. A British Civil Affairs Officer, feeling that it would be easier to build this road than to correct the cartography, began work from the Mizda end, but it was never completed.[27]

NOTES

1. Smyth (whose description of Ghirza is contained in F. W. and H. W. Beechey, 504–12) dismissed the whole residential quarter of ancient Ghirza as "some ill-constructed houses of comparatively modern dates".

2. G. F. Lyon, 65–7; D. Denham and H. Clapperton, "*Narrative of Travels and Discoveries in Northern and Central Africa*", London, 1826, 305; F. W. and H. W. Beechey, *passim*.

3. H. Barth, (2), I, passim; G. Rohlfs, (2), 112.

4. H. S. Cowper—an excellent work marred only by the false conclusions as to the date and purpose of the "senam" monuments. M. de Mathuisieulx, x, 245–77; xii, 1–80; xiii, 73–102.

5. A. Belardinelli; G. Bauer, 33–51.

6. Reference must be made to Professor Caputo's important archaeological discoveries in the Fezzan, described in the

Italian Royal Geographical Society's publication "Il Sahara Italiano—Fezzan e Oasi di Gat", Rome, 1937, 303–30. These revealed a native society, probably the ancient Garamantes, using Roman pottery but otherwise completely unromanised (*cf. Annali Istituti Orientali di Napoli*, iii (1949) 11–33). [See now C. M. Daniels, *Antiquaries Journal* L (1970) 37 f. and *The Garamantes of Southern Libya* (Oleander Press, 1970).]

7. [See below pp. 21 f. and 76 f.] The ruins at Medina Doga (Medina er Ragda) were first reported by W. H. Smyth in 1817 (Smyth, 486), but Cowper failed to find them (Cowper, 241) and they were subsequently forgotten. The Roman Gebel road passes through the centre of the site.

8. Ghirza, the "city in the desert", is in fact a particularly large group of self-contained fortified farms (cf. D. E. L. Haynes, 154–6).

9. [See now David Oates, *PBSR* xxi (1953) 88 f.]

10. [*IRT* 863.]

11. H. Vischer, 63, records that at the time of his arrival at Mizda in 1906, it had not rained there for twelve years. Rainfall must always have been low in this part of the Sofeggin, for there are no traces of ancient cultivation in its bed.

12. It is difficult to ascertain how often the Wadi Beni Ulid floods. Bauer (40) cites only the years 1914, 1925 and 1932; but in 1819 Lyon (61) remarked on the frequency of such floodings.

13. Quoted by the Beechey brothers, *loc. cit.* The fabulous Ras Sem has more recently been identified by Aurigemma (*Rivista della Colonie Italiane*, 2 (1928) 565–73 and 733–42) as the fossiliferous zone of Maaten Rasim, between Augila and Agedabia, where Professor G. Petrocchi has recently found many remains of Mastodon. Thus the legend of "petrified cities" in Libya arose from two sources; from the Romano-Libyan sculptures of the *limes* zone, and from the fossil remains of extinct mammals at Rasim. Only a year ago the writer was asked by an intelligent Libyan driver whether the statues in the museum at Sabratha were men turned to stone, or "statues like Mussolini used to make". The legend dies hard.

14. Tenente G. Bacchetti, quoted in Itinerario No. 41 of the *Manuale Itinerario*, 26.

15. [The dated text is from Gasr Duib (*IRT* 880), see below p. 27 f.] For further details of the historical problems see R. G.

Goodchild and J. B. Ward Perkins, below p. 17 f.

16. The church in question, Gasr es Suq el Oti, lies in the Wadi Busra, near Beni Ulid, was first discovered by Capt. T. Hillyard in 1946 (in the course of a series of local reconnaissances carried out on behalf of the Antiquities Dept. in Tripolitania) and was examined by Mr. Ward Perkins and the writer in 1948; [see now J. B. Ward Perkins, 25 f. and J. B. Ward Perkins and R. G. Goodchild, *Archaeologia* xcv (1953) 54 f.].

17. [See now David Oates *PBSR* xxi (1953) 81 f.; *PBSR* xxii (1954) 91 f.]

18. In 1949 we discovered and planned a small Roman fort near Mselleten in the Wadi Merdum. Measuring only 22 m. square it was no larger than many of the fortified farms, yet it was an exact replica of the large forts found so abundantly in Numidia. [See below p. 38 f.]

19. For the region of the Syrtica there exists an excellent but little-known monograph L. Cerrata, *Sirtis*, full of geographical and archaeological information. Systematic study of the *limes* in this region remains to be initiated.

20. The inset map of cartographic cover [fig. 2] shows that of the area of permanent Romano-Libyan settlement more than a half lies in the region covered only by unrevised Italian 1/400,000 maps. Preparation of 1/100,000 maps for this area is greatly to be desired and would be of great value to scientists and administrators alike.

21. No less an authority than Field-Marshal Lord Alexander refers to this situation in his Dispatch on the final phase of the Libyan campaign, published as *Supplement to the London Gazette*, 5 February, 1948, 862.

22. For the correct (italianised) forms of the place-names it is essential to consult the two lists, each entitled *Elenco dei nomi di località della Tripolitania Settentrionale*, published in 1916 and 1936 as supplements to the 1/400,000 and 1/100,000 map-sheets respectively. The lists are not however comprehensive.

23. An eighteen-seater "autopullman" with bar and radio used to leave Tripoli for Gadames every week, returning after four days.

24. For these and other milestones in Tripolitania, see my paper "The Roman roads and milestones of Tripolitania", 21.

25. Bir Dreder, a group of wells in the bed of the Wadi Dreder, has adjoining it

the site of a large cemetery of Libyan "tribunes", officers who commanded native levies for the defence of the Roman frontier during the fourth century A.D., [see below p. 59 f.].

26. Our ground party enjoyed the hospitality of this gentleman for several days during the summer of 1949, when nearby ruins were being examined. Rues et-Tabel

has become the main centre of the Ulad Bu Seif, in place of the Italian-built village of Bir Nesma, which was less favourably situated and has now been abandoned. [In 1969 the Ulad Bu Seif were back in Nesma.]

27. To this same officer, Captain C. Tower, we owe the fast motor route from Mizda to Bir Scedeua, via Bir Dreder.

2

THE *LIMES TRIPOLITANUS* IN THE LIGHT OF RECENT DISCOVERIES

Written with J. B. Ward Perkins
[From *JRS* xxxix (1949)]
Plates 8–15

The *Limes Tripolitanus*, the easternmost of the series of *limites* protecting the Latin provinces of Roman Africa, ran for some 1,000 km. from Turris Tamalleni (the modern Telmine, on the edge of the Chott el Djerid) to its eastern terminus at Arae Philaenorum ([Ras el-Aáli], near "Marble Arch" [see below p. 155 f.]) on the border of ancient Cyrenaica. Of this total length the western 300 km. lie within the confines of the French Protectorate of Tunisia, and for this sector Cagnat's admirable summary of the archaeological evidence, although written in 1912, has not been seriously outdated by any more recent explorations.[1] The eastern sector, also of 300 km., from the great salt-marsh of Sebcha Tauorga to Arae Philaenorum, is still completely unknown, and its character cannot be profitably discussed until exploration has been carried out: it should, however, be observed that in this eastern zone the *limes* must have followed the bleak shores of the Greater Syrtis, where there were few coastal centres of importance, and virtually no Romanised hinterland.[2]

The central sector of the *limes*, between the Tunisian frontier and the Sebcha Tauorga (fig. 3), is historically and geographically the most important, since it provided the effective rear defence of the prosperous coastal cities of Sabratha, Oea, and Lepcis against the Numidian tribes of the interior, and at the same time protected an area of great agricultural importance, the olive-bearing zone of the Tripolitanian Gebel. Our knowledge of this vital part of the *limes* has hitherto been based entirely on the observations of Méhier de Mathuisieulx who, in the years 1901–4, traversed the interior plateau of Tripolitania and devoted special attention to the problem of the Roman military frontier.[3] Although certain of the archaeological conclusions reached by this pioneer traveller must be rejected in the light of more modern knowledge, the accuracy of his geographical observations and the general value of his exploration remain uncontested.

The origins of the *Limes Tripolitanus* are most obscure, and literary sources provide no definite information about its initial establishment as a coherent defensive system. Archaeology and epigraphy have hardly been more informative for the period of the first two centuries A.D. In the reign of Tiberius, under the proconsul L. Aelius Lamia (A.D. 15–16) a road was cut for 44 Roman miles in a south-westerly direction from Lepcis. Near its western termination, on the

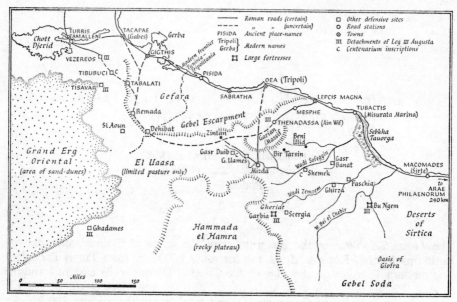

Fig. 3

Tarhuna plateau, a Numidian tribesman erected and dedicated, in the same period, a small sanctuary of Ammon, which had evidently been designed by Roman architects.[3a] Although Aelius Lamia's road was later incorporated in a strategic route garrisoned by military detachments (below, p. 75 f.), there is no evidence that it served a predominantly military function during its earlier years.[4] Indeed, Roman policy in the immediate interior appears to have been directed more, during the first two centuries A.D., to the control of tribal affairs than to the establishment of military frontiers. This attitude is illustrated by the Domitianic boundary stone of Sirte,[5] and a similar stone of Trajan from Bir Soltane, in Tunisia.[6] Not until the reign of Commodus, when garrisons were in existence at Vezereos (Sidi Mohamed ben Aissa) and at Tisavar (Gasr Ghelan), both at the western and Tunisian extremity of the future *limes*, do we find certain traces of the creation of a military frontier zone.[7] Indeed, we have no evidence of the existence of a continuous *limes* until the accession of Septimius Severus, the Lepcis-born Emperor.

In the absence of clear evidence to the contrary, and in view of the relatively abundant traces of the military activity of Severus on the Tripolitanian frontier, we are perhaps justified in regarding him as the founder of the *Limes Tripolitanus*. It is uncertain what motives dictated the final and complete abandonment of the former policy of controlling the desert areas by means of long-distance expeditions from the coastal cities. We have, however, literary evidence that campaigns were conducted in the time of Severus against the tribes of the hinterland of the Tripolis, and the new arrangements attributable to his reign accord well with the general pattern of Severan frontier policy elsewhere in Africa.[8] It may well be that the end of the second century was marked by increasing pressure from the nomadic peoples of the interior, and that the *Limes* was organised to meet an actual rather than a potential threat. Such an interpretation receives strong confirmation from the abundant traces of the care devoted to the African frontier, even by comparatively short-lived emperors of the third century; and one hesitates to accept a recently advanced hypothesis to the effect that from Commodus to Gordian III the Sahara "remained generally peaceful".[9]

The first documentary evidence of the newly established frontier system is provided by the *Antonine Itinerary*, generally attributed to Caracalla, which describes an inland route from *Tacapae* (Gabes) to *Lepcis Magna* under the head "Iter quod limitem Tripolitanum per Turrem Tamalleni a Tacapis Lepti-magna ducit". This itinerary lists eighteen road-stations between Turris Tamalleni and Lepcis, of which one only—Vezereos—can be certainly identified.[10] The newly discovered inscription from Gasr Duib (below, p. 27, pl. 13) gives a clue to the area in which Tentheos (less correctly Thenteos in the text of the *Itinerary*) stood, although it does not help to identify its exact site; whilst the sites of Thenadassa and Mesphe seem, despite lack of epigraphic evidence, to be identifiable with Ain Wif and Medina Doga respectively (below, pp. 21 f. and 76 f.). For the sites of the remaining fourteen road-stations we have virtually no evidence, although similarity of names has suggested the identification of Tabalati with the modern Ras el-Ain Tlalat.[11]

The *Notitia Dignitatum*, compiled nearly two centuries later, appears to con-fuse rather than simplify the problem. It shows a "Dux provinciae Tripolitanae" in command of two field units, the "milites fortenses in castris Leptitanis" and the "milites munifices in castris Madensibus", and of twelve "praepositi limitis", representing the static and territorial elements of the *Limes* garrisons. The twelve zones under *praepositi* are clearly not arranged in geographical order, and only four of them correspond with any of the road-stations listed in the *Antonine Itinerary*.[12] This fact is less perplexing than it might appear, as will be seen when we come to examine the *Limes* system in the hinterland of Sabratha, Oea and Lepcis. Moreover, the clear division between the civil and military authorities attested in the *Notitia*, while it no doubt represents the situation at the moment of its compilation, need not be considered typical of the whole post-Diocletianic organisation of the *Limes*. Several inscriptions referring to a "comes et praeses provinciae Tripolitanae" of the fourth century show that this official had definite military responsibilities in addition to his civil ones. It was a *praeses*, who built the Centenarium Tibubuci (Gasr Tarcine, in Tunisia), and another *praeses*, a certain Flavius Nepotianus who is praised in a Lepcis inscription "quod bar-barorum insolentiam exercitio scientiae militaris adtriberit (*sic*) quod limitis defensionem tuitionemque perpetuam futuris etiam temporibus munitam securam-que ab omni hostile incursione praestiterit".[13] Thus the "dux provinciae Tripolitanae" must have been a relatively late creation, instituted at the end of the fourth or beginning of the fifth century, when it was becoming increasingly difficult for the civil *praeses* to exercise efficient control over the military frontier. With the Vandal occupation of the coast in about 445 this defensive organisation ceased from the Roman point of view to exist, and there is no evidence that it was revived by the Byzantines,[14] but the economic and social structure of the *Limes* was, as we shall see, to survive for many centuries, to be a menace rather than an aid to the Byzantine regime, and to have its influence on the life of interior Tripolitania well into the medieval period.

From his study of the Tunisian sector of the Tripolitanian *Limes* Cagnat concluded that this whole frontier consisted of three types of defences: (1) large forts, connected by less important posts, along the whole length of a linear frontier; (2) a "fosse" and wall in the valleys and at the crossing points; (3) fortresses along the main caravan routes to the south. The latter features, represented by the three isolated posts at Ghadames, Gheria el-Garbia, and Bu Ngem, are already sufficiently known, and need not be discussed here: all were garrisoned by detachments of III Augusta.[15] Linear defences of the "fosse" and wall type, so far as is known in the whole 1,000 km. length of the frontier, exist only in the Gebels Tebaga and Matmata of Tunisia where, in one case at least, they lie well behind the frontier road described in the *Antonine Itinerary*; their date and purpose are equally uncertain.[16] As for the large forts presumed to be scattered along the frontier road, it can only be said that no trace of them has yet been encountered in modern Tripolitania, whereas an incalculable number of small defended buildings exist not only along the full extent of the Tripolitanian Gebel escarpment, but also—in the sector between Zintan and the Sebcha Tauorga—over an area extending up to 150 km. to the south.

Except between the Tunisian frontier at Dehibat and the area of Zintan, between which places the desert approaches to within 50 km. or less of the escarpment and the *Limes* road and defended zone formed a relatively narrow strip, the *Limes* in Tripolitania appears to have been far more complex than Cagnat envisaged. The cause lies in the existence of the vast Sofeggin basin, a complicated network of ravines cut by Quaternary torrents. These ravines, or "wadis" as they are more generally known, vary from steep-sided narrow cuttings to broad shallow troughs, and their beds absorb sufficient water during the rainy season to provide extensive pasture and permit cultivation. Though desert in the less accurate sense of the term, the zone is capable—in good climatic conditions —of supporting a large sedentary population, and even today has a small nomadic one. To the south of the Sofeggin basin, the Wadi Zemzem has similar characteristics on a reduced scale, and it is only in the region of the Wadi Bey el-Kebir that true desert is encountered.[17]

The road which, in the phrase of the *Antonine Itinerary*, "limitem Tripolitanum ducit", has been rightly identified by previous investigators as following close to the Gebel escarpment in the course of its passage through modern Tripolitania. De Mathuisieulx, it is true, suggested that the road swung slightly southwards between Garian and Lepcis to pass by the sites which he examined at El-Edjab and Gasr Anessa; but the recent discoveries at Ain Wif (pp. 21 ff.) destroy this hypothesis; and milestone discoveries in the Tarhuna area make it certain that the Gebel road traversed no part of the Sofeggin basin.[18] This fact, considered in relation to the traces of another military road defended by *centenaria* in the Upper Sofeggin area, and to the widespread remains of *limitanei* settlements in the main Sofeggin and Zemzem basins, shows that the Gebel road must be considered as a *Limes* only in the earlier and narrower sense of the term. Meeting the coast at Lepcis, it could not effectively protect the hinterland of that city. It was never, from Severan times onwards, so fortified throughout its length as to provide a self-contained and effective barrier between the coastal cities and the tribes of the interior. Its military function between Zintan and Lepcis was that of a rear line of communication, garrisoned by military detachments as at Ain Wif; at the same time it presumably marked the approximate line of division between the province of Africa and the military zone of eastern Numidia.

The *Limes Tripolitanus*, in the wider sense of the term, was a defended zone or series of zones which, south of the line Zintan-Lepcis, extended as far as the Wadi Zemzem, embracing the full extent of the Sofeggin basin. In marginal areas, where local cultivation could not support a resident population, its outposts were small isolated posts (*centenaria*) of the character of Gasr Duib, manned presumably by local levies but maintained by the military authorities. Where, however, the beds of the wadis were capable of growing good crops, *limitanei* were settled in fortified farmhouses modelled after the *centenaria*, to form an entirely territorial fighting force. How far this territorial system was leavened, after the disbandment of III Augusta, by a sprinkling of field-force detachments remains obscure; but it is perhaps significant that no such detachments, and indeed no *numeri*, appear either in the *Notitia Dignitatum* (except on the coast) or in inscriptions hitherto found in the *Limes* area within the confines of modern Tripolitania. Future discoveries may, perhaps, throw some light on this problem. Historically, the earliest traces of Roman military activity south of the Gebel occur under Septimius Severus, when the outlying forts at Ghadames, Bu Ngem and Gheria el-Gharbia were established; but though military roads were marked out as far south as Mizda under Caracalla,[19] [it is not until Severus Alexander (if we accept the evidence of *SHA*, see n. 41)] that we have indications of a policy of *limitanei* settlement. Thereafter the development of settlement was rapid, and the disbandment of III Augusta in 238 could be offset by the division of the *Limes* area into local zones under *praepositi* without the necessity of deploying new field-forces in this relatively unimportant sector of the African frontier.

THE MILITARY ROAD-STATION AT AIN WIF (THENADASSA)

Ain Wif lies 2 km. south of the Tarhuna–Garian motor-track, at a point approximately 15 km. west of Tazzoli village centre. The Wadi Wif, near the head of which the spring (*ain*) lies, is a tributary of the Wadi Hammam, which itself eventually runs into the Wadi Megenin, reaching the coast in the immediate neighbourhood of Tripoli city. The area is desolate but not desert. Its hills produce a good crop of esparto grass (*halfa*), for which Ain Wif is an important collecting centre; and remains of a group of Roman oil presses on an ancient site $2\frac{1}{2}$ km. to the north-east show that olives were once grown in the area. The site is much frequented by nomads for its abundant water which rises through fissures in the rocky bed of the wadi and collects in shallow pools. Around these pools is a small oasis of palm-trees (pl. 14). The presence of this water, providing an assured supply throughout the dryest summers, was no doubt the determining factor in the selection of the Roman road-station; for the site is dominated by the surrounding hills and not militarily ideal.

Immediately [east] of the pools, which lie at 385 m. above sea-level, rises a steep cliff surmounted by a fairly extensive plateau at 420 m. It was on this plateau, and at the edge of the cliff overlooking the spring, that the Roman settlement was established, its remains covering an area 350 m. square (fig. 4). In general, the site is today a low heap of rubble, in which lines of walls are dimly recognisable, and occasional standing stones indicate orthostat-and-rubble constructions (pl. 8). At the south-eastern end of the site a larger mound, with central cavity,

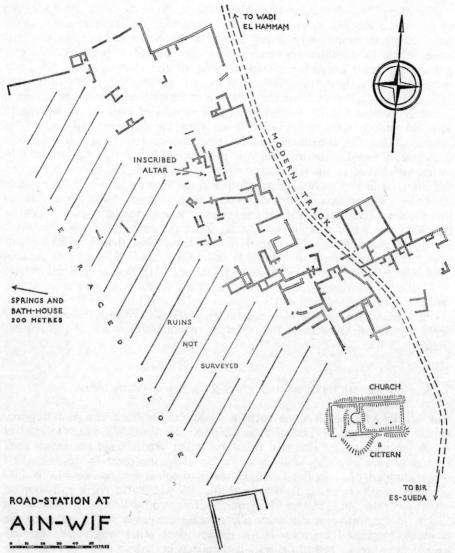

TO WADI
EL HAMMAM

MODERN TRACK

INSCRIBED
ALTAR

TERRACED SLOPE

←
SPRINGS AND
BATH-HOUSE
200 METRES

RUINS

NOT

SURVEYED

CHURCH

B
CISTERN

TO BIR
ES-SUEDA ↓

ROAD-STATION AT
AIN-WIF

0 10 20 30 40 50
METRES

Fig. 4 (after survey by Alan Wells)

marks the site of a Christian church.[20] The surface survey (fig. 4) indicates the
approximate limits of the settlement and reveals a conspicuous absence of systematic planning. In particular it should be noted that there are no perimetral
defences of any sort.

Lying exposed amidst the ruins of an orthostat-and-rubble building towards
the centre of the built-up area was found in 1948[21] an altar of soft brown limestone, the surviving height of which is 0·78 m., the upper moulding being
destroyed. This altar (pl. 10), now in Tripoli Castle, is inscribed as follows, in
letters of 4·5 cm., with many ligatures [IRT 868]:

> [I(ovi)] O(ptimo) M(aximo) D(olicheno)
> [pr]o salute et uictoria [dom]
> inor(um) nostror(um) imp(eratorum) L(uci) Sep[t(imi)]
> Seueri Pii Pert(inacis) Aug(usti) et M(arci) Aurel[i]
> Antonin(i) Aug(usti) Aug(usti) n(ostri) f(ili) et P(ubli)
> S[eptimi Getae] Aug(usti) Aug(usti)
> n(ostri) fil(i) Aug(usti) n(ostri) fratr(is) et Iuliae
> Aug(ustae) matr(is) castr(orum) M(arcus) Caninius
> Adiutor Faustinianus praef(ectus)
> coh(ortis) II H(a)m(iorum) praep(ositus) vex(illationi) le[g(ionis)]
> [III] Aug(ustae) p(iae) u(indicis) aram po[su]
> it et dedicauit

This inscription evidently belongs to the period between the proclamation of Caracalla as Augustus (198) and the death of Septimius Severus (211). The fact that Geta is also described as Augustus cannot be pressed;[22] and it is to be noted that in line 3 the abbreviation is IMPP, rather than IMPPP. The cohort represented by the abbreviations COH II HM (possibly THM) cannot readily be identified. *Hamiorum* is proposed here, as this cohort is known from an inscription in Algeria.[23] Finally, it must be noted that the obliteration of the [number] of the legion, if deliberate, results from the disbandment of that legion in 238; but the damage to the stone may be accidental. M. Caninius Adiutor Faustinianus is not known from any other source, and the cohort which he commanded is presumably one of the units sent to the Numidian frontier from Syria by Septimius Severus.[24]

The presence of a detachment of III Augusta at Ain Wif during the reign of Septimius Severus indicates that the site played some part in the Severan reorganisation of the frontier zone, and this is confirmed by the discovery, amidst the ruins of a substantial bath-building close to the springs, of an inscription recording the repair of the baths by a *centurio princeps*. The inscription (pl. 9) cut in letters of 2·5 cm. on a block of yellow sandstone, is now in Tripoli Museum. It reads [*IRT* 869]

> M(arcus) Coeli[us . . . *16 letters* . . .]
> ninus [. . . *12 letters* . . .]
> balneum u[etustate corrup]
> tum restituendum [curauit]
> eidem assam cellam a so[lo]
> fecit et cylisterium institu
> it curante Iunio Sucesso
> c(enturione) principe

Although *ninus* in line 2 is preceded by an ivy-leaf, this feature may be purely decorative, and the rare cognomen Ninus need not necessarily be accepted; it is unfortunate that the remaining twelve letters of the second line are missing, as these might have given the rank and unit of M. Coelius . . . ninus. It is evident from the text that this individual, very probably himself the *praepositus* of a vexillation, repaired the existing bath-house and constructed anew an *assa cella* or sweating-room, and an unidentifiable feature named a *cylisterium*.[25] The significant fact is that the bath-house had been in use long enough to require repair, whence we may suppose that a garrison remained at Ain Wif for some considerable time. Without the excavation of the bath-house the date of this inscription, and of the initial construction of the building cannot be determined, although a date not later than the third century would appear the most probable. A fragment of a third inscription, in which only the letters . . . NOS . . . (*IRT* 870) are legible was also found in 1948 on the hillside between the main settlement and the bath-house.

From these inscriptions the military character of the occupation at Ain Wif is evident, but that the site must be considered as a road-station rather than a *Limes* outpost is indicated by its lack of defences. The road itself which, like all Roman roads in Tripolitania, must have been an unpaved track, has left no certain traces of its course in the vicinity of Ain Wif, but there can be little doubt that it is the road described in the *Antonine Itinerary* as linking Lepcis with Turris Tamalleni. This road can be traced from Lepcis to the area of Tarhuna, via Cussabat, by means of several Roman milestones found along its line. The first road-station, named Mesphe in the *Itinerary* and placed at 40 Roman miles from Lepcis, can be recognised in the extensive site named Medina Doga, close to the well-known mausoleum of Gasr Doga (fig. 3).[26] From Medina Doga to Ain Wif, following the line of the traditional caravan route, the distance is approximately 45 km., which tallies with the distance of 30 Roman miles from Mesphe to Thenadassa, as given in the *Itinerary*. Despite the lack of milestone evidence between Tarhuna and Ain Wif, we need not hesitate to identify the latter site as Thenadassa.[27] This identification shows clearly that the Gebel road ran on the seaward side of the Garian massif, which separates the escarpment from the Sofeggin basin. Only by occupying this massif and establishing outposts which would control the Sofeggin area could the Gebel, with its rich olive plantations, be militarily secure; and that this policy was carried out is attested by the presence at Bir Tarsin, some 60 km. to the south of Ain Wif, of an inscription of Septimius Severus,[28] by traces of a fortified road in the Upper Sofeggin basin, belonging to the period of Caracalla and his successors (pp. 28 ff.); and by the widespread establishment east of Mizda of *limitanei* settlements having their origins very probably in the third century A.D. (pp. 29 ff.).

GASR DUIB AND THE UPPER SOFEGGIN *Limes* (*Limes Tentheitanus*)

A Roman road, not shown in any Itinerary but documented by milestones, branched from the Gebel road in the area of Giado or Zintan (its point of departure is still uncertain) and ran south-eastwards, following the depression of the Upper Sofeggin to Mizda, where it met the important highway from Oea to the Fezzan. In 1904, several years before Roman milestones were first discovered on this route, de Mathuisieulx examined a small Roman fort named Gasr Uames, some 10 km. west of Bir Sceghega, and correctly identified it as an outpost on a Roman road from Zintan to Mizda: it stands, in fact, beside this road, as the milestones show.[29] The French explorer erred, however, in asserting that Gasr Uames was the only ancient building in the region of the Upper Sofeggin. Twenty-five km. to the west of Uames and 40 km. south of Zintan lies Gasr Duib, a building of precisely the same character. Gasr Duib was visited by F. Coró

GASR DUIB (SANIET DUIB)
GROUND FLOOR

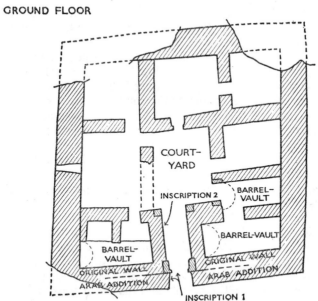

FIRST FLOOR

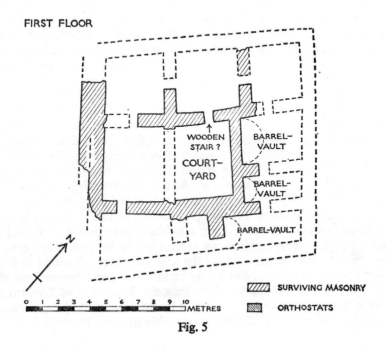

SURVIVING MASONRY

ORTHOSTATS

0 1 2 3 4 5 6 7 8 9 10 METRES

Fig. 5

during the early years of the Italian occupation; but the first report of Roman inscriptions on the site was received in 1948 by the Antiquities Department of the British Administration in Tripolitania; and in August, 1948, the writers were able to visit this remote ruin.

Gasr Duib stands on a small, detached hillock beside the Wadi Duib, a right-bank tributary of the Sofeggin. Beside it lies Saniet Duib, an important water-point for the nomadic tribesmen who keep their herds in this desolate area of the upper Sofeggin.[30] The building is a typical "gasr",[31] a square, tower-like structure, standing in a commanding position on a low knoll (pl. 11). The plan (fig. 5) is simple and consists of a series of rooms grouped about a small central courtyard, with a single entrance in the middle of the south-east face. A sufficient part of the upper storey remains to show that it followed the same general lines as the ground floor, except that here the rooms were disposed in a circuit, with access to the courtyard by a single door in the side facing the entrance. This no doubt opened on to a wooden staircase, a feature which can be traced in many of the *gsur* of central Tripolitania. There are indications of a tower rising clear of the upper storey over the entrance corridor: this is also paralleled at Gasr Uames and other similar sites.

Although the main lines of the building are those of the original structure, it has been considerably modified in detail at many points by later occupants; and without clearance of fallen debris and a thorough structural survey, it is not in all cases possible to distinguish the exact form of the earlier work. It is clear, however, that from the outset some of the rooms were vaulted, while in others the ceiling was carried on timber beams; and that in at least one instance, over the entrance corridor, the original timbering has been replaced in Arab times by the vaulting visible in plates 11 and 12. The tendency to substitute vaulting for timber is characteristic of "gasr" architecture in Tripolitania, and it is no doubt to be attributed to the increasing difficulty of obtaining suitable timber. The outer walls, too, show signs of later modification; but here the evidence is more confused. The south-west side, the best preserved, appears to be Roman work throughout, save for a short stretch of very late work at the north-west end, built after the west corner had already fallen. There is at one point a vertical joint in the thickness of the wall (pl. 11 and fig. 5); but either this is a structural feature or it represents a modification in Roman times; for the masonry on both faces is characteristically Roman, and there is no trace of any alteration or strengthening in the section exposed by the collapse of the west corner. The south-east face, on the other hand, was certainly strengthened in Islamic times. As can be seen in plate 12, the Roman door, of which the left half only is original, is now set back behind some 80 cm. of buttressing masonry, into the left jamb of which is built the broken right half of the original entrance inscription (pl. 13): the left half of the inscription is still *in situ*. A second inscription, set in a similar frame, but now largely illegible, is built into the left wall of the corridor within the doorway. It is not clear whether the later buttressing along this face was everywhere as thick; for the original outer wall would in that case have been surprisingly flimsy, and it may be that the actual doorway was slightly recessed. Both from the character of the masonry, however, and from the stucco cable-ornament on the associated vaults, it is certain that the present outer face is entirely of Arab date. Of the masonry visible in plate 12, only the left-hand part of the inner, original door, and the coursed walling in the upper background are Roman work.

The Roman masonry was of the simplest. The jambs at either end of the entrance corridor, and of one of the doors opening off the courtyard, consist of single, squared limestone orthostats; and in addition to the entrance, with its monumental inscription over the doorway, the corresponding doorway opening into the courtyard consists of an arch of carefully dressed voussoirs springing from a simple projecting moulding. With these exceptions, however, the building has few architectural pretensions. The walls are built throughout of rubble set in mud-plaster, with a facing of roughly squared limestone blocks. These blocks, which average 15–18 cm. in height and 18–25 cm. in length, are laid in courses, here and there packed with chips or interspersed with larger blocks to achieve regularity. Near the west angle, where the footings of the outer wall are exposed, these can be seen to rest upon two courses of massive limestone blocks, very roughly dressed and together rather over a metre in height. Of the outer angles one only, to the east, is preserved, and that is now buried in rubble; but enough is visible to show that the quoins, if any, were of very modest dimensions. Of the doors, some have a flat lintel, others are arched with small, roughly-shaped voussoirs.

By any architectural standards it is a work of modest quality. The wall-surface has nothing to tie it into the core; and the bond at the wall junctions is haphazard in the extreme: indeed, the normal practice is to butt the one wall face against the other, bonding only the core, and in the event of settlement it is usually the angles that are the first to go. These building methods, however rough though they be, possessed also certain obvious advantages: the materials were to hand, and they required the minimum of skilled labour; and judged by the practical test of survival, it must be admitted that it was an architecture adequate for its purpose. In a country with a scanty rainfall and free from serious earthquakes it is common enough to find the mud-and-rubble core of one of these walls standing long after the collapse of its dressed faces; and buildings of the same materials and workmanship can, in the pre-desert areas, be seen standing two, even three, storeys high, 1,500 years from the day they were built.

Of three inscriptions found in the "gasr", one, now walled into the left-hand wall of the corridor within the entrance, could not be read owing to its mutilated state and the short time available. Another, now in Tripoli Museum, is a mere fragment, the sense of which is obscure [*IRT* 882]. The third, however, the original entrance inscription of the building, despite deliberate and accidental mutilation, is still substantially legible [*IRT* 880]. It is inscribed in a panel (pl. 13) which originally measured 0·96 m. by 0·39 m. but is now, as described above, broken into two halves. The letters, 4–5 cm. high with many ligatures, are clearly cut, but worn and pitted in parts. It reads:

Imp(erator) Caes(ar) [M(*arcus*) *Iulius Ph*]*ilippus* inuictu[s Aug(ustus)]
et M(*arcus*) *Iul*(*ius*) P[*hilippus* Ca]es(ar) n(oster) regionem limi[tis Ten]
theitani partitam et [eius] uiam incursib(us) barba[ro]
rum constituto nouo centenario [/////?////]
//A/S prae[cl]useru[nt] Cominio Cassiano leg(ato) Augg(ustorum)
pr(o) pr(aetore) Gallican[o...7 *letters*...] u(iro) e(gregio) praep(osito)
    limitis cura
Numisii Maximi domo [... 4 *letters*...]sia trib(uni)

Despite its mutilated state the date and the sense of this inscription are sufficiently clear. The AUGG in line 5 is evidently an error of a type commonly
found, since Philip junior was still Caesar: the date of the inscription must be
244–6. By the erection of this new *centenarium*, the topographical name of which
is unfortunately obliterated,[32] the Emperor and his son closed (*praecluserunt*),
it seems, the region of the *Limes* [*Ten*]*theitanus* and its road to barbarian
invasions. The *Limes* region is further defined as *partitam*, a reference presumably to the splitting up of the Tripolitanian sector of the Numidian *Limes* into
a series of local zones, of which the *Limes* [*Ten*]*theitanus* was one. Although
the first three letters of this place-name are missing, the restoration seems certain:
Tentheos (recorded in the *Antonine Itinerary* as Thenteos) was a road-station in
the area of Zintan, the exact site of which remains unknown: the form *Limes
Tentheitanus* or *Tenthettanus* is found in the *Notitia Dignitatum*, and—as the
Gasr Duib inscription shows—is apparently the correct one. It has been claimed
that the modern topographical and tribal name Zintan is a survival of the ancient
name.[33]

It is no surprise to find a "legatus Augustorum pro praetore" still in charge of
the Numidian frontier after the disbandment of III Augusta in 238; for Momm-
sen's hypothesis that Numidia was, as a result of this event, reduced to the status
of a procuratorial province has been disproved by discoveries in French North
Africa.[34] It is, however, a little disconcerting to find that the Legatus in 244–6
was named Cominius Cassianus; for the M. Aurelius Cominius Cassianus recorded in inscriptions at Lambaesis has been dated to the year 208. Unless there
has been an error in the reading of the consular names on the significant
Lambaesis inscription, we can only conclude that the Cominius Cassianus of
the Gasr Duib inscription was a son or relative of the earlier Legatus.[35] Of
Gallicanus, the *praepositus,* and Numisius Maximus nothing is known, and it is
only curious that a *centenarium* should have been constructed not, as one might
expect, by a *centenarius,* but by a *tribunus.* The researches of Leschi and others
have already established that the name *centenarium* applied to a small *limes*
outpost, frequently encountered in Roman Africa, derives from the rank of its
commander; and that a *centenarius* was the equivalent, in a static and territorial
force, of a centurion.[36] The significance of the Gasr Duib inscription is that it
shows not only *praepositi limitis,* but *centenaria* (and, by inference, military
centenarii) in existence much earlier than was previously suspected. It is now
apparent that the late *Limes* organisation shown in the *Notitia Dignitatum* as
under the command of a "dux provinciae Tripolitanae" is substantially the same
as the organisation which existed under a "legatus Augusti pro praetore" shortly
after the disbandment of III Augusta, a century-and-a-half earlier. In the eight
years which elapsed between the disbandment of the legion and the construction
of Gasr Duib the Roman staff had already worked out and set into operation a
plan of decentralisation which replaced scattered detachments of III Augusta
by a system of local zones, each under its *praepositus,* defended mainly by
limitanei. That the new order of battle survived until the end of Roman rule in
Tripolitania is sufficient indication of its adaptability.

The *Limes Tentheitanus,* which the new *centenarium* served to protect, must be
the region of the Upper Sofeggin; and Gasr Duib takes its place as a defended
post, one of several, on the military road which linked the Gebel escarpment on
the north-west with the frontier zones of the main Sofeggin and Zemzem basins.

Some 25 km. to the east on the same road lay Gasr Uames; and 40 km. again beyond Gasr Uames, at Mizda, the upper Sofeggin road joined the central road from Oea (Tripoli) to the Fezzan. Here, at Mizda, buried beneath one of the twin Berber villages, it is reasonable to suppose that there was in Roman times a military post of some importance, but of this no trace is now visible above ground. Thanks to the peculiar geography of the frontier zone, the forts on the upper Sofeggin road may be held to have served a double function. They were defensive posts on the fringe of the Romanised area of Tripolitania, limes outposts in the strictest sense; and at the same time they were links in the chain of military roads which served the related, but more complex, defensive system which lay beyond Mizda to the south and east.

THE Limes ZONE BETWEEN MIZDA AND THE SEBCHA TAUORGA

East of Mizda we no longer find the evidence of milestones to indicate Roman roads not listed in the Itineraries; nor have we, except at Bir Tarsin (above p. 24), inscriptions of an official and military character. Yet fortified buildings of substantially the same character as Gasr Duib and Gasr Uames are to be found scattered through the whole basin of the Sofeggin and in several areas of the Zemzem. These buildings do not stand isolated in grim and barren areas, as do the Upper Sofeggin outposts: they are found in chains along the banks of the more fertile wadis, and sometimes grouped together as embryonic villages at the junction of several tributary wadis.[37] Their density varies according to the size and fertility of the wadi beside which they stand: sometimes we find a long series scattered at intervals of only 1 km. but more often the interval is considerably greater. Many of the buildings are accompanied by elaborate and well-built mausolea, which contrast vividly with the austere simplicity of the "gsur" themselves; and they are invariably associated with a complex system of terrace walls across the width of the wadi, and with catchment channels and cisterns.

The fact that these buildings are structurally indistinguishable from the official "centenaria" of the Upper Sofeggin leads one to conclude that their primary function was similar; but the associated tombs and the extensive agricultural installations reveal that we are dealing not merely with a series of military outposts, but with a widespread and uniform structure of society. We enter, in fact, once we move eastward of Mizda, an area of limitanei settlements which in their extent, uniformity of pattern, and degree of preservation are perhaps unique in the Roman world. Their main area extends for some 200 km. east to west, and for 150 km. north to south, the bed of the Zemzem representing approximately their southern boundary. The outer fortress at Gheria el-Garbia marks the southwestern corner of the zone of settlement, whereas the equivalent fortress at Bu Ngem lies rather to the south of the zone which, meeting the coast, then becomes a narrow strip running eastwards along the shores of the Syrtis.

The earliest date of these settlements cannot easily be determined, but it is significant that the inscriptions so far discovered in the "gsur" and their mausolea are, with one possible exception, no earlier than the third century.[38] The great majority of the "gsur" are of the same type of construction as that of Gasr Duib, though many of them show more care in the trimming and coursing of the blocks in their wall faces (cf. the example near Bir Scedeua, pl. 15).[39] The rectangular plan, with central courtyard, is normal, and the presence of one or more upper storeys and a tower over the single entrance doorway is attested in many cases. Three of them, Gasr Banat in the Wadi Nfed, Gasr Faschia in the Wadi Zemzem, and Gasr Gheria esc-Scergia, are "gasr"-type buildings which, while conforming to the general pattern, have exterior walls built of large, carefully cut ashlar blocks; and that these three buildings (all of which have distinctively inset rounded corners nowhere else encountered)[40] represent an early, official stage of "gasr" construction, can hardly be doubted. Moreover, as the "gasr" of this early type at Gheria esc-Scergia lies within the range of the fortress [completed by] Severus Alexander at Gheria el-Garbia, we may tentatively date these three buildings to Alexander's reign (222–35), thus providing a *terminus post quem* for the settlement of this region. This dating, hypothetical as it is, receives historical confirmation from the biography of Alexander in the *Augustan History* in which we find described the Emperor's policy of *limitanei* settlement in frontier areas[41] and it may well prove to be applicable to the whole of the Sofeggin and Zemzem basins east and south of Mizda.

These earliest fortified farmhouses were clearly designed and constructed by Roman military architects, as one would expect in the initial stages of such a programme of settlement. The later "gsur" are generally the work of indigenous hands following the approved model, as is shown by the Libyan inscriptions (in Latin characters) frequently found in monumental *tabellae ansatae* above their doorways. One such inscription from a "gasr" at Shemek is of interest as containing in its Libyan text—not yet intelligible—the word CENTEINARI.[42] Whether this refers to the building as a *centenarium*, or to its occupant as a *centenarius*, is immaterial: it shows, at least, that in the mind of its Libyan constructor the "gasr" was no less a part of the *Limes Tripolitanus* than, for example, the official *centenarium* at Gsar Duib.

From the reliefs carved on the mausolea, and especially those at Ghirza, we can obtain a vivid picture of the daily life of these *limitanei*. Horses and camels are portrayed ploughing the wadis, corn and vines are being harvested, the master of the estate (no doubt the *centenarius* himself) sits in a camp-chair directing the operations of his servants and labourers. Reliefs of palm trees show that date cultivation was possible in some of the more favoured wadis; but the olive does not seem to be depicted and the olive-presses found so frequently in the Fergiani area of the Tarhuna plateau and in other Gebel areas very rarely appear among the ruins of the wadi farmhouses. Hunting scenes are particularly common, and in one Ghirza relief a *limitaneus* is portrayed spearing a naked victim (fig. 6) whose features so closely approximate to those of the Garamantes in the amphitheatre scene in the well-known Zliten mosaics that we can hardly doubt his racial origin.[43] Such military scenes are rare, a fact which indicates the general peacefulness of these wadis for some time after the initial settlements, but also rather ominously foreshadows the increasing absorption of the *limitanei* in their agricultural activities.

How the *limitanei* settlements of this vast zone fitted into the general pattern of the official defensive scheme is obscure. At first, no doubt, each farmer-soldier was recognised as a *centenarius* or *tribunus* (in a local sense bearing no rigid relationship to the official meaning of these ranks outside the zone of settlement[44]) and was responsible to the *praepositus* of the zone of the *Limes* in which his fortified home was situated. Such zones would have consisted of groups of wadis with good internal communications; but it is impossible, in the present state of knowledge, to identify the zone names which appear in the *Notitia* with the actual physical features of the area. The prosperity brought to these wadis by systematic methods of cultivation led, however, to an increase of population which must have complicated rather than simplified the defensive arrangements, and there are clear traces—in the form of clusters of crude huts around individual "gsur"— of an incipient feudalism. This tendency, together with the economic self-sufficiency of the settlements, was in the long run bound to be inimical to the purpose for which the policy was first conceived. Good harvests and full grain-stores coupled with the isolation of the settlements must have led first to a feeling of independence, and then to a sense of indifference towards the fate of the coastal cities. The great invasions of 363 in which Sabratha was destroyed and Lepcis

Fig. 6 Ghirza: funerary relief showing a *limitaneus* spearing a naked victim

sorely threatened could scarcely have occurred without neglect, or even con-nivance, on the part of the *limitanei*.[45] After the Vandal occupation of the coast the final link with Rome was irrevocably broken, and it is hardly surprising that in the *Johannis* of Corippus we find the Byzantine generals fighting peoples whose homes were in the former *Limes* areas, and that the names of some of the tribal leaders listed by Corippus as the most redoubtable enemies are to be found, at an earlier period, on the tombs of the *limitanei*.[46]

As a social organisation, however, the *Limes Tripolitanus* outlived Roman and Byzantine Africa. The climatic conditions which had made possible the first *limitanei* settlements, and which had brought prosperity and expansion to these settlements, continued long after the coastal civilisation had fallen into decay. Many of the "gsur" yield traces of early Islamic occupation in the form of cable-work ornamentation and Arabic inscriptions, rendered in stucco in the vaults of the building: others were evidently constructed in the same period. These facts seem to indicate that static farming continued in many of the wadis long after the first Arab invasions and the conversion of the wadi inhabitants to Islam. Yet an increasing deterioration in the climatic conditions, coupled with a neglect of the natural and artificial resources which had brought this form of farming to success, eventually made sedentary agriculture no longer possible in the more arid areas.[47] The population, still predominantly Berber, either reverted to nomadism—its form of life long before Roman frontier policy had revealed the virtues and rewards of static farming—or concentrated in the most favoured wadis in impoverished villages, each clustered around a central "gasr". The twenty-kilometre length of the Wadi Beni Ulid, in the Orfella region, with its villages spaced evenly on either side of a terraced and planted wadi bed, is today a living survival of the *Limes Tripolitanus* as a social and economic phenomenon.

NOTES

1. R. Cagnat, *Mém. Acad. Inscr.* xxxix (1914) 77, incorporated verbatim in the same author's *L'Armée romaine de l'Afrique*, 524–68. Subsequent references are to this edition. See also A. Merlin, *CRAI* 1921, 236-48.

2. For the ancient topography of the coast of the Greater Syrtis see L. Cerrata. Cerrata's identifications of the Roman road-stations are to be treated with reserve.

3. de Mathuisieulx, x 245–77; xii 1–80; and xiii 73–102.
[3a see below, p. 79 f.].

4. For this road see P. Romanelli, (1), 110, where a military character is postulated; and R. Goodchild, *Roman Roads*, 11–13, where the economic significance of the route is stressed.

5. *IRT* 854.

6. Cagnat-Merlin, 30.

7. *CIL* viii 11048 (Gasr Ghelan) and Cagnat-Merlin, 26 (Sidi Mohammed ben Aissa).

8. *SHA Severus* 18, 3; Aur. Victor, *Caes.* xx, 19. For the general frontier policy of Severus in Africa cf. G. Ch. Picard, *Castellum Dimmidi* (Alger-Paris, 1946) 55–6.

9. J. Guey, 243.

10. ed. Cuntz, 11. For the identification of Vezereos, cf. Merlin, *loc. cit.*

11. Cagnat, 531. [For subsequent discussion of identifications see the summary by N. Hammond, *JAA* xxx (1967) 1 f.]

12. *Not. Dign.* (ed. Seeck), 186–7 (*Occ.* xxxi). The four sectors of the Tripolitanian *Limes*, which occur both in the *Notitia* and the *Itinerary* are as follows: Talatensis (=Talalati); Tentheitani (=Thenteos);

Bizeretani (=Vezereos); and Tillibarensis (=Tillibari).

13. *CIL* viii 22763 (Tibubuci); *IRT* 565 (Lepcis).

14. Diehl, *L'Afrique byzantine* (1896), 228–30, argued effectively from the evidence of Corippus and from other literary indications against a Byzantine occupation of the interior of Tripolitania. No structures of official character and post-Justinian date have yet been identified in the interior.

15. Cagnat, 553–7, where the plan of the fortress of Bu Ngem is inaccurate in detail; and R. Bartoccini, *Afri. Ital.* ii (1928–9), 50–8. [See also below, p. 46 f.]

16. Cagnat, 546. Extensive stretches of "fossata" have also recently been discovered in Algeria, cf. L. Leschi, *Rev. africaine*, nos. 412–3 (1947), 201–12; but their purpose and relationship to the *limes* are still far from clear. See, however, Baradez, *passim*.

17. On the accompanying map (fig. 3) are indicated the differing types of "desert" which lay outside the *Limes Tripolitanus*. It will be seen that the Roman outposts avoided the completely sterile areas of the Grand Erg and the Hammada el-Hamra.

18. *Roman Roads* 11–13 (inscriptions 12–13).

19. *ibid.* 14–20 (Central Road), and 21–3 (Upper Sofeggin road).

20. This church and others recently discovered and surveyed in Tripolitania were published in a separate paper [*Archaeologia* xcv (1953) 44].

21. The altar was first seen in 1925 by Tenente M. Orano. Prof. R. Bartoccini, formerly Superintendent of Antiquities in Tripolitania, courteously communicated the

report to the British School at Rome, and the site was investigated by the writers in 1948. The survey (fig. 4) was carried out by members of the BSR Sabratha expedition, under the direction of Mr. A. Wells.

22. On Severan inscriptions from Bu Ngem (*IRT* 913–15) Geta is similarly described as Augustus while still in fact only Caesar.

23. We owe this suggestion to Mr. Eric Birley, who refers us to Gsell, *Inscr. latines de l'Algérie* 3675. There are difficulties in accepting an alternative reading H(e)m-(esenorum).

24. J. Carcopino, *Syria*, 1925, 30–57 and 118–49; 1933, 20–55.

25. *Cylisterium,* not otherwise recorded in epigraphy, is presumably derived from the Greek κυλιστήριον, a place in which one rolls. Its exact significance in the context of the Ain Wif bath-house is obscure.

26. The road-station at Medina Doga lies precisely at the 42nd Roman mile from Lepcis: it is slightly larger than Ain Wif, but of the same general character. Surveyed in 1949. [A Severan inscription and military tiles subsequently found at El-Auenia west of Jefren, must indicate another road station, see O. Brogan and J. Reynolds, *PBSR* xxvii (1960) 51 f. and J. Reynolds and G. Simpson, *Libya Antiqua* iii–iv (1966–7) 45 f.]

27. Gasr Anessa (or Hanesh), equated by de Mathuisieulx with Thenadassa, lies near Uestata and appears to be of early Islamic date: the distances do not accord with those of the *Itinerary.*

28. *IRT* 887, reported in 1925, but the full text is still to be recorded. A dedication to the Emperor at this remote site is almost certain to be military in character. Attempts to retrace this inscription in 1949 were unsuccessful.

29. de Mathuisieulx, xiii, 73–102. For the Roman milestones (Caracalla and Maximinus), first observed by Coró, cf. *Roman Roads* 21–3.

30. We are indebted to A/Supt. J. Colman, of the Tripolitania Police, for drawing our attention to the inscriptions at Gasr Duib. The site is mentioned briefly by Coró in *Atti del II Congresso di Studi Coloniali* ii (1935), 69–75.

31. The name "gasr" (plural "gsur") is applied locally in Tripolitania to any castle-like building, whether it be a Roman mausoleum or a Turkish fort. As the great majority of the "gsur" in the southern area are fortified dwellings of the Roman period, uniform in plan and constructional technique, we use the word in this paper to denote these buildings.

32. The obliteration of the name following *centenario* appears to be intentional, and may indicate that the outpost was named after a member of the imperial house.

33. de Mathuisieulx, xii, 13–14. Although the inscription appears to confirm the identification of Zintan with *Thenteos*, it must be noted that the tribal name Zintani occurs as far south as Mizda.

34. Carcopino, *Syria* 1925, 31.

35. *PIR²C* 1265. Cf. *CIL* viii, 2611. [See now E. Birley, *JRS* xl (1950) 60 f.]

36. L. Leschi, *CRAI* 1941, 163–76, and *Rev. africaine,* nos. 394–5 (1943); R. Goodchild, "Tripolitanian Inscriptions" 32–4.

37. Small groups of this type occur at Gasr es-Suq el-Oti in the Wadi Bosra, Faschiet el-Habs in the Wadi Merdum, and Gasr Chanafes in the Wadi Scetaf. The extensive site at Ghirza in the Wadi Zemzem, best known for its elaborate mausolea, is a group of some thirty "gsur" set close together without communal planning or defences: it is, in fact, a *reductio ad absurdum* of the whole "gasr" system.

38. None is precisely dated, but the palaeography affords a clear *terminus post quem.* The only inscription in the frontier zone which might be earlier than the third century is from a small temple at Tininai, between Mizda and Beni Ulid (*IRT* 888). The Ammonium at Tarhuna (above p. 18, 79 ff.) shows, however, that the construction of Romanised sanctuaries for the deities of the Libyan tribesmen was undertaken long before extensive *limitanei* settlements were planned. [See now G. Levi Della Vida "Le iscrizioni neopuniche di Wadi El-Amud", *Libya Antiqua* i (1964) 57–63].

39. Plate 15 illustrates a well-built and exceptionally well-preserved "gasr" at the junction of the Wadis Dreder and Sofeggin, near Bir Scedeua, on the road from Beni Ulid to Mizda. Other "gsur" of similar construction exist in the same area and would appear to belong to a relatively early phase in the settlement of *limitanei.*

40. Angle-moulding of the "gasr" at Gheria esc-Scergia illustrated in P. Romanelli, (2).

41. *SHA, Sev. Alex.* lviii, 2. *Cod. Theod.* vii. 15 1, contains a rescript of Honorius and Theodosius II addressed to the *Vicarius* of Africa ordering the ejection of tenants of *limitaneus* land who do not observe their military obligations.

42. *IRT* 889. The word *centenare* also occurs in an inscription of the same type from the Breviglieri area of Tarhuna (*IRT* 875).

43. The Ghirza reliefs are illustrated, in part, by de Mathuisieulx, xii, pl. vi–xiv, and by Bauer, *Afr. Ital.* vi (1935) 61–78, figs. 2–14. A complete and definite illustration of these important documents of *limitaneus* life, which have suffered injury and dispersal during the last century, is [in preparation by Olwen Brogan and David Smith; for an interim report see *JRS* xlvii (1957) 173 f.].

44. The title *tribunus* occurs frequently in Latino-Libyan inscriptions from Africa (cf. *IRT* 886; Chabot, 85, 145, 252). Further examples have been discovered during 1949 in a Romano-Libyan cemetery at Bir ed-Dreder [see below, p. 59 f.]

45. Ammianus, *Hist. XXVIII*, 6. [By 1967 Goodchild had accepted the case made by A. di Vita in *Libya Antiqua* i (1964) 134 f. that the destruction at Sabratha was more probably due to earthquake than to barbarian assault.]

46. Corippus, *Johannis* ii, 80, mentions the former *Limes* station Tillibari; and the names Macurasen (iv, 955) and Cullen (iv, 791, 961), both of which seem to appear on the Ghirza mausolea (*IRT* 898).

47. The problem of climatic changes in the interior of Tripolitania is too complex to be discussed here. The writers would merely place on record their opinion that there has been, in historic times, a small but significant reduction of rainfall.

3

THE *LIMES TRIPOLITANUS* II

[From *JRS* xl (1950)]
(Plates 16–21)

In a previous article in this *Journal*[1] the writer and Mr. J. B. Ward Perkins gave a summary historical and archaeological sketch of the Roman *Limes* in Tripolitania, illustrated by the two sites, Ain Wif and Gasr Duib, investigated in 1948. Further evidence of the character of this *Limes* was obtained in the summer of 1949 when air and ground reconnaissances were made over a considerable area of the frontier zone, with the aid of the Royal Air Force and of the military authorities in Tripolitania.[2] Since this new information relates particularly to the indigenous elements in the Tripolitanian frontier army, and to the types of fortified homesteads occupied by the *limitanei*—aspects which were referred to very briefly in the former article—it has seemed desirable to incorporate it in a supplementary paper, preceded by a note on the historical *regio Arzugum*, which is evidently to be identified, at least in part, with the Tripolitanian frontier zone.

THE *Regio Arzugum*

Orosius,[3] describing the various parts of Roman Africa, gives the boundaries of "Tripolitana provincia quae et Subventana vel regio Arzugum dicitur, ubi Leptis Magna civitas est, quamvis Arzuges per longum Africae limitem vocentur". Although Orosius includes the *regio Arzugum* in the Tripolitan province, the records of the early church councils show that the Arzuges or Arzugitani were considered, from an ecclesiastical viewpoint, as distinct from the Tripolitani. At the Council of Carthage in 397 the primate, Aurelius, drew attention to the fact that the Arzugitan bishops could not be expected to participate in the elections for the Tripolitan sees, as barbarian tribes lay between the two areas. At the same Council he excused himself from visiting the Mauretanian churches on the grounds that if he complied with this request the Tripolitan and Arzugitan churches might expect similar visits. Romanelli[4] has suggested, with great probability, that the barbarian invasions had the effect of making the Arzugitan Christians keep in closer touch with Byzacium than with the coast of the Tripolis. A letter of 419 is in fact addressed jointly "episcopis provinciarum Byzacenae et Arzugitanae".

That the *regio Arzugum* lay rather to the south of the coastal areas is also attested by a letter of St. Augustine[5] who, referring to contemporary schisms, pointed out that the Arzuges might have a stronger claim than the people of Byzacium and the Tripolis to being the southernmost Christian community in

Africa. Two other letters in the correspondence of St. Augustine refer specifically
to the existence of a Roman frontier organisation in the territory of the Arzuges:
the significance of these letters will be discussed later. Despite the slight ambiguity
implied by the phrase "quamvis Arzuges per longum Africae limitem vocentur",
there can be little doubt that Romanelli is right in placing the *regio Arzugum* in the
area of the *Limes Tripolitanus*, although by accepting the old interpretation of
the *Limes* as a line of forts along the Gebel crest, he has greatly underestimated
the extent of this *regio*.[6] It may therefore be accepted that Subventana and *regio
Arzugum* were not, as the text of Orosius might imply, alternative names for the
whole *provincia Tripolitana*: they were rather the two basic areas into which the
province was divided. Subventana was, as a later passage in Orosius[7] confirms,
the coastal region of the province, with its large cities and civil administration;
Arzugitana, or *regio Arzugum*, was the interior plateau with its essentially
military organisation, but with a sufficiently large and static population of
Christian *limitanei* to justify its status as an ecclesiastical area. Since these two
areas, elsewhere separated by the plains of the Gefara, meet in the vicinity of
Lepcis Magna, Orosius was correct in associating that city with both zones.
Whether this division was an official one is more obscure: it is certain, at least
from the evidence of the *Notitia Dignitatum*, that for military purposes the
provincia Tripolitana was a single entity.[8] Yet the entirely different administrative
problems of the fully Romanised coast with its large cities and villas, and of the
interior with its scattered fortified homesteads, may have necessitated a political
division which is reflected in the ecclesiastical organisation.

In the correspondence of St. Augustine there are two letters,[9] previously
referred to, which throw some light on everyday life in the *regio Arzugum*. In
398 a certain Publicola wrote that he had heard that it was customary, among
the Arzuges, for barbarians to take a pagan oath in the presence of the
"decurion"[10] or tribune in charge of the frontier whenever they entered the
territory under engagement to act as crop-watchers or as porters. The acceptance
of such an oath troubled Publicola's Christian conscience; but St. Augustine
wisely pointed out that "it was worse to swear falsely by the true God than to
swear truly by false gods" and reminded Publicola that "not only on the frontier
but throughout all the provinces the security of peace rests upon barbarian
oaths."

This glimpse of frontier life is instructive: it reminds us that the function of
the *Limes* and of its garrisons was not solely to stand ready for large-scale
barbarian invasions, but also to exercise an effective control over the movements
of individual barbarians who, for one reason or another, wished to enter the
frontier zone. These barbarians may have belonged to the Gaetuli, Nathabres or
Garamantes who are recorded by Orosius as lying beyond the southern limits
of the Tripolitan province: the Arzuges themselves, many of them already
Christian by the end of the fourth century, and serving as *limitanei* in the frontier
zone, were not apparently classed as barbarians. The Decree of Anastasius,[11]
relating to the military defences of the Cyrenaican Pentapolis, where frontier
problems were very similar to those in Tripolitania, shows that the movement
of "Romans" into the territory of the barbarians was equally rigorously controlled. It is no less clear from the writings of Synesius[12] that considerable damage
and confusion was caused by quite small bands of barbarian marauders. Control
of individual movement was the best method of preventing the ingress of these

bands; and it is to the credit of Libyan paganism that an oath of loyalty seems to have sufficed to distinguish the bona-fide labourer from the intending bandit.

Despite the abundance of reference to the Arzuges in later literature, their ethnological origins remain obscure. Bates[13] has suggested that they may be related to the Astacures of Ptolemy and to the Aus(t)uriani of Ammianus and Synesius. The geographical position of the Astacures certainly coincides with that of the Arzuges; but the Aus(t)uriani should more probably be identified as migrants from the desert of the Syrtica, since they appear as invaders both of the Tripolis and Pentapolis. Our final glimpse of the Arzuges appears in Corippus[14] where the epic poet, describing the opponents of the Byzantine occupation and their geographical background, writes "nutrit quos horrida tellus Arzugis infandae". "Horrida tellus" is an apt description of the bleak wastes of the Sofeggin and Zemzem basins which, for the reasons given above, may be considered to have formed part of the regio Arzugum.

THE Tribuni OF BIR ED-DREDER

Bir ed-Dreder is a group of wells lying in the bed of the Wadi Dreder (a southern tributary of the Sofeggin) some 50 km. south-east of Mizda. The existence of ancient inscriptions on this site has been known for some years,[15] but until the summer of 1949 there had been no systematic investigation. On examination the site at Bir ed-Dreder proved to be a necropolis containing some 50 stelae of square section originally surmounted by capitals of debased classical types. Some of the stelae bore reliefs of characteristic Romano-Libyan type portraying soldiers and eagles, and no less than nineteen were inscribed in Latin characters, but in an apparently Libyan language, recording the names and other particulars of the deceased. Whilst the full meaning of these texts, many of which are fragmentary, is obscure, the personal names are readily identifiable, and are Libyan, although preceded in some cases by the Roman nomina Flabius and Julius (now used as praenomina), In seven instances the Libyan surname is followed by the military rank tribunus.[16]

The date of these inscriptions is uncertain, but the praenomen Flabius applied to some of these Libyan tribunes strongly suggests that they obtained their commissions during or after the Constantinian period. Indeed, the fact that Flabius and Julius are the only Roman praenomina found at Bir ed-Dreder may indicate that the officers thus named were recruited during the joint reign of Constantius II and Constans (340–50). By this period the rank of tribunus had been generally adopted throughout the Roman army, and was regularly applied to the leaders of purely barbarian detachments. St. Jerome[17] lists the grades of promotion from tiro to tribunus in a cavalry unit, and in African inscriptions of late date tribuni are frequently encountered.[18]

Despite the superficial Romanisation of the funerary monuments of these officers at Bir ed-Dreder, and their Roman praenomina, it is evident that they were essentially native in character, and probably even unacquainted with Latin. Their relatively high rank illustrates the extent to which the frontier army of Tripolitania had become barbarised by the fourth century; and we can well understand why the pagan oaths described by Publicola were accepted from "barbarians" by officers who were not in truth far removed culturally from the "barbarians" themselves. The concentration of tribunes' tombs at Bir ed-Dreder is curious and not easily explicable. There appear to be no Roman fortified buildings in the immediate vicinity of the necropolis, although a large group exists at Bir Scedeua some 10 km. to the east. The tribunes of Bir ed-Dreder were most probably the commanders of mobile detachments which patrolled the less populous areas, and they were evidently senior in rank to the *centenarii* who played a more static role as cultivators and defenders of the Wadi settlements.[19]

THE FORT AT MSELLETIN

Prior to 1949 there had been no evidence of any orthodox military constructions in the whole area between the Gebel escarpment and the outer *Limes* forts at Bu Ngem and Gheria el-Garbia; and this fact confirmed the impression that the normal unit of defence was the fortified watch-tower or farm of Gasr Duib type. Last summer, however, a small fort of conventional design was discovered in the Wadi Merdum, close to the obelisk-tombs of Mselletin. Yet its particular character and size confirm rather than refute the conclusions which had previously been drawn. This fort, known to the local nomads who have built huts against its outer walls as Gasr Bularkan, is situated at the eastern extremity of a sector of the Wadi Merdum which was highly cultivated during the later Roman and early Islamic periods, but is now desiccated (pl. 16; fig. 7). It stands on the right bank of the wadi, on the edge of the rocky plateau, and is remarkably

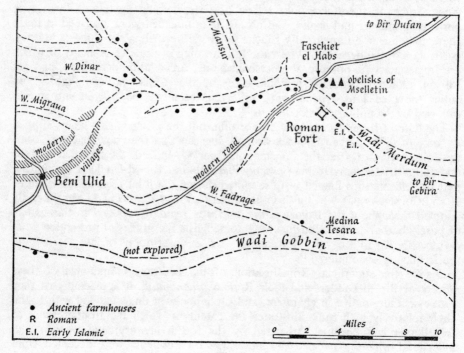

Fig. 7

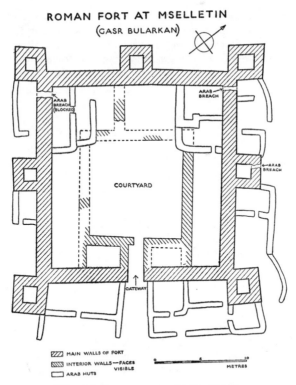

Fig. 8 (after survey by E. D. Oates)

well-preserved (pl. 16–18). It had, none the less, escaped the notice of earlier travellers.[20]

The main walls of the fort, 1·5 m. wide, have, bonded into them, projecting bastions with walls of 1 m. width (fig. 8). The outer faces of both main and bastion walls are of large freshly-quarried blocks of local limestone, only roughly trimmed and coursed: the inner faces are, however, of smaller stones, as found in the majority of the fortified farms. The bastions occupy each of the four corners, and the centres of three of the sides. On the fourth (SE) side, however, the centre of the wall is occupied by the entrance gateway, and there are neither projecting gate-house nor flanking towers. The entrance corridor 1·8 m. wide narrows to 1·1 m. at its entrance to the inner courtyard: this narrowing is original and not due to any later modification. The courtyard, only 10 m. square, was surrounded by barrack-rooms or stables built up against the fort walls, a common practice in later Roman defence works (cf. fig. 9). The partition walls of the individual rooms could not be determined on the surface, owing to fallen rubble. In general, however, the amount of fallen rubble was small, and there can be little doubt that the existing height of the walls (3 m. at the highest point) represents approximately their original condition. The structure is therefore quite different from the high towers of the Roman period more usually encountered in inner Tripolitania.

Despite its orthodox military appearance, typical of the fourth century A.D.,[21] this fort has several curious features. In the first place its dimensions (22 m. square excluding the projection of the bastions) are so small as to place the bastions far too close together; and it was evidently for this reason that the builders refrained from giving the gateway flanking towers such as we find in most African forts of the period. Secondly, the bastions themselves, although hollow and well faced internally, have no communication with the body of the fort, and no loopholes. They could have served only as magazines or, conceivably, as prison cells. If we compare the fort with the similar but larger structures found elsewhere in North Africa, we can see at a glance its meagre proportions (fig. 9).[22]

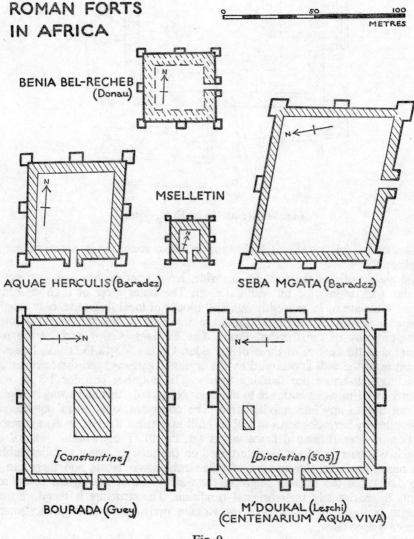

Fig. 9

Gasr Bularkan is far too small to have served any important strategic function in the organisation of the *Limes*. Most probably we should interpret it as a post of essentially local character, related only to the zone of *limitanei* settlements on the eastern edge of which it stands. The standard Roman structure in this zone is the fortified farm, which, by virtue of its superior height, offered better observation across the surrounding plateau. These farms could hardly have benefited militarily from the presence of this little fort near by. On the other hand, routine police-work, of the type suggested by Publicola's letter to St. Augustine, could not conveniently have been carried out by the occupants of the fortified farms, who were normally busy in their fields and would be mobilised only in an emergency. Thus, it is fair to interpret Gasr Bularkan as a police-post, garrisoned by a very small detachment (perhaps not more than twenty men and horses), but deliberately designed to look more impressive than it really was. Its occupants would have had a double function: primarily their task must have been to control the movements of barbarians into the zone of frontier settlement, and to extract those oaths of loyalty to which reference has already been made; but we may also suspect that the presence of this small garrison served to remind the *limitanei* themselves of their military responsibilities. The *dux provinciae Tripolitanae*, who was responsible for the military state of the frontier zone, and his subordinates the *praepositi limitis* were obliged, as the Constitution of Honorius and Theodosius II[23] shows clearly, to eject any persons who held land allotted to *limitanei*, but who shirked the military obligations attached to these holdings. Only by unfailing vigilance on the spot could this law be enforced.

THE FORTIFIED FARMS OF THE *Limes*

In conclusion it may be useful to give some further details of the types of fortified farmhouses which are encountered so frequently in the *Limes*-zone of Tripolitania, and which were, as has already been emphasised, the backbone of the defensive system. Since 1946 many examples of these buildings have been examined and, although surface study rarely yields conclusive dating evidence, a provisional chronology and typology can now be offered. These farmhouses are found both in the olive-growing areas of the Gebel, and in the pre-desert regions farther to the south. In the former area the higher rainfall has caused the collapse of the upper storeys and formed a mound which usually obscures the ground-plan; the southern specimens are better-preserved and more informative to the surface investigator. Apart from the fact that the Gebel specimens are more frequently surrounded by a ditch than the southern ones (due probably to the fact that naturally defensive sites were easier to select on the rocky sides of the southern wadis) there is no fundamental difference between the two.

In the absence of more reliable dating evidence, the type of masonry encountered in these buildings provides the best basis for chronological classification. We can, in fact, distinguish three main periods, as follows:

Period I. Fortified buildings in large well-dressed masonry (pl. 20), occasionally with inset rounded corners. This early type of fortified farm was referred to in the previous article (p. 29 f.) and tentatively assigned to the earlier part of the third century. Very few examples are known in the southern region, and only one complete ground-plan has yet been obtained.[24]

Period II. Fortified buildings in small masonry (pl. 21), moderately well-coursed and trimmed, and with doorways generally of large well-cut blocks and voussoirs. The angles of the buildings are usually, but not invariably, rounded with large roughly-dressed quoins. These structures, generally very similar to Gasr Duib, are extremely plentiful, and show a great diversity of ground-plans, although the principle of a central courtyard or light-shaft is normally maintained. The most carefully-built specimens of this period are probably of the second half of the third century, but the majority are likely to be of the fourth century and to belong to the most intensive phase of the settlement of *limitanei*, contemporaneous with the building of defensive circuits in the coastal cities.

Period III. Fortified buildings in small irregular masonry, uncoursed, and with a pronounced batter to their sides—due, no doubt, to the danger of having vertical walls of such inferior materials. The absence of the central courtyard or light-shaft, and the presence of early Islamic stucco decoration (apparently original) on the surfaces of the dark ground-floor vaults suggest that most of these buildings are of the early Islamic period. Their interest from the viewpoint of Roman studies is that they reproduce, within the technical limitations of their architects and builders, the form and defensive character of their Roman predecessors, and show the survival of a romanised yet Saharan architectural tradition well into the Middle Ages.

Most of the fortified buildings encountered in the Tripolitanian *Limes*-zone can readily be assigned to one or other of these periods, but there are many marginal cases which might belong either to Period II or III. There is no reason to suppose that the construction of these buildings (which provided as much security to their actual inhabitants as they did to the frontier zone as a whole) was suspended during the Vandal and Byzantine periods, even though the *Limes* had then ceased, as such, to exist. Future research may well establish that many of the worst structures of Period II and the best of Period III do, in fact, belong to the years between the Vandal invasion of the coast and the first Arab invasions.

A selection of ground-plans of undoubtedly Roman Period II fortified farms is illustrated here (fig. 10).[25] The types vary, as will be observed, from simple three-roomed towers (Type I) to elaborate structures with projecting towers and large central courtyards (Types V and VI). The overall dimensions normally range between a minimum of 8 m. and a maximum of 25 m. It must be emphasised, however, that the ground-floor plan alone is not an adequate indication of capacity. Our example of Type II (Gasr "D" at Bir Scedeua, also illustrated on pl. 15) is a three-storey tower, whereas Type IV (Gasr "E" at Bir Scedeua) was probably originally of not more than two storeys. The capacities of these two buildings were therefore approximately the same, the nature of the terrain having determined the ground dimensions.

There is no reason to suspect a strict typological development from the simplest to the most complex structures. Indeed, Type IV, which has the plan and proportions of the official third-century *centenaria* of the Upper Sofeggin road (cf. the plan of Gasr Duib, fig. 5, p. 25; and the air photograph of Gasr Uames, pl. 19) probably represents the prototype, the smaller and larger types being parallel developments. In this type the central courtyard is approached by an entrance corridor which was surmounted by an internal tower; but in the more developed types (V and VI) the tower becomes external, and a system of double

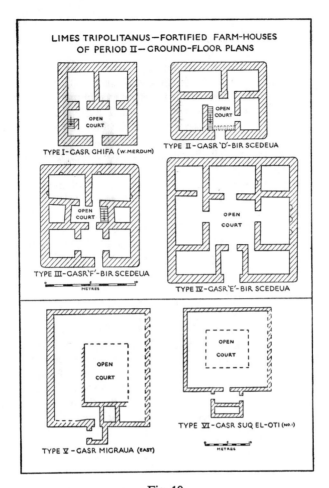

Fig. 10

doors prevented direct assault by battering ram. Henscir Suffit, excavated by Bartoccini in 1926, is an example, in Period I masonry, of a Type IV building later given an external tower.[26]

The function of these fortified buildings is reflected in their siting. In the Gebel area they normally occupy the higher ground in the zone of olive-plantation; further to the south they stand on the rocky sides of the cultivated Wadi-beds. That they were the homes of farmers is certain from the adjacent traces of terrace-walls and olive-presses: in some instances the olive-presses are actually built into the inner walls of the farmhouses.[27] Yet the strong outer walls, lack of outer windows, surrounding ditches, and protected doorways all emphasise the essentially military character of these buildings. The great height of these towers allowed good visibility across the countryside, and it can hardly be doubted that a system of light or smoke signals was in operation during the heyday of the *Limes*.[28]

3—LS * *

GENERAL CONCLUSIONS

The general history of the Tripolitan *Limes*, as revealed by literary and epigraphic evidence, has already been discussed, and it is necessary here only to emphasise the relatively late date of all the known monuments. It is perhaps too soon to affirm that the emperors who preceded Septimius Severus made no attempt to establish an organised frontier, but the fact remains that no traces of a pre-Severan *Limes* have yet been found. In this respect it may be significant that the linear "fossata" which Baradez has proved to constitute the central feature of the Numidian *Limes*, and which he tentatively attributes to the Hadrianic period, have not yet been found in the area of modern Tripolitania.[29]

Apart from the small fort at Mselletin, which seems to have been an attempt to scale down an orthodox frontier outpost to the dimensions of a fortified farmhouse, and the outer fortresses of Gheria el-Garbia and Bu Ngem which are related to oases and caravan routes rather than to any linear frontier, the military works of the *Limes Tripolitanus* seem to have consisted almost exclusively of fortified farmhouses occupied by Libyan *limitanei*. The growing importance of this indigenous element in the frontier army may perhaps explain the absence of traces of official military activity in the *Limes* zone during the fourth century: for it can hardly be an accident that the official inscriptions at present known (of Septimius Severus, Caracalla, Severus Alexander, Maximinus, Gordian III, Philip, Gallienus and Aurelian) are all of the third century.[30] For the fourth century the character of the *Limes*-organisation is shown by the crude epitaphs of the Bir ed-Dreder tribunes and by the fortified homes of the *limitanei*. It was this growing barbarisation of the defensive system which enabled the *regio Arzugum* to survive, socially and economically, the disasters of the fifth century and become the "horrida tellus Arzugis infandae" of Corippus.

ADDENDA

(1) A typical small cluster of fortified farmhouses in a small wadi south of Beni Ulid has been described by Mr. J. B. Ward Perkins, 25–30.

(2) In fig. 9 (above, p. 40) the shaded areas represent the barrack accommodation which, in these late forts, was normally ranged along the inner faces of the main walls. The fourth-century fort of Der el-Kahf in the southern Hauran (Butler, *Princeton Expedition to Syria in 1904–5*, Div. IIA, 145–8) is a well-preserved Syrian example of this same type of military architecture.

(3) Describing ancient buildings along the coast of the Greater Syrtis, the brothers H. W. and F. W. Beechey, (132) wrote: "They seem to be too numerous and too close together to have been forts, though their form very closely resembles them; and they are by no means well calculated for dwelling-houses unless we suppose it to have been necessary that each family should have its castle, unconnected with that of its neighbour, in which it was regularly entrenched." It is evident, indeed, that settlements of *limitanei*, of the same type as those encountered in the interior of Tripolitania, extended along the shores of the Syrtica and into the interior of Cyrenaica.

The writer is indebted to Mrs. Wain-Hobson for redrawing the plans published with this paper.

NOTES

1. [See above, p. 17 f.]

2. The writer must record his great indebtedness to these authorities, and to the Oxford Craven Committee for a travelling grant. As in previous campaigns, every assistance was given by the British Administration in Tripolitania.

3. Orosius i, 2, 90.

4. *Rend. Pont. Acc.* iv (1926), 155–66, where the evidence of the Councils for the episcopal sees of Tripolitania is fully documented and discussed.

5. Augustine, *Epist.*, 93.

6. *Rend. Pont. Acc.* iv (1926), Tav. ix.

7. Orosius i, 2, 100. In this passage the Subventani are sited on the coast adjoining the Lesser Syrtis.

8. *Not. Dign.* Occ. xxxi (*dux provinciae Tripolitanae*).

9. Augustine, *Epist.*, 46–7.

10. St. Augustine clearly refers to the military rank rather than to the municipal office.

11. Oliverio, *Doc. Ant. Afr. Ital.* ii, 135–63 [=*SEG* ix. 356 from Ptolemais in Cyrenaica].

12. Cf. Synesius, *Epist.*, 104.

13. O. Bates, 68, n. 7; cf. Ammianus, *Hist.* xxvi, 4, 5; xxviii, 6, 2.

14. Corippus, *Johannis* ii, 148.

15. A. Belardinelli, pl. opp. p. 24; cf. F. Beguinot, 14–15.

16. [For a fuller publication of the discoveries at Bir ed-Dreder, see below, p. 59 f.]

17. Jerome, *ad Pammachium* i, 19.

18. *CIL* viii. 17317, 17393, 5217; Merlin, *ILTun.*, 1199. Cf. the fifth-century "tribune" of Verulamium: Collingwood and Myres, *Roman Britain and the English Settlements*, 306.

19. For these *centenarii* [see above pp. 28, 30 and "Tripolitanian Inscriptions", 32–4.]

20. Messrs. E. E. D. M. Oates and R. M. Bradfield made the survey on which fig. 8 is based.

21. No dating evidence was found during the course of the surface examination, but the building is closely akin to dated fourth-century forts found in Numidia (cf. n. 22).

22. Fig. 9 is based on the following site-plans: Benia bel-Recheb—Donau, *BAC* 1903, 358 (fig. 7); Aquae Herculis and Seba Mgata—Baradez, 10, 223; Bourada—Guey, 193; M'doukal (Aqua Viva)—Leschi, *Revue africaine* nos. 394–5 (1943), 9.

23. *Cod. Theod.* vii, 15, 1.

24. Bartoccini, *Afr. Ital.* ii (1928–9), 106–10, illustrates Henscir Suffit, an example of this type near Jefren. The type of masonry may be a less reliable indication of period in the Gebel areas which were more highly Romanised than the regions further to the south.

25. These plans were obtained during the 1949 campaign and, in the case of the Bir Scedeua specimens, are largely the work of Mr. M. H. Ballance. Mr. M. H. de Lisle has obtained a similar series of plans from the hinterland of Misurata.

26. Bartoccini, l.c., explains the indirect entrance of Henscir Suffit as intended "to shield the intimate life of the house from extraneous eyes". There is no evidence that the early Libyans had such Islamic scruples about their womenfolk, who are portrayed unveiled on contemporary funerary monuments. The doorway systems encountered in these buildings are patently defensive in purpose.

27. As in a building at Faschiet el-Habs, close to Mselletin; but in general the main area of ancient olive-presses is in the Gebel, where there was always higher rainfall and more abundant topsoil.

28. For light signals, cf. Synesius, *Epist.*, 130. Apart from their residential function, the Tripolitanian towers may be compared with those depicted on Trajan's Column.

29. Baradez, 161. The Numidian *fossata* have still to be conclusively dated.

30. Of these emperors only Septimius Severus, Severus Alexander, Gordian III and Philip are recorded on building inscriptions. The other names are from milestones.

OASIS FORTS OF *LEGIO III AUGUSTA* ON THE ROUTES TO THE FEZZAN

[From *PBSR* xxii (1954)]
Plates 22–30

The two well-preserved Roman fortresses to be described in this paper have been known for many years. They were first brought to European notice by the British-sponsored geographical expeditions of the nineteenth century, when Tripoli was the spring-board for repeated attempts to find a route into Central Africa. Although important discoveries have been made in one of these forts (Bu Ngem) in more recent years, no detailed ground-plans have previously been published.

The following notes and illustrations[1] are primarily intended to fill this lacuna in the documentation of the African *limes*; but it is hoped that they may also serve to increase our knowledge of early third-century trends in Roman military architecture. The European frontiers of the Roman Empire have yielded, and are still yielding, numerous examples of first- and second-century forts, and equally numerous examples of the forts erected during the later-third and early-fourth centuries, when barbarian invasions threatened the whole Roman world.

The Severan period, so notable in many aspects of Roman art and archaeology, is relatively poorly represented in the sphere of military architecture. The great fortress of *Legio II Parthica*, built near Rome by Septimius Severus, is too obstructed by medieval and modern Albano to be very informative;[2] and the latest discoveries on that site await definitive publication.[3] We must therefore look further afield for well-preserved forts built *ab initio* under the Severi; and Africa is in this as in so many other matters a rewarding area of enquiry.

The forts with which we are here concerned mark the southernmost limit of Roman territorial occupation in Africa west of the Nile valley. They lie close to the thirtieth parallel, and together with Gadames—where a similar fort must once have existed—form a straight line marking the theoretical boundary between Roman-controlled Tripolitania and the kingdom of the Garamantes, who occupied the scattered oases of the Fezzan.

Roman policy towards the Fezzan is only summarily recorded in history. The campaigns of Cornelius Balbus[4] in about 20 B.C. appeared, at the time, to have crushed the Garamantes decisively; but by A.D. 68 that warlike race was again in condition to invade the coastal region, and to necessitate the punitive expedition led by Valerius Festus[5] in the following year. Thereafter the Garamantes appear to have behaved, for a time, in a manner more befitting their status as a client kingdom, for it is recorded that Julius Maternus (not otherwise known, but probably *legatus Augusti pro praetore* in Numidia) marched to Garama, and there joined forces with the King of the Garamantes in a four-month expedition to the lands of the Ethiopians, "near Agysimba, where the rhinoceros is found."[6]

Whilst, therefore, the Romans cannot be accused of lack of interest in the interior of Africa, their closer acquaintance with the terrain, following these expeditions, did not persuade them of the utility of extending their territorial occupation into the Fezzan. The only Roman monument hitherto found south of the thirtieth parallel is an isolated mausoleum, which still stands near Germa (ancient Garama) and which was probably the tomb of a merchant engaged in importing the Roman pottery and glass often found in Garamantic tombs.[7]

We next hear of campaigns in this part of Africa during the reign of Septimius Severus, who "by defeating very warlike tribes rendered the Tripolis, his birth-place, completely safe".[8] On this occasion there is no specific mention of the Garamantes, but one may suspect that they had once more been making mischief; and it is surely significant that the forts with which we are here concerned were erected in the first half of the third century on the three main routes leading from Roman into Garamantic territory. Whether earlier outposts existed on the same sites, we cannot say; but there is no trace of them, apart from a possible vestige of an earlier ditched camp at Gheria el-Garbia.

The fact that Gadames, Gheria el-Garbia, and Bu Ngem form a straight line on the map is, in the main, an accident. There are no indications of any minor defensive works in the vast desert areas that separate them,[8a] and their own siting was clearly conditioned by the proximity of strategically-positioned oases. The oasis of Gadames is still important today, whilst that of Gheria el-Garbia could be so, were it not plagued by malaria. Bu Ngem is the smallest and most wretched of the three oases, but intrusive sand-dunes may have caused a decline in its size and amenities since Roman times.

BU NGEM (pls. 22, 24, 25; fig. 11)

The oasis of Bu Ngem lies 200 km. due south of Cape Misurata (the ancient *Cephalae promontorium*, marking the western edge of the Syrtic Gulf), and occupies the bed of the Wadi Bey el-Kaib, a tributary of the Wadi Bey el-Kebir. It consists of some 150 palm-trees, and about twenty wells from 5 to 15 m. deep, most of which yield a rather unpalatable water. Here, in 1843, the Turks established a small fort, which the Italians reconstructed during their occupations of 1914 and 1927–42. For all its inadequacy, Bu Ngem is the main staging-point between the oases of the Jofra (where lie the villages of Hon, Socna, and Waddan) and the Tripolitanian coast.[9]

The Roman fort, which lies about 1 km. [east] of the now derelict Italian redoubt, is in a desolate area swept by mobile sand-dunes; but its outlines are clear both from the air (pl. 22) and on the ground. When Captain G. F. Lyon[10] visited the site in 1819 there was more to be seen than there is today, the high-standing gateway-towers having later been stripped of their upper parts to build the Turkish fort. Lyon's drawing (pl. 25) of one of these towers is therefore an important record, and the surviving remains indicate that we may have confidence in its accuracy. Cagnat[11] published a sketch-plan of the fort compiled by the explorer Duveyrier, who visited Bu Ngem in 1869; but whilst its proportions are correct, the details of the gateways and curtain-wall are misleading.

In plan (fig. 11), Bu Ngem is a rectangular fortress of orthodox pre-Diocletianic type, measuring 91 by 136 m. externally, and having rounded corners with, presumably, internal corner-turrets. As is usual in such forts, the gateways in the two longer sides are set east of centre, so as to allow the cross-street to skirt the front of a centrally-placed *principia* or headquarters-building. Three of the gates are of identical pattern, with a single arch flanked by rectangular towers; but the eastern gate (pl. 24) is larger and has the side walls of the towers cut away, a feature which occurs also at Gheria el-Garbia.

The exposed faces of the gateways and their towers are all faced with blocks of a hard black limestone, drafted at the edges, but left extremely rough towards the centres. This is merely a skin concealing walling of limestone rubble and mortar, which same material was used, with an exterior rendering of plaster, in the curtain-walls of the fort. As Lyon's drawing shows, this ashlar facing was confined to the lower part of the fort gate, the upper storey being built throughout in rubble and mortar; but we need not accept Lyon's view that this superstructure is of early Islamic date, for Gheria el-Garbia provides an analogy which can hardly be post-Roman. In the case of Bu Ngem, however, there may have been a change of plan during the Roman period, for the drawing of 1819 shows two arched windows, later blocked up, in the ashlar facing of the tower only a little lower than the windows of the upper storey. And one might be tempted to conjecture that the superstructure belongs [about a generation later,] the original fort having had lower gate-towers; but Turkish demolition makes it impossible to check this. One thing is completely certain, that the fortress and its gates, as originally designed, were the work of the legate Quintus Anicius Faustus in the year 200–1.[12]

Air photographs show that the interior of the fortress was divided up in orthodox fashion. The site of the *principia* is marked by high-standing orthostats, some provided with projecting brackets. Immediately to its north are the remains of a bath-house, in which Italian soldiers found in 1927[13] the well-known metrical inscription of Quintus Avidius Quintianus, a centurion of Legio III Augusta, extolling the goddess Salus. Another inscription[14] found in the same building records its erection in 201–2 by a *vexillatio* of the same legion. The bath-house was roofed with barrel-vaults constructed from bottle-shaped terra-cotta tubes, which were interlocked, neck to base, to the required diameter, and then filled with liquid cement. Such lightweight and utilitarian vaulting occurs also in a bath-house adjoining the theatre of Sabratha.

Air survey shows scattered buildings, probably of *canabae*, extending for 150 m. to the north-west and north-east of the fort walls; and a dedication to Jupiter Hammon,[15] found a kilometre to the north, suggests the presence of a small shrine. To the south there was an extensive cemetery, which has yielded two funerary inscriptions, neither of distinctively military character. From what source the fort and its baths were supplied with water is uncertain. A well noted by Lyon and by Duveyrier near the south gateway, and now no longer visible, can hardly have been adequate for all purposes. Three kilometres to the north-east of the fort lies a small lake set in a deep natural hollow mantled with lush vegetation; and it is not impossible that these waters were utilised by the Roman garrison at Bu Ngem.

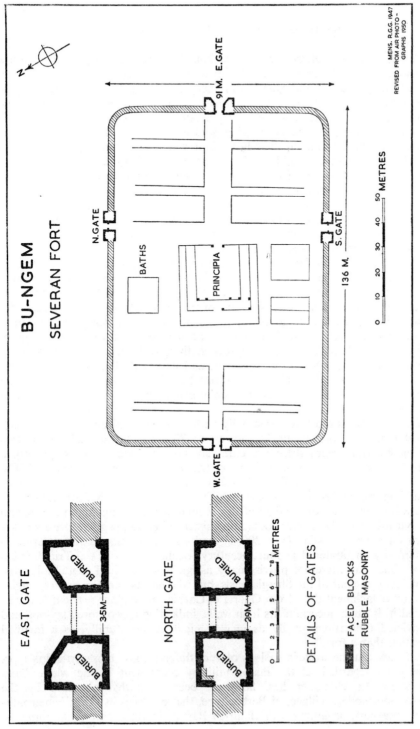

Fig. 11

GHERIA EL-GARBIA (pls. 23, 26–30; figs. 12–14)

In the region of the Gheriat, some 300 km. due south of Tripoli, there are a number of oases of varying sizes, the two largest being known as Gheria el-Garbia ("the western") and Gheria esh-Shergia ("the eastern"). These oases lie at the heads of tributary wadis that run eventually into the great Wadi Zemzem, and to their west is the desolate rock-plateau of the Hammada el-Hamra. In antiquity, as today, travellers heading southwards from Tripoli towards the Fezzan found in the Gheriat their last major water-points and their last chance of obtaining dates, cereals, and vegetables, before crossing the bare Hammada.

The eastern Gheria, lying on the modern motor-track to the Fezzan, is the better known of the two main oases, and it was there that the Italian colonial garrison of 1928–43 established a large redoubt. The western Gheria, although larger and more populous, is too malarial for European habitation; but this fact does not seem to have influenced the Romans, who established there their largest fortress in the whole of Tripolitania.

Before describing this fortress, some reference must be made to the very much smaller Roman fortified building at Gheria esh-Shergia, which has sometimes been confused with it.[16] It stands on the edge of a steep cliff overlooking the oasis and is incorporated within the walls of the modern redoubt. Adaptation for modern military use has removed all traces of its interior walls, but the outer faces of its main walls are well-preserved on three sides, and form a rectangle of 38 by 19 m. The latter dimension may originally have been as great as 25 m., as the eastern wall has toppled over the cliff, and its precise line is uncertain. The original entrance into the building must also have been in this lost wall, for the masonry on the other three sides rises uninterruptedly to a maximum height of about 7 m.

These outer walls are faced externally with faultlessly cut and coursed blocks of local limestone, of varying heights up to 70 cm.; and at each of the two surviving exterior angles there are curiously inset rounded corners (pl. 30), a feature that occurs in two other similar structures in inner Tripolitania.[17] The inner faces of these main walls, and probably also the interior partition walls of the building, were of rubble masonry, which has almost entirely fallen away.

There is no evidence of the date of this Roman fortified building in the eastern oasis; but it is unlikely to have come into existence before the great fortress in the western oasis was in being [A.D. 200–1], and its construction is far superior to that normally encountered in fourth-century fortified farms of the Tripolitanian interior. One may therefore provisionally assign it to the third century. Its role was evidently to control the Shergia oasis, but whether its garrison was of regular troops, on detachment duty from Gheria el-Garbia, or whether resident *limitanei* occupied it, is quite uncertain. Its high walls, indicating a two-storey lay-out, and its restricted dimensions justify us in classing it, architecturally, as a fortified farm rather than a fort.[18]

The fortress in the western oasis is of very different, and more orthodox type, and may be regarded as the major military monument in the whole *limes Tripolitanus*. Its character has, however, been somewhat obscured by the medieval and modern village, of Berber type, that occupies its ruins. Nineteenth-century travellers, beginning with Heinrich Barth[19] in 1850, were mainly impres-

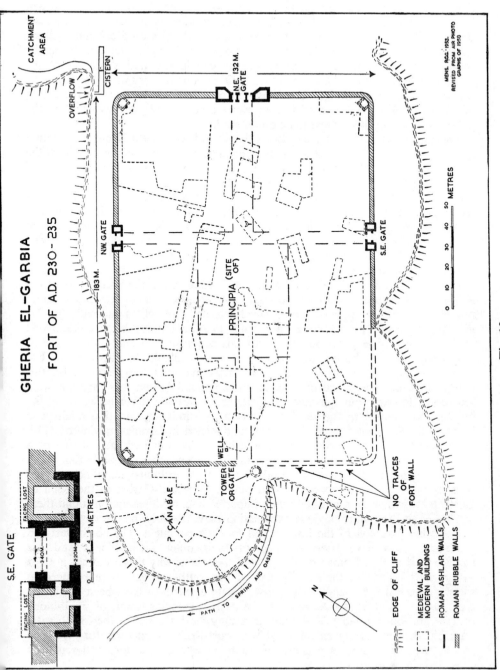

GHERIA EL-GARBIA

FORT OF A.D. 230-235

Fig. 12

sed by its fine triple-arched gateway (pl. 26-8; fig. 13), and were surprised by the absence of any similar ashlar masonry to indicate the outlines of the fort itself. Cagnat, writing in 1912 from Barth's description, concluded that "Le reste de la fortification a complètement disparu sous les sables ou a été employé par les indigènes à la construction du village voisin".[20] A flight over the site in the summer of 1950 proved the falsity of the conclusion, and showed that the modern village (now almost completely abandoned) occupied the rectangle formed by the fort walls (pl. 23). Closer inspection on the ground in the spring of 1953 revealed the traces of two or three other gateways, thus enabling the general outlines of the fortress to be established.

The fortress (fig. 12) is exactly twice the size of that at Bu Ngem, its external dimensions being 183 by 132 m. It occupies a narrow spur running out from the main plateau towards the oasis, and the ground falls away with a very steep cliff on all except the north-east side. On this side is situated the triple-arched gateway observed by so many previous travellers, which has the inner flanks of its projecting towers cut away as at Bu Ngem. One of these towers is still standing to almost its original height, its upper storey being pierced by round-headed windows in the two surviving faces. A similar window must certainly have existed in the third face, so as to have commanded the curtain-wall.

The main façade with its triple arches is impeccably constructed and comparable with the finest Severan work at Lepcis Magna, but the lower parts of the high-standing south-east tower, although of identical stone, are much more roughly coursed. The upper storey is faced externally as well as internally (pl. 27) in small masonry; but, although a rebuild may reasonably be suspected, one must be chary of leaping too rapidly to this conclusion so long as the base of the tower remains buried in rubble and not available for inspection. The construction of the gateway arches must have required the presence, on this remote spot, of very skilled masons. It is not impossible that these artisans were sent down to carry out the more intricate work, leaving the completion of the building-programme to the resident garrison. A similar explanation might also be applied to the gateway at Bu Ngem, as depicted in Lyon's drawing of 1819. Certainly climatic conditions alone would hardly have caused the collapse of a gateway-tower so solidly built, and one may doubt whether the barbarian tribes of the Fezzan would have undertaken any very arduous demolitions. That restorations of some sort were carried out at Gheria el-Garbia in the reign of Gordian III is, however, attested by an imperfectly-copied inscription found there in 1914;[21] and the more obvious explanation may, possibly, be the correct one.

The other gateways of the fortress call for little comment. The north-west and south-east gates have been stripped of their outer facing-blocks and are incorporated in post-Roman dwellings, which explains why they were not noticed by previous visitors to the site. A plan of the south-east gate is reproduced to show its general form, and the north-west gate appears to have been of similar type. On the south-west side, towards the oasis, a circular tower, of small-block construction but probably of Roman date, may mark the site of the fourth gateway; but the area is too encumbered with post-Roman structures for certainty, and in any case there are reasons for doubting whether the fort wall was ever completed in its southern sector.

The curtain-wall, 2·5 m. broad, is of very inferior construction by comparison with the gateway; but we have already noted a similar situation at Bu Ngem.

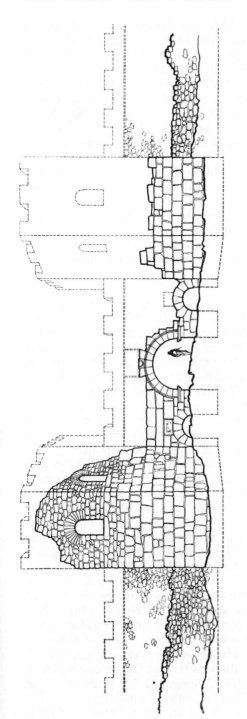

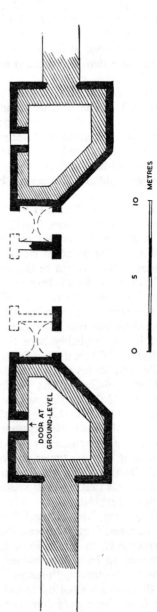

Fig. 13 Gheria El-Garbia: north-east gate

The only part of its course still standing high is at the northern corner of the fort (pl. 30), where there was evidently an internal turret, a round-headed arch appearing above the projecting cornice that seems to mark the level of the rampart-walk. Below this cornice the fort wall is faced with irregular stones of medium size, uncoursed and thickly pointed; whilst above it the facing is of even smaller stones, and very similar to that in the tower of the main gateway. It is this similarity that most strengthens the view that the latter tower belongs to the original lay-out of the fort, rather than to a reconstruction, for there is no reason to suppose that the rounded northern corner of the fort has also been completely rebuilt.

The most puzzling feature at Gheria el-Garbia is the apparent absence of any fort wall at the southern corner; here the ground is largely clear of modern structures, and there is no reason why a 2·5 m. wall should have left no trace on the hard rock surface. Reference to the plan will show that the surviving sectors of the fort wall end at or near the very points where the steep cliff comes closest to the wall-line, and we may perhaps infer that the fortress was never completed, the steep-sided cliff having been deemed a sufficient natural defence in this southern corner of the site.

Within the walled area there are no ancient features of note visible today, apart from a square-sectioned well, which is said to be 35 m. deep and to communicate by a 300 m. horizontal gallery, now collapsed, with the spring of El-Gaba el-Kebira in the adjacent oasis. There are also traces of a catchment area on the slopes of the plateau to the north of the fort, which diverted winter rainfall into a 20 m. long cistern, formerly protected from evaporation by a vault. A channel, later blocked, seems to have formed an overflow over the side of the cliff.

The small semicircular area lying outside the south-west fort wall contains numerous remains of buildings, some of which may be of the Roman period; and it was probably here that *canabae* were situated. The spring of El-Gaba el-Kebira, 100 m. distant from the cliff-edge, can provide up to 40,000 l. of water daily, and serves to irrigate the adjacent oasis of some 4,000 palm-trees.

Gheria el-Garbia has yielded fewer inscriptions than Bu Ngem. The central keystone of the north-east gateway bears a laurel wreath containing the enigmatic text: PRO/AFR/ILL,[22] but the real dedicatory inscription of the fortress should have stood above this keystone, as at Bu Ngem. An inscribed block of the appropriate size and character was in fact discovered by Barth built into the doorway of a small circular tower, of post-Roman date, which still stands a mile north-east of the fortress. This inscription[23] gives the titles of Severus Alexander (A.D. 230–5) and records that the *praepositus* of a detachment (*vexillatio*) of Legio III Augusta built the fort (*burgus*).

The term *burgus*, used it seems, in the German *limes* to describe a small watchtower,[24] may appear inappropriately applied to Gheria el-Garbia, which corresponds, in dimensions, to a cohort fort. These military expressions seem, however, to have been rather loosely applied by the Romans (just as the terms "fort", "fortress", "redoubt", etc., are loosely used today). An inscription[25] of the Antonine period found recently in Bulgaria records that in one region of the *limes* there were constructed 4 *praesidia*, 12 *burgi*, and 109 *pruri*, and these statistics may imply that burgi were sometimes forts of medium dimensions.

As there is no smaller structure that might be termed a *burgus* at Gheria el-Garbia, we [might assume] that the inscription in question refers to the fortress,

which must therefore have been constructed (*a solo . . . instituit*) in the reign
of Severus Alexander. Against this conclusion there is, however, the remarkable
resemblance that Gheria el-Garbia bears to Bu Ngem, which latter fort was
unquestionably built in A.D. 200–1, thirty years earlier; and the fact that it is
precisely double the size. One receives the strong impression of a single Severan
programme of military construction in which Gheria el-Garbia was destined to
play a larger role than Bu Ngem.[26]

These considerations tempt one to conjecture that Gheria was first planned and
laid out under Septimius Severus, but was only completed and dedicated thirty
years later; and, in support of this conjecture, one may quote those structural
peculiarities of the main gateway to which we have already referred, which give
the impression of a work begun by one team of builders and completed by
another. For how long after the reign of Severus Alexander the fortress remained
occupied is uncertain, but there is epigraphic record of a repair under Gordian III.
Whether these outermost defences of the *limes Tripolitanus* had a part to play in
the post-Diocletianic organisation is uncertain. The absence of fourth-century
milestones on the roads of the interior, and the omission of *Cidamae* (Gadames)
from the Notitia Dignitatum rather suggests that such large official forts were
abandoned, the responsibility for defence being delegated to locally-recruited
limitanei or perhaps to *foederati*.

Two other features of Gheria el-Garbia remain to be described—the first a
curious relief (fig. 14), now much mutilated, over the keystone of the left-hand
side-arch of the main gate. The lower part of this relief has been deliberately
erased, probably in antiquity; and Barth's "trace of a chariot and a person in
curious attire following it" is pure fantasy. All that is distinctively visible is the
pair of victories flanking a pair of eagles at the top of the relief, and an altar with
tripod base and a fire burning on it in the bottom right-hand corner. The left-
hand bottom corner seems to have been occupied by an object of slightly different
shape, whilst the remainder of the relief—whatever it may have depicted—
occupied the centre of the panel.

Fig. 14

The other point of interest, still to be investigated, is the appearance on the air photograph of some features suggestive of ancient fortification on the opposite side of the oasis to the main fortress. Here, in an area partly occupied by modern Arab houses, there seem to be (*a*) a ruined wall cutting off a small triangular promontory; and (*b*) an L-shaped ditch enclosing the edge of the plateau a little south of (*a*). The wall itself may be a native construction, but the ditch suggests Roman work, and it would be interesting indeed if it were to prove to be a temporary marching-camp thrown up during one of the earlier Roman expeditions into the Fezzan.

GADAMES

The third and westernmost of our outer fortresses is that which must have existed in the oasis of Gadames, although no traces of its outline have yet been detected. Gadames is over 400 km. south-west of Sabratha, and was probably linked with that port by a caravan route, which has not, however, yielded any milestones. It is a large oasis boasting some 20,000 date-palms and a number of copious springs. Fragmentary inscriptions[27] show the presence of a Roman garrison at Gadames under Septimius Severus and Caracalla, and attest work of construction or reconstruction under Severus Alexander by a centurion of *Legio III Augusta*. One need not, therefore, doubt the former existence of an orthodox fortress of the Bu Ngem or Gheria el-Garbia pattern.

The flourishing life of Gadames both in late antiquity and in the Middle Ages was evidently inimical to the survival of the Roman fort which may have lain on the same site as the present irregularly laid-out village. The only ancient remains *in situ* at Gadames are the so-called *asnam*, which are rubble cores of funerary monuments in which a strong native influence is present. Excavations[28] carried out around the bases of the *asnam* have brought to light numerous graves of late antique date, together with pagan funerary inscriptions. It was only under Justinian[29] that the inhabitants of Gadames were converted to Christianity, as part of the Byzantine policy of entrusting to barbarian but Christian *foederati* those frontier areas which could not be conveniently garrisoned by regular troops.

GENERAL CONCLUSIONS

The historical setting of these three outer fortresses has already been discussed, and it need only be reiterated that all three fall within the period A.D. 201–35. Bu Ngem was certainly constructed and fully equipped at the earlier date, and one may suspect the same of Gadames. At Gheria el-Garbia, however, the work was only completed by the later date, and then one angle of the fort walls appears to have been left unfinished, it having been decided that the natural features of the site offered sufficient protection in this quarter.

Far more surprising than the failure to complete the fort walls is the very attempt to place a conventionally-planned fortress of such dimensions on this restricted site. The two gateways in the longer sides of the fort lie only a few yards from the cliff-edge, and served very little purpose. Moreover, the whole area of the fort is dominated by higher ground to the north, on which post-Roman occupants of the oasis very sensibly erected a circular watch-tower. As at

Bu Ngem, the Gheria el-Garbia fortress was sited solely with a view to controlling the adjacent oasis, and had little other tactical value. Large caravans could have passed, unobserved from its walls, along the plateau to the north.

It is also noteworthy that the two surviving fortresses both have very elaborate gates and relatively simple curtain-walls. The use of an elegant ashlar facing on the exposed surfaces of the gates seems to reflect a desire to make these fortresses as impressive as possible. It was perhaps intended that the traveller on the caravan routes should become immediately aware that he had entered Roman-controlled territory, and that his liberty of action was now under definite restrictions. "Prestige" forts of a very similar type were erected by the Italians throughout Libya.

In terms of architecture, these Roman oasis forts of the third century show conservative trends. Their rounded corners, internal turrets, and disposition of *principia* and barrack-blocks, look backwards to the first and second centuries rather than forward to the post-Diocletianic era. Since they were built by detachments of *Legio III Augusta*, guided no doubt by long-accepted manuals of military engineering, this fact need not surprise us. The absence of a bank behind the walls, such as occurs even in the third-century Saxon Shore forts of Brancaster and Reculver,[30] may reflect new tendencies in fort-construction, but more probably results from the lack of any suitable heavy soil that could be used for this purpose. The new conceptions of military architecture that characterise the end of the third century and the whole of the fourth, more especially the emphasis on closely-spaced projecting bastions, were not to be diffused through the medium of conservative-minded legionaries. They resulted, more probably, from the army reforms linked with the names of Diocletian and Constantine, and from third-century experience in constructing small outposts manned by static *limitanei*, and in defending cities.

NOTES

1. I must here express my indebtedness to Lt.-Col. P. J. Sandison, Sudan Defence Force, and to Capt. J. James, 14/20 King's Hussars, for enabling me to visit Bu Ngem in 1947 and Gheria el-Garbia in 1953; to Air Headquarters, R.A.F. Malta, for arranging an air reconnaissance of these sites in 1950, and allowing me to fly in a Lancaster aircraft (pilot: Fl./Lieut. Hillier) to obtain air photographs; to Mr. Duncan Black for the restored elevation of the main gateway of Gheria el-Garbia; and to Cpl. Day, 14/20 Hussars, and the Department of Antiquities of Tripolitania for some of the photographs here reproduced.

2. G. Lugli, "Castra Albana I-II", *Ausonia* ix (1919), 211-65, and x (1921), 210-59. Recent air photographs suggest that the plan of the legionary fort reproduced as pl. IX in the first of these articles is slightly inaccurate, the outline of the walls being more regular than is shown. The overall dimensions of the fort are 435 by 230 m.

3. The *Porta Praetoria* has been fully revealed by war damage. See *Fasti Archaeologici* i (1946), no. 1932.

4. Pliny, *Hist. Nat.* V, 5, 35-7. Cf. P. Romanelli in *Rendiconti Acc. Lincei*, 1950, 472-92.

5. *Ibid.* V, 5, 38. Solinus 29, 6-7. The "iter praeter caput saxi" followed by Festus cannot be identified with certainty. It may well have been the central route, Tripoli-Mizda-Gheriat.

6. Marinus of Tyre, cited by Ptolemy, I, 8-9; I, 10, 2. Agysimba cannot be precisely located.

7. G. Caputo, "Scavi Sahariani", *Monumenti Antichi* xli (1951), 201-442; [C. M. Daniels, cited p. 15 above, n. 6].

8. *SHA Severus* 18, 3. Cf. Aur. Victor, *Caes*, xx, 19.

[8a. But see now the Severan structure at

Gasr Zerzi, O. Brogan *Libya Antiqua* i (1964) 43 f..]

9. Under the Karamanli rulers of Tripoli in the early nineteenth century, Bu Ngem was recognised as the northern boundary of the Fezzan, and slaves who died beyond this point during their journey to the coast were held to be the loss of the Pasha of Tripoli, and not of the ruler of the Fezzan; G. F. Lyon, 66.

10. *Ibid.* 65–6, with plate.

11. R. Cagnat, 555 *et seq.* [A French expedition directed by R. Rebuffat began to excavate the site in 1967; for results see R. Rebuffat, J. Deneauve, G. Hallier, *Libya Antiqua* iii–iv (1966–7) 49 f.]

12. *IRT*, 914–16.

13. R. Bartoccini, "La fortezza romana di Bu Ngem", *Africa Italiana* ii (1928), 50–8. *IRT*, 918–19.

14. *IRT*, 913.

15. *Ibid.* 920.

16. Cf. P. Romanelli, (2), 13 and pl. IVB. Another small fortified building adjoins the small oasis of Mago, 7 km. north-west of Gheria el-Garbia.

17. In the well-preserved fortified building of Gasr el-Banat, in the Wadi Nfed (D. E. L. Haynes, 149); and in a very ruinous building at Faschia, in the Wadi Zemzem.

18. These fortified farms, so common in Tripolitania, are discussed summarily above, p. 41 f.

19. H. Barth, (2), i, 126–31. H. Vischer (78–80) gives a description and a photograph, showing that the ruins have changed little in the last half-century.

20. Cagnat, 555.

21. *IRT*, 896. We could not find this text in 1953.

22. *IRT*, 897. The reading is certain, but the meaning entirely obscure.

23. *Ibid.*, 895.

24. *CIL* xiii, 6509; cf. *O.R.L.* Strecke 10 (Lief. 44), 85. The meaning of *burgus* is also discussed by Wolff in *Röm.-Germ. Berichte* viii (1917), 80–1.

25. V. Beshevlyev, *Epigraphic Studies* (Sofia, 1952), 33, no. 55.

[26. Discovery of an inscription of Septimius Severus at Gheria el-Garbia, *Libya Antiqua* ii (1965) 136 and pl. 64b, now shows that the impression was correct; the *burgus* must be a subsidiary building.]

27. *IRT*, 907–9.

28. By Pavoni in 1913 (*Rivista Coloniale* viii (1913), 2, 315) and by Bilotti 1935 (MS. report in archives of Antiquities Department of Tripolitania). A scientific re-examination of the *asnam* is badly needed.

29. Procopius, *De aedif.* VI, iii, 10.

30. J. K. S. St. Joseph, "The Roman Fort at Brancaster", *Antiquaries Journal* xvi (1936), 444–60.

5

THE ROMANO-LIBYAN CEMETERY AT BIR ED-DREDER

[From *Quaderni di Archeologia della Libia* iii (1954)]

[This article, written in English, was published in Italian which has been translated back into an English that is, it is hoped, clear, though it lacks Goodchild's own touch. The material in it is of importance in itself and of interest as marking a step further in the understanding of Latino-Libyan texts, which, in 1963 were recognised by Professor Levi Della Vida as essentially a debased neo-Punic (*Oriens Antiquus* ii (1963) 71 f.; see also iv (1965) 59 f.).]

Bir ed-Dreder (The Wadi Dreder Well) lies about 45 km. south-east of Mizda from which it may be reached by a recently constructed motor track, branching off the Mizda-Gheriat road near the derelict fort in the Wadi Gelela (fig. 15).

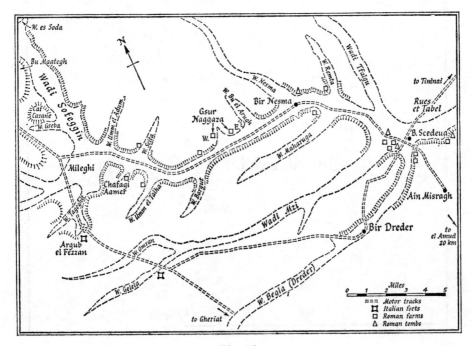

Fig. 15

Neither Barth, nor de Mathuisieulx, the two pioneers of exploration in the Sofeggin area, ever visited it and the first reports of ancient remains there came from Italian army officers during the Italian occupation of Tripolitania. Lieut.-Col. A. Belardinelli published a photograph of an inscription from Dreder in his important monograph on the region of the Ghibla (South);[1] and a squeeze of another inscription was sent to the late Professor Francesco Beguinot who wrote a brief note on these and other "Latino-Libyan" inscriptions of Tripolitania.[2]

During the summer of 1949 I decided to undertake a brief archaeological expedition, with the assistance of the British Military authorities in Tripolitania, to examine some of the ancient monuments in the Sofeggin area. A small military party was organised under the command of Capt. Lord Leven of the Coldstream Guards, and this made it possible to visit a large number of sites. Bir ed-Dreder was included in the itinerary in the hope of discovering new inscriptions there; and in fact a total of twenty new texts, complete or fragmentary, was found in a Romano-Libyan cemetery on the edge of the plateau near the wells (fig. 16). The texts were transcribed and photographed as well as possible during this first

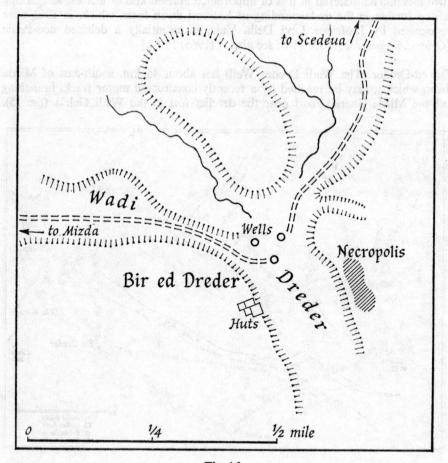

Fig. 16

visit, but it soon became clear that really accurate copies could not be made quickly. It was decided therefore, with the agreement of Professor Giacomo Caputo, then Superintendent of Antiquities in Tripolitania, and with financial help from the appropriate British authorities, to remove the monuments to the Museum in Tripoli Castle, as was done in August of the same year, under my own supervision and with the invaluable assistance of Signori Santino Gaudino and Mario Fabbri. In the Museum careful squeezes of each inscription were taken from which Mr. Antony Clark traced the facsimile drawings reproduced here. The Superintendency's draughtsman, Sig. Carmelo Catanuso drew the capitals and reliefs which were taken to Tripoli at the same time as the inscriptions. The photographs are by Sig. F. de Liberali.

The importance of the Bir ed-Dreder inscriptions is twofold. In the first place they constitute the largest group of the Latino-Libyan inscriptions which are a feature of the Tripolitanian frontier zone so far found on any site; and they must inevitably make a serious contribution to the interpretation of the still unknown language of these inscriptions. Secondly they are of particular interest for the study of the *Limes Tripolitanus*, since they refer to "*tribuni*", half-barbarous officers of the frontier army in the late Roman period.

In the article cited above, Professor Beguinot made a first attempt at solving the enigma of the Latino-Libyan texts. I have ventured to disagree with some of his hypotheses in a note on them which is concerned with archaeological rather than linguistic considerations;[3] but I think that the time has not yet come for a definitive interpretation of their language, although we can already recognise in them both Latin and Punic elements on a substratum which is probably essentially Libyan. It is to be hoped that future discoveries will permit further progress in this new branch of epigraphy. Meanwhile it is important that the texts should be published in as accurate a form as possible, together with accounts of the archaeological context in which each was found. I am very grateful to the editors of the *Quaderni* for their offer of hospitality in these pages and to Signora F. Bonaiuto who translated these notes from English into Italian.

THE SITE

The Romano-Libyan cemetery of Bir ed-Dreder stands on a limestone platform on the left bank of the Wadi Dreder about 300 m. east of the wells (fig. 16). It is on two levels and immediately above the cliffs, 15 m. high, which run along the Wadi edge. As at many other sites in the Sofeggin area there is no accumulation of earth on the platform and no likelihood therefore that more inscriptions remain buried there. A number of stones, among them one with an inscription (no. 19, now in Tripoli), had fallen or been pushed from the cliffs and lay, when found, on the ground below them.

In the Wadi bed, below the cemetery, there are some rough walls, while the outline of a small building, probably ancient, can be seen on the top of the cliffs which form the right bank of the wadi; but these remains are modest in size and unimportant. We failed to find any trace of genuine habitation in the neighbourhood and a subsequent air survey, from a plane kindly made available by the R.A.F., revealed no ancient settlement. We must conclude, therefore, that the cemetery lay at some distance from the homes of those buried in it. The nearest ancient habitations that we noted are the fortified farms near Bir Scedeua (fig. 15), but the tombs in which their inhabitants were buried are close by them.

THE FUNERARY MONUMENTS

The tombs of Bir ed-Dreder show very little variation of type. Each has the following characteristics:

1. A small grave (length 60–90 cm.) defined by a single line of unsquared stones, like those of modern Beduin tombs.
2. A stone base set in the ground in front of the grave, containing a socket to take the inscribed stele (cf. fig. 17 for the stelae carrying inscriptions, no. 4–6, 8–11, 15).
3. A stele, rectangular in section (varying from cm² 16–35) and, when complete, 1–1·55 m. in height. Most stelae were monoliths but on the lower terrace we found one which was more elaborate and included a shaft made of blocks measuring 16 x 16 x 21 cm. The inscription of Masigama (no. 4) came from this monument.
4. A roughly shaped capital crowning the stele, also rectangular in section so as to fit on to it (fig. 17).

Bases, stelae and capitals are all of the local yellow-brown limestone, whose surface, usually very hard, has become worn and cracked as a result of centuries of exposure.

Not much can be said of the individual graves. Most of them are invisible on the surface but what little appeared showed that their outline was rectangular. Their modest size suggests cremation burials rather than inhumations; and in fact excavation of one of them confirmed this, producing nothing but a few fragments of calcined bone. In this tomb there was no trace of an urn to hold the ashes; but it is very likely that the majority of the tombs were opened long ago by Arabs in search of treasure. The chances of finding an intact tomb or objects of artistic or historical interest are small.

The graves and the bases of the stelae are all that remained, in a strict sense, *in situ*. The stelae themselves and their capitals were found scattered around on the surface or used in rough modern walls.

DECORATED ELEMENTS

The majority of the stelae were plain "rectangular" shafts without mouldings or ornament of any kind. But one of them—carrying inscription no. 10—has on the reverse face a panel containing a relief of a human figure armed with two staves or spears and below it a Roman eagle; a second—with illegible inscription —shows a relief of a human figure armed with a single spear (cf. fig. 17, no. 12); a third has a relief of an unidentified object perhaps meant to represent a military *vexillum* (cf. fig. 17, no. 13); and on two there are very simple incised rosettes of a type common on the lintels of doors in Tripolitanian fortified farmhouses (fig. 17, nos. 11 and 12).

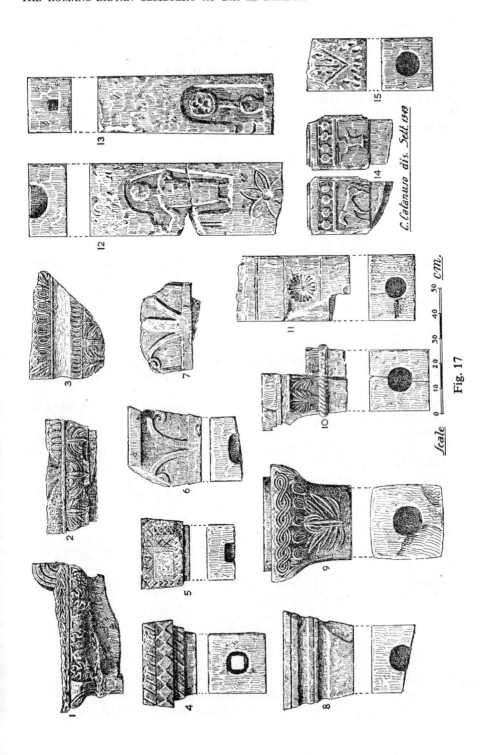

C. Catanuso dis. Sett. 1949

Fig. 17

Scale

The crowning capitals are decorated with ornament which varies from crude geometric pattern (fig. 17, no. 4) to quite elaborate compositions with bunches of grapes and acanthus leaves (fig. 17, no. 1). The great variety of decorative schemes apparent in fig. 17 indicates the range of tastes and of resources available to those who erected these monuments. Granted that the tombs appear to belong to a single and quite brief period, we have here a demonstration of the difficulty of dating individual examples of this provincial art solely on the basis of stylistic criteria.

<h3 style="text-align:center">THE INSCRIPTIONS[4]</h3>

The lettering is very roughly cut. In some cases (e.g. nos. 2, 8) the mason has dismally failed to keep his lines straight; in others he has only saved himself by cutting a series of horizontal guide-lines (e.g. nos. 1, 3, 5, 7, 12, 13, 20). The Latin alphabet is used, with the addition of two non-Latin characters, Σ and 8 both of which appear in similar inscriptions elsewhere in Tripolitania (e.g. *IRT* 889, 892). The absence of the letter P may be an indication of Semitic influence on the language. The spelling of the word BYN or BVN, used indifferently to indicate paternity, shows that Y and V represent the same vowel.

The catalogue below gives the dimensions of each monument and the recognisable elements in the texts. Where no facsimile is reproduced the complete legible text is given.

1. Complete stele, 35 by 35 by 155 cm.; letters, 3·5–4·5 cm., cut between horizontal guide-lines. FLABISAICHAM BN MACARCUM TRIBYNVS . . . . . MACHRVΣ (fig. 18).
2. Complete stele, 33 by 33 by 128 cm.; letters, 5–6 cm. IVLLVS MASTHALVL BYN CHVRDI . . . . (fig. 19).
3. Damaged stele, 33 by 33 by 60 cm.; letters, 2–5 cm., cut between horizontal guide-lines. FLABIVS MAC[A]RCVM . . . . TRIB[VNVS] . . . MACARCVM TRIBVNVS (fig. 20).
4. Block, 46 by 50 by 21 cm., inscribed within a *tabella ansata* 33 by 16 cm. with raised borders; letters, 4–4·5 cm. MAΣIGAMA BYN ISACHV TRIBVNVS (fig. 22).
5. Complete stele, 35 by 35 by 120 cm.; letters, 4 cm. IVLIVS . . . . . IBITVA . . . . MACHRVΣ BYN ROGATE (fig. 23).
6. Stele, 26 by 26 by 80 cm.; letters, 2·5 cm. IVLIVS NASIF TRIBVNVS . . . . (fig. 24).
7. Fragment, 25 by 20 by 48 cm.; letters, 4–5 cm., cut between horizontal guide-lines (not illustrated).

. . . . . .
IMNVS
NIMIRA
BVN / / / / /

8. Fragment, 22 by 22 by 55 cm.; letters, very irregular, 2–5 cm. Nothing can be made of the text except perhaps a name DOMBASSA (fig. 25).
9. Fragment, 25 by 25 by 64 cm.; letters, 3–5 cm. . . . . YRIRABAN BYN ISICVAR (fig. 26).

Fig. 18 Stele no. 1

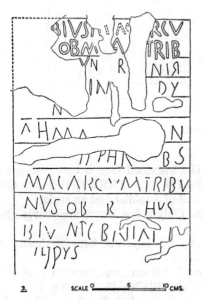

Fig. 20 Stele no. 3

Fig. 19 Stele no. 2

Fig. 21 Stele no. 14

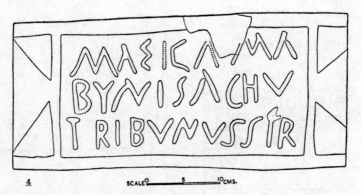

Fig. 22 Stele no. 4

10. Complete stele, 32 by 32 by 80 cm. The inscribed face is badly worn and the only words legible are ....]MIRATH ... TRI[BV]NVS ... (Not illustrated.) On the reverse face is the relief of a soldier and an eagle.

11. Stele, 20 by 20 by 68 cm.; letters, 3 cm. Only a few letters are visible. (Not illustrated.)

12. Fragment, 25 by 25 by 30 cm.; letters, 2·5 cm., cut between horizontal guide-lines. Totally illegible. (Not illustrated.)

13. Fragment, 16 by 16 by 27 cm.; letters, 4–4·5 cm., cut between horizontal guide-lines. FLABIVS MASIN[TH]AN TR[I]BVNV [S . . . . . (fig. 27).

14. Fragment, 25 by 25 by 48 cm.; letters, 3–4 cm., last line 8 cm. FLABIUS ISIGVARI TRIBYNYS BYN IARNVHAN . . . . (fig. 21).

15. Stele, 25 by 25 by 95 cm.; letters, 2–3 cm. The inscribed surface is badly damaged and only a few isolated letters are visible. (Not illustrated.)

Fig. 23 Stele no. 5

Fig. 24 Stele no. 6

Fig. 25 Stele no. 8

16. Rectangular base carrying a colonette, total height 62 cm., base 28 by 28 by 37 cm., inscribed within a panel (22 by 31 cm.) with diagonal ornament along the edge. The text is considerably damaged but the second line may read BVN IEDO . . . . . (Not illustrated.)

17. Stele, 23 by 23 by 60 cm.; letters, 3·5 cm. . . . BVN VASARA BABAR TIMSI (fig. 28).

18. Stele, 28 by 28 by 78 cm.; letters, 4·5 cm. Badly damaged, with only a few letters surviving. (Not illustrated.)

19. Stele, 33 by 33 by 55 cm.; letters, 1·5–2·5 cm., very irregular and badly formed. The inscribed face has been hacked and damaged. (Not illustrated.) The following lines may be read in part:

> . . . . KAYSNISMV.
> . . . . BEATINOM
> . . . . EKYC . . . .
> . . . . DVC (vacat)

20. Stele, 25 by 25 by 98 cm.; letters, 4 cm., cut between horizontal guide-lines. Illegible. (Not illustrated.)

21. Inscribed stele, with surface badly damaged and the upper part of the text completely lost (see fig. 29).

I do not propose to discuss here the interpretation of the individual texts—but the following list of recognisable elements in them may be useful:

1. Names and Latin words
Flabius nos. 1, 3, 13, 14.
Iulius nos. 2, 5, 6.
Rogate no. 5, cf. *IRT* 855 (Sirte) [the Latin root has been given a Punic ending].
Tribunus nos. 1, 3, 4, 6, 10, 13, 14.

2. Libyan names attested in other Tripolitanian inscriptions
Isiguar nos. 9, 14; cf. *IRT* 867 (Bir el-Uaar).

Fig. 26 Stele no. 9

Fig. 27 Stele no. 13

Issicuar cf. *IRT* 902 (Ghirza).
Masinthan no. 13, cf. *IRT* 884 (at Mizda).
Nimira no. 7, cf. *IRT* 898, 899 (Ghirza).
Nasif no. 6, cf. *IRT* 899, 901 (Ghirza).

3. Presumed Libyan names not attested elsewhere
Saicham or Isaicham no. 1.
Macarcum nos. 1, 3.
Machrus nos. 1, 5.
Maσigama no. 4.

4. Common words or phrases repeated in several texts
BYN *passim.*
TYRIRABAN nos. 1, 9.
BABARTIMSI nos. 9, 17.
VSEB nos. 1, 5.

GENERAL CONCLUSIONS

Although the language of the inscriptions on the funerary stelae is unknown, they contain elements which identify the character of the cemetery and its relation to the general archaeological picture of the Sofeggin area.

It can be said with reasonable certainty that the tombs contained cremation burials of individuals who were pagans and in many cases officers (tribunes) of the Tripolitanian frontier army in the late Roman Empire. These officers spoke a native language but had undergone some Roman cultural influences as shown by their assumption of Roman *nomina* and their burial with funerary monuments which, however debased in form, seem to derive from classical practice. Their native names appear to be Libyan rather than Punic but their cremation of the dead and their use of the word byn (bun) to indicate paternity (assuming that this is the correct interpretation) prove that there were Punic influences too.

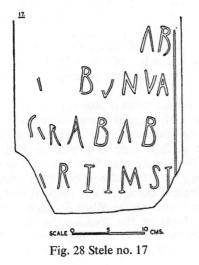

Fig. 28 Stele no. 17

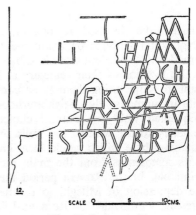

Fig. 29 Stele no. 21

Like the majority of the part-Romanised inhabitants of the Tripolitanian frontier zone the tribunes of Dreder might be described as Liby-Phoenician.

Exact dating evidence for the erection of the monuments is lacking but the frequency of the name *Flabius* (*Flavius*) provides an important clue. From the reign of Constantine onwards, and very especially in the second half of the fourth century—the period to which we can assign the military cemetery at Concordia on the Adriatic—the name *Flavius* was widely adopted by barbarians enrolled in the Roman Army, and by public officials, as a *praenomen*.[5] The Dreder cemetery can therefore be placed in the fourth century or the early fifth. If we recall the measures undertaken by Justinian to convert the tribesmen of the interior of Tripolitania to Christianity a date after the Byzantine re-conquest becomes unlikely;[6] and in any case there are good grounds for doubting that the Byzantine government ever organised a frontier so far to the south.

We can perhaps advance a little further. Beside the four examples of *Flabius* there are three of *Iulius* and these are the only Roman *nomina* appearing in the surviving inscriptions of the group. It seems probable that they were taken in honour of a reigning emperor or emperors and if so there are good grounds for conjecturing that the period concerned was the joint reign of Iulius Constans and Flavius Iulius Constantius, after the death of Constantine II, i.e. 340–350. The imperial *nomina* were probably taken on enrolment in the Roman Army rather than given at birth.

The rank of *tribunus* in the Roman Army of the late Empire indicated the commanding officer of a unit.[7] A tribune normally commanded a *numerus* of 500 men and was senior to a *centenarius* or a *ducenarius*. From the *Notitia Dignitatum* we know that the *limes Tripolitanus* was divided into regional sectors each commanded by a *praepositus limitis*.[8] A tribune therefore was the immediate subordinate of the *praepositus* of his region.

It is surprising that the cemetery contains no memorial to any officer below the rank of tribune; and still more so that it is so distant from any Roman fort known to us. Recent work has shown, however, that the normal *castellum* in the Tripolitanian frontier zone was a small building which served as a fortified farmhouse and might be commanded by a *centenarius*[9]—there are several such buildings in a good state of preservation at Bir Scedeua (fig. 15). It seems a plausible hypothesis therefore that the tribunes of Bir ed-Dreder were not commanders of such strongpoints but tribal chieftains, leading semi-barbarous *foederati* who guarded the deserted regions on the extreme edge of the settled territory. They could perhaps be compared with the irregular native troops who often served with the Italian army in Libya.

The location of their cemetery at Bir ed-Dreder poses a problem. But if I am right in conjecturing them to be commanders of irregular troops recruited from Libyan nomads, the neighbourhood of an important and therefore much-frequented well is a natural choice; and in fact there is a modern Beduin cemetery to the west of the wells. Alternatively there may have been a Libyan sanctuary here which would have given the area a special religious significance.

Its remoteness from the main area of ancient occupation is perhaps understandable. In the Roman period the entire region of the Wadi Sofeggin, from the depression of Mileghi to the neighbourhood of Bir Scedeua (fig. 15) was intensively cultivated by Romano-Libyan *limitanei*. Their buildings are still quite well preserved and include the well-known building of Gasr Nagazza with its elaborately sculptured doorway, the church of Chafagi Aamer and pagan tombs such as the Mausoleum of Bir en-Nesma.[10] The permanently settled *limitanei* would be likely to view with prejudiced eyes the presence of nomad *foederati* in their midst and the *praepositus limitis* will therefore have taken steps to ensure that the latter remained on the borders of the settled zone, both in life and in death.

NOTES

1. A. Belardinelli, 23.

2. F. Beguinot, 14–19.

3. R. G. Goodchild, "Latino-Libyan inscriptions" 135–44.

4. *IRT* 886.

5. E. De Ruggiero, III, 161 (s.v. "Flavius").

6. Procopius, *De aedif.* VI, 2–3.

7. R. Grosse, Die Rangordnung der römischen Armee des 4–6 Jahrhunderts, in *Klio*, xv (1918), 148.

8. *Not. Dign.* Occ. I, 39: XXXI.

9. See above p. 26 f. and p. 30 f.

10. I. Gentilucci, Resti di antichi edifici lungo l'uadi Soffeggin, in *Africa Italiana*, v (1933), 172–87.

ROMAN SITES ON THE TARHUNA PLATEAU OF TRIPOLITANIA

[From *PBSR* xix (1951)]

Plates 31–40

During the years 1895–6 the late H. Swainson Cowper visited the Tarhuna plateau of Tripolitania and examined in considerable detail a large number of ancient sites. The results of this exploration, first published in the *Antiquary*, were later embodied in a monograph published in 1897.[1] Cowper was not the first European to visit the ancient monuments of the Tarhuna region: he had been preceded by Smyth (1817), Barth (1850), Von Bary (1875), and Rohlfs (1879).[2] His own work was more detailed, and geographically more concentrated, than that of his predecessors, and his publication, amply illustrated by photographs and drawings, remains today an indispensable companion for any investigator of ancient sites in the eastern Gebel.

Cowper's main thesis, which occupies a predominant place in his book, was that the trilithon-shaped "senams" (arabic for "idols") of the Tarhuna plateau were prehistoric monuments of a religious character. This conclusion was immediately challenged by Sir John Myres and the late Sir Arthur Evans, who demonstrated conclusively that these megalithic structures were in fact the frames of Roman olive-presses.[3] In consequence general interest in the Tarhuna plateau declined, and even the researches of de Mathuisieulx (1901–4), which resulted in the discovery of the important neo-Punic inscription of Ras el-Haddagia, failed to counterbalance the lost repute of the "senams".[4] On the eve of the Italian occupation Professors Salvatore Aurigemma and Francesco Beguinot carried out an archaeological mission in the Gebel and visited the Tarhuna; but it was not until 1940, when Professor Giacomo Caputo began the excavation of the great mausoleum of Gasr Doga, and of a church and fortified building lying to the east of Breviglieri village [now El Khadra], that the archaeological interest of the zone once more attracted attention.[5]

Although increased knowledge of the Tarhuna plateau has deprived it of its prehistoric monuments, it still retains an archaeological importance as a zone of intensive Roman olive-cultivation, containing ancient monuments ranging in date from A.D. 15 to the end of the classical period. These monuments consist primarily of Roman-Libyan farmhouses with associated olive-presses and mausolea; but they also include pagan and Christian places of worship, and traces of a ceramic industry. Urban development, on a modest scale, is represented by the road-station at Medina Doga, the largest site in the region.

When Cowper visited the Tarhuna plateau fifty years ago, the only tree in the whole zone was an ancient batum named "el-Khadra", a landmark for many miles, the roots of which grow out of a small Roman mausoleum (pl. 37).[6] Though surviving, and venerated by the Arabs as a *marabut*, this tree is today hardly noticeable among the extensive olive and almond plantations, and the high eucalyptus rows planted as windbreaks. The intensive agricultural development carried out in the Tarhuna area by Italian enterprise during the last twenty years has had, inevitably, an adverse effect on the condition of some of the ancient monuments. It has also resulted in the gradual abandonment of old Arab place-names and great difficulty was encountered in identifying the Ras el-Haddagia of the neo-Punic inscription (see p. 79 f. below). Fortunately Cowper's topographical descriptions are so exact that one can still identify on the ground most of the places to which he refers in his monograph.

Owing to his preoccupation with the supposedly religious character of the "senams", Cowper said little about the Roman farmhouses to which these olive-presses belonged; and though his exploration gave an idea of the intensity of the Roman agricultural settlements, it did not provide much information as to their character and distribution. Today, with the existence of good maps,[7] we are in a better position to study these aspects; and at various times during the period 1946–9 the present writer was able to visit many of the Tarhuna sites, including some unknown to Cowper. The area selected for general study measures 26 by 21 km. (fig. 30) and includes the majority of the sites which Cowper visited. Excellent air photographs, taken by the R.A.F. for operational purposes in 1942, cover a strip of 20 by 5 km. in the heart of this area, and it is in this inner area that the writer's investigations have been mainly concentrated. It is not the intention of the present paper to correct or amplify the observations on the olive-presses already published by Cowper, but rather to concentrate on certain sites of special interest and importance, of which two—the sanctuary at Ras el-Haddagia, and the pottery-kiln at Ain Scersciara—were excavated by the writer in 1947. The mausoleum at Gasr Doga, and the church and fortified building near Breviglieri, both excavated by Professor Caputo, [were] published elsewhere,[7a] and are therefore only referred to in the present article.

The writer is indebted to Professor Caputo for his advice and encouragement at all stages of the work, and for his hospitality at the Concessione Catarella on many occasions; to Professor Giorgio Levi Della Vida for his appendix (pp. 93–6) on the inscription of Ras el-Haddagia, incorporating the evidence of the additional fragments found in 1947; to Messrs M. H. Ballance and M. H. de Lisle for their help in the survey of Medina Doga; to Sig. Santino Gaudino, an intelligent and capable foreman during the two small-scale excavations, and to Sigg. Carmelo Catanuso and F. de Liberali for drawings and photographs.

THE GEOGRAPHICAL SETTING (fig. 30)

The name Tarhuna [a tribal name] belongs, in its wider sense, to a plateau some 40 km. in length from west to east, and some 20 km. from north to south. Its eastern and western limits are marked approximately by the wadis Gsèa and Wif (both outside the limits of the accompanying map). The northern limit is the edge of the steep escarpment which looks towards the Gefara; whilst the southern limit is not closely defined, the fertile soil of the Tarhuna gradually giving way to the rocky desert of the Orfella region. Today the name Tarhuna is

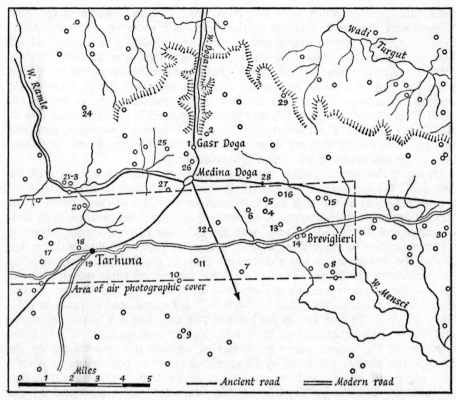

Fig. 30

commonly applied to the modern village which has grown up around the wells of El-Ubberat, where the Turks constructed a fort and named it "Gasr Tarhuna", after the region. Before the construction of this fort visiting Turkish officials camped at Ain Scersciara. In Cowper's day there were no permanent dwellings anywhere on the plateau, the population living either in tents, or in underground houses, and moving seasonally to other areas.

The plateau averages 450 m. above sea-level, falling slightly from the Gebel escarpment (where some of the hill-tops exceed 500 m.) in a south-easterly direction. It is a water-shed, the important wadis Ramle, Doga and Turgut running northwards towards the coast, and the upper tributaries of the Tareglat, of which the wadi Mensci is the most important, running south-eastwards. The Tareglat itself, bearing first eastward and then northward to meet the sea between Homs and Zliten, is named Wadi Caam in its lowest sector and is clearly identifiable with the Κίνυψ (*Cinypus flumen*) of antiquity. It was because the *Cinypus* has its origins in the Tarhuna plateau that Cowper identified the latter as the "Hill of the Graces" (λόφος ὁ χαρίτων) of Herodotus, described by that writer as "thickly covered with trees, though all the rest of Libya is bare". With the merits of this identification we are not, however, concerned here.[8]

Geologically, the plateau consists of limestone, of which bare outcrops appear on the hill-tops; but over the greater part of the area there exists a deep layer of fertile sandy soil. Beneath the upper limestone strata are to be found seams of good-quality clay, the outcrop of which at Ain Scersciara gave rise to the siting of a pottery industry there in Roman times.

Rainfall (normally 300 mm. per annum) is above the average for the rest of Tripolitania, excluding the fertile Menscia oasis of Tripoli, and important perennial springs exist at Ain Scersciara and Ain Doga.

ANCIENT COMMUNICATIONS

The plateau is traversed by a complex network of caravan tracks, many of which are now interrupted by the Italian agricultural settlements and replaced by hard roads. Most of these tracks radiate from El-Ubberat (Tarhuna village) and belong to the post-classical period; but there are faint traces of an earlier lay-out radiating from Medina Doga, which was undoubtedly the nodal point of local communications during the Roman period. In all, five ancient tracks seem to have converged at Medina Doga, of which two were marked out by Roman milestones, but none were apparently paved. Two, possibly three, represent routes recorded in the Roman itineraries. These five tracks are as follows:

(a) The Eastern Gebel road, the earliest of which we have dating evidence, was laid out in A.D. 15–17 by L. Aelius Lamia, proconsul of Africa, and linked the Tarhuna zone with the port of Lepcis.[9] Although the earliest milestones found in the Tarhuna area are of the third century, there can be little reason to doubt that they follow that first-century line. At Mile XXX, in the Wadi el-Mé, Mr. David Oates has recently found two milestones (of Maximinus and Gordian III); two more (of Caracalla and an unidentified emperor) were found by Professor Caputo in 1940 in situ near the Zavia el-Medeni, and bear the mileage figure XXXVIIII.[10] The alignment of these two mile-stations points directly towards Medina Doga, which by measurement, must have stood at the 42nd mile from Lepcis. The first-century terminal milestone, near the Arch of Septimius Severus at Lepcis [IRT 930], gives the length of the road as 44 miles, and its destination as in mediterraneum. Bearing in mind that the road was probably not marked out at every mile until the reign of Caracalla, the discrepancy of two miles is insignificant; and the fact that no precise destination is named on the Lepcis milestone probably indicates that Medina Doga was not, in the reign of Tiberius, of sufficient importance to be specifically named.[11]

(b) Although the mileage figures preclude any possibility that Aelius Lamia's road continued further westward from Medina Doga, that such a continuation was later established is shown by the Antonine Itinerary, and by recently-discovered milestones. The Itinerary[12] describes a road from Turris Tamalleni to Lepcis via the interior, and gives the following as the road-stations west of Lepcis: Lepti Magna—XL—Mesphe—XXX—Thenadassa. The identification of Medina Doga as Mesphe (see below p. 76 f.) seems certain, even though the mileage figure should be 42 rather than 40; and Thenadassa has recently been identified at Ain Wif, 30 Roman miles from Medina Doga, where there are the remains of an important road-station with evidence of military occupation.[13] During 1950 the first Roman milestones came to light on the road from Mesphe to Thenadassa, at the 53rd and 57th miles from Lepcis. These columns, with inscriptions of Gordian III and Gallienus, show that the Roman road from Tarhuna to Ain Wif passed about 2 km. south of Tazzoli village centre, and did not follow the line of the modern motor track from Tazzoli to Ain Wif.

(c) Running due north from Medina Doga a trackway of undoubted antiquity passes the mausoleum of Gasr Doga and the adjacent Roman cisterns, and continues along the bed of the Wadi Doga (the upper reach of the Wadi el-Msabha) to meet the Gefara plain at Sugh el-Giumaa. Thence it probably communicated with the Roman coast-road in the vicinity of Gasr Garabulli.[14]

(d) The direct route from *Mesphe* to *Oea* ran due west for 5 km. from Medina Doga to Ain Scersciara, and then followed the bed of the Wadi Ramle to the Gefara, which it crossed in a direct line to Mellaha in the Tripoli oasis. This track became the "Trigh Tarhuna", constantly used before the construction of the modern road from Tarhuna to Tripoli via Castel Benito. This may well be the inland route from *Lepcis* to *Oea* shown in the Peutinger Map, where the road-stations and distances are given as follows: *Lepti Magna*—XXV—*Subututtu*—XV—*Cercar*—XX—*Flacci Taberna*—XVI—*Oea*. This hypothesis would involve placing *Cercar* either at, or near, Medina Doga; and it may be questioned whether that site would have had two alternative ancient names. On the other hand, the simpler hypothesis that the inland route marked on the Peutinger Map ran parallel, and close, to the coast road involves even greater topographical difficulties.[15]

(e) Finally, there are faint traces, visible on air-photographs,[16] of a trackway running southwards from Medina Doga, passing the mausoleum of El-Khadra, and then apparently continuing towards the Orfella region. Although the exact route and destination of this trackway have still to be determined, it would be reasonable to suppose that Medina Doga was, during the later Roman period, at least, linked by a recognised route with the intensively occupied wadis of the Orfella.

Thus Medina Doga was an important meeting-point of tracks used in the Roman period, and the area selected for study may be considered as having been exposed, throughout the classical period, to cultural and political influences penetrating both southwards from the coast, and northwards from the Sahara. It is hardly surprising, therefore, that the epigraphy[17] of the region records Libyan, Punic and Roman names, and that a few luxury villas with mosaic floors stood in a zone where the more common type of Romanised habitation was the austere fortified farmhouse. Moreover, the fact that the road from Lepcis through Medina Doga to Ain Wif is described in the Antonine Itinerary as *iter quod limitem Tripolitanum ducit* reminds us that military influence must have been strong, even in this area of intensive agricultural development.

MEDINA DOGA (pl. 31; fig. 31)

The Roman road-station at the head of the Wadi Doga, the meeting point of the five trackways listed above, is the most extensive ancient site in the area selected for study: it is also, after Ghirza, the largest site so far encountered in the interior of Tripolitania, and the one most closely approximated to a small town. It lies inconspicuously among the recent olive plantations of the Concessione

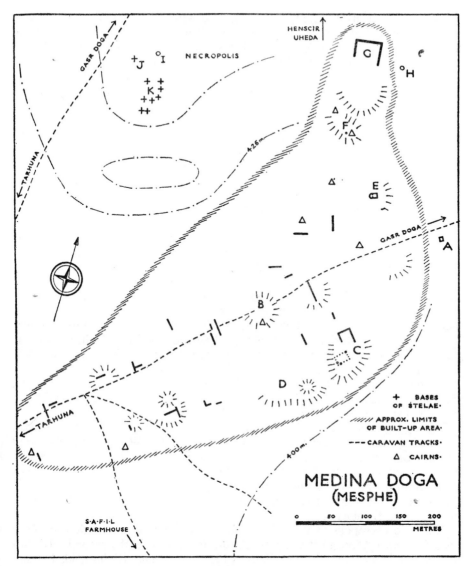

Fig. 31

S.A.F.I.L., in a natural bowl, a fact which distinguishes it from the majority of the ancient sites of the Tarhuna, and may explain why its ruins have attracted so little attention. Commander (later Rear-Admiral) W. H. Smyth seems to have been the first to record the antiquities of this site, but he exaggerated its extent, probably through including some of the adjacent but isolated ruins. Rohlfs, visiting the site in 1879, wrote "Südöstlich von diesem Grabdenkmal (Gasr Doga) welches einer genauern Untersuchung würdig ist, liegt etwa 2 km entfernt das grossartige, wahrscheinlich ebenfalls aus der Römerzeit herstammende Ruinenfeld einer ganzen Stadt", and added that the Arabs found coins and "intagli" in the ruins. Cowper seems to have visited the site but says little about it; and, although an Italian official at Tarhuna interested himself in the necropolis, there seems to be no further published reference to Medina Doga, which is not even marked as an ancient site on the 1/100,000 map.[18]

The site (fig 31) is today covered by a geometrical "grid" of olive-trees laid out in straight lines at intervals of 20 m., but the mass of masonry and rubble has hindered the growth of many of the young trees. Industrious farmworkers have collected into cairns the smaller stones lying on the surface, but large numbers of squared orthostats and occasional columns protrude from the low mounds which mark the area; and from these and the scatter of stones, tiles and pottery, the approximate limits of the ancient settlement can be determined.

A caravan track enters the site from the east, passing the base of a small mausoleum (A), and continues over the highest mound (B), which probably covers a building of some importance. The most substantial visible remains lie south of this track and include a colonnaded building (C) with limestone columns of 60 cm. diameter, and the probable site of a bath-building (D), marked by flue-tiles on the surface. Another bath-building—perhaps the main one—lay north of the track (E), and its apsed frigidarium was partly uncovered in 1949. On the north-east side of the site the area of ruins runs up the gentle slope of the hill, includes another colonnaded building (F) and terminates in a large enclosure (G) with walls of larger ashlar blocks, in contrast to the orthostat-and-rubble masonry used elsewhere on the site. Some 300 m. further north, an isolated ruin, called Henscir Uhéda and surrounded by a ditch, crowns the hilltop. Fragments of a marble statue were found here on the surface in 1949, and a limestone panel with the Constantinian monogram, now in Tripoli Museum, was brought from this ruin in 1914.[19] On the western side of the built-up area, the ruins continue as a thin strip along the caravan track for a little distance towards Tarhuna, and extend almost to the site of another ditched building.

It is evident that Medina Doga had no perimetral defences, in which respect (as in many others) it resembles the road-station at Ain Wif. Its general lay-out suggests the gradual development of a settlement beside an ancient road that ran more or less on the line of the trackway which now crosses the site. The wall-alignments are consistently parallel or at right-angles to this track, except in the north-eastern sector, where there seems to have been a northward extension on a different alignment.

The main necropolis of this roadside community lay on the north side of the residential area. Close to the large enclosure (G) a hole in the ground (H) leads to a series of underground chambers, which were inspected in 1949, but not surveyed. They appear to run for some distance westward under building G, from which a vertical shaft, now blocked, apparently gave access to them. These tomb-chambers have been previously entered, and without removal of the deep deposit of soil which has washed into them, it is difficult to judge their date and character. Further to the west a recent subsidence in the ground (I) marks another group of underground tomb-chambers. Nearby (K) are scattered on the surface numerous bases of Libyan funerary monuments.[20] One complete stele (J) with pointed top, bears a Latino-Libyan funerary inscription.[21]

Trial pits dug in 1949 revealed that the ruins of Medina Doga are well preserved beneath the surface, but at a depth which would necessitate fairly extensive excavations to obtain useful results. The moulded base of a column of building C was found to rest on a pavement of stone flags 1·50 m. below the surface. In the case of the northern bath-building (E), the *opus signinum* floor of the apsed frigidarium was found at 1·30 m. below the surface. A bench ran around the curve of the apse, and was interrupted by a cement lavabo, which was originally fed from an external cistern and had an outlet pipe, cased in cement, running across the floor of the room (pl. 31).

Our general picture of Medina Doga is that of a *vicus*, which developed gradually at the intersection of several important trackways and eventually became a fully romanised centre of some importance. Whether a small community already existed on the spot in A.D. 15–17, when Aelius Lamia's road was cut, remains to be determined; but the fact that the road (at least, as marked by later milestones) headed straight for this site in the last 12 miles of its course may not be without significance. It is equally uncertain what part this site played in the organisation of the *limes*: the irregular lay-out argues against a distinctively military origin; but the case of Ain Wif shows that the lack of defences cannot be held to disprove the possibility of its having, at some period, contained a small garrison. The large enclosure (G) may be military in character, and a mausoleum which lay further to the north and is now demolished, contained an inscription recording a *veteranus*.[22] It can hardly be doubted, at least, that Medina Doga, the *Mesphe* of the Antonine Itinerary, remained the local administrative centre of the Tarhuna plateau throughout the Roman period; but the elucidation of its detailed history must await excavation.

THE SANCTUARY OF AMMMON AT RAS EL-HADDAGIA (pls. 32–4; figs. 32, 33)

The earliest dated building on the plateau is the Ammonium of Ras el-Haddagia. Cowper visited this site (his no. 31, which he calls "Kom el-Khadajieh") in 1895, but observed on the surface nothing of apparent significance. de Mathuisieulx, in 1901, was more fortunate, for in the intervening years Arabs had unearthed a large block, in two pieces, on which was inscribed a long neo-Punic text. A squeeze was sent to Clermont-Ganneau, who was able to determine that the inscription referred to the construction of a sanctuary of Ammon, built during the proconsulship of L. Aelius Lamia (A.D. 15–17). The inscription, rediscovered by Aurigemma and Beguinot in 1911, was transported to Tripoli Museum three years later,[23] and the site of the discovery was soon forgotten, so much so that in 1935 the contractors who built Breviglieri village-centre quarried much of their stone from the ancient walls.

The name Ras el-Haddagia, recorded by Aurigemma as the site of de Mathuisieulx's discovery, appears on no modern map, and considerable difficulty was experienced in 1947, when the writer, in collaboration with Prof. Caputo, sought to identify it. Cowper's topographical indications gave a clue, and eventually an elderly Arab was found who remembered the place-name and ascribed it to a hill 2 km. south of Zaviet el-Medeni, and 1 km. west-north-west of Breviglieri village-centre (fig. 32). Examination of the air photographs covering this region revealed some dim outlines of what appeared to be walls on this hill-top (ht. 432 m.); and a visit to the site established that these "walls" were in fact robber-trenches, still open, from which the stones of ancient walls had been extracted within the memory of local Italian peasants. Excavation was decided upon in

MAP OF BREVIGLIERI AREA

RR = ROMAN REMAINS

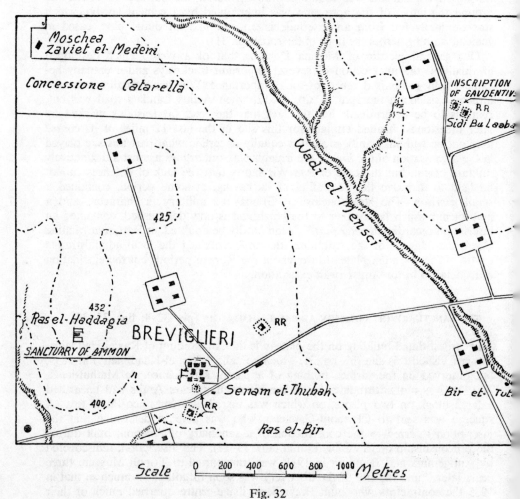

Scale   0   200   400   600   800   1000 Metres

Fig. 32

order to obtain such information as had survived the stone-robbing; and in the
course of this excavation, the lowest courses of the Ammonium were found
almost intact, together with further fragments of the neo-Punic dedicatory
inscription, thus confirming the identification of the site beyond any discussion.

The surviving remains of the Ammonium consist of three features: (a) the
Shrine; (b) the Portico; and (c) late walls, representing a farmhouse of the
Christian period or later, which had occupied the whole site after its desecration
and destruction. Associated objects were few. Two small fragments of white
marble, one representing a palm trunk, were all that had survived of the cult-
statues. The angle of a Corinthian pilaster-capital in grey limestone was the only
relic of the original architectural ornamentation. The only two coins found were

both illegible; whilst the relatively abundant coarse pottery was found, unstratified, in soil disturbed by the stone-robbing. In one or two areas, where pre-Sanctuary humus layers were found undisturbed, they contained no occupation material of any kind. A single post-hole, found just outside the south-west corner of the shrine, was probably cut to receive a scaffold-pole or a fence-stake associated with the stone building, and cannot be considered to prove the existence of a timber predecessor. In these circumstances, the dated dedicatory inscription may be held to indicate the beginning of occupation on the site; whilst a lamp of late form, found in the ruins of the rough walls of the later farmstead, represents the latest period.

(a) *The Shrine* (pls. 33, 34) is represented by the lowest course of finely-cut and tooled limestone blocks, forming a rectangle of 7·05 by 2·95 m., with a partition wall towards the west end of the rectangle. To ensure stable foundations, the natural rock, which rises to within 40 cm. of the present surface outside the area of the shrine, had been levelled off at a depth of 80 cm. over the whole area of the structure. On this solid and level bed of rock was laid the foundation course of blocks 44 cm. high and normally 51 cm. in width. Some of the blocks, however, were trimmed only on their outer face, which indicates that the structure was of podium type, its original floor-level being close to, if not above, present ground level. The earth filling of the podium was entirely disturbed, a large pit (fig. 33; Pit 1) having been dug in the eastern half of the building; it contained mixed soil, potsherds and damaged limestone blocks. Another pit (fig. 33; Pit 2) was found outside the north wall of the podium, and ran obliquely under the wall foundations: it was 2·20 m. deep and contained much mortar, wall-plaster, and a fragment of the neo-Punic dedicatory inscription. Both these pits evidently post-date the abandonment of the sanctuary. The only other feature of note relating to the Shrine was a rectangular cutting recessed into the rock outside the east face of the podium. This can hardly be other than the site of an altar that was completely dismantled when the sanctuary was desecrated. It should also be remarked that the wide foundation-bedding cut for the east podium wall probably marks the site of a flight of steps.

(b) *The Portico* is the most damaged part of the whole site, the stone-robbers of 1935 having removed all but four blocks. Its walls were, however, marked either by the bedding-level cut in the rock (fig. 33: "imprint"), or by robber-trenches in the upper strata. Thus the complete plan of the structure could be ascertained. The greater width (0·90 m.) of the inner wall, in contrast to that of the outer walls (0·60 cm.), suggests that it served as a stylobate for a colonnade open towards the shrine. If this hypothesis is correct—and it would seem to be supported by the fact that the neo-Punic inscription mentions "porticoes"—we must interpret this part of the building as a covered shelter for visitors awaiting their turn to pay their vows at the shrine.

The portico was structurally secondary to the shrine, the foundation trench on its west wall being 13 cm. higher than that on the podium, and its outer wall inset by 12 cm., but it need not necessarily be inferred that it was later in date: its few surviving blocks, though less neatly trimmed, were of the same character as those of the podium. It may be stated categorically that no corresponding portico existed on the south side of the shrine. The rock and topsoil south of the south-west angle of the podium were undisturbed, and neither foundations of the

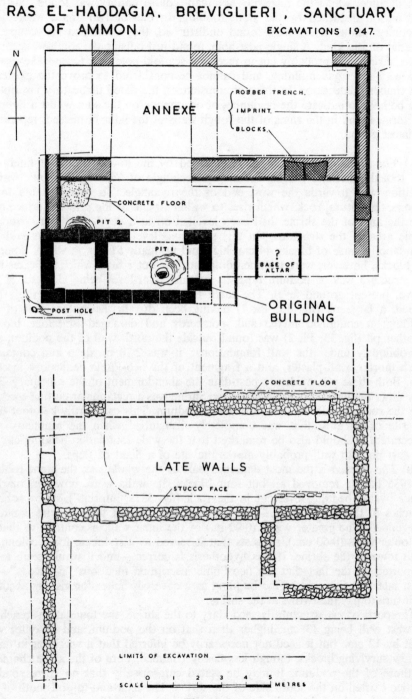

RAS EL-HADDAGIA, BREVIGLIERI, SANCTUARY
OF AMMON.   EXCAVATIONS 1947.

N

ANNEXE

ROBBER TRENCH.

IMPRINT.

BLOCKS.

CONCRETE FLOOR

PIT 2.

PIT I

?
BASE OF
ALTAR

POST HOLE

ORIGINAL
BUILDING

CONCRETE FLOOR

LATE WALLS

STUCCO FACE

LIMITS OF EXCAVATION

SCALE 0 1 2 3 4 5 METRES

Fig. 33

pagan period nor robber-trenches marking their site were encountered anywhere south of the shrine.

(c) *The late farmhouse*. The walls of the building consisted of small chips of blocks and columns, with occasional large blocks to give strength to angles and wall-junctions. Later disturbance had been extensive throughout its area, and the plan as recovered by the excavation is incomplete. In one place a rough concrete floor was found; but towards the south, where the natural rock approaches the surface, the rock itself, pitted and uneven, served as a floor. It may be assumed that, in its original state, this late farmhouse extended northwards across the ruins of the shrine and portico, the pits under the podium probably being associated with it. The general impression conveyed by these sorry remains is one of abject poverty, and although classed here as a farmhouse, this ramshackle structure must be sharply distinguished from the well-built, if austere, fortified farms of the Tarhuna plateau. Chronologically, the building must belong to the final phase of settled occupation on the plateau, and it was perhaps the home of a simple herdsman and his family.

The general character of the Sanctuary of Ammon, before its demolition in the Christian period, is not entirely clear from the few surviving remains. It seems to have been a small countryside shrine, of podium type, with steps and altar on the east; and with a small square chamber at the west end of the podium. It was in this chamber that we may assume that the cult-statue, referred to in the dedicatory inscription, stood. The exact position occupied by the inscribed lintel is uncertain; but since its length (2·19 m.) is slightly less than the width of the podium, we may imagine that it stood above the entrance to the cult-chamber. Close parallels for this small countryside sanctuary are difficult to find, if only because our knowledge of temple architecture in Tripolitania is largely confined to the coastal cities. The little temple at Sghedeida, on the outskirts of the Tripoli oasis, excavated by Professor Renato Bartoccini in 1921,[24] has certain affinities, including a floor-level raised 0·50 m. above the ancient ground-level and an altar in front of the building. It is interesting to note that the cult-chamber at Sghedeida could only be entered "per mezzo di un'apertura rialzata dal suolo, simile ad una finestra attraverso la quale il devoto poteva anche passare la propria offerta". It is very probable that at Ras el-Haddagia, as at Sghedeida, the cult-statue was intended to be seen but not closely approached. The architectural form of the shrine is, however, more closely paralleled by Senam Tininai, between Mizda and Beni Ulid, a structure sometimes incorrectly described as a mausoleum, but certainly—as both its architecture and inscription confirm—a small temple.[25] Here, as at Ras el-Haddagia, the cult-chamber was fronted by a pronaos, a feature absent at Sghedeida. The measurements of these three shrines, the only rural examples at present known in Tripolitania, may be tabulated as follows:

	Internal dimensions of cult-chamber m.	Overall external dimensions m.
Ras el-Haddagia	1·85 by 1·7	7·05 by 2·95
Sghedeida	1·20 by 1·00	2·25 by 2·05*
Senam Tininai	2·45 by 2·20	6·80 by 3·40

(* Excluding precinct wall.)

If we compare the plans of these Tripolitanian shrines with the two best-known Romano-Punic rural sanctuaries in Tunisia—the Sanctuary of Baal and Tanit near Siagu, and the Sanctuary of Tanit at El-Kenissia, near Sousse[26]—we cannot fail to be struck by the simplicity of the Tripolitanian shrines and the complexity of the Tunisian. The only point of similarity would seem to lie in the use of extremely small chambers to house the cult-statues. It is hardly possible, however, in the present state of knowledge, to recognise in the surviving ruins of the Ras el-Haddagia Ammonium any features that can be said to reflect the nature of the cult.

It is safe, perhaps, to say that in outward character the building is essentially Roman; and Levi Della Vida has already pointed out that the excellent palae-ography and the separation of individual words prove the dedicatory inscription of the Ammonium to have been cut under Roman influence.[27] That the architect and the builders of the Ammonium were skilled craftsmen from the coast seems indisputable; and it may be doubted whether they would have been influenced in their choice of design by any native Libyan tradition.

The most pertinent question which may be asked is whether the divinity described as "the Lord Ammon" in the dedicatory inscription is to be identified with the Libyan Jupiter Ammon, whose cult spread westwards from the oasis of Siwa, or with the Punic Baal-Hammon, identified with Saturn in the Roman pantheon. Clermont-Ganneau suggested the former interpretation; whilst Lidz-barski, on purely linguistic grounds, preferred the second.[28] In considering this problem it must be borne in mind that the dedicator at Ras el-Haddagia, bears a Libyan and not a Punic name (see Appendix I); and that whereas the cult of Saturn is not attested in any literary or epigraphic documents relating to the area of modern Tripolitania, that of Jupiter Ammon is. A road station *ad Ammonem* stood 16 Roman miles west of Sabratha (Peutinger Map); an Ἄμμωνος (πόλις) is recorded by Ptolemy (IV, 3, 42) somewhere in the interior of Tripolitania; an inscription to *Jupiter Hammon* (*IRT* 920) has been found at Bu Ngem; whilst traces of the cult are no less frequent in Cyrenaica.[29] Finally, it is not perhaps without significance that a fragment of wall-plaster found in Pit 2 at Ras el-Haddagia bears the painted letters ... AMM ..., which would suggest that the divinity of this sanctuary bore the name Hammon, and not Saturn, under the *interpretatio romana*.

THE VILLA AND POTTERY-WORKS AT AIN SCERSCIARA

It would be expected that at Scersciara, as at Gasr Doga and Ain Wif, there should be traces of Roman settlement in the vicinity of the perennial springs; and Barth, who camped on this pleasant site in February, 1850, noted the ruins of a massive building of large stones on the hillside some 200 m. north of the water-fall.[30] This building, reconstructed as a fort during the Turkish period, and consequently much mutilated, has traces of a surrounding ditch, and was in origin probably a Roman fortified farm of the usual type: it does not appear to be of exceptional interest. More unusual, for the region in which they occur, are the remains of a mosaic floor exposed in a road-cutting made shortly before the war, on the west side of the cascade, and some 50 m. from it.

(a) *The portico and mosaics* (fig. 34)

During 1947 this mosaic was examined, to discover the character of the structure to which it belonged, and to decide on the best measures of protection. Owing to the presence of a plantation of young eucalyptus trees, the exploratory trenches were of necessity irregular and intermittent (fig. 34). They revealed that the exposed section of mosaic belonged to a series of rectangular panels, separated by guilloche borders; these panels formed the floor of a narrow portico closed by a continuous wall on one side, with a colonnade opening northwards towards the hollow of a small tributary wadi. The borders of the individual panels conform to the intercolumniation of the colonnade, the bases of which were 2·60 m. apart, centre to centre. The columns were of strongly cemented rubble, with a stucco surface, an unusual method of construction in this Gebel area, where good quality limestone is abundant: they rested on a continuous stylobate of limestone blocks. The variety of the geometrical designs in the various panels (in red, white and blue tesserae), their competent execution, and the material used in the columns and back wall of the portico all testify to construction by artisans familiar with the constructional features of coastal villas, and perhaps less skilled in handling heavy materials.

It is clear that the portico was not an organic part of a villa lay-out. There are no traces of rooms opening off it, and its line, following the edge of a natural hollow, diverges from the straight. The portico was traced for some 25 m. southwards from the first surviving mosaic panel, and for some 12 m. northwards towards the waterfall, to which it seems to have descended by a series of terraces; but in this latter area the mosaic floor had completely disappeared, the stylobate alone surviving. In the southern part of the excavated area, where the portico was covered by a metre of wind-blown sand, and had not suffered interference, the mosaic was found covered by a thick layer of white mortar representing the collapsed terrazzo-roof of the portico. This interpretation was confirmed by the absence of roof-tiles. Between the layer and the mosaic itself there was no occupation material, a fact which indicates that the portico was not lived in.

The purpose of the portico seems to have been to provide covered communication between an as yet unlocated villa and the waterfall. Possibly this villa lies beneath a conspicuous mound some 50 m. beyond the southernmost trench dug in 1947; but time and funds did not permit its investigation. To judge from the quality of the mosaics in the portico, it would seem that this supposed villa must have been a rich one, and it would not be surprising if its owners had felt the need to connect it, by a covered portico, with the waterfall itself where there may have been a shrine or a nymphaeum. The mosaics themselves are of a type one would tentatively date to the second century A.D.

(b) *The potters' works* (pls 35, 36; figs. 35, 38)

Only 100 m. north of the waterfall, and close to the steep cliff of the main wadi bed, quantities of potsherds and blocks of baked clay were noticed on the surface during the investigations of 1947. A trial excavation brought to light a small circular pottery kiln, in poor state of preservation, of a type known on other sites in Tripolitania (see Appendix II). A short distance from this first kiln, an isolated mound attracted attention for the remains of a clay-built structure which protruded from it. When completely cleared of superficial sand, this mound

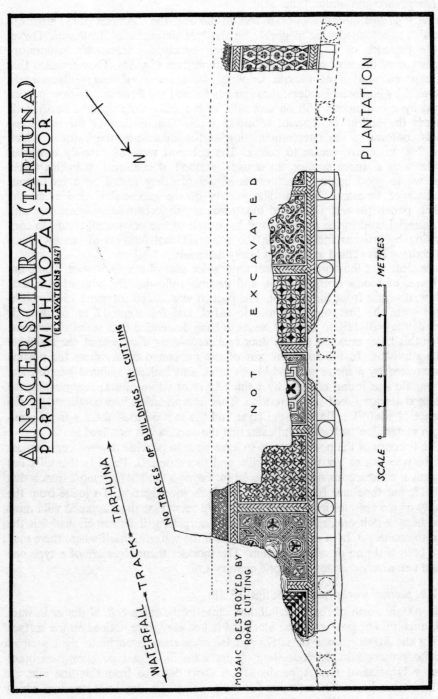

AIN-SCER-SCIARA (TARHUNA)
PORTICO WITH MOSAIC FLOOR
(EXCAVATIONS 1947)

PLANTATION

NOT EXCAVATED

NO TRACES OF BUILDINGS IN CUTTING

WATERFALL TRACK TARHUNA

MOSAIC DESTROYED BY ROAD CUTTING

SCALE 0 1 2 3 4 5 METRES

Fig. 34

POTTERY-KILN AT SCERSCIARA

(EXCAVATIONS 1947)

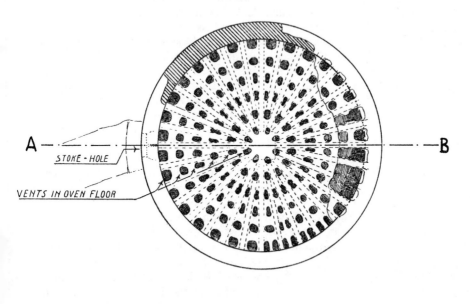

A ————————————————— B

STOKE - HOLE

VENTS IN OVEN FLOOR

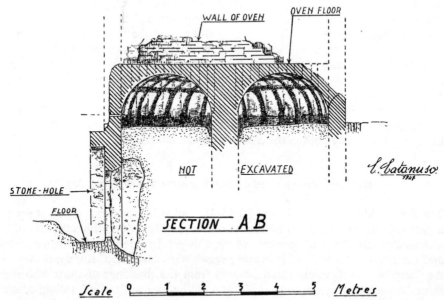

WALL OF OVEN

OVEN FLOOR

NOT   EXCAVATED

E. Catanuso
1947

STOKE - HOLE

FLOOR

SECTION A B

Scale   0   1   2   3   4   5   Metres

Fig. 35

proved to contain two large circular kilns, one almost completely destroyed, the other in a remarkable state of preservation. Measuring over 6·00 m. in diameter, it must rank as one of the largest Roman circular kilns yet brought to light.

The kiln (pls. 35, 36; fig. 35) was of up-draught type, its perforated oven floor being supported on a central pillar. The identification of the stoke-hole arch proved the depth of the combustion chamber to be $4\frac{1}{2}$ m. but it was not possible to remove all the soil from this chamber without risking the collapse of the whole structure. The outer walls of the kiln were of clay blocks which, not being completely fired, were friable; the inner structure, lined with clay daub, had been fused by the heat to the solidity of cement. The vent-holes, arranged in six concentric circles, were cut in the oven floor in the spaces between the thirty-two ribs that, springing from the central column, supported that floor. Of the walls of the oven proper only a small segment remained intact, and there is no evidence of how the oven was covered during firing. This type of kiln, in which the perforated oven floor is supported by a central pillar, rather than by transverse walls or a longitudinal rib, seems to have been rare in the European provinces of the Roman empire, and the closest parallel known to the writer is presented by two kilns found in the Byzantine potteries of Corinth in 1936–7.[31] The smaller and better preserved of these two kilns presents a profile remarkably similar to that of Ain Scersciara. The Corinth kilns, although of the eleventh century A.D., probably represent a survival of a type which was widely diffused in the Mediterranean during the later Roman period. Yet we know so little about the character of Roman kilns in the Mediterranean area that it would be rash to generalise. (See Appendix II). No remains of the kiln's last load were found in the oven, and the industry can only be dated from the indirect evidence of the pottery sherds and wasters, all of coarse ware, found throughout the site. These suggest, though they can hardly be said to prove, a late date—perhaps in the fourth century[32]: it may well be that by this period the villa and portico on the other side of the waterfall had already fallen out of use, for the smoke and activity of the industrial site must have reduced the residential charms of Ain Scersciara. The siting of the ceramic industry at this place is easily explained. Water and good-quality clay were both available in abundance, and wood for fuel was probably easily obtained locally. The road-system already described, of which one branch passes the Scersciara site, enabled the products of the kilns to be exported easily both to the coast and to the interior.

THE FORTIFIED FARMS OF THE TARHUNA PLATEAU (pl. 38)

The sites at Medina Doga, Ras el-Haddagia and Ain Scersciara represent special aspects of the romanisation of the Tarhuna plateau. More characteristic of its archaeology are the olive-presses, which Cowper has described in some detail, and the farmhouses with which these presses were associated. Rarely, if ever, do the "senams" of Tarhuna stand isolated from the dwellings of those who used them. Sometimes they are found built into the interior walls of a farmhouse, itself surrounded by a ditch; more often, in the area under review, the olive-presses are found on the outer edge of the ditch, or a little distance beyond it.

On the Tarhuna plateau the great majority of the ancient farm sites are surrounded by a broad ditch, which neither time nor agriculture have been able to efface, and they are therefore easily identifiable on air photographs, even when surface indications are scanty. The low, rectangular mounds, which these ditches surround, represent the ground-floors of the farmhouses filled in with the collapsed rubble from one or more upper storeys. The olive-farms of this area were therefore, at least during the period of their greatest expansion, tower-like structures of a type still to be found in very nearly perfect condition in the arid zones of the Sofeggin basin. In the Tarhuna area the higher rainfall has caused the collapse of the upper storeys.

Some fifteen sites of this type can be identified on the air photographs of the 20 by 5 km. strip in the heart of the area under review, and they are equally abundant outside the area of photographic cover. In most cases, however, surface study reveals little more than their overall dimensions, which vary from 10 to 30 m. square. In one instance only, Henscir Salamat (see below), is it possible to recover the interior plan, without excavation. Normally these farmhouses stand alone, and on the highest ground, but occasionally one finds two set close together. An example of this is to be found at Sidi bu Laaba, a little north-east of Breviglieri village-centre, where two ditched farmhouses, only a few metres apart, have produced curious late reliefs, and a Christian inscription recording the erection of a *turris*[33]—to be identified no doubt with one or other of these buildings. Another technical name applied to these tower-like structures was *centenarium*, which is attested by an inscription found by Caputo in the building of this type south of Sidi Ali ben Zaid.[34]

Of these sites, Henscir Salamat (fig. 36) alone merits detailed description, for the reasons already stated. It occupies a hill-top (ht. 486 m.), some 2 km. north-west of Medina Doga; and some 100 m. to its north-west is a group of olive-presses, which no doubt belonged to the same estate. On the south edge of the broad ditch that surrounds the farmhouse is a smaller installation that is best interpreted as a wine-press, since it has a pressing-floor and a tank, but lacks the characteristic monolithic uprights typical of the olive *torcularia*. The pressing-floor (2·34 by 1·64 m.) communicates by a spout with a deep tank, cement-lined, measuring 1·30 by 1·70 m., of which the bottom is 1·20 below the level of the pressing-floor.

The farmhouse proper is 17 m. square externally, and is entered by a doorway, flanked by monolithic jambs, on its south side. A small entrance hall, to the east of which a room contains what appears to be the base of a staircase, leads into the central courtyard, in which a cistern-mouth is visible. The rooms to east and west of the court have not been excavated, and it is uncertain whether they were each sub-divided into two smaller rooms. The north side of the building is occupied by three rooms, of which the central one also has a cistern in the floor. Henscir Salamat is, like the majority of the later fortified farmhouses, a building of no great architectural pretensions, its walls consisting of outer and inner faces of small irregular stones, with a central core of earth and rubble. Yet the amount of cut stone used for door-jambs and similar features, and the small but well-built wine-press show that Roman building techniques were well-known to its constructors. To judge from the surface remains visible on the similar sites in the Tarhuna plateau, the general arrangements of Henscir Salamat may be taken as typical of these fortified buildings.[35]

HENSCIR SALAMAT
(TARHUNA)

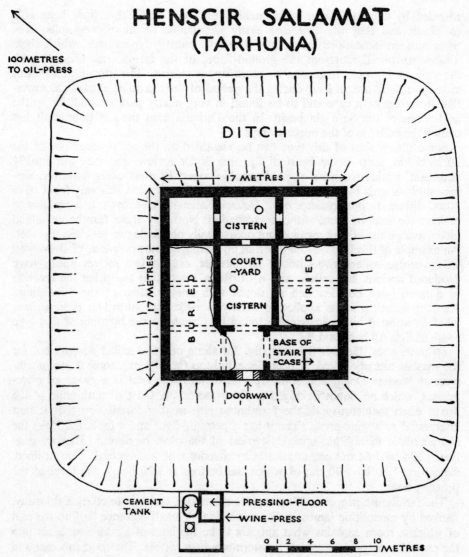

Fig. 36 Henscir Salamat: plan of fortified farm

GENERAL CONCLUSIONS

Our picture of the Tarhuna plateau in the Roman period, as illustrated by the archaeological evidence, is necessarily incomplete. Until one or more olive-farm sites have been stratigraphically excavated and dated by the material found in significant layers the economic history of this fertile and important region will remain obscure. Yet the existing evidence is not without a certain historical value.

For the pre-Roman period archaeology is still completely silent: Carthaginian coins are not infrequently found on the plateau,[36] but not in association with structures that could be considered contemporaneous. Aelius Lamia's road, and the sanctuary of Ammon on Ras el-Haddagia may reasonably be considered as marking the first influx of Roman influence into this eastern Gebel region, during the reign of Tiberius. The monuments of Lepcis Magna show that Romanisation was already effective in that city under Augustus, and the extension of this process into the hinterland, at a slightly later date, would have been a logical step. Romanelli has suggested that the construction of the road was an essentially military undertaking: *si lanciava invece audacemente proprio nel cuore del paese nemico.*[37] Against this interpretation, however, it may be argued that the construction of the Ammonium of Ras el-Haddagia, contemporaneous with the road, would have been an anomalous undertaking if the road was at that time serving as a *limes*. The dedicatory inscription of the Ammonium and the remains of the sanctuary itself show clearly that it was erected by Romanised craftsmen on behalf of a Libyan notable, a "sheikh" of the "Beni Masinkaw". The neo-Punic title "chief of the army in the territory of the Libyans", applied to Aelius Lamia is, as Levi Della Vida points out below (Appendix I), a standard formula for *proconsul Africae*, and no implications should be drawn from it.

In these circumstances, while we must allow that Tiberian policy in the Tarhuna plateau may have been influenced by military considerations, we must not overlook the political and economic implications of the policy. As early as the middle of the first century B.C. Lepcis had been able to draw on the produce of "hundreds of thousands" of olive trees, according to Gsell's computation[38]; and this substantial figure could only have been reached if the Tarhuna as well as the Msellata region came within the economic orbit of that city. The construction of the Tiberian road from Lepcis to the Tarhuna would have served to facilitate the export of olives to the expanding emporium, and at the same time to strengthen political control over the interior. Road and Ammonium alike suggest a negotiated agreement between the authorities on the coast and the native leaders of the Eastern Gebel; and if military operations were envisaged at all, they must have been intended to take place to the south or to the west of the road-head at Medina Doga.

For the first and second centuries A.D. archaeological evidence is scanty, but we may perhaps assume a gradual extension of Roman influence and increased agricultural development. The tombstone of a veteran from near Gasr Doga (Appendix III, no. 1) and the remains of mosaics at Scersciara and El-Ubberat suggest the presence of a few immigrant settlers; but there is no evidence whatsoever of the large imperial or private estates of the type which existed in other parts of Africa, to which the famous inscription of Henscir Mettich in Tunisia[39] refers. Indeed the later healthy development of small self-contained olive-farms, with homesteads of semi-military type, argues against there ever having been a depressed class of coloni in the Gebel region.

During the third century A.D. the organisation of a deep limes zone, stretching southwards to the Wadis Sofeggin and Zemzem, gave the Gebel region an increased military importance as a base for military activities. Although there is no evidence that large forts were established in the Gebel, detachments of the Third Legion are recorded at Ain Wif on the Gebel road,[40] and it is not improbable that similar detachments were to be found at Medina Doga. Milestones of Caracalla, Maximinus and Gordian III show that the Eastern Gebel road was, in common with the other official routes of Tripolitania, kept in regular repair throughout the century.[41] It is to this period that we can perhaps attribute the beginnings of the widespread establishment of fortified farmhouses, of which Henscir Salamat, described above, is a typical example. The density which these homesteads eventually reached suggests that a well-developed olive-farm of some 200 hectares (500 acres) could adequately support a Romanised Libyan family and its servants.

The spread of Christianity is sufficiently documented by the later inscriptions (Appendix III, nos. 3 and 4), and by the Chi-rho monograms of Constantinian type found both at Henscir Uhéda and at Sidi bu Laaba. It seems probable that by the end of the fourth century paganism was on the decline among the settled farmers of the Tarhuna; and that at some later, but uncertain, date the Ammonium of Ras el-Haddagia could be dismantled in accordance with the Theodosian laws, without offence to local feelings. The only church at present identified is that excavated by Caputo on the south side of the modern road near Sidi Ali ben Zaid: this has an added baptistry, which Ward Perkins has identi-fied as of Justinian date, and the building itself must therefore be earlier.[42] Its decorative elements testify to a vigorous tradition of Christian art surviving throughout the fifth century and possibly later.

It is more difficult to judge the repercussions in the Tarhuna area of the political events that were taking place elsewhere in the province. One inscription (Appendix III, no. 2) seems to record the thanksgiving of a Christian family for the safety of its sons and estate after a barbarian raid: the text cannot be dated with precision, but certainly belongs to the latter part of the fourth century or to the opening years of the fifth. If, as has been suggested,[43] the Austuriani who raided the coast in the years 364–7 came from the desert areas south of the Gebel, it might be assumed that the Tarhuna plateau felt the first impact of their on-slaught, and the inscription in question could be associated with that event. On the other hand, it seems more likely that the Austuriani were of Syrtic origin; whilst the events of 364–7, which happened to be recorded in detail by Ammianus, were certainly repeated during the subsequent half-century.[44]

For the closing decades of the Tarhuna's ancient history there is, in fact, a great scarcity of documents. The region was Christian, populous, and agricul-turally prosperous at the end of the fourth century, as seems attested by the archaeological evidence; and there is reason to believe that these conditions continued for at least another century and a half. It need not be assumed that the Vandal occupation of the coast after A.D. 455 had any serious effects on the life of the Tarhuna, which was no longer dependent on the prosperity of the coastal cities. The frontier organisation of the closing years of Roman rule had been so native in character, and so closely interwoven with the agricultural economy of the region, that its disbandment posed no particular problems, and resulted only in a greater measure of autonomy for the interior.

That the Tarhuna plateau was included in the zone known as the *regio Arzugum*, or the ecclesiastical *provincia Arzugitana*, is suggested by a number of late sources, and Corippus included the *Arzuges* among the enemies of Byzantine rule against whom John Troglita waged his Libyan campaigns.[45] It is probable, however, that relations between the Byzantine regime and the interior, after the Vandal defeat, were initially cordial, and that it was only at a later date, after experience of Byzantine mismanagement, that open conflict broke out. How far

the Christian farmers of the Tarhuna plateau shared in the conflict, or were the
victims of the pagan tribesmen who led the resistance, is obscure; but it is safe
to assume that John's campaign brought no benefit to the countryside. It was
in these years of the mid-sixth century, no doubt, that the social and economic
decline of the interior first became pronounced. Later events and conditions
accelerated the process, and in due course reduced the once-prosperous plateau
to the condition in which Cowper found it in 1895.

APPENDIX I

THE NEO-PUNIC DEDICATION OF THE AMMONIUM AT RAS EL-HADDAGIA* (pl. 32)

By Professor Giorgio Levi Della Vida

The dedicatory inscription of the Ammonium (fig. 37) is cut on a single block of
hard pink limestone, measuring 2·19 by 0·43 by 0·42 m. On the inscribed face the
three lines of lettering lie within a slightly recessed die, 1·93 by 0·31 m., and the
larger letters are uniformly 7·5 cm. high. The other faces of the block are well
trimmed, but not finely tooled, and give the impression that the block was built into
a structure, and not in any sense free-standing.

As found by de Mathuisieulx in 1901, the inscription consisted only of the two
main pieces of the block, but three additional fragments, not known to Clermont-

* [For subsequent publication see H. Donner and W. Röllig, *Kanaanäische und
Aramäische Inschriften* (Wiesbaden, 2nd ed. 1966–9)].

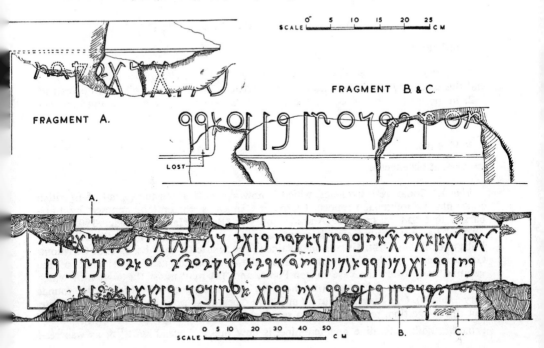

Fig. 37

Ganneau, the first editor, have since been found. Fragment C was found by Aurigemma and Beguinot in 1910 and appears (slightly displaced from its correct position) in the photograph published by the former in *Notiziario Archeologico*, i (1915), 41, fig. 1. Fragments A and B were both found during the excavations of 1947, the former in Pit 2, the latter close to the surface on the south side of the Ammonium.

The following remarks aim only at a correct understanding of the wording of the inscription. The basic interpretation still remains that which was given more than forty years ago by the great Semitic epigraphist Clermont-Ganneau (*Recueil d'archéologie orientale*, vii, 86–114, cf. *Répertoire d'épigraphie sémitique*, no. 662); nothing essential was added by Lidzbarski (*Ephemeris für semitische Epigraphik*, iii, 60–1), and some of the latter's criticism of Clermont-Ganneau's suggestions proves now to be unfounded. The few remarks jotted down by the present writer in *Libya* (*già Rivista della Tripolitania*) iii, 95–6, can be disregarded without inconvenience, as they have been superseded by further findings and research. Although Clermont-Ganneau was unable to evince a continuous sense from the text, most of his brilliant suggestions, which lacked documentary evidence at the time when they were first made, are now supported by fresh material and a closer examination of the stone. To be sure, a few passages remain unexplained, as is too often the case with neo-Punic inscriptions; however, the general meaning of the inscription can be considered as well ascertained.

The text follows, transliterated in Hebrew letters:

1. לאדן לאמן מאש אלם שפער סת ומקדש בתאי וח[ע]רפאת אש באֹנֹא ואיקדֹש

2. בשת רב תאחת רב מחנת בשד לובים לוקי עילי לעמיע לְכסף בן

3. שׁעֹסֹידועסֹתְ בן נְמרר אש בבנא מעסנכעו . בתצאתם בתם

Translation:

1. To the Lord Ammon, this (is the) beautiful(?) idol (*literally*: statue of a god) and the sanctuary of his temples and the porticoes, which were built and dedicated[46]
2. in the year of the proconsul over Africa (*literally*: the territory of the Libyans), Lucius Aelius Lamia, by $_N^T$ K S F son of

3. Shasidwasa $_n^t$ son of $_N^T$ amrar, who belongs to the Sons of Masinkaw, with their annexes, at his expense.

Line 1. Some fresh evidence, which is now available about the spread of Egyptian cults into Tripolitania, supports Clermont-Ganneau's contention, opposed by Lidzbarski, that אמן means here Ammon and not (Ba'al) Hammon. Since 1905 ש(א)מ "statue" has been found elsewhere, as early as the tenth century B.C. (inscription of Eliba'al of Byblos). שפער is still unexplained. The first letter may be, as both Clermont-Ganneau and Lidzbarski assumed, the relative pronoun used as a mark of the genitive, as is often the case in neo-Punic, and פער may mean the matter of which the idol was made (although (*marmor*) *parium*, as suggested by Lidzbarski, sounds very unlikely). One may think of an adjective, "beautiful", on the analogy of Aramaic, but this suggestion, too, is far from satisfactory. Evidence for סת as a demonstrative pronoun, both masculine and feminine, is now bulky. Instead of בְא, as was read by Clermont-Ganneau, the stone has undoubtedly בְתָאי, which can only be the plural of a noun followed by a possessive suffix of the third person masculine singular: "of his temples" (instead of "de son temple", as Clermont-Ganneau has it). Why the plural was used, while the temple was obviously only one, is not entirely clear. וחערפאת "and the porticoes", doubtfully suggested by Clermont-Ganneau, is sure: ח as an article instead of ה is due to assimilation to the following 'ayn (see *Africa Italiana*, vi, 23). The following words, to the end of the line, read undoubtedly באנא ואיקדש; the upper apices of the broken *alif* in באנא have been supplied by the recently discovered fragment A. The verbal form איקדש (ifil), of which Clermont-Ganneau was not entirely sure, is now well-established (inscription of Bir Tlelsa, in *Ephemeris für semitische Epigraphik*, iii, 288; Tripolitana 13 in *Libya*, iii, 105–7, *Journal of Biblical Literature*, lxiii, 5; Tripolitana 30 in *Africa Italiana*, vi, 104).

Line 2 is preserved in its entirety, and was correctly read and explained by Clermont-Ganneau. תאחת, corresponding to *pro-*, as in *proconsul*, must have been a regular term of the language of administration: it is found in another inscription (Tripolitana 27, in *Africa Italiana*, vi, 4, where the first two letters are restored) in the same meaning as here, although its Latin counterpart is slightly different (*tribunicia potestate*). רב מתנח, "the chief of the army", as a standard translation of *consul*, has been discussed at length elsewhere (*Africa Italiana*, vi, 8), and it was shown that the emphasis which the Punic term puts on the military aspect of the Roman consulate matches the Greek translation of consul, στρατηγὸς ὕπατος. No implications concerning Lamia's office in Libya should be drawn from it. Another instance of שד לובים, "the territory of the Libyans", obviously corresponding to *provincia Africa*, has been pointed out by Clermont-Ganneau in a neo-Punic and Libyan bilingual inscription from Maktar (*apud* J.-B. Chabot in *Journal Asiatique*, 1918, 1, p. 280 = *Punica*, p. 220 = *Receuil des inscriptions libyques*, no. 31; cf. J. Février in *Journal Asiatique*, 1949, pp. 87–8). The dedicator's name is Libyan, as well as the names of his father and grandfather. To the best of this writer's knowledge, none of them has been met with so far in Libyan, Punic, or Latin inscriptions. The initial letters of T K S F have been compared by Clermont-Ganneau to the beginning of the well-known name *Tacfarinas*. Names beginning with T K . . . . . are by no means scarce in Libyan inscriptions (see Chabot, *Recueil*, p. xxii), but names with an initial N K . . . . . are no less frequent (*ibidem*, p. xx), and *t* and *n* are not differentiated in the neo-Punic script.

Line 3. The patronymic, which was mutilated on the stone when first studied by Clermont-Ganneau, has been entirely restored by the finding of fragments B and C. The signs of the latter were not quite correctly read by the writer in *Libya*, iii, 96; but the reading is now sure, as even the broken letters are unmistakable, except for the last letter, which of course may be *t* or *n*. Shasidwasan or Shasidwasat (fully vocalised) is a new name, as is the grandfather's Tamrar or Namrar (the second vowel may also be *i* or *u*); the numerous Libyan names beginning with N M R . . . (Chabot, *Recueil*, p. xx) and, on the other hand, T M R N (*ibidem*, p. xxii) may be mentioned for the sake of comparison. Clermont-Ganneau was certainly right in assuming that the words בנא מעסנכעו mean "the sons of . . .", and refer to a tribe. It should be added that the preceding letters . . . ב אש mean "belonging to . . ."; a similar expression is found in an inscription from Sabratha (Tripolitana 35, in *Rendiconti dell'Accademia dei Lincei*, Ser. VIII, iv (1949), pp. 411–12), where one reads אש בעם אופקי, "who belongs to the people of Lepcis". The last two words, which are only slightly damaged, were correctly read by Clermont-Ganneau, who however failed to grasp their meaning, and thought of תצאת as meaning "borders". The present writer endeavoured to prove that בתצאתם, which occurs frequently and is almost always followed by בתם means "with their external parts" (from the stem *yṣ'*) and refers to the accessories, or annexes, of the buildings or monuments mentioned in the inscriptions (*Atti dell'Accademia delle Scienze di Torino* lxx, 191). Professor

J. Février, in a paper read in July, 1948, at the International Meeting of the Orientalists in Paris and partially published in *Actes du XXIᵉ Congrès International des Orientalistes*, Paris, 1949, pp. 103–4, denied the correctness of that explanation and suggested a different one, "at their expense", which would fit the meaning of הוציא in late Hebrew. However, the personal suffix *-m*, being in the plural, cannot refer to the donor, who is single.[47] Therefore, one should assume an objective genitive, namely, "at the cost of them". Should Février's explanation be correct, בתם would have here its literal meaning of "completely"; otherwise, it would mean "at his expense", as in two bilingual inscriptions from the Theatre of Lepcis Magna (Tripolitana 30 in *Africa Italiana*, vi, 107, and Tripolitana 32 in *Rendiconti dell'Accademia dei Lincei*, Ser. VIII, iv (1949), pp. 404–6), where it matches *de pecunia sua* of the Latin text.

APPENDIX II

CERAMIC INDUSTRIES IN ROMAN TRIPOLITANIA

Roman coarse pottery has been found in abundance during the Italian excavations at Sabratha and Lepcis Magna, and also during the more recent excavations of the British School at Rome: large quantities of pottery, most of it rather characterless, can also be picked up on the surface of the ancient sites in the interior of Tripolitania. It is evident that many, if not most, of these wares must have been manufactured locally, but the character and chronology of the Tripolitanian ceramic industries have still to be studied. The publication by Miss K. M. Kenyon of the abundant pottery found in stratified levels at Sabratha will no doubt establish a firm base on which a dated typology can be built up. Meanwhile, however, it may be useful to place on record some Tripolitanian sites at which Roman pottery was made.

The only Roman kiln-site in Tripolitania which has hitherto been published is that found in 1925 under the Centrale Elettrica of Tripoli (outside the walls of ancient Oea), and described by Professor R. Bartoccini in *Africa Italiana*, ii (1928–9), 93–5. On this site, a workshop-enclosure was brought to light containing four circular kilns and some cisterns. Associated pottery, including one kiln-load still *in situ*, has been dated by Bartoccini to the second half of the fourth century A.D., and the abandonment of the workshops attributed to the barbarian raids of that period.

The Tripoli kilns all had central pillars, which Bartoccini interpreted as having supported a dome, and their circular interior was divided into two levels: the lower level, elliptical, was close to the furnace, while the upper level, "three-quarter-moon"-shaped, lay more distant from it. According to Bartoccini the furnace communicated with the oven itself by a high-level flue: *Le camere di cottura si aprivano verso il forno vero e proprio con uno stretto canale rettangolare, superiormente rialzato ad angolo acuto.* The general arrangements of the Tripoli kilns are closely paralleled by those of the Scersciara and Tazzoli kilns recently excavated by the writer; the main point of difference (unless there has been some error of interpretation) would seem to be that in the latter kilns the furnace opens directly into the low-level compartment of the oven.

Since the war three additional kiln-sites have been identified in Tripolitania, and kilns have been excavated on two of them. On all three sites large mounds of sherds and wasters surround the kilns, and some representative specimens of pottery have been collected and deposited in Tripoli Museum: they are almost exclusively thick-necked jugs of the type which were found on the Tripoli kiln-site, but a closer study of the material is to be desired.

The first of these additional sites lies on the north side of the main Tripoli-Homs road, at Kilo 102, between Fondugh en-Naggaza and Homs. It is on high ground at the head of the Wadi Giabrun es-Seghir, and marked by a high mound, consisting almost entirely of pottery sherds, on the verge of the modern road. Large masses of Roman concrete nearby seem to represent cisterns. This site was first observed in 1943 by Mr. J. B. Ward Perkins, at whose suggestion the writer dug out one of the kilns in 1947. The kiln (fig. 38, *right*) proved to be remarkably similar to those described by Bartoccini. It was circular, with an inner diameter of 2·60 m., and its low-level compartment, heavily marked by burning, communicated directly with the exterior furnace by a flue 40 cm. wide. In the centre of the oven, and resting on the edge of the upper floor, was the base of a central pillar of rectangular section. The outer walls of the kiln were built of clay blocks, but their width was not ascertained. No remains of the last load were found in the kiln, the filling of which consisted of ashes and wasters from the surrounding dumps. Two amphora-handles found on the surface of this potter's works both bear a potter's stamp (fig. 39, A), which can reasonably be accepted as the trade-mark of this particular establishment, although its exact meaning is obscure.

The second kiln site to be identified recently is that at Ain Scersciara, which has

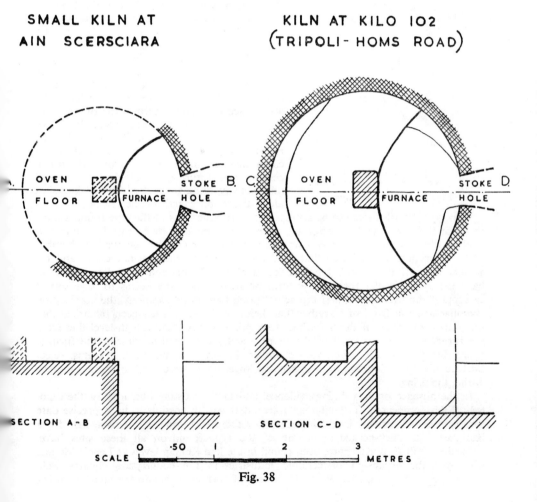

Fig. 38

already been described above (p. 84 f.). In addition to the large kiln there illustrated (fig. 35), the remains of a small kiln of the Tripoli type were also uncovered. Although much damaged, its plan and section (fig. 38, *left*) show it to be of basically the same type as that excavated on the Homs road at Kilo 102. Here again the furnace communicated directly with the lower chamber, and it is clear that this lower chamber must be considered as a combustion chamber and not as a part of the oven: pottery stacked in it would have been badly distorted by the heat.

The third site, identified in 1948, lies some 25 km. to the south-west of Ain Scersciara, and 4 km. west of Tazzoli village centre. The rough track (used largely by esparto-grass lorries) from Tazzoli to Ain Wif crosses the deep Wadi el-Kadra and then climbs to a ridge on which stands the cistern Magen Burnia. About 800 m. before reaching Magen Burnia this track cuts through a horse-shoe shaped bank which consists entirely of pottery sherds. Large quantities of burnt clay blocks testify to the existence of kilns, but none have yet been excavated. Heavy amphora-rims of the type found on all the other kiln-sites abound, and one handle bore a potter's mark (fig. 39, B), probably to be related to this workshop.

These three pottery-works all lie in what may be described as "Gebel country", and

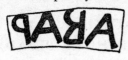

A.   KILO 102 (HOMS)

B.   MAGEN BURNIA (TAZZOLI)

0   1   2   3   4   5
CM.

Fig. 39 Potters' stamps

their siting is probably to be explained by the presence of clay seams in the limestone outcrops. At Ain Scersciara this clay is still exposed, and appears to be of excellent quality. The Homs and Tazzoli sites do not seem to have a good water-supply, but this difficulty could probably be overcome by the use of cisterns and wells. When one considers the abundance of fortified farmsteads of the later Roman period scattered throughout the Gebel and further to the south, it will readily be understood why these ceramic industries often came into existence so far from the urban centres, and future archaeological survey will undoubtedly bring to light additional kiln-sites along the whole length of the Gebel.

Two types of kilns seem to be represented: (*a*) large kilns of the type found almost intact at Scersciara, with a perforated oven floor supported by a central column and vaulted ribs; unfortunately it was not possible to clear out the combustion chamber of the Scersciara example, so that its detailed arrangements are not clear; and (*b*) smaller kilns of the Tripoli type, as found also at Homs and Scersciara. Here we have the same circular form and central pillar, but the latter seems to have served to support the oven dome, and the actual firing had no perforations, the combustion chamber being in front of it, rather than below it. It has already been remarked that the Tripoli examples, if the published description is exact, had a high-level flue from the furnace, whereas in both of the more recently excavated specimens, the furnace opens directly into the combustion chamber. In any case, we must, it seems, reject Bartoccini's suggestion that both upper and lower floors were used to contain pottery during the firing.

In the absence of firm dating evidence, and in the existing obscurity of the typological development of Tripolitanian wares, it is hardly possible to fix a precise date for these Gebel ceramic industries. Certainly there is a good *prima facie* case for a late date, for thick-necked amphorae of the type found on all these sites have, according to Professor Caputo, been found in the late Roman levels at Lepcis Magna. Moreover, the expansion of ceramic industries in the countryside equates well, historically, with the increasing establishment of fortified farms in the interior during the late third and fourth centuries, and with the gradual decline of the coastal cities and their imports.

The wares manufactured on these Gebel sites are not, in themselves, of a character to stimulate great archaeological interest. Superficial examination appears to reveal no trace of a local ceramic art comparable, say, to the New Forest and Castor wares of Britain: the products of the Tripolitanian potters were strictly utilitarian. Yet a detailed excavation of these kilns, and examination of their products, would prove of the greatest utility for investigators of the occupation-sites in the interior, where the problem of establishing an absolute chronology is always acute. The three sites described above are all easily accessible, and it is to be hoped that some student of Roman ceramics will devote to them the attention which they clearly merit.

APPENDIX III

THE CLASSICAL EPIGRAPHY OF THE TARHUNA REGION

In the area of the Tarhuna plateau covered by the zone map (fig. 30) the ancient inscriptions at present known total nine. On other parts of the Tarhuna plateau, outside the limits of the map, there are a few additional texts, none of any great importance. Of these nine inscriptions, one, the dedicatory inscription of the Ammonium on Ras el-Haddagia, is in neo-Punic: it is fully described and translated by Professor G. Levi Della Vida in Appendix I above. Of the remaining eight, five are in Latin (in some cases of a rather rudimentary type), and three are of the type best described as "Latino-Libyan", being inscribed in Latin characters in an indigenous language which seems to contain both Libyan and Punic elements, but which cannot yet be confidently translated. Inscriptions of the latter type are relatively abundant in the interior of Tripolitania, and are discussed by the present writer (above, p. 69 f.).

The Latin and Latino-Libyan inscriptions of the interior of Tripolitania [were] included, with measurements and full bibliographical references, in the collection of *Inscriptions of Roman Tripolitania*, edited by Miss J. M. Reynolds and Mr. J. B. Ward Perkins and published by the British School at Rome. It will therefore suffice, for present purposes, to list those inscriptions which have been found in the area under review, and to give the texts of the more interesting specimens, with such commentary as is appropriate to the problems already discussed above in our description of the Tarhuna zone. The evidence of the milestone inscriptions has already been considered (p. 75 f.) in dealing with the ancient communications of the Tarhuna plateau, and need not be repeated here.

(a) *Latin inscriptions*

1 (=*IRT* 872). Inscription in good lettering of the first or second century A.D., recording the erection of a funerary monument, for himself, by C. Clodius Paulus, of the tribe Col(lina), a *veteranus*. This inscription, published by Cagnat and Merlin (p. 2, no. 3), was reported by M. Hegly as having stood in the facade of a small mausoleum, since demolished, some 800 m. south of the large mausoleum of Gasr Doga (*BAC*, 1910, ccvii). It is now in Tripoli Castle Museum. Although the exact find-spot is no longer identifiable, the mausoleum of this veteran must have stood on the northern outskirts of Medina Doga.

2 (=*IRT* 875). Inscription (pl. 40) in lettering of the late fourth or fifth centuries A.D., found on an unidentified site in the Breviglieri–Tarhuna area. When seen by the writer in 1947, the inscribed stone was in the garden of a colonist's cottage below the eastern slopes of Ras el-Haddagia. Inquiries made by Professor Caputo have ascertained that the stone came originally from an uncertain site close to the modern road from Breviglieri village centre to Tarhuna. It reads:

> Flavii Sebentius c(en)t(e)n(arius)
> et Stiddin eius con
> iunx hunc locum
> didicarunt O bonum [i]ni
> tium natisqui filiis concil
> ium saluis libiris
> cum filicitati trium
> fanti Binaitir possissu

The abbreviation CTN in line 1 is not, apparently, paralleled elsewhere, but its expansion into *centenarius* seems certain (cf. R. G. Goodchild, "Tripolitanian Inscriptions", 34). The name Stiddin is recorded elsewhere in Africa (*CIL* viii 10686; *IRT* 236) and is presumably of native origin. The O following *didicarunt* probably represents an intended monogram cross, similar to that which we find in the following inscription (3), but never completed. The meaning of the remaining part of the text is obscure, but the intention seems to have been to record that the dedication of his *locum* (whether farmhouse or church is uncertain) was to be a *bonum initium* for the sons of the family. Binaitir was presumably the name of the estate. Although *salvis* may be intended in a Christian sense, it seems possible that the general tone of the inscription, with its emphasis on the safety of family and estate, may be an indirect reference to some danger happily averted, in which case one would think of a barbarian invasion. On the other hand, the acclamatory nature of these Christian inscriptions must be borne in mind.

3 (=*IRT* 876). Inscription, in lettering of the late fourth or early fifth centuries, very similar in form and content to (2). It was found, about 1935, in the course of removing stones from the ruins of two adjoining ditched buildings at Sidi Bu Laaba, 2 km. north-east of Breviglieri village centre. The discovery was reported to the Superintendency of Antiquities at Tripoli by Professor Aurigemma, who was at that time visiting Tarhuna. The stone is now in Lepcis Magna Museum, together with two crude bas-reliefs of hunting-scenes, and a large Christian monogram found on the same site. The hunting reliefs, each of which includes a Roman eagle, are closely paralleled by a relief seen by de Mathuisieulx (xii, 30 and pl. xxi, 1–2) *in situ* beside an inscription over the doorway of a fortified farmhouse at Muagen Tuansia, in the Wadi Merdum a little west of Bir Gebira. The contemporaneity of the Sidi Bu Laaba and Muagen Tuansia sites can hardly be doubted. The inscription reads:

> Fl(avius) Gaudentius
> bono tuo proce
> das et i(n) nomine
> (C)hristi omnes genus
> Seberi bibant (*monogram cross*) va(le)
> hec turis fabric
> ata est ANOTAP LSA (or LGA)
> ETRAVLIHORDETFOLXXX

The inscription clearly records the erection of a *tur(r)is*, no doubt one or other of the two ditched buildings on the site of which it was found, by Flavius Gaudentius, who must presumably have belonged to a family of *Severi*. It is interesting to note that an inscription at Mizda (*IRT* 884) appears to record the repair of the tomb of Iulius Severus son of Masinthan by a certain Gaudentius. Although the Mizda inscription is of the same period as that at Sidi Bu Laaba, it would be rash to assume that the same Gaudentius is recorded in both texts; but it would seem that the name Gaudentius was connected with a family of Severi (perhaps native Libyans settled as *limitanei* under the Severan emperors) in Tripolitania.

The meaning of the last part of the inscription, following *fabricata est*, is highly obscure. Although the letters LSA occupy the right-hand ansa, it is clear that they are meant to follow on after ANOTAP: so, too, the figure XXX presumably follows FOL. At first glance the latter suggests a sum of money, *fol(les)* XXX; but it is difficult to see why so insignificant a sum should be mentioned in a building inscription (H. Mattingly, *Roman Coins* (1928), 229, n. 3, quotes St. Augustine in illustration of the low value of the *follis* at that period). An alternative explanation would be to interpret the first three letters after *fabricata est* as *an(n)o*, and to assume that the tower was built in the 30th year of TAPLSA, RAULIHORD and FOL.... But these names are not recognisable as Libyan, and it is difficult to imagine why so cumbrous an era should ever have been devised. Until further evidence is forthcoming, the meaning of the final part of this text must remain obscure.

4 (=*IRT* 874a). Fragmentary inscription in late lettering similar to that of 2 and 3, found by Professor Caputo at Sidi Bu Zeriba, an ancient site on the edge of the plateau some 8 km. due north of Breviglieri village centre. Unfortunately the stone was broken by the Arabs who dug it out, and the only intelligible part of the text is the opening phrase:

> In nomine pa[tris et fili]
> et sp(i)r(itus) sanct(i)
> . . . .

The seven lines which follow are too mutilated to be restored, but they were probably of similar content to 2 and 3.

5 (=*IRT* 874). Fragmentary inscription seen by Cowper (238, n. 1) 200 yards north of Gasr Doga, and now lost. No information as to the shape of the stone or the type of lettering is given by Cowper, and it is impossible to judge its character. The last line, recorded as MXXXV, suggests a milestone fragment; but this may be a misreading of *vixit an]n xxxv*.

(b) *Latino-Libyan inscriptions*

(Texts of Latino-Libyan type [are] published in facsimile in *Inscriptions of Roman Tripolitania*, since the forms of the letters are often far from clear, and at least two non-Latin letters are used.)

6 (=*IRT* 873). Inscription cut in a recessed die of *tabella ansata* type on a pointed stela, 2 m. high, lying on the surface in the northern necropolis of Medina Doga (above, p. 78). The text, of five lines, appears to record the erection of this monument to a certain Muthunilim, by members of his family. The name Muthunilim (cf. *CIL* viii, 10525, 23904) is of Punic origin.

7 (=*IRT* 877). Inscription, flanked by low reliefs of an eagle and a lion, in late letters similar to those of 2 and 3 (pl. 39). It originally stood over the doorway of a fortified building, with adjacent church, excavated by Caputo on a hill-top close to the south side of the Breviglieri–Marconi road, some 8 km. east of Breviglieri village centre. It is now in Lepcis Museum. The text (cf. "Tripolitanian Inscriptions", 33, p. 30) has, as its first line, the word CENTENARE which is evidently to be identified with the military term *centenarium* applied to a small frontier outpost. The remaining part of the text is obscure except for what appears to be a name *Marci C(a)ecili Bumupal*, perhaps, like the Sebentius and Gaudentius of 2 and 3, the owner of the estate of which this homestead was the centre.

8 (=*IRT* 877a). Inscription or graffito in late letters cut on a block which formed part of the architectural ornament of the church on the same site as 7. Apart from the word *bibas*, the text is quite unintelligible, and it probably contains Libyan elements. This inscription was not visible when the block was in position, so it was presumably cut by a mason.

Although the tally of inscriptions from the Tarhuna plateau is relatively small, it will be noticed that these texts come from some seven different sites, none of them of great extent and importance. The high proportion of late texts is in the main attributable to the fact that it became customary, from the fourth century A.D. onwards, for the construction of farmhouses, etc. to be recorded epigraphically by their owners. This custom, originating probably from the example of the purely military constructions of the Severan period (cf. the inscriptions over each of the four gateways of the fort at Bu Ngem) became widespread in Tripolitania, as it did also in Northern Syria during the same period. It can hardly be doubted that a fair proportion of the ditched farm-sites described above (p. 88 f.) would yield, on excavation, their original dedicatory inscriptions.

The problems raised by the use of Latin and Latino-Libyan inscriptions in the same area are too complex to be discussed here; for some initial comments, the reader is referred to the paper quoted at the beginning of this appendix. One fact seems clear, that the two types of inscriptions were being cut simultaneously during the fourth century; and it is noteworthy that those texts which show clear signs of Christianity are invariably in Latin, even if of a rather rudimentary type. It seems probable, therefore, that the Latino-Libyan texts are predominantly (though not exclusively, as the case of inscription 8 shows) pagan.

APPENDIX IV

A SHORT LIST AND CONCORDANCE OF ANCIENT SITES ON THE TARHUNA PLATEAU

Approximately one hundred ancient sites are marked on that section of the Italian 1/100,000 map of the Tarhuna area (Sheet 1475 of the Istituto Geografico Militare's survey of Libya) which is the subject of the present study (cf. fig. 30). The density of ancient occupation is therefore considerable and the compilation of an archaeological inventory is handicapped by the very abundance of surface remains. The frames of olive-presses and the outlines of ditched farmhouses are easily recognisable, but there are many other sites, the character of which can be determined only by excavation. In these circumstances it is hardly possible, as yet, to compile a definitive and classified list of ancient sites. More extensive archaeological reconnaissances are required on the ground, and relatively complete air photographic cover would be needed to achieve the best results.

Meanwhile, however, it may be useful to give the exact topographical locations of those sites already described by Cowper in the *Hill of the Graces*, and those other sites more recently recorded. It has already (p. 73) been pointed out that Cowper's topographical descriptions are extremely reliable, but the map which he published is, of course, entirely superseded by the modern large-scale surveys. Since the place-names printed on the modern maps are not always the same as those recorded by Cowper, and since the formation of the Breviglieri village settlement and of the adjacent private "concessioni" has completely changed the face of the Tarhuna countryside, it is not easy for any person unfamiliar with the terrain to identify on the map those places described in Cowper's book. The following concordance may help to overcome this difficulty.

The map-references given in the last column of the inventory are obtained from the grid printed on the British editions of the Italian 1/100,000 maps: the original maps are not gridded. The *Libyan Grid*, adopted during the war for this purpose, is based on Longitude 18° East, and consists of large 100-km. squares (denoted by letters of the alphabet) sub-divided into 1-km. squares, each numbered by two figures of "eastings" and two of "northings". Thus the full map-reference consists of one letter followed by two groups of three figures, the last figure of each group representing the distance in hundreds of metres from the south or west margins of the small squares. It is to be hoped that future editions of these Libyan maps may combine the cartographic quality of the Italian originals with the convenience of the metrical grid, which—as the Ordnance Survey has already recognised in Britain—is of value for the activities of peace, as well as those of war.

(a) *Sites recorded by Cowper*

(Note: The numbers in brackets, after the inventory number, are those used by Cowper in listing the sites he examined. His sites 1–9 and 35–59 fall outside the limits of the region under review: a few other of his sites have not yet been securely identified on the ground. Place-names in *italics* are marked on the modern 1/100,000 maps: in such cases the form of the place-name shown on the map has been adopted in preference to Cowper's.)

In this and the following list the following abbreviations have been adopted: O.P. (olive-presses); D.F. (ditched farmhouse); Inscr. (inscription).

1 (10).	*Gasr Doga.* Large mausoleum; cisterns; inscr.	.	.	L 958 227
2 (11).	Hill *495*, 1km. NE of Gasr Doga. O.P. .	.	.	L 967 235
3 (12).	Miscellaneous ruins (? Medina Doga)	.	.	(Site 27, below)
4 (16).	Sajit-el-Haj Ibrahim. D.F.; O.P. .	.	.	L 998 192
5 (17).	*Sidi Mahmud* (Ras el-Id). O.P. .	.	.	L 998 194
6 (18).	Hill *460*, 1 km. SW of Si. Mahmud (Ras el-M'shaaf). Large farmhouse, without ditch	.	.	L 990 190
7 (20).	*Sidi Ahmed el-Uhesci* (Kom es-Las). O.P.	.	.	L 985 155
8 (25).	*Ras el-Maeghel.* D.F.; O.P.	.	.	M 035 155
9 (26–7).	*Sidi Ahmed ben Dachil* (Senam el-Jereh). D.F.; O.P.	.	L 947 120
10 (28).	*Sidi el-Hag Said* (Kom el-Lebet). O.P.	.	.	L 946 151
11 (29).	*Sidi Com Saud.* D.F. .	.	.	L 957 164
12 (30).	El-Khadra. Mausoleum and batum tree	.	.	L 968 180
13 (31).	Ras el-Haddagia. Temple of Ammon. pl. 31; inscr.	.	M 010 180
14 (32).	*Breviglieri* village square (Senam el-Thubah). D.F.; O.P..	M 019 175
15 (63).	*Sidi bu Laaba* (Ras el-Benaieh). D.F.; inscr. .	.	M 036 195
16 (64).	*Zaviet el-Medeni.* D.F.; O.P.	.	.	M 008 198

(b) *Sites not recorded by Cowper*

17.	*Ras Gassciut.* D.F. (pl. 38) .	.	.	L 863 167
18.	*Tarhuna* village. D.F.	.	.	L 890 172
19.	*Tarhuna* village. Christian catacomb? (Roman building with mosaic in this area)	.	.	L 891 168
20.	*NE of Sidi el-Garib.* D.F. .	.	.	L 892 197
21–3	*Ain Scersciara.* Portico with mosaic; pottery works; D.F.	L 885 207
24.	*Bu Tuil.* Mausolea; stone relief	.	.	L 900 250
25.	Henscir Salamat. D.F. (fig. 36) .	.	.	L 944 228
26.	Henscir Uhéda. D.F.; Christian monogram .	.	L 957 220
27.	Medina Doga. Road-station (Mesphe). (fig. 31)	.	L 957 211

28.   1 km. NW of *Zaviet el-Medeni*, Milestones   .   .   . M 002 204
29.   *Sidi bu Zeriba*. Inscr.   .   .   .   .   .   . M 010 255
30.   1½ km. SW of *Sidi Ali Ben Zaid*. Farmhouse; Christian
             church; inscr.   .   .   .   .   .   . M 095 176

(Note: To the east of Site 30 is the head of the Wadi el-Mé, which has a well-preserved series of Roman dams. These, and other remains in the area of the Wadi el-Gsèa, [were] investigated by Mr. E. D. Oates, Rome Scholar at the British School [see *PBSR* xxi (1953) 81 f., xxii (1954) 91 f.]. Cowper has described some of the Wadi Gsèa sites, 268–74 (sites 44–9).

The distribution of the sites on the Tarhuna plateau calls for brief comment. It will be seen from fig. 30 that, in general, the ancient sites bear little relationship to the water-courses. The springs at Ain Doga and Ain Scersciara gave these areas a special importance, but elsewhere the ancient farms and their associated olive-presses tend to occupy the higher ground. The siting of the tower-like farmhouses on high ground was, no doubt, influenced by considerations of security and the importance of good observation over the whole of the estate. In the areas of the Sofeggin basin south of the Tarhuna Gebel, the Roman farmhouses invariably occupy the sides of the wadis, the beds of which were terraced and cultivated, and the intermediate plateau between the wadis is barren of ancient remains (cf. the sketch-map of the Wadi Merdum area, (above p. 38). One is therefore perhaps justified in calling the homesteads of the Gebel area "Hill Farms", and those of the Sofeggin basin "Wadi Farms". In the latter areas olive-cultivation was the exception rather than the rule, as is shown by the scarcity of olive-presses.

NOTES

1. *The Antiquary*, February–March, 1896; H. S. Cowper.
2. W. H. Smyth, 486; H. Barth, (2), I, 65–76; E. von Bary, *Zeitschrift für Ethnologie*, viii (1876), 378–85; G. Rohlfs, 104–7.
3. *Proc. Soc. Antiq. Lon.* 2nd Ser. XVII (1897–9), 280–93. Cowper subsequently admitted, with very good grace, that his theories "have proved to be radically wrong" (*Ibid*, 297–300).
4. de Mathuisieulx, x, 269–72.
5. A preliminary account of these excavations, by Professor Caputo, appears in *Bulletino del Museo dell'Impero Romano*, xii (1942), 151–4.
6. Cowper (256) incorrectly describes the stones around the roots of this tree as having been "collected and placed there". They are, in fact, *in situ*.
7. Sheet 1475 (Tarhuna) of the series of 1/100,000 maps, surveyed by the Istituto Geografico Militare in 1933, covers the greater part of the plateau, and marks all the more important ancient sites. The original Italian edition of this map is much easier to read than the British war-time

edition; but the latter has the advantage of a metrical grid (see Appendix IV).
[7a Gasr Doga: S. Aurigemma, *QAL* iii (1954) 13–31; Breviglieri: G. Caputo, *Bull. Mus. Imp. Rom.* xiii (1942) 151 f., Ward Perkins and Goodchild, *Archaeologia* xcv, 44 f.]
8. Cowper, 122–30. Herodotus (IV, 175) describes the λόφος δ χαρίτων as being 200 stadia (35 km.) distant from the sea. The head of the Wadi Mensci, most distant tributary of the Wadi Caam, is actually 32 km. from the sea, as the crow flies, and twice that distance following the course of the Tareglat.
9. For this road see Romanelli, (1), 104–10, and Goodchild, *Roman Roads*, 11–13.
10. Goodchild, *op. cit.*, 13 (nos. 12–13). The writer is indebted to Mr. Oates for information on the two newly discovered milestones [*IRT* 936, 937, without texts].
11. An alternative explanation might be that the original *caput viae* was at Ain Scersciara rather than Medina Doga, in which case the distance of 44 miles would be correct.
12. Cuntz, 10–11.

13. For Ain Wife, see above p. 21 f. The writer is indebted to Prof. Caputo for information of the new milestone discoveries in the Tazzoli area [IRT 939a and b; see also now p. 109 f. below].

14. The inscription (Appendix III, no. 5) seen by Cowper 200 yards north of Gasr Doga might have been part of a milestone on this route, but the existing record is insufficient to establish the character of the inscription. So, too, the Caracallan milestone (*IRT* 928) from near Gasr Garabulli could possibly belong to a road leading from the coast to Medina Doga.

15. Romanelli, (1), 107, adopts the latter interpretation, but it is difficult to see what purpose would have been served by such a route, as there were few centres of importance in the Gefara.

16. It should be noted that the road from Lepcis to Medina Doga does not show up at all on the air photos of the Tarhuna plateau, even though its course is known from the milestones. In cultivated terrain those unpaved routes that fell out of use soon after the Roman period were rapidly obliterated by wind-blown sand or by cultivation.

17. For the epigraphy of the area see Appendix III, and the relevant sections of *IRT*.

18. Smyth, 486; Rohlfs, 106. Cowper (240 (Site 12), and 241, note 1) refers to "a large mass of ruins, consisting chiefly of Roman work, such as fragments of columns, wells, baths or cisterns" which lay a half-hour south-east of Gasr Doga, and is probably to be identified with Medina Doga; but he saw no recognisable city, and for that reason thought he had missed Smyth's "Medina Dugha".

19. G. Nave, "Frammenti indigeni d'arte cristiana a Tarhuna ed Henscir Uheda, Tripolitania", *Bolletino d'Arte*, viii (1914), 96–104.

20. These bases include stones with rectangular hollows cut in their upper surfaces, and presumably intended to receive funerary offerings. Professor Caputo, who has found similar stones in the Fezzan, is studying these objects.

21. Appendix III, no. 6. Since removed, together with some of the bases, to Lepcis Museum.

22. Appendix III, no. 1.

23. Cowper, 256; de Mathuisieulx, x, 272 and xiii, 93 (where the site of the discovery is called "Es-Sailat", a name not recorded elsewhere); Aurigemma, *Notiziario Archeo-logico*, i (1915), 39, gives the correct name, Ras el-Haddagia.

24. *Africa Italiana*, i (1927), 213–14.

25. de Mathuisieulx (xii, 21), and Gentilucci (*Africa Italiana,* v (1933), 187, and figs. 20–1) both describe the Senam structure as a mausoleum; but its remains, surveyed by the writer in 1949, and an inscription found on the site (IRT 888), indicate that it was a small temple.

26. *Siagu*: A. Merlin, "Le Sanctuaire de Baal et de Tanit près de Siagu", *Notes et Documents de la Direction des Antiquités et Arts* (Tunis), iv (1910), pl. I. *El-Kenissia*: Carton, "Le Sanctuaire de Tanit à el-Kenissia", *Mém. Acad. Inscriptions*, xii, i (1908), pl. I.

27. G. Levi Della Vida, *Libya (già Rivista della Tripolitania)*, iii, 96.

28. See Levi Della Vida's remarks in Appendix I (p. 93 f.).

29. L. Vitali, *Fonti per la storia della religione Cirenaica*, Padua, 1932, 4–10.

30. H. Barth (2), I, 67.

31. *Corinth*, xi (C. H. Morgan, *The Byzantine Pottery*), Harvard, 1942, 15–17, and fig. 9.

32. See Appendix II. These surface finds have been deposited in Tripoli Museum.

33. Appendix III, no. 3. The site has been much mutilated by stone robbing, the inscription having been found in the course of those operations, during the laying out of Breviglieri colony. An eye-witness of the discovery pointed out the exact site to the writer.

34. Appendix IV, site no. 30; Appendix III inscription no. 7. [For another, see p. 111 f. below].

35. Although there is some variety in the size of the buildings and the disposition of the rooms, the fortified farmhouses of Tripolitania almost invariably have upper storeys, an inner courtyard, and a single doorway in the outer walls (see some representative plans published by the writer above p. 43, fig. 10).

36. Information from Professor Caputo. A bronze Carthaginian coin was found in 1949, lying with a miscellaneous collection of useless articles left by local Arabs as offerings at the *marabut* of El-Khadra. It was removed, but to avoid offence to the *genius loci* a nickel lira coin was left in its place: the latter has since disappeared.

37. Romanelli, (1), 110.

38. S. Gsell, "L'huile de Leptis", *Libya (già Rivista della Tripolitania)*, i (1924–5), 41–6.

39. J. Toutain, "L'inscription de Henchir Mettich", and E. Cuq, "Le colonat partiaire dans l'Afrique romaine", *Mem. Acad. Inscriptions*, xi, (1897) p. 31 f.

40. See above p. 21 f.

41. R. G. Goodchild, *Roman Roads*, 11–13.

42. This church, together with others in Tripolitania, [was] published by Mr. Ward Perkins in *Archaeologia*, xcv.

43. R. Bartoccini, "La curia di Sabratha", *QAL* i (1950), 33.

44. It is important to recall that the detailed record of events compiled by Ammianus ceases in 378, and that there is no chronicle of comparable quality for the years that followed. The fact that an inscription (*IRT* 480) from Lepcis, belonging to the period 408–23, praises the *comes et dux* Ortygius for the measures taken against the Austurians shows that the invasions of 364–6 were only the beginning of a whole series of disasters. The events in the Pentapolis, recorded so vividly by Synesius, confirm this conclusion.

45. See above p. 37.

46. The passive has been used, instead of the active of the neo-Punic text, in order to preserve the word sequence of the original.

47. Février assumes that the suffix -*m* may refer to the singular; however, this point is still controversial (see the article in *Rendiconti dei Lincei*, cited above, p. 96).

7

INSCRIPTIONS FROM WESTERN TARHUNA

Plates 41–4

[Six pages of typescript, under this title, forming the major part of an article incorporating new inscriptions, were found among Goodchild's papers. He wrote them after 1951 and before the death of Professor Vergara-Caffarelli in 1961, but held them back, presumably because he was not satisfied that he had extracted all that was possible from the Sidi Sames text (p. 111 f.)—he had in fact asked me to look at it too when I was next in Tripoli.

Olwen Brogan and I (with generous help from Mr. Awad Sadawiya and members of the Department of Antiquities in Tripoli) have checked the texts of the inscriptions on the stones and added some additional information and illustration. In addition I have chosen between alternative versions of some paragraphs, provided a few connecting and concluding sentences (printed in square brackets) and added my own reading of the Sidi Sames text and footnotes. All map references are to the American Army 1/50,000 map of Libya.]

Archaeological explorations carried out in recent years between Cussabat and Tarhuna[1] have still to be extended westwards into the broken country that lies between Tarhuna and Garian. Much of this country was too rugged for extensive agricultural exploitation in antiquity; but the more cultivable part of the Tarhuna plateau continues westward at least as far as the Wadi El-Gadra (map ref.: sheet 1574.5574), and is occupied today by the semi-abandoned Italian colonists' village of Tazzoli.

The village-centre stands close beside the prominent hill-top of Henchir Bu Drehiba (423 m. above sea-level), which is capped by the great square mound of a collapsed fortified farm or watch-tower of the type already familiar in the Tripolitanian Gebel. Another fortified building, called Henchir el-Abiad and of some architectural pretensions, lies *c.* 6 km. to the north-east, close to the modern road from Bir Miggi to Tazzoli.

In this paper we are concerned not with the general archaeology of the Tazzoli region, which awaits study, but with certain epigraphic discoveries made in recent years. Two new inscriptions relate to the Roman "Gebel Road",[2] which traversed the zone on its way to Ain Wif and Garian. A third text, included in *IRT* (no. 871), but now more fully published, refers to the defensive measures taken by the land-owners of the later Roman period.

In publishing these inscriptions, I must express my gratitude to Signor Santo Gaudino who brought the milestones to my notice, to [the late] Dott. E. Vergara-Caffarelli, for his help and encouragement, and to the 14/20 King's Hussars who solved for me the problem of transporting the heavy stone of Sidi Sames from its hill-top site to Tripoli Museum where it could more conveniently be studied.

The accompanying map (fig. 40)[3] shows the precise find-spots of the new milestones. Since they may, at some later date, be removed to Tripoli Museum, it is the more important that their site should be accurately recorded, so that the Roman Road which they mark may eventually be traced westwards towards Garian.

[Two inscribed milestones in this region were found in 1950 and published as *IRT* 939a, erected at Mile 53 in the reign of Gallienus, and *IRT* 939b, erected at Mile 57 in the reign of Gordian III.] The intelligent interest displayed by the fourteen-year-old son of an Italian colonist formerly living at Tazzoli has now brought to notice two more, marking the 56th and 57th miles. As we shall later observe, the new stone from Mile 57 was found at a considerable distance from the one brought to light in 1950.

The course of the Gebel road—which, like the other roads of Roman Tripolitania, was an unpaved track with perhaps a few minor artificial improvements—is represented by a surviving but little-used caravan route running south-westwards from Tarhuna village. It passes Henchir El-Hagial, Marbuaet Amor ed-Debu, and the twin hills of Ras Gummam and Ras el-Gleb: immediately west

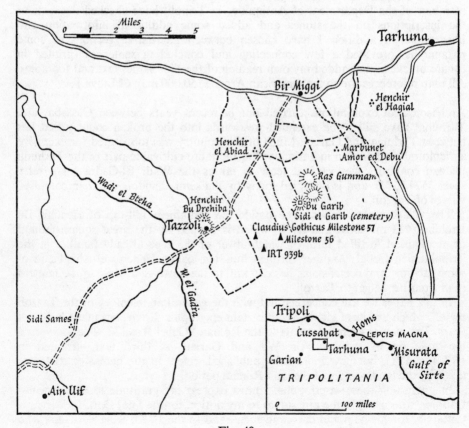

Fig. 40

of these hills it traverses the sandy plain of Ed-Dahar, a favourite camping-area for local Bedouin. Its precise course beyond Mile 57 has still to be ascertained.

MILE 56. LOCALITY EL-GARIB [map ref. 618780] (pl. 41)

Here [the track runs across a shallow valley west of the low hill Bu Garib on which there is a Moslem cemetery. Roman pottery of the fourth to fifth centuries was picked up there in 1971, identified by John Hayes as Tripolitanian Red Slip Ware, Forms 3 and 4. Just below the hill], on rocky ground with very scant vegetation, are the remains of two milestone bases, with characteristic circular recesses. Two corresponding columns lie beside the bases [though it may be noted that the lower part of the inscribed column is badly cut and would not have fitted easily into its socket]. One column, of 1·57 m. in height and 38 cm. in diameter, has long had its [presumably] inscribed surface exposed to the wind, with the result that nothing is legible. The other is in good condition [but by 1971 showed serious weathering on the left half of the inscribed face].

Column (1·67 m. by diam. 0·36), inscribed within a recessed die (0·94 by 0.45). Letters, [III cent. capitals, quite well cut]: 1.1, 0·065; ll. 2–5, 8–10, 0·06; ll. 6, 7, 0·04; l. 11, 0·06; l. 12, 0·05; [A without a cross-bar.]

	IMP CAES	
	M. IVLIVS FILIPVS	*sic*
	PIVS FELIX AVG PO	
	NTIFEX MAXIMVS	
5.	TRIBVNICIE POTES	*sic*
	STATE///PATER PAT	*sic*
	RIE ET M. IVLIVS	*sic*
	PHILIPPVS NOBIL	
	ISS[I]MVS CESAR	*sic*
10.	FILIVS AVGVSTI	
	u. NOSTRI *u.*	
	M. P. N̄. LVI	

[L. 6, it is not clear whether the number for the tribunician power was ever inserted.]

This text, which belongs to the years A.D. 244–9, calls for no particular comment except to note the mis-spelling of the imperial name, and the fairly common use of *E* for *AE*. It is, however, historically interesting as the first milestone of the emperor Philip to be found in Tripolitania. The now well-known inscription of Gasr Duib (*IRT* 880, see above p. 27 f.) shows that this ruler undertook works of fortification in the Tripolitanian *limes*, and it is therefore not surprising that his name should also be associated with road-improvements.

MILE 57. TAZZOLI PODERE NO. 127 [map ref. 603782] (pl. 42)

On a low hill adjoining the modern farmhouse, agricultural operations have brought to light a column 0·90 m. in height and 0·40 m. in diameter. It is in good condition[4] and was probably covered by sand fairly soon after its erection. The inscription, in capitals of 4–5 cm. height, runs as follows:

IMP CAES
M AVRELIO
CLAVDIO VIC
v. TORI AVG
TRIBVNIO   *sic*
ET POTESTATE
PATRIAET P R   *sic*
RIE M LVII   *sic*

[L.4 I is faint, rather as if it had been added by an afterthought.]

The inscription evidently refers to Claudius II (Gothicus) and is the first milestone of this emperor to be found in Tripolitania.[5] It belongs to the years A.D. 268–70, but the title *"victor"* is unusual, *"invictus"* being the normal epithet used on milestones of this emperor. Clearly the lapicide was working from a copy which he hardly understood, for *"tribunio et"* is obviously a blunder for *"tribunicia"*, whilst the two final lines are meant to represent *"patri patriae M LVII"*. It would seem, therefore, that the arduous task of inscribing new milestones was, at some stages of the third century in Tripolitania, entrusted to illiterate persons.

But the real problem raised by this milestone is topographical rather than epigraphic, for, as has been said, another milestone erected under Gordian III equally marking the 57th mile from Lepcis Magna was earlier found almost 1,000 m. to the south-east [map ref. 607775]. Both columns are approximately one Roman mile (1,480 m.) from mile-station 56 below El-Garib; but the fact that they are so distant from one another is remarkable. The most obvious and simple explanation is that one or other stone has been moved; and if that is the case, the heavier stone of Gordian III must be considered as the one *in situ*, and the smaller and more manageable column of Claudius Gothicus must be the stray. But against this view there remains the mint condition of the latter column,[6] and the fact that it does not appear to have served any secondary function on the site on which it was found. For what purpose would anyone have carried a stone 1,000 m., partly up-hill and left it there undamaged?

An alternative explanation, which is interesting for its relevance to the problem of soil-erosion, is that both milestones lie *in situ*, and that the Roman road had shifted its course between A.D. 249 and 268, with the result that the milestone-erection team sent out under Claudius Gothicus found no earlier column at the 57th mile. In this case one must assume that the terrain through which the road ran was as sandy and wind-swept in antiquity as it is today. Since the road itself has left no surface traces one cannot check this hypothesis by any normal archaeological process; but the eventual discovery of columns at the 58th mile, still further to the west, would perhaps provide confirmation one way or the other.[7]

The new milestones are not, in themselves, of very great epigraphic interest; but they do, at least, provide further confirmation of the already very evident interest of the third-century Roman emperors in milestone erection in Africa. Of the milestones hitherto found in Tripolitania all, with one [exception (*IRT* 930, the *caput viae* of this road, which is Tiberian), are of the third century, when the road was an essential feature in the military dispositions for the defence of the province].

It remains only to draw attention to the unexpected occurrence on this sector of the Gebel road, of columns of two emperors not represented previously in the corpus of Tripolitanian milestones, and to the absence from it of the far more familiar inscriptions of Caracalla and Maximinus, so abundant on other sectors of this road itself and on the other Roman roads of the province.

THE INSCRIPTION FROM SIDI SAMES [map ref. 721479] (pls. 43, 44)

About 10 km. south-west of Henchir Bu Drehiba (and Tazzoli village-centre), and a few hundred metres north of the modern Bir Miggi–Ain Wif motor-track, there are the remains of a small watch-tower in which lies the tomb of a Moslem saint named "Sidi Sames" [from whom the whole area is named]. The tower measures 16 by 11 m., has outer walls of large dressed stones, and is surrounded by double ditches, now largely silted up.

In the summer of 1948 John Ward Perkins and the writer [visited this site together and saw an inscribed block lying beside it. The text, cut on a badly damaged surface, seemed at that time hardly legible and what was published in *IRT* (no. 871) gave no sense. On removal to Tripoli however it was available for photography and study in varying lights, see plate 44. From this emerged the following reading]:

```
    IN HIS [P]RED[IIS] . . CIN . . . RBENTI . . . RONSIX . . .
    N . . . . L . . . . . . . . . . . . . NE . . . . . . . INCVR[S]I[O]
    NI BARBARORUM SEV GENTILI[VM . . . . . . . . . . ] NTIS
    IMPENSIS IN . . . . TE . . . . . . . . . . . . . RISFIDIL . . . .
5.  QVADRA . . . . .
    . . . . . (nothing legible)
    . . . . . (nothing legible)
    L . . NSV . TME . . RIVSCO . . . . . . . . . RIDEFICA . .
```

Despite the gaps the gist of the inscription can be safely inferred from what remains, and from analogous inscriptions found elsewhere in Africa.

The opening formula *In his pr(a)ediis* is a common one, and the Tripolitanian limes (inside modern Tunisia) has provided a well-known example in *CIL* viii, 22774, from Henchir el-Guecirat. Similar texts have come from Mauretania (*CIL* viii, 9725, from Ammi Musa) and from Numidia (*CIL* viii, 19328, from Ain et-Tin). All these texts refer to the construction of a fortified building within a private estate (*praedia*). At Ammi Musa the building in question was *castra*, on the other sites they were *turres*.[8] Since our Sidi Sames text is actually from a small fortified building on a hill-top, we need not doubt that the inscription records its erection within a private estate.

The name of the landowner must have followed in line 1, and the first part of line 2 must have described the building constructed. Lines 2–3 refer specifically to an invasion, actual or [foreseen and this calls to mind the well-attested incursions of the Austuriani recorded by Ammianus Marcellinus and in an inscription of Lepcis Magna in the late fourth and early fifth centuries,[9] which certainly created the kind of conditions in the country to which private construction of this sort was the natural response.]

[After further study of the stone in Tripoli Castle and on the photograph I would tentatively suggest some additions and revisions of Goodchild's readings to give the following text:

        IN HIS [P]RED[IIS . .]ÇIN[. . .]RBENTI[. . .]TORIS ẸX[ST]
        RVÇT[OR]ISTO[. . c.8 . .]NI[. . c.7 . .]INCVRSI[O]
        NI ḄARBARORVM SEV GENTILIVM[. .]N[. . . .]ẸNTỊ Ṣ[VIS]
        INPẸNSISÇONṢ[.]NTE[. . ? . .]DẸÇẸMẸṬ[. . . .]
5.   QVADRAGIN[TA]ỊDỊAỊỊẸ[. . .
        [. . c.7 . .]ON[. . ? . .   ]NẸ[. . c.6 . .]
        [. . c.6 . .]ONO[. . ? . .   ]TE[. . c.6 . .]
        L·RNỊÇIVỊTMEL[. .]RIVS ṢẸ[.]P[. . c.10 . .]AEDEFỊCA[. . .]

Thus in ll. 1/2, I would suggest that the name of the owner (e.g. *Asinius or Licinius Urbentius*) ended with the cognomen *Victor* and was followed by the description *exstructor* on the analogy of *CIL* viii, 27551 where the owner and his sons are described at this point in the inscription as *exstructorum et dedicatorum*. In 1.2, the letters TO may suggest that the building was called a *turris*, although NI might indicate the presence of the word *munitionem* used in a Tripolitanian inscription which must be concerned with similar building (*IRT* 884, 1. 2). In ll. 4,5 there seems to have been a statement of the costs incurred in the building, cf. the costs of buildings of comparable date recorded in *IRT* 876, 898, 900 and 906.

In l. 8, the first word appears to be a verb, cf. *constituit* in this position in *CIL* viii, 19328, 1. 5. It was probably followed by the name of the owner's agent, cf. *Numidius ser. act.* in *CIL* viii, 19388, 1. 6, *Vitalis, ser. act. eorum* in *CIL* viii, 22774, 1. 5, *Thiasus proc.* in *CIL* viii, 25990, 1. 4; it would in fact be possible to read *Mee[. .]rius se[r.] p[roc.]* here or even, if I am wrong to see P where Goodchild saw N, *se[r.]aç[t.]*, perhaps followed by *eorum. The* letters at the end suggest part of the verb *aedificare*—the sense of the line being, I conjecture, *instituit Me[. .]rius ser. act. eorum et aedificavit.*

The reference to danger from *gentiles* as well as *barbari* contained in 1. 3 suggests that the natives settled in the *limes*-zone (see above, p. 35 f.) may have shown some tendency to make common cause with the invaders from whom they should, in theory, have protected the province.]

NOTES

[1. David Oates, *PBSR* xxi (1953) 81 f., *PBSR* xxii (1954) 91 f.]

[2. See above p. 19 f.]

[3. Goodchild noted that "the existing 1/100,000 maps of Tripolitania do not include the whole area of Tazzoli and are faulty as regards the layout of the modern colonists' settlement"; it was his intention to illustrate this paper with a map drawn from recent air photographs. Unfortunately we cannot find that he carried out this intention and since we do not have the air photographs concerned can only give a drawing from the faulty maps.]

[4. It is, however, unusually short for a Tripolitanian milestone and may therefore have been cut down at some unknown date.]

[5. There is as yet no record of operations in the *limes* area during his reign, but he may have been honoured at Sabratha (*IRT* 51) and if so this would suggest that he did take an interest in the province.]

[6. But see n. 4. If the truncation suggested there occurred in antiquity, the stone could have been rejected and broken up because of the poor quality of its epigraphy —though *IRT* 939a, which is similarly illiterate, indicates that there was a high tolerance of this kind of thing.]

[7. In an alternative version of his comment on this stone Goodchild put forward yet another possibility—that while the new stone marks the line of the main road "the column of Gordian (*IRT* 939b) stands on a *diverticulum* leading more to the south".]

[8. Although the formula with *in his praediis* is here recorded for the first time within the area of modern Libya, the construction of fortified buildings on private estates is well attested there and epigraphically indicated e.g. by *IRT* 865, 875, 876, 877, 889, 894a; see also above, p. 88 f.]

[9. Ammianus, *Hist.* XXXVII. 6. 10 f., *IRT* 480; for discussion see P. Romanelli, *Storia delle Province Romane dell'Africa*, (Rome, 1959) 565 f.]

HOARDS OF LATE ROMAN COINS IN THE MARKET OF LEPCIS MAGNA

[This manuscript, found among Goodchild's papers, must have been written after the death of Dr. Milne in August, 1951, but perhaps not long after. I have printed it as it stands; no other interpretation of this important material seems to have been published.]

During the course of Professor Guidi's excavation of the Roman Market of Lepcis Magna, numerous coins, mainly of late Roman date, came to light. The "assistente", Finelli, who was in charge of the actual digging, listed these coin-finds in his weekly "relazioni" sent to Guidi, and the coins themselves were given an inventory-number and deposited in the magazzini of Lepcis Museum, where some of them were later cleaned. The stratigraphic contexts in which the coins were found are not recorded; and the individual specimens do not therefore assist the dating of the various constructional phases. But the several hoards of late Roman coins which were found—especially in the year 1930—are of importance for the light they throw on the final phase of the Market's life.

In the weekly "relazioni", the coins in question are usually described as "Byzantine", but this description is only generic, as the following notes will show. Finelli was not a trained numismatist, and his descriptions of the coins, although intelligent, are not sufficiently accurate to be used for historical purposes. For instance, one hoard of over 2,000 coins of the Vandal period ("Hoard 1458", below) was described as of the period of "Constantine II and Procopius".[1]

Happily, the coins themselves are still preserved, and the principal hoards can be identified by comparing their quantities and the dates of their registration, as recorded in the accession register of Lepcis Museum, with the information given in the "relazioni". It is on this basis that the following notes have been compiled, the identifications having been made by the actual re-examination of the coins themselves, particularly of the cleaned specimens which appear to be representative of the general content of the hoards. To facilitate any future and more detailed study of these coins, I quote the Museum accession-number (e.g. "Hoard 1317") in each case.

Hoard 1317. Found during the week ending 7 January, 1930, close to the internal colonnade (quadriportico) at the north angle of the building, underneath a "mensa ponderaria". The hoard totalled 535 coins, all AE3, of which 58 cleaned specimens can be identified as follows:

Constans	2
Constantius II.	4
House of Constantine	5
Julian	1
Valentinian I	2
Valens	2
Gratian	2
House of Valentinian	2
Valentinian II	3
Theodosius I	4
Arcadius	5
Honorius	2
House of Theodosius	3
Uncertain	21

Hoard 1352. Found on 24 January, 1930, on the north-east side of the Market (exact site not stated). The hoard consists of 114 coins, all AE3, which have yet to be cleaned and examined. Preliminary examination indicates that the contents of the hoard range from the later issues of the House of Constantine to those of the House of Theodosius. It is therefore comparable with hoard 1317.

Hoard 1362. Found on 1 February, 1930, in the street on the north-east side of the Market, resting on the street-level, below the fallen wall of the Market. 39 coins, all AE3, as follows:

Third-century "radiate"	1
Constantinopolis	1
Constantius II	2
House of Constantine	6
Julian	1
Valens	2
House of Valentinian	1
Gratian	1
Theodosius I	2
Uncertain	22

Hoard 1574. Found on 20 July, 1930, close to the fallen south-west wall of the Market (exact site not stated). 138 coins, all AE3, of which 29 have been cleaned and can be identified as follows:

Constans	3
Constantius II	10
Julian	2
Valentinian I	2
Valens	2
Uncertain	10

These four coin-hoards all seem to belong to approximately the same period. The absence of coins of Theodosius I and his family in Hoard 1574 is probably accidental, and should not be stressed. Hoard 1317, with its issues of Arcadius and Honorius, is perhaps the most representative of the hoards, and indicates that these deposits of bronze coins were being hidden in the Market in the first half of the fifth century. At that period, the Market was still evidently in fair condition, its outer walls not yet collapsed (cf. the case of Hoard 1362); but it must be assumed that the building had already fallen out of use, as it is unlikely that the owners of the coins would have hidden them in a Market which was still being used and kept clean. The presence of these coin-hoards is not, therefore, a reflection of commercial activity on the Market site in the early fifth century. On the contrary, it is more probable that the hoards were deposited by the inhabitants of the late huts which were built on the ruins of the Market, more especially on the site of the limestone *tholos*.[2] The walling-up of this *tholos* can only have occurred after the breakdown of organised municipal life at Lepcis; and the cessation of municipal epigraphy after about A.D. 410 accords well with the evidence of the coin-hoards themselves. It is conceivable, of course, that the occupants of the late structures were engaged in commerce, and that the presence of these four hoards is to be accounted for in this way; but at the time of their deposit, the Market, as an organic structure, had ceased to exist.

The fifth hoard is of very different date and composition, and requires separate consideration. I am indebted to the late Dr. J. G. Milne, of the Ashmolean Museum, Oxford, for examining it and providing a report on which the following notes are based. Dr. Milne was the foremost authority on the class of coinage in question, which he had studied extensively in Egypt (cf. J. G. Milne, "The Currency of Egypt in the Fifth Century", *Numismatic Chronicle*, Ser. 5, vi (1926) 43–92). His opinion on this Lepcis hoard is therefore particularly valuable.

Hoard 1458. Found on 25 April, 1930, during the excavation of one of the "botteghe" on the north-east side of the Market, outside the original perimeter wall, and beside the side-street which bounds the Market *insula*. The hoard consisted of 2,115 small coins (AE4) most of which measured 7–8 mm. in diameter. During the interval between the withdrawal of Italian troops and entry of the Allied army the Museum of Lepcis was broken into by Arabs and some of its contents (including this hoard) were disturbed. It was possible, however, to recover some 1,671 specimens out of the original 2,115.

Many of the coins bear extremely crude impressions, and belong to a class which Wroth (*British Museum Catalogue of the Coins of the Vandals, Ostrogoths and Lombards*, London 1911, xviii–xxi—quoted hereafter as BMC) has assigned to the Vandal period, but to issuers who "would seem to have been some tribe or people less civilised than the Vandals and who understood less well the art of coining". Milne (*op. cit.*, 54–5) has, however, pointed out that similar coins occur in Egypt, which the Vandals never occupied. It is safest, therefore to consider the Lepcis hoard as consisting of local currency of the Vandal period, in which Byzantine official issues, and local copies are mixed. The contents of the hoard, as analysed by Dr. Milne, are as follows:

House of Theodosius (all worn and many fragmentary)	26
Probably of this period, but corroded	64
Copies of Theodosian types other than Victory or Cross	10
Anastasius. Reverse ЄB (5 *nummia*)	2
Monograms or letters—thirteen varieties, including one Leo (BMC 31/110) and one Zeno (BMC 32/119–22)	14
Victory types (more or less degraded)	317
Monogram of Anastasius (BMC 32/128–31)	70
Λ in wreath (BMC 34/141–8)	56
Cross in wreath (BMC 41/195–200)	14
Unidentifiable (many completely worn)	1098

	1671

Dr. Milne concluded "that the hoard was buried in the reign of Anastasius". He stated: "The latest official coins are the two of his 'fives' (i.e. 5 nummia pieces), and the minims with Ⱥ in wreath are on the whole better preserved than those of other groups, and may be referred to him, taking the place of his monogram-coins. I do not think any of the monograms can be referred to Justin or Justinian ... The hoard is of much the same composition as the latest of those described in my article (*Numismatic Chronicle, loc. cit.*) on the currency of Egypt in the fifth century. In all these fifth-century hoards the proportion of barbarous issues grows as the date advances: there was very little official bronze struck after the first quarter of the century, and as it grew scarcer the provincials had to do the best they could for small change."

Hoard 1458 has, therefore, a special interest. It represents a period in the history of Lepcis Magna for which other archaeological evidence is almost completely lacking. At the time of its deposit, in the reign of Anastasius (491–518), Tripolitania was still under Vandal rule, and the city of Lepcis, its defensive-walls dismantled by the Vandals, was exposed to attack by the Libyan tribes of the interior. We learn from Procopius (*De Aedif*. III.4.1) that at one time in this unhappy period the city was completely empty of inhabitants. But life must have continued in the calmer moments between the barbarian raids; and, for reasons which we shall never know, one inhabitant of Lepcis buried his savings in the ruins of the Market. Whether the late structures on the site of the limestone *tholos* and elsewhere in the Market area were at this time still occupied, we cannot tell; but the absence of similar coins among the scattered finds argues against this possibility. When the new Byzantine city-walls were built, after the reconquest, the Market area was finally excluded from the inhabited zone, and its history comes to an end.

NOTES

1 See N. Degrassi, *QAL* ii (1951) 46.   2. *Loc. cit.*, 30–31, figs. 4, 5.

9

THE UNFINISHED "IMPERIAL" BATHS
OF LEPCIS MAGNA

[From *Libya Antiqua* ii (1965)]
Plates 45–49

Of the monuments of Lepcis Magna excavated during the last decade, one of the most imposing—and also most perplexing—is the complex usually referred to either as the "Terme tarde sul mare" or the "Edificio Stellare". This complex was excavated in 1955–6 by the Department of Antiquities, under the direction of the late Professor Ernesto Vergara-Caffarelli, and under the immediate supervision of Sig. Francesco Russo.

Owing to the premature death of Professor Vergara-Caffarelli in 1961, no detailed scientific report on this excavation has been published, and the first plan and analysis of it have been given by Professor Giacomo Caputo in the recently published volume *Leptis Magna*.[1] Nor did Vergara-Caffarelli leave any notes from which his own definitive conclusions might be extracted, although some of his provisional views regarding the edifice can be gleaned from writings compiled during the course of the excavations.[2]

With the authorisation of the Directorate-General of Antiquities in Libya, and in agreement with Professor Antonino Di Vita, who succeeded Vergara-Caffarelli as Antiquities Adviser in Tripolitania, the present writer offers the following structural analysis of the "Terme tarde sul mare". Although nothing can take the place of an excavator's own report, the monument in question speaks largely for itself. Moreover, the writer, in the course of frequent visits to Lepcis Magna at that period, was able to observe the excavation in all its phases, and thus to have early cognisance of the peculiarities which the monument offers.[3]

I hope to show, in the following pages, that these peculiarities are mainly the result of the edifice having been constructed around a pre-existing nucleus, and then abandoned before the intended work had been completed. Interpreted in this sense, the "Terme tarde" fall into place in the general run of Roman thermal architecture, as exemplified by the great "Imperial" baths of the city of Rome. Their special interest, in the context of the history of Lepcis Magna, lies in the fact of their abandonment, the reasons for which—whether political or economic—are still uncertain.

I also hope that this present paper may serve as a tribute to the memory of Ernesto Vergara-Caffarelli, who was for eight years my esteemed colleague in the Libyan antiquities service.

As their name indicates, the "Terme tarde sul Mare" lie close to the sea, in the waterfront quarter of Lepcis Magna that runs westward from the Old Forum. They are, however, separated from the sea by a street that runs more or less parallel to the ancient shore-line. Too little has been excavated to reveal when this quarter of the city was first developed, but one would logically expect that its development would have been early—certainly not much later than that of the Old Forum itself, the earliest monuments of which are Augustan.

Whether the site had any particular significance in the later town-planning of Lepcis is uncertain, and the fact that the large domed hexagonal hall (the "Edificio Stellare") marks the beginning of a minor *decumanus* leading to the major portal of the Severan Forum may be fortuitous. This fact was, however, one of the circumstances which gave rise to the excavation in 1955, as Vergara-Caffarelli has himself explained.[4]

"The Department of Antiquities has been induced to concentrate its own investigations at this point both for the fact that on the top of a high sand-dune there appeared remains suggestive of a buried building preserved to an exceptional height, and for the particular position in which these ruins lay relative to the other monuments of Lepcis. For, in fact, that cross street of the Triumphal Way which on one side leads to the principal entrance of the Forum Severianum, on the other side terminated up against this very sand-dune: which led one to suppose that the buried building must have had a considerable importance if it was constructed in topographical correspondence to the most important monument of Lepcis."

However, if the interpretation of the complex which I give below is correct, the great hexagonal hall was never meant to be entered from this street, and its position was dictated by the pre-existence of a bath-house (and attendant water-conduits) on this site. Therefore it would perhaps be prudent to defer any general topographical conclusions until the western quarters of Lepcis have been more fully excavated.

THE EXCAVATION

The excavation was begun in September, 1955 by the removal of sand from the ruins of the hexagonal hall, and was continued until the middle of February, 1956, by which time the latest floor-levels throughout the edifice had been exposed. Later in the same year, after the fallen remains of the dome had been removed, the excavation of the hexagonal hall was continued down to foundation level.[5]

In May, 1957, at the invitation of Vergara-Caffarelli, Professor Furio Fasolo, head of the Faculty of Architecture of Rome University, brought to Libya a group of students to survey these Late Baths, and a number of detailed architectural drawings were prepared, including a plan of the whole complex.[6]

During the course of the excavation various urgent tasks of "first-aid" conservation were carried out to the more ruinous walls, and in addition the columns of the "Old Vestibule" were re-erected, as also a single column in the "New

Frigidarium". Much, however, remains to be done, if the monument is to stand up to the erosion of the sea-winds.

GENERAL DESCRIPTION

A short general description of the "Late Baths" was given by Vergara-Caffarelli in a communication to the *Fasti Archeologici*, which it may be useful to reproduce here.[7]

"An excavation of much larger proportions has been carried out close to the sea-shore at the end of the street which leads to the western doorway of the Severan Forum. There has come to light a fairly complex building which displays various constructional phases.

"In this edifice, which presents in some places evident installations for hot baths, there can be recognised a colonnaded courtyard preceded by a small latrine, a three-aisled hall with lateral apses of interesting architectural construction, and on the opposite side another hall, even more interesting, hexagonal externally and with radial plan internally. This room was covered by a great cupola in pumice-stone concrete with brick courses.

"These rooms may be considered among the latest constructions of Lepcis Magna prior to the Vandal invasion, built with material almost entirely second-hand. Very rich is the series of inscriptions which seem to be re-used in the construction, and from which it is possible to obtain interesting information regarding the public and private life of the city. Also noteworthy is the number of statues, although almost all in a bad state of preservation."

For the purposes of our present analysis, the constituent parts of the complex may be listed, from east to west, in the following order, giving the major halls the letters marked on the accompanying plans, and the interpretations of their functions which result from the more detailed discussion given below: (see plan, fig. 41).

(A) The Hexagonal domed hall ("Edificio Stellare"), which I propose to call the "New Caldarium", since it was added to a pre-existing bath-building, and constructed in a manner only explicable if we assume that it was meant to contain a hypocaust in its centre and hot-baths in its recesses. Never completed, it later served as a "New Vestibule" to (B).

(B) The "Old Baths", being the hot rooms (Tepidarium and Caldarium) of a pre-existing suite of baths, the *frigidarium* of which was levelled when (A) was constructed.

(C) The "Old Vestibule", which was originally the *apodyterium* of the "Old Baths", with which it was linked via the (later-demolished) *frigidarium*. After the construction of (A) it became isolated from the Baths, and was remodelled to serve an entirely different function.

(D) The "New Frigidarium", intended as a lofty vaulted hall, with plunge baths in its corners. It was never completed (doubtless for the same reasons— whatever they may have been—that prevented the completion of (A)) and was therefore completely abandoned. Later, crude blocking walls were constructed to divide its space into small rooms (pl. 49).

(E) Uncompleted wall-footings, representing a northern extension of (D),

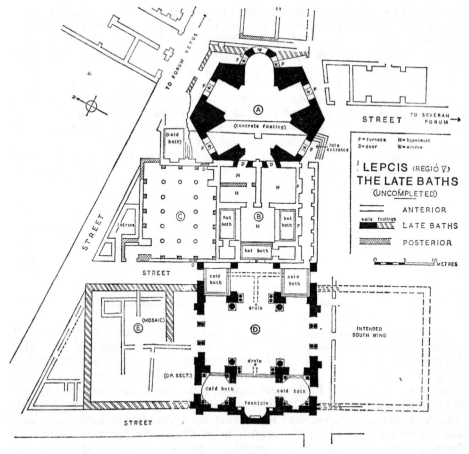

Fig. 41

which was intended to be matched, on the south, by a similar extension, thus forming a symmetrical bath lay-out characteristic of the great Imperial baths of Rome and of the major provincial cities.

DETAILED ANALYSIS OF THE COMPLEX

1. The Earlier Baths

As already noted above, the elements (B) and (C) of the complex belong to a set of Roman baths that had existed long before the elements (A), (D) and (E) had been added. The walls of this earlier period are clearly identifiable as being constructed of newly-hewn sandstone blocks. This material, in the context of building trends at Lepcis, suggests a date not later than the end of the first century A.D.

The edifice was rectangular, measuring approximately 34 by 22 m., and with irregularities on its north side due to the oblique course of the street that ran parallel to the seashore. It is apparent that both eastern and western walls of the building rested on exceptionally broad (2 m.) concrete foundations, perhaps intended to take the thrust of vaulting and overhead cisterns. Many fragments of fallen vaulting were, in fact, found in (B) when it was excavated. The whole suite of these early baths can be distinguished as follows:

Entrance and Apodyterium. Hall (C) was evidently the original vestibule, entered probably by a doorway in its west wall, close to the later junction with Hall (D). This doorway, found blocked by the excavators, has since been re-opened. The exact original lay-out of the *apodyterium* is not clear, although there are traces of a marble floor, the slabs of which were removed before the time the room received its final form. A doorway in the north-west corner led to a latrine of a triangular plan necessitated by the line of the adjacent street. A second internal doorway, in the east wall of the *apodyterium*, led to the

Frigidarium, which had the form of a long narrow room with a cold plunge bath at its north end. The later construction of the hexagonal hall (A) caused the demolition of most of this frigidarium, leaving intact only the plunge-bath, which is marble-lined and entered by three steps. The fact that the doorway from the *apodyterium* was then blocked (since reopened by excavators) shows that this cold bath then ceased to function, its walls probably being deliberately levelled. The east wall of the frigidarium, although demolished down to its lowest foundations, can still be recognised among the footings of (A). Two door-ways in the west wall of the *frigidarium* led into the

Tepidarium and Caldarium, which together constitute part (B) of the whole complex. They are not completely cleared of soil and of very late intrusive walls, but their general character is sufficiently apparent. There can be little doubt that early entrances from the *frigidarium* existed on the same site as the surviving doorways, which belong to the period of construction of the Hexagon (A); for the wall dividing the *tepidarium* into two equal halves appears to be original. The main service corridor, used for stoking the hypocausts of both *tepidarium* and *caldarium*, runs along the south side of the block; but there were also furnaces for heating water-boilers situated in the twin tower-like alcoves in the north-western and south-western corners of the *caldarium*. All the floors in this part of the building have marble paving over the *suspensurae*, and hollow flue-tiles lining the walls. The three hot baths of the *caldarium* are arranged as in most of the medium-sized Roman baths of Africa. Noteworthy is the large window (later blocked: blocking removed by excavators) that stands immediately behind the westernmost hot-bath: also the heavy projecting cornice that runs along the whole length of the wall outside this window and shows that this was an external wall of the whole original block.

In his analysis of the complex Caputo has rightly stated[8] that "the bath nucleus with its water-tanks on an upper storey, is situated in the centre of the whole *insula*, and is the part which lasted longest and goes furthest back in time". Where I must disagree with him is in his interpretation of the secondary additions (A) and (D), the former as a sixth-century Byzantine church, and the latter as a late Roman governor's palace.

2. The uncompleted Late Baths

The imposing structures that were added to the eastern and western sides of the pre-existing Baths both belong to a single and identical phase of constructional activity. This is demonstrated by the following features common to both (A) and (D):

(a) *Materials*. Medium-sized blocks re-used from earlier monuments, including a number of inscribed stones. It is probable that the buildings were intended to have an external plaster rendering.

(b) *Mortar*. Normally containing much charcoal or ash, which gives a speckled core, and a greyish-black outer surface.

(c) *Dimensions*. The simple linear walls have a consistent width of 110–20 cm.

(d) *Incomplete state*. In the exterior angles of the Hexagon (A) the alternate courses overlap, simply because the re-used blocks have not yet been cut down to accommodate the obtuse angles. In (D), as we shall see, drains and other features all testify to incompletion.

THE HEXAGONAL HALL (A)

The so-called "Edificio Stellare" is in fact a double hexagon: an external hexagon interrupted only by a projecting apse on the east, and an internal hexagon from the arched sides of which open off rectangular recesses. The west side of the external hexagon is firmly knitted to the pre-existing fabric of the Early Baths (B), with the vaulted and heated chambers of which it intercommunicates and is co-axial.

The four remaining sides of the hexagon—two on the north and two on the south—have broad windows, each about 2·70 m. wide and of uncertain height. Three of these have been blocked up with large stones at a second period. The fourth, on the south and at the point of junction of the old and new buildings, has been narrowed to form a doorway accessible from street-level by three steps rather awkwardly contrived. This is the only apparent entrance to the hexagon from outside; and it is a mean and ignoble approach to a structure of considerable architectural pretensions.

Inside the doorway, and at a slightly lower level, corresponding to that of the sills of the twin doorways leading into (B), there extended a crude pavement of stone slabs and blocks covering most of the hexagon. It rested on made soil without any mortar bed, and was clearly an improvised floor belonging to the latest phase of the hexagon's life. Immediately above it lay large concrete fragments of the fallen dome, constructed—as Vergara-Caffarelli described—of lightweight pumice-stone with tile courses (pl. 46).

The insubstantial character of this floor, and the fact that the round arches of seeming doorways were visible immediately below the window-sills, persuaded the excavators that the effective floor-level of the hexagon, as first designed, must have been considerably lower than that of the late slab pavement. A sounding was therefore made which reached a lower level corresponding to the sill of the supposed arched doors. Subsequently the whole of the hexagonal hall was cleared down to this lower level, after the remains of the concrete dome had been broken up and removed, and the late slab pavement had been dismantled.[9] Thus the seeming "floor-level" of the hexagon now appears a good 3 m. below the level of the adjacent streets!

In fact, this lower level is not a floor at all: it is a platform of stone blocks from which the walls of the hexagon rise, and in its midst—as we have already seen—are embedded the concrete foundations of the demolished east wall of the Early Baths. It was obviously never intended that users of the Hexagon should circulate at this low level; and the impossibility of such an assumption is made clear by the level of the two doorways leading into (B). These doorways are so well constructed as to leave no doubt that they were meant to serve an essential part in the function of the hexagonal hall. Yet today, following the clearing of the earth filling, they are suspended meaninglessly in the air, 3 m. above the supposed "floor" (pl. 47).

Caputo, interpreting the Hexagon as a Byzantine church, hints that these doorways may have communicated with a raised *matroneum*;[10] but the suggestion is hardly convincing when we bear in mind that the rooms into which they open are heated bath-rooms.

I venture to suggest that these difficulties and perplexities vanish once we accept that the "Edificio Stellare" is an uncompleted building, in the sense that the initial labour of construction (walls, window-openings, and dome) was not followed by the essential work of refinement, which would have included, of course, the elimination of these protruding blocks on the outer angles of the outer hexagon. Viewed in this light, the "doorways" (six in number) at the lower level are merely furnace stoke-holes for heating hypocausts and hot-baths, although they would also have facilitated the movement of men and materials into the building during the work of construction.[11] Certainly they were never intended to be visible, except—externally—to the service staff who fed the furnaces. For use of the latter was provided a low-level external corridor, divided into two sections, each of which served three furnace openings. The northern corridor was nearly completed (except at its east end, where the massive concrete of the early frigidarium impeded digging): the southern one seems to have been only just begun when work came to a standstill.

Of the six stokeholes thus provided, two were intended to heat the easternmost recess of the hexagon, which has an apsidal projection eastwards surmounted by the triple window previously referred to. Here the hottest of the baths in the intended "New Caldarium" should have been sited, the arrangement of the windows being exactly paralleled in other great bath-houses of "Imperial" type.[12] The four minor recesses, which must equally have been intended to contain hot baths, were each fed by a single furnace. The large central area of the hexagon was obviously intended to hold a hypocaust with brick pillars supporting a floor at the level of the sills of the two doorways leading into (B).

With reference to the Hexagon as a whole, Caputo has written that "there is no detail indicating hot-baths", and this is true as regards the complete lack of the brick and mortar work necessary to construct a functioning Caldarium. But once we reject the low-level arched doorways as real entrances and accept them as furnace-holes—as I think we must—the whole character of the Hexagon reveals its *intended* function as a Caldarium. Clearly the highly specialised bricklayers and plumbers necessary to complete the building never arrived to start work. The hexagon remained as it had been left by the first team of builders—the stone-masons and concrete-mixers.

Thus the earth filling and the high level stone pavement removed by the excavators represent an attempt to bring back into use the Old Baths (B) after it had become apparent that the grandiose new Caldarium was never going to be completed. This modification, including also the blocking of most of the broad windows of the outer hexagon, and the improvisation of a doorway in one of these windows, served to create a spacious—if somewhat rudimentary—*apodyterium* to replace the one that had been cut off by the construction of the Hexagon. This would seem to show that the demand for steam-baths continued long after the failure of the more grandiose schemes of reconstruction.

THE RECTANGULAR HALL (D)

On the west side of the complex, and precisely co-axial with both (A) and (B) is the large rectangular Hall which I propose to identify as the "New Frigidarium". It measures 23 by $17\frac{1}{2}$ m. internally, and has in its centre four masonry piers of L-plan, which give the main body of the hall a cruciform shape, by isolating the four corners. The shorter axis of the Hall was evidently the major one, since along its line each of the piers is fronted by a lofty column of cipollino marble, topped by a Corinthian capital. On this same axis, too, are the only apparent entrances to the Hall, in the form of broad portals subdivided by two pairs of white marble columns set on re-used limestone bases. A similar use of columns in pairs is found on the longer axis of the Hall, where they are built up against the L-shaped piers, and presumably supported cross-arches.

To define this Hall as "three-aisled" is to suggest a basilican character which it does not possess. Its plan is that not of an audience hall but of a large vaulted *frigidarium* such as we find in the great "Imperial" Baths of Rome, and even at Lepcis itself, in the Baths of Hadrian.[13] Traces of concrete vaulting (even in fallen form) are absent, and it may well be that the walls of the Hall were never completed to sufficient height for the pouring of the roof-concrete to begin. But that it was on the builders' programme can hardly be doubted.

Further proof that this was meant to be a *frigidarium* is provided by the uncompleted plunge-baths in the four corners (and also, more unusually, in the centre of the west side of the Hall). Lack of the plaster rendering which, alone, could have made these plunge-baths hold water has obscured their real character, but the presence of drains is a decisive indication of their intended function. The three baths on the west side of the Hall are interconnected, and a single drain—on the longer axis of the Hall—was provided to drain them. On the east side, where there were two baths only, a T-shaped drain was constructed, also on this same axis. Both drains head towards the centre of the Hall, where they were doubtless meant to communicate with a major drain running north and south: but of this drain there is no trace, and it was evidently never constructed.

It is the western interior façade of the Hall which is most ornamental, for the two plunge-baths in the angles have circular foundations, whilst the central "piscina" lies in front of an elaborate apse, in the centre of which is a projecting platform for a statue. Two smaller statue-niches, crowned by monolithic arches, flank it. Caputo has described this as "a front arranged with one large statue between two small ones, or with a large throne (seggio), between two small ones", and has preferred the second interpretation which would make the Hall into a governatorial hall of audience.[14]

The presence of the drains, uncompleted as they are, shows that the area in front of this facade was intended to hold water, so it is clear that statues rather than living men would have occupied the niches. The central statue was probably meant to be in the form of a fountain from which flowed cold water: the flanking ones would have been purely ornamental. But it is improbable that suitable statues were ever mounted here, before the completion of the concrete vaulting. Indeed the top cornice of the central statue-niche shows clear signs of not having been completed.[15]

It is not only as regards its vaulting and internal fittings that the New Frigidarium is patently incomplete, but also in two other important respects: its lateral communications with a necessary entrance and *apodyteria*, and its axial interconnection with the heated rooms that culminated in the New Caldarium.

The two identical portals, each divided into three openings by a pair of marble columns, are not external doorways, for there is no means of closing them. They are simply internal passages designed to connect the New Frigidarium with other parts of the New Baths, as planned. Indeed on the north side of the Frigidarium hall there extend contemporaneous wall-footings 110 cm. broad enclosing a hall or court measuring 18 by 17 m. This feature, on which the work of construction had hardly begun, extended across an area previously occupied by private houses, to which belonged mosaic and marble floors still visible.[16] The walls of these houses had been stripped down to their lowest courses, doubtless to provide building stone for the new walls, but the latter are raised only to a uniform height corresponding more or less to the intended floor-level of the new constructions. Here the interruption of the work of construction is particularly clear.

On the south side of the New Frigidarium, a similar hall or court was intended, as is shown not only by the character of the triple portal, but by projecting stones left at the south-west outer corner of the Frigidarium on the line where the wall should have run. These stones are patently left in anticipation of a second phase of construction which, in fact, never took place.

The lack of any doorway connecting the New Frigidarium with (B) (the Old Baths) is the feature most perplexing to the modern visitor who seeks to understand the whole complex; and it is doubtless this lack which persuaded Caputo to regard the "Edificio Stellare" (A) and the great Hall (D) as distinct monuments, having no functional interrelationship. Yet the fact that the two are co-axial is significant enough, and the difficulty disappears once we accept that the hot rooms of the "Old Baths" (B) were intended to be remodelled to serve as a *Tepidarium*. The cutting of a doorway through the west wall of (B) to link it with (D) would, logically, have taken place when (B) was remodelled; and this necessary remodelling was never to take place.

Thus the whole nature of the new buildings in the complex of the "Terme Tarde" seems to indicate that a grandiose project was being implemented piecemeal, perhaps because of shortage of funds or shortage of skilled labour. The whole programme may have been divided up into separate contracts, the first one being concerned with the basic construction of the two great vaulted halls, (A) and (D). The former, the "Edificio Stellare", was completed and given its dome; the latter was nearly completed (except for the vaulting) when the work was halted. The secondary, but highly skilled work of installing hypocausts and hot baths in (A), and cold baths and drains in (D), was never begun. Nor was the remodelling of (B). In such an incomplete condition has the monument come down to us.

3. Later use of the Old Vestibule (C)

It has already been stated that the vestibule (C) must have been the *apodyterium* of the earlier baths. Of its floor in this first period there remain the impresses of marble slabs that were subsequently removed. Over this was laid the latest floor, consisting of small square slabs of a yellow stone, of a type found in the Market and other public buildings at Lepcis, more especially in the fourth century A.D.

The twelve columns of the Corinthian order, and with monolithic shafts of varying marbles, that constitute its inner peristyle—if such it is—have their bases resting on the lower floor level: but it is by no means certain that the colonnade was there from the beginning. Indeed, the disposition of the columns is related to a series of rectangular piers built up against all four walls of the room, and incorporating re-used statue bases in their lowest parts. One such base, re-used upside down, bears a mutilated dedication to Caracalla in A.D. 215–16 (Trib. Pot. XVIII), which provides a *terminus post quem* for the reconstruction of this hall.

The colonnade (and, possibly, also the wall-piers) supported arcades of rubble masonry, of which substantial fragments still lie within the hall. It is quite possible that the whole of (C) was roofed over, and was more of a basilica than a peristyle or "cortiletto". Its reconstruction provided a new entrance at the north-west corner, and a total rebuilding of the north-east corner.

Clearly, Hall (C)—in its latest form—has nothing to do with either the Earlier Baths or the uncompleted Late Baths. The very fact that it is a completed building with a floor and with marble revetments to its walls distinguishes it from the latter. We must therefore assume that after the project of rebuilding the Baths on a grandiose scale had been abandoned, this part of the site was brought back into use for quite different purposes. What these purposes were cannot easily be judged, as none of the inscriptions found within (C) appear to be relevant. Perhaps it was an assembly-hall for some commercial or professional group, for it is clearly too small to have played any very important part in municipal affairs.

INSCRIPTIONS AND SCULPTURES

The present article is concerned only with the structural character and intended function of the various parts of the "Late Baths" complex; and the inscriptions and sculptures found during the excavation need only concern us here insofar as they may throw light on the function and history of the complex. More detailed analysis may be left to specialists in art-history and epigraphy.[17]

The walls of Halls (A) and (D) contain numerous blocks bearing fragments of monumental inscriptions, of which the lettering seems to be mainly of the first-century A.D. Of the same period, presumably, is a single fragment of Neo-Punic text, found loose in the excavations, but probably coming from the fallen stones of the late walls.[18] On the northern outer face of the "Edificio Stellare" (A), low down in the wall, is a rectangular base of brown limestone bearing an almost-illegible inscription, the letters of which suggest a post-Severan date.

The inscriptions built into the fabric of the Late Baths therefore do little more than indicate a post-Severan date for the edifice, and such dating is already sufficiently apparent from the extensive re-use of material from earlier buildings, and from the slipshod methods of construction.

Two other inscriptions, both in honour of the emperor Gallienus and both precisely dated to the period 10 December, 267 to 9 December, 268 (*tribunicia potestate xvi, imperatori xv, consuli vii*), were found within the area of the New Frigidarium. One, a large moulded base of white marble, bears a dedication by the *Lepcitani Saloniniani* and was found beside the uncompleted drains in the eastern part of the Hall (D): it is in damaged condition, and may have been brought in to be cut down for re-use. The other,[19] a limestone base of smaller dimensions, was dedicated to the same emperor by C. Servilius Marsus, *curator reipublicae regionis Tripolitanae*: the top of the base is missing, suggesting that re-cutting was in progress.

Since the New Frigidarium has no floor, and its drains were left uncompleted, it is inconceivable that either of these bases ever stood within the building. Like the other inscriptions previously referred to, they provide only a *terminus post quem*, and not an entirely secure one at that: for it is possible that they were dumped on the abandoned building site at a later date.

The same possibility applies to the sculpture, although some items may have come from the Frigidarium of the Early Baths, and have been removed when that structure was demolished to make way for the great hexagonal New Caldarium. Thus a fine and complete Aesculapius was found in the street immediately north of the Old Vestibule (C); and from the same street came a torso of Hercules. Within (C) was found a headless female statue, possibly a Hygeia.

What is noteworthy is that no sculpture of any kind was found in the Hexagon (A), and only damaged and incomplete material in the sand and rubble overlying the Hall (D), so that it seems unlikely that in either part of the New Baths had the work of construction ever reached a point at which statues would have been introduced. Certainly no contractor would have exposed valuable sculpture to the risk of staining by lime mortar dripping from newly-laid roofs.

Therefore, by and large, the inscriptions and sculpture found during the excavation of the "Terme tarde sul mare" have no direct relevance to the history of this monument or to the character of its intended ornamentation. However, a closer study of the fragmentary inscriptions built into the fabric of the Hexagon and the Hall may reveal which monuments of Lepcis were quarried to provide building stone.[20]

PARALLELS FOR THE NEW CALDARIUM AND NEW FRIGIDARIUM

We do not need to search far for parallels to support the proposed identification of (A) and (D) as intended bath-rooms, the former hot and the latter cold. In the case of (A), the so-called "Edificio Stellare", the door-like hypocaust stoke-holes below the intended floor level, and the broad windows above the recesses meant to contain hot baths, are alike clear pointers to the intent of the architect. These features appear in numerous public baths of the Roman period, but are best documented in the Imperial Baths at Trier, thanks to Krencker's fundamental study of that monument.

Where the unfinished Imperial Baths of Lepcis differ from the general run of such buildings is in the *hexagonal* plan adapted for the Caldarium. Most frequently, in such vast edifices, the caldarium was rectangular, sometimes with apsidal recesses. But at Rome, in the Baths of Caracalla and also in the Baths of Constantine we have circular caldaria which must have been domed.[21]

The hexagonal plan adopted at Lepcis allowed the possibility of constructing a dome, while at the same time conforming to the adjacent street-plan. Moreover, since the only available building materials (apart from the concrete core) were rectangular blocks taken from earlier buildings, a hexagonal structure could be thrown up more rapidly than a circular one.

We do not know what form the tepidarium was intended to take, as the work of construction never reached the point of remodelling the Early Baths (B) to serve this new function. However, the fact that the earlier east wall was retained and bonded into the Hexagon seems to imply that no drastic structural changes were planned. One has the strong impression that the planners of the new Baths were working with a limited budget and anxious to avoid unnecessary expense. A point of interest is that the twin doors leading into the Hexagon are exactly paralleled at Rome in the Baths of Caracalla, of Diocletian and of Constantine. It would seem that the builders at Lepcis were deliberately copying certain features of the metropolitan prototypes.

The Frigidarium, as we have already seen, follows the Roman models, the principal difference being that it has no axial communication with a *natatio* further to the west, the place where such communication would normally exist being blocked by the central piscina on the west side, with its fountain and statue-niches. The absence of a *natatio*—for it seems to be deliberately omitted from the design—may indicate a falling-off of the city water-supply; or it may merely be that available space was limited and funds not available for further expropriations. However, such a fresh-water swimming-pool, within a stone's throw of the sea, may have seemed an unnecessary luxury at the period when the Late Baths were planned.

It is also clear that work had never even begun on the construction of a south wing to the New Frigidarium to balance the partly-constructed wing (E) on the north. In the present state of the excavations it is difficult to judge whether the necessary demolition of private dwellings had begun.

THE DATE OF THE LATE BATHS, AND CAUSES OF THEIR ABANDONMENT

We now come to the two major problems regarding the unfinished Late Baths at Lepcis. When was their construction (or, more precisely, the reconstruction of the earlier bath-house) begun? Why was the work never completed?

The extensive use of re-used blocks in Halls (A) and (D) persuaded Vergara-Caffarelli to define these Baths as "one of the latest constructions at Lepcis Magna before the Vandal invasions", and it is evident that he rejected any possibility of their belonging to the period of the Byzantine re-occupation (sixth century A.D.). With this conclusion the present writer is in the fullest agreement, for the testimony of Procopius is explicit: "He (the Emperor Justinian) has left the buried portion of the city just as it was, covered by the sand heaped up in mounds; but the rest of the city he has surrounded with a very strongly-built wall".[22] Since the line of the circuit-wall of Justinian is known,[23] and since these Late Baths lie well outside it, it is difficult to attribute to them so late a date.

There is another, more technical, reason for denying a Justinianic date to any part of the Late Baths. For the greyish mortar, previously described, used in their construction is quite different from that used in the Byzantine city walls, where the builders mixed a high proportion of broken *murex* shells (from refuse piles of purple-dye works, as Professor Alberto Blanc has shown)[24] into their white lime mortar.

Moreover, it is inconceivable that the sadly shrunken and impoverished Lepcis that Justinian restored to life could have felt the need for a bath-establishment planned on this truly monumental scale. The same is probably true of Lepcis during the first half of the fifth century, where the dwindling number of public inscriptions attests the breakdown of organised municipal life.

Thus the choice of dates seems to lie between the third and the fourth centuries A.D. when, despite a sad decline from the exaggeratedly high hopes of the Severan age, Lepcis still had its moments of renovation and optimism, as attested by the fulsome language of public inscriptions.

The earliest possible date would seem to be the reign of Gallienus (A.D. 253–68) when the city added the name of his consort Salonina to its official titles,[25] and set up numerous statues and dedications in his honour. Indeed, at first sight, the presence of two such dedications to this emperor amidst the ruins of the Late Baths might seem to confirm such a date. But reasons have already been given above for doubting the relevance of these two texts to the actual history of the Baths.

A more probable date for the monument would be in the fourth century when Lepcis was enjoying its new status as capital of the Tripolitan province, and when a considerable amount of reconstruction was in progress in the city. Several of the *praesides* who had their seat of office at Lepcis are described as *instauratores moenium publicorum*, including the governor Flavius Archontius Nilus (A.D. 355–60).[26] Had the construction of the Late Baths begun about 360, it would be understandable if the Austurian threat of 363, and the subsequent political scandal described by Ammianus[27] halted the work. Again, the dome of the half-completed hexagonal Caldarium might have fallen in the earthquake of 365, the effects of which in Sabratha have recently been noted by Professor Di Vita.[28]

Alternatively, the construction of these new "Imperial" Baths may have been motivated by some unrecorded disaster that put out of action the Baths of Hadrian beside the modern bed of the Wadi Lebda. The collapse of the great dam that diverted the flood waters into the "Monticelli" diversionary canal may have occurred at an earlier date than is generally supposed: the Hadrianic Baths could have been irreparably damaged. These, however, are mere speculations; and, as multiplicity of bath-buildings in the larger Roman cities is a normal feature, it is not necessary to suppose that the Hadrianic Baths were no longer functioning when the Late Baths were planned.

Tempting as it is to suppose that the abandonment of the project was the result of some known political or seismic event, we must bear in mind that the whole edifice bears signs of parsimonious planning. The retention of the walls of the Old Baths in the midst of the new ones, the absence of a *natatio*, the slipshod construction, all alike suggest that means were not commensurate with grandiose aims. A financial crisis, or the death of an imperial patron, are no less likely causes for the halting of the project.

These are merely conjectures, but they are the best that can be offered in the absence of relevant inscriptions; and the very fact that the Baths were never completed makes it unlikely that any inscriptions were ever set up in them.

Stratigraphic excavation in and around the complex may, one day, resolve the problem of date; but before such work can be attempted, it will be necessary to remove or replace the masses of stone that still encumber the New Frigidarium.

While leaving this precise determination of date to future research, the essential character of the "Edificio Stellare" and its adjacent parts seems certain. The great Hexagon is not a church, but an uncompleted Caldarium; whilst the ornate Hall that lies on the same axis is an even more incomplete Frigidarium. No fires ever burned in the furnaces of the former, and no water flowed in the plunge-baths of the latter. Events, whether political or economic, conspired to bring to a halt the last great municipal project of pre-Vandal Lepcis Magna.

NOTES

1. *Leptis Magna* (Presentazione di Ranuccio Bianchi Bandinelli. Testo di Ernesto Vergara Caffarelli e Giacomo Caputo. Fotografie di Fabrizio Clerici), Rome, 1963, 107–10 (by Caputo).

2. See articles in the newspaper *Giornale di Tripoli*: 6 April, 1956 and 10 December, 1956; also *Fasti Archeologici*, xii (1959), 351.

3. Summary reports of the work (*Giornale di Scavo*) for the months September–December, 1955 and January–February, 1956 exist in the archives of the Department of Antiquities, and have been consulted. I am indebted to Sig. Francesco Russo for much additional information; to Sig. Carmelo Catanuso for drawings on which the accompanying plan is based; and to Sig. Flaminio De Liberali and Ess. Hassan Hassuna for photographs. The original survey of the monument was made by students of the Architectural Faculty of the University of Rome under the direction of Professor Furio Fasolo.

4. *Giornale di Tripoli*, 6 April, 1956 (my translation).

5. The technical resources of the Department of Antiquities at that time did not allow the possibility of cutting up the enormous concrete masses of the dome and replacing them *in situ*, by the technique which Giacomo Caputo so successfully applied in his restoration of the Theatre at Lepcis Magna.

6. This plan was revised by C. Catanuso for publication in the volume *Leptis Magna*, and has been further modified for the present paper.

7. *Fasti Archeologici*, xii (1959), p. 352 (my translation).

8. Caputo, *loc. cit.*

9. Also dismantled was a circular furnace (limekiln or oven?) installed in the northernmost recess of the hexagon, and resting on another stone-slab floor (pl. 48). This presumably belonged to an intermediate period between the abandonment of work on the hexagon and the re-use of the Old Baths.

10. Caputo, *Leptis Magna*, 108 (my translation).

11. It is the *height* (2·50 m.) of these "doorways" which has concealed their real nature as intended furnaces; but we must remember that this height would have been reduced had the floor of the hypocaust been laid in the Hexagon. In any case, the height is not unparalleled. Cf. D. Krencker and E. Kruger, *Die Trierer Kaiserthermen* (Augsburg, 1929), 73, Abb. 87a. Professor A. Di Vita has pointed out to me that the furnace openings in the "Seaward Baths" at Sabratha are equally high.

12. Krencker-Kruger, *op. cit.*, 69, Abb. 83b.

13. Krencker-Kruger, *op. cit.*, Abb. 394 (Baths of Nero); Abb. 397 (Baths of Trajan); Abb. 400 (Baths of Caracalla); Abb. 412 (Baths of Diocletian); Abb. 422a (Baths of Constantine).

14. Caputo, *loc. cit.*, 108.

15. The gaps between the three moulded stones that form the top cornice should have been filled with rubble or concrete; but this was never done.

16. In Catanuso's plan (*Leptis Magna*, 109) this northern extension of the New Frigidarium is dissociated from the rest of the structure, its walls being shown in outline only. But their width and materials leave no doubt that they belong to the Late Baths, and have nothing to do with the remains of earlier houses which they enclose.

17. I understand that the inscriptions will be published by Signora Ginette Di Vita-Evrard.

18. This is being studied by Professor Giorgio Levi Della Vida.

19. On this stone the name of the emperor is missing, and the imperial titles could refer to Diocletian; but the palaeography leaves no reasonable doubt that Gallienus was intended.

20. Professor Di Vita informs me that some of these re-used fragments unite with fragments found at the West Gate (Porta Oea), thus suggesting that Late Baths and Late Roman City Wall were contemporaneous. But as the date of the latter is still uncertain, this does not resolve the immediate problem.

21. Krencker-Kruger, *op. cit.*, Abb. 400 and Abb. 422a.

22. Procopius, *De aedif.*, VI, iv 3.

23. R. G. Goodchild and J. B. Ward Perkins, "Defences of Lepcis Magna", 54, fig. 4.

24. A. C. Blanc, *Residui di manifatture di porpora a Leptis Magna ed al Monte Circeo*, Appendix to R. Bartoccini, *Il Porto Romano di Leptis Magna* (Rome, 1958) 187 f.

25. R. G. Goodchild, "Tripolitanian Inscriptions", 31.

26. *IRT* 562 and 563.

27. Ammianus, *Hist.* XXVIII, 6.

28. Di Vita, 134, note 8.

10

MEDINA SULTAN

(Charax, Iscina, Sort)

A PRELIMINARY NOTE

[From *Libya Antiqua* i (1964)]
Plate 50

Of the many ancient sites that lie in the Syrtic region of Libya the greatest in extent, and the most long-lived in its history, is Medina Sultan, the site of the Punic, Roman and Early Islamic settlements known respectively as *Charax, Iscina* and *Sort*. In anticipation of the excavations which the Libyan Antiquities Department hopes shortly to initiate on this important site,[1a] it may be useful to set out our existing knowledge regarding the history and archaeology of Medina Sultan, including the results of an air survey made by the present writer in 1952.

THE SITE

The principal ruins of Medina Sultan lie between the coastal Highway and the sea at the 55th Kilometre-stone east of modern Sirte, and are approximately 51 km. from Sirte by the more direct ancient caravan-track along the shore. Five km. further to the east is the small oasis of Sultan, where there are some twelve wells of excellent water, and a small palm-grove immediately behind the coastal dunes. Five km. to the south of Sultan oasis, on a low hill, is the well named Bir esh-Shakshakia, near which are some ancient ruins isolated from the main group at Medina Sultan itself. The Shakshakia ruins are not included in the air survey of 1952, and cannot therefore be discussed in the present article.

PREVIOUS EXPLORATIONS

The first modern description of Medina Sultan is the very summary one given by the brothers Beechey following their visit in 1821, in the course of their geographical and archaeological survey of the Syrtic region. The Beecheys mention two distinct sites: "Medinet Sultan" where "the remains of several strongly-built fortresses" seemed to indicate "an important military position"; and, two miles to the south-east, "the decided remains of an ancient town, called Medina". It is clear that the second site must be the Shakshakia to which we have already referred, and that the generic name "Medina" was applied to it by the Beecheys' guides. The fortresses at "Medinet Sultan" are evidently the ones still visible today incorporated in the wall-circuit of Islamic Sort, to which we shall refer later: the plans which the Beecheys made of these structures were unfortunately omitted from their published volume.[1]

In 1846 Heinrich Barth visited Sultan, but his account adds little or nothing to the Beecheys', except the observation that the two forts at Medina Sultan were interconnected by a rampart. He did, however, arrive at the important conclusion that these remains represented the successive sites of *Charax, Iscina* and *Sort*; and his lengthy discussion of the ancient topography of the Syrtic region was more scholarly and precise than the Beecheys' previous contribution to this subject.[2]

The next visitor to leave some notice of Sultan was another German, G. A. Freund, who passed the ruins in May, 1881. He claimed to have seen the remains of an ancient theatre: "the stage is rectangular, and the ramp leading to the orchestra thirty feet long." There is no other record of such a building at Sultan, and there is reason to doubt the reliability of Freund's observation.[3]

In 1931 an Italian officer, Captain Luigi Cerrata, made extensive geographical and archaeological reconnaissances in the Syrtic region, and his monograph, published in 1933,[4] is still the best available description. Of Medina Sultan he gives a sketch-plan (not entirely reliable) and some photographs; but his narrative tends to assume that the visible ruins were all of Roman date, representing the site of *Iscina*.

In 1950, during the course of the "Map of Roman Libya" expedition led by the present writer,[5] Sultan was visited and a compass-survey made of the principal part of the site. Its general character, together with the typical Islamic potsherds found on the surface of the "Medina" left little doubt that this was the site of an Islamic city rather than a Roman one; although it was evident that Iscina, too, must have stood hereabouts.

While looking through the air-photographic cover of the Syrtic region, provided by the R.A.F., the writer came across some high-level photographs taken in 1949 and showing what appeared to be a most complex series of walls and enclosures extending along the coast for 2 km. westward of Medina Sultan. More detailed photographs were required, and through the kind assistance of the R.A.F. Malta, these were obtained in 1952.[6] As the accompanying map—based on these air photographs—shows, the archaeological area of Sultan extends far beyond the limits of the medieval city of *Sort* and leaves little doubt that the complex of enclosures, barely visible to a ground observer, forms part of *Iscina*.

THE ANCIENT GEOGRAPHERS

It was, as we have noted, Barth who first proposed that Medina Sultan represented the successive sites of *Charax, Iscina* and *Sort*. His conclusions were adopted and developed by Karl Müller in his edition of the *Minor Greek Geographers*,[7] and it may be useful to set out briefly the main arguments.

Charax

Strabo (XVII, iii, 20) describes *Charax* as lying east of *Turris Euphranta* which, at one period of Ptolemaic rule, had been the boundary of Carthage and Cyrenaica. The "Stadiasmus"[8] gives the name as *Korax*, and the distance from *Euphranta* as 200 stades (35 km. approximately). Ptolemy records a *"Pharax* village" in the same area.[9]

Because the total of distances from port to port listed in the Stadiasmus falls short of the true length of the coastline, some of the figures must be corrupt, and Müller therefore proposed that 200 should be corrected to 290 stades (50 km. approximately) which is the true distance from *Euphranta* (modern Sirte) to Sultan. This also places *Korax* at its correct distance of 150 stades (26 km.) from *Eperos* (probably En-Naim).

Whilst, therefore, the identification of *Charax/Korax* with Medina Sultan rests on learned ingenuity rather than on precise figures of distance, it is likely enough that the flourishing medieval port of *Sort* had a Punic predecessor; and in default of a better site at the 200-stade distance actually given by the "Stadiasmus", we may accept the Barth-Müller hypothesis.

The main interest of *Charax* lies in Strabo's assertion that it was used by the Carthaginians as an "emporium", wine being taken there and exchanged for silphium and silphium-juice smuggled from Cyrenaica.[10] This clandestine commerce would have brought into existence a resident community, as indicated by the title "village" attributed to *Pharax* by Ptolemy.

Iscina

This place-name appears in the Roman road-itineraries, the Antonine Itinerary[11] placing it 34 Roman miles (50 km.) east of *Macomades*, which itself occupied the site of earlier *Euphranta* (modern Sirte). The Peutinger Map[12] gives the same distance, and adds after the name *Iscina* the enigmatic phrase "locus Iudaeorum Augusti", presumably indicating an Imperial settlement of Jews. Whether this was in existence before the Jewish Revolt that devastated Cyrenaica in A.D. 115, or whether it represented a subsequent transfer of population, is uncertain.[13] It is noteworthy that a Jewish inscription at Rome refers to a native of "Iskina", which can hardly be other than the Syrtic settlement of this name.[14] That other Jewish settlements existed in the Syrtica is shown by Procopius' reference to the Jews of *Boreum* (Bu Grada, near Marsa Brega) whom Justinian converted to Christianity, converting their ancient synagogue into a church.[15]

Sort

The Arabic place-name *Sort* was presumably derived from the ancient name *Syrtis*, which Procopius[16] explains as having its origin in the Greek word "suresthai" meaning "to be drawn" in reference to the action of currents on ships trapped in the Syrtis.

El-Bekri describes *Sort* as being one day's journey from *Maghmedas*, which latter place is described as an "idol" (senam) standing on the edge of the shore, and surrounded by several other "idols".[17] There can be no reasonable doubt that *Maghmedas* was derived from the Roman name *Macomades* (Sirte), and that the "idols" were either columns or, perhaps more probably, funerary obelisks of the type commonly erected both in Tripolitania proper and in the Syrtica during the Roman period. (One intact specimen survives today at El-Garrush near the roadside 40 km. east of Sirte, and bases of others can be seen in the hills behind Sirte itself.)

Edrisi[18] does not give the name *Maghmedas*, but the locality he calls *El-Asnam* ("the idols") is clearly the same place; and he gives the distance from here to *Sort* as 46 Arab miles, which should be equivalent to about 78 km. This is greatly in excess of the true distance from *Macomades* (Sirte) to Sultan which, as we have seen, is in the neighbourhood of 50 km. only. We need not, however, be unduly concerned by this discrepancy, as few of Edrisi's mileage figures will bear close scrutiny.

THE MODERN PLACE-NAME "SIRTE"

Modern commentators[19] on the geography of the Syrtic region have sometimes confused medieval *Sort* with modern *Sirte* ("Sert" in arabic); and it may therefore be useful to explain how the latter name came into being.

After the decline and abandonment of *Sort*, its name came to be applied loosely to the whole region (just as the name "Barka" has been transferred from a single city to a whole region). Until the Turkish re-occupation of Libya in 1835, following the fall of the Karamanli dynasty, the Syrtic region had no recognised administrative centre, and was infested by bandits. To remedy this, the Turks erected a fortress at Marsa Zaafran (modern Sirte) completing it in 1842, and nominated a "Bey of Sert" to represent the government.[20] The fortress, at first called "Qasr Zaafran", later came to be more generally known as "Qasr Sert"—and thus a regional name came to be re-localised, although not in the place of its origin. The Turkish fortress was repaired by the Italians in 1912, and around it has grown up the modern township of Sirte.

ISLAMIC ACCOUNTS OF SORT

Of the medieval city that succeeded Charax and Iscina some account is given by the Arab geographers and historians. In common with Agedabia it served as an important staging-point on the overland route from Barka to Tripoli, and had the additional advantage (lacking at Agedabia) of a harbour in its immediate vicinity. El-Bekri,[21] writing in the eleventh century, described Sort as:

> "A large city situated beside the sea, and enclosed by a wall of bricks, containing a mosque, a bath and several bazaars. It has three gates, of which one faces the south, another the north, and the third—a small one—leads to the sea. This city has no suburbs but possesses date-palms, gardens, sweet-water springs, and a large number of cisterns."

The inhabitants of Sort, at this period, had an ill-repute for avarice and sharp commercial practice, and El-Bekri says that they were nick-named the "Abid-Kirilla" (servants of the Kirilla) in reference to a voracious Asiatic bird. He adds that their character was entirely the opposite of that of the inhabitants of Tripoli "who are the most likeable men in their social relations, and the most honourable in their commercial transactions, and the most polite towards strangers".

These men of Sort spoke "a kind of jargon which is neither Arabic, Persian, Berber or Coptic", and nobody except their own people could understand them.

One of their typical sharp practices was to conceal any shortage of basic com-
modities so as to defeat the laws of supply and demand. Thus when a ship
bearing olive-oil came into harbour at a time of shortage of this commodity,
they would inflate skins with air and hang them prominently in shops and houses
to suggest that there was no scarcity, thereby persuading the visiting traders to
sell at a low cost.

Edrisi,[22] writing a century after El-Bekri, described Sort as "a town surrounded
by a wall of earth, and situated two miles from the sea". It was then surrounded
by sand, and its palm-trees were no longer sufficient for the needs of the inhabitants: grass was rarer here than at Augila. At this time Sort and Agedabia were
both "in a miserable condition and containing only a few inhabitants".

In the first half of the thirteenth century Ibn Sayd (quoted by Abulfeda[23])
stated:

> "Sort is one of the ancient cities mentioned in books. The Arabs have
> destroyed it, and there remain only some castles in which the Arabs have
> established their residence."

It seems clear, therefore, that the flourishing if dishonest city recorded by
El-Bekri gradually decayed after the invasion of the Beni Hilal and Beni Suleim
(c. 1050), and that by the thirteenth century there remained only a few Arab
squatters in the fortified buildings within its site. This course of events was not,
however, peculiar to Sort. Agedabia and Barka both suffered the same decline
which resulted in the elimination of sedentary life throughout the Syrtica and
Cyrenaica.

THE ARCHAEOLOGICAL REMAINS

(A) *The walled Islamic city of Sort* (fig. 42)

The most prominent remains at Medina Sultan are the two forts standing at the
south-west and south-east angles of a polygonal enclosure the maximum dimensions of which are 500 m. from west to east, and 600 m. from south to north.
The two forts are connected, as Barth first noticed, by a rampart forming the
southern defences of the city; and the same rampart can also be traced northward from each fort, forming a continuous circuit which falls just short of the
prominent hillock (the "north fort") overlooking the sea. Thus the wall-circuit
is heavily fortified, and on rising ground, on its inland course; whilst towards the
sea it is in the plain and dominated by the "north fort" which, although extra-
mural, can hardly have failed to be garrisoned.

The forts are stone-built, the west fort having a double enclosing wall measuring about 40 by 60 m. and the east fort a large outer enclosure 100 m. square.
The central "keeps" are reduced to mounds of crumbling stone: although no
doors are visible, they are probably concealed by fallen debris, and the suggestion
of the Beecheys[24] and Barth that the forts were doorless is highly improbable.

The rampart-circuit, however, shows no surface signs of stone construction, and
is visible only as a low and broad mound, with some traces of a ditch fronting
it at several points. El-Bekri describes Sort as having ramparts of "brick"; and
the present remains probably represent the collapse of mud-brick walls, which
Edrisi described as of "earth".

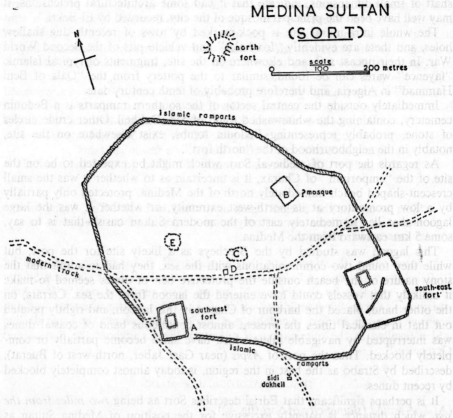

Fig. 42 Medina Sultan: site of the Islamic city

Of the three gateways mentioned by El-Bekri, none are visible; but it must be noted that his description of the principal gates being to north and south is improbable, since the main Syrtic caravan route runs from east to west through the middle of the city. Likewise, as the sea is to north, the smaller gateway leading to it must have been on this side. This error in orientation is perhaps due to the fact that any traveller in the Syrtic Gulf has the impression of going from north to south, towards the foot of the gulf, even when he is in fact travelling from west to east.

Within the wall-circuit, most of the low-lying area is cultivated today and there is only a thin scatter of stone and potsherds on the surface, except at one or two points where more massive buildings have resisted the cultivator. One such building (C on plan, fig. 42) lies immediately north of the east-west track that traverses the site, and is approximately in the centre of the city. Another (B on plan) lies close up against the north-east line of the ramparts, and is the largest recognisable structure in the intra-mural area. Some fragments of stucco decoration found on the surface of this building, together with a hexagonal column shaft of small dimensions, indicate that it had some architectural pretensions; it may well have been the principal mosque of the city, recorded by El-Bekri.

The whole intra-mural site is pock-marked by rows of recently-dug shallow holes, and these are evidently "fox-holes" and vehicle pits of the Second World War. In their upcast soil, and elsewhere on the site, fragments of typical Islamic "fayence" wares can be found, similar to the pottery from the "Qala of Beni Hammad" in Algeria, and therefore probably of tenth century date.

Immediately outside the central sector of the southern ramparts is a Bedouin cemetery, containing the whitewashed tomb of Sidi Dakheil. Other crude circles of stone, probably representing Bedouin tombs, exist elsewhere on the site, notably in the neighbourhood of the "north fort".

As regards the port of medieval Sort, which might be expected to be on the site of the "emporium" of Charax, it is uncertain as to whether it was the small crescent-shaped beach immediately north of the Medina, protected only partially by a low promontory at its north-west extremity, or whether it was the large lagoon that lies immediately east of the modern Sultan oasis—that is to say, some 5 km. eastward from the Medina.

This lagoon was studied by the Beecheys as a likely site for the port; but while they found two communications with the sea, they had to admit that the stony nature of the beach outside the protective belt of dunes seemed to make it unlikely that vessels could have entered the lagoon from the sea. Cerrata, on the other hand, placed the harbour of Charax in this lagoon, and rightly pointed out that in classical times the present almost continuous band of coastal dunes was interrupted by navigable inlets which have since become partially or completely blocked. Thus the port of *Aspis* (near Gasr Jaber, north-west of Buerat), described by Strabo as the best in the region, is today almost completely blocked by recent dunes.

It is perhaps significant that Edrisi describes Sort as being *two miles from the sea*, which distance is patently excessive for the position of Medina Sultan as regards the beach to its immediate north, but would be nearer the truth if sea-farers entered the lagoon and landed near the modern Sultan oasis. This problem needs to be studied in greater detail, because—for the reasons already set out above—where the port of medieval Sort stood, there we must seek the remains of Punic *Charax*.

(B) *The traces of Iscina* (fig. 43)

As has been previously stressed, the most prominent remains of Medina Sultan, interpreted by the Beecheys as a Roman military station, and by Cerrata as the site of the town Iscina, must now be regarded—beyond any reasonable doubt—as the site of medieval Sort. This does not, of course, exclude the possibility that the remains of Iscina lie buried beneath the medieval city.

The results of the air-survey of 1952 seem to convert this possibility into a probability, since they reveal an extraordinary complex of enclosures extending for 2 km. westward of the medieval Medina, and for 1 km. at least to its south and to its east. These enclosures are virtually invisible to the ground observer, as they occur in a plain that is normally covered with pre-desert vegetation. Only here and there, where the motor-tracks of the Second World War (little used today) cross the enclosure walls, is it possible to see clearly the whitish

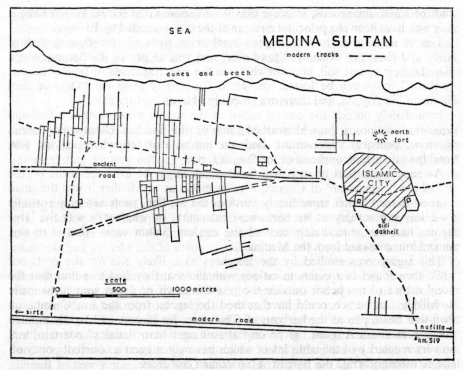

Fig. 43 Medina Sultan: ancient enclosure-walls to the west of the Islamic city

"pisé" with which they are constructed: it is easy to mistake them for natural outcrops of limestone.

From the air the enclosures are most conspicuous and coherent on the west side of the Medina, and the accompanying plan shows their lay-out. A dark strip, 25–30 m. broad, uninterrupted by walls, marks the old coastal highway leading directly to the centre of the Medina. Both to the north and south of this road the enclosure-walls run in straight lines, for the most part forming long narrow strip gardens, with occasional divisions across their shorter axis. In one or two places house-sites may be suspected, but such instances are not frequent.

South of the main ancient highway a narrow lane runs diagonally through the area of enclosures to meet the highway a short distance outside the wall-circuit of the Medina; and this would seem to indicate that the settlement to which these enclosures belonged lay on or near the Medina site.

There is, therefore, no immediate proof that the enclosures are not contemporaneous with the surface remains of the Medina, marking the gardens of the inhabitants of Sort; but it may be noted, first that their extent seems to be disproportionate to the size of the Medina itself, and second, that the material used—the characteristic white "pisé"—is not represented in the surface remains of the Medina. Moreover, the remains of the enclosures get fainter as we approach the ramparts of the medieval city, as though to indicate that they have been obliterated by subsequent occupation and cultivation.

In these circumstances it seems justifiable to suppose that the enclosures belong to a much earlier phase of history, and since the small Punic emporium of Charax is unlikely to have possessed such extensive areas of plantation, it is surely to *Iscina*, the "locus Iudaeorum Augusti" to which we may provisionally assign them.

GENERAL CONCLUSIONS

From the evidence at present available, it is hardly possible to draw any definitive conclusions; and such must await the outcome of future excavations. But from the superficial appearance of the site, both on the ground and from the air, we may make the following tentative deductions:

(*a*) of Punic *Charax* there are no obvious traces, but this is hardly surprising if we bear in mind the modest character of the early emporia in Tripolitania. The site of Charax must have adjoined the sea; and we may therefore choose between the small and ill-sheltered beach immediately north of the Medina and the shore of the large lagoon some 5 km. to its east.

(*b*) Roman *Iscina* appears to be represented by the extensive enclosure-walls revealed by air-survey; but the centre of the Roman-period town may lie beneath the Medina, and it is conceivable that the two forts incorporated in the medieval town-wall belong to an earlier period. The exact significance of the description "locus Iudaeorum Augusti" given on the Peutinger Map remains uncertain; but the very regularity of the complex of enclosures may suggest a coherent policy of land-settlement carried out by one of the Roman emperors.

(*c*) Medieval *Sort* is clearly recognisable from its circuit of ramparts, and although not as large as El-Bekri's description might give one to believe, holds out interesting possibilities to its future excavators. It is, in fact, the only major early Islamic site between Tripoli and the Egyptian border that has escaped the ravages of the stone-seeker; and within its walls we may expect to find the mosque, bath and bazaars referred to by El-Bekri. But the fact that mud-brick is likely to have been used extensively, not only in its ramparts but also in some of its intra-mural buildings, will necessitate the most careful excavation methods.

NOTES

[1a. See the reports of M. Mostafa in *Libya Antiqua* iii–iv (1966–7) 145 f. and A. Abdussaid, ibid. 155 f.]

1. F. W. and H. W. Beechey, 169–71.

2. H. Barth, (1), I, 334–5. His conclusions regarding the ancient topography of the Syrtic area are in a lengthy footnote, 364–77.

3. G. A. Freund, 171.

4. L. Cerrata, 209–12.

5. I am indebted to Messrs. M. H. Ballance and D. J. Smith for their contributions to the survey and the study of the pottery during this campaign.

6. I was permitted to fly in a Lancaster aircraft fitted with both oblique and vertical cameras, and was thus able to obtain fairly comprehensive air cover of the site.

7. *Geographi Graeci Minores* I.

8. *Stadiasmus Maris Magni* in Müller.

9. Claudius Ptolemaeus, *Geographia* (Ed. Müller).

10. *Strabonis, Geographica* (Ed. Müller and Dubner).

11. (Ed. Cuntz).

12. *Tabula Peutingeriana* (ed. C. Miller). In fact, the Tabula gives a total distance of 39 Roman miles between Macomades and Iscina; but Cerrata (208) rightly places "Ad Speluncas" at the mouth of the Wadi

Henewa, and corrects its distance from Iscina from "XIII" to "VIII" Roman miles. This brings the two itineraries into concordance and seems plausible.

13. Barth, (1), 374, assumes that the Jewish settlement at Iscina dated back to the third century B.C.; but there seems to be no evidence for this.

14. J.-B. Frey, *Corpus Inscriptionum Iudaicarum*, i (Europe) (Rome, 1936) 12, n. 7, from a tomb under the Villa Torlonia. It is the tombstone of a certain A(d)iutor, a "grammateus" of the CEKHNWN. [For a discussion of this interpretation and alternative suggestions see H. J. Leon, *The Jews of Ancient Rome* (Philadelphia, 1960) 149 f.]

15. Procopius, De aedif, VI, ii, 21. The

remote antiquity of the Jewish settlement is here attested.

16. Procopius, *ibid.* VI, iii, 4.

17. El-Bekri (trans. de Slane), 21.

18. Edrisi (trans. Dozy and De Goeje), 160.

19. Cf. *Encyclopedia dell' Islam* (first edition) s.v. SYRTE. Ettore Rossi, who compiled this item, was evidently uncertain as to the relationship of modern *Sirte* to ancient *Sort*.

20. H. Barth, (1), 330.

21. El-Bekri, 17.

22. Edrisi, 143, 155.

23. Abulfeda, ed. Reinaud (1848), 204.

24. Beechey, 170.

CYRENAICA

Goodchild's Cyrenaican work is illustrated mainly by topographical papers, since he had only just begun to publish detailed results of his excavations in the cities. Moreover in the last years of his life he was mainly concerned with material from Apollonia, the port of Cyrene, which will be included in a volume on that city now in preparation under the editorship of Professor Donald White of the University of Michigan.

MAPPING ROMAN LIBYA

[From *The Geographical Journal* cxviii (1952)]
Plates 51, 52

Our Libyan expeditions of 1950–1 were a continuation, over a rather wider area, of the archaeological reconnaissances described in a previous paper in the *Journal*.[1] They differed mainly in that their aim was the collection of information for a map of Roman Libya, and that they were therefore concerned as much with the coastal regions as with the interior. In both years a summer programme of field-work was organised under the auspices of the Map of Roman Libya Committee (under the Chairmanship of Professor R. E. M. Wheeler) of the Society of Antiquaries of London, and with the financial support of several universities and learned societies, including the Royal Geographical Society.

During the two seasons' work, small parties of investigators[2] examined scores of ancient sites scattered between Sirte (Tripolitania) and Ain el-Gazala (Cyrenaica) and in several inland areas. We enjoyed the greatest possible help from the British military authorities in Cyrenaica, including the use for a fort-night each season of a small column of desert-worthy vehicles.[3] To Lieut. A. Weston-Lewis, 16/5 Lancers, who commanded this column on both occasions, and to the officers and other ranks who participated in Exercises "Roman Swan" I and II, we are deeply grateful. The co-operation of H.Q., R.A.F., Malta[4] enabled us to fly over part of the desert frontier area, and to obtain air photo-graphs of some of the ancient sites. Our main work was however on the ground. To the Governments of Tripolitania and Cyrenaica we are indebted for many facilities.[5]

It should first be explained that the term Roman Libya is used here to describe those parts of the Roman Empire which are now included within the boundaries of the recently constituted Kingdom of Libya. This is an arbitrary definition, accepted for reasons of convenience. The Romans themselves used the name "Libya" either in a general sense, to describe the whole of North Africa, or in an administrative sense, as an official name for the regions between Alexandria and Cyrenaica.[6] From the viewpoint of history and culture Tripolitania was an eastern extension of the realm of Carthage and became a Latin-speaking province with a strong Punic tradition. Cyrenaica was colonised by Greeks from Thera (Santorin) and gravitated, culturally and politically, towards Egypt: it remained Greek-speaking until the Islamic invasions.

Despite these differences, there is much to be said for treating the whole of northern Libya as a single unit in historical geography. Tripolitania and Cyrenaica were both isolated from their neighbours by coastal deserts, and both had a desert hinterland at a relatively short distance from the coast. In both cases a coastal plain with oases gave rise to large cities, whilst a well-watered plateau at its rear provided opportunities for agricultural development based on village and farm rather than on urban units. The more abundant vegetation of the Cyrenaican plateau, due to heavier rainfall and a stiffer soil, gives the superficial impression that this was the better of the two territories; but Tripolitania has greater water resources in the steppe and "pre-desert" areas, and has always been able to support a larger population. During the later period of Roman history, when North Africa was being invaded by savage tribes from the edges of the desert, Tripolitania and Cyrenaica had both to face the same problems and to co-ordinate their defensive policy in the face of a common menace; but it was not until the second half of the sixth century A.D., in the final phase of Roman rule, that the eastern and western halves of Libya actually came under a single administration.[7]

Our tasks, for the purposes of compiling the map of Roman Libya, were those of examining as many ancient sites as possible, of ascertaining which of them belonged to the Roman period, of recording their visible remains by plan and photograph, and of identifying them, where possible, with the localities listed in the ancient geographies. The latter include, in the case of Libya, the Geographies of Strabo and Ptolemy, the Roman road itineraries (Antonine Itinerary and Peutinger Map), and that invaluable "Mariner's Guide" of antiquity, the *Stadiasmus Maris Magni*.[8] Needless to say, the identification of an ancient place-name is only possible when the classical texts give some firm indication of its locality; and for this reason it has proved difficult to identify places which are not on the coast, or which do not appear in the road itineraries. Ptolemy's map of Libya does not inspire confidence. Small coastal reefs are shown as miles out to sea, and localities which were on the plateau only 20 miles from the coast are marked as being in the heart of the desert.[9]

Our investigations took place in two distinct areas: in the Syrtica, along the shores of the Gulf of Sidra, and in Cyrenaica proper, between Benghazi and the Gulf of Bomba. Of these two regions, the Syrtica was the least known to archaeologists, the report of the Beechey brothers (1821) representing the latest available information.[10] In Cyrenaica proper, much important work had been done by the Italian government on the sites of the great Graeco-Roman cities, but the interior, which had been in a state of rebellion up to 1930, had not been investigated.

The Syrtic coast road from Misurata to Benghazi, built by Marshal Balbo in 1935, is over 800 km. long and traverses an area which is in places notoriously barren. It is however an exaggeration to say that Tripolitania is separated from Cyrenaica "by a 500-mile strip of desert",[11] for the region around the little town of Sirte is well watered and fertile, and in years of drought the herds of Tripolitania are transported to these lush pastures. One can, in fact, divide the shores of the Syrtic Gulf into four regions of differing character, as follows: (a) Misurata–Buerat (Kilo. 211–377)[12]—barren plains on the edge of the Sebcha Tauorga; (b) Buerat–Nofilia (Kilo. 377–601)—good pasture, decreasing after es Sultan (Kilo. 524); (c) Nofilia–Marsa Brega (Kilo. 601–795)—very barren plains with large salt-marshes at the foot of the gulf; (d) Marsa Brega–Benghazi (Kilo. 795–1033)—fair pasture. In area (a) water is extremely scarce; areas (b) and (d) offer numerous wells of good capacity and quality; area (c) offers a few wells of brackish water, and one good and abundant series of wells (which the ancients named the "springs of Ammon") at Maaten Bescer (Kilo. 773), east of Agheila.

We found, as might be expected, that the extent of ancient settlement in the Gulf varied according to the availability of water. In area (a) there were virtually no ancient remains, whereas in (b) we found a great concentration of Roman farmhouses in the coastal belt, for some 50 km. each side of Sirte. In (c) ancient settlement was limited normally to a few road-stations and coastal landing-places, and in (d) there were scattered farms in favoured areas. Two types of Roman farm are encountered in Libya, the "open" and the "fortified"; and in the area around Sirte we found numerous examples of each type. Accompanying the "open" farms were pagan funerary monuments which, like the farmhouses themselves, were built of strong concrete, no doubt because of the shortage of good building stone in that area.[13] Around Marsa Brega, in area (d), the farms were all fortified, and probably belong to the period of Justinian who took energetic steps to defend that part of the Gulf.

The ancient geographies show that there were a number of small village settlements scattered around the Gulf, and some of these expanded in the Roman period and became important. *Macomades* (which Greek mariners had called *Euphranta*) was the centre of the agricultural region of area (b), and its site is represented by modern Sirte (Kilo. 474), where there is an interesting Christian catacomb. Farther to the east there was a village called *Iscina*, with a Jewish community, which must have stood near modern es-Sultan; but the remains of an ancient city at Medina Sultan, usually identified as *Iscina*, we found to be early Islamic in date, and to be identifiable with the city of *Sort* mentioned by several early Arab geographers.[14]

A large fortress on the promontory of Ras Ben Gawad (Kilo. 620) is very probably the *Zacasama praesidium* of the Peutinger Map, and some 3 miles inland, in the Wadi Hariga, there are extensive remains of what was probably the small town of *Digdiga*, which ranked as a municipium. From Ras Ben Gawad eastwards to the area of Agedabia, there is no difficulty in identifying the successive road-stations or coastal localities recorded in antiquity; the very scarcity of ancient sites makes the task the easier. First one encounters the small settlement of *Tugulus* (Gasr Haddadia) beside the modern road at Kilo. 670 and next, some 40 km. further on, the site of the famous *Arae Philaenorum*.

The story[15] of the Philaeni brothers, worthy representatives of Carthage, who elected to be buried alive to secure a favourable boundary for their country, is well known. The modern traveller, however much he may admire the noble spirit of the Philaeni, must remain a little astounded that so desolate a tract of country should have inspired such devotion. The "Altars" which the grateful Carthaginians erected to their heroes had disappeared even in Strabo's day,[16] but the name of the place remained as a memorial to the Philaeni throughout the Roman period. *Arae Philaenorum* was in fact the official boundary between Tripolitania and Cyrenaica.

During our 1951 expedition we had the good fortune to be able to establish, beyond reasonable doubt, the site of this provincial boundary. At Kilo. 709, near Bir Umm el-Garanigh, we found a small Roman fort, and 4 miles inland of it, close to the foot of the Gebel el-Ala, we encountered the bases, drums and capitals of four 25-foot high Corinthian columns, each of which had originally been surmounted by a statue. The name of the emperor Diocletian on one of the

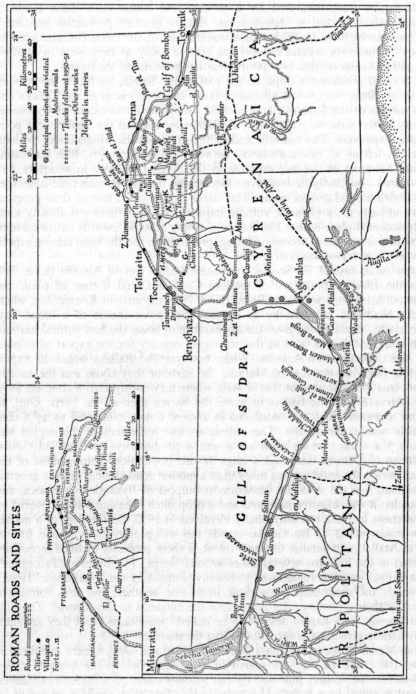

Fig. 44 Modern routes and ancient sites in Libya

drums hinted that here, as in the Roman camp at Luxor, the four emperors of the Tetrarchy were honoured by a column and statue each. Such honorific columns, when erected in desert areas, usually marked provincial frontiers,[17] and there can be little doubt that such was the case at Bir Umm el-Garanigh. The "Altars" themselves remain however as elusive today as they were in Strabo's time, and one suspects that two natural features gave rise to the legend.

On a small promontory opposite the reef of Bu Sceefa, we found the remains of a small village which was almost certainly the *Automalax* of the Greeks and the *Anabucis* of the Romans, and marked the westernmost extent of Cyrenaean territory in the same way that *Arae Philaenorum* marked the easternmost point of Punic expansion. The seaward end of the great Sebcha Mugtaa was, perhaps prudently, left as a "no-man's-land" between the rival powers. It is interesting to note that most of the major places in the Syrtic Gulf had, in antiquity, two place-names—one indigenous and one Greek, and that the Roman road-itineraries usually give the indigenous name. The Greek sailors often named their promontories and harbours arbitrarily, without inquiring whether there was already some locally accepted place-name. The Romans, whose attitude towards native customs and traditions was more accommodating, preferred to use the local names, especially where land travel was concerned.

A few miles east of Bu Sceefa, the ruined Italian fort of Agheila (Kilo. 750) marks the effective boundary of modern Cyrenaica, and a tract of plain and salt-marsh brings one to Marsa Brega (Kilo. 795), the ancient *Kozynthion*, where a rocky headland, crowned by an ancient fort, gives shelter to a broad bay. Superficially, Marsa Brega gives the appearance of being the best natural harbour in the Gulf, and it was used in the nineteenth century for the export of sulphur from the deposits near Agheila. When however the Italians began to export carnellite from the marshes of Marada, the harbour they chose was the ancient one of *Arae Philaenorum*, at Ras el-Aali, where they constructed a concrete jetty.

At Marsa Brega one begins to leave the barren area of the Syrtic Gulf, to re-enter a region which was inhabited in ancient times; it has still today a considerable nomad population. The largest ancient settlement in this region was *Boreum*,[18] a village which grew up round a promontory castle at Bu Grada, 8 miles east of Brega, and had a large Jewish population. During most of the Roman period, Boreum was no more than a modest road-station, but the generals of Justinian selected it as the westernmost outpost of Byzantine Cyrenaica, and surrounded it with massive ramparts and a deep ditch. The site was discovered by the Beecheys in 1820, but only finally identified in 1950. On the edge of a marsh, a few miles inland of Bu Grada, stands the well-preserved Byzantine fort of Gasr el-Atallat; and smaller outposts (most of them probably fortified farms) are scattered in the hills for several miles around Brega. The historian Procopius[19] has explained why this region was so heavily fortified by the Byzantines. "Here," he wrote, "the mountains press close upon one another, and thus forming a barrier by their crowding effectively close the entrance to the enemy." The hills of the Boreum area hardly deserve to be called "mountains", but they are sufficiently high to give good observation across the marshes.

From Marsa Brega to Benghazi there are two routes. One, a mere camel-track, follows the coast, passing the marsh of Ain Agan, which the ancients called *Krokodeilos*. The other, followed by the modern road, goes through Agedabia. The latter place, now a flourishing and expanding town, was in antiquity an important watering-point on the caravan route to the oasis of Augila, and was garrisoned by the Romans in the first century A.D.[20] Its ancient name seems to have been *Corniclanum*. It was still prosperous in the eleventh century, when El Bekri described it as having a mosque built by the Fatimid Caliph al-Qā'im (934–45), baths and bazaars. By the nineteenth century however, it was completely abandoned, and was only re-occupied after its establishment in 1921 as the capital of a Senussi emirate. All that has survived of ancient Agedabia is a small vaulted building which has often been described as a Christian church, but is in fact a fragment of a large fortress-palace, presumably Fatimid, which was still well preserved in the nineteenth century.[21]

Between Agedabia and Benghazi there are a number of fortified structures, including an interesting series of "Romano-Libyan" forts scattered around Ghemines[22] (the ancient *Chaminos*), and an orthodox Roman fort with angle towers at Zavia et-Tailimun. The general character of ancient settlement in these plains gives the impression of a native society, barely touched by Greek or Roman culture, settled here in the Roman period to serve as a cushion against the attacks of savage Syrtic tribes; but excavation is required before the Ghemines forts can be reliably dated. Whilst Agedabia marked the spearhead of the Roman *limes* in the Syrtica, its rear defences seem to have been on the line Tailimun–Sceleidima–Msus. The fort at Sceleidima is buried beneath an Italian successor, but we found the outpost at Zaviet Msus well preserved, its walls covered with the names of Graeco-Roman soldiers.[23] Although it is only 60 miles from the coast, it was the furthest outpost of Roman Cyrenaica, and members of its garrison evidently felt moved to leave a record of their stay in this bleak place. A trooper of the 16/5 Lancers, out on a desert patrol, had pencilled his name on the ancient walls only two hours before our own arrival, and in so doing had followed unwittingly a 2,000-year-old tradition.

The Pentapolis proper, extending from Benghazi (Berenice) to Derna, took its name from the five principal ancient settlements within its confines: *Berenice*, *Tauchira* (Tocra), *Ptolemais* (Tolemaide), *Cyrene* and *Apollonia* (Marsa Suza). The sites of these cities and of ancient *Barka*, the predecessor of Ptolemais, had long been known, and excavations had been carried out by Italian archaeologists on some of them. What remained uncertain was the extent of Graeco-Roman penetration into the desert and the ancient topography of the habited areas, including the road-system, the *limes* and the distribution of villages and farms. One of our first tasks was therefore to ascertain whether there had been, as in Tripolitania, a flourishing series of frontier settlements deep in the interior. Cartography indicated that the southernmost line along which ancient buildings had been found was the track El Abiar–Charruba–Mechili, but a reconnaissance (in 1950) along this route showed an absence of Graeco-Roman remains, and indicated that we were well outside the area of effective ancient occupation. We did however encounter a series of mud-brick forts which we are inclined to attribute to the early Islamic period rather than to the Romans. One of these forts, at Gasr Tecasis, occupied the site of a native Libyan farm of the Roman period, and had been adapted as a turret in an Italian redoubt.[24] Close to Gasr Tecasis we found a puzzling archaeological feature, a wall of rough stones, only 70 cm. broad, which crossed the Wadi Sammalus and then ran across open desert for some 3 miles. One can only guess that it may, like a similar wall in Transjordan, have served as an ancient tribal boundary.[25] Another mystery was a well-preserved village site, of native character, at Medinet Bu Hindi on the track from Mechili to Derna; neither pottery nor architecture have yet provided any basis for dating its impressive ruins which are certainly of considerable antiquity.

During our 1951 season we kept closer to the forest area of Cyrenaica, and followed another west–east route, the *Tariq Aziza*, which links the southernmost springs and wells of the plateau on the line El Abiar–Maraua–Buerat (Gherrari)–Chaulan. Here we found numerous stone forts, of which the majority are roughly built and probably early Islamic, but some (Gasr Remteiat, Gasr Maragh, etc.) undoubtedly classical. There can in fact be little doubt that the *Tariq Aziza*, marking the division between forest and steppe and between springs and cisterns, also represents the approximate southern limit of Graeco-Roman occupation.[26]

In our quest for traces of the ancient routes of Cyrenaica we were as successful as we could reasonably expect to be in the limited time at our disposal. The task was not an easy one, as the old roads were not normally paved and Roman milestones are very rarely found. The routes are however marked by deeply worn wheel-ruts wherever the line of a road or track crosses a rocky outcrop, each pair of ruts being invariably one and a half metres apart, centre to centre. In many places shallow cuttings have been made, and some of the wheel-ruts give the impression of having been deliberately cut to assist traffic. Their standard gauge certainly suggests that they were not entirely accidental. From the combined evidence of these wheel-ruts, and of the Roman road-itineraries, we have been able to plot the general outline of the ancient routes in the Pentapolis. From Berenice to Ptolemais there was a single route, not far from the shore; but at Ptolemais the road forked, and there was a choice of two routes to Cyrene—a lower one crossing the wadis Meghiunes, Giargiarummah and Kuf, near their seaward extremities, and an upper one following the watershed at their heads.[27]

Apart from the two routes from Ptolemais, three other Roman roads converged at Cyrene, all from the east. One was the road from Cyrene's port, Apollonia, and another the road from Derna (*Darnis*) crossing the fertile Cyrenaican plateau. The third road, recorded on the Peutinger Map, ran in an almost direct line from the Gulf of Bomba to Cyrene, and was the shortest route from the latter city to the Egyptian frontier. *Agabis* (Ghegab) was one of its road-stations, and *Mandis* (Gasr Carmusa) another. The latter site, on the plateau of Dahar el-Ardam, 20 km. south of Derna, is marked by some massive Greek tombs, and a small pseudo-peripteral temple. The main road-station in the Gulf of Bomba was *Paliurus*, which must have been situated near the mouth of the wadi Tmimi. We were not however able to visit and identify it.

The plateau, both to east and west of Cyrene, is full of ancient sites, some of them extensive villages, others fortified farms and towers. There are several Christian churches, as at Lamluda (ancient *Limnias*) and Mtaugat, near Tert, where ditches and thick revetment walls show these buildings to have been strongly fortified. It is evident that in the days of Bishop Synesius, when the Pentapolis was ravaged by savage Libyan tribes, the church of each small village, by virtue of being its most substantial building, became its citadel. Life in the Pentapolis must have been difficult and dangerous then, for the invaders, anticipating the tactics of Omar Muktar in 1925–30, infiltrated into the deep ravines of the wadi Kuf and cut the province in two.[28]

In one of his letters Synesius describes a journey which he made from his

see of Ptolemais to the area of Derna, in order to settle an ecclesiastical dispute.
The Bishops of Derna and Erythrum were, it seems, contesting the ownership
of an old fort at a place called *Hydrax*, and Synesius was obliged to intervene, as
Metropolitan of the province. It is evident that Hydrax lay inland somewhere
mid-way between Erythrum and Darnis, and the most likely site seemed to be
Ain Mara, the abundant springs of which place would explain its ancient name.
On visiting Ain Mara we found on a hill above the springs a massive Roman
fort, its walls twisted and overturned by an earthquake exactly as described by
Synesius in his letter.[29]

On the coast of Cyrenaica there were a number of small villages and harbours,
the approximate sites of which can be determined from the distance figures
given in the *Stadiasmus Maris Magni*, and in most instances there are archaeological remains to support the identification. The site of *Erythrum* lies at the
mouth of the wadi el-Atrun where "springs of pure, sweet water gush forth on
the very shore", as described by Synesius. There we found the remains of a small
church, with marble columns and capitals. *Phycus*, the small port which Synesius
used for the despatch of letters to his numerous overseas friends, is represented
by extensive ruins at Zaviet Hammama north of El-Hania. The promontory of
Phycus, which the ancients considered to be the northernmost in Cyrenaica, was
not the modern Ras Aamer, but the small headland which shelters the bay of
Zaviet Hammama.[30]

One or two major sites are still rather elusive. *Hadrianopolis*, a settlement
founded by the emperor Hadrian in his attempt to repopulate Cyrenaica after
the heavy casualties of the Jewish revolt, is usually supposed to have been at
Driana, a small village between Benghazi and Tocra. Despite the suggestive
place-name, we could find no convincing remains of an ancient settlement at
Driana, and have been forced to the conclusion that the real site was at
Tansoluch, 5 miles nearer Tocra, where there are at least the remains of an
extensive village.[30a] It seems in fact that attempts to establish new urban units in
the Pentapolis during the Roman period failed to meet with success; even the
original five cities never expanded beyond their Ptolemaic city walls. On the
other hand, rural settlement became much more intensive during the later Roman
period, and it is certainly mistaken to interpret the history of Roman Cyrenaica
as one long period of decline.[31]

Our general conclusions may be summarised as follows:

1. The lines of communication in ancient Cyrenaica ran from east to west, rather
   than from south to north. Professor Cary is correct in saying that "Cyrenaica
   in ancient times was never the terminal region of a caravan route".[32]
2. The scarcity of water south of the forest belt on the Gebel el Akhdar discouraged the Romans from establishing settlements deep in the interior.
3. The greatest menace to the peace of Cyrenaica during the Roman period
   came from the Syrtic region, and the approaches from that region were
   guarded both by forts and by settlements of *limitanei*.
4. Invaders who had breached the outer defences could take advantage of the
   deep wooded ravines of the wadi Kuf area to penetrate into the most fertile
   and populous regions. The massive late Roman forts (Gasr Beni Gdem, Gasr
   Sciahden, etc.) in the Kuf area represent an "inner *limes*" designed to prevent
   the province being cut into two.

Despite the gloomy predictions of Synesius, whose initial attitude of courageous resistance later turned to despair,[33] Libya did in fact survive the attacks of her African invaders. The Austurians overran the country in 410 and 450, the Mazices in 510; yet the cities remained occupied, and Byzantine administration continued. It was only in A.D. 643 that the new Arab invaders, under the command of Amr ibn al Asi, put an end to Roman rule in Libya.

It need hardly be stressed that the two expeditions of the Map of Roman Libya Committee have been sufficient only to give a broad overall picture of the extent and character of Roman occupation in eastern Libya. It would require many years of work, and many workers in the field, to produce a detailed archaeological survey of the whole area; and, in the absence of inscriptions, excavation is required if we are to be able to date the numerous forts and farms scattered throughout the countryside. Meanwhile however the compilation and publication of a provisional map of Roman Libya, based on previous discoveries and on our own rapid long-range reconnaissances, may serve as an aid to students, and as a stimulus to further research.

NOTES

1. *GJ* cxv (1950) 161–78; [p. 3 f. above].

2. Mr. M. Ballance (1950) and Mr. D. Smith (1950–1) were my principal assistants, and the under-named also took part in the work of visiting and recording sites: Messrs. M. de Lisle, J. Eames, R. McGregor, J. Spaul, P. Titchmarsh (1950); R. Bradfield, V. Hancock, D. Strong (1951). Mr. A. McK. Frood, Lecturer in Geography at Reading University, accompanied us during the 1950 season, as did also Mr. C. Musgrave.

3. For army assistance we were particularly indebted to Brigadier E. G. Andland, C.B., C.B.E., M.C.

4. Air co-operation was kindly arranged by Group Captain J. C. Larking, D.F.C.

5. We received the greatest help from Mr. Stewart Perowne and Mr. C. N. Johns of the Government of Cyrenaica; and from Mr. R. Goddard-Wilson of the British Residency at Benghazi.

6. From the administrative reforms of Diocletian (A.D. 297) until the Arab invasions, the area of Cyrenaica was split into two provinces, Upper and Lower Libya.

7. The "Descriptio orbis Romani" of George of Cyprus shows Tripolitania under the Diocese of Egypt, whereas previously it had formed part of the African Diocese, Cyrenaica alone coming under Egypt.

8. The best edition of the *Stadiasmus* is Müller's (*Geographi Graeci Minores*). His Atlas is a little out of date, but his identifications have, in the main, been confirmed by our own archaeological findings.

9. Ptolemy also places the towns of Neapolis and Chaerecla in the Pentapolis, near Ptolemais, whereas the historian Ammianus Marcellinus states specifically that they were in Lower Libya, i.e. east of Derna.

10. F. W. and H. W. Beechey. The archaeological information contained in Heinrich Barth's *Wanderungen* is repeated verbatim from the Beecheys' report. L. Cerrata gives useful information for the western half of the gulf.

11. M. Cary, 219.

12. The kilometre figures given here are the "official" Italian ones which appear on the kilometre stones, many of which have been mutilated or destroyed in recent years. Place-names, with one or two exceptions, are reproduced in the Italian forms which appear on all available maps of Libya.

13. The best-preserved specimen of these Syrtic mausolea is the obelisk of Eluet el-Garoosh (Kilo. 504) which Della Cella, in 1817, mistook for an ancient boundary mark between Cyrenaean and Carthaginian territory. (P. Della Cella, 79.)

14. El Bekri, 17 f.; Edrisi, 155 f. The line of the mud-brick town-wall of Sort can still be traced, and there is much glazed pottery of early Islamic date on the surface. [See now p. 137 f. above.]

15. Sallust, *Jug.* LXXIX.

16. Strabo, *Geog.*, III, 5, 6.

17. [For the site see now p. 156 below.] Cf. the column of Trajan at Kheurbet el Bilaas, on the frontier of Palmyrene territory (Schlumberger, 43–73).

18. [See below, p. 187 f.]

19. Procopius, *De aedif.* VI, 2 (translation by Dewing in the Loeb series).

20. Close to Agedabia lies the remarkable rock-cut fort of Gasr el-Heneia, described in *Antiquity*, xxv (1951) 133–41. [See below, p. 173 f.]

21. J. R. Pacho, 268 and Pl. xc. [See now David Whitehouse, *Third Annual Report of the Society for Libyan Studies* (1971–2) 12 f.]

22. [See below, p. 181 f.]

23. The inscriptions at Msus were first reported to us by Dr. W. Hagemann, who had observed them while serving as a staff officer under General Rommel. [Partially published in *JRS* xliii (1953) 76; a fuller account by J. M. Reynolds in a forthcoming number of *Libya Antiqua*.]

24. Mud-brick was used in the construction of some Roman forts in Egypt and in southern Algeria, but in Cyrenaica and the Syrtica the use of mud-brick seems to be characteristic of the early Islamic period. The evidence of date is however still slight.

25. Sir A. Kirkbride, "Shebib's Wall in Transjordan", *Antiquity*, 22 (1948) 151–4.

26. It is probable that the semi-arid region south of the *Tariq Aziza* was left to the native Libyan population, traces of whose simple hutments can be observed between El-Abiar and Charruba.

27. The modern route from Barka to Cyrene, crossing the wadi Kuf near Gasr Beni Gdem, does not follow any well-defined ancient track. Most of the wheeled traffic of the Greek and Roman periods must have reached Cyrene via Maraua and Slonta, as did Italian wheeled traffic before 1925.

28. The wadi Kuf region is admirably suited for guerrilla warfare, and General O. Mezzetti's remarks in his memoir *Guerra in Libia* 156–9, should be read by anyone interested in the military problems of the period of Synesius.

29. Synesius, *Epist.*, 67. We were unable to identify with confidence the village of *Palaebisca* which shared a bishop with *Hydrax*. It could have been at Bet Tamer or at Zaviet Marazigh, at both of which sites there are extensive remains. [See below, p. 251 f.]

30. The ruins at Zaviet Hammama, and elsewhere in the little-known region between Cyrene and Ras Aamer, were examined during our 1950 season by Messrs. D. Smith and P. Titchmarsh. See also Freya Stark, "The Coast below Cyrene," *Geographical Magazine*, December 1950, 342, [and below, p. 249 f.].

[30a. See now below p. 227, n. 15.]

31. The cultural decline of Cyrenaica was mainly due to the rise of Alexandria as the intellectual centre of the Levant; but the country did play a large part in the development of the Arian heresy. Arius himself is said to have been of Libyan origin, and he was supported by several Cyrenaican bishops.

32. M. Cary, 218. The caravan track from Augila to Benghazi, via Agedabia, was never as important commercially as the routes which linked the Fezzan with the ports of the Tripolis.

33. Synesius, *Essays and Hymns* (Ed. Fitzgerald), Vol. II, "Catastasis". Invaluable and attractive as they are, the writings of Synesius give only one side of the situation in the Pentapolis. His portraits of contemporary officials and generals are coloured by personal animosity.

12

ARAE PHILAENORUM AND AUTOMALAX

[From *PBSR* xx (1952)]
Plates 53–58

From antiquity down to the present century the shores of the Greater Syrtis (the modern Gulf of Sidra) have had the ill fame of constituting the most desolate and inhospitable part of the Mediterranean seaboard. Absence of landmarks, scarcity of water, and abundance of venomous serpents are all attested by the ancient writers, who spared no pains to paint as terrifying a picture as possible of this unhappy region. The child-devouring Lamia did well to select as her residence a cave in this very area, somewhere not far west of *Automalax*.[1]

Yet where horror is greatest there will heroism shine the most brightly, and we may recall that the Syrtic Gulf was the scene not only of the epic marches of Ophellas and of the younger Cato,[2] but also of the supreme sacrifice of the Philaeni brothers,[3] who gave their lives to secure for Carthage a favourable eastern frontier against the rival claims of Cyrene, and whose tombs later served to mark the political and cultural boundary between the eastern and western halves of the Roman Empire.

From the promontory of *Cephalae* (Cape Misurata) on the west to that of *Boreion* (Ras Taiunes) on the east, the Syrtis is 425 km. wide across the chord, and 740 km. long around the arc, but its shores are not so uniformly desolate as some recent commentators[4] have implied. On the contrary, a 100-km. strip, of which the modern town of Sirte (ancient *Macomades*) is the centre, enjoyed sufficient rainfall during the Roman period to permit intensive cultivation, and is still an important grazing area today. Bleak desert, in the strictest sense of the word, occurs only between Misurata and Buerat, and again, at the very bottom of the gulf, between Nofilia and Agedabia. It is with the second of these two desert areas that we are here concerned.

The nineteenth-century travellers, who were the first modern Europeans to follow the Syrtic land-route, have left a picture of this region not unlike that of the classical authors. Dr. Paolo Della Cella,[5] who accompanied the Pasha of Tripoli's army to Cyrene in 1817, wrote of extensive sand-dunes at the bottom of the gulf, and feared lest the Pasha's troops should suffer the same fate as the ancient Psylli and be overwhelmed by mobile dunes: it is clear, however, that his imagination was stronger than his sense of geographical accuracy. The Beechey brothers, who followed the same route four years later, left a very much more balanced description of the terrain, and pointed out some of the absurdities of Della Cella's narrative; but they agreed, at least, that the zone was bleak. "We had now arrived", they wrote, "at the most southern point of the Gulf of Syrtis, and few parts of the world will be found to present so truly desolate and wretched an appearance as its shores in this neighbourhood. Marsh, sand, and barren rocks alone meet the eye and not a single human being, or a trace of vegetation, are to be met with in any direction . . ."[6] As recently as 1930, a young Danish traveller, attempting to follow the coast by car, was saved from an unenviable fate only by the intervention of one of the scattered Italian garrisons.[7]

All this was changed in 1936 by the construction, at vast expense, of Marshal Balbo's "Litoranea Libica", a bitumenised road which enables traffic to flow swiftly and safely through the Syrtic area; and in the war years 1940–3 the number of human beings who traversed the region on military duty probably exceeded the total traffic of the previous millennium. The classical horrors of the Gulf could not survive this revolution, but land-mines and barbed wire took the place of the Lamia and the serpents. Even today, nine years after the end of the fighting in Libya, war-time explosives in the area of El-Agheila and Marsa Brega take a heavy toll of life and limb among the Bedouin and their herds.

Of the ancient settlements recorded by the classical geographers as having been situated in this part of the gulf, two stand out as of particular interest and importance: *Arae Philaenorum* and *Automalax*. Their sites have hitherto been a matter of speculation and conjecture; but it is now possible, as a result of the Map of Roman Libya expeditions of 1950–1, to produce more concrete evidence for their exact location.

ARAE PHILAENORUM

The "Altars of the Philaeni", traditionally erected by the people of Carthage in honour of their two young heroes, occupy a considerable place in classical literature. The evidence of the texts relating to them has been fully discussed by Windberg in the *Real-Encyclopädie*,[8] and need not be re-examined in detail here. Windberg's topographical conclusions are, however, confused and misleading, since he attempts to identify the anchorage of *Arae Philaenorum* with the harbour of *Aspis*[9] (which lay some 300 km. further to the west), and at the same time accepts as ancient the boundary-cairns of relatively recent date that the Beecheys saw near Mugtáa.[10]

The testimony of ancient geographers for the site of *Arae Philaenorum* is, however, remarkably clear and consistent; and no less than three sources (the *Stadiasmus Maris Magni*, the Antonine Itinerary, and the Peutinger Map) give measurements that seem free from serious corruption. The only major complication lies in the fact that *Automalax*, well-attested in the Greek sources, is replaced in the Roman itineraries by an *Anabucis*, which was either on the same site or within a few miles of it: this problem will be discussed later (pp. 163–6). But all sources agree that the "Altars" were situated some 35 km. (M.P. XXV = km. 37; 185 stades = km. 33) to the west of *Automalax-Anabucis*, which was itself at the very foot of the Gulf.[11]

Müller, whose edition of the *Stadiasmus*[12] offers the most recent scholarly study of the problem, assumed (no doubt rightly) that the important wells of Maaten Bescer represent the Ἀμμωνίου Πηγαί of the *Stadiasmus*; and by measuring westward on the best maps then available, he sited *Automalax* at the seaward end of the *sebach* (salt-marsh) of Mugtáa, and the ἀκρωτήριον of *Arae Philaenorum* at the small headland called today Ras Lanuf. He recognised, however, that the evidence of the road-itineraries suggested a site further to the east, and he therefore marked a second *Arae Philaenorum* close to the small promontory of Ras el-Aali.

It was the Ras Lanuf site that commended itself to the Italian builders of the imposing "Arch of the Philaeni", erected by order of Marshal Balbo in 1936 to commemorate the completion of the new coast road. The arch itself, which British soldiers nostalgically dubbed "Marble Arch", bears colossal bronze figures of the Philaeni brothers; and a small travertine "shrine" built near by is inscribed with Sallust's description of their sacrifice, and with a note stating that this was the "traditional" site of their burial place. There are, however, no ancient remains of any significance at "Marble Arch", and we may suspect that the choice of site was influenced by a desire that the Arch should be visible from a long distance.[13]

The accurate maps and charts that are available today show that Müller's uncertainty sprang largely from the defects of the cartography of his times. If we follow his own method, and measure westwards from Ἀμμωνίου Πηγα at Bescer, we find that the site of *Automalax* (180 stades) falls a little west of Agheila, close to the reef of Bu Sceefa, whilst the promontory of *Arae Philaenorum* (185 stades) coincides with that of Ras el-Aali. Thus the evidence of the *Stadiasmus* is, in fact, perfectly compatible with that of the road-itineraries, and Ras el-Aali must be preferred to Ras Lanuf.

We can, however, check this conclusion in a manner that was not possible to Müller—by measurement eastwards from the road-station *Tugulus* (Ant. Itin.) or *Tagulis* (Peut.). Until the present century there was no convincing evidence of the site of this place, and Müller wisely refrained from speculation. Ancient remains have, more recently, been reported as Gasr Haddadia, at Kilo. 670 of the modern road, and a visit to this site in 1950 showed it to be a small hill liberally scattered with Roman pottery and crowned by a small early Islamic fort.

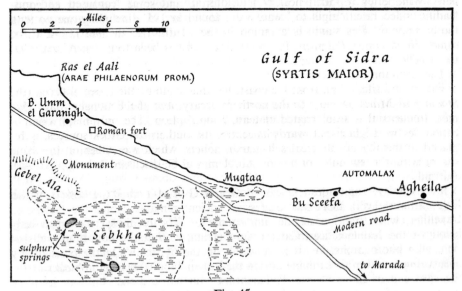

Fig. 45

An air photograph (pl. 53) taken by the R.A.F. in 1951 revealed what was not apparent on the ground—the outline of a Roman camp some 60 m. square, one of the largest in the Syrtic region.[14] Assuming, as we must, that Gasr Haddadia is the site of *Tugulus*, a distance of M.P. XXV eastward brings us to the neighbourhood of Ras el-Aali, and to the *Banadedari* of the Antonine Itinerary, which scholars have agreed in identifying with *Arae Philaenorum*.[15] The Peutinger Map, which gives the latter place-name in its more usual form, shows this distance as M.P. XXX, but a corruption of the final figure from V to X is probably to be inferred.

It may be said therefore that Ras el-Aali has far stronger claims than Ras Lanuf to be the approximate site of the famous "Altars", and study of the purely archaeological and topographical evidence reinforces these claims. First, it may be noted that the sheltered bay of Ras el-Aali was selected in 1940 by the Italians for the loading on to coastal vessels of minerals from the oasis of Marada, and has near it the slightly brackish well of Bir Umm el-Garanigh.[16] It therefore answers the description of the *Stadiasmus* as a "good summer anchorage with water". Second, although no ancient remains have yet been reported on the actual promontory (the suspected presence of land-mines discouraged a close investigation in 1951), there are two notable ancient sites in the immediate vicinity (fig. 45).

The first of these, 2·5 km. east of Bir Umm el-Garanigh, is a small Roman fort conspicuously placed on a low ridge, which runs parallel to the sea. It is, beyond doubt, the "Ruin" which the Beecheys marked on the map,[17] but to which they do not refer in their text. Measuring 35 by 32 m. externally, it has dry-built walls 2 m. wide, of untrimmed local stone. An entrance gateway in the centre of the landward (SW) side, gives access to the interior, in the centre of which there seems to have stood a building. The remains[18] are, however, too encumbered with sand and rubble to reveal any plan. On the slopes of the hill outside the gateway much pottery is scattered, and some fragments of good-quality undecorated "sigillata" ware were found in 1951, including one potter's stamp: **S.M.F.** This stamp is common in the Mediterranean area (J. H. Iliffe, *Quart. Dept. Antiq. Palestine*, ix (1942), 54), and has been found in Africa (*CIL* viii, 10479, 32); it is well represented at Pompeii (*CIL* x, 8055, 25a) and cannot be later than the first century A.D.

The second site, 6 km. from the coast, lies due south of Bir Umm el-Garanigh, and in a slight hollow close to the northern escarpment of the Gebel el-Ala. This *gebel* (mountain) is an elongated plateau, 7 km. in length, the outline of which is broken by two slight rises towards its centre. Its southern slopes fall away into the western extremity of the great salt-marsh, Sebcha Mugtaa or Chebira, in which are situated the sulphur springs of Ain Umm el-Gelud, Ain Rabaia, and Ain el-Braghi.

In this hollow, appropriately named Graret Gser et-Trab ("the hollow of the little earth-castles"), there are impressive ancient remains, which the Beecheys, travelling closer to the coast, did not encounter. The credit for their discovery belongs to an Italian officer, Capt. Luigi Cerrata, who published a brief description, with photographs, in his monograph on the Syrtica.[19] On the basis of his observations, and of those made during the Italian 1/400,000 geographical survey, the site is marked as "Arae Philaenorum" on some maps; but no accurate description of these ruins has hitherto been published.[20]

The remains at Graret Gser et-Trab (fig. 46) consist of four well-defined structures, and of a number of scattered wall-foundations and stones indicating a
small village community. Of the four main structures, two are probably Roman,
whilst the other two are evidently later and incorporate re-used architectural
elements of the Roman period (pl. 54).

The building A, of which only the north-west corner stands above ground-
level (pl. 57), is of rubble masonry solidly concreted with a mortar containing a
high charcoal content, and pointed with a finer white plaster. The walls are 0·75
m. wide, and the surviving corner has large quoins of white limestone, rather im-
perfectly squared. The south and east walls appear to have fallen outwards, and
some large blocks, now lying flat, indicate a doorway in the centre of the east
wall. A stone base stands against the inner face of the west wall. The building
seems originally to have consisted of a room, 6 by 8 m. internally, fronted on
the east by a masonry platform extending eastward for another 10 m. There are,
however, traces of other walls running southwards from the main structure, and
the building may have been more complex than appears at first sight; yet the
superficial resemblance to a small rural shrine is striking.[21]

Building B, parallel to and north of A, is a simple rectangle of mortared
rubble masonry, plastered externally and measuring 2·60 by 5·20 m. It could have
been a subsidiary shrine or altar.

Buildings C and D, further to the north, contain the architectural elements
that make the site noteworthy. C is a dry-built strip building, of rubble masonry,
entered by two doorways from an outer enclosure composed entirely of re-used
column drums, bases, and capitals. This enclosure is entered by a doorway on

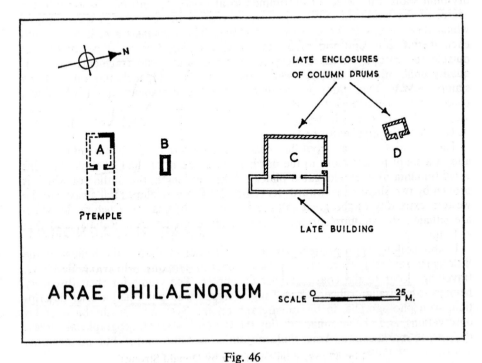

Fig. 46

the north, which, like the other two doorways, has large monolithic jambs. D is a much smaller enclosure formed of column drums only, and with a doorway on the east.

The architectural elements incorporated in C and D are as follows:

Four Corinthian capitals; each 70–90 cm. in bottom diameter and about 1·00 m. high.

Four base drums, including base mouldings and part of shaft. Diam. 1·10–1·20 m.; ht. 0·56–0·66 m.

Three top drums, with remains of astragal. Diam. 0·72–0·92 m.; ht. 0·38–0·44 m.

Forty-two plain intermediate drums. Diam. 0·75–1·10 m.; ht. 0·46–0·60 m.

It is evident that no more than *four* columns are represented by these elements, and that one top drum and an indeterminate number of intermediate drums are missing. One of the latter, damaged and abandoned by the constructors of the late enclosures, lies in the sand some 50 m. to the west of the site; but there seems no reason to suspect that many others are buried or destroyed. If we assume an equal number of intermediate drums for each column, their total would be forty-four, or perhaps forty-eight. Taking the former figure, we may easily arrive at the minimum original height of the columns to which the drums belonged. It must have been in the neighbourhood of 6·85 m., or, including the capitals, 7·85 m. (fig. 47).

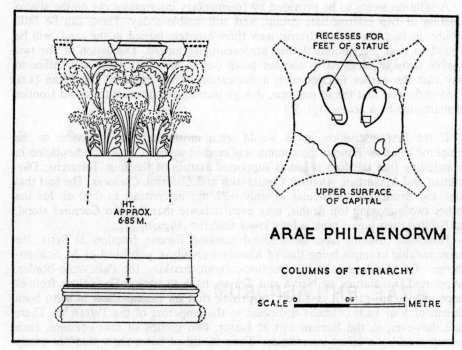

RECESSES FOR
FEET OF STATUE

UPPER SURFACE
OF CAPITAL

HT.
APPROX.
6·85 M.

ARAE PHILAENORVM

COLUMNS OF TETRARCHY

SCALE 0 ————— 0·5 ————— 1 METRE

Fig. 47 (based on a drawing by Donald Strong)

Where did these four lofty columns stand, before they were dismantled to form the late enclosures? No bases are visible, and the problem cannot be resolved without excavation; but the following points may be noted:

(a) The astragal and base moulding of the drums have been deliberately trimmed, showing that they were rolled a little distance to their present site. They are unlikely, therefore, to have come from a structure on the site of buildings C and D.

(b) Whilst they could well have come from A, their proportions are far too large for them to have formed a portico fronting that building, the walls of which could hardly have stood as high as 8 m. They could, conceivably, have stood as a free-standing tetrapylon monument on the platform fronting the east side of A.

(c) The complete absence of any elements of an architrave, a pediment, or of pilaster responds, makes it difficult to interpret the columns as embodied in a structure.

(d) Each of the capitals has, in its upper surface, a pair of oval recesses, splayed outwards, as though to receive the feet of a statue, and backed by a single recess as for a vertical support.

These circumstances seem to justify the conclusion that the columns were free-standing and supported statues (probably of bronze) which have since disappeared. Statues of whom? If of the Philaeni brothers, one would have expected two statues rather than four, since the unsuccessful and anonymous Cyrenaean rivals of the Philaeni are hardly likely to have been honoured.

A solution seems to be provided by fragmentary inscriptions cut on the stucco coating of two intermediate drums, and still visible today. There can be little doubt, in fact, that other drums, now three-quarters buried in the sand, will be found to bear inscriptions if they are eventually moved. Discussion of the two visible texts is relegated to another place (see Appendix), but it will suffice to say that the earlier inscription is a dedication to the emperor Diocletian (A.D. (284–305), and that the second one, though incomplete, appears to record frontier demarcation by a *praeses* (pl. 55).

If the first inscription is, as would seem most likely, a dedication to the emperor in whose honour the column was erected we need have little hesitation in concluding that the four columns supported statues of the four Tetrarchs; Diocletian and Maximian, *Augusti*; Constantius and Galerius, *Caesares*. The fact that one top drum has a diameter of only 0·72 m., in contrast to 0·90 m. for the other two surviving top drums, may even indicate that the two *Caesares* stood, as befitted their junior rank, a little lower than the *Augusti*.

Honorific columns have been found marking Roman frontiers in Syria, the most notable example being that of Kheubert el-Bilaas, published by M. Schlumberger. On this latter site the frontier column, marking the Palmyrene border, supported two statues, of Nerva and Trajan, back to back.[22] Since these frontier monuments are rare, it is hardly surprising that no example has hitherto been found of four such columns dedicated to the emperors of the Tetrarchy. There are, however, in the Roman fort at Luxor, two groups of four columns, each group marking a street intersection. Their inscribed bases show that one group was dedicated to Diocletian, Maximian, Constantius, and Galerius in A.D. 300, and the other to Maximian, Licinius, Constantine, and Maximinus in 308–9.[23] A similar group of four columns, but supporting statues of the Four Evangelists rather than of emperors, stood in the main colonnaded street of Ephesus.[24] Although the tetrastyle monument of Graret Gser et-Trab stood detached, and not at any street-intersection, there need be little hesitation in accepting it as erected under the Tetrarchy to mark the frontier between the Dioceses of Africa and Oriens, and between the newly established provinces of Tripolitania and Libya Pentapolis.

Whether the columns and their capitals actually belong to the period of Diocletian is more obscure. On the top of the capital illustrated (pl. 56; fig. 47), two earlier mortice holes can be seen underlying the larger recesses cut for the feet of the statue. These, and similar holes in the other capitals, suggest that the columns did originally support an architrave before they were adapted to receive the statues of the Tetrarchs. It is unlikely, however, that this earlier phase of their service took place at the foot of the Syrtic Gulf. More probably the columns and capitals were taken from some pre-existing building in the Pentapolis and shipped to Arae Philaenorum for their new function. Their stone is certainly not local, and closely resembles that found in the ancient cities of *Tauchira* (Tocra) and *Ptolemais*.

The date at which the four columns were dismantled and their elements used to form the enclosures C and D cannot be determined without excavation. The narrow building to which enclosure C is attached, thus providing an open forecourt, could equally be of Byzantine or of early Islamic date. Although this part of the Syrtica seems to have been even more sparsely populated in the medieval period than in Roman and Byzantine times, the small early Islamic fort at Gasr Haddadia shows that constructional activity was not entirely lacking after the Arab invasion. That the columns were pulled down in order to obtain the (presumably bronze) statues which they supported seems inherently probable: it is unlikely that the toil of demolition would have been undertaken merely to make use of the drums and capitals in a structure of such crude type. It may be mentioned, by way of analogy, that the modern bronze statues of the Philaeni, at "Marble Arch", have been mutilated by souvenir-hunters and metal-robbers, and will—if conditions of public security deteriorate in this desolate region—go the same way as those of the Tetrarchs.

The area of Ras el-Aali presents, therefore, three features that are consistent with its identification as *Arae Philaenorum*: (1) a promontory and safe anchorage, as recorded by the ancient sources; (2) a Roman fort, not later than the first century A.D., guarding the well of Bir Umm el-Garanigh, and perhaps serving as a police and customs post on the boundary; (3) a village, 6 km. inland, containing a probable temple, and an impressive frontier monument. As regards this third feature, it may be recalled that Ptolemy mentions specifically a "village of the Philaeni", whilst Scylax refers to a temple of Ammon at or near the "Altars".[25]

All that is lacking, from the archaeological viewpoint, is any trace of the "Altars" erected by the Carthaginians to their heroes; and this is hardly surprising when we recall Strabo's statement that the "Altars of the Philaeni no longer remain, yet the place has taken on the appellation", and Pliny's rather enigmatic remark that these Altars were "made of sand".[26] There is, indeed, plenty of sand at Ras el-Aali, but its main concentration is in the form of a narrow ridge of dunes immediately behind the sea-shore: in the plains between the sea and the Gebel el-Ala there are no dunes, and in such a wind-swept area no one in his right senses would pile up mounds of sand to mark the graves of heroes.

What Pliny probably meant to imply was that the "Altars" were natural features, and not man-made: sand would have suggested itself to him as the most likely element in the Syrtic region. We must therefore consider if some conspicuous geographical feature could have suggested "Altars" to the mariners and land travellers of antiquity. The small promontories of Ras Lanuf and Ras el-Aali are low and almost indistinguishable, and without the help of a "Mariner's Guide" like the *Stadiasmus*, they would be difficult to identify from either land or sea. But a more imposing landmark is not lacking. The frontier monument of Arae Philaenorum stood, as we have seen, close to the foot of the Gebel el-Ala, which the Beecheys aptly described as a "remarkable table land". In this region of marshes and coastal dunes the Gebel catches the eye of every land-traveller, and must appear equally prominent to the crews of coasting vessels, provided they are sufficiently far off-shore to see over the top of the intervening dunes. Is it too much to suggest that this conspicuous plateau, its silhouette broken by two natural rises, gave birth to the legend of the "Altars"? Or did the Philaeni really elect to be buried in the one place where nature had already provided a marker for the limits for Carthaginian expansion?[27]

AUTOMALAX

The problem of *Automalax* is closely linked with that of *Arae Philaenorum*. Whereas the latter site marked the limit of Carthaginian expansion into the Syrtica, the former became the effective western boundary of Ptolemaic Cyrenaica. At one period, it is true, the Cyrenaican boundary was pushed forward westward to *Turris Euphranta*[28] (the later *Macomades*, modern Sirte), but this seems to have been an ephemeral change, and it is *Automalax* that is named, together with *Catabathmus* (Sollum), in the famous *Diagramma*[29] of Ptolemy I, defining the frontiers and constitution of the Cyrenaican state. Other classical sources support *Automalax*, rather than *Turris Euphranta*, and it may be noted that the archaeology of the Syrtica links the area of Sirte with the Punic rather than the Greek sphere of influence.[30]

Logically, one would have expected *Arae Philaenorum* to have been accepted as the boundary of Cyrenaica, and during the Roman Empire this seems to have been the case; but previously the Cyrenaeans evidently found it convenient to place their frontier a little further east, leaving a "no-man's-land" between themselves and the Carthaginians. A glance at a modern map of the area (fig. 45) will explain why this arrangement was preferred. Only a few miles east of Ras el-Aali the desolate salt-marshes of the Sebcha Mugtaa run down to the seashore, impeding communications by land, and isolating the area of Ras el-Aali from that of El-Agheila. This marsh was probably more formidable in ancient times than it is today,[31] and security of communications would have demanded that the westernmost Cyrenaican outpost should lie east of it.

The ancient sources that refer to *Automalax* are listed by Pietschmann in the *Real-Encylopädie*;[23] and it need only be noted here that the more recently discovered *Diagramma* gives the place-name as Αὐτάμαλαξ, which closely approaches the form recorded by Ptolemy (iv, 4, 2) and adopted in this paper. Strabo described *Automala* as a fort, containing a garrison, and situated at the very foot of the Gulf; and Ptolemy also lists it as a fort. The *Stadiasmus*, usually so full of topographical detail, gives the place-name without a word of description. In the two Roman itineraries *Automalax* has no place, but an *Anabucis* occupies approximately the same site. Although Müller[33] marks the two sites as distinct, Mannert, followed by most recent writers,[34] has assumed that they are simply Greek and Libyan place-names for the same site. As we shall see, this is the most acceptable view.

Attempts to locate *Automalax–Anabucis* have hitherto been unsuccessful. The Beecheys thought that the fort and bay at Marsa Brega were the strongest claimants, although they had to admit that the Gulf had already begun to curve northwards at that point. According to their observations, "there is no (ancient) place of any kind at the bottom of the Gulf before Brega."[35] Müller, as we have already seen, placed *Automalax* at the point where the Great Sebcha joins the sea, and *Anabucis* a little further east, near the reef of Bu Sceefa; but he had no archaeological evidence to support this hypothesis. Most Italian commentators have sited *Automalax–Anabucis* at El-Agheila which site was unheard of prior to the construction of the Italian fort there in 1928: here again, archaeological proof is lacking.

Following the identification of *Arae Philaenorum* in 1951, inquiries were made at the *mudiriya* of El-Agheila in order to ascertain if any ancient remains were known to exist in the area. Information was received that there were remains of an ancient landing-place on the beach opposite the reef of Bu Sceefa, and a visit to the site rapidly confirmed the accuracy of this report. The site is on a small promontory backed by high sand-dunes, and separated from the modern coast-road by two parallel limestone ridges. As the promontory is shielded from these ridges by the intermediate dunes, it is easy to understand why the Beecheys failed to observe it.

The promontory of Bu Sceefa, which is little more than a step in the coast-line, lies 8 km. west of the fort of El-Agheila, and is the nearest part of the coast to the island or reef of Bu Sceefa, which is itself 2 km. off shore. The promontory is flat, but rocky at the water's edge: it is partly covered by sand interspersed with bushes. In this sand are visible numerous walls of rubble masonry, very similar to those that are to be seen in the walled village of *Boreum*,[36] at Bu Grada, east of Marsa Brega. The settlement at Bu Sceefa is also walled on the landward side, but by a narrow dry-built wall of limited defensive value unless originally backed by a stockade. A large fragment of fallen wall, externally plastered, at the south-west corner of the site, probably represents a tower guarding the angle. Gaps in both west and south sectors of the wall possibly represent entrances. The buildings within this perimeter wall seem to have consisted of small rectangular rooms, but a larger building, which can be described as a castle, and is surrounded by a shallow ditch, stands beside the sea at the northern end of the site. It is almost completely covered by a high dune obscuring its inner arrangements.

One of the small rectangular rooms at the south end of the site was cleared of sand in 1951, and found to have no paved floor: its walls were dry-built with a single course of diagonally pitched stones, as found also in the perimeter wall of the settlement. Much pottery is scattered over the site, including a

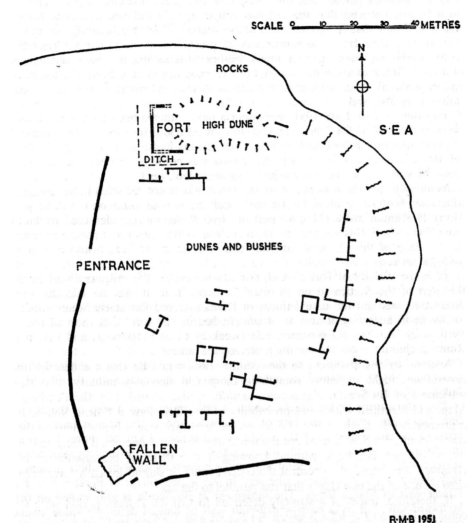

AUTOMALAX

SCALE 0   10   20   30   40 METRES

ROCKS

N

SEA

FORT   HIGH DUNE

DITCH

DUNES AND BUSHES

ᴘENTRANCE

FALLEN WALL

R·M·B 1951

Fig. 48 (based on a survey by R. M. Bradfield)

large quantity of native hand-turned ware, some wheel-turned "ribbed pottery" characteristic of the later Roman period, and one fragment of Byzantine green-glazed fabric. Pottery of undoubted Greek date was entirely absent on the surface.

The Bu Sceefa site is situated precisely at the bottom of the Gulf, and the fact that it stands on the only promontory on this part of the coast leads one to conclude that it must—despite the superficial absence of early pottery—represent the site of *Automalax*. The distances given by the *Stadiasmus*, from the promontory of *Arae Philaenorum* on the west, and from ᾿Αμμωνίου Πηγαί on the east, coincide exactly with the actual distances from Ras el-Aali and Maaten

Bescer[37] respectively. It cannot be claimed that the walled settlement is earlier than the Roman period, but the fort itself may well be more ancient; and it must be remembered that the ancient sources merely indicate that *Automalax* was a fort, not that it was a centre of population. The fort is small, not more than 16 m. square, but there is no reason to presume that the "garrison" referred to by Strabo was more than a small coastguard detachment. The maintenance of a large Greek garrison on this part of the coast would have been an expensive and unprofitable undertaking; communications must normally have been by sea rather than by land, and only the smallest vessels could use the anchorage. During our visit of July, 1951, we found a small sponge-fishing craft anchored close to the reef of Bu Sceefa, and greatly tossed about by waves. The selection of promontories for the Greek forts and settlements in the Syrtica is well attested (cf. the case of *Boreum*);[38] and if *Automalax* was not at Bu Sceefa, then at least there is nowhere else where one might reasonably look for it.

As already remarked (above, p. 164), *Automalax* is not recorded in the Roman itineraries, both of which show *Anabucis* (defined as *praesidium* on the Peutinger Map) 25 Roman miles (37 km.) east of *Arae Philaenorum*. Measured by land from Ras el-Aali, this distance brings one close to Bu Sceefa, but measured from the "Village of the Philaeni" at Graret Gser et-Trab, 37 km., brings one to a point rather nearer El-Agheila. Yet we do not know the exact route of the coastal track in the vicinity of Ras el-Aali, nor can we expect the mileage distances in this part of the Syrtica to be absolutely precise. Thus it may be said that the distance-figures and the actual traces of Roman occupation at Bu Sceefa would justify us in accepting it also as *Anabucis*, bearing in mind that most of these Syrtic sites had two place-names, one Greek and one indigenous, and that the Romans, characteristically, usually preferred the latter.[39]

A more serious objection to the identification would be that the description *praesidium* ought to imply something more conspicuously military than the settlement of Bu Sceefa. *Zacasama praesidium*, also recorded by the Peutinger Map, and identified with great probability at Ras Ben Gawad,[40] near Nofilia, is a promontory fort, with a broad ditch on the landward side, which dominates the coastal route. Bu Sceefa does not dominate anything, and one could easily pass it by, as did the Beecheys, without knowing it was there. If the *praesidium* of *Anabucis* was intended to control the coastal route, it should logically have been sited on one of the two ridges that run parallel to the sea.[41]

If, therefore, traces of a strongly defended fort of the Roman period were to come to light on the hills between Bu Sceefa and El-Agheila, or at El-Agheila itself, one would have no hesitation in accepting their site as *Anabucis*. But they have not come to light, and until they do, we are perhaps justified in assuming with Mannert and later writers, that *Automalax* and *Anabucis* are one and the same site, and in interpreting the Roman "*praesidium*" as a coast-watching post, similar to its Greek predecessor. The nearest real *praesidium* seems to have been the fort, already referred to, at Bir Umm el-Garanigh, 30 km. to the west. Is it possible that the copyist of the Peutinger Map placed the word "*praesidium*" after *Anabucis*, instead of after *Arae Philaenorum*, in error? The alternative explanation, that *Anabucis praesidium* was in fact at Bir Umm el-Garanigh, makes nonsense of the evidence of the Itineraries, evidence which in every other respect is consistent with the topography and archaeology of this region.

GENERAL CONCLUSIONS

It may be useful to recapitulate briefly the conclusions at which we have arrived in the course of this inquiry. They are as follows:

1. Ras el-Aali is the only acceptable site for the promontory and anchorage of *Arae Philaenorum*.
2. The "Village of the Philaeni" recorded by Ptolemy is presumably represented by the ruins at Graret Gser et-Trab, which include a possible temple of Ammon (cf. Scylax) and an imposing group of honorific columns, of the Tetrarchy, marking the Roman provincial frontier.
3. Although firm evidence of pre-Roman date is lacking, the ancient settlement at Bu Sceefa is the only acceptable site for *Automalax*.
4. *Anabucis* is most likely to have been on the same site as *Automalax*, and to be represented by the visible remains at Bu Sceefa; but in this case its description as a *praesidium* must be interpreted with reserve. Alternatively, it may have been a separate place and stood nearer El-Agheila; but archaeological evidence for a site in the latter area has still to be found.
5. A *praesidium* did in fact exist, during the first century A.D., at Bir Umm el-Garanigh, 30 km. west of Bu Sceefa.

Finally, a few remarks on ancient communications in the Gulf may not be out of place. First, as regards sea communications, it is interesting to note that the *Stadiasmus* gives shorter stages, and far more topographical detail, in the eastern sector of the Syrtis than in the western. The landmarks described between *Berenice* and *Arae Philaenorum* are nowhere more than 200 stades apart, and usually much less. Westward of *Arae Philaenorum* the stages are often of 350 stades, and sometimes even more. This difference is not attributable to the existence of a greater number of landmarks and coastal settlements in the eastern (Cyrenaican) sector: on the contrary, the Tripolitanian part of the Syrtis can boast such promontories as Ras Ben Gawad, infinitely more important to the mariner than some of the places named in the Cyrenaican section of the *Stadiasmus*. We can only conclude that the compiler of *Stadiasmus* had, at his disposal, more detailed records of the Cyrenaican coast: and this is not altogether surprising if the sources of the *Stadiasmus* are mainly of Cyrenaic origin of pre-Roman date. Carthage was singularly jealous of her Syrtic possessions, and would have sternly discountenanced Greek commerce west of *Arae Philaenorum*.

There may, however, be a supplementary reason for the surprisingly detailed description that the *Stadiasmus* gives of the coast from *Berenice* to the foot of the Gulf. Not only was the outpost of *Automalax* probably supplied by sea, but we may suspect that there was considerable coastal trade carried on by small boats and lighters, which hugged the coast, and needed detailed information of every reef and headland. Windberg has suggested that it was the export of sulphur from Mugtaa deposits that gave importance to the harbour of *Arae Philaenorum*. In antiquity, as today, sulphur was extensively used in the cultivation of vines, and Greek farmers in the Cyrenaican Gebel may well have received their supplies from the Syrtic area. The modern use of these deposits, for the same purpose, has been proposed recently.[42]

Of land communications, little need be said. There were no paved Roman roads along the shores of the Syrtis, but the caravan routes presented no particular difficulties except, perhaps, at the crossing of the Great Sebcha between *Arae Philaenorum* and *Automalax*. The wells and cisterns scattered along the Syrtic shores were sufficient to meet the needs of normal caravans, and the increased use of the camel[43] during the Roman period must have had its effect on the development of land traffic. Wheel-ruts of ancient date have been observed near El-Agheila, which would indicate that vehicular traffic was not unknown in these parts.[44] The relative accuracy of the mileage figures in the Antonine Itinerary shows that the Syrtic route was carefully surveyed by the Romans.[45]

In antiquity, as more recent times, the ease with which the land-route could be followed depended largely on the degree of local security. So long as the Nasamones, and other raiding tribes, remained uncontrolled, the journey along the Gulf must have been perilous; but after the crushing of the Nasamones by Suellius Flaccus under Domitian[46] and the establishment of outposts at Gasr Haddadia and at Bir Umm el-Garanigh, the Syrtis must have lost much of its ill repute. That the *pax romana* remained undisturbed in these parts up to the end of the third century A.D. is attested by the frontier monument at *Arae Philaenorum*. Only later, towards the end of the fourth century, did the route once again became arduous and perilous, as a result of the barbarian invasions.

APPENDIX

THE INSCRIPTIONS AT ARAE PHILAENORUM

During our brief visit to the ancient site of Graret Gser et-Trab, in July, 1951, we observed fragmentary Latin inscriptions carved on two of the column drums that form the late enclosures C and D (p. 159f. and fig. 46). Careful copies were made by Mr. David Smith and the writer, and are here reproduced (fig. 49). There is every reason to suspect that the removal of the sand that has blown up against the enclosure walls would reveal further inscriptions, and perhaps the missing part of no. 2; but such a task was beyond our resources at the time of the visit.

Both inscriptions are cut into the white stucco with which the standing columns were coated, thus concealing the joints between the individual drums. The dismemberment of the columns has damaged this stucco, and where it has fallen away from the stone the letters are normally missing. In the case of no. 1, however, some of the letters were cut sufficiently deeply to leave traces on the underlying stone.

Inscription no. 1 is evidently earlier than no. 2, since it was plastered over before the columns were dismantled, whereas no. 2 shows no signs of having been obliterated in this manner. It is reasonable to assume that no. 1 was plastered over at the time that no. 2 was cut, even though there are no grounds for presuming that both drums belong to the same column.

1. On a drum now forming part of the west side of enclosure C. Letters: 7–8 cm. high, widely spaced and tolerably regular.

[Domino] nostro
Diocletiano imp(eratore)

It is to be noted that there are no traces of letters below l. 2, even where the surface of the stone is intact. It is unlikely, therefore, that the name of the emperor was followed by that of the dedicator. If, as we have suggested (p. 161), each of

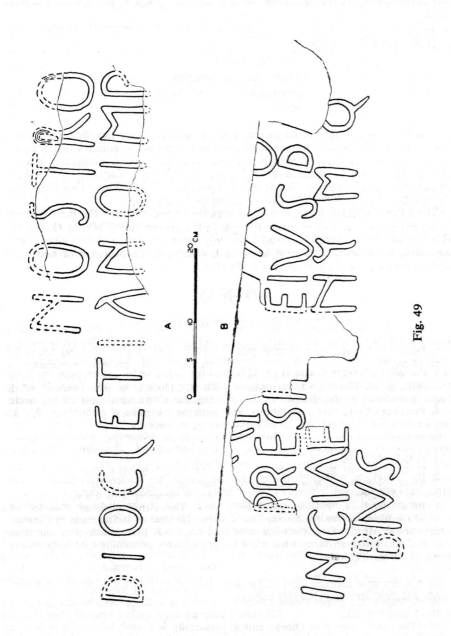

Fig. 49

the four columns supported a statue of one of the Tetrarchs, it may be supposed that the name of the emperor in question was carved on the column at the eye-level, the circumstances of the dedication being inscribed elsewhere, perhaps on a separate base.

2. On a drum now forming part of the north side of enclosure D. Letters: 6 cm. high, closely set and irregular (pl. 55).

/ / / /(illegible)/ / / /

/ / /pr(a)esid[e] eiusde[m]

[prov]inciae   NÝ M Q

BIVS

The remains of l. 1 are too fragmentary to be restored: they recorded, presumably, the name of the *praeses*. The use of *eiusdem* in l. 2 probably indicates that the name of the province occurred earlier in the text, whence we may conjecture that the inscription referred to the demarcation of the provincial boundary. The use of Latin, rather than Greek, suggests that it was the *provincia Tripolitana*, rather than *Libya Pentapolis*, which took the initiative of cutting the inscription.

The letters indicated by capitals cannot easily be restored; but the most probable interpretation is that a D occupied the gap in the plaster before NY M Q, and that this part of the text should be read [d(evoto)] nu(mini) m(aiestati)q(ue) eius. It must be noted, however, that the first letter of l. 4 has every appearance of being a B, which might suggest the personal name [Fla]bius.

NOTES

1. Diodorus XX, 41. There are in fact no known caves in the area in question.

2. Diodorus, *loc. cit.* for Ophellas; Plut. *Cato Minor*, 56.

3. Sallust, *Jug.*, LXXIX, where the featureless character of the terrain (*neque flumen neque mons erat*) is exaggerated.

4. Professor Cary, 219, dismisses the Syrtica with the statement that "a 500-mile strip of desert separates Cyrenaica from the coastal oasis of Tripolitania".

5. P. Della Cella, 90.

6. H. W. and F. W. Beechey, 210.

7. Knud Holmboe, *Desert Encounter* (London, 1936), 95–176.

8. *RE* xix, 2098, s.v. "Philaenorum Arae".

9. The evidence of the *Stadiasmus Maris Magni* shows clearly that *Aspis* lay near the modern Buerat el-Hsun, west of the town of Sirte, the ancient *Euphranta* or *Macomades*.

10. H. W. and F. W. Beechey, *loc. cit.*

11. Strabo *Geog.* II, 123; XVII, 836.

12. C. Müller, *Geographi Graeci Minores* i, 456–7; and Tab. XX.

13. [The arch has now been pulled down.] The official description of the Italian coast-road and its arch (*La strada litoranea della Libia*, Mondadori, 1937) states (134): "A pochi passi dell'Arco eretto sulla Litoranea, sono infatti gli avanzi di antichissimi ruderi, che hanno la forma di tomba, entro la quale una tradizione mai interrotta, dal periodo preromano ad oggi, vuole siano stati sepolti i fratelli Fileni." There is no other evidence of this remarkable "tradition", nor of any ancient tomb near the site of "Marble Arch". The only archaeological feature visible today is a rough field-boundary wall, of a type to be encountered throughout the Syrtic region.

14. I am indebted to Group Captain J. C. Larking, D.F.C., of Air Headquarters, Malta, for air photographs of this and other Syrtic sites. The identification of *Tugulus* with Gasr Haddadia was first made by Cerrata in his *Sirtis*, 220, in which the Roman and early Islamic remains are not differentiated.

15. Windberg, *RE* xix, 2098, where *Banadedari* is accepted as a Libyan form of the place-name, and not as a corruption from a Greek or Punic name.

16. The wells between Nofilia and Bescer are all more or less brackish, but they are none the less used by the local bedouin, whose palates are less sensitive than those of Europeans.

17. H. W. and F. W. Beechey, frontispiece.

18. The ancient sites of the Agheila and Bir Umm el-Garanigh areas were visited during the 1951 field campaign of the Map of Roman Libya Committee. Transport and other amenities were generously provided by the British military authorities at Headquarters Cyrenaica District. I am especially indebted to Lieut. A. Weston-Lewis, 16/5 Lancers, and to 2/Lieut G. Carpenter, R.E., who accompanied our party; and to my archaeological assistants, Messrs. R. M. Bradfield, V. Hancock, D. Strong and D. Smith. The last-named has kindly allowed me to reproduce his photographs (pls. 54, 55.)

19. Cerrata, 227–9. The importance of this discovery appears to have escaped the attention of the builders of "Marble Arch" who, as we have seen, selected a site near Ras Lanuf as the "traditional" burial-place of the Philaeni.

20. Cerrata's account is vague, especially as regards the character of building A, and the period of buildings C and D. Although the latter are patently post-Roman, he thought that they represented the two structures shown on the Peutinger Map.

21. Very few rural shrines have hitherto come to light in Libya. The small sanctuary of Jupiter Ammon, at Ras el-Haddagia in Tripolitania [above, p. 79 f.] may be cited as a parallel.

22. D. Schlumberger, 43.

23. P. Lacau, "Inscriptions latines du temple de Louxor", *Annales du Service des Antiquités de l'Egypte*, xxxiv (1934), 17–46. Cf. U. Monneret de Villard in *Archaeologia* xcv (1953), 85 f.

24. *Forschungen in Ephesos* (Vienna, 1906), I, 132–40. The Ephesus columns appear to have been erected in the Christian period, but it may be conjectured that in other instances columns of the pagan Tetrarchs may have been re-dedicated to the Evangelists after the triumph of Christianity.

25. Ptolemy IV, 3, 4; C. Müller, i, 85 (*Scylacis periplus*, 109). The text of Scylax is corrupt, and it is uncertain whether ἀλοῦς should be read as ἄλσος. It is clear, at least, that there was a sanctuary of "Syrtic Ammon" in the neighbourhood of Arae Philaenorum. Were it not for the remains at Graret Gser et-Trab one might prefer to site it at Maaten Bescer where there were the Ἀμμωνίου Πηγαί recorded in the *Stadiasmus*.

26. Strabo *Geog.* III, 171 XVII, 836 Pliny, *Hist. Nat.* V, 4 (*ex harena sunt hae*).

27. It is interesting to note that Dr. William Smith, in his *Dictionary of Greek*

and Roman Geography (London, 1854), anticipated the conclusions to which the new archaeological evidence leads. He stated (i, 186, s.v. "Arae Philaenorum") that the legend of the Philaeni "has all the character of a story invented to account for some striking object, such as *tumuli*", and that Gebel "Allah" (= Ala) seen by the Beecheys "has very likely as good claims . . . to be considered one of the so-called Altars, as any other hill or mound seen or imagined by the ancients."

28. Strabo *Geog.* XVII 836. The date at which this frontier was effective is uncertain. (F. Strenger, *Strabos Erdkunde von Libyen* (Berlin, 1913), 121–2.)

29. *SEG* ix (Leyden, 1938), 1.

30. In the Roman period the mausolea of the farmers who cultivated the fertile area around Macomades were of the obelisk form that prevails in inner Tripolitania but is completely absent in Cyrenaica.

31. The problem of post-classical desiccation in Libya is too complex to be discussed here; but there is reason to believe that the marshes of the Syrtic region were wetter in antiquity.

32. *RE* ii, 2604, s.v. "Automala".

33. C. Müller, Tab. XX.

34. Schmidt in *RE* i, 2016, s.v. "Anabucis".

35. H. W. and F. W. Beechey, 229.

36. [See below p. 187 f.].

37. Arae Philaenorum to Automalax: 185 stades = 32·8 km. Actual sea-distance from Ras el-Aali to Bu Sceefa = 34 km. Fontes Ammonis to Automalax: 180 stades = 31·9 km. Actual sea-distance from Bescer to Bu Sceefa = 31·5 km.

38. [See below p. 187 f.]

39. The Greek mariners whose information is embodied in such documents as the *Stadiasmus* seem to have been somewhat arbitrary in giving their own names to landmarks in preference to local names. The naval hydrographers of the nineteenth century were similarly inclined, and named Geziret el-Maracheb, in the Gulf of Bomba, "Seal Island".

40. The Peutinger Map gives the place-name as *Zagazaena*, but *Zacasama*, as listed in the Ravenna Cosmography (iii, 5) seems closer to the *Sacazama* of Ptolemy (IV, 3).

41. Air photographs of the area of El-Agheila have so far failed to reveal any indications of a Roman fort; but it must be admitted that blown sand could have obscured such traces.

42. Windberg in *RE, loc. cit.* I am in-

debted to Mr. K. R. Butlin for information relating to the sulphur deposits of the Syrtic Gulf. The sulphur is formed by microbiological action, which is now being studied in English laboratories.

43. Cato's army used donkeys in its epic march through the Syrtica (Plut., *Cato Minor*, 56), but by the third century A.D. the camel was widely used in Libya.

44. G. A. Freund, travelling from Benghazi to Tripoli in May, 1881, observed the wheel-ruts of an ancient road at a place called "Egelte Sania" situated between the wells of Bescer and the Sebcha Mugtaa (168). Although this report has not been subsequently confirmed and the exact site is uncertain, Freund was an acute observer, whose archaeological notes are generally reliable. In the Cyrenaican *gebel* ancient wheel-ruts are commonly encountered.

45. The Antonine Itinerary gives the distance from *Macomades* (Sirte) to *Boreum* (Bu Grada) as 221 Roman miles (= 327 km.). The actual distance, as measured on the latest maps, is 343 km. In such terrain, and on so ill-defined a route, the margin of error is astonishingly small.

46. Of this campaign we have only the record of Zonaras (xi, 19), and a brief allusion in the geographical poem of Dionysius Periegetes (209–10). That Suellius Flaccus marched through the Syrtic region is confirmed by a boundary-inscription found near Sirte (*IRT* 854).

13

"LIBYAN" FORTS IN SOUTH-WEST CYRENAICA

[From *Antiquity* xxv (1951)]
Plates 59–61

In his comprehensive study of the *Eastern Libyans*, published in 1914,[1] Oric Bates devoted several pages to the discussion of certain forts, seen in south-west Cyrenaica by nineteenth-century travellers, the architecture of which seemed to indicate a native Libyan origin, entirely free from Greek or Roman influence. After repeating the descriptions given by these travellers, and reconstructing plans and sections of two of the forts from the recorded measurements (always a perilous undertaking), Bates concluded that these structures, typified by Gasr el-Heneia near Agedabia, and by several examples near Ghemines, belonged to the ninth or eighth century B.C., "the great era of polygonal masonry".

That the ancient Libyans had no cities, but only fortified strongholds, situated at water-points, is attested by Diodorus, who adds that these strongholds were used as deposits for surplus crops.[2] It would be surprising, however, if a semi-nomadic race, as backward as Diodorus paints the ancient Libyans, had the inclination and competence to build such massive forts as those which Bates discusses. If such competence had in fact existed, we might be led to conclude that classical writers had not done justice to the early Libyans, and that Greek colonisation followed by Roman political absorption had stifled a native culture of considerable promise.

Bates himself urged that these Cyrenaican forts should be further investigated, but various factors, including the unsettled political situation in Cyrenaica,[3] prevented any such investigation from being carried out during the years of Italian occupation (1912–42). It seemed necessary, therefore, during the 1950 field campaign of the Map of Roman Libya committee,[4] to test this hypothesis of Bates by a re-examination of the actual structures on which it was based. If these structures appeared to be as early as was claimed, they would clearly have to be omitted from the Roman map; if, on the other hand, they were to prove to be of Roman date (as certain comparative evidence from Tripolitania suggested), they would have to be included. As the full programme of the expedition was an extensive one, ranging over the whole area of ancient settlement from Sirte to Derna (a distance of some 500 miles), it was clearly impracticable to attempt excavations on the sites in question. It was hoped, however, that a study of the surface remains might throw some light on the problem.

The first of these sites to be visited was Gasr el-Heneia, which stands on a slight rise in a desolate plain of typical Syrtic character, 5 miles south of Agedabia. Hamilton had visited this ruin in 1852, and had described it as "a strong fortress of very early architecture, and by far the most curious construc-

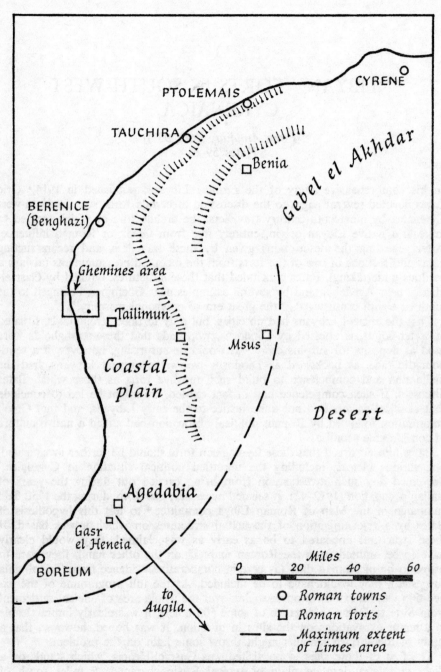

Fig. 50 Western Cyrenaica

tion I had met with in these countries ... I have no hesitation in ascribing it to a date coeval with the best monuments in Cyrene".[5] Rohlfs, visiting Heneia in 1868, decided that the fort "was neither a Greek nor a Roman construction, but of Libyan origin",[6] which conclusion, as we have already seen, was taken up by Bates and introduced into his book, together with supposedly confirmatory evidence from other sites at Ghemines. The only other first-hand record of Heneia appears to be that published in the report of the Bodrero topographical mission which explored large areas of Cyrenaica in February–March, 1919, after the first ephemeral Italo-Senussi pact.[7] This description is a summary and non-committal one, but is accompanied by some good photographs, one of which has been reproduced, without comment, by Fantoli in his collection of ancient geographical texts relating to Libya.[8] No plan of Heneia, other than Bates' hypothetical reconstruction, appears to have been published, nor are these earlier descriptions sufficient to give a clear idea of the character of the structure. A full description may therefore be useful.

Gasr el-Heneia appears from the distance as a low mound, from which protrude some fragmentary walls, not more than 2 m. high. Only when one approaches close to the site does its defensive character become evident, the mound proving to be an "island" 23 m. square surrounded by a vertical-sided rock-cut ditch, 4–4½ m. wide (fig. 51). This ditch must originally have been about 5 m. deep, as is shown by the level of the doorways which open into it, but it is now much silted up (fig. 52). The rock wall of its inner face is pierced by small triangular light-slits which served to illuminate the rock-cut basements which lie beneath the fort. These slits may also have served as loop-holes.

Hamilton describes how the fort "was approached by means of a wall, hardly fifteen inches broad, which is built across the moat on one side. This wall was, perhaps, once the support of a movable bridge." The wall in question, which still spans the northern ditch is in fact rock-cut and not of built-up masonry; and Hamilton's explanation of its function is entirely wrong. The actual entrance to the fort consisted of a wooden bridge,[9] supported on twin stone arches, spanning the southern ditch. The recesses for the horizontal beams, and for the lower voussoirs of the arch, are still clearly visible in both faces of the ditch (plate 59). One of the voussoir recesses on the outer face of the ditch cuts rather awkwardly into a rock-cut chamber and it is possible that the supporting arches were a later addition to a simple wooden bridge; but this possibility should not be unduly stressed.

The outer walls of the fort, 1·50 m. wide,[10] form a square of 16 m. externally; they are built of medium-sized stones, reasonably well coursed, but have largely fallen or been robbed, so that only the north-east and south-west corners are visible. Between the outer face of these walls and the inner edge of the ditch is a berm 3·50 m. wide with a low revetment wall on the edge of the ditch: it was probably the large, irregular, blocks of this revetment wall which gave Rohlfs the impression of an archaic form of architecture. Of the inner arrangements of the fort at ground-level nothing is now visible owing to fallen masonry, the most conspicuous feature being the rectangular staircase well, serving also as a light shaft, which penetrates into the basements. A rock-cut staircase descends from ground-level on the west side of this well, and there are indications of another narrow staircase descending from the east side. The cutting of these stairs

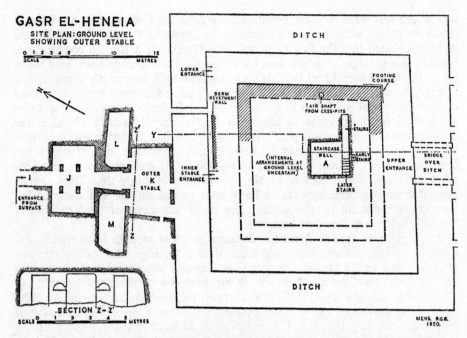

Fig. 51 (the "outer stable" and connected rooms are below ground-level)

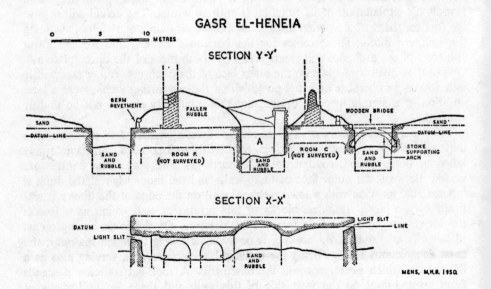

Fig. 52

put out of use an earlier staircase which had descended from the south side of the well (plate 60).

It is only when we descend the staircase into the basements that we begin to appreciate the complexity of the lay-out (fig. 53) of Gasr el-Heneia, and the justice of Hamilton's description of the fort as "the most curious construction" he had encountered during his long travels in Libya. Opening off the bottom of the well, by doorways which are now damaged and partly blocked by sand and

GASR EL-HENEIA
BASEMENT PLAN

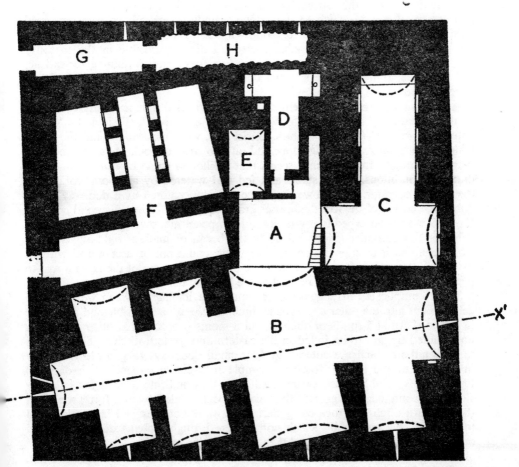

MENS. J.E.H.S.
1950

Fig. 53

fallen stone, are a number of remarkable chambers, all cut in the living rock, which occupy the whole basement area of the fort. Although the rock-walls of these chambers are cracked by earth-tremors, and have been pierced in places by treasure-hunters, the general arrangements of these basements are reasonably clear. The lay-out was doubtless intended to be rectangular but, as so often happened in ancient rock-cutting, the alignments were gradually lost, with the result that the long gallery (B) is considerably askew to the axis of the fort.[11]

This gallery is now heavily blocked with sand, but must have been impressive in its original condition. The division into vaulted bays, each lit by a light-slit opening into the ditch, was no doubt dictated by the necessity of supporting the weight of the rock ceiling. In all probability the gallery provided the barrack and messing accommodation for the horsemen whose mounts, as we shall see, were stabled close at hand. A smaller, T-shaped, room (C), the walls of which had semi-circular niches cut in them[12] may have served as office or officers' quarters. Most remarkable is the latrine (D)—perhaps the only ancient rock-cut example still preserved intact—which has two stone seats in opposite bays, each equipped with small semi-circular niches for lamps (fig. 54). At the foot of each seat were cess-pits covered with stone slabs; a vertical airshaft, visible in the masonry of the east wall, may have served to ventilate these pits. Adjoining the latrine, but with a separate entrance into the staircase-well, was a small chamber (E) of uncertain purpose.

Also forming part of the basements, but approached independently by means of doors leading from the ditch, were the "inner stables" (F) and the "lower entrance corridor" (G). The stables consist of a vestibule leading into the stalls, which have a flat rock ceiling supported on two rows of rock piers. Between the piers are troughs, from which it seems that six horses could be stabled, in rather cramped conditions, in the stalls, and fed and watered by a groom working in the central corridor.[13] The lower entrance corridor, entered by a doorway in the north-east corner of the fort ditch, rises gradually and leads into a second corridor (H) into which the expedition was not able to penetrate, owing to later blocking. Whether this second corridor led up to the berm, or made a right-angled bend which enabled it to enter inside the fort walls, could not be ascertained without extensive excavation. It is certain, however, that the purpose of the lay-out was to provide access between the main part of the fort and the ditch.

These complicated arrangements become more intelligible when we study the galleries cut into the outer edge of the ditch. These are still visible and accessible in the northern and southern ditches, and it seems probable that other chambers, now sanded up, are to be found in the eastern and western ditches. The galleries in the southern ditch are entered by four small doorways ranged symmetrically in relation to the bridge: they are simple rock-cut chambers which offer no features of special interest, except insofar as they indicate a need for living or storage accommodation greater than could be provided by the fort proper. In the northern ditch, the rock-cut galleries are more complex and interesting, and incorporate the passage by which horses were brought down from ground-level outside the fort into the ditch, and thence into the inner stables.

Some 16 m. from the outer edge of this ditch a depression in the ground (fig. 51, I) marks the sloping ramp which led down into a rectangular underground chamber (J) with its roof supported on four rock piers. From this chamber a passage leads into the outer stable (K) in the ceiling of which are stone bosses

GASR EL-HENEIA. ROCK-CUT LATRINE.

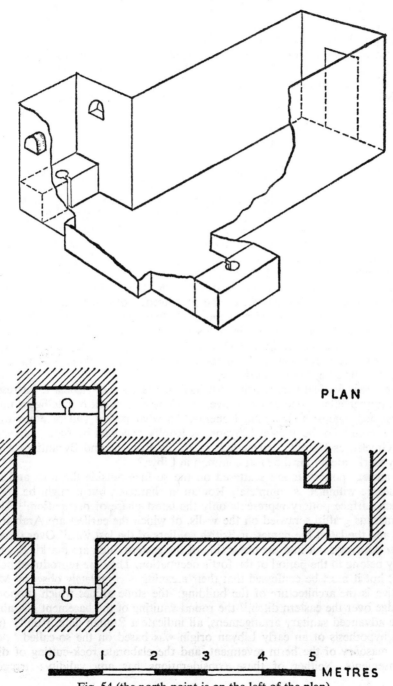

PLAN

Fig. 54 (the north point is on the left of the plan)

perforated to receive halters. The inner face of the doorway leading from J to K has curious semi-circular slots in each jamb, which suggests an elaborate system of barricading this door against attack from outside. On each side of the door are guardrooms (L and M) communicating with the outer stable. Two doorways lead from the stable into the ditch.

When we correlate these features in the outer side of the ditch with those of the fort basements, we begin to appreciate the ingenuity of the whole defensive system of Heneia. Despite its small size the fort could accommodate mounted detachments, and could, in time of emergency, resist siege. The dismounted members of the garrison entered the fort by the bridge across the southern ditch, but horses were brought in, at a lower level, from the north side and tethered either in the outer stable or in the ditch itself, in conditions of excellent security. In an emergency a limited number of horses could be stabled in the basement of the fort.

Since so much of the daily life of the fort was carried on in the deep flat-bottomed ditch, it was essential to provide access from the ditch to the interior of the fort. Direct access through the inner stable would have been perilous, since the outer stable offered attackers the best means of penetration into the ditch. By leaving a rock-barrier across the whole width of the ditch to the east of the outer stable entrance, and by cutting the lower entrance beyond this barrier, close to the north-east corner of the ditch, this danger was avoided. Attackers who had managed to fight their way, through the outer stable, into the ditch could possibly penetrate into the inner stable,[14] but they were still far from penetrating into the bowels of the fort itself. To achieve this they would have had to go round three sides of the ditch, exposed all the way to fire either from the parapets, or from the light-slits of the basement. The lower entrance could also be used by the defenders as a "sally-port" from which to clear the ditch of any attackers who had penetrated into it: the blocking wall protected their rear in the course of such sallies.

These defensive features, which must have made Gasr el-Heneia a fortress as nearly impregnable as one can conceive, are clearly the work of intelligent minds and designed against a determined enemy. To what period and race are we to attribute them? To the ancient Libyans, as Rohlfs, followed by Bates, supposed; to the Greeks, as Hamilton suggested; or to the Romans and Byzantines whose military works are by far the most common in Libya?

The ancient pottery found scattered on the surface outside the fort, and to a lesser degree within it, is completely Roman in character, but it might be argued that such surface pottery represents only the latest phase of occupation.[15] There are numerous graffiti scrawled on the walls, of which the earliest are Arab tribal marks, and the latest the names of British soldiers of the last war.[16] Over three of the four doorways cut into the outer side of the eastern ditch are markings which possibly belong to the period of the fort's occupation. They are reproduced below (fig. 55) but it must be confessed that their meaning is completely obscure. More suggestive is the architecture of the building: the stone arches which supported the bridge over the eastern ditch,[17] the round vaulting of the basement chambers, and the advanced sanitary arrangemens, all indicate a Roman date. Rohlfs' (and Bates') hypothesis of an early Libyan origin was based on the so-called "polygonal" masonry of the berm revetment, and the elaborate rock-cutting of ditch and basements. Neither of these considerations has any validity: irregular

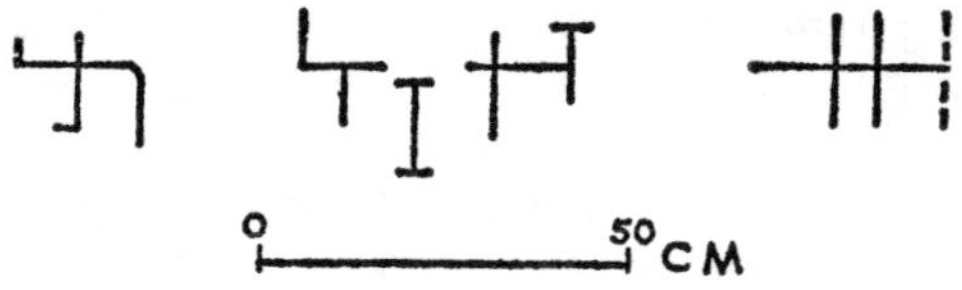

Fig. 55 Detail of graffiti

masonry is frequently found in Libya in revetment walls of the Roman period; rock-cutting was prevalent in Cyrenaica in both the Greek and the Roman periods.[18] Fortified buildings with vertical-sided rock-cut ditches are quite often encountered in the Cyrenaican Gebel, and there is no reason to doubt that most of them belong to the Roman period. At Ain Mara, between Cyrene and Derna, there is, for example, a fort of typical Roman masonry which is surrounded by a rock-cut ditch, with chambers in its outer face, exactly as found at Gasr el-Heneia.[19] The basements of Heneia are, however, apparently unique.

In considering the probable date of Heneia we must take into account its strategic role. The site itself has little local significance: it is in open desert and offers neither water nor agricultural facilities. Its importance lies in the fact that it controls the southern approaches to Agedabia, and sits astride one of the main caravan routes from the distant oases of Augila. In antiquity, as today, Agedabia was a key point on the caravan route from the coastal plains of Cyrenaica to the oases of Augila and Gialo. Inscriptions published by Ferri in 1926 show that Agedabia (which can be identified with the *Corniclanum* of the Peutinger Map) had a Roman garrison between A.D. 15 and 51: several of the soldiers who carved their names on the rocky outcrop near the modern village were of Syrian origin.[20] The fort which they garrisoned has not been positively identified, but probably lies beneath the ruins of an early Islamic fortress which has, in turn, been enclosed within the walls of an Italian "fortino".[21]

In these circumstances we need have little hesitation in interpreting Gasr el-Heneia as a frontier outpost, probably of the first century A.D., dependent on the Roman fort at Agedabia. How long it retained a garrison we cannot judge, but it may well have been brought back into use under Justinian, when the Syrtic *limes* was reorganised, and the city of *Boreum* (Bu Grada, near Marsa Brega) fortified.[22] Although its defensive arrangements are not of the pattern encountered in the northern *limites* of the Roman empire, Gasr el-Heneia is in size and function a typical desert outpost of Roman Libya. The elaborate rock-cutting of ditch and basements merely reflects the influence of the Cyrenaican rock-cutting tradition on the planning of such military works.

Having disposed of Gasr el-Heneia as a possible relic of native Libyan military architecture, let us now consider the group of fortified buildings in the area of Ghemines for which Bates also claimed a Libyan origin. Of these the only published description is that given by the Beechey brothers who travelled along the Syrtic coast in 1821, and subsequently surveyed the ancient cities of the Pentapolis.[23] Unfortunately the Beecheys never published the plans which they had drawn in the Syrtica, and which would undoubtedly have been most useful, so we can only quote their description.[24] After speaking, in general terms, of the fortified buildings which they had encountered all the way along the Syrtic coast, and which they rightly attributed to the Roman period, the Beecheys go on to say: "At Ghemines, which is a day's journey to the northward of Carcora, there are several interesting remains of ancient forts, some of which are altogether on a different plan from those [previously] described. They are built of large unequal-sized stones, put together without cement, and made to fit into one another in the manner which has been called Cyclopian. Their form is a square with the angles rounded off, and some of them are filled with earth, well-beaten down, to within six or eight feet of the top; the upper part of the wall being left as a parapet to the terrace which is formed by the earth heaped within it." They then describe one unusual example of these forts, which had projecting towers in the centre of each of its walls.

During the summer of 1950 the Libya expedition was able to work for two days in the Ghemines area, examining several of the best-preserved forts in the group to which the Beecheys refer. The fort with the projecting towers, of which Bates gives a reconstructed plan and section, was not in the group which was examined, and its site could not be identified on the ground; but it was later rediscovered, near Suani Tica, 20 km. south of Benghazi, in the course of an air reconnaissance. It is, in fact, much less "Libyan" in appearance than the Ghemines examples and need not be considered here.

The largest and best-preserved of the Ghemines forts is called Gasr el-Ataresh by the local population and lies 2 km. north-east of the centre of Ghemines village. During the Italian occupation it had been incorporated in a fort built by the Italian army, the massive walls of the ancient structure being repaired in order to support an observation tower. The Italian fort has since been entirely demolished for its stone, but the ancient structure has survived almost intact, thanks to its heavy and intractable materials. Gasr el-Ataresh measures 38 by 36 m. externally, and has corners so rounded as to give the impression that the plan is oval. Its outer walls, the only ones visible, consist of large irregular stones, roughly coursed, but with little or no attempt at facing or trimming. A barely perceptible depression, running outside these walls, marks the site of a shallow ditch, as found with the other Ghemines forts.

Although the inner arrangements of Gasr el-Ataresh are not visible, the outer wall contains, in the centre of its east face, the northern jamb and three voussoirs of the arched entrance doorway, which originally gave access to the interior. It is curious that the Beecheys failed to observe this feature, which completely destroys their strange hypothesis that these forts were intentionally filled with earth, and that their occupants were "drawn up" into the upper part of the building by ropes or similar tackle! The internal filling of stones and earth in these Ghemines buildings is due entirely to the collapse of upper storeys which, in some cases, may have been built of mud-brick. They must all have had, as at El-Ataresh, a single doorway at ground-level; but these doorways are either buried beneath fallen rubble, or—more often—the wall containing the doorway, being the weakest side of the building, has collapsed.

Examination of the exposed masonry of the outer wall of Gasr el-Ataresh and the other Ghemines Forts shows the inaccuracy of the term "Cyclopian" used to describe them. The large stones which form the outer facing (the inner facing, not visible, was probably of small materials) are not "made to fit into one another" as the Beecheys state. On the contrary there are numerous interstices which have been filled with small stones. The arched doorway of Gasr el-Ataresh is probably sufficient refutation of the "ancient Libyan" date attributed to these buildings; but it may be added that both at El-Ataresh, and at the nearby

fort of El-Chel, well-trimmed orthostats (probably door jambs) can be seen
built into the original "Cyclopian" masonry. Thus it must be presumed that the
builders of these forts drew not only on rough untrimmed boulders, but also on
the materials of pre-existing buildings, sufficiently sophisticated to have well-cut
door jambs.

Of the sites examined by the expedition in 1950, some (including a pair of
forts at El-Frascit, 5 km. south-east of Ghemines) have collapsed into almost
shapeless mounds, and are not informative without excavation. Plans of the three
best-preserved (El-Ataresh, El-Chel, and Bu Msceili) are reproduced here (fig.
56) for comparative purposes, although in no instance is any interior plan visible.
In most cases these buildings are surrounded by the ruins of crude hutments of
more or less contemporaneous date, which include orthostat door-jambs similar
to those built into the walls of El-Ataresh and El-Chel. At El-Chel this adjoining
settlement is extremely extensive, and at El-Frascit a massive rotary olive-crusher
points to the agricultural character of some of these settlements. The pottery

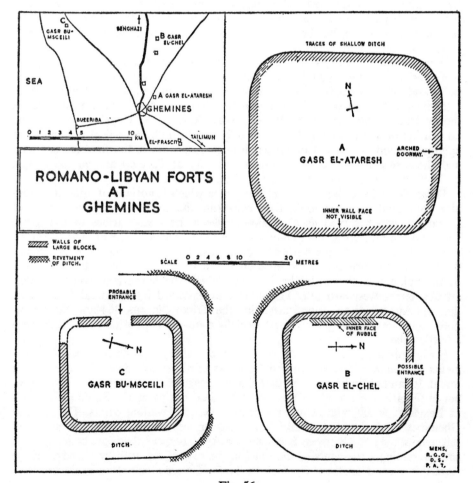

Fig. 56

scattered among these ruins is not very informative, as much of it has been dropped by the Bedouins, but there is nothing noticeably archaic, and there is a considerable proportion of recognisable Roman forms. At Bu Msceili, which lies near the sea, the main feature of note is the fact that the rough blocks of the outer walls bear the remains of a thick coating of uneven white plaster which seems, from its appearance, to be an original feature.

Although an ancient Libyan origin for these Ghemines forts is to be rejected, it must be admitted that there is a strong native influence apparent in their architecture. There are several orthodox Roman fortified buildings in this part of Cyrenaica, including a fort with angle-towers at Tailimun, some 10 km. south-east of Ghemines, and a small but well-built fortified farm at Gsur el-Galida, on the roadside 17 km. south of Benghazi. These Roman structures are, like Gasr el-Heneia, well-built of dressed and coursed masonry, very different from that encountered at Ghemines. The most probable interpretation of the Ghemines structures is that they are native buildings of the Roman period, influenced by the architecture of the fortified farms, but inferior in materials and structural technique. This inferiority is reflected in the rounded corners, which were built thus not from choice, but because a right-angled corner, dry-built of such crude materials, would soon collapse.

If we accept the suggestion that these forts belong to the Roman (or Byzantine) period, we have still to ascertain the actual century in which they were built; and, without excavation, it is difficult even to make a guess. The history of settlement in the coastal plains between Benghazi and Agedabia is most obscure, the evidence produced by the Italian excavations in the Gebel regions having no bearing on the problem. There are only two firm chronological pointers—the epigraphic evidence of a Roman garrison at Agedabia in the first century A.D., and the historical record of Justinian's activity at *Boreum* and in the Augila oasis. For the intervening five centuries history is silent.

These plains have, however, an importance which historians of ancient Cyrenaica have tended to overlook; they constitute the south-western *limes* zone of Cyrenaica, which served as a cushion between the savage tribes of the Syrtic zone and the Graeco-Roman civilisation of the Cyrenaican Gebel. The historical sources which refer to the barbarian invasions of Libya during the later Empire do not reveal the origin of the invaders;[25] but there can be little doubt that the Syrtic region was the spring-board from which the barbarians launched their attacks, either westward into Tripolitania or eastward into Cyrenaica. The fact that the Austuriani are found attacking the Tripolis in A.D. 364 and the Pentapolis some forty years later is best explained on the supposition that they were a Syrtic tribe.

In Tripolitania, as has been described elsewhere,[26] a deep zone of settlements of *limitanei* was established from the third century onwards, to meet the threat. It can hardly be doubted that similar measures were adopted in Cyrenaica, not in the arid zone south of the Gebel Akhdar, but along the Syrtic plain south of Benghazi which offered water resources to any invading bands. The forts at Ghemines, and the vast number of more or less similar structures scattered throughout the plain between Benghazi and Agedabia, can therefore be interpreted as representing settlements of *limitanei* in the rear of the military outposts of the Agedabia area. That these Cyrenaican *limitanei* were much more backward than their opposite numbers in Tripolitania is evident from the character of their forts, and of the settlements adjoining them. They were recruited, no doubt, from the more docile Libyan tribes of Cyrenaica, from those who in Italian colonial terminology would have been called the "sottomessi"—the submitted.[27]

The purpose of these settlements was to block the main route from the bottom of the Syrtic gulf to the coastal cities of the Pentapolis. The policy of playing off one barbarian tribe against another, of using "foederati" to defend areas which had no adequate military garrison was, of course, a common feature of later Roman history. In some cases the policy succeeded, but there was also a danger that the "foederati" might throw in their lot with the invaders, or, at the best, adopt a neutral attitude. That such actually happened in Cyrenaica can perhaps be inferred from a passage in a letter of Synesius, in which it appears that a "half-barbarous" tribe called the *Macetae* informed the barbarians of the defenceless condition of the province, whereupon the latter "came countless like the leaves and the flowers in spring".[28]

If the Ghemines forts, and the others of this type in the coastal plain, can be proved by excavation to belong to the latter part of the fourth century A.D., then there will be good grounds for interpreting them as constructed by the *Macetae* under Roman direction. If they belong to an even later period, they may result from the policy of Justinian who, as Procopius attests, took energetic steps to establish security in south-west Cyrenaica. Whatever their date may be, these forts seem to mark the impact of Roman policy on a primitive society whose only spontaneous architecture is represented by the crude huts which are to be found scattered in many parts of Cyrenaica.[29] The native strongholds to which Diodorus refers have still to be identified.

NOTES

1. Oric Bates, 160 f.

2. *Diodorus Siculus*, III, 49.

3. The area between Ghemines and Agedabia was not brought effectively under Italian control until 1923, whilst the bottom of the Syrtic gulf was only pacified in 1928.

4. The archaeological surveys of Gasr el-Heneia and the Ghemines forts were carried out by Messrs. M. Ballance, R. McGregor, D. Smith, J. Spaul, and P. Titchmarsh in July, 1950, under the direction of the writer. We are indebted to the Government of Cyrenaica for many facilities, including accommodation at Agedabia and Ghemines, and to the British military authorities.

5. J. Hamilton, 175–6.

6. G. Rohlfs, (1), II, 39.

7. *Itinerari della Cirenaica (Note ed appunti della missione Bodrero, Feb.–Mar. 1919)* (Rome, 1920), 76 and fig. 99–101.

8. A. Fantoli, *La Libia negli scritti degli antichi* (Rome, 1933), pl. opp. p. 140.

9. The ditches which surround the Roman towers and fortified farms of Libya are usually uninterrupted, and bridges must have existed in most cases. Gasr el-Heneia does, however, provide the first evidence of their existence.

10. The thickness of these walls probably indicates that the building had an upper storey, and was a high watch-tower.

11. The plan (fig. 53) was made by Mr. John Spaul in conditions of considerable difficulty, owing to lack of light, and to intrusive sand and rubble. The alignments of rooms C, D, and E could only be ascertained approximately.

12. Niches of this type are frequently found in the Roman fortified farms of the Tripolitanian desert area. They probably held lamps.

13. It is, perhaps, unlikely that this small and unlit stable was ever used except in an emergency.

14. A diagonal loop-hole, at the north end of room B, effectively covers the entrance from the outer stable to the ditch.

15. In the absence of any dated tomb-groups or stratified series the coarse wares of Roman Cyrenaica remain relatively uninformative. Mr. David Smith, of Durham University, is studying the sherds collected

during the Libyan Map expeditions of
1950–1.

16. One pencilled graffito gives the name
of Oberleutnant Friederich Von Freiharth
and the date 1916. This German Officer
must have been one of the enemy agents
landed by submarine during the Great War
in order to stir up the Senussi against the
Italian and British allies.

17. The possibility of these being secondary must be borne in mind. See above,
p. 175.

18. Not only the Greek tombs of Cyrene,
but also the Roman tombs of Tocra, are
almost entirely rock-cut. This rock-cutting
tradition seems to have died out during the
later Roman period and has not yet been
found in a Byzantine context. [There
appears now to be a Byzantine instance at
Bir-Tarakenet near Ain Mara, *PBSR* xxx
(1962) 41 f.]

19. The Ain Mara Fort is evidently the
one referred to by Synesius in his description of *Hydrax* (*Epist.* 67). [See pp. 152 and
251.]

20. S. Ferri, 363–86 (= SEG ix, 773–95).

21. The so-called "Christian basilica" of
Agedabia (Romanelli, (3), fig. 31) is actually

the only surviving fragment of the great
early Islamic fortress-palace seen at
Agedabia by Pacho and other nineteenth-
century travellers. [See also pp. 150 and
154, n. 21.]

22. Procopius, *De aedif.* VI, 2. [For
Boreum see below p. 187.]

23. H. W. and F. W. Beechey, 244–6.

24. In the Beecheys' report there are
frequent references in the text to illustrations
which were not actually published. It
appears that H. W. Beechey proposed to
publish these in a separate monograph,
together with drawings made in Nubia; but
this publication never saw the light of day.

25. Ammianus, *Hist.* XXVIII, 6; Synesius
Catastasis and *Letters* (*passim*).

26. [See above pp. 29 f. and pp. 35 f.]

27. The equivalent Latin term would
probably be *pacati* (cf. Procopius, *De aedif.*
VI, 3) or *foederati*.

28. Synesius. *Epist.* 130 (ed. Fitzgerald).

29. During the 1950 expedition native
sites, with few traces of Romanisation, were
found between El Abiar and Charruba,
and also near Martuba, south-east of Derna.
The later prehistory of Libya has been
sadly neglected, and merits investigation.

14

BOREUM OF CYRENAICA

[From *JRS* xli (1951)]
Plates 62–5

Two localities of ancient Cyrenaica bore the name Βόρειον The first,[1] recognised by the ancient geographers as the eastern extremity of the Greater Syrtis, was a promontory and harbour which, from the evidence of the *Stadiasmus Maris Magni*, lay 131 stades (23·5 km.) south of the city of Berenice. It has been convincingly identified with the modern Ras Taiunes, a small headland at precisely that distance from Benghazi. There is no evidence that this promontory was ever the site of permanent settlement in the form of a village or fort.

The second Βόρειον[2] lay further to the south, not far from the bottom of the Syrtic gulf (fig. 57). The *Stadiasmus* describes it as a village with a deserted castle, a landing-place, and a supply of fresh water. The *Antonine Itinerary* records Boreum as a road-station, 37 Roman miles (55 km.) north-east of Anabucis, which was itself situated in the vicinity of the modern El-Agheila [see p. 164]. It is, however, Procopius who gives us the fullest information about this southern Boreum. He describes it as "the last city of Pentapolis towards the west", and

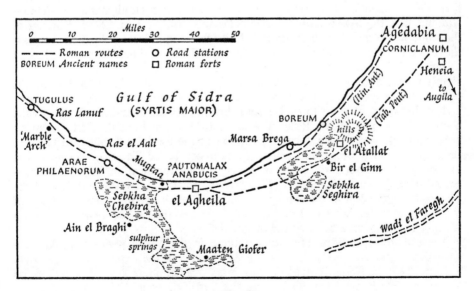

Fig. 57

goes on to explain that "Here the mountains press close upon one another, and thus forming a barrier by their crowding effectively close the entrance to the enemy. This city, which had been without a wall, the Emperor (Justinian) enclosed with very strong defences, thus making it as safe as possible for the future, together with the whole country round about it."[3] Procopius also states that Boreum "which lies near the barbarian Moors, has never been subject to tribute up to the present time, nor have any collectors of tribute or taxes come to it since the creation of man", and he adds that it had a Jewish community whom Justinian converted to Christianity, transforming their synagogue (traditionally built by Solomon) into a church.

It is evident, therefore, that Boreum had become recognised in the sixth century A.D. as a frontier town, the last bulwark between the Pentapolis and the barbarians of the Syrtic gulf. Indeed, this recognition probably goes back to the fifth century, since Sozomen[4] quotes Boreum as the westernmost place in those African regions which were subject to Constantinople. This fact indicates that the Greek frontier outposts of Automalax, and its Roman successor Anabucis, which must have both stood near El-Agheila,[5] had declined in importance, owing to the breakdown of security in the Syrtic region following the barbarian invasions of the later fourth century. The traditional western boundary of the Pentapolis lay at Arae Philaenorum, some 40 km. west of El-Agheila,[6] but the plains and salt-marshes of that area made it impossible to organise any effective system of defences there. The fact that the coastal route of the Syrtis was commanded at Boreum by the hills to which Procopius refers made it a key point in the Byzantine defensive system.

It may seem curious that Boreum does not appear in the town-lists of Hierocles and George of Cyprus. It is known that the place was a bishopric even before the conversion of its Jewish population to Christianity,[7] and the only walled town between Berenice and Lepcis Magna would surely merit a place in the official lists. The explanation lies presumably in the fact, which Honigmann has demonstrated,[8] that the *Synecdemus* of Hierocles was compiled in 527–8. Boreum at that time was probably still an unwalled village without fiscal obligations towards the Eastern Empire, and would therefore rightly be omitted. The compilers of "George of Cyprus" overlooked the addition of a new city to the Pentapolis; they simply repeated the old list of Hierocles, adding, under the Egyptian diocese, the cities of the Tripolis which had by that time been detached from Africa proper.

The discovery of the site of Boreum (but not its identification) is due to the brothers F. W. and H. W. Beechey who, in 1821, carried out the first systematic archaeological and geographical exploration of the Syrtic gulf. Some distance to the east of Marsa Brega and near a promontory called Tabilba, they observed an ancient castle and "the ruins of a very strong fortification, which was connected with the castle by a wall of five feet in thickness carried quite round the precipice on which it stood. This was defended on the inland side by a fosse of thirty feet in width excavated in the solid rock; and the rubbish extracted from it was piled up to form a bank on the outer side."[9]

These massive fortifications, quite unique in the Syrtic region, should have suggested to the Beecheys the work of Justinian; but the explorers were unduly influenced by the *Geography* of Ptolemy who, in fact, omits the southern Boreum altogether. Barth, who travelled along the Syrtic coast in 1846, made the suggestion tentatively, and it was subsequently incorporated by Müller in his edition of the minor Greek geographers, and repeated (by Sethe) in Pauly-Wissowa-Kroll, *Real-Encyclopädie*.[10] No attempt has, however, been made to corroborate the identification, although an Italian airman, Tenente Castellini, flying over the promontory of Bu Grada in 1927, reported the existence of a great defensive ditch which was presumably part of the ruins described by the Beecheys.[11]

In the absence of any detailed description of these remains, or of any accurate plan which would show their layout, the most recent writers have hesitated to accept this identification. Ghislanzoni, in his excellent article on Cyrenaican archaeology, assumed that Boreum occupied the promontory of Ras Taiunes, which had in antiquity, as we have already seen, the same name. Ferri, describing some inscriptions at Agedabia, admitted that the site of Boreum could not be identified. Romanelli, in his recent study of Roman Cyrenaica, refers to the place and to Justinian's work there, without committing himself as to its actual site.[12]

The exact identification of Boreum is of importance not only for its bearing on the frontier policy of Justinian but also in relation to the general ancient topography of the Syrtic Gulf. The mileage figures given in the Roman itineraries can only be usefully studied if there are a number of firm and indisputable identifications to form a sound basis for map-measurement. A walled town like Boreum ought, logically, to be more easily identified than any road-station or small harbour. It was therefore decided during the summer expedition of the Map of Roman Libya Committee in 1950[13] to re-examine on the ground the ancient remains which the Beecheys had seen at "Tabilba", and which Castellini had observed from the air at Bu Grada. As had been anticipated, these ruins proved to be one and the same.

BOREUM

The site of Boreum (fig. 58), as conclusively established by this recent investigation, occupies the promontory of Ras Bu Grada, a small headland 12 km. north-east of the war-ruined village of Marsa Brega and 4 km. west of the important wells of Maaten Tabilba. On the headland itself (pl. 63) stood a citadel, the castle referred to in the *Stadiasmus*, with extensive rock-cut galleries underneath it. On the edge of the cliff is a cistern which probably provided the water supply for the garrison, although there may have been wells in the adjoining village. There are traces of a ditch across the neck of the promontory.

The village occupied rising ground behind the headland, and was enclosed with massive ramparts (pl. 65) which are undoubtedly those referred to by Procopius. They consist of a wall 1·70 m. wide, of blocks of soft sandstone, fronted by a ditch 10–15 m. wide and originally nearly as deep. The outer face of the wall has crumbled away and spilled into the ditch, which accounts for the fact that the Beecheys did not notice its existence. In the north-east corner of the walled area a prominent fort adjoins the town wall, and projecting bastions stand at the south-east corner and in the middle of the south side of the wall. The remains of a causeway indicate a gateway in the east wall, and an archway near the south-east corner tower probably marks a small postern in the south wall. The soil and rock dug out of the east and south ditches lie scattered in low mounds on the outer side of the ditches. On the north and west the town area is fringed by the sea. The remains of a sea-wall run from the south-west corner to

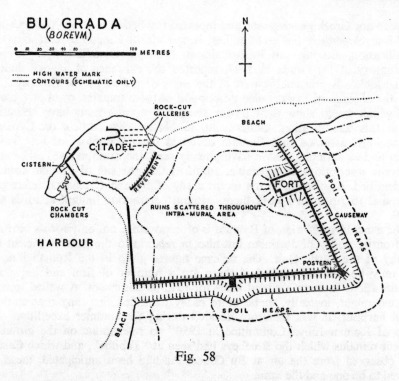

Fig. 58

the neck of the headland, but there are no signs of a corresponding wall on the
north side. Inside the town walls the soil is littered with building stones, but there
are no columns or other architectural features visible on the surface, and one
receives the impression of a settlement very meagrely Romanised.

The built-up area of Boreum, barely 250 by 150 m. in extent, is small by
comparison with the main cities of the Pentapolis, but is sufficiently large to
show that the site was more than a fort. The Roman and Byzantine forts of
Cyrenaica are extremely small, most of them hardly more than 20 m. square,
and few more than 50 m.[14] There can be little doubt that the original nucleus of
Boreum was the citadel on the headland (pl. 63), and that the village which
sprang up in its vicinity was of modest dimensions and minor importance until the
day that one of Justinian's generals decided to make this the westernmost outpost
of the Pentapolis.

THE DEFENCE OF THE AREA

Procopius asserts that the work of Justinian not merely protected Boreum itself
but also "the whole country round about it". It is, in fact, on the low hills
fringing the salt-marshes around Marsa Brega and Bu Grada that we encounter
the greatest number of ancient forts to be found in this part of the Syrtic coast.
Most of them have collapsed into square mounds conspicuous for their surrounding ditches, many have been robbed of stone to build military works during
the Libyan campaigns of the recent war, and some are in areas which are still
heavily mined.

Of these forts, which are referred to briefly by the Beecheys,[15] the best-preserved and most important is Gasr el-Atallat, which stands on a low hillock on the edge of the marsh, 10 km. south-east of Boreum. As it had not previously been planned, it was visited during the course of the 1950 expedition. It proved to be a rectangular structure (fig. 59), 31 by 27 m. externally, with walls 1·70 m. wide built of large carefully coursed blocks of shelly limestone (pl. 62). In the middle of the north-east side a doorway 1·10 m. wide gave access to the interior. The interior arrangements of the fort are not, however, visible, owing to the mass of fallen material; but there is a small vaulted chamber abutting against the inner face of the north-west wall. A wide ditch surrounds the fort and there are extensive remains of buildings outside its north-western side (pl. 64).

Like most of the ancient forts in Cyrenaica, Gasr el-Atallat bears no inscription to show when, and by whom, it was built. The masonry is, however, remarkably similar to that of the town-walls of Boreum, and it seems reasonable to conclude that this fort, and most of the smaller ones in the same group, are the work of Justinian. The fortification of Boreum would not, alone, have kept the

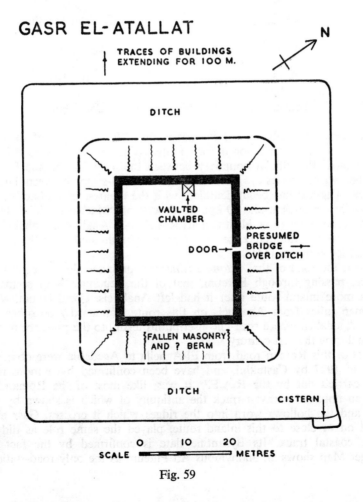

Fig. 59

barbarian tribes of the Syrtic region from penetrating north-eastwards towards the heart of the Pentapolis; but by forming a defensive cushion of fortified farms and watch-towers, with its nerve-centre at Gasr el-Atallat, this aim was achieved.

TOPOGRAPHY AND HISTORY

The firm identification of Bu Grada as the ancient Boreum throws useful light on the ancient topography of the foot of the Syrtic gulf, and on the courses of the Roman roads shown in the itineraries (fig. 57). The evidence of the itineraries is as follows:

Antonine Itinerary	Peutinger Map
Tugulus	Tagulis
XXV	XXX
Banadedari	Arephilenorum
XXV	XXV
Anabucis	Anabucis praesidium
XXV	XXX
Tiniodiri	Ad Puteum
XII	XXX
Boreo	Priscu taberna
XXIII	XVIII
Tincausari	Corniclanu

It has been generally agreed by critics that "Banadedari" of the *Antonine Itinerary* must be a corruption of, or an alternative name for, Arae Philaenorum, which marked the official boundary between the Tripolis and the Pentapolis.[16] Thus, the two itineraries are coincident for the road-sector between Tugulus and Anabucis. Tugulus has been identified, with the greatest of probability, at Gasr el-Haddadia, an ancient site 10 km. north-west of "Marble Arch".[17] The site of Arae Philaenorum is [now identified at] Ras el-Aali. Anabucis, probably identical with the ancient Automalax, seems to have been situated near the modern El-Agheila. [See above p. 164].

Whereas the road of the *Antonine Itinerary* continues along the coast towards Berenice, passing through Boreum, that of the Peutinger Map seems to have taken a more inland route after it had left Anabucis. Corniclanum, which was 78 Roman miles from Anabucis on this route, can hardly be other than the modern Agedabia, where rock-cut inscriptions testify to the presence of a Roman garrison during the first century A.D.[18]

Traces of this Roman road from El-Agheila to Agedabia were observed from the air in 1927 by Castellini, and have been confirmed by a more recent air survey carried out by the R.A.F.[19] It was, like most of the Roman roads in Libya, an unpaved caravan track the antiquity of which is shown by its direct course and the hollows worn into the ridges which it crosses. Gasr el-Atallat, situated on or close to this inland route, played the same role as did Boreum for the coastal track. Its Byzantine date is confirmed by the fact that the Peutinger Map shows an anonymous Ad Puteum as the only road-station in the area.[20]

Comparison of the Syrtic *limes* of Cyrenaica under Justinian with that of the first century A.D. shows how little change there had been in the geographical definition of the main frontier area. Agedabia had been the key-point of the earlier *limes*, no doubt because of its commanding position beside the best wells on the caravan route to Augila. South-westward of Agedabia the Syrtic coast was garrisoned only by isolated detachments at Anabucis *praesidium* and, inside Tripolitan territory, at Zacasama *praesidium* (Ras Ben Gawad, near Nofilia).[21]

Justinian's policy was only a slight modification of this earlier system. He extended imperial control into the oases of Augila, converting to Christianity their pagan population, and thus reduced the importance of the Agedabia base. On the other hand, he pushed the *limes* area 80 km. further towards the bottom of the gulf, and by fortifying Boreum and its surrounding district made it no longer necessary to keep an outpost at El-Agheila. This policy presumably involved the virtual abandonment of the Syrtic shores between Marsa Brega and the easternmost outposts of the reconquered Tripolitan province; land communications between the Tripolis and the Pentapolis must have remained at the mercy of those Syrtic tribes whose 'chef-lieu" Digdiga had formerly ranked as a *municipium*, but was now a hot-bed of revolt.[22]

ADDENDUM

A vivid description of a small Christian community in this part of the Syrtic Gulf is to be found in Sulpicius Severus *Dialogue* I, 3–6, which confirms the assertion of Procopius that these areas were exempt from taxation.

NOTES

1. *Stad. mar. magn.* 62–3; Strabo *Geog.* XVII, 836; Mela I, 37; Pliny, *Hist Nat.* V, 28; Ptolemy IV, 4, 2; Ammianus *Hist.* XXII, 15, 2. Cf. *RE* iii, 730 s.v. "Boreion 2" (Sethe).

2. *Stad. mar. magn.* 78–9; *Itin. Ant.* 66, 1. Cf. *RE* iii 730, s.v. "Boreion 3"; and Müller, I, 452, and Tabulae I, xx.

3. Procopius, *De aedif.* VI, 2.

4. *Hist. eccles.* II, 3.

5. [At Bu Sceefa, see above, p. 166.]

6. [At Ras el-Aali, see above, p. 157.]

7. Sentianus, Bishop of Boreum, was one of the several ecclesiastics of the Pentapolis who supported Arius (cf. Nicetas Choniata, *Thesaurus* 7, quoting a lost fragment of Philostorgius). He did not, however, attend the Council of Nicaea. Although listed by Lequien, *Oriens Christianus* II, 627, Boreum does not appear as a bishopric in A. H. M. Jones, ed. 1 [but was added ed. 2, 498 and Appendix IV, Table 49].

8. E. Honigmann, 2; but cf. Jones, Appendix III.

9. F. W. and H. W. Beechey, 233–5.

10. H. Barth, (1), 349. (His description of the site is a repetition of the Beecheys'.) *RE loc. cit.*

11. *Bollettino Geografico* (Governo della Cirenaica, Ufficio Studi) no. 5, July-Dec., 1927, 20 (with unscaled sketch-plan).

12. Ghislanzoni, "Notizie arch. sulla Cirenaica", *Notiz. Arch. Min. Col.* i (1915), 72; Ferri, 363; Romanelli, (3), 120, 173, 204.

13. The expedition was carried out under the auspices of the Society of Antiquaries of London, with generous contributions from learned bodies, including the Roman Society. I am indebted to Messrs. Ballance, McGregor, Smith, Spaul, and Titchmarsh for the survey of Boreum (fig. 58), and to the first-named for photographs (pls. 62, 63).

14. Numerous examples of these forts were visited and surveyed in the course of the 1950 expedition [See e.g. pp. 172 f. and 204 f.].

15. Beechey, 230, note. There are at least twelve of these forts within a radius of 5 km. of Boreum.

16. Cf. Windberg in *RE* xix, 2098–101, s.v. "Philaenorum Arae", [and above p. 156f.].

17. See above, p. 157f. Gasr el-Haddadia, first recorded by Cerrata (Sirtis 220), is a much more satisfactory identification for Tugulus than the Wadi Matratin ("Teratin") proposed by Miller. Cf. Treidler in *RE* (2) iv, 2024–5, s.v. "Tagulis".

18. Ferri, *loc. cit.* = *SEG* ix, 773–95.

19. I am indebted to Air Headquarters, R.A.F. Malta, for the air photographs (pls. 64, 65) of Boreum and Gasr el-Atallat, taken by Flying Officer MacGillivary at my suggestion. During the same air reconnaissance the line of the Roman road was observed and photographed.

20. Ad Puteum must have been at, or near, the well which supplied the Italian village at Marsa Brega, some 15 km. west of Gasr el-Atallat.

21. Miller (892) proposes this identification which is entirely acceptable. There is a large fortress on the headland of Ben Gawad, which dominates the coastal route.

22. Digdiga, described as Municipium Selorum on the Peutinger Map, is referred to by Corippus (*Johannidos* II, 119) as one of the centres of the African revolt. Its site has been identified by Cerrata, with great probability, in the Wadi Hariga, near Marsa el-Ihudia (220).

15

THE ROMAN AND BYZANTINE *LIMES* IN CYRENAICA

[From *JRS* xliii (1953)]
Plates 66–76

Although Cyrenaica ranked, under the earlier Empire, as a senatorial province, it was too exposed to barbarian attack to be left undefended; and there is ample evidence that it had its own garrison—probably a small one—from the first century A.D. onwards.[1] This garrison was evidently inadequate to prevent the outbreak of the Jewish Revolt of A.D 115, and may consequently have been strengthened; but it was the crisis of the mid-third century that showed all too clearly the insecurity of the isolated Cyrenaican plateau. The Marmaric tribes invaded the province, and Cyrene itself seems to have been overwhelmed.[2] The Diocletianic reforms resulted in the creation of a new "middle-eastern" command under the *Dux Aegypti Thebaidos utrarumque Libyarum*,[3] but the loss of the chapter of the *Notitia Dignitatum* enumerating the units stationed in the two Libyas makes it difficult to reconstruct the military organisation of these provinces at the end of the fourth century. The works of Synesius help to fill the lacuna and at the same time provide a vivid picture of life in an invaded area.[4]

From A.D. 390 onwards, Cyrenaica seems to have had little respite from barbarian invasion. The gravest threat came from the Ausuriani or Austuriani, a savage race probably from the hinterland of the Syrtic Gulf. They first appear in Roman history in 363–5, when they invaded Tripolitania;[5] but by 399 or thereabouts their incursions ranged over both sides of the Syrtica, giving rise to the lamentable situation recorded by Synesius. We hear of their invading Libya again in about 450[6] when the Roman general Armatius campaigned against them. Early in the sixth century the main threat seems to have come from the Mazices, who had installed themselves in the oases west of the Nile valley and Cyrenaica suffered from their inroads on at least one occasion.[7]

The fact that the provinces of Upper and Lower Libya survived these prolonged barbarian attacks, and fell only to the Arab invaders of the seventh century, shows the tenacity of the military commanders to whom their defence was entrusted. The gloomy account given by Synesius of the corruption and cowardice of the Roman generals of his time—an account distinctly coloured by his own personal animosities—gives only one side of the picture. To assess the problems with which these commanders were faced, and which they seem eventually to have solved with some measure of success, we must appeal to the topographical and archaeological evidence.

Of the physical character of the Roman *Limes* in Cyrenaica there has been little or no previous discussion.[8] Although the nineteenth-century explorers who first brought Cyrenaica to European notice[9] encountered many ancient fortresses in the course of their travels, they left no detailed descriptions of these structures. Nor has the first half of the present century yielded much additional information. As an initial step towards remedying this situation, the Map of Roman Libya expeditions of 1950–1[10] undertook the visiting and surveying of a large number of forts scattered between the Syrtic Gulf and the Gulf of Bomba. The following notes are based on the results of these surveys, but it must be stressed that limitations of space make it possible to refer only to the more important and interesting sites, and that firm chronological conclusions must await the execution of more detailed study and excavation.

The most common type of ancient fort encountered in Cyrenaica is a simple square stone-built structure, usually surrounded by a ditch, and without projecting towers. Except where otherwise stated, this basic pattern is to be assumed in the following descriptions, in which the overall external measurements of the fort walls are normally given. Usually, these walls are constructed of newly-quarried and well-coursed ashlar masonry; and it is common to find, in the later forts, a revetted "skirt" of dry-built masonry forming the scarp of the ditch. This talus is structurally independent of the fort walls and may sometimes be a secondary addition.[11] Certain mud-brick forts lying on the fringes of the area of Graeco-Roman occupation seem to be mainly of Islamic date and are excluded from consideration in the present paper.

THE SYRTIC APPROACHES

The approaches to the Cyrenaican plateau from the Syrtic region were strongly defended in antiquity, and constituted a desert *Limes* of Syrian or Numidian type. The westernmost outpost within the confines of Cyrenaica was a small (35 by 32 m.) undiched fort situated on a hillock at Bir Umm el-Garanigh, close to the legendary site of the "Altars of the Philaeni".[12] This post was occupied in the first century A.D., and was certainly abandoned before the age of Justinian, when the western defences of the Pentapolis lay around the walled city of Boreum (Bu Grada, near Marsa Brega). In this latter area there is an extensive group of small ditched forts, with its centre at Gasr el-Atallat.[13]

Agedabia, the ancient Corniculanum, was garrisoned in the first century A.D. by troops of Syrian origin, whose outpost probably lay beneath the Fatimid fort, of which some surface remains still exist today. The presence of important wells at the junction of the Syrtic coastal route and the caravan track to the oases of Augila made Agedabia a key-point in the frontier organisation. A short distance to its south is the small but ingeniously-contrived watch-tower of Gasr el-Heneia, which has been fully described elsewhere.[14]

Between Agedabia and Benghazi (Berenice) there are a number of small fortified buildings, perhaps fortified farms rather than official forts, scattered along the two parallel Roman caravan routes; and there are also, around Ghemines, many roughly-built forts surrounded by villages of native character. These were perhaps constructed and occupied by friendly Libyan tribes, such as the Maci, under Roman or Byzantine supervision.[15] Of more official type is the small and well-preserved fort of Gasr Haddumah, situated near Magrun. Its walls (20 m.

square) have carefully-coursed faces of large blocks, and are fronted by a ditch 7 m. broad.

Forming a west–east line from near the coast to the barren steppe of the interior are three important forts at Zauia et-Tailimun, Esh-Sheleidima, and Zauiet Msus. This line probably marked the innermost defences of the Syrtic *Limes*, and it is interesting to note that Italian colonial military posts occupied precisely the same sites.

The fort at Tailimun (fig. 60) was visited by Hamilton in 1854,[16] and stands at an important track-junction: a *zauia* (convent) of the Senussi order now occupies part of its site, and has consumed some of the ancient materials. Although parts of only three outer walls, and of two angle-towers, remain above the ground, the fort appears to have measured 38 by 44 m., and to have been divided internally by two walled streets or intersecting corridors meeting at right-angles. An arched doorway gives access to the north-western angle-tower from the inside of the fort; and the main entrance to the fort itself was probably on the east or south. There are no definite traces of a surrounding ditch.

Of the ancient fort at Esh-Sheleidima little can be said, as a large Italian redoubt occupies its site, but a length of 38 m. of ancient large-block stonework incorporated in the modern walls shows that it was no smaller than Tailimun. A broad and irregularly-shaped ditch, much modified by Italian military engineers, surrounds the hill-top on which the fort stood. This hill dominates a valley (appropriately named El-Bab, "the gate") which gives easy access from the coastal plain to the higher ground beyond the Gebel escarpment.

At Zauiet Msus, too, the Roman outpost is incorporated in an Italian fort, but it has escaped serious injury, and may be considered one of the most interesting sites of the Cyrenaican *Limes*.[17] Its form (fig. 61) is that of a simple watch-tower (7½ by 6 m.) and a surrounding outer, unditched, enclosure (19½ m. square), walled with well-laid drafted masonry of hard limestone (pl. 69). A flat lintel caps the single doorway opening into the west side of the enclosure (pl. 66). The inner faces of the enclosure walls consist of rubble masonry which may be in part ancient; but it is not certain that the internal cross-walls springing

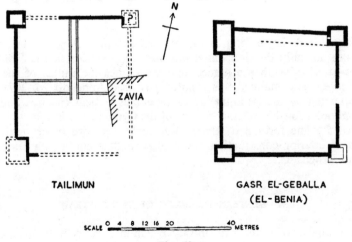

TAILIMUN   GASR EL-GEBALLA
                              (EL-BENIA)

SCALE 0 4 8 12 16 20   40 METRES

Fig. 60

WATCH TOWER AT ZAVIET MSUS

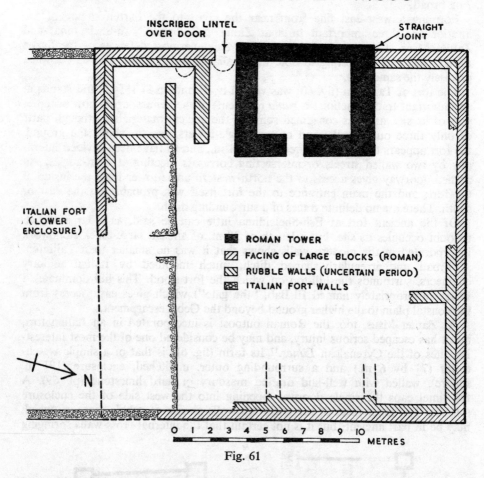

INSCRIBED LINTEL
OVER DOOR

STRAIGHT
JOINT

ITALIAN FORT
(LOWER
ENCLOSURE)

- ■ ROMAN TOWER
- ▨ FACING OF LARGE BLOCKS (ROMAN)
- ▨ RUBBLE WALLS (UNCERTAIN PERIOD)
- ▧ ITALIAN FORT WALLS

N

0 1 2 3 4 5 6 7 8 9 10
METRES

Fig. 61

from this rubble facing belong to the original scheme. Of particular interest is the fact that not only the door-lintel but also large sectors of the Roman wall-facing are inscribed with the names, and sometimes the ranks, of the Graeco-Roman soldiers who manned this isolated post (see Appendix, p. 207). Msus is much frequented by the Bedouin for its capacious ancient cisterns, and appears to be a vital point for the effective control of the Cyrenaican hinterland.

North of the line formed by these three forts there are other small fortified structures of inferior construction and uncertain date continuing almost to the outskirts of Benghazi.

THE WESTERN DEFENCES OF THE PLATEAU

Although a number of small forts, mostly Byzantine, are to be found scattered in the coastal plains[18] between Benghazi and the site of Ptolemais, these alone could not have ensured the security of the cultivated areas. Of particular importance in antiquity, as also today, was the broad and fertile plain of Merj, the *terri-torium* of Barka, Cyrene's former rival. It is therefore hardly surprising to find that the western and southern approaches to this plain were controlled in ancient times by a number of forts and fortified farms. Some of these lie on the sides of the vale which runs from El-Abiar to Merj; but the most interesting are those situated due south of Merj, along the sheltered route which, in 1941, allowed members of the Long-Range Desert Group to strike at Axis aircraft on Merj airfield.

Especially important, for its size and dominant position, is the fortress of Gasr el-Geballa, at El-Benia (fig. 60, right).[19] It occupies an isolated hill at the junction of several valleys, and must have effectively controlled the surrounding country-side. It is square (39 m. each side, but with a slight irregularity in its lay-out), and has rectangular angle-towers of varying sizes (pl. 67). The entrance was probably on the east, but the curtain-walls appear to have fallen in late antiquity, and have been rebuilt in inferior masonry. Of the interior arrangements nothing is visible, except for traces of minor structures, perhaps barracks, built up on the inner side of the main walls. There is no ditch; but the steep slope of the hill makes one unnecessary.

Of very different character, and probably of much later date, are a number of fortified farmhouses scattered along the edges of a cultivable valley close to the edge of the escarpment overlooking the plain of Barka. This group of defen-sive structures, which may conveniently be named after Zauiet el-Gsur ("convent of the castles"), includes the exceptionally well-preserved fortlet of Sidi el-Chadri, and is clearly a para-military settlement of *limitanei* of a type well represented in Tripolitania.[20] Each homestead has strong outer walls which were of two storeys' height. Internally, the buildings consisted of a number of rooms opening, by arched doorways, off a central courtyard. In structures of this type, which are extremely common throughout the Cyrenaica plateau, the heavy voussoirs of the arches have survived better than the rubble-built interior partition walls; and it is no exaggeration to say that seemingly isolated arches protruding from fallen masses of stone are the most prominent features of ancient sites in Cyrenaica. An indication of date is provided by a cross of Byzantine type carefully cut on one of the corners of Gasr Sidi el-Chadri.

THE OUTER DEFENCES OF THE CYRENE PLATEAU

East of Gasr el-Geballa (Benia) there is no very clearly-defined outer line of ancient forts, and many of the *gsur* marked on existing maps appear to be of early Islamic date;[21] but as one approaches the borders of the Cyrene plateau, a coherent defensive lay-out becomes more apparent. The most important and impressive of the forts in this area belong to what we may term the Wadi Kuf group, and will be described later. For the moment, we must consider the forts which protected the southern and eastern approaches to the plateau; and it is convenient to list them from east to west, beginning with the fort at Ain Mara, an important group of springs on the eastern edge of the plateau.

This structure[22] is 34 m. square, and is surrounded by a deep vertical-sided ditch, in the outer faces of which there are rock-cut chambers—a feature occurring also at Gasr el-Heneia, near Agedabia. Beneath the centre of the fort, the original internal arrangements of which are obscure, there is a large rock-cut cistern. Although much damaged by later occupation (including a Senussi *zauia*), the Ain Mara fort is exceptionally interesting, in that it can be linked with a well-known episode in the life of Synesius, which also provides a valuable *terminus ante quem* for this type of vertically-ditched fort. In his sixty-seventh letter Synesius refers to a dispute between the Bishops of Erythrum (El-Atrun) and Darnis (Derna) over the possession of the fort at Hydrax. At that time (c. A.D. 400) the fort was "an abandoned heap of ruins", having been destroyed by an earthquake. Not only does Ain Mara conform to the geographical position of Hydrax, as given by Ptolemy, but the fort itself is in extremely ruined condition and its outer walls are twisted and bulged in a manner which can only have been caused by a severe earth-tremor.

Ain Mara marks the eastern end of a series of fortified structures 15 km. or less apart, forming an outer ring of outposts for the protection of the Cyrene plateau. These outposts include Gasr Bu Hassan and Gasr Uertig, situated near the track which ran south[east]ward from Cyrene to the Gulf of Bomba, and Gasr el-Maragh and Gasr er-Remteiat, both 35 km. due south of Cyrene. Of these forts, Gasr er-Remteiat is the most notable, and probably the most ancient, having some of the characteristics both of El-Heneia and of Ain Mara. It is 33 m. square, and surrounded by a vertical-sided rock-cut ditch, spanned on the south by a causeway giving access to the fort, and on the north by a narrow rock-wall, the function of which can be deduced by reference to the arrangements of El-Heneia. There are remains of various internal partition walls, but they give little idea of the original plan.

Gasr el-Maragh is clearly of later date, and conforms more to the pattern of the small Byzantine forts that lie nearer the ancient areas of occupation in the Gebel. It is a simple watch-tower, 15 m. square, with a high revetted talus on the inner side of a very broad surrounding ditch. We may reasonably infer, from the juxtaposition of Remteiat and Maragh (only 5 km. apart), that this outer defensive circuit of the Cyrene plateau remained garrisoned over a long period of time.

West of Remteiat there is another small late tower above the wells of Buerat (Gerrari), and a small fort of uncertain date at Sira. Beyond this point we enter the southern edges of the Kuf area, where some of the finest forts of Cyrenaica are to be encountered.

THE DEFENCES OF THE KUF REGION

Between the plain of Barka, situated on the lower Cyrenaica plateau, and the high plateau of Cyrene, there extends a large area of very broken country traversed by a complex series of deep ravines and their minor tributaries, and mantled with undergrowth and occasional dense forest. Invaders from the south can, by taking advantage of this region of the Kuf,[23] cut Cyrenaica into two and have sheltered access to the western end of the Cyrene plain. This was, no doubt, the area "infested by the enemy" which Synesius had to pass through on his way from Ptolemais to Hydrax; and in more recent days the guerilla bands of Omar Muktar continually interrupted land communications between western

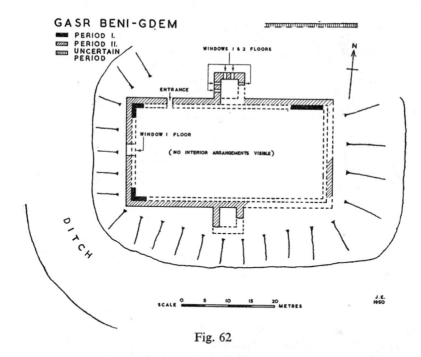

Fig. 62

and eastern Cyrenaica by blocking this zone through which Italian engineers had, audaciously but perhaps imprudently, constructed their main lateral road.[24]

There are countless fortified buildings in the Kuf region, which Italian generals aptly termed the "triangle of the castles"; space permits the description of only a few of the most interesting examples.

Well-known to the nineteenth-century explorers, and to many more recent visitors, is the great fortress of Gasr Beni Gdem, a magnificent specimen of late Roman military architecture (pl. 68).[25] It is an oblong structure (44 by 23 m.) of two storeys, with projecting towers in the centre of each of the two longer sides (fig. 62, pl. 70). The large windows in each storey of the well-preserved north tower were, no doubt, provided for *ballistae*. The outer walls are of double thickness (pl. 71), the existing facade having been built up against that of an earlier fort, apparently of the same basic plan, but perhaps of lesser height. The inner arrangements cannot be made out, owing to fallen material, but the lower chamber of the north tower retains traces of its vaulting (pl. 70). The only visible entrance is an arched door in the curtain wall a little west of this tower. This massive fortress was clearly intended to dominate one of the most dangerous areas of the Kuf region. It bears no particular relationship to the main Roman lines of communication.

Less prominent and almost unknown,[26] but more complex and better-preserved internally, is the fort of Gasr esh-Shahden, situated on a hill-top in the heavily wooded country some 8 km. south-east of Beni Gdem. The fort proper is a keep standing in the centre of an irregular ditched enclosure (fig. 63) embracing the whole hill-top, and containing a number of minor buildings, the functions of which are obscure. Numerous rock-cut chambers open off from the inner edge

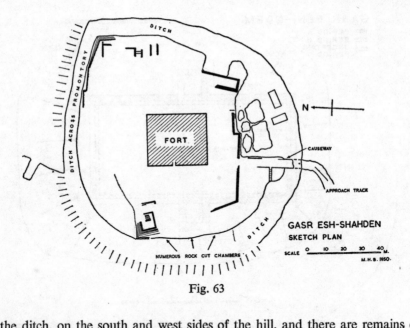

Fig. 63

of the ditch, on the south and west sides of the hill, and there are remains of a causeway by which the ditch was crossed.

Three building periods are evident in the keep at Shahden. It began as a simple isolated tower (14 by 13 m.) with three vaulted chambers (fig. 64, C, D, and E) approached through a vestibule (B), at ground-floor level. Later, a strong but rather irregularly-coursed outer wall (pl. 73) was built around the keep. Finally, in the third constructional phase, the interval between the tower and the outer wall was built up into long vaulted galleries on both ground-floor (F, G, and H) and upper storey (J, K, L, and M). The method of access between the two levels is uncertain, but a staircase may lie in the still inaccessible north-west corner of the fort.

The date of the stronghold remains largely hypothetical, owing to lack of

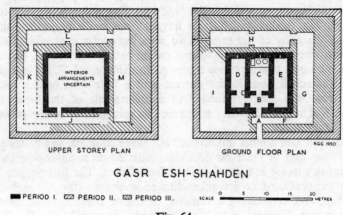

Fig. 64

inscriptions. The hill-top may have been fortified even before the Roman occupation of Cyrenaica, but the existing masonry of the keep is probably entirely Roman and Byzantine. Nor has the first-period tower any characteristics which would justify one dating it earlier than the fifth century A.D. On the other hand, the considerable number of Greek quarry-marks on the masonry of the third period makes it difficult to accept a post-Islamic date for that phase. It seems most likely, therefore, that the whole structural history of Shahden falls between the fifth and seventh centuries A.D. Indeed, the drastic additions of the third period may well be the work of Justinian, who is known to have fortified two "monasteries" in the interior of the Pentapolis.

Finally, mention must be made of the small (13 by 15 m.) unditched watch-tower of Gasr Ushish (pl. 74), situated on the southern fringes of the Kuf area. not far south-west of Slonta. Its austere but well-built walls, pierced by narrow loop-holes, show what the castle of Shahden must have looked like in its earlier days. Here, too, there are indications that the ground-floor chambers were vaulted over—a marked characteristic of late Roman military architecture in Cyrenaica.[27]

THE EASTERN APPROACHES TO THE PENTAPOLIS

In marked contrast to the abundance of fortified structures in the Syrtic region, and on the upper Cyrenaican plateau, there is a curious scarcity of forts guarding the eastern approaches to the Pentapolis. On the high ground around Martuba there are a few small military buildings, such as the example at Siret el-Medaanat (16 by 19 m.) which protected the route from Darnis inland towards Mechili; but further east, towards the Gulf of Bomba, they are rare.

At Mechili, a watering-point and track-centre comparable in importance with Msus, one would have expected to find a Roman outpost; and there was, indeed, an early Islamic fort,[28] of which the internal mud-brick walls can still be traced today. Possibly the walls of the Roman structure, if such existed, lie buried beneath the mounds of the medieval site.

Tobruk, the ancient Antipyrgus, was fortified by Justinian, who established troops there, and the outlines of his fort—a square with projecting towers—survived into the present century.[29] Whether an earlier fort and garrison had existed at Antipyrgus is entirely uncertain.

Future archaeological exploration may well throw useful light on the manner in which the coastlands of Lower Libya were protected from barbarian attack: but the evidence at present available suggests that the *Limes* in this Marmaric region never reached the same development as it did in the Pentapolis, or towards the Syrtic Gulf. "Dry Libya" contained too few centres of habitation to attract the predatory instincts of the invader, or to necessitate any large-scale measures of defence.[30]

THE INTERNAL DEFENCES OF THE PLATEAU

The forts previously described belong, in the main, to the outer defences of the Pentapolis; but it would be erroneous to suppose that the province remained, throughout its history, guarded only by forts and watch-towers scattered in the mountains and steppe some distance from the zones of intensive occupation and cultivation. On the contrary, the castles of Cyrenaica occur with equal frequency in the cultivable areas and close to the great cities. They stand even along the shores of the Mediterranean. It is therefore quite clear that from the fifth century onwards the whole province had become a *Limes*, and that there was no longer any clear distinction between civil and military zones.

Similarly, it is almost impossible to distinguish, in the more densely habited areas, between the fort and the fortified farm. The fortified structures are, almost invariably, small (usually about 15–20 m. square) and surrounded by ditches (cf. Gasr Tectana, pl. 72). Christian crosses sometimes incised on their walls show the lateness of their date. Their wall masonry, normally well-built, is of the same character as that encountered in the larger fortresses, with projecting string-courses of "headers" bonding the inner and outer faces of the wall. A few typical plans are given on fig. 65. Forts built of re-used materials are relatively rare.

More remarkable are the fortified churches which occur in some of the villages. These have not previously been recognised as such, although Pacho noticed that many of the "castles" had apses at their extremities.[31] Recent explorations have shown clearly that in many of the villages the church became the citadel during the barbarian invasions: its walls were strengthened, and a ditch was dug round them. The best examples occur at Lamluda (the ancient Limnias) and at Mtaugat, near Tert, both sites being on the plateau east of Cyrene. Since these villages rarely had wall-circuits, the selection of the most substantial building as a citadel was a logical result of the general lack of security.

The distribution of the smaller fortified buildings in the cultivated areas of the Pentapolis appears to have no special tactical significance, and the view, sometimes expressed, that they represent staging-points along the ancient routes[32] cannot be maintained. It is, however, interesting to note that in the area of ancient Barka (modern Merj) they occur not on the fertile plain, but in the more broken country along the edges. This fact probably reflects not only the military importance of controlling the more sheltered terrain—always an attractive hiding-ground for outlaws—but also the economic fact that the *limitanei* were granted marginal ground tax-free in return for their services. It was the more fertile terrain that yielded the taxes necessary to support the regular army and the administration.

THE DEFENCES OF THE CITIES

The defences of the Cyrenaic cities raise particular problems which can only briefly be discussed in this paper. Detailed archaeological surveys of the urban wall-circuits have yet to be made. Meanwhile, it must be noted that each of the five principal cities of the Pentapolis was given, in Hellenistic or early Roman times,[33] a strong circuit of walls which remained standing throughout the first four centuries of Roman occupation. The reduced urban man-power of the later Roman period often made the manning of these extensive circuits an impossible task, and there is clear evidence of a policy of retrenchment both at Cyrene and at Ptolemais. On the former site the Roman Forum [Caesareum] became, probably during the course of the [third] century,[34] a citadel and fortress, with loop-holes cut in its outer walls, and surrounding buildings (including a small theatre on the south) levelled to the ground to clear the field of observation. There are

FORTS IN CYRENAICA

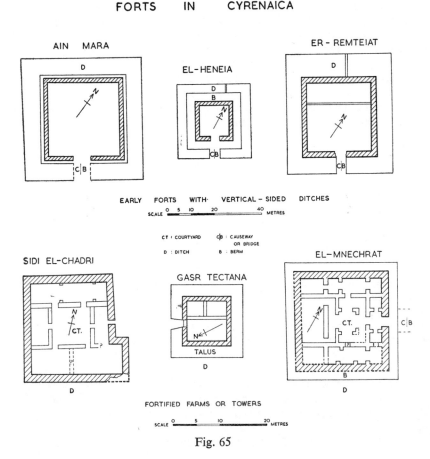

Fig. 65

no signs of late repairs to the main city wall-circuit, which probably ceased to be manned.

Ptolemais offers even clearer indications of this same policy. The inner sector of its original wall-circuit lay dangerously close to the foot of the escarpment, and reduced manning would have enabled the city to be stormed by surprise. At some date before the reign of Anastasius, this wall-circuit was completely dismantled, leaving only the West Gate standing as an isolated redoubt, and a new wall was built closer to the harbour.[35] In the abandoned area of the city between the two walls was constructed a large fortress (pls. 75, 76) on which was inscribed (not necessarily at the moment of its construction) the now famous Decree of Anastasius, relating to the military organisation of the Pentapolis.[36] The architecture of this fort, so closely akin to that of Gasr Beni Gdem, Gasr Shahden, and a host of smaller outposts, is our principal clue to the dating of these latter buildings.

Of the three remaining cities of the Pentapolis, Berenice was refortified by Justinian, but nothing remains of its walls, and it is not known how far the Hellenistic and Byzantine circuits coincided.[36a] The walls of Apollonia, which—under its alternative name of Sozusa—seems to have replaced Ptolemais as capital of the Pentapolis,[37] appear to be of early date, and it is significant that Procopius makes no reference to them. The walls of Tauchira, on the other hand, were extensively repaired by Justinian, and the towers are almost entirely his work. Here, however, the earlier wall-circuit was retained by the Byzantines, which fact made this one of the largest walled cities of the sixth-century Pentapolis. Finally, mention must be made of the walls of Boreum,[38] which Justinian erected for the defence of the western extremity of the Pentapolis, and of those of Darnis, which are of uncertain date.

GENERAL CONCLUSIONS

It is apparent, from this topographical survey—incomplete as it may be—that the effective limits of the Roman defensive system in Cyrenaica did not vary greatly between the first and sixth centuries A.D. Certain outlying posts, such as Msus, were probably abandoned long before the end of the Roman period; but the Byzantines spared no pains to keep a firm grip on the fertile Cyrenaica plateau. Whereas in Tripolitania the Byzantine government was content to hold the coast and its main cities, and to control the interior only through the medium of friendly tribes,[39] in Cyrenaica there was no such compromise.

The most notable feature of the late Roman *Limes* system, as illustrated by the surface remains, is the multiplicity of small, closely-spaced defensive buildings, ranging from official fortresses like Gasr Beni Gdem to small fortified farms and defended churches. The whole province of Libya Pentapolis had become, by the reign of Justinian, a land of castles, and almost every hill-top was surmounted by a fort or tower in visual communication with a score of other towers. In the present state of archaeological exploration it is hardly possible to make an estimate of the number of these structures; but the total must run into several hundreds.

This thick crust of late fortifications naturally obscures the character of the earlier *Limes*, and much excavation will be required before the successive strata of military occupation can be distinguished. For the moment, it can be said that a first-century *Limes* certainly existed in south-western Cyrenaica, covering the approaches from the Syrtic Gulf; and some of the earlier forts on the fringes of the Cyrene plateau may well belong to the same era. We have yet to learn, however, whether the settlement of *limitanei* to increase the official defences, began in Cyrenaica, as it did in Tripolitania, in the third century. We have also to learn whether the simple square fort or tower so frequently encountered in Cyrenaica developed from the similar forts with which the *limes Tripolitanus* was equipped, or had independent origins in the Hellenistic period.[40] It seems, however, clear that this type of military structure, so typical of the Roman frontiers in Libya, was the prototype of the mud-brick towers with which the Coptic monasteries of Egypt were so often provided. The fact that St. Anthony installed himself in an abandoned Roman fort was not without its influence on later monastic architecture in the east.[41]

APPENDIX

INSCRIPTIONS AT ZAUIET MSUS

As already described (above, p. 198) the ashlar facing of the walls at Zauiet Msus is inscribed, in a number of places, with the names of Graeco–Roman soldiers who garrisoned this outpost. The inscriptions vary from rough, hardly legible, graffiti, to reasonably well-cut capitals; but the heavy weathering to which the walls have been exposed makes it difficult to read most of the texts. The following texts and fragments were observed in the course of a brief visit made in August, 1950; a more leisurely examination, in more favourable conditions of light, would doubtless yield further information.[42] The palaeography of the inscriptions is akin to that of the Agedabia inscriptions copied by Ferri (*Rivista della Tripolitania* ii (1926), 363–86 = *SEG* ix, 773–95) and a first-century date is probable. The architecture of the building itself, with its flat lintel doorway, instead of an arch as encountered in the later forts of Cyrenaica, confirms this early dating. As at Agedabia, the letters Ω and Σ are often inscribed in the forms   and C.

On the lintel of the doorway. Irregular letters of 3–6 cm.

1. ᾽Αλέξανδρος Πανταλέ/οντος στρατιώτης

On the walls of the tower

2. Letters: 4 cm.   ᾽Επίγο/νος τεσ/σεράρι[ος]
3. Letters: 7–8 cm.   ΚΑΛΛΙΕΤΙ . . . . .
                          Συμμ[. . . . .
4. Letters: 2–5 cm.   ᾽Ιούλιος ΑΜΛΥ. . . . . . .

On the east wall of the enclosure

5. Well-formed letters of 7 cm.   Δάχις Χαλδαις Ερν[. . .
6. Letters: 4 cm.   Λόκος/ ῾Ηρακλ/ίδα

On the north wall of the enclosure

7. Letters: 5 cm.   ᾽Ανδρόνικος / ῾Ηλιοδώρου
8. Letters: 3–5 cm.   Θεύδωρος Κρίσπο(υ) στρατιώτης

On the west wall of the enclosure

9. Letters: 5–8 cm.   [᾽Ι]ούλιος Τέρτιος ΤΟΡΙ. . . . . .

The only major problem which these fragmentary texts raise relates to no. 1, inscribed over the door-lintel. The prominent position of this text might seem to indicate that Alexander, son of Pantaleon, built this outpost; but the lintel does not give the impression of having been intended to bear an inscription, and it is more probable that this soldier merely selected a conspicuous part of the structure on which to record his stay in this lonely place.

NOTES

1. E. Ritterling, "Military forces in the senatorial provinces", *JRS* xvii (1927), 29. Cf. the inscriptions *SEG* ix, 773–95.

2. *SEG* ix, 9, recording the re-foundation of Cyrene as Claudiopolis by the prefect Probus (= Tenagino Probus, cf. A. Stein, *Die Präfekten von Ägypten* (Berne, 1950), 148–50). It is significant that the latest

imperial dedication hitherto found in the excavated areas of Cyrene is one (unpublished) of Gordian III. The absence of later dedications, especially in the Forum, can only mean that the city never really recovered, despite its "re-foundation". [This view was much modified by subsequent discoveries, see Goodchild, *Kyrene und Apollonia* 45 f.]

3. *AE* 1889, 152; 1934, 7–8. A separate Duchy of the Two Libyas came into existence about 381, following the creation of the Egyptian Diocese. By 470, at the latest, Libya Pentapolis had its own Duke (*Cod. Iust.* XII, 59, 10).

4. For a useful summary of the evidence provided by Synesius, see J. C. Pando. For the chronology of his works, see P. Lacombrade. The military units in the Pentapolis at this time included Arabian cavalry, Dalmatae, Marcomanni, Thracian cavalry, and Unnigardae. [See also below, p. 241 f.].

5. Ammianus, Hist XXVIII, 6. This Austurian invasion, which happens to be recorded in some detail owing to its connection with the scandal of Count Romanus, has perhaps been given undue weight by some modern commentators.

6. An Austurian invasion of Tripolitania at the end of the fourth century is attested by a Lepcis inscription (*IRT* 480): it is probably to be identified with that *coniuratio* of "Saturiani" and "Sub-Afrenses" recorded in *Cod. Theod.* vii, 19, 1. For the invasion of 449, see Priscus Panites, frag. 14, in Müller, *Frag. Hist. Graec.* iv (Paris, 1851), 98.

7. Johannes Antiochenus, frag. 216, in Müller, o.c. iv, 621. E. Stein (105) dates this invasion about 513.

8. P. Romanelli's account (3), (197–205) is topographically incomplete, and misleading in that his map (fig. 17) shows the modern roads, not the ancient ones.

9. The major works are those of J. R. Pacho, F. W. and H. W. Beechey, R. M. Smith and E. A. Porcher, and J. Hamilton. A summary but well-illustrated narrative of the Halbherr expedition of 1910 is published in *Africa Italiana* iv (1930), 229–90.

10. These expeditions, sponsored by the Society of Antiquaries of London, were supported by British universities and learned bodies, including the Roman Society. A preliminary account appeared in *Geogr. Journ.* [see above p. 145 f.]. I am indebted to a number of helpers, including Messrs. M. H. Ballance, J. Eames, D. Smith, D.

Strong, and P. Titchmarsh, for the fort-plans here reproduced.

11. This defensive feature, which also occurs in fifth and sixth-century forts and towers in Syria, is sometimes inaccurately termed a "glacis". The word "talus" is used in this paper. Apart from its strictly military function, it may also have served as a reinforcement against earthquake shocks.

12. See p. 158.

13. See p. 149.

14. The Agedabia inscriptions are to be found in *SEG* ix, 773–95. The Fatimid (?) fort has recently been excavated by Mr. C. N. Johns. [See also the fuller work reported by David Whitehouse *op. cit.* p. 154, n. 2.] For Gasr el-Heneia, see p. 175 f.

15. See p. 173 f.

16. Hamilton, 168.

17. It is curious that this fort at Msus has escaped attention. It was brought to my notice by Dr. W. Hagemann, a former staff officer in the German Afrikakorps.

18. The coastal forts, including the notable example at Gasr el-Mtanneb, near Tocra, were probably constructed or strengthened after the Vandal conquest of the African provinces.

19. Visited by Hamilton (24) but not hitherto planned.

20. They are closely akin to the examples illustrated above, p. 43 fig. 10 and, like those examples, are sited in relation to the cultivable bed of the adjacent wadi.

21. The outlying forts of Gasr Bu Gassal and Gasr Abd el-Crim have yet to be surveyed; but others, such as Gasr Mgiahir (South) and Gasr Mushtashi, seem to be Islamic.

22. Pacho (110) described this fort as "Saracenic", but the only post-classical features are some small chambers built inside its walls. [See p. 251 below for further discussion of the identification.]

23. The name Kuf applies, strictly speaking, only to the upper reaches of the great Jarjarummah valley; but it is usually, and conveniently, used to describe the whole region.

24. O. Mezzetti, 144, describing events in 1927. There does not appear to have been any important ancient road through this difficult and dangerous terrain.

25. First accurately described by Smith and Porcher (22, and pl. 8).A rough sketch-plan appeared in *Bull. Arch. Inst. Amer.* ii (1910), pl. XXXVIII.

26. We are indebted to Mr. Wilkes, of the Cyrenaican Administration, for bringing this site to our notice.

27. In Cyrenaica, unlike Tripolitania (cf. p. 26 above), there is no reason to suppose that vaulting came into vogue owing to lack of timber.

28. El-Bekri, 13, referring to the "Wadi Makhil". His description leaves no reasonable doubt that this is Mechili.

29. Procopius, *De aedif.* VI, 2, 2. The fort was described as "Saracen" by nineteenth-century travellers. Its remains, exposed by war-time bombing, have recently been studied by Mr. Christopher Musgrave. [For a brief account and a plan see Goodchild, "Fortificazioni", 237 f.]

30. Justinian (*Edict XIII, De dioecesi Aegyptiaca,* ed. Zacharias von Lingenthal, Leipzig, 1891) allocated two regular units (*numeri*) to a "Duke of the Libyan *limes*" stationed at Paraetonium (Marsa Matruh). The view (cf. Romanelli, (3), 171) that this Duke also defended the Pentapolis is difficult to accept.

31. Pacho, 120. His "Kasr Chendireh" (pl. XI, 3) is clearly a Christian church.

32. The fact that one encounters buildings of this type at intervals along the modern highways of Cyrenaica is purely accidental. They are so common that they occur on almost any route one may choose to follow in the Pentapolis.

33. The exact date of these walls is still uncertain, as Hellenistic and early Roman masonry cannot easily be distinguished in Cyrenaica. The Acropolis of Cyrene was, however, restored by Q. Lucanius Proculus, proconsul, in the reign of Augustus: *Doc. Ant. Afr. Ital.* i, 2, 181, no. 49.

34. The excavation of the [Caesareum] is still unpublished; and the partition walls comprising the inner arrangements of this fortress have been cleared away. [The text originally read "fifth"—for Goodchild's later view on the date see p. 239 below and *Kyrene und Apollonia,* 44.]

35. Observations by the writer. Only a few traces of the later wall-circuit still re-main. [See also p. 246 f.; but writing in 1966 (in "Fortificazioni", 235) Goodchild noted that the Chicago expedition (Kraeling, *Ptolemais*) had found no clear evidence for construction of a new circuit wall after the dismantling of the Hellenistic Roman one.]

36. *SEG* ix, 356; translation and commentary by Oliverio in *Doc. Ant. Afr. Ital.* ii, 2, 135–63. Since a fragment of the same text has been found at Tocra, there is no reason to assume that Ptolemais was still, under Anastasius, the military headquarters of the province. [Still more significant is the copy, carefully cut on marble, found at Apollonia, F. Chamoux, *CRAI* 1955, 333 f.]

[36a. Excavation in 1971–2 shows that a defensive wall was built hurriedly in the mid-third century, see T. W. T. Tatton Brown, *Third Annual Report of the Society for Libyan Studies* (1971–2) 11.]

37. J. Honigmann, 47 and 61.

38. See p. 187 f.

39. [See above, p. 56.]

40. It is unfortunate that, superficially at least, inscriptions are completely lacking in these Cyrenaican forts of the interior. Excavations at a type-site like Gasr el-Heneia are greatly to be desired.

41. U. Monneret de Villard, *Deyr el-Muharraqah* (Milan, 1928), 31–5. While admitting that these Coptic towers derive from fortifications on the Roman *Limes*, Monneret de Villard seeks an eastern origin, claiming that Roman architects did not construct towers divided into rooms at each floor-level. Such towers were certainly being built in the third century on the African frontiers (cf. the case of Gasr Duib), and may well have been adapted from the simpler watch-towers of the European frontiers.

[42. Expeditions made in 1969 and 1970 did in fact obtain more texts, see J. M. Reynolds in a forthcoming volume of *Libya Antiqua.*]

16

THE FORUM OF PTOLEMAIS (CYRENAICA)

[From *Quaderni di Archeologia della Libia* v (1967)]

The outline of the street-plan of ancient *Ptolemais* (Tolmeita in Cyrenaica, Libya), is now well known, thanks to the excavations of Caputo in 1935–42[1] and to the surveys of Kraeling in 1956–8.[2] It is a plan of remarkable regularity, indicating that the whole area of the ancient city was laid out at the time of its foundation, towards the middle of the third century B.C.

The major public monuments of the Hellenistic and Roman city have remained more elusive, largely—no doubt—because of the extensive demolitions that were carried out in late antiquity, in order to provide building materials for a series of massive Byzantine fortresses. Dismantled column drums from the earlier monuments form late enclosure walls on many parts of the site, and the bases to which these belonged lie buried beneath rubble and plough soil.

The site of the principal Agora or Forum has hitherto remained undetected. Halbherr,[3] it is true, interpreted as an Agora the spacious mosaic-paved platform, surrounded by porticoes, overlying the largest group of cisterns in the ancient city; and Caputo, identifying this monument as of Roman date, changed its designation to "Forum". Kraeling's team from Chicago Oriental Institute have re-named this monument "The Square of the Cisterns", rejecting any function as a major civic centre.[4]

Kraeling, summarising the existing state of knowledge of the city's topography, has stated: "What is needed above all is the discovery and excavation of the agora of Ptolemais and its surrounding buildings", and has suggested a site near the harbour. "Whether Ptolemais or any other Greek city ever had a forum is questionable."[5]

Certainly an early commercial Agora might be sought near the harbour—although there are absolutely no surface remains to guide such a search—but by the Roman period there must have been a civic centre situated more centrally within the city walls. In a city where bi-lingualism was very marked, this civic centre might well have been officially designated a "Forum" (as at Roman Antioch and other cities of Hellenistic origin) although referred to more commonly as an Agora by the Greek-speaking citizens. Synesius, in fact, refers to it by the latter name, in accordance with his normal literary tendency to avoid non-Greek words wherever possible.[6]

For the existence of such a Forum at Ptolemais there is, indeed, epigraphic evidence, hitherto unpublished. The Ptolemais Museum contains, amongst other objects discovered during the pre-war Italian excavations, three fragments of a Latin inscription cut, in letters of 1 cm. height, on a soft limestone slab. These

Fig. 66

(fig. 66) evidently belonged to a copy of an emperor's or governor's letter, the subject-matter of which cannot easily be conjectured.

The major fragment (A), which measures 29 by 18 by 3 cm., contains traces of nine lines of text, which may be transcribed as follows:

(A)

... i]nstrum[ent ...
... as nostrarum ...
... pr]oprium negotium ...
... ut inspiciant et fidem ...
... s de is quae adversus ...
... int huius epistulae in foro ...
... tionibus claris litteris ...
... rum quotien[s ...
... s in po ...

Two minor fragments, B and C, clearly from the same text, but not contiguous with the major fragment, read as follows:

(B)

> ... EXV inplic ...
> ... ientes di ...
> ... IOTOP ...

(C)

> ... RVMVS ...
> ... m de eo ...
> ... qu ...

The major fragment, which alone concerns us here, appears to contain the concluding section of the letter, ordering its display "in clear letters" in the Forum of the city. Instructions of this kind for the public display of new legislation are not unparalleled[7] and as we do not know whether the letter was addressed exclusively to Ptolemais, or whether it was sent to a regional authority, we cannot be sure that the writer was specifically aware of the existence and the location of a Forum at Ptolemais.

What we can be sure of, however, is that the document would have been displayed in the principal public square of Ptolemais, whether it was locally named Agora or Forum; and, therefore, the precise find-spot of this inscription must be considered as the principal clue to the location of that public square.

At first, inquiries made by the present writer failed to reveal the find-spot of this "Forum" inscription. A photograph of the major fragment taken at Tolmeita before 1942 gave no indication of provenance. Nor could my friend, Professor Giacomo Caputo, provide an immediate answer when I showed him the stone in December, 1964.

In February, 1965, however, he wrote to me confirming that while he had not himself previously seen the inscription, it might have been the one referred to in a manuscript report (relazione di scavo) written by the assistente G. Torelli who was the foreman in charge of the excavations at Ptolemais in July, 1937. Caputo generously enclosed a copy.[8]

This report, describing the excavations of the small theatre (so-called "Odeon") referred first (on 1 July 1937) to the colonnade on the western side of the Odeon, which fronted the principal Cardo of the street-plan, and has a water conduit of terracotta pipes running along its length. Later (on 3 July 1937) it stated:

"In the same (portico) fronting the theatre, inside the portico immediately adjoining the southern angle column, 30 centimetres below ground level, were found various fragments of sculpture and a fragment of a limestone slab broken into two pieces and bearing nine lines of an inscription in latin. The dimensions of the letters are one centimetre square."[9]

Although there is no transcription of the text in this report, and no mention of the dimensions of the fragment itself, the description is sufficient to leave no doubt that this is the stone with which we are here concerned. Latin texts inscribed in small letters on local limestone are rare at Ptolemais, and *this is the only one containing nine lines and broken into two pieces.*

It therefore follows that our text referring to the Forum of Ptolemais was found at the southern end of the portico that fronts the Odeon on the west; and as the inscribed stone is fragmentary and of a soft material having no value for building purposes, it is unlikely to have travelled far from the place where it was originally set up.

The portico in which it was found is structurally part of the Odeon, and we should not seek the Forum on this western side of the monument. But on the north side of the Odeon, only 30 m. distant, there are visible the bases of a series of widely-spaced, fluted, columns, of 80 cm. diameter. These, as the present writer stated in his published description of the Odeon following its complete excavation in 1955,[10] are "too distant from the Odeon to have any direct structural relationship," and seemed to mark a colonnaded street or piazza lying north of the Odeon. But as the now well-known street-plan of the city does not allow for a major street in this direction, a public square would be the more likely solution.

Following up the important clue thus provided by Professor Caputo's information of the provenance of the "Forum" inscription, the writer arranged, in the autumn of 1965, for a series of soundings to be made to ascertain the extent of the portico on the north side of the Odeon.[11]

The area previously excavated contained the emplacements of five columns (one completely missing) at intervals of 5·10 m. (centre to centre). Soundings dug at this same interval eastwards brought to light the bases, or sub-bases of eight additional columns, of which the easternmost lay 5·20 m. within a well-built wall running south to north, marking the edge of an insula of the town plan. This same wall supported, in late antiquity, an aqueduct supplying water to the Byzantine Baths, situated in the "Street of the Monuments".

As the colonnade clearly did not extend further eastward, a further series of soundings were made in a northerly direction, at the same intervals, and at the same distance from the enclosing east wall. Once again, bases were found, this time of smooth, unfluted columns, of 80 cm diameter. Seven full columns were found, north of the terminal column of the southern colonnade, and north of these, at the same interval, was found a half-column, indicating the presence of a structure projecting westward from the colonnade.

We thus have, on the south side of the public square, twelve intercolumniations of 5·10 m. each, giving a minimum length of 61 m.; and on the east side eight intercolumniations representing 41 m. Assuming that the structure represented by the terminal half-column occupied the middle of the eastern portico, the total length must have been considerably more than double this extent, some 90 m. at least (fig. 67).

Within the eastern part of this large enclosure there are some massive concrete remains, perhaps representing substructures of a temple podium; but without excavation, it is not possible to indicate them on the map.

It is clear, then, that within 30 m. of the find-spot of an inscription nominating the Forum of Ptolemais, we have a large colonnaded square measuring some 60 by 100 m., flanked by major streets on two sides, and situated in the very centre of the city. It could, conceivably, have been the temenos of a large temple; but it seems far more probable that it is the Roman-period Forum of Ptolemais; and as the basic topography of the city remained little changed between Hellenistic and Roman times, it may mark the site of the Hellenistic Agora.

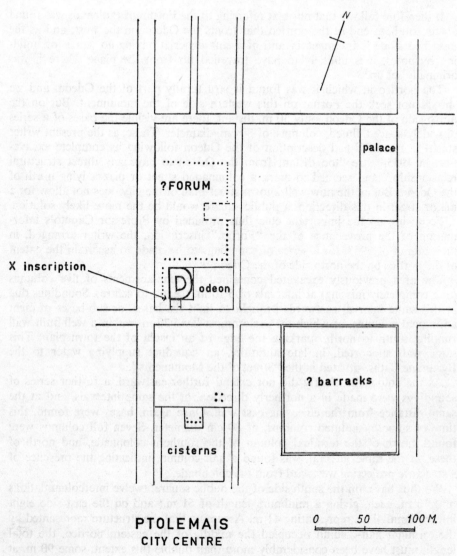

PTOLEMAIS
CITY CENTRE

Fig. 67

More than this we cannot say, until excavations have been carried out in this area, which obviously should attract the attentions of future excavators at Ptolemais. If it is, in fact, the Forum there may come to light in this area important documents regarding the municipal life of the city, still too-little known. Whatever future investigation may reveal, it is now more than ever evident that major public monuments of Ptolemais—hardly distinguishable by surface indications—lie buried beneath the soil. They should tell us much of the development of Hellenistic and Roman architecture within the cultural orbit of Alexandria.

NOTES

1. G. Caputo, 33–66.
2. C. H. Kraeling, *Ptolemais, city of the Libyan Pentapolis.*
3. G. Oliverio, "Federico Halbherr in Cirenaica", *Africa Italiana* iv (1931) 229–89.
4. Kraeling, 62. It must be borne in mind, however, that the cisterns may have been inserted into a pre-existing building. The whole monument requires closer investigation.
5. *Ibid.* 115–16.
6. Synesius, *Epist.* 3 and 57. Letter 57 refers to a "Royal portico" (τὴν στοὰν τὴν βασιλείαν) which served as a law-court, and therefore may have been a civil basilica, adjoining the Forum.
7. M. W. Frederiksen, *JRS* lv (1965), 184.
8. All recent workers at Ptolemais have cause to be grateful to Professor Caputo for the liberal supply of information derived from his pioneer excavations there.
9. Translated from the Italian.
10. Kraeling, 90.
11. The work was directed by Ess. Abdussalam Bazama, the site supervisor at Tolmeita.

17

THE DECLINE OF CYRENE AND RISE OF PTOLEMAIS: TWO NEW INSCRIPTIONS

[From *Quaderni di Archeologia della Libia* iv (1961)]
Plates 77–9

The literary sources for the history of Roman Cyrenaica are very scanty, and for the period between the Jewish Revolt of A.D. 115 and the Austurian Invasion of *c.* A.D. 390, we must rely largely on epigraphic and archaeological material. Between these two events Cyrene ceased to be capital of the province and was replaced by Ptolemais, where Synesius later took up residence as metropolitan Bishop of the Pentapolis.

The two inscriptions published here for the first time do not close this gap in history, but they may help to bridge it. They indicate that the shift of administrative centre from Cyrene to Ptolemais was neither a consequence of the Jewish Revolt nor a reflection of events in the fourth century. In Cyrenaica, as throughout most of the Roman Empire, it was the third century A.D. which had the most profound effects on the administrative and social order, and the policies crystallised in the reforms of Diocletian often had their origin at an earlier date. We can only hope that continued excavation in all the ancient centres of the Pentapolis may eventually elucidate the course of events during that crucial but elusive third century.

That I am able to publish these two inscriptions together is due to the generosity of my friend and colleague Prof. Giacomo Caputo, the first excavator at Ptolemais, and discoverer of the Triumphal Arch to which our second inscription belongs. Thus the present paper, although it does not bear his name, is no less a fruit of a happy collaboration which began in Tripoli in 1946. I must also express my gratitude to Prof. Pietro Romanelli for his invitation to contribute, a second time, to these "*Quaderni*"; and to Miss Joyce Reynolds for her advice on various epigraphical problems arising from the texts here discussed.

A DEDICATION TO COMMODUS BY CYRENE, "METROPOLIS OF THE HEXAPOLIS"

When large-scale excavations of Cyrene were resumed in 1954 by the Department of Antiquities, it was decided to concentrate on the "Valley Street" or principal *decumanus* of the Roman city which ran from the East Gate of Cyrene down to the North (or Apollonia) gate adjoining the Sanctuary of Apollo. This decision was motivated partly by a desire to increase our topographical knowledge of ancient Cyrene, and principally by the necessity of impeding any further develop-

ment of the modern village of Shahat which sits astride the centre of the archaeological zone.[1]

The Severan Market and Late Roman Theatre were excavated in 1954–5, and
the large Christian Basilica or "Cathedral" in 1955–6. In 1956 work was transferred to the central part of the valley, between the modern Post Office [now a
Youth Club] and the "Casa Parisi" antiquarium, where it is still in progress. A
continuous sector of some 200 m. of the "Valley Street" has now been cleared,
together with its paved sidewalks and the buildings on either side.

Prior to 1956 the only monument visible in this area was the "Grande Ginnasio," so called because a Hadrianic inscription referring to the city's gymnasium had come to light during soundings made in 1930. In 1933 the late Prof.
Gaspare Oliverio re-erected six marble columns of the facade of the "Ginnasio"
without, however, establishing the building's character or topographical
situation.

The new excavations have so far only exposed the frontage of the "Ginnasio"
(Building E on plan, fig 68), and have shown that the columns belong to a late (?
fifth-century A.D.) reconstruction. The exact character of the edifice in both its
earlier and later phases has still to be determined; but it may be noted that its
identification is still entirely conjectural, the inscription itself being a copy of an
imperial letter[2] in which the gymnasium is only incidentally mentioned, and the
stone being reused in a late pavement. The principal gymnasium of Cyrene was
certainly situated elsewhere, near the Caesareum.[2a]

On the south side of the Valley Street, immediately opposite Building E, three
adjoining temples occupy the whole frontage of an *insula*. The flanking temples
(A and C) are of orthodox plan, with pronaos and cella: Temple A cannot be
completely excavated owing to an adjacent modern house, but it is evident that

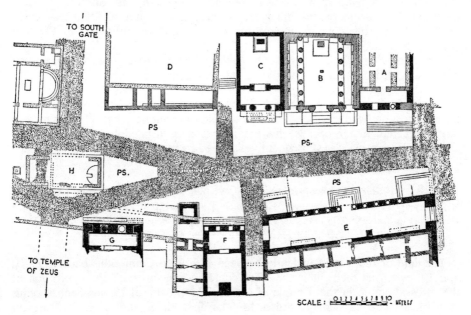

Fig. 68 Cyrene: plan of Valley Street excavation

it was extensively remodelled in Byzantine times to serve some secular function, and of its original arrangements little is visible. Temple C was fully dismantled and purified by fire[3] at the end of the fourth century A.D.; but its large base for the cult-statue is remarkable for having a series of water-channels cut into it. We therefore believe that it was dedicated to the nymph Kurana, and that the cult-statue was in the form of a fountain, the water emerging from the mouth of the lion being strangled by the nymph. An aqueduct ran at a high level behind the temple, and part of a life-size statue of Kurana and the lion was found in the street nearby.[4]

We are, however, concerned here with the central temple, B, which—like C—had been dismantled and burned out by the early Christians. It is obviously later than the two flanking shrines, and is of "basilical" plan having two internal rows of five columns with capitals of Pergamene type. The large base for the cult-statue stood close against the back wall, and was flanked by two smaller bases for minor statues. The latter were of imperial personages, heads and torso fragments being found of statues of Trajan and Hadrian.[5]

The statue that stood on the central base has perished, but as the inscription fixed to this base refers to the emperor Commodus in the accusative, it seems likely that this ruler was represented, perhaps in his favourite role of Hercules. Fragments of a colossal Hercules statue have in fact been found in the vicinity though it cannot be proved that they came from this shrine.

The inscription was found lying face downwards in front of the base from which it had fallen. It was broken into small fragments and damaged by burning. Although the greater part of the text was found in this manner, it seems that the inscription was not complete when it fell; and indeed part of its right-hand end was subsequently identified among the epigraphic fragments preserved in Cyrene Museum, and derived from pre-war excavations. Where these additional pieces were found is not on record, but it may be suggested tentatively that they came to light during the construction of the nearby modern buildings, in the first years of the Italian occupation.

The inscription (pls. 77–9) was cut on three contiguous plaques 4–5 cm. thick with roughened backs, and when complete measured 3 by 0·35 m. The letters are 4–5 cm. high and rubricated: stops between letters are painted with the exception of the ivy-leaf at the end of line 1. Parts of the name and titles of Commodus have been superficially erased, after his *damnatio memoriae*, but this erasure was not completed, either because his memory was re-instated by Severus, or because the inscription was subsequently plastered over.

The text reads:

Αὐτοκράτορα Κα[ίσα]ρα Λούκιο[ν Αἴλιον Αὐρ]ήλιον Κ[όμμοδ]ον Εὐ[σ]εβῆ] Εὐτυχῆ Σεβ[α]στὸ[ν Σ]αρματικὸ[ν Γερμανικὸν] μέγισ[τον Βρε]ταννικὸν | τὸν Σωτῆ[ρα] καὶ Εὐεργέταν ἁ π[όλις ἁ Κυρανάων] ἁ μα[τρόπολι]ς τᾶς Ἑξα | πόλιος [ἁ]φιερώσαντος Λ(ουκίω) Σεμ[πρ]ωνίω [. . . c. 13 . . . τ]ῷ κρατίστω | ἀνθυπάτω (v.) Ἐπ'ἀγαθῷ [?τῷ κυρίω] (v.)

The date of the text is evidently between 185 when Commodus became *Felix*, and 192 when he died: it is therefore contemporaneous with the dedication of the colossal statue in the Temple of Zeus.[6] The proconsul Lucius Sem[pr]onius (cognomen lost) is here recorded for the first time, and is not at present identifiable.

The extensive restorations to religious buildings carried out at Cyrene in the reigns of Marcus Aurelius and Commodus are already attested both in the Temple of Zeus and in the Sanctuary of Apollo.[7] Some of this work represented the making good of damage suffered during the Jewish Revolt, but we need not doubt that new temples were also being constructed, and our Temple B has every appearance of being a creation of the Commodan era: its "Pergamene" capitals anticipate those which occur so lavishly in the Severan buildings of Lepcis Magna.

The main interest, however, of the Commodan inscription from the statue-base of temple B is its description of Cyrene as ἁ μα[τρόπολι]ς τᾶς Ἑξαπόλιος. Cyrene acquired the title *metropolis* either at the end of Hadrian's reign, or under the Antonine emperors,[8] and in recent years numerous examples of its use have been found in inscriptions of the later second century.

The expression Ἑξάπολις has first appeared in a dated context in our Commodan inscription, although Miss Joyce Reynolds has convincingly restored it in a damaged text of Marcus Aurelius and Lucius Verus (c.A.D. 165–6) recording the construction of the great public cisterns at Cyrene.[9] The word does, however, appear in the form [Ἑ]ξαπόλεως in [a damaged] context in the margin of an inscribed mosaic in the pronaos of the "Temple of Jason Magnus" in the Sanctuary.[9a] This inscription, itself probably Commodan, refers to work carried out by Marcus Aurelius Euphranor, a priest of Apollo.

In the first century A.D. the five cities constituting the Cyrenaican Pentapolis were Berenice, Tauchira, Barka-Ptolemais,[10] Cyrene and Apollonia. Therefore unless Barka and Ptolemais were subsequently each given separate status, which is most improbable,[11] the new name "Hexapolis" must have been coined in recognition of the creation of the new city Hadrianopolis, situated on the coast between Berenice and Tauchira.

Of this city we know little except the bare fact of its existence, as attested by the road-itineraries of the second–third centuries, and the Byzantine city-lists of the sixth century.[12] It is reasonable to suppose that its creation resulted from the influx of new settlers (including veterans) after the Jewish Revolt;[13] and it may be significant that it was sited midway between Berenice and Tauchira, both of which had large Jewish populations.[14] Thus Hadrian may have intended that it should be a centre of Hellenism in those parts of the Pentapolis where Jewish influence was strongest.

How Hadrianopolis fared in later years is not known. Its survival down to the Arab invasions is proved by the Byzantine town-lists, but it is remarkable that so few archaeological traces have remained.[15] We do not obtain the impression of a successful and highly-developed settlement. Certainly, by the age of Diocletian the name Pentapolis had returned into currency and we hear nothing more of a Hexapolis.

INSCRIPTIONS ON THE TRIUMPHAL ARCH IN THE
"VIA MONUMENTALE" OF PTOLEMAIS

The excavations initiated on the site of ancient Ptolemais by Prof. Giacomo Caputo in 1935 brought to light some 200 m. of a major *decumanus* together with adjacent edifices of such character as to justify the name "Via Monumentale" given to this street.[16] It is evident that the thoroughfare was particularly important in the later centuries of the city's life, and the inscriptions found along its course fall mainly in the period Diocletian-Anastasius.[17]

At the western end of this *decumanus*, and at the point where it was crossed by a *cardo* running northwards from the so-called "Forum" [now called "Square of the Cisterns", see p. 210] towards the sea, stood a Triumphal Arch with three portals (fig. 69). This arch had evidently been stripped down to its lowest courses by the Byzantine stone-seekers who were so active throughout Ptolemais; but although only the bases of the four piers remained *in situ*, the fallen architectural elements were sufficient to permit a graphical reconstruction in the main features of which we may have complete confidence.[18] The use of spirally-fluted columns set into the corners of the piers is an unusual feature, and reminds one of the Arch of Theodosius at Constantinople.[19]

A few surviving blocks from the attic of the Arch bear remains of a Latin inscription of monumental character, although rather irregularly incised. This inscription, to which we shall refer again later, lacks the names of the emperors and of the *praeses* who dedicated it, and is therefore of little assistance in establishing the date of the Arch. More informative, although not without their own perplexities, are a series of marble plaques found by Caputo among the debris of the monument and in its vicinity.

These plaques represent an inscription which must have run across a large part of the Arch's facade. The plaques were uniformly 63 cm. high, but of differing lengths and thicknesses: on all of them are incised setting-out lines for

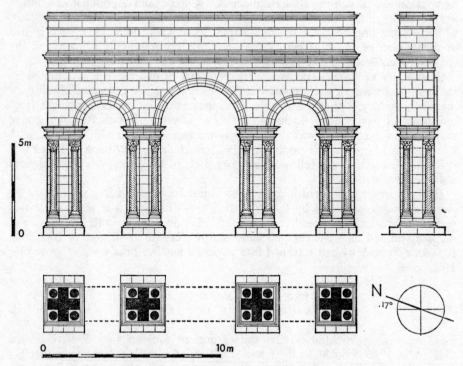

Fig. 69 Ptolemais: reconstruction of the Triumphal Arch
[redrawn by Miss S. Gibson from the design of Luigi Turba]

four lines of text, each line being 9–9½ cm. high. The total length of the inscription could have been as much as 15 m.; but epigraphic considerations suggest that it was shorter—perhaps in the neighbourhood of 10 m.

All the marble plaques had been broken into small fragments, and it is evident that the greater part of the original text is missing. During the excavations of 1935 the major fragments were brought to the Museum and pieced together under Caputo's direction; but during the disturbances of 1941 these restorations were again broken. Fortunately the actual losses were slight, and from comparison with notes kindly supplied by Caputo, only one letter seen in 1935 seems now to be lost. By measure of compensation a number of additional letters have been identified in the course of recent studies; and, in consequence, it is now possible to give a closer analysis of the inscription's content.

The plaques represent two inscriptions, and three texts (fig. 70). The principal text which we may call Text B, was later modified by the cancellation of certain imperial names, and the substitution of other words, thereby producing Text C. Texts B and C are, of course, on the same side of the inscribed plaques; but three of the latter also bear, *on their reverse faces*, remains of another inscription which we propose to call Text A. This, as I hope to demonstrate, is in fact a preliminary draft of Text B, rejected either because of its poor draughtsmanship, or for other reasons not immediately apparent.

Text A can be distinguished from B-C not only by its more irregular letters, but also by the vividness of the rubrication still surviving on it. This shows that the text was not long, if at all, exposed to the weather. In Texts B-C on the other hand, the rubrication is very faint, and the whole face of the marble considerably weathered. We may therefore suppose that Text B, modified into C, remained on the Arch until its ruin.

Text B

The principal fragment (B.1) measures 125 by 63 cm, and is approximately 10 mm. thick. The following features must here be noted:

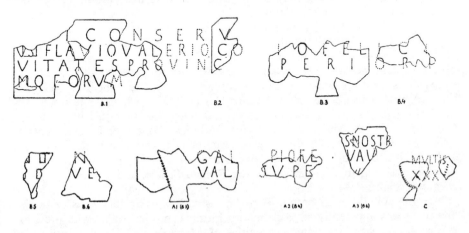

Fig. 70 Ptolemais: inscriptions from Triumphal Arch

Line 1: Following the letters ... ICO was an N read by Caputo in 1935, but now lost: the wide spacing of the letters in this first line is noteworthy. I propose to restore here not an affiliation, such as *Diu]i Con[stantii*, but rather an opening acclamation of the type much in favour in fourth-century epigraphy, such as *Liberatoribus orbis Roman]i con[seruatoribus rei. p.* etc.[20] At this late date, the affiliation normally follows rather than precedes the emperor's own name.[21]

Line 2: The first two letters ... VS are re-cut over an erased two-letter word, which is completely illegible but most likely to have been ET.

Line 3: The *ci]uitates pro[uinciae* are evidently the dedicators of this text.

Line 4: This is the common formula [*deuotae n(umini)*] *m(aiestati)q(ue) eorum*, and shows that more than one emperor was named.

For the name of the surviving emperor, and of the province whose cities thus honoured him, we must seek the aid of other fragments. Fragment *B.2* is small, but the single letters of its first and third line accord so well with the restorations previously proposed (i.e. *conseruatoribus* and *prouinciae*) that we are surely justified in reading the ... CO ... of its second line as referring to either Constantius I or Constantine the Great, both of whom were *Flauii Valerii*.

Fragments *B.3* and *B.4*, taken together, give us [*p]io felici* in the second line and *su]periori[s* in the third: thus the emperor was an *augustus*, and the cities were of the *pro[uinciae Libuae Su]perioris*. Now we have already seen that the part of the second line immediately preceding the name of the surviving emperor has been erased and reinscribed with a word terminating in ... *VS*. This can only mean that in Text *B* another emperor was named before *Flauius Valerius* ..., and that his name was later cancelled and replaced by an extension of the opening acclamatory formula, ending perhaps in [*imperatorib]us*.

The fragments that survive from the left-hand part of the inscription are small and discontinuous yielding no sequences of letters; only one (fragment *B.5*) is worthy of reproduction here because it reveals erasures in both the second and third lines, with re-cutting only in the case of the former. From this we may further deduce that two imperial names have suffered a *damnatio memoriae*, one of which preceded *Flauius Valerius* ..., and the other followed.

Now in the confused years that intervened between the disintegration of Diocletian's "Tetrarchy" and the emergence of Constantine the Great as sole ruler of the Roman world, there seems to be only one brief period during which a Constantius or Constantine occupied second place in an imperial college of three *augusti*. This period was the years 311–13, during which we normally find these three *augusti* listed, on milestones and other inscriptions,[22] in the order: Galerius Valerius Maximinus, Flavius Valerius Constantinus and Valerius Licinianus Licinius. Maximin II (Daia) was, in fact, junior to both Constantine and Licinius, but he is known to have usurped the senior rank. This was later formally assigned to Constantine by the Roman Senate, and was acknowledged even by Licinius.[23]

Interpreted in this manner, our Text *B* presents few major difficulties. In the first line there was apparently an acclamatory formula, not restorable with precision; in the second were the names and titles of Maximin and Constantine; and in the third the name of Licinius followed by the identification of the dedicators, the cities of Libya Superior. The right-hand third of the bottom line following the formula of devotion was vacant; but it is not possible to say whether the left-hand third of the same line was equally blank. To the right-hand part of the text I would provisionally assign a further, rather enigmatic, fragment (*B.6*) which has the letters .. VE.. in its third line: this might conceivably be part of *uel Pentapoleos*, following the provincial name.[24]

The name of Maximin was obliterated after he had been defeated at the battle of Adrianople in 313, the erasure being covered by an expansion of the opening acclamations; so that Constantine now had the first place. The name of Licinius would have remained untouched until his removal from office in 323, after which it was cancelled without any replacement. The inscription, in its mutilated condition, remained on the Triumphal Arch as a mute witness to Constantine's struggle for unchallenged power.

Text A

We must now consider the earliest text, *A*. which is represented only by three major fragments preserved on the reverses of *B.3*, *B.4* and *B.6*. The largest fragment, *A.1* (on *B.3*), is from the left-hand edge of the inscription, as shown by the palm-branch in its left margin. The names GAL ... and VAL ... mark the beginning of lines 2 and 3. In fragment *A.3* (on *B.6*) the letters are more closely spaced; but I think this is merely because the lapicide was approaching the right-hand end of the text. *Domini]s nostr[is*[25] presumably followed after an acclamatory formula of the same type as in Text B; and *in]u(icto) au[g(usto)* followed the name and titles of an emperor. In fragment *A.2* (on *B.4*) we have these titles *pio fe[lici]*, and under them, in the third line, *supe[rioris]*.

The latter item shows us that we are dealing with a text of the same character as Text *B*, namely a dedication to emperors by the cities of Libya Superior; and at first thought, one might seek to identify a group of emperors who were in office before 311–13, and whose inscription was removed from the Arch to make way for that of Maximin, Constantine and Licinius. But on further consideration, it seems certain that Text *A* is, to all intents and purposes, a duplicate of Text *B*— in short, a first draft that was later rejected. For the GAL ... and VAL ... at the beginning of its second and third lines can hardly be other than Galerius Valerius Maximinus and Valerius Licinius Licinianus, the same colleagues of Constantine in 311–13.

It is not difficult to see why this first draft should have been rejected. The letters are badly formed and irregularly spaced, and the whole lay-out would have looked very shoddy on a Triumphal Arch which was, architecturally, quite competently constructed. The fact that the letters are rubricated seems to suggest that the rejection took place after the inscription had been put in place—or, at least, while it was being erected. The new text (*B*) that replaced it may not seem of high calligraphic standard; but at least it was a substantial improvement.

It may now be useful to set out the presumed text of the inscription, using the elements provided by both *A* and *B*: the former are here italicised, the latter in capitals, missing parts being shown in small type. It must be stressed, however, that this composite reconstruction may be partly misleading: in particular, the opening formula could have been changed when A was rejected in favour of B.

?liberatoribus orbis romanI CONserVatoribus ... dominiS *NOSTRis/GALerio ualerio maximino pio felici inv. aug.* et FLAVIO VALerio COnstantino pIO

FELICI in*V. AVg.* et/*VAL*erio liciniano licinio pio felici inv. aug. ciVITATES
PROuinciae libuae SVPERIORIs . . / . . . . . . ? ? . . . . deuotae n M Q EORVM

In our present state of knowledge Text *C* cannot usefully be set out in the
same manner. The first line presumably remained unchanged from that of *B*,
and acclamatory additions were made in the first half of the second line in place
of the name of Maximin. The first half of the third line was completely obliterated and nothing added in its place: the second half of the third and all of the
fourth line remained unchanged.

We should also consider two additional fragments which whilst of slightly
different character,[26] seem to belong to the same group of texts. Together they
constitute a circular wreath containing the words:

MV[lt]IS
XX[x]

This is clearly a reference to the future *tricennalia* of an emperor, and would
probably have been accompanied by a similar roundel inscribed *uotis xx.*
Numismatic studies have shown that the pious hopes for a thirty-year reign could
be expressed even before twenty years had been completed.[27] On the other hand,
an emperor should have completed more than ten years, if not fifteen, before
his subjects looked ahead to the *tricennalia.* Now in 311–13 none of the three
augusti of our Triumphal Arch inscription had completed ten years; and I therefore suggest that this roundel may have been added to the Arch in 323, when
Constantine had completed seventeen years' rule, and at the same time that the
name of Licinius was erased. Constantine's Arch at Rome had already set a pre-
cedent for the display of such vows.

Finally, we must speak of the inscription that was carved on the sandstone
masonry of the Arch itself, probably in the attic. Caputo found seven inscribed
blocks, some of which are clearly adjoining, thus giving us four fragments of the
text. The latter was long and probably extended across most of the front of
the Arch: that it was in two (or more) lines is shown by the fact that some blocks
have a simple cornice and belong to the first line, whilst others are on plain
blocks and must have stood below. The letters are very irregularly cut and also
rubricated: they average 20 cm. in height.

(*a*) *From the upper line*:

1. . . .]num uic[t]ores ac triumfatores semper A[ugusti . . .
2. . . .]ius u(ir) p(erfectissimus) praeses statuit e[t . . .

(*b*) *From a lower line*:

3. . . .]eorum semper[. . .
4. . . .]imum dedic[auit . . .

Clearly, very little can be gleaned from these fragments which represent only
a small proportion of the former text. The palaeography and the imperial title
uictores et triumfatores alike indicate a fourth-century date, but it is hardly possible to be more precise. Whether the text refers to the construction of the Arch,

or to its later embellishment with statues or other new features, it is hardly possible to judge. We can only await future excavations in the area, which might possibly bring to light additional inscribed blocks.[27a]

CONCLUSIONS

As has already been suggested at the beginning of this paper, the key to the later developments in Roman Cyrenaica must lie in the poorly-recorded events of the third century A.D. Under Commodus, as we have seen, Cyrene was still the "Metropolis of the Hexapolis", enjoying unchallenged supremacy in the province. It seems reasonably sure that this situation remained unchanged under the dynasty of Severus: the great Propylon erected in the Valley-Street of Cyrene in honour of Severus, "benefactor of the whole world", is surely the homage paid by a provincial capital, even though the accompanying inscription is [incomplete].[28]

An inscribed base of *c.* A.D. 209–11 recently found in the Valley Street records the devotion of the prefect of the Macedonian Cohort (then stationed at Cyrene) to Caius Pomponius Cordius, a *procurator Augustorum* who is also described as *praeses*: this latter title may be purely honorific, or it may indicate an interim governor of the province.

The same Cohort figures again in an unpublished dedication to Gordian III found in the Agora area of Cyrene during the pre-war Italian excavations. Whether this cohort was permanently stationed in Cyrene after the Jewish Revolt has still to be determined, but it seems probable that the Cyrenaican garrison was reformed and strengthened after that unhappy event.

A milestone of the emperor Philip (244–9) found in 1959 at El-Beida, on the Roman highway between Cyrene and the Sanctuary of Aesculapius at Balagrae, shows that the roads of the upper plateau continued to be maintained: it gives the distance figure A CYRENIS X.

The last relevant Cyrenean text, before the age of Diocletian, is the well-known inscription of the reign of Claudius Gothicus (268–70) recording the campaigns of Tenagino Probus against the Marmaridae, and the foundation of the city named "Claudiopolis". It is hardly to be doubted that this name refers to Cyrene itself which, either through gradual economic decay or in direct consequence of barbaric invasion, needed re-foundation.[29] The new name was, however, to be ephemeral; we do not hear of it again.

Diocletian is recorded at Cyrene[30] but only in modest texts which do not reveal the city's status. At Ptolemais, on the other hand, we find the only known Cyrenaican copy of that emperor's Price-Edict, and also a Triumphal Arch dedicated to Maximinus, Constantine and Licinius by the cities of the Province of Libya Superior. Such a dedication would only be appropriate in the provincial capital, and if Ptolemais was the capital by A.D. 311–13, it can hardly be doubted that it had assumed this status at the time of the Diocletianic administrative reforms in Egypt and the adjoining lands (A.D. 297).

These are the facts, as at present known; but their explanation is still elusive. The episode of "Claudiopolis" seems to show that Cyrene was, under Claudius Gothicus, in such a bad way as to need official help. On the other hand there is little evidence to show that Ptolemais was particularly flourishing in the same period. It had been a somewhat artificial creation of the Ptolemies, with a very inferior harbour, and dependent on aqueducts for its water-supply. Part of the area within its over-extensive wall-circuit seems never to have been built up.

In selecting Ptolemais as capital of Libya Superior or Pentapolis, Diocletian may have been influenced by the poverty rather than the wealth of that city. It may have been felt that a new province needed a new capital, and that this was an opportunity to revive a grandiose but moribund city. Or again, since the Diocletianic military command in Libya was—initially at least—unified over both Upper and Lower provinces,[31] it may have been decided that Cyrene should remain the military headquarters, the civil administrations being moved to other centres.

All these are mere speculations, but the one fact that seems certain is that Cyrene always enjoyed an extraordinary vitality due to its central position in the fertile upper plateau. It suffered severely in the Jewish Revolt of 115 and in the earthquake of 365, but Ammianus' description of it as *"urbs antiqua sed deserta"* refers only to the immediate aftermath of the latter event. In his speech before the Emperor Arcadius, in 399, Synesius described Cyrene as "now poor and downcast, a vast ruin, and in need of a king";[32] but dead cities do not send embassies, and from the later letters of Synesius we obtain the impression of a Cyrene seething with activity, if not all of it to that writer's taste. Recent archaeological research has confirmed the vitality of Cyrene's life in the early fifth century, even when it was no longer the administrative centre of Pentapolis.[33]

So, too, Cyrene survived as a populous centre long after the age of Synesius. Its Cathedral was rebuilt in the sixth century, and another church newly constructed then. In the early Islamic period, its population seems to have become even more dense if somewhat disorganised; for dwelling-houses of this late age have recently been found extending across the Byzantine ramparts and into the now abandoned Cathedral.[34] It was not the first Arab invasion, but the mass migration of the Beni Suleim and Beni Hilal in the eleventh century, that finally put an end to Cyrene's life.

Ptolemais, despite the advantages of its new status after Diocletian's reforms, does not seem to have had such a continuous and intensive occupation. After a revival which lasted until the time of Honorius and Arcadius, it again fell on hard times. The Byzantines stripped its most notable buildings of stone to build a series of fortresses, of which the largest bore the well-known Decree of Anastasius. By that emperor's reign, or under Justinian at the latest, Ptolemais ceased to be capital of Libya Pentapolis, its supremacy passing to Apollonia-Sozusa.[35] Even the repair of its aqueduct by Justinian himself did not fully revive its fortunes; and the new Arab masters of the seventh century found it expedient to make their own capital at Barka, leaving Ptolemais its original function as a dependent port.[36]

NOTES

1. The Department's programme of work at Cyrene has been closely co-ordinated with that of the Italian Archaeological Mission directed by Prof. Sandro Stucchi. Since 1957 the Mission has carried out important tasks of *anastylosis*, and of stratigraphic sounding, principally in the area of the Agora and

Caesareum. (*Bollettino d'Arte*, 1959, 57–61). This harmonious collaboration of Department and Mission has become one of the most essential and profitable features of post-war work at Cyrene.

2. The inscription, a letter of Hadrian of A.D. 134–5, has been published by P. M.

Fraser ("Hadrian and Cyrene", *JRS* xl (1950) 77–87). Additional fragments have recently been found and will be published by [J. M. Reynolds].

[2a. See now S. Stucchi, *Cirene 1957–1966* in *Quaderni dell'Istituto Italiano di Cultura di Tripoli* 3 (1967) 99 f.]

3. The Christian purification of pagan temples by fire is best attested at Cyrene by the present condition of the great Temple of Zeus. (R. G. Goodchild, J. M. Reynolds, C. J. Herington, "Zeus", *PBSR* xxvi (1958) 39–40.)

4. E. Paribeni, *Catalogo delle sculture di Cirene*, Roma, 1959, 75, no. 176, tav. 102.

5. E. Rosenbaum, *A Catalogue of Cyrenaican Portrait Sculpture*, London, 1960, nos. 24, 33, 36, pls. XX. 1–3, XXV, XXVI 1–2, XXVII. 1–2, XXVIII. 1–4.

6. Goodchild-Reynolds-Herington, 34–5.

7. *SEG* ix, 172 and 173; *Africa Italiana* i (1927), 335.

8. The earliest dated text mentioning this title is *SEG* ix, 170 (*Notiziario Archeologico* ii (1916), 183–4), of A.D. 161. Hadrianic inscriptions hitherto found at Cyrene refer to the city simply as ἁ πόλις, [but the word ματρόπολις is now known to occur in the Hadrianic inscription referred to in no. 2.]

9. Reynolds, "Four Inscriptions from Roman Cyrene", *JRS* xlix (1959) 98–9.

(9a. See J. and L. Robert in *REG* lxxv (1962), *Bulletin Epigraphique* no. 366 resolving ἰς ἐῶνα [τὸ κοι]νὸ[ν Ἐ]ξαπόλεως].

10. Romanelli, ((3), 28, n. 1) has pointed out that whereas Strabo includes Barka and omits Ptolemais, Pliny does the reverse.

11. Barka was, in the Roman period, only a small country town situated off the main coastal highway.

12. Tabula Peutingeriana, Antonine Itinerary; Synecdemos of Hierocles, George of Cyprus.

13. S. Applebaum, (*JRS* xl (1950), 87–8) shows that the re-settlement began under Trajan, with 3,000 veterans. Orosius (VII, 12, *b*) refers to "colonies" founded by Hadrian himself.

14. The only three public inscriptions of Roman date found on the site of Berenice all refer to the Jewish community. (Roux, *REG* lxii (1949) 281–5; Caputo, *Parola del Passato*, 1957, 132 f.) At Tauchira the funerary inscriptions in the necropolis contain a high proportion of Jewish names. (Gray, *Cyrenaican Expedition, 1952* (Manchester, 1956), 43 f.; cf. Reynolds in *JRS* xlvii (1957) 273).

15. Until recently the only traces of

Hadrianopolis consisted of the modern place-name Driana, and some inscribed tombs in a quarry near this locality. Recently (1959) marble columns and capitals have been found at the Zawiya, near the shore. Even allowing for a depth of wind-blown sand over the ruins the presumed site of Hadrianopolis is unimpressive. [See now notably G. D. B. Jones and J. H. Little, *JRS* lxi (1971) 67 f., but they had missed this indication that Goodchild had discovered the site.]

16. For the position of the "Via Monumentale", and an account of the work carried out at Ptolemais in 1935–42, see Caputo, 33–66 and fig. 2.

17. The major fragments of the Price-Edict of Diocletian were found re-used in a marble pavement fronting a small apsed hall on the south side of the street: they may originally have been displayed within this hall. (Caputo and Goodchild, "Diocletian" 106–15.) The Decree of Anastasius (*SEG* ix, 356), now in the Louvre, was originally carved on the face of the great fortress in the eastern sector of the "Via Monumentale".

18. Caputo, "Arco Trionfale in Cirenaica", *Atti III Congr. Studi Colon.* (Firenze, 1937), 133–7; Romanelli, (3), 255–6, and fig. 38.

19. *Jahrbuch des Deutschen Archäologischen Instituts*, 44 (1929), 325–38.

20. *ILS* 737 (of A.D. 351–4): this is cited here as an example only—there are infinite possibilities of variation in such opening formulae. *Conservatoribus* might well be followed only by *provincialium*, in our present instance.

21. Cf. *ILS* 692, 699, 702, 703, etc.

22. *ILS* 663 and 664; *Eph. Epig.* V no. 1404; Diehl, *ILCV*, 1.

23. De Ruggiero, II, 644 (s.v. Constantinus), IV, 1029 (s.v. Licinius).

24. Another possibility is a debased genitive [*Lib*]*ue;* but it seems wiser to exclude this fragment from any restoration of the text, until its position can more certainly be established.

25. These letters are very closely spaced in *A*, but in *B* they may have been abbreviated to the initials *DDD NNN*, and perhaps carried forward to the second line.

26. The letters of the "vota" inscription are smaller than those of the main texts *A-B-C*, but the fact that the plaque bears the same setting-out lines as the latter seems to demonstrate its association.

27. Cf. J. Pearce, "The *Vota*-Legends on the Roman Coinage", *NC*, 1937, 112–23.

[27a. For (a) 1 Goodchild printed . . . in aeter]num etc. but in discussion later had agreed to reject this and suggest that . . .]num was the conclusion of an imperial name, probably Valentia]num or Gratia]num, which provides a date.]

28. *Fasti Archeologici* x (1957), 268–9.

29. *SEG* ix, 9. Romanelli ((3), 130–1) considers the identification of Claudiopolis with Cyrene as uncertain; but the inscription (which is from a building, and is not merely a commemorative stele), is not otherwise explicable. I suspect that some of the late defensive walls at Cyrene, called generically "Byzantine", may belong to the third century; and that this text stood over a gateway. Unfortunately its exact provenience within Cyrene is not known. [See p. 233 f. below for a suggestion that Cyrene's condition was due to earthquake].

30. *SEG* ix, 266–8, 270, 274–5 (all from the "Nymphaeum" of the Sanctuary of Apollo); also one inscription recently found in the Valley Street.

31. Inscriptions at Luxor (*ILS* 701; *AE* 1889, 152; *Ibid.* 1934, 7–8) show the "Two Libyas" joined with Egypt and the Thebaid under a single *dux*; subsequently there was a *Dux Libyarum*, and by the second half of the fifth century a *dux* in each of the two Libyas, (cf. Romanelli, (3), 136, n. 1). I must here express disagreement with Professor Romanelli on the subject of Justinian's Edict *de dioecesi Aegyptiaca* (*ibid.* 170): in my view the "Libya" of that Edict is Lower Libya, exclusive of Pentapolis, and its *dux*—resident at Paraetonium—was concerned only with the defence of the former Marmaric regions.

32. Synesius, *De Regno* (Fitzgerald (2), I, 109). Lacombrade, 84, dates the embassy of Synesius to the years 399–402.

33. Cf. Reynolds, *JRS* xlix (1959) 100.

34. The silence of El-Bekri and other Arab geographers on the subject of Islamic Cyrene is perhaps due to the fact that the city lay neither on the coast nor on the main caravan route from Egypt to the Maghreb. In any case its population then must have been predominantly "Berber".

35. That Sozusa was the sixth-century "metropolis" of Pentapolis is shown not only by the geographical texts (Synecdemos of Hierocles; George of Cyprus) but also by its fine series of churches of this period, and a Byzantine Governor's Palace, identified in 1959 [see Goodchild, *Antiquity* xxxiv (1960) 246 f. and the forthcoming volume on Apollonia being produced by archaeologists of the University of Michigan].

36. Although Edrisi, writing in the early twelfth century A.D., described Tolmeita as "a very strong place, surrounded by walls of stone", it is unlikely that the Hellenistic and Roman wall-circuit was still in existence at this late date. The early defences had probably been dismantled in Byzantine times, and replaced by a more modest circuit around the harbour.

18

A COIN-HOARD FROM "BALAGRAE" (EL-BEIDA), AND THE EARTHQUAKE OF A.D. 365

[From *Libya Antiqua* iii–iv (1966–7)]
Plate 80

During the excavation of the Roman Theatre which forms part of the Sanctuary of Aesculapius at *Balagrae* (El-Beida) there was found, in May, 1956, a small hoard of bronze coins of the fourth century A.D.[1] The circumstances of this discovery and of another made forty years previously in its immediate vicinity, indicate that the coin-hoard lay on the floor of a late dwelling which had been improvised in the *ambulacrum* of the Theatre after its disuse, and which was later destroyed in an earthquake which tumbled down masses of masonry and trapped at least one human victim.

The composition and date of this hoard of coins are therefore indicative not only of the disuse of the Sanctuary Theatre, but also of a great seismic disaster which has left its traces also at Cyrene and Apollonia. The present writer, having referred to this disaster in several published papers,[2] feels that it is desirable to place on record the archaeological and historical evidence which justifies our considering it as one of the major events in the history of Cyrenaica.

THE BEIDA COIN-HOARD

The Roman Theatre of the Sanctuary of Aesculapius lies immediately east of the peristyle enclosure in which the main Temple stood; and the principal gateway of this Temenos faced a corridor running under the cavea of the Theatre and into the centre of the orchestra (fig. 71). Although separated from the Temenos by a narrow paved street or corridor, which also formed a tunnel under the cavea, the Theatre was structurally a part of the Sanctuary and was constructed—as an inscription shows—by the emperor Hadrian, whose name also appears on the peristyle architrave of the Temenos.[3]

Of the Theatre, there remained relatively intact, in 1956, only the southern half: the northern half had been stripped of stone in 1915–18 to build a massive colonial fortress, despite the protests of the then Superintendent of Antiquities, Ettore Ghislanzoni, and of his Assistant, Senesio Catani.[4] The latter made soundings at various points in the area which showed clearly the monumental character of the remains, although they were not extensive enough to reveal their identity as part of a Theatre.

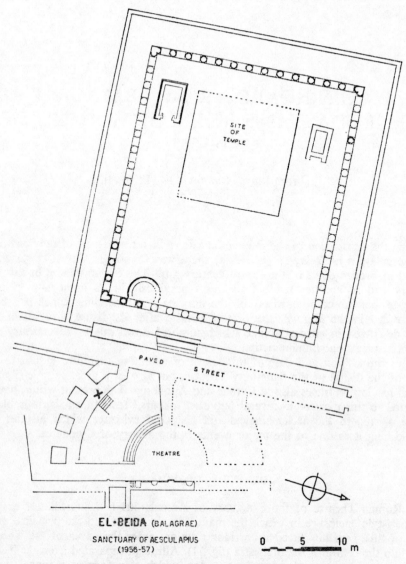

Fig. 71 Balagrae (El-Beida): theatre of Sanctuary of Aesculapius
(X=coin-hoard, May 1956)

The more extensive excavations of 1956 uncovered the semicircular *ambula-crum* which lay under the southern half of the *cavea*, and exposed four massive piers of masonry which had supported arcades forming the external facade of the Theatre. Between two of these piers a sounding had been made by Catani in May, 1917, and a photograph taken at that time[5] shows the remains of a late doorway inserted between the piers, and fragments of a human skeleton, accompanied by bronze and terracotta domestic vessels, crushed by the fallen stone.

No photograph could illustrate more graphically the results of an earthquake (pl. 80).

In the *ambulacrum* itself, immediately in front of the site of the skeleton and only 3 m. from it, the excavations of 1956 brought to light, at the same level, a hoard of 259 small bronze coins (fig. 71). They were not contained in a jar, but were spread over an area about 2 m. square and could have been shaken out of a perishable container—such as a box or purse—by the same shock that had destroyed the adjacent rooms. It is evident that at some period between the Theatre's disuse and the earthquake, a family had taken up residence in the *ambulacrum* and had constructed partition walls and doorways to form a humble dwelling which also extended beyond the Theatre, towards the south.

Some of the coins of this hoard are illegible,[6] and many have been clipped, thus obliterating their obverse legends. It is therefore preferable to classify them by their reverse types, listing the names of emperors represented in each type.

Type		*Number*
CONSTANTINOPOLIS	obv : helmeted head to l.	
	rev : victory to l.	2
Legend VN MP	Emperor, veiled, standing r.	1
GLORIA EXERCITVS	rev : two soldiers and 1 standard	7
GLORIA EXERCITVS	rev : two soldiers and 2 standards	1
	Emperors: Constantine I	
	Constantius II	
	Constantine II	
VOT XX MVLT XXX	in wreath (341–61)	8
	Emperors: Constantius II	
	Constans	
SPES REIPVBLICE	Virtus helmeted to r., holding globe and spear (355–61)	67
	Emperors: Constantius II	
	Julian Caesar	
FEL TEMP REPARATIO	(Falling horseman) (351–61)	124
	Emperors: Constantius II	
	Julian Caesar	
VOT X MVLT XX	Emperor: Julian Augustus (360–3)	1
SECVRITAS REIPVBLICAE	Victory to l., holding wreath and palm	
	Emperor: Valentinian I	1
Illegible		47
	TOTAL	259

As can be seen, the great majority of the legible coins belong to the two series SPES REIPVBLICE and FEL TEMP REPARATIO which were issued in the period 350–61 under Constantius II, Constans, Gallus and Julian Caesar. But the presence of a single coin of Valentinian I (from 364) takes us just into the beginning of his reign. Assuming that this group of coins was in current use when the building containing it collapsed, this event must have occurred about A.D. 365.

A COIN-HOARD FROM THE AGORA AT CYRENE

The circumstances in which the Agora of Cyrene came to be excavated have been fully described by Professor Sandro Stucchi in a recent monograph;[7] for the earliest discoveries we are largely dependent on an excavation journal compiled by the same assistant Catani who made the soundings, previously referred to, at El-Beida. Catani was an acute observer and conscientious recorder, although not equipped for the detailed analysis of coin discoveries.

Under the date 14 October, 1916,[8] Catani recorded the discovery of 243 small bronze coins in a terracotta vase lying in the corner of one of the small rooms which had been constructed, at a late date, on the previously open Agora square. He described the coins as varying from 11 to 18 mm. in diameter and consisting —so far as he could tell without cleaning them—of two main types: (1) obv: DN CONSTANTIVS NOB CAES, rev: soldier spearing fallen enemy, FEL TEMP REPARATIO; (2) obv: ... CONSTANTIVS PF AVG; rev.: two soldiers with standard. Legend illegible.

These coins cannot now be identified in the coin collection of Cyrene Museum; but a fragmentary list from the Museum archives[9] gives further details of forty-nine coins described as being part of the "Tesoretto dell'Agorà" which is clearly the hoard found in 1916, more precisely identified after cleaning. Four types are described, but the list is obviously incomplete:

(a) DN CONSTANTIVS PF AVG rev: soldier spearing horseman (20)

(b) DN FL CL IVLIANVS NOB C rev: emperor standing, legend SPES REIPVBLICE (6)

(c) FL CONSTANTIVS P F NOB CAES rev: soldier spearing fallen soldier, legend FEL TEMP REPARATIO (6)

(d) DN CONSTANTIVS P F AVG rev: emperor standing, legend SPES REIPVBLICE (17)

The precise composition of the 1916 hoard from the Cyrene Agora cannot be determined from the fragmentary records cited above. It is not impossible that individual coins of Julian Augustus and of Valentinian escaped Catani's notice but were later identified and included in the lost portions of the Museum list.

However, it can be said that this Cyrene hoard must have consisted mainly of issues of Constantius II and of the reverse-types FEL TEMP REPARATIO and SPES REIPVBLICE, as in the case of the Beida hoard, and must have been accumulated at approximately the same period. As also at Beida, it was not a large and valuable hoard hidden for recovery at some future date, but a modest collection of loose "change" needed for everyday use and therefore kept in the corner of a room. How did it come to be abandoned in one of the mean houses that had been constructed in the previously open space of the Agora of Cyrene?

Catani himself had noticed in the Agora area clear traces of a collapse of buildings ("crollo") due probably to an earthquake, and he remarked in his Journal that "the coins found in the terracotta urn and those others which are found, now and then, in the excavations here, being of the same emperor, lead one to believe that the collapse happened at this period". Human remains were not found, it seems, in the Agora square; but they were found when the excavations were extended, in the same year 1916, to the northern Stoa of the Agora. There, crushed beneath the fallen drums of one of the inner colonnades, lay several skeletons.[10]

In his recent monograph, Professor Sandro Stucchi has rightly accepted the evidence of the Agora coin-hoard as indicating that some of the late houses in the Agora square were destroyed in the earthquake of 365,[11] but he has postulated a subsequent partial reconstruction of the Agora buildings and an occupation continuing into the fifth century, and terminated early in that century either by the threat or actuality of barbarian invasion, or by another earthquake in which the victims found in the North Stoa lost their lives.[12]

The present writer is not entirely convinced that life did continue in the Agora after 365, for no coins of later date seem ever to have been found in occupation levels there. Moreover, the nearby 'House of Hesychius"—which once appeared likely to be of the age of Synesius—has, in the most recent excavations, yielded no coins later than Constantius II.[13] The ceramic material associated with the latest levels in the Agora itself was mainly removed during the excavations of 1916, and it is not yet clear whether the few residual sherds found recently by Stucchi in these same levels are necessarily later than 365.[14]

The Cyrene that existed in the period when Bishop Synesius wrote his letters was apparently concentrated along the sides of the *Decumanus Maximus* of the city which ran along the central valley and emerged from the North Gate to join the highway linking Cyrene with Apollonia. Along this main street stood the two known Christian churches of the city, one of which certainly was in existence in the fifth century.[15]

EARTHQUAKES AT CYRENE

In contrast to Asia Minor, Crete and Syria, the Cyrenaican region has no continuous record of earthquakes, and archaeological exploration has not yet detected traces of any such disaster earlier than the middle of the third century A.D.[16]

That some major disaster did overwhelm the city at the latter period is suggested by an increasing body of archaeological evidence. Stucchi has suggested that damage to the North Stoa of the Agora, in its penultimate period, might have been caused by an earthquake which is said to have devastated Crete in 251 A.D.[17]

In support of this hypothesis of a third-century seismic disaster at Cyrene, it may be mentioned that the small Roman Theatre west of the Caesareum, the so-called "Odeum", was certainly destroyed by fire towards the middle of this century. The statues that had adorned its stage, including a fine series of the Muses, were found broken and burned in a layer of ash underlying rough houses belonging to the second half of the third century. The outer walls of this Theatre, on the south side, have also evidently been displaced by an earth tremor— although this might have happened in 365, after the Theatre had long been out of use.[18] In all probability the destruction of the adjacent "House of Jason Magnus" took place in the third rather than the fourth century, as it was excluded from the area enclosed by city walls constructed before A.D. 300.[19]

Since exact evidence of date for this earlier disaster is not yet available we must await the results of further explorations; but it seems probable to the present writer that it took place in 262 rather than 251. For Libya is known to have suffered in the former year, as a passage in the life of Gallienus testifies:

Trebellius, *Gallienus* (*Scriptores Historiae Augustae*)[20]

"In the consulship of Gallienus for the 5th time and Faustinianus ... amid so many calamities of war there was also a terrible earthquake and a darkness for many days. There was heard, besides, the sound of thunder, not like Jupiter thundering, but as though the earth were roaring. And by the earthquake many structures were swallowed up together with their inhabitants, and many died of fright. This disaster, indeed, was worst in the cities of Asia; but Rome, too, was shaken and Libya also was shaken. In many places the earth yawned open, and salt water appeared in the fissures. Many cities were even overwhelmed by the sea . . . ."

If Cyrene had, in fact, been severely damaged at this time, it would explain why it had to be re-founded, with the new name of Claudiopolis some six years later, by Tenagino Probus, the general of the emperor Claudius Gothicus who had just defeated the Marmaric tribesmen.[21] Of course, it must be recognised that damage by fire could have been caused during an attack on Cyrene by these same tribesmen; but it is, at least, unlikely that they would have overturned walls and columns.

Much more substantial is the evidence for a major disaster in 365 which affected the whole of the central and eastern Mediterranean region, and destroyed —if we are to believe Libanius—"all and every one" of the Libyan cities. As this was the earthquake which caused the loss of the two coin-hoards described above, it may be useful to discuss it in some detail.

It seems that ominous rumblings had occurred in several regions a few years prior to the main disaster, for the historian Ammianus Marcellinus records that in 358 there were terrible earthquakes in Macedonia, Asia Minor and Pontus which overthrew many cities. The worst blow was in Bithynia where the city of Nicomedia was entirely ruined on 23 August, in circumstances which Ammianus described in some detail, following up with a short treatise on the causes of earthquakes and their various types.[22]

Seven years later, on 21 July, 365 (during the first consulship of Valentinian I and Valens), there occurred a seismic disaster of even greater magnitude which seemed to have affected the "whole world", meaning, of course, the whole Mediterranean basin. On this occasion, to the widespread damage caused by the shock itself were added the ravages of a tidal wave which engulfed the coastal regions and of famine and pestilence following the disaster.

No less than thirteen late antique historians[23] refer to this earthquake, of which the two most contemporary and most reliable were Ammianus Marcellinus and Libanius, whose accounts are worth reproducing here:

Ammianus Marcellinus *XXVI, 10, 15–18*[24]

"While the usurper (Procopius), whose various acts and death we have been relating, was still alive, on the 21st of July, in the first consulship of

Valentinian and his brother, fearful dangers suddenly overspread the whole world, such as are related in no ancient fables and histories.

For a little while before sunrise there was a terrible earthquake, preceded by incessant and furious lightning. The sea was driven backwards, so as to recede from the land, and the very depths were uncovered, so that many marine animals were left sticking in the mud. And the depths of its valleys and the recesses of the hills, which from the very first origin of all things had been lying beneath the boundless waves, now beheld the beams of the sun.

Many ships were stranded on the dry shore, while people straggling about the shoal water picked up fishes and things of that kind in their hands. In another quarter the waves, as if raging against the violence with which they had been driven back, rose, and swelling over the boiling shallows, beat upon the islands and the extended coasts of the mainland, levelling cities and houses wherever they encountered them. All the elements were in furious discord, and the whole face of the world seemed turned upside down, revealing the most extraordinary sights.

For the vast waves subsided when it was least expected, and thus drowned many thousand men. Even ships were swallowed up in the furious currents of the returning tide, and were seen to sink when the fury of the sea was exhausted; and the bodies of those who perished by shipwreck floated about on their backs or faces.

Other vessels of great size were driven on shore by the violence of the wind, and cast upon the housetops, as happened at Alexandria; and some were even driven two miles inland, of which we ourselves saw one in Laconia, near the town of Mothone, which was lying and rotting where it had been driven."

Libanius, *Funeral oration upon the Emperor Julian (Oratio XVIII) 291–3*[25]

"Earth truly has been fully sensible of her loss, and has honoured the hero (Julian) by an appropriate shearing off of her tresses, shaking off, as a horse does his rider, so many and such great cities. In Palestine several; of the Libyans all and every one. Prostrate lie the largest towns of Sicily, prostrate all of Greece save one; the fair Nicaea lies in ruins; the city, pre-eminent in beauty, totters to her fall, and has no confidence for the time to come. 'These are the honours paid to him by Earth, or if you choose, by Neptune himself; but on the part of the seasons, famines and pestilences, destroying alike man and beast, just as though it were not lawful for creatures upon earth to enjoy health now that he has departed' "

By referring to the two divinities, Earth (*Ge*) and Neptune (*Poseidon*), Libanius was evidently alluding to the twofold character of the disaster: earthquake followed by tidal wave. This Oration is not dated, but Foerster[26] has convincingly argued that it was written towards the end of 365, while memory of the earthquake was still fresh in men's minds.

Later historians have somewhat confused the chronology. The Christian writer Sozomen,[27] anxious to demonstrate that "God gave manifest tokens of his displeasure" at the religious policies of Julian, attributed the tidal wave at Alexandria to the reign of that emperor. Socrates,[28] another Christian historian, gave the main earthquake and tidal wave their correct date (365), but assigned the destruction of Nicaea to an earthquake which shook Bithynia only on 11

October 368. This city was constantly plagued with earth-tremors, and had been struck already in 362: it presumably suffered again in 365 and in 368.

The only city of Greece that was spared in 365 was, presumably, Athens; for the pagan historian Zosimus[29] informs us that when the cities of Greece, the Peloponnesus and Crete were overwhelmed by earthquake, Athens and the Attic region were saved by a priest named Nestorius who made sacrifices to Achilles, in response to a divinely-inspired dream. But Zosimus placed this event, without precision, towards the end of the reign of Valentinian, and is silent regarding an earthquake in 365.

The Byzantine chronicler, Georgius Cedrenus[30] has increased the confusion by recording a "world-wide" earthquake, with tidal wave at Alexandria, in 368, and also a similar disaster at an uncertain date in the reign of Gratian (375–83). The latter event is said to have drowned 50,000 people who had flocked to observe the retreat of the sea at Alexandria, and to have destroyed a large part of Crete, Achaia, Boeotia, Epirus, and Sicily.

Despite these chronological variations in some later histories, the testimony of Ammianus and Libanius is confirmed by Orosius,[31] Hydatius[32] Paulus Diaconus[33] and the Chronicon Paschale,[34] and there can be no reasonable doubt that although localised earthquakes occurred both before and after 365, the major and universal disaster (*per universum orbem*) occurred only at the latter date.

As we have seen, Libanius asserted that of the "Libyan" cities *all and every one* was destroyed. Unfortunately we cannot tell whether he was using "Libyan" in its broadest geographical sense to mean North Africa generally, or whether he referred only to the two Libyan provinces, i.e. Libya Inferior and Libya Pentapolis. Certainly the cities of the two Libyas must have been devastated; but for Tripolitania and regions further west we must seek other evidence than that provided by the Roman chroniclers.

The destruction of the principal cities of Sicily shows, however, that the earth-quake extended to the central Mediterranean region. Striking confirmation of its effects on the southern shores of Italy has been provided by an inscription found in 1912, recording that the public baths of *Regium*, which had "collapsed through old age and earthquake" (*thermas vetustate et terrae motu conlapsas*) were restored and re-dedicated in 374.[35] That the cities of Tripolitania were similarly damaged seems indicated by a growing body of archaeological evidence.[36]

The extent of the destruction in Cyrenaica in 365 cannot easily be assessed. Apart from the testimony of Libanius that "each and every city" perished, some retrospective allusions by Synesius,[37] and a funerary inscription in a tomb at Cyrene itself,[38] we are dependent entirely on archaeological evidence. Here we must be cautious lest we attribute to the earthquake of 365 damage which was sustained in the similar disaster of 262 (see above), or even in the Jewish Revolt of 115.

Ammianus Marcellinus, writing soon after 378, but referring to events that took place in Egypt in 362, described Cyrene as "an ancient city, but now deserted" (*urbs antiqua sed deserta*).[39] It is conceivable that he was referring to the depressed condition of the city before 365—if we allow for some exaggeration —but more probably he was describing the situation immediately after the earth-quake.

That reconstruction of the city was delayed seems indicated by the speech made by Synesius at Constantinople in 399, when sent as official ambassador to the court of Arcadius. He referred to his native city as "a great ruin, in need of a King".[40] Yet his letters, written before 413, imply that Cyrene was still an important social and economic centre, even though it had ceded to Ptolemais its function as a provincial capital.

Of other earthquakes that shook eastern Libya after the great disaster of 365, we have no direct evidence; but that does not necessarily mean that they never occurred, for the historical sources are altogether too few to permit of an *argumentum ex silentio*.

On the other hand, it seems clear from the literary evidence that the earthquake of 365 was exceptionally destructive and terrifying throughout the central and eastern Mediterranean region. This fact, and the evidence of the coin hoards at Beida and Cyrene as described above, surely justifies us in considering this to have been a major event in Libyan history.

NOTES

1. These coins are now preserved in the Museum at Cyrene.

2. *Cyrene*, (1963), 25.

3. For a short description of the Sanctuary see H. Sichtermann, in *AA* 1959, 326–35.

4. The quarrying of stone also yielded some statues, and fragments of inscriptions naming Aesculapius, thus confirming Hamilton's earlier identification of the site as *Balagrae*. Hamilton, 123.

5. *Cyrene Photographic Archives*, no. F. 101 dated 8 May, 1971. Further excavations were carried out on the site in 1920 by Prof. Silvio Ferri but were in the area east of the Theatre.

6. The cleaning and identification was carried out by the writer in primitive conditions. Laboratory cleaning would probably reduce the number of "illegibles".

7. S. Stucchi, *L'Agorà di Cirene* I.

8. I am indebted to Prof. Stucchi for the opportunity of consulting the Catani Journal.

9. The original archives and registers were largely destroyed during World War II, and only fragments remain.

10. Stucchi, Tav. LXV, I, 323. A manuscript report by Ghislanzoni dated 1 April 1916 records the discovery, amidst blocks from the walls, column drums, and blocks with triglyphs, etc., of three skeletons "which are evidently those of victims of the earthquake which destroyed Cyrene in the second half of the fourth century A.D." The photograph shows one of these skeletons lying trapped under a fallen column.

11. Stucchi, 294.

12. Stucchi, 307.

13. My own remarks in *Cyrene* (1963), 47 therefore need correction.

14. Stucchi, 330.

15. The eastern church or "Cathedral" seems to have been constructed in the fifth century; but it was greatly modified during the sixth century, when the mosaic floors were laid.

16. The fall of the outer columns of the Temple of Zeus was attributed by Pesce (*BCH* lxxi–ii (1974–8) 349) to an earthquake which occurred before A.D. 185; but recent researches have shown that they were overturned by Jewish rebels in 115. (*PBSR* xxvii (1958) 41).

17. Stucchi, 293 (quoting Platakis). Professor Stucchi informs me that this notice is derived from a Hagiography of the "Holy Ten".

18. Information from the excavator, Ess. Abdulhamid Abdussaid.

19. See my review of Prof. Mingazzini's book.

20. Translation by D. Magie, *Scriptores Historiae Augustae* III (Loeb edn.) 27.

21. *SEG* ix, no. 9. Despite Romanelli's caution (in (3), 130) there can be no reasonable doubt that the *Claudiopolis* of this inscription was Cyrene itself.

22. Ammianus, *Hist.* XVII, 7, 1–13.

23. Clinton, *Fasti Romani* i, 470. Cf. N. Putorti's article cited below.

24. Translation by C. D. Yonge, *The Roman History of Ammianus Marcellinus*, London 1862, 434.

25. Translation by C. W. King, *Julian the Emperor*, London 1888, 213.

26. Libanius (ed. Foerster) Vol. II, 1904, 223–4.

27. Sozomen VI, 2.

28. Socrates IV, 3 and 11.

29. Zosimus IV, 18.

30. Migne, *Patr. Gr.* Vol. 121, 591 and 599.

31. Orosius VII, 32.

32. Hydatius, *descriptio consulum*, an. 368.

33. Paulus Diaconus, *Historica*, A.U.C. 1118.

34. Migne, *Patr. Gr.* Vol. 92, 755.

35. N. Putorti, "Di un titolo termale scoperto in Reggio di Calabria", *Rendiconti dell' Accademia Nazionale dei Lincei*, xxi, 791.

36. A. Di Vita, 134.

37. In his *Catastasis* (Fitzgerald, (2), II, 363) Synesius refers to an earthquake as the first of a series of disasters that had over-taken the Pentapolis. In Letter 67 he refers to earthquake-damage at Hydrax. In neither case need it be assumed that this earthquake had taken place very recently.

38. See D. Comparetti, 161.

39. Ammianus, *Hist.* XXII, 16, 4.

40. Synesius, *De Regno* (Fitzgerald, (2), I) 109.

19

SYNESIUS OF CYRENE: BISHOP OF PTOLEMAIS

Plates 81, 82

[Three unpublished manuscripts containing archaeological and topographical commentary on the writings of Synesius were found among Goodchild's papers. The unfinished *Country Estate of Bishop Synesius* must have been written last of the three since it refers to the first post-war resumption of excavation at Cyrene and Ptolemais (in 1954) which is not envisaged in the other two; it is printed here virtually as it stands with the addition only of a few notes. The other two, headed *Synesius and the Pentapolis: some archaeological notes* and *Synesius and the Defence of the Pentapolis: an archaeological and topographical enquiry*, both include some discussion of Cyrene and Ptolemais in Synesius' time together with accounts of country sites, and where they overlap it is not altogether easy to tell which is the later or the preferred version. Much of what is said about Cyrene is outdated as a result of subsequent excavation—thus Goodchild argued here, largely on the analogy of Ptolemais, that the conversion of the Caesareum to use as a fort and the abandonment of the Hellenistic/Roman city wall for a new and much shorter defensive circuit were probably developments of the early fifth century, but after excavation he decided that they should be dated in the later third century, as stated in his last work, *Kyrene und Apollonia*, 74, 144/5; in consequence nothing on the late defences of Cyrene is printed here. As far as is known, however, he continued to regard his argument concerning the late defences of Ptolemais as substantially valid, pending further excavation, and had not changed his mind on any important point in the sections on minor localities, which constitute a valuable contribution to Cyrenaican topographical studies. I have selected the fuller version for printing as far as possible but for Ptolemais it has been necessary to make some conflation of the two versions since at least one page is missing from one manuscript. A few notes have been added. The result very obviously lacks Goodchild's final polishing—but should nonetheless be useful.

All references to Synesius are to Fitzgerald's translations.]

THE COUNTRY ESTATE OF BISHOP SYNESIUS

One of the fullest and most interesting pictures of country life in North Africa during late antiquity is provided by the letters of Synesius of Cyrene, the pagan philosopher (and sportsman) who was later to be ordained as Bishop of Ptolemais. Kingsley, who portrayed the "Squire-Bishop" in his novel *Hypatia*, defined him as "a man of magniloquent and flowery style, not without a vein of self-conceit; yet withal of overflowing kindliness, racy humour and unflinching courage, both physical and moral". This assessment may be allowed to stand, subject to the important reservation that virtually everything we know about the man derives from his own writings, including letters that were doubtless hand-picked for publication.

During the past century scholars of several nations have studied and analysed the writings of Synesius, attempting to determine their chronological sequence.[1] A number of firm points have been established, but it may be doubted whether much more remains to be argued from the letters themselves until we can obtain some new independent evidence in the light of which they may be re-assessed. Archaeology may well prove helpful if the recently-resumed excavations at Cyrene and Ptolemais can be continued: for in both cities the monuments of the age of Synesius are plentiful, and may yield inscriptions which could illuminate our textual information.

For the moment, however, I am concerned neither with the birthplace of Synesius nor with his bishopric, but with the country estate from which he wrote most of his letters. No previous attempt has, so far as I know, been made to localise it, probably because the majority of commentators have tracked down Synesius in their libraries rather than on his native hills. Where literary sources are vague, geography can often be summoned to their aid, and I think that by process of elimination one can decide on the area in which any hunt for the villa of Synesius should be made.

Cyrene was the native city of Synesius, where the names of his reputed ancestors "back to Eurysthenes who settled the Dorians in Sparta" were engraved on the public monuments (*Epist*. 57). There, too, were the "Dorian tombs" of his family in which, at one moment of alarm inspired by barbarian invasion, he feared that he would find no final resting-place (*Catast*.). Certainly there must have been a family house within the walls of Cyrene, and it was perhaps used by his brother Euoptius on occasions when affairs took him to the city (*Epist*. 50). But Synesius himself, during the most productive period of his letter-writing, preferred to live away from it. This may have been, as he asserts (*Epist*. 50), due to dislike of his fellow-citizens; or it may be that it was a means of escaping the heavy financial burdens that fell on any *curialis* in his home town.

Yet whilst Synesius chose the country life, it is clear that the estate on which he spent most of his time before election to the bishopric was not very distant from Cyrene. As Coster has pointed out,[2] the remote residence (? called "Anchemachus") described in *Epist*. 148 was not the only one at the disposal of Synesius. That estate was far from the sea, in "the southern extremity of Cyrenaica", but a considerable group of letters show him as sending and receiving regular letters from his overseas friends; and in three of them (*Epist*. 51, 101, 129) we learn that the little port of Phycus [fig. 73] was the place where these letters were posted.

Now Phycus [see also pp. 152, 249 f.] was "a harbour of the Cyreneans" (*Epist*. 101), but not, as one modern commentator has claimed, "the harbour of Cyrene from the time that Apollonia became a separate city". Its site can be identified, beyond controversy, with the little bay of Zaviet el-Hammama, sheltered by the promontory of Kheshem el-Kelb, some 25 km. west of Apollonia. Between Cyrene and Phycus there lay broken country traversed only by rough mule-tracks,

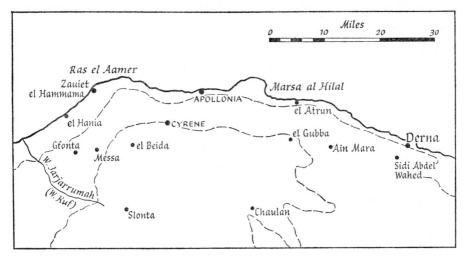

Fig. 72

whereas Apollonia lay at only half the distance from Cyrene and was linked by a first-class highway.

If Synesius so frequently entrusted his letters to the "oarsman of Phycus" it was simply because that was the nearest port of call for the coastal shipping of the day. Had he been resident when those letters were sent on the immediate outskirts of Cyrene or in the area eastward of it, he would surely have despatched and received his mail through Apollonia.

When the barbarian invaders penetrated into the heart of Cyrenaica, and began to menace the isolated homesteads, Synesius was brisk in building up a local "home guard", and it may be said that his whole attitude to the regular Roman forces in the country was tinged by a distinctly "home guard" prejudice. It was they who were pampered, cowardly and ill-led, whilst the irregular units which he represented shone with valour and energy. But the Phycus sailors, we learn (*Epist.* 132) were no good in a home guard role, and the mere fact of their mention shows that the estate of Synesius could not have been greatly distant from that part of the coast.

Another topographical clue is provided by two references (*Epist.* 104, 132) to campaigning with the "Balagritae" who were originally mounted troops, but later had their horses taken away by Duke Cerialis (who probably needed remounts for his regulars). Balagrae was a small township some 15 km. south-west of Cyrene [on the site of modern El Beida], which enjoyed a pagan fame for its great Sanctuary of Aesculapius, founded from Epidaurus.[3] Even after the Temple had been dismantled it flourished as a Christian community; and it seems clear that a territorial unit had been recruited from its citizens. The Balagritae evidently operated within a restricted field of action and occupied an intermediate role between the completely irregular forces levied by landowners like Synesius and the regular units which had the traditional names of Marcomanni, Dalmatae, etc.

It seems clear that since Synesius campaigned with the Balagritae it was

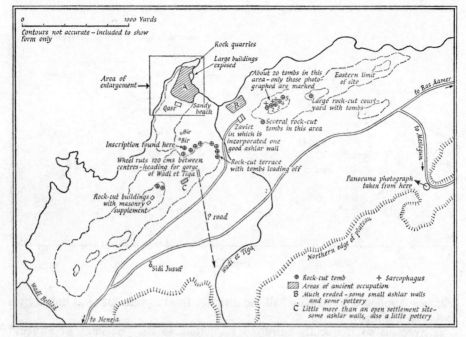

Fig. 73 Phycus (after the survey by D. J. Smith and P. A. Titchmarsh, 1950).
For inset see fig. 74.

because his own estate was reasonably close to Balagrae, and we can therefore draw a line between Zaviet el-Hammama and El Beida as a theoretical axis on which the Synesian estate should be sought [fig. 72]. The seaward part of this line can, however, be immediately rejected, for in a letter (*Epist.* 114) addressed to his brother Euoptius, Synesius entreats him to leave the unhealthy area of the coastal marshes and come up to the hills. "Here you can go under the shadow of a tree... You can step across a rivulet... All things are fragrant with perfume, the aromas of a healthy soil." Now Balagrae stood on the northern edge of the upper plateau, and was separated from Phycus by a lower plateau devoid of running water. If rivulets existed on or near the lands of Synesius, these must have lain on the upper plateau somewhere between Zavia Gfonta on the west and El Beida itself on the east. A whole series of springs with adjacent streams occupies this narrow strip of plateau.

Although Euoptius was a frequent visitor to Cyrene, where he had relatives (cf. the mother-in-law mentioned in *Epist.* 93, addressed to Hesychius, who was certainly resident at Cyrene), his favourite resort was a country estate "in the country of the Phycuntians" (*Epist.* 114), where he had a garden in which the near-extinct silphium was grown (*Epist.* 106). Nearby were marshes containing stagnant salt water, which Synesius, probably quite erroneously, considered as injurious to the health of his brother (*Epist.* 114). Such marshes do not exist in the immediate vicinity of Phycus itself but begin at the modern Hania and extend westwards as far as the mouth of the Wadi Jarjarumah (the lower course of the Wadi Kuf). We must therefore conclude (unless the letters of Synesius are pure rhetoric, in which case our present inquiry, and all previous discussions of Synesius' life, must be abandoned) that Euoptius had his Phycuntian estate somewhere near the coast west of Hania. In this area the narrow coastal strip below the lower escarpment contains numerous patches of cultivable soil, and there are scattered indications of ancient settlement. Since Synesius, on one occasion when his horses and donkeys were at pasture, contemplated walking down to his brother and was only restrained by relatives who thought that would seem undignified (*Epist.* 109)—there is no suggestion of exhaustion!—it is clear that our proposed geographical limits, Gfonta–Beida, for his own estate are valid.

Can we go closer than this, on the literary evidence alone? I rather doubt it, but must draw attention to two slender pieces of evidence which might be adduced, one in support of the western end of the Gfonta–Beida strip, and the other in favour of Beida itself, the eastern limit. A letter (*Epist.* 122) to Euoptius gives an account, clearly based on eye-witness reports, of the courageous action of the "priests of Axomis". These clerics led some peasants "from the very church door" down into the "Myrtle Valley", a long deep ravine covered with forests. There they encountered barbarian invaders of whom many were killed with stones by the deacon Faustus.

Now the site of Axomis is not certainly identifiable, and there are, needless to say, many ravines in the area with which we are here concerned. Yet, of them all, the modern Wadi Kuf, upper reach of the Wadi Jarjarummah, is the deepest and most heavily wooded. That it was found convenient by barbarian invaders as a means of concealed penetration is shown by the forts which the Byzantines built nearby. Gasr Beni Gdem and Gsar Sciaden [Shahden] are the most massive defensive works in the whole of the ancient Pentapolis.[4] Therefore one is tempted to identify Axomis either with Messa, an important village site, or with the smaller ancient centre at Sidi Abdel Wahed, between Messa and the Kuf valley. There are remains of Christian churches visible on both sites.

The other letter (*Epist.* 126), one of the latest ones in the whole collection since it was compiled after the death of Synesius' third son, states that the bishop was engaged in building a monastery "beside the river Asclepius". It is not at all certain that this was in the vicinity of Ptolemais, and the river-name would have been appropriate in the vicinity of Balagrae, where Aesculapius had his great sanctuary.

How long after his ordination as Bishop of Ptolemais Synesius kept his estate in the vicinity of Balagrae, there is little evidence; but it is certainly incorrect to assume that he spent all his time at his See. *Epist.* 79, addressed to Anastasius, includes the remark: "I see my house faring ill. I am compelled to dwell in my native city at a time of distress." It was for this reason, his non-residence at his See, that he confessed himself unable to be of assistance to his flock; and one may suspect that "dwelling in my native city" also included long sojourns in that country estate which he loved so much. It may even be that he kept at Balagrae the wife whom he had refused to renounce on his appointment as Bishop (*Epist.* 105).

Here we may end these speculations, for that is all they are; and we must rest content with the certainty that the principal and most-used country residence of Synesius was in that area which we have geographically defined, at the western end of the upper plateau. Can we go further and identify the actual building?

Unfortunately the Cyrenean plateau is over-rich in ancient ruins, and there are at least 50 potential sites in the small zone which we have selected.

[The manuscript breaks off here; for a further point see p. 253.]

SYNESIUS AND THE PENTAPOLIS:
ARCHAEOLOGICAL AND TOPOGRAPHICAL NOTES

The history of Cyrenaica between its short-lived Hadrianic renaissance and the Arab invasions of the seventh century A.D. is most meagrely documented. The clouds of uncertainty only lift for the relatively short period (c. A.D. 390–415) covered by the works of Synesius; and even for that period our picture of events in the Pentapolis is far from clear.

The importance of the writings of Synesius, as illustrating the social, political and economic conditions of his times, has long been recognised. The bibliography of *Synesiana* is already extensive and English readers have had the benefit of Fitzgerald's translations, and of Pando's admirable summary of the life and times of the Bishop of Ptolemais. Fitzgerald and Pando have both given brief but useful sketches of the geography of the Pentapolis, but neither they, nor previous writers, have attempted to use topographical and archaeological evidence to illustrate the events which are described so vividly in the Catastasis and the Letters.[5]

In the absence of any independent literary source for the history of the events which Synesius describes, commentators have been led to accept the Bishop of Ptolemais at his own valuation; the heroes of his account have been applauded and the villains uncompromisingly condemned. The figure of Synesius commands, and will always command, respect: quite apart from his literary abilities, so highly esteemed in the Middle Ages, his letters and essays reveal him as a man of high moral principles, and a patriot. His delight in country pursuits, and his distaste for generals and government officials have particularly endeared him to English readers. Yet the most high-minded and worthy public figures are not always balanced observers of the events through which they live; and it is hardly fair to the memory of the personal and political enemies of Synesius if we accept his version of events, without recourse to any other evidence which may be available.

During the last thirty years such evidence has gradually been coming available, as a result of the excavations which were carried out at Cyrene and Ptolemais by the Italian government, and of the archaeological reconnaissances made more recently in Cyrenaica. Excavations were in progress at Cyrene from 1920 to 1942, and at Ptolemais from 1935 to 1942. Unfortunately the published reports on these excavations are few, and, in the case of Cyrene, of little relevance to the period of Synesius. Yet the excavated parts of both cities contain abundant remains of that period, study of which gives at least a general picture of the conditions of the fifth century.[6]

In many instances, however, the clearing and reconstruction of the monuments of Cyrenaica has resulted in the complete removal of those levels which represent the period of Synesius. Certainly the archaeology of the fifth century A.D. is not, in Libya, a very rewarding subject, and the magnificent Italian reconstructions of ancient monuments were only made possible by the demolition of late walls containing architectural fragments from the earlier buildings. Few archae-ologists, and certainly no tourists, will lament the fact that the barrack-buildings were cleared out of the Caesareum at Cyrene. We must hope, however, that future excavators will give close attention to these remains, and will date and document them adequately before permitting their demolition.

In addition to the archaeological evidence of fifth-century A.D. conditions in Cyrene and Ptolemais, we must also consider the topographical background of the events which Synesius described. Unfortunately many of the places to which he refers have not yet been identified, and are not likely to be identified for many years. The ancient topography of the Cyrenaican coast is well documented, and the Roman road itineraries also give the names of a few inland places; but those ancient towns or villages which lay inland and off the line of the Roman roads are most difficult to identify. In Cyrenaica, as in Tripolitania, Ptolemy is not a very trustworthy source for the topography of the interior.

Yet we can, as we shall see, identify some of the places which are mentioned by Synesius, and these identifications are helpful in studying the meaning of his correspondence. We shall find too that there is some evidence of the actual area in which Synesius had his country retreat, and from which he wrote many of his most interesting letters. Although the military operations described by Synesius cannot yet be assigned to specific battle-grounds, they become much more intelligible when we study the general character of the terrain and of the frontier organisation.

Discussion of the chronology of Synesius' life, and of his letters, is outside the scope of the present article. It is unfortunate that the excavations in Cyrenaica have not yet yielded epigraphic evidence of any of the military or civil officials who figure in his works. If such discoveries are made in future years it will then be opportune to review the whole problem which at the moment rests mainly on the ingenious (but not altogether convincing) reconstruction made by Druon. For the moment we are concerned only with the external evidence for the condition of the Roman Pentapolis at the time of its best-known historical figure.

Cyrene

Although the works of Synesius contain many references to Cyrene, and to their author's pride in his birthplace, they do not provide a very clear picture of the contemporary condition of this once-famous city. Most of the references are in fact of a rather disparaging character. In his essay *De Regno* addressed to Arcadius in 399 (so Druon), Synesius speaks of Cyrene as "now poor and down-cast, a vast ruin, and in need of a king" (§ 40). This description is not unlike that given by Ammianus (XXI, 16, 4) two decades earlier: *urbs antiqua sed deserta*. On the other hand, random references in the letters of Synesius show that Cyrene was still sufficiently alive for certain aspects of its society to rouse his displeasure. Although in philosophy the city had "fallen lower than any of the cities of Pontus" (*Epist.* 103), its law-courts and their frequenters were so active as to induce Synesius to live away from them. (*Epist.* 50). There were still in-fluential people in Cyrene to whom he occasionally wrote (*Epist.* 60, 93).

Excavations carried out at Cyrene by the Italians from 1920–42 uncovered most of the area of the Apollo Temple, a large part of the centre of the city containing Forum [Caesareum] and Agora, and several outlying structures. In all

these areas the remains of late dwellings were found overlying or occupying the
earlier structures, but their date was not established by the excavators, who
refer only generally to them as "tardo-romano" or "bizantino". As public inscriptions of the fourth and fifth centuries A.D. are almost entirely lacking, it is
difficult to reconstruct even a summary chronology of the later history of the
city ...

....

... But Cyrene was already, by Synesius' time, in a very sorry state. We may
hesitate to accept Ammianus' adjective *deserta* (see p. 226) as a literal description, but there can be no doubt from the archaeological evidence that there had
been a steady deterioration of Cyrene's fortunes from the third century onwards.
An inscription of Claudius Gothicus (A.D. 268–70) recording the re-founding of
Cyrene as "Claudiopolis" probably indicates an attempt to arrest the decay in
its early stages (*SEG* ix. 9); its failure is reflected in the rarity of later dedications
to emperors. Once the provincial administrative centre had been transferred to
Ptolemais in the early fourth century [see p. 225], the decline of Cyrene became
irrevocable.

To the political and economic factors which brought about this decline were
added natural disasters. Synesius refers twice to earthquakes as having devastated the country (*Epist.* 58, 67), and although he gives no clear evidence of date,
it would seem likely that one at least of these earth tremors occurred in the last
decade of the fourth century. A Christian inscription of the same period, in a
tomb outside Cyrene, records the death of a mother and her son in an earthquake,[7]
whilst the fallen columns of the Apollo and Zeus temples, and the tumbled walls
of other public buildings all tell the same story. We have no evidence of when
these earth tremors first began on a serious scale in the Pentapolis [but see p.
234 for a major one in 262], nor of their effect in terms of human lives. It would
seem, however, from the archaeological evidence at Cyrene and at Apollonia
(where large parts of the ancient city are submerged beneath the sea) that the
central area of the Gebel was the zone most seriously affected.

Large numbers of isolated buildings in the countryside, churches, as well as
fortified farms, have sloping revetments built up against their outer walls for a
considerable height ...

Ptolemais

In contrast to Cyrene, Ptolemais has yielded ample evidence of continued, and
indeed increased, prosperity during the last half of the fourth century ...

....

Early travellers were often puzzled by the fact that the West Gate of Ptolemais
still stands high and isolated, whilst the curtain wall on either side was hardly
visible on the surface. The Italian excavators uncovered a large sector
of these walls adjoining the West Gate, and there can be no doubt that they had
been deliberately demolished during antiquity, and their materials carted away
... presumably to be used elsewhere in the city. Only the seaward end of the
western city wall was still standing, 12–13 feet high, in 1822, when the Beechey
brothers visited Tolmeita. This fact is, as we shall see, significant.

When were these defences of Tolmeita levelled? At first sight, Edrisi's description of Tolmeita as "a very strong place, surrounded by a stone wall, and much
populated"[8] suggests that the original defensive circuit was still standing in the

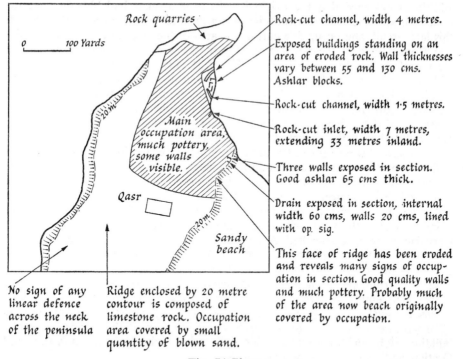

Rock-cut channel, width 4 metres.

Exposed buildings standing on an area of eroded rock. Wall thicknesses vary between 55 and 130 cms. Ashlar blocks.

Rock-cut channel, width 1·5 metres.

Rock-cut inlet, width 7 metres, extending 33 metres inland.

Three walls exposed in section. Good ashlar 65 cms thick.

Drain exposed in section, internal width 60 cms, walls 20 cms, lined with op. sig.

This face of ridge has been eroded and reveals many signs of occupation in section. Good quality walls and much pottery. Probably much of the area now beach originally covered by occupation.

No sign of any linear defence across the neck of the peninsula

Ridge enclosed by 20 metre contour is composed of limestone rock. Occupation area covered by small quantity of blown sand.

Fig. 74 Phycus

twelfth century. If this had been the case, however, it would be most difficult to explain when and where the masonry from the city wall was removed. Over the main part of the ancient city there are no recognisable remains of substantial medieval Islamic buildings, and not a single inhabited building existed in 1822 at the time of the Beecheys' visit. Even in 1911, when the Italians landed here, a small Zavia was the only recent structure, the modern village of Tolmeita being entirely later than 1911.

Study of the topography suggests, however, a different interpretation. The Beecheys observed, in 1822 "a wall running round the small port within the town". Although the port area has suffered severely from stone-robbing since 1911, one small fragment of this wall is still visible, and it is evidently a late Roman wall of defensive character.[9] This fact, taken together with the survival of the seaward end of the main west wall, is suggestive. It seems to indicate that at Ptolemais, as at Lepcis Magna in Tripolitania, the city had contracted at a late period to within a small defensive circuit around the port. It was to this reduced circuit that Edrisi presumably referred.

One would be tempted, on the analogy of Lepcis, to attribute this secondary wall circuit to Justinian, were it not that Procopius is completely silent on the matter. As he specifically records the erection or repair of city walls at Tauchira, Berenice and Boreium, and the provision of an aqueduct for Ptolemais, his silence on the subject of the defences of Ptolemais must surely indicate that Justinian did not find it necessary to carry out any new work of that kind. Indeed, there is

additional evidence that the original walls of Ptolemais had already been demolished, and the new reduced circuit constructed, at an earlier date. Outside
this late circuit, and occupying part of the area of the original city, is the massive
late Roman fort, in the northern facade of which was found the now famous
Decree of Anastasius (*SEG* ix. 356). The fort must therefore be contemporary
with, or—more probably—earlier than the reign of Anastasius; and the wall on
which the inscription was cut is in fact secondary, there being clear evidence of
an earlier fort, built of re-used stones, some inscribed with earlier graffiti. The
character of this indicates that it stood as an isolated redoubt in an undefended
area, rather than as the citadel of a walled town.

For a *terminus post quem* for the demolition of the original defences of Ptolemais, we must turn to the excavated monuments within the city area, but outside
the later wall-circuit; for it can hardly be believed that organised municipal life
continued to be vigorous in that part of the city abandoned when the new circuit
was built. In this abandoned area excavations were carried out by the Italians
from 1935 until the final British occupation of Cyrenaica. In addition to a fine
Christian church, a so-called Agora, and the splendid "Colonnaded Palace"
recently published by Pesce,[10] a sector of an important Roman east-west street
was excavated by Giacomo Caputo in 1935. This excavation brought to light the
base of a triumphal arch with a monumental inscription set up in honour of
unidentified emperors, *victores ac triumfatores semper augusti* by. . . *ius v(ir)
p(erfectissimus) praeses* [see above, p. 224]. The text and the style of lettering
alike indicate a late date. In this same street were found the facades of public
buildings with similar monumental inscriptions honouring Valentinian, Valens and
Gratian, and also Arcadius and Honorius.

It is evident, therefore, that public buildings were still being erected and
dedicated in this part of the city in 367–75 and in 395–408, and the contrast
between these late indications of municipal vigour, and the subsequent abandonment of almost three-quarters of the city area is most striking. The changed
fortunes of the city between the beginning of the fifth century and the reign of
Anastasius can only reasonably be attributed to those events described by
Synesius, or to similar events occurring within a century of his death. Yet it was
no barbarian attack that levelled the outer walls of Ptolemais: the demolition was
carried out systematically, and as part of a deliberate policy. We can begin to
understand this policy better when we consider the large extent of the original
circuit[11] and the reduced man-power available in the later Roman period . . .
Without adequate forces to man this vast perimeter, the city wall could be a
menace rather than an aid to the defence of the city.

In Synesius' account of events in the Pentapolis the *praeses* Andronicus is
singled out more than any other individual for the Bishop's disfavour. It was he
who "invested the city with the semblance of one taken by storm" and who "cut
off the fairest part of it . . . making the royal colonnade (? the Basilica), of old
the courts of justice, into a place of execution" (*Epist.* 57). Previous commentators have accepted, without hesitation, the rather one-sided view which Synesius
puts forward: they could hardly do otherwise in the absence of any explanation
of the policy of Andronicus. The highly-coloured description of the enormities
committed by Andronicus is perhaps less acceptable to the critical reader who
bears in mind the archaeological evidence of events in Ptolemais during the fifth
century. That Synesius, who claimed to be born of ancient Greek stock, should

despise the self-made son of a Benghazi fisherman is understandable; that he should condemn the cruelties alleged to have been committed by Andronicus was right and proper; but that he should have portrayed the *praeses* as a stupid ruffian destroying the city without justification merely shows how prejudiced an observer he was of the events which were convulsing his country.

If, as we may suspect, it was Andronicus who pulled down the walls of Ptolemais to build a smaller and more easily defensible circuit around the port, and to erect strong points in the abandoned part of the city, he was merely carrying out a policy which was as inevitable as it was regrettable. Justinian, who pursued a similar policy at Lepcis Magna, was fortunate enough to have a Procopius to justify his action for posterity ... We would be unwise to assume, in the present state of knowledge, that Andronicus was as corrupt, vicious and ineffective as Synesius paints him.

Phycus

After Cyrene and Ptolemais, it is the port of Phycus which claims the largest place in the topographical content of the *Letters*. It is mentioned five times, in contexts which reflect not so much the importance of the place as the closeness of Synesius' associations with it (*Epist.* 51, 101, 114, 129, 132). Not only did his brother live there (*Epist.* 114), but he himself used the port on several occasions for sending and receiving mail, and for embarking for Alexandria (*Epist.* 51, 101, 129). On one occasion, during an emergency, sailors from Phycus served with Synesius in a local militia, but were found to be unsatisfactory (*Epist.* 132).

Ancient sources, other than Synesius, have little to say about Phycus. Of its history we only know that Marcus Cato made an unsuccessful attempt to land there in 47 B.C., when seizing Cyrene for the Pompeian party. To the ancient geographers it was best known for the fact that its promontory was held to be the northernmost one of the Cyrenaican coast; and all concurred that it lay between Apollonia and Ptolemais, and was rather nearer the former than the latter. Later commentators have therefore usually identified Phycus with the headland of Ras Aamer (incorrectly called "Ras Sem"). In 1860–1 the British explorers Smith and Porcher studied the problem and came to the conclusion that Phycus could only have been at Zaviet Hammama, some 8 km. to the west of Ras Aamer, where there is a small bay and a rocky promontory, but they made no detailed survey of the site.[12]

During the Map of Roman Libya expedition of 1950, Messrs. D. Smith and P. Titchmarsh re-visited Zaviet Hammama, and made a rough survey of the surviving ancient remains [figs. 73, 74]. From this survey, and from the absence of any other harbour between Hammama and Apollonia, it is evident that Smith and Porcher were correct in their identification. The small village of Phycus lay mainly on the west side of the bay, although there are also traces of ancient buildings along the shore east of the wadi. Lying inland of the bay, which served as the harbour, are numerous rock-cut tombs and sarcophagi. Wheel-ruts heading southwards represent minor tracks linking Phycus with Balagrae, and perhaps with Cyrene.

The importance of the identification of Phycus as Zaviet Hammama lies in the hint which it gives as to the location of Synesius' country estate, from which many of the earlier letters must have been written. The port of Cyrene was Apollonia, with which it was linked by a well-engineered highway, 13 Roman miles, *c.* 20 km., long. It is inconceivable that Synesius would have used the port of Phycus for his correspondence if he were residing either in Cyrene or on its outskirts. To reach Phycus from Cyrene by horse or mule would have meant a [longer] journey across most difficult country. On the other hand, any country landlord living near Balagrae would have found it convenient to send and receive his mail from Phycus, which was only *c.* 20 km. distant.

Balagrae

The small town of Balagrae lay 12 Roman miles west of Cyrene on the main road to Ptolemais, and was noted for its temple of Aesculapius, referred to by Pausanias and other writers. Hamilton correctly identified the site of this temple at Zavia Beida, where some massive foundations were uncovered in the course of building the Senussi "zavia", and excavations were carried out by Italian troops in search of stone in 1915, and, more methodically, by the Italian Antiquities Service in 1920. Of the latter work no report has been published.[13]

Although Synesius does not mention the town of *Balagrae*, he twice refers to the *Balagritae*, an armed militia recruited, no doubt, from the inhabitants (*Epist.* 104, 132). In one letter we have a detailed account of operations against the barbarians, in the course of which John the Phrygian behaved discreditably (*Epist.* 104). In another we find Synesius soldiering with a detachment of dismounted Balagritae and some Phycuntian sailors (*Epist.* 132). Oliverio, following Druon, has assumed that this letter was written from Cyrene; but if this were the case, it is curious that no reference should be made to the regular troops who were stationed at Cyrene, or to the sailors of Apollonia who might more reasonably have been called to the defence of Cyrene than those of Phycus. It is perhaps more reasonable to suppose that Synesius is referring here, as in many other instances, to a "Home Guard" operating in the Gebel west of Cyrene.

Erythrum

The little village and harbour of Erythrum lay outside the main orbit of Synesius' activities.[14] It was on the coast midway between Apollonia and Darnis (modern Derna), and being away from the main Roman roads of the province relied on coasting vessels for its communications. Synesius called there once on a journey to Alexandria, and noticed the "springs of pure, sweet water" which "gush forth on the very shore" (*Epist.* 51). Later in his life, as Bishop of Ptolemais, he was called on to arbitrate in a dispute which had arisen between the bishops of Erythrum and Darnis, for the possesion of the fort at Hydrax (*Epist.* 67).

The Beechey brothers and Pacho, working quite independently of one another, both identified the site of Erythrum at the mouth of the Wadi El-Atrun, a few kilometres east of the great bay of Marsa el-Hilal (the ancient Naustathmus). The Beecheys described the remains at El-Atrun as "much decayed and mutilated, apparently those of an ancient town of small dimensions". Pacho also noticed the remains of an aqueduct. The ruins at El-Atrun still survive, although they have been even more mutilated by stone-seekers engaged in building the Italo-Arab colony of Fiorita. They lie on the top of a cliff on the west side of the mouth of the Wadi El-Atrun, where, exactly as described by Synesius, abundant spring-water runs down to within a few yards of the beach.

Survey shows that the area of habitation at Erythrum is very small: part of it may have fallen into the sea through the undermining of the cliffs. The most conspicuous feature is a ruined castle on a headland, separated from the mainland by a deep ditch. Behind this lies the small settlement area, also ditched on its south side. Among the mounds of ruins can be recognised a Christian church, with eastern apse, which was equipped with marble capitals and columns. These may have been re-used from some earlier building, but one capital has a Greek cross carved on it.

The identification of Erythrum may be considered as certain. It was a small coastal village blessed with an abundant water supply, but with relatively little cultivable soil in its vicinity. It is not surprising that its bishop should have attempted to lay hands on property at Ain Mara on the plateau some 13 km. inland. Erythrum, like Phycus, was an isolated place which had little chance of expansion during the Roman period. Yet it became an episcopal see and had, as Synesius tells us, several villages in the interior as its dependencies.

Hydrax

In one of the longest and most interesting letters, addressed to Theophilus, Patriarch of Alexandria, Synesius describes his visit to the villages of Palaebisca and Hydrax, in order to arbitrate at a disputed episcopal election (*Epist.* 67). These villages were in the Pentapolis (Libya Superior), but on the boundary of Libya Inferior or Sicca, the province which included the former area of Marmarica. The provincial boundary ran inland from the sea a little to the west of Darnis, which was for some time the capital of the lower province. At the time of Synesius' visit (which Druon dates to 411) the country between Ptolemais and these villages was "infested by the enemy", and it is quite evident that the Bishop of Ptolemais did not enjoy his mission.

Of these two villages, Palaebisca is recorded only by Synesius, and cannot yet be identified.[15] Hydrax, however, is recorded by Ptolemy as being situated inland, approximately midway between Erythrum and Darnis, which is what the evidence of Synesius would lead one to suppose. Its name suggests the presence of water, in sufficient abundance to be a matter of note. The most copious springs which lie inland between Erythrum and Darnis are those of El-Gubba (Giovanni Berta) and Ain Mara. El-Gubba is, however, too far west to have been situated close to the boundaries of the territory of Darnis, and Ain Mara seems the more likely site.

The springs of Ain Mara lie in a valley 3 km. south of the modern road from El-Gubba to Derna. This valley is one of the greenest and most fertile in the whole Cyrenaican Gebel, although it is fringed on the south by a rugged treeless plateau. The traveller arriving from the west would feel that he was literally, as well as administratively, on the borders of Libya Sicca. The identification of this place as Hydrax requires, however, archaeological support if it is to be convincing. Such support is not hard to find.

In his report to Theophilus, Synesius describes how there was, in the highest part of the village, a strong fort which had been destroyed by an earthquake, but which could be repaired and would be of value in the prevailing conditions of barbarian invasion. In this derelict fort the Bishop of Erythrum had irregularly consecrated a small room in the hope that he would thus be able to deprive the legal owner, the Bishop of Darnis, of possession, Synesius adds that the fort could only be approached by crossing the whole plateau, and that there were vineyards and olive plantations in its vicinity.

Although fortified farmhouses are abundant on the plateau west of Derna, true forts are relatively scarce. The only one yet recorded does in fact stand on a spur on the east side of the springs of Ain Mara: it was surveyed by Mr. M. H. de Lisle during the 1950 expedition [plan illustrated p. 205 above]. This fort is 34 m. square, and has outer walls 1·40 m. wide, of small, well-coursed blocks. Surrounding the fort, but almost completely filled by fallen masonry and rubble, is a vertical-sided rock-cut ditch. Ditches of this type are frequently encountered in Cyrenaica; rock-cut chambers opening off their sides served as store-rooms, stables, and living accommodation in times of peace. In the centre of the walled area at Ain Mara, a rock-cut cistern, with a small opening from the surface, held the emergency water-supply.

In all the forts and fortified farms of Cyrenaica, the heavy rainfall has caused the partial collapse of walls, but at Ain Mara there are signs of a more violent destruction, not even attributable to the hand of man. The north-west and north-east walls both have outward bulges, and in the latter case a large slice of the inner edge of the ditch has caved in. Nothing short of an earth-tremor could have had this result, and we need have little hesitation in identifying the Ain Mara fort as the one referred to by Synesius. Outside the fort ditch a labyrinth of rough stone walls represents a small village community; but the main occupation of ancient Hydrax should probably be sought in the valley, closer to the springs.

GENERAL CONCLUSIONS

The archaeological and topographical evidence discussed above may serve to illustrate the physical environment in which Synesius lived and worked. It is, of course, impossible to reconstitute a clear and consecutive narrative of events from letters which are undated, and which in any case can only represent a fraction of his total correspondence. Yet the evidence of the letters, considered topographically, may help us to see more clearly some of the salient points of Synesius' life in the Pentapolis.

Although Synesius took pride in the fact that he was born at Cyrene, of ancient stock, he seems to have spent a great deal of his recorded life living in the countryside some distance from the city. [Modern commentators] have rightly concluded that Synesius had more than one country estate, but they have not ventured to suggest where these were located. The country residence about which we have most information is described in a single letter: it lay far from town or road, and was apparently midway between the coast and the salt-marshes (baltets) which lie beyond the wooded Gebel (*Epist*. 148). This place, which was perhaps called Anchemachus, must have been situated somewhere on the southern edge of the forest belt, perhaps towards Chaulan or Slonta.

Most of his letters from the countryside seem, however, to refer to another estate, which was sufficiently near Cyrene to be used on one occasion by the barbarians as a base to menace that city, but sufficiently far away to enable Synesius to escape the company of those latter-day Cyreneans for whom he felt such contempt (*Epist*. 95, 114). We have already discussed (p. 241) the significance of the fact that Phycus played so prominent a part in Synesius' life; and it seems reasonable to assume that his country villa lay west of Cyrene in cool wooded country not far from Balagrae [for more detail, see above p. 242].

This area is full of ancient buildings, but it is hardly possible to single out any one of them as having belonged to Synesius. It would be erroneous, too, to suppose that he lived, like the great writers of the earlier Empire, in a large, luxuriously-equipped country mansion. In the Cyrenaica of his day, the unit of rural habitation seems to have been the fortified homestead, a building in which comfort was sacrificed to defensibility.

There is little reason to doubt that it was while resident in this latter estate that Synesius first experienced the impact on the countryside of the barbarian invasions. When we study his remarks on the military situation, and his criticism of the strategy of the military commanders, we must always remember that Synesius saw events through the eyes of a country gentleman serving in a "home guard" (so e.g. *Epist.* 78). If he criticised the policy of keeping the regular troops "shut up within walled towns", it was largely because he was a country-dweller by temperament, and had experienced the devastation wrought on crops and herds by marauding invaders. The forces available in the Pentapolis were very limited, and the *dux* had to decide whether to save the towns at the cost of the countryside, or to sacrifice the towns for the sake of keeping an intact field-force with which to search out and rout the enemy. The peculiar geography of the Cyrenaican Gebel is, however, invariably on the side of the guerrilla, as the Italians found during the period 1922–30. The deep wooded ravines of the Wadi Kuf allow small bands to penetrate, unseen, into settled areas, to cause havoc and confusion, and to withdraw to safety. The Gebel countryside is not favourable for the deployment of large field forces, and given their limited resources, the Roman generals were perhaps right in deciding to save the cities and to leave the defence of the rural area to such local militias as the Balagritan yeomanry, and the Phycuntian sailors. There is, at least, no evidence that any of the cities fell to the barbarians.

The final glimpse which Synesius gives us of the military situation in the Pentapolis is in the *Catastasis*, which Druon dates to A.D. 412. In this essay Synesius declares that the province is entirely lost, and that he himself would have escaped to some distant island, had a ship been available. That having proved impossible, he was obliged to wait for the expected attack on Ptolemais, resolved to meet death at the altar of his church. Whether the military authorities in Ptolemais shared this defeatist view is not known; but from the archaeological evidence already discussed it seems more likely that a drastic policy of retrenchment was carried out. The eastern government at Constantinople had no intention of abandoning the Pentapolis, and at some later date reinforcements must have been sent to remedy the situation. Learning from the experience of the Austurian invasion, the military leaders in Libya erected massive block-houses on the sides of the ravines of the Wadi Kuf area; and these block-houses—such as Gasr Beni-Gdem and Gsar Shahden [see plates 68, 70, 71, 73] were kept garrisoned until the end of Byzantine rule. The Pentapolis was saved eventually by professional soldiers, not by the *curiales* whom Synesius represented.

NOTES

[1. See p. 244.
2. C. H. Coster, *Byzantion* xv (1940–1) 10 f.
3. See p. 250.
4. See pp. 201–2.
5. A. Fitzgerald, (1) and (2). For the Greek text of the letters see R. Hercher, *Epistolographi Graeci* (Paris, 1873) 638 f. and for the other writings Migne, *Patrologia Graeca*. J. C. Pando; cf. also H. Druon, cited below on chronology. More recently C. H. Coster, in *Byzantion* xv (1940-1) 10 f. and C. Lacombrade.
6. For the sites of Cyrene and Ptolemais see now Goodchild, *Kyrene und Apollonia* and C. H. Kraeling et al., *Ptolemais*.
7. D. Comparetti, 161 f.
8. Jaubert, *Géographie d'Edrisie* I. 293.
9. The Chicago expedition, however, found no clear evidence for such a wall, see Kraeling, *loc. cit.* n. 2, 26 f. and Goodchild, "Fortificazioni", 235, but it is "the supposed sea-wall" briefly examined in 1972, see R. Yorke, *Third Annual Report of the Society for Libyan Studies* (1971–2) 4. While it remains uncertain whether or not Goodchild was right in his interpretation of its date and function, the main lines of his account of the defences of Ptolemais in the fifth century are unaffected and his hypothesis of the part played by Andronicus deserves consideration.

10. G. Pesce, *Il Palazzo delle Colonne in Tolemaide di Cirenaica* (Roma, 1950).
11. Goodchild left space for a figure here but none seems to have been published since the Chicago expedition added a considerable length of wall on the Gebel to the total perimeter; a rough computation from their plans (in Kraeling, *loc. cit.* n. 2) suggests a length of some $4\frac{1}{2}$ km. on the landward side.
12. Smith and Porcher, 61. A brief account of Phycus was recently published by G. D. B. Jones and J. Little in *JRS* lxi (1971) 73 f. Ancient references to it are to be found in Lucan, *Pharsalia* ix. 300; Strabo, *Geog.* xvii 837; Ptolemy, *Geog.* iv. 4; Scylax, *Periplus* 108; *Stad. Mar. Magn.*, 54.
13. See now p. 229 f., and Hamilton 123).
14. See now Jones and Little, *loc. cit.* in n. 7, 76. Two churches have recently been excavated here, Goodchild in *Corsi di Cultura sull' arte Ravennate e Bizantina* (Ravenna, 1966) 218 f.
15. See also above p. 152; Jones and Little, *loc. cit.* in n. 7, 76, identify Palaebisca with Bet Tamer, but without argument.]

20

BYZANTINES, BERBERS AND ARABS IN SEVENTH-CENTURY LIBYA

[from *Antiquity* xli (1967)]

The extraordinary rapidity of the Arab conquest (fig. 75) of the north African coastlands between Alexandria and Tripoli has often evoked comment, even in an age which has seen modern armies advancing still more rapidly over the same route. One recent writer, exceptionally well qualified to discuss Arab warfare, has affirmed that "the welcome offered to the Arabs in the Western Desert and Barka seems to suggest that the people in this area were themselves partly Arab."[1]

Of the actual course of events during the first campaigns (A.D. 642–5) we have, however, only the most rudimentary knowledge. The Arab documentary sources, relatively detailed in their account of the conquest of Egypt, dry up almost completely once the army of 'Amr ibn el-Aasi moved westward from the Delta. We have little more than a mention of the capitulation of Barka, and only slightly more circumstantial accounts of the storming of Tripoli and Sabratha. There is certainly no mention of a "welcome" in Cyrenaica, but equally there is no reference to prolonged armed conflict before the Arabs reached Tripoli. How, then, was this notable victory achieved?

Perhaps we shall never know the whole truth regarding this initial Arab campaign in Africa, which was to secure a firm bridgehead for future successes in the Maghreb and in Spain. Yet a new analysis of the documents, both Arab and Coptic, in conjunction with study of the increasing body of archaeological evidence for conditions of life in seventh-century Libya, seems called for.

When Butler wrote his masterly *Arab Conquest of Egypt* more than a half-century ago little was known of the Byzantine archaeology of neighbouring Libya. The splendid surveys made by the Beechey brothers in 1821 had revealed the presence of numerous Byzantine churches in the cities of the Pentapolis, as was only to be expected;[2] but subsequent travellers had done little to document the extraordinary wealth of Byzantine constructions, military as well as ecclesiastical, scattered throughout the countryside.

Today, the picture of Byzantine Cyrenaica, on the eve of the Arab conquest, is far more complete: we know that there was a pattern of settlement as intense as in any part of Syria or Asia Minor. Churches have been excavated in the cities and country villages, the latter being very numerous indeed. Castles and watchtowers, constructed in most solid and competent stonework—in most cases, newly quarried—have been surveyed. At Apollonia-Sozusa, the capital of Libya Pentapolis from Anastasius to Heraclius, the Governor's Palace has been identified and

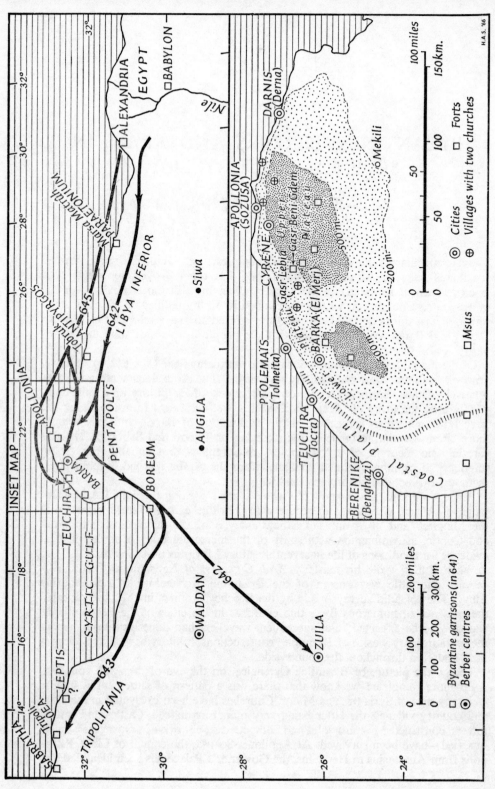

Fig. 75 Map to show the Arab conquest of Libya

explored.[3] At Tauchira, where the Byzantine garrison made its last stand, a vast fortress-palace of late Byzantine or early Arab date is coming to light.[4]

The Arab conquerors are, unfortunately, less easily identified by the archaeologist than the Byzantines whom they displaced. Cavalry actions, without extensive siege-works, do not leave traces on the landscape. Moreover, at the time of the conquest of Libya, there were no distinctive Islamic coins in general circulation, and no distinctive Islamic pottery in extensive use. An early Arab occupation site is therefore hardly likely to be distinguishable from a late Byzantine one: the abundant coins of Heraclius are common to both.[5]

Whilst, therefore, we cannot reconstruct the course of the Arab campaigns from archaeological indications alone, we can at least assess their probable impact, in terms not only of the military defences with which they had to reckon, but also of the political and religious structure of the invaded population.

Such assessment may help to explain certain peculiarities in the Coptic accounts of the Arab invasion of Libya, including a statement by the chronicler John of Nikiu which has seemed so improbable that modern translators have distorted or ignored it (see Appendix). It may also illuminate the strategy that underlay 'Amr ibn el-Aasi's dash to Barka in 642.

THE FIRST ARAB EXPEDITION INTO PENTAPOLIS (Summer 642)

It is reasonable to assume, as all commentators have done, that an Arab expedition into the Pentapolis would not have been put into motion prior to the capitulation of Alexandria (8 November, 641). There is only doubt as to whether 'Amr ibn el-Aasi awaited the Byzantine evacuation of that city (17 September, 642) before moving westwards. Butler[6] took the view that full possession of Alexandria was a prerequisite for conquering the Pentapolis; but Brooks,[7] and Caetani[8] have both suggested that the campaign took place in the summer of 642, while the hand-over of the city was still awaited.

This latter view seems inherently more probable, for 'Amr ibn el-Aasi—assuming that he was well informed as to climatic conditions in eastern Libya—would surely have chosen to launch his offensive long before the winter rains, which begin in November. Heat would have been less handicap to the hardy Arab horsemen than the winter mud and flooded wadis which could have impeded their progress. There were ample cisterns in the coastal regions containing, even in summer, a residue of water from the previous winter's rains.

The Arab sources that refer to the expedition give no details of its execution. The fullest and most reliable account is that of Ibn Abd el-Hakam (ninth century A.D.)[9] who, after stating that the Luwatah Berbers had long previously occupied Antabulus (Pentapolis) or Barka, adds:

> 'Amr ibn el-Aasi now entered the land with his horsemen and reached Barka, with whose inhabitants he made a treaty: they agreed to pay a tribute of 13,000 dinars, with the stipulation that they could sell their children to pay the tax.

Another source[10] states that the Arab general had besieged the city of Barka for some time before this treaty was made; and all seem to agree that the annual

tribute was subsequently paid with the greatest regularity, it never being necessary to send tax-collectors to Barka. Its inhabitants were, in consequence, deemed
to be the most generous and pacific in North Africa.

On the Coptic side, which we must now take into consideration, the Chronicle
of John of Nikiu makes a brief reference to the invasion of Pentapolis, but
mentions neither the city of Barka, nor the peace treaty made between the Arabs
and the Berbers. Indeed, the Chronicle, as translated literally from the Ethiopic
text (which is our only source),[11] gives a very different account of the campaign:

> 'Amr (ibn el-Aasi) oppressed Egypt. He sent its inhabitants to fight the
> inhabitants of Pentapolis, but after having obtained a victory, he did not let
> them remain there. He took from this country plunder and captives in
> abundance.
> And Abulyanos the prefect of Pentapolis and his troops and the rich
> men of the province withdrew into the city of Dushera (Tauchira)—now its
> walls were strongly fortified—and they closed the gates. So the Moslems
> returned to their own country with the booty and the captives.

This account appears in the Chronicle immediately before the mention of the
death of the patriarch Cyrus (March, 642); but it is not excluded that the campaign actually took place a few months later, during the course of the summer.
What is noteworthy is the fact that John of Nikiu seems to imply that Egyptians
(i.e. Copts) were sent into the Pentapolis to help the campaign there, but that
they were deprived of the fruits of their collaboration with the Arabs, who kept
for themselves the booty and the captives.

Moreover, despite the initial victory to which John of Nikiu refers, the Byzantines were not completely routed but remained in possession of Tauchira—and
possibly, also, of other places further to the west. Until these were eliminated
there would remain the danger of Byzantine reinforcements arriving by land
from Tripolitania or by sea from Crete or Constantinople. The former possibility
was reduced by the lightning dash to Tripoli in 643, which will be discussed later.
The latter was impeded by a second expedition to Pentapolis, which seems to
have taken place in 644 or 645.

THE SECOND EXPEDITION (A.D. 644–5)

The Arab sources provide no clear reference to this second campaign.[12] We know
of it only from a passage in the "History of the Patriarchs of the Coptic
Church", which is generally attributed to Bishop Severus of Ashmunein (tenth
century A.D.), but which embodies parts of an earlier chronicle compiled by Abba
George, archdeacon and secretary of the Patriarch Simon (A.D. 689–701), "on
the mountain of St Macarius in the Wadi Habib".

This chronicle states[13] that 'Amr ibn el-Aasi arranged with a "Duke Sanutius"
(of whom we shall have more to say) to arrange for the recall of the Coptic
patriarch Benjamin, who had long been in hiding from Orthodox repression. At
their first meeting, 'Amr addressed the patriarch:

> "Resume the government of all thy churches and of thy people, and if
> thou wilt, pray for me, that I may go to the west and to Pentapolis and

take possession of them, as I have of Egypt, and return to thee in safety and speedily." Then the holy Benjamin prayed for 'Amr, and pronounced an eloquent discourse.

And after that, 'Amr and his troops marched away from Alexandria, and the Christ-loving Sanutius marched with them. . . .

The narrative continues with an account of miraculous happenings when the baggage-ships of the expedition were about to set sail from Alexandria. The vessel on which Sanutius himself had embarked refused to sail because its captain had clandestinely brought on board the head of St. Mark, stolen from his tomb which had been broken open during the Arab occupation of the city. Sanutius therefore "anchored the ship in which the commander 'Amr was" and returned to search his own vessel. The saint's head was found and returned to its tomb (which Sanutius arranged to have restored at his own expense), and the fleet then sailed away without further difficulty.

Despite the miraculous episode, there is no reason to discount the basic historical truth of this narrative. The reconstruction of the shrine of St. Mark is likely to have been remembered in the Coptic church, and to have been associated with a personage and with an occasion. The personage Sanutius, is—as we shall see—an historical figure; and if 'Amr had decided to use ships, he would have needed the services of a Copt to command this fleet. Moreover, as it is generally agreed that Benjamin returned from his thirteen-year exile in the autumn of 644, this expedition can hardly have been confused with the one of 642, which, as already shown, probably took place while Alexandria was still in Byzantine possession, with the tomb of St. Mark unviolated.[14] Moreover, the fact of the survival of the Byzantine garrison, in its "last stand" fortress at Tauchira, necessitated a further campaign with the aid of a fleet which could hardly have been assembled at the time of the first campaign.

Who was the "Duke Sanutius" thus associated with the second campaign? He is presumably the same man as the "Sinoda" mentioned by John of Nikiu[15] as having been selected by the Arabs to serve as governor of the province of Al-Rif (part of Lower Egypt). He was at that time hated by the Copts for what seemed excessive pro-Arab sympathies; and this hatred was enhanced by the fact that he was himself—as his name indicates, and as the title "Christ-loving" confirms—a Copt. The name Shenouti or Shenoudi is common in the prosopography of Coptic Egypt, and survives even today. It is not necessary to assume, as Butler did[15a] that the military title *Dux* proves that Sanutius had begun his career in the Byzantine administration: the title could have been assumed automatically with the governorship, conferred by the Arabs.

Whatever his origins, Sanutius was clearly an opportunist, well suited to play the part of collaborator with the invaders. If we wish to be charitable, we may suppose that his collaboration was inspired by the desire to free fellow-Monophysite believers from orthodox oppression. If the Patriarch Benjamin could pray for 'Amr ibn el-Aasi, Sanutius was surely entitled to fight for him!

The achievements of this expedition of 644–5 are not recorded. We may perhaps assume that Tauchira and other pockets of Byzantine resistance were finally liquidated. Whether 'Amr himself led the campaign throughout its course, or delegated command to his Arab and Copt subordinates, is uncertain. The

Arab commander-in-chief was, at this time, beginning to have troubles of his own, resulting from criticisms of his administrative and fiscal policies. These were to culminate in his replacement of Abdallah ibn Sa'd.

Despite the many uncertainties inherent in these Coptic chronicles, it does seem certain that the Arab conquest of Pentapolis was a more complex operation than is generally believed to have been the case. John of Nikiu implies—if we have accurately interpreted his testimony—that the Coptic participation in 642 was very considerable. "The History of the Patriarchs" shows that a leading Copt commanded a fleet supporting the expedition of 644–5.

It therefore follows that the siege and submission of Berber Barka, by a purely Arab force, as recorded in the Arab chronicles, was only a part—if, no doubt, the most important part—of the operations in eastern Libya.

THE CAPITULATION OF BARKA

From the moment of the Arab invasion of Libya down to the present day, the whole area of ancient Cyrenaica has borne the name Barka. This regional name is derived from the name of the city (Barka or Barcae) that had been founded by dissident Greeks from Cyrene in the reign of king Arkesilaus II (sixth century B.C.). The old town of El Merj (partially destroyed by earthquake in 1962) occupies the site of Barka.[15b]

Barka had been an important centre in the earlier centuries of Greek settlement in Cyrenaica, and is known to have had a strong Libyan element in its population and culture; but in Hellenistic, Roman and Byzantine times it was eclipsed by its own port, Ptolemais, which had been grandiosely laid out in the third century B.C. Barka, being neither on the sea nor on the main network of Roman roads,[16] declined and became little more than a village. It was a bishopric in the fifth and sixth centuries, but so were several other obscure villages of the Pentapolis.

During the second half of the sixth century, Barka seems to have enjoyed a revival of its fortunes—perhaps after the population of waterless Ptolemais drifted back to it. But it appears to have become a Berber settlement, increasingly alienated from Byzantine rule. It is significant that when the Berbers of Tripolitania and the Syrtica revolted against the Byzantines in the sixth century, the general John Troglita—according to Corippus—found them supported by "the 'Barcaei', who have left their own land and are already heading for ours"[17]

We do not know whether Barka ever came back under direct Byzantine control, following this revolt. Perhaps their chieftains continued to receive the customary insignia of office from the hands of the governor,[18] and perhaps they paid tribute. But their loyalty had worn very thin, and in the coming struggle between Byzantines and Arabs they could be considered as "unaligned".

It is evident, therefore, that these Berbers of Barka, members of the extensive Luwatah tribe or group of tribes,[19] were a key factor in 'Amr ibn el-Aasi's plans for the conquest of the Pentapolis. They controlled the rich wheat-growing area of the lower Cyrenaican plateau, and their alliance—or, at least, neutrality— would enable the Arabs more easily to crush the Byzantine resistance in the coastal garrisons. Moreover, since their degree of Christianity was very slight and superficial, and confined to the areas bordering on effective Byzantine occupation, these Barkans could be considered as the most promising future converts to Islam.

Thus, the cavalry dash to Barka, followed by its siege and surrender, as described in Arab sources, was the key action of the whole campaign. But it was not, as some modern writers have assumed, the only action. The populations of the old cities of the Pentapolis—decrepit and impoverished as these may have been—and the rural populations in the upper plateau around Cyrene, were not to be considered as Luwatah Berbers. They were fully Christianised and unlikely to welcome the Arab invaders, unless the invasion could be presented in some manner as a liberation. And it was, no doubt, to create the image of such a liberation that the Coptic part in the campaign was so substantial.

RELIGIOUS DISSENSIONS IN THE PENTAPOLIS

Long before the Arab invasion, the Libyan provinces of the Eastern Roman Empire (Upper Libya or Pentapolis, and Lower or "Dry" Libya (equivalent to the Marmarica)), had proved fertile ground for the development of schismatic movements within the Church. As early as the reign of Valerian the city of Ptolemais had produced Sabellius whose heretical doctrines became widely diffused. In the following century Arianism flourished most vigorously in the areas west of Alexandria. Bishops Secundus of Ptolemais and Theonas of Marmarike (supported also by Sentianus of Boreum) had been among the leading exponents of the Arian doctrine, and thereby lost their sees after the Council of Nicaea.[20]

The "Two Libyas" had, from the earliest days of the Church, been recognised as being subject to the see of Alexandria, and this dependence was specifically reconfirmed by the Council of Nicaea.[21] Therefore it was only to be expected that the religious controversies that were later rife in Egypt would have their repercussions in the Libyas, tending after the Council of Chalcedon towards the creation of a local Monophysite church, in rivalry to the official Orthodox church. It is surely no accident that the Emperor Zeno's *Henotikon*, an ill-fated compromise designed to heal the discords created by Chalcedon, is addressed to the Libyan clergy as well as to the Egyptian.[22]

Leaving aside the purely doctrinal aspects of the struggle between the orthodox and Monophysite communities, there was also a deep-rooted political and economic motivation. Orthodoxy, as Stein has pointed out,[23] was the faith of the aristocracy—the landowners—whose loyalty to Constantinople was not uninfluenced by material considerations. The masses, and more especially the peasants, favoured Monophysitism. It may not therefore be insignificant that when the governor Apollonios,[24] during the first Arab-Copt campaign in Pentapolis in 642, withdrew into the strongly walled city of Tauchira, he took with him not only the Byzantine officials, but also the "rich men" of the province.

Historical testimony for the existence, in the Libyas, of the two rival Churches hardly exists; but that is not surprising when we recall that there were no large outbreaks of violence, such as occurred so often in Egypt. Archaeological evidence, accumulating in recent years, is beginning to fill the void.

It has long been known that the old cities of the Pentapolis each contained

several churches (four at Apollonia and at least three at Tocra, for example):
by itself, this fact is of no significance. What is remarkable is that even in the
smallest villages of the countryside, it is normal to find two churches, one of
which is usually a massive fort-like building, often surrounded by a ditch, and
the other an undefended church.

This is not the place for a catalogue of church sites in Cyrenaica,[24a] and it will
suffice here to mention the twin churches at Lamluda (Limnias), at Mgarnes, at
Gasr el-Lebia and at Gasr Silu. We do not yet know enough about the internal
fittings of these churches to be able to decide which were Orthodox and which
Monophysite; but it seems at least likely that the more heavily fortified churches
were the Orthodox ones, erected by government inspiration and subvention, and
designed to have a military role as well as a religious one.

THE MILITARY DEFENCES AND GARRISONS

We have seen that the impact of the first Arab-Copt campaign in 642 caused the
provincial governor to retire, with his troops, into the walled city of Tauchira.
This lies in the western half of what was then the more populous part of
Cyrenaica, and its selection for a "last stand" against the invaders implies that
the areas to the east had already fallen, or were no longer tenable.

By the seventh century, the two capitals of the Libyan provinces were Darnis
for Lower Libya and Apollonia-Sozusa for Pentapolis.[25] Recent excavations on
the latter site make it certain that the city was occupied and flourishing down
to the eve of the Arab invasion of 642: the Governor's Palace, in particular, has
yielded evidence of intense activity in the first quarter of the seventh
century.

To reach these two cities from Alexandria, an invading army had first to pass
the two fortress towns of Paraetonium (Marsa Matruh) and Antipyrgos (Tobruk),
both of which had been set up as garrisoned frontier posts by Justinian.[26] Then,
as in more recent campaigns, it was not, of course, difficult to bypass these
fortresses. But it is inconceivable that they could have been bypassed without
their garrisons receiving information and passing on warnings to the other
garrisons further to the west.

The Cyrenaican mountains (the Gebel el-Akhdar of today) were protected in
Byzantine times by a highly complex system of forts, fortified churches and
watchtowers, normally sited on the highest points, and intervisible. The massive
sixth-century fortress of Gasr Beni Gdem—the most imposing of the series, and
originally intended to prevent Libyan tribesmen from infiltrating into the ravines
of the Wadi Kuf region—has intervisibility with at least a score of minor outposts. No doubt the approach of invaders could be signalled (by fire, smoke or
heliograph) across the whole mountain area with great rapidity.

These mountain strongholds were probably garrisoned mainly by irregular
troops—local levies of the type mentioned by Synesius two centuries earlier, and
the *kastresianoi* who are referred to in Byzantine documents.[27] In addition there
were at least five regular units, *arithmoi* (Latin *numeri*), each presumably
stationed in one of the five principal cities of the Pentapolis. Very probably, the
strength of the *arithmoi* had been reduced by the dispatch of relieving forces to
Egypt to help arrest the first Arab advance.[27a] But the strongholds garrisoned

by irregular troops who cultivated the lands adjoining their posts can hardly have been left empty at the moment of the invasion of 642.

To reach the heart of the Pentapolis, the agriculturally rich upper plateau around Cyrene, scattered with numerous villages especially populous in Byzantine times, the invaders had no need to occupy either Darnis or Apollonia-Sozusa, the provincial capitals. Both these cities lay on the shore below the plateau, and had very indifferent lateral communications. Their isolation from the plateau had been an advantage during the long period of Libyan raids (by Austuriani or Mazices) from the southern deserts. But in the face of a determined and well-organised attack from Egypt, it would have been folly to keep the military command in such isolated places.

We may therefore suppose that the withdrawal of the Byzantine commander Apollonios (presumably Dux of the Pentapolis) from Apollonia to Tauchira was not merely a hasty evacuation in the face of overpowering forces, but was a planned strategic withdrawal. Certainly Tauchira was, as the Chronicle of John of Nikiu indicates, a strongly walled city. But Apollonia itself was no less strongly walled, as archaeological remains show. It could certainly have resisted an attack by nomads unskilled in siegecraft.[28]

Tauchira, however, had a great strategic advantage. It stood at the beginning of the vast coastal plain that extends south-westwards towards Benghazi and thence southwards to the foot of the Syrtic Gulf. In this plain there was room for manoeuvre; reinforcements could arrive by land from Tripolitania, and, if necessary, a withdrawal could be made by land towards Tripolitania. In Apollonia, by contrast, there was no way out except by sea, and no hope of receiving reinforcements except by sea.

Thus the decision was made to evacuate Apollonia, and was put into effect before the Arab-Copt forces arrived. This much is clear from the archaeological evidence, since neither the Governor's Palace nor the walls show signs of violent assault. The officials and troops marched out, leaving the civil population to make their own terms with the invaders. The history of Cyrene's once-flourishing port came virtually to an end.[28a]

At Tauchira the incoming Byzantine authorities set about improving their defences. The old Hellenistic city walls had been extensively repaired and re-modelled already in the age of Justinian, and been given a series of rectangular turrets set at close intervals around the circuit. There are also grounds for supposing that the seaward side of the city was first walled by Justinian or one of his successors.[28b]

In the interior of the city, on the south side of the former *Decumanus maximus*, recent excavation has brought to light a vast Byzantine fortress, subdivided into courtyards and barrack rooms. Unlike the massive fortresses of the age of Anastasius and Justinian which survive elsewhere in Cyrenaica, this Tauchira citadel has no foundations at all. Its broad walls, constructed of stones stripped from earlier edifices, rest only on compacted earth, with the result that some interior walls are visibly tilted. This surely denotes a fortress constructed in haste in an open space cleared of all earlier edifices. Coin finds are not inconsistent with a Heraclian date, and we may perhaps identify this citadel as the last monument of Byzantine rule in Cyrenaica.

While his troops manned the outer defences of Tauchira, Apollonios and his headquarters staff probably installed themselves within this inner citadel during the years 642–5. With the Berber inhabitants of nearby Barka already tributaries of the Arabs, and the Christian population of the coast subverted by religious schism, the prospects of a prolonged "last stand" must have seemed slight—unless reinforcements could arrive from the west. Since, as we shall see, two at least of the cities of Tripolitania fell to the Arabs not long after the treaty of Barka, the chances of reinforcement were slight indeed.

How and when the Tauchira strongpoint finally collapsed we do not know; but it seems at least likely that it survived until the campaign of 645 when 'Amr had—as we have already shown—a naval element commanded by Duke Sanutius. No scattered weapons or bodies of slain defenders have yet come to light within the citadel, but there would have been a cleaning-up after the Arabs had taken possession.[28c] It may be significant that the door pivots of the citadel gateway show signs of heavy burning, as if to suggest a military assault. But Apollonios may have slipped away by sea before the Arabs and their allies arrived, leaving only an empty and gutted city.

THE ARAB DASH TO TRIPOLITANIA

The success of the cavalry attack on Barka in 642, and the relatively rapid submission of the Berbers there, must have convinced 'Amr that he could risk his best forces in a lightning assault on Tripolitania, without even awaiting the final reduction of the Byzantine base at Tauchira. In the same year that Barka fell, 'Amr sent Okba ibn Nafi on a brilliant cavalry raid to Zuila in the Fezzan, and made a treaty with the Berber people of that region.[29]

Such Byzantine bases as remained south of Berenice (Benghazi), notably the fortress-city of Boreum (near Marsa Brega), were easily bypassed. The rest of the Syrtic coastlands as far as Cape Misurata were no longer under Byzantine control, the scattered Berber population having already shown itself hostile during the Berber revolt of 543. The problem was one of logistics rather than tactics, but the predatory Arab horsemen did not need lavish supply columns.

It was in A.H. 22 (December, 642–November 643), according to most Arab sources,[30] that 'Amr reached the city of Tripoli (ancient Oea) and laid siege to it. As at Tauchira, the defensive walls proved impregnable, and a month passed before an adventurous group of seven Arabs found a way of penetrating into the city along its western seashore. The Arab war-cry "Allahu Akbar" shouted in the main church was enough to cause the flight of the Byzantine garrison to their ships in the harbour. Before the news of the capture of Tripoli reached the nearby city of Sabratha, 'Amr's forces were already there and entered by an unguarded gateway.

What is notable in the record of this campaign is the absence of any mention of Lepcis Magna, the former capital of Byzantine Tripolitania. Had it previously fallen, or was it no longer an occupied city in 643? It seems at least unlikely that 'Amr would conduct a prolonged siege of Tripoli while leaving an active Byzantine garrison in Lepcis in his rear. More probably the Luwatah Berbers of the area around Lepcis had already succeeded in extinguishing life in a city which bore odious memories for them.[30a]

CONCLUSIONS

This analysis of the Arab campaigns in Libya in 642–5 is necessarily speculative, since the historical sources are altogether too slight to permit of certainty. The essential problem is how the Arabs broke through the Byzantine defences of the Cyrenaican mountains, defences which are, even today, extraordinarily impressive. There is certainly no known fact, or even probability, to support Sir John Glubb's suggestion that the Arabs were "welcomed" in the Western Desert and Barka by their own kinsmen. But they were welcomed, in Libya as in Egypt, by a Christian population of Monophysite doctrine which had been led to believe that these new and powerful allies could destroy their Orthodox oppressors [see note 31].

If the fortresses of the Cyrenaican mountains put up no resistance to the invaders, it was not merely because of a supposed general corruption and inefficiency of the Byzantine regime. With 'Amr came influential Copts, like Duke Sanutius, probably holding out the promise of a "popular" Monophysite church independent of Constantinople. Such a promise could have subverted the hard-core Christians of the Cyrenaican coast; whilst the "marginal" Christians of the purely Berber regions, simple men uninterested in—and probably bewildered by —the hair-splitting of Christian theologians, rapidly found in Islam an attractive new faith, suited to their daily needs.

The disillusionment of the hard-core Christians finds expression in John of Nikiu's Chronicle, although the very survival of the Coptic church in Egypt is testimony to the good faith of 'Amr ibn el-Aasi. In Libya the Berbers newly converted to Islam rapidly gained possession of the areas previously occupied by Monophysite Christians, so that the total extinction of Christianity in Cyrenaica, soon to follow,[30b] can be attributed to Berber conquest rather than to Arab policy.

The hero of the whole episode is, of course, 'Amr ibn el-Aasi, one of the most remarkable men of history who, in addition to being a genial personality and a most skilled and courageous warrior, was also an adroit politician.[31] He would have been the first to realise that his brave Arab horsemen could hardly reduce the massive fortresses of Cyrenaica without the aid of a popular Monophysite insurrection. There is no reason to suppose that his use of "collaborators" like Duke Sanutius was in any way cynical: he would no doubt have been willing to grant the Monophysite church the same freedom in Libya as it enjoyed in Egypt. His genius lay in recognising that the Berbers were the real power in North Africa, and that the immediate success of Islam depended on their submission and conversion.

APPENDIX

JOHN OF NIKIU AND THE FIRST EXPEDITION TO PENTAPOLIS

Some justification is required for the version given above (p. 258) of John of Nikiu's account of the first expedition to the Pentapolis. The most recent editions of his Chronicle all give translations which imply that 'Amr ibn el-Aasi sent a purely Arab force against the Pentapolis in 642.

Thus, in Zotenberg's definitive edition of 1883 (*Chronique de Jean, Évèque de Nikiou*, in *Notices et extraits des manuscrits de la Bibliothèque Nationale*, tome xxiv) his translation reads: " 'Amr envoya les troupes de ce pays" and his note 1 on p. 578 comments: "C'est-à-dire les Arabes qui étaient en Egypte. Ce n'est pas probable que l'auteur ait voulu parler des Egyptiens."

In his *Annali dell'Islam* (iv, 294 (20 A.H.), 165) Caetani translated as follows: " 'Amr mandò le genti che teneva in questo paese contro gli abitanti della Pentapoli", and gives no further explanation. Likewise, R. H. Charles (*The Chronicle of John, Bishop of Nikiu, translated from Zotenberg's Ethiopic text* (London, 1916) reads: "34. And 'Amr subdued the land of Egypt, and sent his men to war against the inhabitants of Pentapolis."

It is probable that both Caetani and Charles were influenced by what Zotenberg had said in his footnote in the edition of 1883; but it is interesting to observe that in an earlier version published in the *Journal Asiatique* in 1879 (septième serie, tome xiii, no. 2. pp. 376–7) Zotenberg had given a variant translation: " 'Amr opprima l'Egypte. Il envoya ses habitants combattre les habitants de la Pentapolis, et, après avoir remporté la victoire, il ne les y laissa demeurer."

In view of the fundamental difference between Zotenberg's first and second versions, it seemed important to obtain expert opinion regarding the wording of the Ethiopic text. The writer therefore sought the help of Professor Giorgio Levi Della Vida, to whom all students of Libyan history and archaeology are deeply indebted, and has received the following reply (19 March, 1965):

> I have consulted Enrico Cerulli, who is the greatest contemporary authority in matters of language, history and literature of Ethiopia, and with him I have carefully examined, yesterday morning, the passage of the Chronicle of John of Nikiu which interests you. ... The Ethiopic text (p. 334, lines 27–28), translated literally, says: "After having subdued the country of Egypt, ['Amr] sent *the men of it (la-sab'a zi 'ahà)* to fight against *the men of the five cities*—Pentapolis (*sab' a 5 ahgurat*)." The word sab', which strictly means "men", is currently used in the sense of "inhabitants"; the fact that the same term is used to indicate the men whom 'Amr sent into Pentapolis and those who were already there (that is to say, naturally, the inhabitants) seems to be in favour of your thesis. But it must not be forgotten that the Chronicle of John of Nikiou is the Ethiopic translation of the Arabic version of a Greek or Coptic text, and that it is therefore somewhat perilous to try to detect subtle shades of meaning.

NOTES

1. Sir John Bagot Glubb, *The Great Arab Conquests* (1963), 261.

2. F. W. and H. W. Beechey.

3. For a preliminary report see R. G. Goodchild, "Palace at Apollonia", 246–58.

4. Excavation in progress (1964–5).

5. No examples have yet been found in Cyrenaica of the Arab-Byzantine coins classified by J. Walker, *A Catalogue of the Muhammedan coins in the British Museum*, II (1956).

6. A. J. Butler, 427.

7. E. W. Brooks, *Byzantinische Zeitschrift*, iv, 1895, 435.

8. L. Caetani, iv, 532.

9. L. Caetani, iv, 533, §124.

10. L. Caetani, iv, 534, §127 (Bakr ben al-Haytham, quoted by Baladzuri).

11. For bibliography and discussion of the translation see Appendix.

12. A. J. Butler (441, n. 1) refers to a second expedition to Pentapolis taking place in A.H. 25. He probably had in mind the cavalry raid into the Maghreb made in that year by Abdallah ibn Sa'd ibn Sarh (Al-Waqidi in Caetani, vii, (1914), 137). But we are here concerned with a naval-supported expedition from Alexandria, which must have left that city before the brief Byzantine reconquest by Manuel early in A.H. 25.

13. R. Graffin and F. Nau (Arabic text edited and translated by B. Evetts), *Patrologia Orientalis*: "History of the Patriarchs of the Coptic Church of Alexandria" (Paris 1947–8), I, 2; I, 4; V, 1.

14. A. J. Butler (441) claims that Severus of Ashmunein "seems to refer, however wrongly, to the first expedition"; but this is not necessarily the case, even if we allow for a certain confusion in the minds of the, Coptic chroniclers.

15. John of Nikiu, 120[29] (trans. R. H. Charles, London and Oxford 1916); cf. L. Caetani, iv, 293 and A. J. Butler, 363.

[15a. Butler (427) calls Sanutius a Melkite; but elsewhere (440), he rightly recognises him as a Copt.]

[15b. The site of Barka has yielded Greek tombs as well as Kufic inscriptions of the Fatimid period; and there is no doubt that the classical and medieval cities were on the same site.]

16. R. G. Goodchild, *Tab. Imp. Rom.* (Cyrene).

17. Corippus, *Johannidos*, II, 123–4 (ed. Mazzucchelli, 1820): translation by J. Alix, *Revue Tunisienne*, vi, 1899, 315.

18. For these insignia bestowed on Berber notables, cf. Procopius, *De aedif.* IV, 21.

19. For the Luwatah (Leuathae), cf. Oric Bates, 67. In this article the Arabic name is preferred.

20. P. Romanelli, (3), 232.

21. J. Stevenson, *A New Eusebius* (1957), 360. (The Canons of Nicaea: 6. "Let the ancient customs hold good which are in Egypt and Libya and Pentapolis, according to which the Bishop of Alexandria has authority over all these places.")

22. Evagrius, III, 14 (ed. J. Bidez and L. Parmentier, 1898): "To the reverend bishops and clergy and monks and laity in Alexandria and Egypt and Libya and Pentapolis . . ."

23. E. Stein, 162.

24. J. Maspero (24, n. 5) suggests that the name "Aboulyanos" given by John of Nikiu should be read as "Flavianus". It seems, however, more likely that it was Apollorios, a common enough name in Cyrenaica.

[24a. These churches will be listed in a forthcoming paper in collaboration with Mr. J. B. Ward Perkins.]

25. J. Honigmann.

26. J. Maspero, *loc. cit.*; Procopius, *De aedif.* VI, ii, 2.

27. J. Maspero, 60.

[27a. According to the Byzantine historian Nicephorus, the emperor Heraclius sent John, Duke of Barca or Barcaina, against the Arabs in Egypt. This suggests that troops may have been withdrawn from garrisons in Pentapolis; but the designation "Duke of Barca" is strange and seemingly anachronistic. Cf. Butler, 207 and Caetani, iv, 183.]

28. For the walls of Apollonia, see J.-Ph. Lauer, "L'enceinte d'Apollonia", *Revue Arch.*, 1963, 129.

[28a. There are archaeological traces of impoverished life continuing at Apollonia for some time after the Byzantine evacuation. The churches of the city were subsequently deliberately destroyed, and their columns overturned.]

[28b. Recent excavations have brought to light the north-east corner tower of the wall-circuit of Tauchira, and a stretch of the sea-wall. All appear to be of Byzantine date.]

[28c. Circular corner towers were added to the fortress, probably by the Arabs who seem to have occupied Tauchira for a little time before shifting their new Cyrenaican capital to Barka itself.]

29. L. Caetani, iv, 536.

30. L. Caetani, iv, 698.

[30a. Lepcis Magna had previously been seized by the Luwatah Berbers and left deserted, during the closing years of Vandal rule. (Cf. Procopius, *De aedif.*, VI, iv.) The Byzantine reoccupation was superficial, and the slaughter of eighty Berber notables in the palace of Duke Sergius in 543 was not likely to be forgotten by the Luwatah.]

[30b. No sure indications of prolonged Christian survival have yet been found in Cyrenaica. The Cathedral of Cyrene had been converted into dwelling houses by the ninth century A.D., and the geographers El-Bekri and Edrisi (eleventh and twelfth centuries) do not mention Christian communities. A precise date for the submergence of the Christian church has still to be determined.]

31. L. Caetani (iv, 85) rightly emphasised the "passive sympathy" of the Copts for the invading Arabs, and concluded that "there is no doubt that the Copts greatly facilitated the Arab conquest". Here he differed from Butler's strongly worded opinion that there had been no alliance between the Copts and the Arabs until after Manuel's recapture of Alexandria (Butler, 480). Our present interpretation of the conquest of Pentapolis, if correct, surely weakens Butler's contention.

A HOLE IN THE HEAVENS

[The major part of a book under this title—a popular but scholarly history of the site of Cyrene—was found in two copies among Goodchild's papers. It was written at least eight years before his death, although some corrections, as well as notes indicating where more were needed, had been added to the top copy at a much later date. Chapter I was missing from both copies, probably because he had removed it to form the basis of the introduction to *Cyrene and Apollonia; an historical guide*. With the permission of Mrs. Goodchild the opening section of this introduction has been inserted in place of the missing chapter—enough to explain the title of the book; and I have added a paragraph to link this to what follows in Chapter II. Chapters II–IX are printed substantially as they stand in the manuscript, with only a few changes where he himself had indicated the need for them. He had clearly intended to add detailed footnotes, but it has seemed better to offer instead a short basic bibliography to each chapter. Goodchild had read so widely in books not always easily obtained in this country and had drawn so much of his account from unpublished material in the Cyrene archives that provision of full documentation would involve a considerable research project. Chapter IX already gives the impression of incompleteness. Chapters X and XI were probably never started, for they cover the period of Goodchild's own long service in Cyrene and he would have left them to write after his retirement. Notes for Chapter XII exist and show that in this he would have described the problems of excavation in Cyrenaica and explained his own methods; but the notes are in too rudimentary a form for publication. I have appended a very brief postscript indicating in outline some of the points that I think would have appeared in the final version of chapters IX–XI—but it is, of course, sketchy in the extreme.

It should perhaps be pointed out that the book is concerned with the rediscovery of Cyrene and not of Cyrenaica as a whole so that it contains little or no reference to certain notable early travellers who, like James Bruce, visited Cyrenaica but are not known to have taken an interest in Cyrene. It may also have ignored a few visitors whose accounts, like that of Père Pacifique, were nugatory.]

CHAPTER I

THE FOUNDING OF CYRENE

The story of the founding of Cyrene as a colony of Greek immigrants from the island of Thera (modern Santorin) has been handed down to us as a mixture of legend and historical tradition. The date usually assigned to this event is 631 B.C., and there can be little doubt that this is approximately correct. It seems that towards the middle of the seventh century B.C. a crisis due to over-population arose in the small Aegean island, and a seven-year period of drought caused such distress that forced emigration seemed the only solution. Before deciding on so drastic a step the leaders of the community consulted the famed Oracle of Apollo at Delphi, and were told to found a colony in Libya. An expedition was organised and entrusted to a certain Aristoteles, who took the name Battus and became first King of Cyrene. Some 200 young men were nominated to accompany Battus, and from Thera they sailed to Crete where they found a pilot to lead them to the shores of Africa. They founded their first settlement on a small island called Platea in the Gulf of Bomba, on the eastern outskirts of the fertile Cyrenaican plateau.

According to legend it was Battus himself who had consulted the Delphic Oracle, in order to seek a cure for a stammer. He was a little perplexed when the Oracle replied: "Battus, thou camest for a voice, but the lord Apollo sendeth thee to found a city in Libya, which giveth good pasture to sheep." The advice proved, however, to be less irrelevant than it first seemed, for after his arrival in Libya Battus encountered a lion and was so frightened that he yelled loudly and clearly, and never had trouble with his voice thereafter.

The first settlement on the island of Platea was not a success. The island was no larger than the later walled city of Cyrene, and there was but little water on the mainland. After two years the settlers decided to consult the Oracle again. "We have dwelt in Libya," they protested, "but have fared no better for our dwelling there." The Oracle replied sarcastically to their leaders: "If thou knowest Libya, which giveth good pasture to sheep, better than I (though I have been there, and thou hast not) then I greatly admire thy wisdom."

Convinced by such expert advice that they had yet to find the true Libya, the settlers returned to Africa and moved their settlement from arid Platea to a more favourable site called Aziris, situated on the mainland between Bomba and Derna (at the mouth of the modern Wadi Khaliji). Here they remained another six years, in the course of which they learned that even better sites lay on the high plateau farther to the west. Friendly Libyans offered to guide them to a place where they could establish their permanent settlement. These guides were, however, anxious to prevent the Greeks from seeing Irasa, the "finest part of the country" (perhaps Derna itself, or Ain Mara), so the march was made at night, and when dawn broke the travellers found themselves on the future site of Cyrene. "Here, O Greeks," said the guides, "ye may fitly dwell, for in this place there is a hole in the heavens."

The Libyans referred, of course, to the abundant rainfall of the Cyrene area. Their own numbers were small, and the country was large: in all probability they themselves were only thinly scattered on the upper plateau, finding its winter climate too harsh for their African blood. But the Greeks were captivated by a landscape not unlike the Greek mainland, and relatively free from those droughts which they had suffered on Thera. There was good arable soil and ample pasture: most important of all, the Libyans were friendly and willing to give their daughters in marriage to these foreigners who had arrived without their own womenfolk.

[Thereafter the city grew in size and wealth, its prosperity reflected in the grandeur and extent of its monuments. Although its history was chequered by periodic setbacks due to bitter feuds among its citizens, to attacks from external enemies, including Libyan tribes, not all of whom remained consistently friendly, and to natural disasters, especially earthquake, there was vigorous reconstruction after each. It was mother city to the four other cities of classical Cyrenaica and to the many Greek villages in its countryside. In the Roman period, although less wealthy, especially after the serious destruction caused by a revolt of the Jewish communities of the territory in A.D. 115, it was capital of the Cyrenaican section of the province of Crete and Cyrene until the time of the Emperor Diocletian. It lost its primacy in his reign but its monuments show that life, and sometimes vigorous life, continued on the site. It did, indeed, survive the Arab invasions of the seventh century A.D. and lasted until the invasion of the Beni Hilal in the eleventh. Goodchild records an old tradition, handed down in the Gebel el-Akhdar, according to which the Hasa tribe, which now occupies the site of Cyrene, derived from the union of a Greek called Iani and a woman called Saada of the Beni Suleim who accompanied the Beni Hilal. The Beni Hilal, however, put an end to sedentary life throughout Cyrenaica; Cyrene's surviving inhabitants took to a nomadic existence, and the city was left to decay.]

BIBLIOGRAPHY

History of Cyrene:

F. Chamoux, *Cyrène sous la Monarchie des Battiades* (Paris, 1953).

P. Romanelli, *Cirenaica Romana* (Verbania, 1943).

A. H. M. Jones, *Cities of the Eastern Roman Provinces*, Chapter XII (second edition, Oxford, 1971).

Monuments of Cyrene:

R. G. Goodchild, *Kyrene und Apollonia* (Zurich, 1971).

CHAPTER II

REDISCOVERY (1706–1859)

Plates 83, 85

The site and ruins of ancient Cyrene were rescued from oblivion not by any single and spectacular feat of discovery, but by a series of explorations and studies which began early in the eighteenth century and were intensified in the nineteenth. Students of the classics knew well enough—in general terms—where Cyrene must have stood, for there survived Ptolemy's map of the second century A.D. (which, before 1820, was still the main authority for the outline of the north-eastern coastline of Africa) and other ancient and medieval geographical sources. The main obstacle to early exploration was Cyrenaica's ill-fame as a *terra incognita* where no government existed, and where the traveller's safety was constantly in hazard.

It was only in 1631 that the Ottoman Turks had extended their dominion eastwards from Tripoli into "Barka", as Cyrenaica was (and still is) called by the Arabs. But whilst Mohammed Bey, the first governor, succeeded in collecting some taxes from his Cyrenaican subjects, and built a castle on the seashore at Benghazi, the Ottoman hold on this wild and warlike land remained somewhat precarious. In the interior the tribal leaders held undisputed command, and were responsible to no one.

In 1706 the French consul at Tripoli, Claude Lemaire, decided to brave these hazards and seek out the site of Cyrene. He was the first European to do so, and although his description of the ancient site leaves much to be desired, it is not without interest:

"Cyrene has been a great and proud city, to judge from the buildings, the debris of which presents a certain splendour. I have seen ten statues in excellent taste, all draped in the manner of the Arabs of to-day, some five and a half feet in height, but all mutilated and headless. There is a most beautiful spring which emerges from a rock and makes a loud murmur: according to the Arabs the spring comes from a considerable distance, and has been found by quarrying into the rock. This spring is abundant and runs impetuously: the water is cool and delightful—it runs incessantly, neither increasing nor diminishing, however great the drought.

The finest houses were, it appears evident, around the spring. Above there is a wall of extraordinary thickness, almost a hundred toises; it is well built. There are some marble columns sixteen feet high. I estimate that the city was four leagues in circumference; there is no sign of a wall-circuit. It is built on a lofty mountain two leagues from the sea ...

In another great valley there are a number of houses cut in the rock, where there are shops and rooms of unusual architecture, and large windows. Here, it seems, the Cyrenean merchants had their habitations ...

The mountains and the ancient monuments are almost uninhabited. There are a few Arabs encamped in the ruins of Cyrene, who live there for six months each year on the milk of their animals, with a little barley: this keeps them in health and gives them longevity. There are some people in the woods who live like wild animals, and have no religion ... The Arabs encamped in Cyrene have more civilized and more kindly manners. Their women are gracious, and have the finest teeth in the world; they are dark-skinned and do all the work, the men being very lazy.

Although this account is reasonable enough, Lemaire's observations entered the field of fantasy when he came to describe the ruins at Safsaf, a few miles east of Cyrene. Here he claimed to have seen a "champ de Mars" containing no less than 25,000 tombs of soldiers, "laid out in order of battle, as with an army". The tombs of the private soldiers were 5 or 6 feet high, laid out in double lines, whilst those of the officers were taller. It is evident that the Consul had mistaken for funerary monuments the standing-stones which the ancients set up to mark out their fields and farm-enclosures.

A quarter of a century later another Frenchman, the surgeon Granger, followed in Lemaire's footsteps. He landed at Derna in 1733 and engaged a "robber-chief" to take him to Cyrene, promising a cash recompense on his safe return to Cairo. This prudent arrangement succeeded, but unfortunately Granger's description of the ancient city, a *Mémoire curieux et très-detaillé*, was lost after being sent to Paris.

We have to wait for nearly a century for the next description of Cyrene, written by another physician, this time an Italian. Agostino Cervelli, a native of Pisa, travelled from Tripoli to Derna in 1811–12, accompanying a military expedition launched by the Karamanli Pasha of Tripoli. Of a brief visit to Cyrene he wrote as follows:

> "After remaining eight days at Safsaf, I went to see the famous city of Cyrene which the local people still call Gren or Gueranna. It is about eight miles west of Safsaf ...
> I saw at Cyrene great buildings, destroyed fortresses, temples nearly com-pletely destroyed, and an infinite number of tombs scattered along the road ...
> The outskirts of the city were protected by great fortresses, a half mile apart, and built on the plain or on its edges. In the middle of this enclosure are fallen arches and great buildings which have the appearance of towers: one sees them when one approaches towards the sea, and along a road or path which twists among the mountains ...
> After having marched two miles, one begins to rise between two flanking hills, and one reaches a fountain of fresh water, coming from one of the caves in the mountain. The Moors who entered into this cave ... seriously assured me that after having gone about a mile, uphill, they were stopped by a wheel turned by the water, and could go no further. This wheel, they said, is armed, all round its circumference, with knife-blades which hold back the greedy people and prevent them from getting hold of the treasures hidden in the interior of the mountain.

Cervelli was unable to check the accuracy of this remarkable story, because his escort came to blows with the local population, accusing them of having stolen a lamb. "This occurrence", he recorded sadly, "prevented me from in-vestigating deeply the antiquities of Cyrene and from copying the inscriptions to be found there." Likewise he was unable to descend to Apollonia, and was only able to quote the assurance of the Bey of Derna that there existed there "the remains of another city of the same kind as Cyrene". Cervelli's account, published many years later (in 1825), included a sketch-plan of the eastern part of Cyrene, but it is unfortunately so schematic as to have virtually no scientific value.

More fortunate was yet another doctor, Paolo Della Cella, a twenty-four-year old Genoese who arrived in Tripoli in 1816 to stay with his cousin the Sardinian consul. The Pasha of Tripoli was then again mounting a punitive expedition against his disloyal Cyrenaican subjects, and the services of a physician were needed. Della Cella volunteered to go, and his series of letters written during the journey (and greatly embellished subsequently) formed a small book which was read throughout Europe. It is an attractive narrative, but does more credit to the doctor's good heart than to the accuracy of his powers of observation. His description of Cyrene is, however, useful, in that he included copies of some Greek inscriptions then visible.

"I still feel my imagination moved by the spectacle which confronted me when I first reached these hills. Their summit forms a plateau, and as far as the eye can see all around, everywhere there are ruins. The ground is covered with remains of towers and walls, here and there raised up by ruins on top of one another, with long stretches of streets flanked by tombs and sarcophagi: in short, so many sorts of ruins show themselves in every direction that nothing lacks to complete the picture of a most splendid city."

After copying the inscriptions still visible among the ruins of the ancient city, and describing the famous Fountain of Apollo, "one of the most abundant springs I have ever seen", Della Cella visited the vast Necropolis, and noted that the majority had been either broken into or destroyed by the weather. "I wandered extensively", he wrote "among the ruins of these tombs, and had my heart moved by that profound sentiment of veneration which the ancient Cyrenaicans felt for the dead. What sort of city, I asked myself, was this where the living shared their living space with the dead, and spent so much care in adorning the streets and most prominent places with their tombs?"

Della Cella, like all others before, and some after him, could not distinguish clearly between the Cyrene of the living and the city of the dead. The city walls which divided the two zones were too damaged to be immediately apparent, and the roads winding through the vast necropolis were too easily mistaken as streets of the actual city. It remained for the Beechey brothers, a few years later, to make this essential distinction. Della Cella did notice that many of the ancient tombs were occupied by "a race of people who find in these hollows a shelter against the aggressions of the Bedouin and the exactions of the Pasha's agents. A state of independence is so attractive amidst so much slavery that, in these caves, leaping up and down the hillside like goats, they pass their days peacefully. Here they have established themselves in family units, and have so multiplied that all these slopes in the northern part of Cyrenaica are fully populated."

Della Cella's account of Cyrenaica, widely diffused a century earlier, was reprinted in the first years of the Italian occupation, and it was then claimed that he was the initiator of the scientific documentation of Cyrene. While giving him full credit for a lively and informative account of a little-known land, and for some useful if amateurish copies of inscriptions, it must be conceded that his publication belonged in spirit to the eighteenth rather than the nineteenth century. The first fruits of truly scientific inquiry were to be picked a few years later, and by a Frenchman and Englishman respectively, Jean Raymond Pacho and Frederick Beechey.

Beechey's expedition (it is more correctly called "the Beecheys'", because Frederick, a junior naval officer was accompanied by his brother Henry, a gifted artist) was sponsored by the British Admiralty, following suggestions made by Commander W. H. Smyth, who had visited Tripoli and Lepcis Magna in 1817. Having been unable to explore Cyrenaica during that visit, Smyth proposed to the Admiralty on his return that a combined land and sea expedition should be sent to survey the Syrtic and Cyrenaican coastlands, and at the same time to study and illustrate the ruined cities of the Pentapolis. The nautical survey would be carried out by H.M.S. *Adventure* under Smyth's own command: the Beecheys would take charge of the land party.

The project was accepted and blessed by both the Admiralty and the Colonial Department, and in July 1821 the *Adventure* set sail from England with her complement of surveyors and antiquarians. She anchored off Tripoli on the morning of September 11th, and the travellers went ashore to meet the British Consul-General, Colonel Hanmer Warrington—a remarkable man who, over a period of thirty years, was the real power behind the shaky throne of the Karamanlis.

At Tripoli Castle the reigning Pasha, Yusef Karamanli, was presented with four brass cannon, whilst his High Admiral, Reis Morat, "made known the friendly disposition of the King of England towards his Highness". Reis Morat was singularly qualified to act as intermediary, being the former Peter Lyell, Scots mate of a merchant vessel and later convert to Islam. The Pasha, whom he served loyally, accepted his recommendation, and promised every assistance to the British party, even to the extent of nominating the Sheikhs who were to escort the land expedition.

Fully equipped with supplies, and wearing the Arab dress which they considered necessary for their journey in parts where Europeans had rarely been seen, the Beecheys set out from Tripoli on 5 November. We need not follow their itinerary in detail, although it was to provide the fullest description hitherto available of the desolate coastlands between Tripoli and Benghazi. Their coastal survey revealed the true shape of the Syrtic Gulf, erasing from the map of the Mediterranean a score of bays and headlands with which earlier and more imaginative cartographers had embellished it.

The journey was eventful, as well as long and tedious. Sheikh Mohammed el-Dubbah, the escort selected by the Pasha, proved to be a wily old patriarch who was playing a double game, and encouraging the camel-drivers to demand extra payments. At Ras Lanuf, where Mussolini's "Marble Arch" sat astride a main highway,* the Beecheys' camelmen staged a sit-down strike. "A more dreary and barren spot could scarcely have been anywhere found than that which our friends here selected," recorded the Beecheys. "... It was imagined that being here without any resources, unable to procure either provisions or water, and far from any inhabited place, we should necessarily be induced to comply with whatever demands it might be advisable to make on the occasion." But the

* The arch had been removed by 1972.

Beecheys firmly refused to be blackmailed and Sheikh Mohammed, realising tardily that these foreigners were of singularly stubborn breed, hastened to move the party onwards.

On 12 January 1822, after nine weeks of travel from Tripoli, the Beecheys reached Benghazi, to find that the winter rains would impede any further travelling for some months. As they needed rest and refitting after their Syrtic ordeals, and Frederick himself was in bad health, they accepted the delay cheerfully. It was not until 17 April that they moved eastwards towards Cyrene, visiting the ancient cities of Tocra (*Tauchira*) and Tolmeita (*Ptolemais*) on the way. On these sites they carried out detailed surveys, and it was only in the first days of May that they finally arrived among the tombs and rock-cut roads on the outskirts of ancient Cyrene. After a much-needed drink at Apollo's fountain, they pitched their tents near the centre of the ancient city.

The Beecheys remained at Cyrene until the middle of July, and made an exhaustive study of the surface remains. Frederick surveyed the ancient city, establishing the lines of its faintly-visible defensive walls and the courses of the main streets. Henry made drawings of the Fountain of Apollo and of certain tombs in the necropolis, and also copied the much-damaged paintings that survived in some of the tombs. Unfortunately a large number of their drawings had to be omitted from the published volume for reasons of economy, and if these unpublished drawings still exist, their present whereabouts are not known.

Whilst their maps and drawings of Cyrene (and of the other ancient cities of Cyrenaica) are excellent and reveal a precision rarely attained at that period, the Beecheys' narrative is less successful. The qualities that make good surveyors and artists rarely lend themselves to literary eloquence: the occasional touches of dry humour that enliven the narrative of travelling through the Syrtica disappear entirely in the description of the Cyrenaican mountain sites. It is typical of the Beecheys' style that a whole page of turgid writing is required to inform the reader that the beauty of Cyrene's site is beyond words! The descriptions of the tombs, which were at that time the most prominent vestiges of Cyrene's past, have recently been described by a competent observer as "banal and inaccurate". The modern investigator of ancient Cyrene would gladly sacrifice nine-tenths of the Beecheys' narrative in return for those plans and drawings which were omitted from the published report.

On the other hand, it must be said that Frederick Beechey's map of Cyrene was an extraordinarily accurate representation of the outlines of the ancient city, and that more than a century has had to pass before it could be bettered. Not only was the whole circuit of the ancient city walls accurately plotted, but the main axial street that ran in the valley between the two hills on which Cyrene stood was identified and given due eminence. In later years it came to be overlooked, and has only been brought back into repute by excavations carried out since 1954.

By singular good fortune the major omissions in the Beecheys' published description of Cyrene were filled by the very detailed drawings made by the French traveller Pacho, who arrived in Cyrene in 1825, apparently unaware that he had been preceded by a major expedition. Pacho, then aged thirty and accompanied by Frederick Müller, a young orientalist, made Alexandria the springboard for his own exploration of Cyrenaica. But at Derna Müller became seriously ill, and Pacho had to continue alone and unaided. He wandered through the eastern part of the upper Cyrenaican plateau, visiting and describing an interesting series of ancient villages and fortresses; but it was at Cyrene, with its vast necropolis, that he found most scope for his artistic talent.

Cassels, in his recent catalogue and analytical description of the Cyrene necropolis states that Pacho's drawings "give an impression of the characteristics of the tombs and their general appearance which is not bettered elsewhere". On the other hand the Frenchman was as unskilled in topographical survey as his English predecessor had been in descriptive writing. Pacho's plan of ancient Cyrene is utterly useless, except in a few points of detail which had escaped other travellers. Thus we can see how the Beechey and Pacho expeditions, although working independently and in ignorance of one another, succeeded in being complementary. Had ancient Cyrene been erased by some natural cataclysm in 1827, later students would still, by study of the published reports, have been able to obtain a fairly reliable outline picture of the lost city.

Yet Pacho himself felt that he had been disastrously forestalled when, on his return to Europe, he learned for the first time of the Beecheys' enterprise. His reactions were akin to those of Scott on finding Amundsen's flag at the South Pole; and this fact, coupled with his own natural trend towards melancholia, led him to commit suicide only a few years later, after his return to France. It was a sad and senseless tragedy.

Following the monumental explorations of 1821–6, the lure of "discovering Cyrene" faded, and it became clear that only by excavation could important new light be shed on the history, architecture and art of the Greek metropolis. But four decades were to pass before any serious excavations could be undertaken. Meanwhile more European travellers came to gaze upon, and wonder at, the surface remains. The first was the German explorer, Heinrich Barth, who in 1846 passed through Cyrene on his way from Tripoli to Alexandria: his notes on what was then visible would doubtless have been valuable, but all the records of his journey were lost when he was attacked by robbers near the Egyptian frontier. In consequence his published account added little, other than learned conjecture, to previous knowledge of Cyrene.

Potentially more informative, but actually quite disastrous, was M. Vattier de Bourville's assault with spade (and saw) in 1848. This gentleman was French consul at Benghazi, and finding his official duties not very onerous, devoted his ample leisure to tomb-robbing. The "gaping sepulchres" long visible in the necropolis of ancient *Berenice* (Benghazi) were largely the result of his work, though other consuls (including a British one, George Dennis) were to follow this bad example. Not content with the vases thus obtained at Benghazi, Vattier de Bourville decided to attack the richer soil of Cyrene. He dug ruthlessly around a temple in what is now known to have been the "Caesareum", narrowly missing the colossal statue of Bacchus which Smith and Porcher were later to recover, and then assaulted some tombs in the Necropolis. Had his activities been confined to digging, the damage might have been forgivable; but, not content with movable objects, he sawed off the painted metopes of a fine tomb in the western cemetery, and sent them to the Louvre together with the great inscription of the Byzantine emperor Anastasius similarly removed from the walls of a fortress at Tolmeita. Needless to say, his memory is not greatly revered at Cyrene today.

Despite all these activities of exploration, illustration and dismemberment which had taken place since Lemaire's initial visit in 1706, Cyrene still lacked an author. Della Cella had written attractively but without accuracy; the Beecheys expressed themselves tediously; Pacho contributed little more than a travel-journal to his excellent plates. The beauty of Cyrene, and the charm of the "Green Mountain" with its then primitive pastoral Arab society had been hinted at but unworthily portrayed in words.

This deficiency in the bibliography of Cyrene was worthily made good by James Hamilton, a British traveller who may also be regarded as Cyrenaica's first tourist. He was evidently a man of ample means, interested in travel for its own sake, and content with his own company for protracted periods. After several tours in Syria, he decided to turn his attention to the ancient Pentapolis, preparing himself by studying colloquial Arabic, and reading all that ancient and modern writers had to say about Cyrenaica.

Hamilton arrived at Benghazi in 1852, and his account of his Cyrenaican travels was published four years later. In it he modestly disclaimed any aim "to write a book full of antiquarian lore or geographical details". "If", he added, "the narrative of my visit should induce others of my countrymen to vary their Egyptian and Syrian tours by a visit to the Pentapolis, the object of my ambition will be gained." At a later place, he reiterated these purely touristic recommendations: "To the traveller who has tarried in Egypt till the spring, who is tired of Syria, and unwilling to go to Europe, a more delightful retreat for summer cannot be suggested. The air is far purer than in any part of Italy, the scenery more beautiful and more varied, and fever and dysentery are unknown."

Although addressed to the well-to-do of a more leisured age when travelling was not impeded by currency regulations, visa formalities, or the vulgar necessity of earning a living, Hamilton's appeal is still valid today. Summer at Cyrene could and should become an essential part of any Middle East tour; though the modern tourist will expect more comforts and amenities than those provided by that "triangular patch of ground beneath a lofty rock" in the Wadi Belgadir, where Hamilton advised future visitors to pitch their tents.

Despite its author's disclaimers, Hamilton's little book is full of "antiquarian lore", and his description of Cyrene's tombs is today acknowledged to be comprehensive and accurate as well as elegant. Only rarely in his narrative does a personal note intrude upon the otherwise purely objective account of things seen and heard, and the most poignant is worthy of quotation:

"My descriptions (of the tombs) such as they are here given, were written on the spot, after repeated visits; and this morning, in no unfitting mood, I began my task. The growling camels around my tent, the bleating sheep at the fountain above, roused me earlier than usual; and I prepared to set out upon my round, while the cool air invited to exertion, and the first rays of the sun gilded the summits of the hills. To most men such bright mornings are exhilarating; and the pursuit of the red-legged partridge, with dog and gun, would seem more suitable to the hour than a walk among the tombs. But to me they are associated with recollections too painfully in unison with my present task... Such a morning was it, this day twelve years ago, when thou, O Marcellus, wert snatched from us, in the springtime of youth, in the force of thy strength, and talent, and manly beauty... Long years have passed since that sad morning, yet I have not learned to forget or ceased to mourn thee... here, in the city of countless tombs, thy image rises to my memory, and accompanies my pilgrimage..."

It required a man of Hamilton's sensitivity and literacy to remind us that the numberless tombs of ancient Cyrene represent equally numberless personal tragedies. The busy antiquarian with his trowels and tape-measures is too easily inclined to forget the human side of his subject-matter.

The glazed vases and corroded jewellery that are sifted out of the tomb-chambers of Cyrene may help to re-create history and to embellish museum showcases, but however tawdry and vulgar funerary customs have been throughout the ages, the essential fact remains that archaeology is concerned with men, and not with things. To a chronicler of the past, an ounce of human character, be it good, bad or indifferent, is worth a ton of potsherds.

Hamilton was also the first visitor to Cyrene to have dealings, and trouble, with the representative of the newly-founded Senussi fraternity. On a hilltop at El-Beida, close to the ruins of a great Sanctuary of Aesculapius, Sidi Mohammed ben Ali Senussi had founded, some eight years previously, the first Libyan convent of his new Islamic brotherhood. It was inevitable that this movement should have been in its earliest days, excessively fanatical, puritanical, and xenophobic, but although the initial force of Senussi teaching has since faded, largely through the conversion of a reform movement into first a Resistance and then an Establishment, it must be acknowledged that the Senussi leaders were pioneers in re-introducing sedentary life into a region devastated by the anarchy of nomadism. It is no accident that the Senussi "zawiyas" or convents, many of them today abandoned and forgotten, were almost invariably planted on ancient Graeco-Roman sites—places which were eminently suitable as nuclei for settled communities.

At Cyrene, in a tomb near the Fountain of Apollo, there dwelt, in 1852, the local "ikhwan" or zawiya-head, according to Hamilton "a fanatic of the first order, who will not defile his eyes by even looking at a Christian". After stones had been thrown at Hamilton by followers of this fanatic, the traveller felt obliged to call for protection from the local representative of such government as existed: this representative was Sheikh Bubaker Hadduds, a notable of the Baraasa tribe, who represented the Ottoman Empire with the title of "Bey", and was still engaged in building a massive castle for himself at Ghegab, south-east of Cyrene. The Sheikh's secretary, "a man of good taste and manners" condemned the stone-throwers to fifty strokes apiece of a *courbash* and the sentence was executed on the spot. "It was really necessary to enforce such punishment," wrote Hamilton, "however painful to one's own feelings". The pain must also have been considerable on the other side, for Hamilton was not further molested during his stay at Cyrene.

Hamilton also complained of much inconvenience from a source of his own choosing—the guide Mohammed El Adouli, whom he had engaged in Benghazi. This "immense man, enveloped in his white barracan, new yellow and red shoes on his feet ... his long gun slung over his shoulder, with a blunderbuss at his saddle-bow" is one of the most picturesque and best-documented figures in the chronicle of nineteenth-century exploration at Cyrene. He was originally from Misurata in Tripolitania, but had married into the Hasa tribe, and while normally resident at Benghazi, made frequent sojourns in the Gebel. He was the escort recommended by the foreign consulates in Benghazi, and had accompanied Vattier de Bourville in 1848: later he performed similar services not only for Hamilton, but also for Smith and Porcher, Dennis and Rohlfs. The last-named traveller, in 1868, confirmed what Hamilton claimed to have experienced sixteen years earlier, that "Mohammed, serving his own, utterly neglected my interests"; but one may suspect that Hamilton expected rather more single-minded devotion than a proud Arab could reasonably give. Smith and Porcher were to testify in El-Adouli's favour; and although their experience of the Middle East was less than Hamilton's, their standards were probably less exacting. Certainly El-Adouli knew how to take advantage of a rich foreign traveller, and how to insert on to his pay-roll that host of impecunious relatives which every Arab of position is, by custom, obliged to support. But Hamilton was hardly in a position to judge how far his guide's influence might have been responsible for the peace and security of his stay at Cyrene, and for the remarkably forceful solution of the contretemps with the Senussi followers. By and large, the balance of evidence is in Mohammed el-Adouli's favour, and the fact that so many Europeans got to their destination and returned to tell their tales entitles us to honour his memory.

A graver error of judgment in Hamilton's otherwise excellent and well-balanced assessment of conditions and persons in nineteenth-century Cyrenaica lies in his having taken too seriously the Arabs' complaints against Turkish rule. He concluded that "the arrival of any Government, Moslem or Christian—so only not the Sultan's—would be hailed with general satisfaction". Other later travellers were led to the same false conclusion that efficient and just European rule would be preferred by the Cyrenaican Arabs to the corrupt and ineffective Turkish administration. Thus it was that in 1911 the Italians arrived in Cyrenaica expecting a simple "passeggiata militare" attended by flags of welcome—but in fact encountered a resistance that was not to be broken until some twenty years had passed and vast sums had been spent on suppressing guerrilla activity amidst the rugged country of the "Green Mountain". The Turks had, in the eyes of their Cyrenaican subjects, many faults; but when it came to facing a threat from a foreign Christian power, these grievances were put aside.

BIBLIOGRAPHY

Ottoman conquest and administration:
C. Bergna, *Tripoli dal 1510 al 1850* (Tripoli, 1925).

The Senussi Movement:
E. E. Evans-Prichard, *The Sanusi of Cyrenaica* (Oxford, 1949).

Travellers:
C. Lemaire, see *Voyage du Sieur Paul Lucas, fait par ordre du Roy, dans la Grèce, l'Asie Mineure, la Macédoine, et l'Afrique. Description de l'Anatolie, la Caramanie, la Macédoine, Jérusalem, l'Egypte, le Fioume, et un Mémoire pour servir à l'histoire de Tunis, depuis 1684.* (Paris, 1712).
Tourtechot—Granger, see *Relation du voyage fait en Egypte par le Sieur Granger en 1730 . . .* (Paris, 1745).
A. Cervelli in M. Delaporte, *Receuille des Voyages et des Mémoires publiée par la Société de Géographie de Paris* (Paris, 1825) 20 f.
P. Della Cella, *Viaggio da Tripoli di Barberia alle frontiere occidentali dell' Egitto* (Genoa, 1819).
F. W. and H. W. Beechey, *Proceedings of the Expedition to explore the Northern Coast of Africa* (London, 1828).

J. R. Pacho, *Relation d'un voyage dans la Marmarique et la Cyrenaique* (Paris, 1827–29).

H. Barth, *Wanderungen durch die Küstenländer des Mittelmeeres* (Berlin, 1849).

Vattier de Bourville, see Letronne in *Journal des Savants* 1848, 370 f., *Rev. Arch.* v (1848) 150 f., 279 f. and Jomard in *Mémoires de l'Académie des Inscriptions et Belles Lettres* xvi (1851) 68 f.

James Hamilton, *Wanderings in North Africa* (London, 1858).

For G. Dennis and G. Rohlfs see bibliography to Chapter IV. For J. Cassels see bibliography to the Postscript.

CHAPTER III

FIRST FRUITS (1860–61)

Plates 86–9

Prior to 1860 the foreign investigators of Cyrene's ruins had merely scratched and surveyed the surface remains. Vattier de Bourville, it is true, had dug some sporadic holes and recovered a few statues, but there is no record of any concentrated attempt at excavation. That some previous unrecorded treasure-hunting had taken place seems indicated by Hamilton's statement that in the Agora area "All this part has been extensively excavated in certain directions, by order of the Grand Vizier, who presented the spoil to France". South of the Agora square there was, in fact, until it was levelled by the Italian excavators in 1937, a high mound consisting entirely of dumped soil from some earlier and unrecorded digging activity. But in this narrative we can only take cognisance of what is on the record; and therefore the year 1860 marks the first serious attempt to excavate ancient Cyrene.

In that year there was stationed at Malta Captain R. Murdoch Smith, an officer of the Royal Engineers who had lately worked at Halicarnassus with the archaeologist Newton. After reading the previous descriptions of Cyrene, Smith felt convinced that a rich haul of ancient sculpture would reward future excavators. He interested a naval friend, Commander E. A. Porcher of H.M.S. *Hibernia*, and the two set about making plans.

They first hoped to persuade the Admiralty to put at their disposal a small sailing vessel which could serve as a base ship; but in the end they had to be content with naval transportation to Tripoli and Benghazi, and with the promise of further help when the time came for them to return. Apart from this aid, and the grants that they later received from the British Museum—when the material results of their enterprise had become evident—the expedition was entirely at their own expense. The Turkish government did, however, issue a Firman authorising their work, and this was presented to the Pasha in Tripoli when Smith and Porcher arrived there on 21 November, 1860. Ten days later, travelling again by sea, they were at Benghazi where they unloaded their tents and stores, which were of modest quantity and included "two dozen tins of preserved meats to be used on emergencies only".

At Benghazi the explorers paid their respects to the Kaimakam who resided in the Castle (since demolished); and they enjoyed the hospitality of the British Vice-consul Frederick Crowe. It was the latter who advised them, against the Kaimakam's offer of a Turkish escort, to entrust their personal safety to an Arab notable from the Cyrene area, one Amor ben Abdi Seyat. Mohammed El-Adouli was, presumably, no longer free to undertake such duties, although he was to give much help some months later when he visited Cyrene and called on the British party.

After buying two horses and hiring camels to transport their stores, Smith and Porcher left Benghazi on 12 December. No sooner were they out of the suburbs than the rain poured down making the track impassable, and the travellers were obliged to set up camp. The bad weather so interrupted the rest of their journey that they did not arrive at Cyrene until the 23rd of the month. Here they spent the whole day in making their quarters as comfortable as possible, their selected residence being a rock-cut chamber on the north side of the main ancient street leading down from the city-centre to the Sanctuary of Apollo.

There is no record of how Smith and Porcher spent Christmas in what they called their "tomb of residence" (although it is unlikely that this particular rock-chamber had ever served as a tomb, being within the ancient walls). An engraving in their published volume, made from a drawing, shows them sitting comfortably in a cave carpeted with reed mats, and with various articles of equipment hanging on the walls. A large cooking-pot is boiling over a charcoal fire, and the scene is one of domestic tranquillity. But as an indication of the coldness of the season it may be noted that their "Union Jack" flag is spread out over a bed as additional cover. Doubtless they were beginning to wonder, as the members of the Norton expedition, a half century later, equally wondered, whether they had chosen the best season to visit "Sunny Africa".

Men like Smith and Porcher were not easily discouraged by climatic conditions. They had not come to Cyrene for winter sunshine, but to seek ancient works of art. The consul in Benghazi had evidently advised them as to local aptitudes for hard work, because they brought with them four negroes to undertake the digging. As their first task they turned their attention to the Necropolis, which had attracted the major attention of previous travellers. Here a great disillusionment awaited them.

They had hoped to find some intact tombs, even in an ancient necropolis so patently robbed in a wholesale manner. But digging soon showed that even those tombs then covered beneath a deep deposit of soil had already been violated. Thus Smith and Porcher turned their attention to the city proper, within its defensive walls, as already accurately defined by the Beecheys. Here they were more successful, and in January, 1861 astonishing fortune attended their excavations in the ruins of a small temple previously partially dug out by Vattier de Bourville. This temple, now known to have stood in the centre of a great portico anciently called the *Caesareum*, yielded to its new investigators "a very perfect marble statue of life size. The head and both hands were gone, but otherwise the figure was uninjured, the surface being almost without a scratch." Two days afterwards the figure was all but completed by the discovery of the head and left hand, near the same place. Thus came to light the fine statue of Bacchus, now in the British Museum.

Finding statues at Cyrene was one thing; moving them to a place of safety was more difficult, for at that time not a single wheeled vehicle existed in the area. Smith and Porcher were obliged to fell a tree (itself somewhat scarce at that period) and to make a rough sledge to which the statue was lashed. It was then hauled out of the excavation and yoked to a camel, which "proved quite successful". In this manner the statue was brought down to the "tomb of residence" and stored in safety.

At the end of January excavations began in the area of the Temple of Apollo, on the terrace below the Acropolis hill, and here again fortune smiled on the excavators. For within a few days there came to light, broken into some 120 fragments, a colossal statue of Apollo with his lyre. When pieced together after arrival in England, the statue was complete except for its fore-arms. But Apollo, unlike Bacchus, did not move easily from his find-spot. "The camel, although an excellent beast of burden, was quite unaccustomed to pulling", and the route was now necessarily uphill. In the end the excavators and their labourers had to drag the sledge themselves.

Meanwhile Smith and Porcher had already informed the British government of their initial successes, and had requested that a man-of-war should be sent, together with the materials necessary for crating the statues for their exportation. They also received a grant of £100 from the British Museum to enable them to continue excavating. The warship arrived off Apollonia before the arrival of the letter announcing its despatch, and owing to rough seas moved eastward to the sheltered bay of Ras el-Hilal where it anchored on 10 May. On hearing of its arrival, Smith and Porcher saddled their horses and rode down, to find H.M.S. *Assurance* under Commander Aynsley carrying wagons, timber and other necessary stores. Two days later, after the storm had calmed, the *Assurance* sailed back to Apollonia and landed thirty bluejackets to assist in handling the heavy statues.

Carpenters were sent up to Cyrene to crate the statues, which were then brought down by wagon to the top of the lower Gebel escarpment, at which point all traces of the ancient road were lost. It was therefore necessary to lower the wagons straight down the vertical face of the hill by tackle, a very hazardous operation in view of the weight that they were carrying. There was a nasty moment when a badly-positioned anchor slipped: "To our horror, away went the wagon at a tremendous pace, and the anchor after it almost flying. For a second the destruction of the wagon and the Apollo seemed inevitable, as it was heading for a precipice 200 or 300 feet in height, when, to our relief, it gave a great bound and landed itself in a large cavity in the rock."

At length, on 8 June, the task of transporting the first load of statues to the shore and of loading them into the ship's boats was terminated. The *Assurance* set sail for Malta, and Smith and Porcher returned to their lonely "sepulchral" residence at Cyrene.

In view of the obvious success of their operations, the explorers could be assured of further help from their own homeland, but there were some of the local residents in the Cyrene area who were beginning to think how they could turn this strange affair of the statues to their own advantage. It is more easy today, than it was a century ago, to understand local feeling in this matter. For centuries these blocks of marble, carved into figures deemed impious by Islamic teaching, had been lying, partly exposed, around the ruins of Cyrene. A few had been taken away as presents from the Sultan to foreign powers, but now—for the first time—a well-organised foreign expedition, acting admittedly with permission from the Sultan's government, but unaccompanied by Turkish troops and not even employing local labour, was taking away these things en masse. Moreover the head of the Senussi Zawiya, Sidi Mustafa Derdefi, was constantly urging the local tribesmen to hasten the departure of the infidels whose operations brought so little benefit to any true Believer.

In the calmer episodes of their narrative, Smith and Porcher give an interesting account of Cyrenaica as it was a century ago. Whilst they do not manage to present such a well-drawn and convincing picture as Hamilton's, there was much good sense in what they had to say. For example, the all-night barking of dogs was then, as still today, a maddening disturbance to the western sojourner. "One would naturally imagine," they observed, "that a dog given to perpetual barking, and in this respect like the boy in the fable who called 'Wolf!', would be of comparatively little value as a watch. The Arabs, however, think otherwise. They say truly that if a dog barks all night he cannot possibly fall asleep, and that the change in his bark on the approach of an intruder is quite sufficient to arouse the soundest sleeper. His usual bark is a warning to the enemy that the sentries within the camp are awake, and to his master it is a perpetual report of 'all's well'. The hoarse voice of the dog, the plaintive grumbling of the camels, and the bleating of scores of lambs and kids, joining with the shrill cries of the surrounding jackals, form a midnight chorus the reverse of musical." A modern resident can confirm all this, but must confess surprise that Smith and Porcher do not include the braying donkey among the members of the "chorus".

Before the arrival of the *Assurance* the two explorers had already made extensive journeys in the Cyrene district, visiting Derna, Apollonia, and even the isolated little harbour of Zaviet Hammama, site of ancient Phycus. In April they went even further, riding down to Tolmeita and Tocra. On this occasion they spent a night at Merj (Barka, Barce) Castle as guests of Haj Ahmed, who had been friendly and helpful to them on their outward journey. Here, too, they met Suliman Captan, "one of the most remarkable men in the country", and a grandson of that Scottish seaman Peter Lyell whom, as "Reis Morat" and High Admiral of Tripoli, the Beecheys had encountered in 1821. Suliman Captan had been Mudir of Ghegab—the nearest Turkish outpost to Cyrene—at one stage in his career, and still bore the scars of a gunfight that had taken place when the Cyrene tribesmen were being pressed to pay their taxes.

That the post of Mudir of Ghegab was no sinecure (and for that reason usually assigned to a local Cyrenaican rather than to a Turk) became even more evident when Smith and Porcher returned to Cyrene. The Turks had recently appointed a weak Mudir, giving him as "adviser" one of the toughest characters of the Gebel el-Akhdar—the Baraasa strongman Bubaker Bey Hadduds whom Hamilton had met and recognised immediately as a shrewd personage. Bubaker Bey coming from the rival Baraasa tribe, deemed it expedient to persuade the new Mudir that the Hasa sheikhs were "a rebellious, turbulent set, whom he should imprison at the first opportunity". The unfortunate Mudir followed this not disinterested advice, clapping into jail the Hasa chieftains who had gone to Ghegab to pay their respects to authority. Infuriated by such treachery the Hasa launched a midnight attack on the Castle, liberated their sheikhs, and incidentally killed two Turkish soldiers.

Fearing grave reprisals from the Turkish authorities, the Hasa leaders pleaded with Smith and Porcher to intervene through the British Consul to obtain a pardon from the Kaimakam or Governor at Benghazi. The necessary overtures were made, and the Kaimakam (who, in any case, must have been disinclined to send a punitive expedition so far away from his base) graciously pardoned the offenders. This affair gave the British excavators a local prestige which was to prove useful—indeed, probably vital—at the time of their departure.

In June the excavations at Cyrene were resumed, the great Temple of Zeus being the main objective. Owing to shortage of local labour, Smith decided to ride down to Benghazi to engage some more negroes, and travelled the whole distance of 160 miles in the record time of three days. Returning with twenty husky Fezzanese a few days later, he had the misfortune to run into an Arab ambush planned with the object of making slaves of the blacks. One of the negroes was kidnapped and taken away, but the remainder arrived safely at Cyrene, where they were to be paid the then princely salary of five Turkish piastres a day plus their food.

By the end of August this increased labour force had already produced notable results. Several temples had been explored and the number of statues found was more than a hundred. In order to move this material to the coast for the expected arrival of a British man-of-war, part of the labour force was put onto repairing the old Graeco-Roman road to Apollonia, long overgrown and in places washed away. On 26 September H.M.S. *Melpomene* arrived off Susa, while Smith was laid up with a severe attack of fever. Porcher therefore rode down to the coast and arranged for wagons and packing materials to be sent up to Cyrene. On the first day of October all was ready for the first load of statues to be taken down to the sea-shore.

But the exit of Smith and Porcher with their spoil was to be more tempestuous than their arrival the previous winter. One of the Hasa chieftains, less grateful than his colleagues, decided that the time had come to levy "harbour dues" (although the port of Apollonia had not been repaired since the end of Byzantine rule), and when this exaction was not forthcoming he blocked the road to the coast with tree-trunks. Whilst the excavators could easily have called their blue-jackets from the *Melpomene* to force a passage, they prudently sought local aid and called on other Hasa elders to remind them of services previously rendered in the matter of Ghegab Castle.

These diplomatic overtures succeeded, and by 11 October the last load of "finds" and stores had reached the shore safely. "Thus fortunately ended an affair which, but for the gratitude of the powerful tribe we had formerly be-friended, would, in all probability, have resulted in a great loss of life". In token of gratitude Sheikh Hussein and Haj Hassan were invited on board the warship and given liberal presents of powder together with certificates of good conduct addressed to the British Consuls at Benghazi and Derna. It is recorded that the ship's band accompanied the last loads to the beach playing, no doubt, nautical airs suitable to the occasion. Amor ben Abdi Seyat, who had helped the explorers throughout their sojourn, inherited their two horses.

At daylight on the morning of 14 October, 1861, H.M.S. *Melpomene* sailed away to Malta, and as the outline of the Gebel el-Akhdar faded into the horizon Smith and Porcher must have felt the lifting of an enormous burden. In terms of the works of art recovered their long sojourn had been triumphantly success-ful, but the troubles that had attended their departure had been a heavy strain. This had been the first large-scale exportation of ancient works of art from Libya, but it was also to be the last. Not until 1910 was another expedition of similar potentiality authorised by the Turkish government; and the fruits of that later exploration, headed by the American Richard Norton, were never to leave the country.

How should we judge the activities of Smith and Porcher from our modern viewpoint? Certainly the pre-war Italian excavators of Cyrene, understandably resentful that much of the cream had been taken off the milk, wrote scathingly on the subject. Oliverio, their doyen, expressed himself in no uncertain terms:

"I certainly cannot find a single word of admiration for those two Englishmen who, from 23 December 1860 to 14 October 1861, turned everything upside down, digging everywhere in Cyrene where there seemed the slightest glimmer of hope of finding precious marbles to take away. Everything else, the excavation for its own sake, which should normally be the one and only preoccupation of the excavator, meant nothing to them and caused them no concern: *trouver c'etait leur bout plutot que de savoir* (Beule) ... England might have reason for being grateful to these two of its sons, but not archaeological science, which was damaged by them and in some respects irreparably."

Giacomo Guidi, who himself dug only briefly at Cyrene (but found that Smith and Porcher had left for him, in the Temple of Zeus, something of exceptional interest: the fine marble head of Zeus) was a little more charitable. He described his British predecessors as "with few resources, inadequate funds, without serious scientific qualifications, but animated by holy enthusiasm for the investigation of the ancient monuments"; and he pointed out how the picture of their "Tomb of Residence", with its sparse furnishings, showed how willingly they had sacrificed over a long period "that 'comfort' so dear to the English."

Of course Smith and Porcher worked unscientifically by modern standards; but the methods of today will seem no less unscientific to archaeologists of tomorrow. Considering the difficulties which they encountered it is surely greatly to their credit that they were able, after their return to England, to compile and publish a magnificent and attractive volume, illustrated with plans of excavated buildings, drawings of inscriptions, and photographs of the major works of art recovered. It is not an entirely scholarly volume, for the Captain and the Commander did not pretend to be scholars; but it presented its readers with a picture of ancient Cyrene, and of its wealth of Greek and Roman sculpture, which could only leave a deep impression.

On the matter of *how* Smith and Porcher dug, and of the degree of destruction they wrought to the ancient buildings, we must take Oliverio's verdict with a grain of salt. If, instead of being exhumed in 1861 by Smith and Porcher's "good strong blacks", the British Museum Apollo had been dug out by the soldiers of General Tassoni's Supply-Depot which occupied the site in 1914, science would not have been greatly the richer. Even if this statue, and the others found by Smith and Porcher, had remained undisturbed underground during the years of Italian military activity at Cyrene, their subsequent excavation in the 1930s would not necessarily have been followed by prompt and detailed scientific documentation. For reasons which we shall later examine, a large part of the work of Oliverio himself and of his colleagues has remained unpublished down to the present day.

It is one of the more disagreeable characteristics of archaeologists of all nations that they too often show scant piety to the memory of their precursors, and feel obliged to lay heavy and exaggerated stress on the "scientific" and "definitive" character of their own work. Nothing at Cyrene is ever definitive: every old problem has to be re-assessed at intervals of time, taking into consideration new facts that have emerged from the soil; every ancient building has to be re-studied years after its initial excavation, since the very processes of decay sometimes serve to reveal new and unsuspected features of earlier date. Even the destructive work of nineteenth-century treasure-seekers, or twentieth-century stone-diggers have their constructive aspects. By breaking through the latest floor of the Temple of Apollo, Smith and Porcher inadvertently helped to throw light on the earlier history of the building. By removing hundreds of tons of fallen stone from all over Cyrene the industrious Italian sappers of 1915–18 inadvertently facilitated the work of later excavators. Let us try to be charitable to all our predecessors—even to the abominable Vattier de Bourville whose busy saw removed from Tolmeita an important inscription which an Italian naval shell might conceivably have shattered during the landings of 1913.

Perhaps the main basis for later criticism of Smith and Porcher lay in the fact that they had *taken away* the objects they found. On the other hand, given the conditions then prevailing in Cyrenaica, they could hardly have done otherwise. It was not that *buried* statues were exposed to any real danger from the local population, but the Beecheys and others had already noticed that anything in which the visiting foreigner had shown any obvious interest tended to be mutilated as soon as his back was turned. It is not profitable to inquire closely into the psychological motives behind such action. We can only note with satisfaction that it is all past history, and that today the people of the Cyrene area normally take pains to preserve, and to hand over to the Museum—*their* Museum—the statues or inscribed stones which they come across in their fields and gardens.

Whether the Cyrenean first fruits gathered by Smith and Porcher and taken to the British Museum will ever return to their place of origin is more problematic. Now that the opportunities of acquiring new antiquities from the Mediterranean area are becoming less and less, the museums of northern Europe are more than ever reluctant to relinquish any of their old holdings. In any event, the national collections of Cyrenaica are perhaps sufficiently rich in sculpture—thanks to the Italian excavations, and to the Italian policy of non-exportation applied rigorously after the initial removal of the "Venus of Cyrene". So far as the Cyrenean collection of the British Museum is concerned, what would be profitable would be an interchange of *disjecta membra* with the Cyrene Museum; for both parties would gain by having their own statues made more complete. But prejudice is always stronger than logic, and a Danish sculptor who made such a proposal a few years ago met with a somewhat frigid response from Bloomsbury.

BIBLIOGRAPHY

R. M. Smith and E. A. Porcher, *History of the Recent Discoveries at Cyrene* (London, 1864); cf. also the brief account by W. S. W. Vaux, in *Transactions of the Royal Society of Literature*[2] vii (1863) 399 f.

CHAPTER IV

MURDER ON THE ACROPOLIS (1904–11)

Plates 90, 91

At 9 a.m. on the morning of 11 March 1911, Herbert Fletcher De Cou, forty-two-year old American archaeologist, climbed up the northern slopes of the Acropolis Hill at Cyrene in order to supervise the Arab workmen then engaged in excavating ancient buildings on the summit. His Director, Richard Norton, had remained in camp to look after a sick colleague, and De Cou had been delegated to take his place for a few hours.

While De Cou scrambled up the slippery hillside, a stocky bearded figure in knickerbocker suit, three Arabs with rifles were hiding behind a ruined wall awaiting his approach. At a range of 25 yards they opened fire, and two bullets found their mark. De Cou dropped dead, and the assassins slipped away un-hampered either by the Arab workmen who were close behind the victim, or by the soldiers of the Turkish guard, seventy-five strong, who were supposed to be protecting the members of the American expedition.

This tragedy, the only one of its kind to find a place in the annals of Cyrene's exploration, constitutes a mystery which seems almost insoluble. Who killed De Cou, and for what motive?

To understand the background of the De Cou affair we must go back many years before Richard Norton's expedition arrived in Libya. The truth is that, after many centuries of almost complete autonomy—inhibited only by a weak and ineffective Turkish administration—the Bedouin of Cyrenaica began to have fears of intended foreign and Christian occupation. In some respects Smith and Porcher were the innocent cause of these suspicions. Already, in 1861, the arrival at Apollonia of the British man-of-war sent out to embark their precious statues had given rise to rumours of intended occupation. Arab suspicions were not unnaturally reinforced by subsequent events in Tunisia and in Egypt, on the two flanks of Libya.

But the travellers who arrived at Cyrene between the departure of Smith and Porcher and the closing years of the century do not seem to have encountered any very marked hostility. Neither Gerhard Rohlfs in 1869, nor Weld Blundell in 1895 found cause to complain of their reception, although the former did note some uneasiness when his photographer set up the heavy plate-camera on its tripod. The technical apparatus of the foreigner was perhaps more to be feared than his person.

Italian interest in Cyrenaica had been dormant since Della Cella's visit of 1817, and for most of the nineteenth century Italian energies were devoted more to the problems of the Risorgimento than to the lures of overseas expansion. It was only after Italian unity was achieved that aspiring imperialists began to cast covetous eyes towards the only tract of North Africa not already engulfed by older and more powerful European nations.

The first Italian explorations of their imperialist era were, in fact, largely commercial, and organised by the Milanese "Society for the commercial exploration of Africa". Captain Manfredo Camperio, this Society's representative, in collaboration with Giuseppe Haimann, visited Cyrene in March, 1881. Only in the area east of Derna (including Tobruk) did they find their movements impeded by the Turkish authorities.

American scientific interest in the antiquities of Cyrenaica, presumably free from commercial or imperialistic motives, began in 1904 when the Chicago millionaire Allison V. Armour brought his luxury yacht *Utowana* from Cyprus to Derna, in the course of a classical cruise in which participated the well-known British orientalist D. G. Hogarth.

Hogarth has left an excellent account of this first American visit to Apollonia and Cyrene (General Eaton, a century earlier, had got no further west than Derna, even though the U.S. Marines anthem still sings vaguely of "the shores of Tripoli"). He describes the "ghostly" Greek highway that gave access from the coast to Cyrene—the same highway that Smith and Porcher had repaired for the transport of their statues—and the sullen and suspicious Hasa tribesmen who clasped their guns and spears while they watched the strange new visitors. The Turkish hold on the Cyrene area was now stronger, in consequence of the settling at Apollonia of Cretan Moslem refugees in 1897: down there on the coast was a small garrison of Turkish peasant-soldiers, whilst up at Cyrene a lonely Stambouli mudir represented the Sultan, living in a small stone-built hut which was the first building there since the Beni Hillal swept through the country nine centuries previously.

Hogarth had the normal prejudices of the conventional classicist: Roman and Byzantine remains were of minor interest to him, and he therefore concluded that Smith and Porcher "did no more than scratch the uppermost skin of Cyrene. All that is most precious there, the spoil of the true Hellenic age, is still to seek." Hogarth also expressed the view that "if it were ever his fortune to search for the earliest Cyrene", he would do so on the Acropolis Hill, and not in the eastern part of the city. Norton, as we shall see, followed this advice, although the results were to be less encouraging than he had hoped. The Acropolis of Cyrene yielded to him not the city of Battus the Founder, but much later remains—and a hideout for assassins.

In the years following this first visit of the yacht *Utowana*, the internal situation in Cyrenaica began—from a foreign visitor's viewpoint—to deteriorate. Local suspicions, already latent, were inflamed by a series of foreign "explorations" of which the political motive was but thinly concealed by professedly scientific aims. In 1905 the Banco di Roma had been encouraged to begin the "economic penetration of Libya", and in the summer of 1907 Senator Giacomo De Martino made a visit to Derna and the Gebel el-Akhdar of which the scope was plainly that of political reconnaissance. Even more ominous—if certainly more scientific—was the expedition in the following year of a British-led expedition working under the auspices of the "Jewish Territorial Organisation".

The "J.T.O." expedition, as it is usually abbreviated, set a high standard of scientific research, and the published report was later used by Italian liberals as a counter to the over-optimistic claims of the imperialists. But although the scientists sent to Cyrenaica by the "J.T.O." rejected the country as unsuitable for mass Jewish immigration, owing mainly to lack of water resources, the mere fact that such a reconnaissance had taken place—and with Turkish approval—strengthened local xenophobia. It was becoming increasingly difficult to distinguish between disinterested scientific interest in Cyrenaica and the now all too patent foreign manoeuvres to grab it.

Despite the increasing tension in Cyrenaica itself, the American interest stimulated by the *Utowana's* first cruise remained unabated. With the backing of the American Institute of Archaeology, and the moral and practical support of Armour, Richard Norton decided to apply for a concession to excavate at Cyrene and—surprisingly enough in the circumstances—the Ottoman government granted him an irade in May, 1910. During the following summer Norton made a brief visit to determine his future programme, and issued a report couched in the most optimistic terms and appealing for collaborators with a spirit of adventure.

The news of the American concession caused some consternation in Rome; and the Italian government hastened to instruct its Ambassador in Turkey to obtain, at all costs, approval for an Italian expedition under the distinguished archaeologist Federico Halbherr to dig in the same country, perhaps at Tolmeita, the site of ancient Ptolemais. The Turks were not prepared to do more than authorise a preliminary reconnaissance by the Italian team. This was better than nothing, and Halbherr hastened to Benghazi where he arrived on 5 July, 1910, taking over all available rooms in the city's only hotel—the notorious Albergo Maffei—only a quarter of an hour before the American party returned from the Gebel. This hardly daunted Norton, who enjoyed not only the confidence but also the hospitality of the British Consul, J. F. Jones.

Halbherr's tour of the country lasted only eleven days, and he had left Cyrenaica long before Norton returned in October with the advance party of his own expedition, and with the equipment transported in Armour's yacht. They disembarked at Apollonia on 11 October, and began to set up camp at Cyrene. By the 24th the whole party was on the site, ready to begin digging five days later.

Norton's staff was well-chosen. The direction of the excavations, supervised by himself, was divided between De Cou (responsible for inscriptions), Joseph Hoppin (vases), and Charles Curtis (lamps, terracottas and coins). Lawrence Mott was to look after photography, and an English physician, Arthur Sladden, was doctor not only for the members of the expedition but also for such local Arab residents as came to seek treatment. The only notable omission in the personnel of the team was an architect to plan and analyse the ancient structures brought to light; and the results of this deficiency are evident in the published report.

De Cou himself was an experienced classicist who had taught not only at the University of Michigan but also at the American Archaeological Schools of Rome and Athens. He was of extremely modest disposition, Dr. Sladden attesting to his "retiring character and natural reserve and self-effacement". With De Cou, Norton had a "long friendship of no ordinary character", and the death of this friend was a severe blow to the expedition leader, who wrote subsequently "Words cannot picture him to those who knew him not, and give but sad satisfaction to those of us who loved and admired him."

If we still do not know why De Cou was shot, or who precisely were his assassins, at least the other circumstances of the murder are well attested. As we have already seen, it was De Cou who led the workmen up the Acropolis hill on the morning of the fatal day, Norton remaining in camp to attend to Dr. Sladden who was himself sick. Shortly after 9 a.m. news reached the camp that there had been trouble on the hill, and shots fired. Norton went up immediately, to find his friend dead.

Somewhat belatedly the Turkish guard took over control of the situation, and had the body of the victim carried down to an ancient rock-cut tomb-chamber adjoining the Mudir's house, where it was guarded by troops. On the following day De Cou was buried on the hillside a little east of the American camp, close to the modern Museum of Sculpture. The rough coffin was draped with the American flag, and Norton himself read the burial service. The tomb was well looked after during the four decades of Italian occupation, and received an inscribed headstone erected by the American authorities after the Second World War.

On 16 March a Turkish investigating judge arrived to make inquiries, and his conclusions—if any—presumably lie buried in the Ottoman archives at Istanbul. American interests in the sad affair were represented by Francis Jones, the British consul in Benghazi, who wrote to Norton on 4 April that the authorities were doing all they could to catch the murderers. There were rumours, plenty of them, but no positive facts were ever communicated to the members of Norton's expedition. On 16 April there arrived at Cyrene a redoubtable English orientalist, Captain (later Brigadier-General Sir) Wyndham Deedes then an Inspector of Turkish Gendarmerie: Sir Compton Mackenzie was later to include an interesting character-sketch of this remarkable man in his "Gallipoli Memoirs". The visit of "Dedez Bey" was a routine one, not connected with the De Cou murder, but he offered to give any help he could.

Because of the unconcealed hostility of the Italians towards the granting of the American excavation concession at Cyrene, it was perhaps inevitable that a political motive began to be attributed to the murder. In his published report Norton wrote: "The Arabs who committed the murder had never had any relations or dealings with us; they did not belong to the neighbourhood, but were hired and sent from more than fifty miles away... As to the instigators of the crime, it need only be said that among all the foreigners settled in the Cyrenaica, and the natives with whom I talked, I never heard a contradiction of the report which was general at the time in the country from Cyrene to Tripoli."

In his conversations, after returning to Europe, Norton was less guarded in his statements, explicitly laying the blame on the Italians. But he did not, as was erroneously stated by Gaspare Oliverio, many years later, specifically accuse the Italian archaeologists of the crime; Dr. Sladden has testified, only recently, that he has "no recollection of the Halbherr expedition ever being discussed by any of the members of our party". The rival teams had, after all, never met one another; and if they had, a gentleman like Richard Norton could hardly have failed to be impressed by the integrity of another gentleman of the calibre of Federico Halbherr.

Needless to say, the Italian archaeologists who worked at Cyrene in later years were distressed by the suggestion that a much venerated colleague might have had anything to do with so dastardly an affair. From their interrogations of the local population they concluded that the motives of the murder were xenophobic in general, and personal in addition. Oliverio, in fact, stated that

De Cou had been killed because "he had too insistently gone after a Bedouin woman". Another Italian archaeologist, Ghislanzoni, wrote as early as 1914 that the assassin had been a certain Saad Eshelmi who "was killed a few months ago near Benghazi by a tribal sub-section which he, implacable enemy of all Europeans and Christians, wished to rob for having submitted to the Italians".

Now Norton had been convinced that the assassins had not been local people, but had come from nearer Benghazi: Sladden records a rumour that they were from Tocra. On the other hand, the then Italian vice-consul at Derna, Sabetta, has stated that the two culprits were in fact members of the Hasa tribe, from the Cyrene area, and that they had sought sanctuary at Gubba, near Derna, where the Sheikhs of the Anakla tribe had resorted to arms to prevent the Turkish Mudir of Cyrene from arresting them. Writing on the eve of the Italian occupation, he asserted that no arrest had been made in connection with the crime; and this seems likely enough if the whole issue had developed from a simple paid assassination into a matter of tribal honour.

From all these contrasting accounts, it is virtually impossible to draw any reliable conclusions today; although something may one day be gleaned from the Ottoman archives, or from the confidential consular reports of Francis Jones. We can only outline the main possibilities: (a) that there was a personal motive, the shy self-effacing De Cou having aroused hatred or jealousy; (b) that De Cou was a victim of mistaken identity, it being presumed by the assassins that Norton himself would be leading the workmen on the fatal day; and in such case the murderers were out to get the leader of the expedition, and did not even know what he looked like; (c) that if (b) is the correct answer, the underlying motive may have been simple xenophobia and suspicion of foreign intentions, or alternatively somebody had given encouragement to cause disturbance in the American camp and these instructions had been carried out with excessive zeal.

In the latter connection it may be noted that there had been pot-shots fired at the American camp throughout their stay: specifically on 31 October, 5 November, 15 and 26 December, 20 January, and 1 March. The fact that one shot, on 15 December, had gone through De Cou's bedroom at 3 a.m. might seem to support the theory of a personal vendetta; but on 26 December, it was the window of Hoppin's room that was shattered. These nocturnal episodes all seem to add up to the idea of a determined attempt to make the Americans leave; and the murder of 10 March may, conceivably, have been a final and desperate attempt to achieve this aim. Whether this was stimulated by patriotic motives, or by a desire to obtain some promised reward, it is impossible to determine.

There is also another aspect of the affair which deserves consideration. What was the Turkish "guard" of seventy-five armed soldiers doing during all this period of nocturnal musketry culminating in daylight murder? Is it possible that the Turks themselves had a hand in the affair? Certainly they must have been justifiably tired of all these foreign caravans passing through Cyrenaica, on one pretext or another; and if diplomatic considerations made it impossible to refuse entry, they could at least speed departure. It has been alleged by other travellers that the Turks made a habit of organising sham "attacks" by Bedouins on the convoys which they themselves escorted.

Whatever its underlying motive, the murder of De Cou was a grave blow to Norton's plans; and his bitterness must have been further increased by the somewhat disappointing results of his first season's work. Despite Hogarth's previous optimism regarding the prospects of discoveries on the Acropolis hill, five months' work by nearly a hundred workmen produced very little of interest in the way of either ancient buildings or associated objects.

The largest building uncovered proved to be a much-damaged courtyard house, which the excavators claimed to date back to the third century B.C. (although many of its characteristics indicate a later date, perhaps even in the Roman period). On the northern slope of the Acropolis hill an apsed building, also probably Roman, had some indeterminate Greek walls beneath its foundations, some 18 feet below the modern surface.

More fruitful was a small clearance made in a garden on the south-western slopes of the hill, which yielded a large number of early Greek statuettes. This site may have been a little sanctuary, but Norton did not have time to investigate it fully, and towards the end of his campaign he transferred his main attention to the Necropolis, and cleared a large area of sarcophagi and rock-cut tombs east of his camp. Here at least one intact sarcophagus came to light, and Norton optimistically declared that "as the seasons go on we shall continue clearing more and more of the Necropolis, for it is probably the place where we are most certain to find vases".

Apart from a fine head of Athena, and some minor sculptures most of which were scattered surface finds and not the results of his own digging, Norton had little to show for his labours and sacrifices. The larger objects remained at Cyrene after the expedition had left, and were seen in April, 1912 by the French doctor Rémond, who was then serving with the Turco-Arab forces against the recently-arrived Italian troops, still beleaguered in their fortified beach-heads at Benghazi, Derna and Tobruk.

All in all, circumstances proved singularly unfavourable to this American enterprise, in contrast to the astounding—if less-merited—fortune enjoyed by Smith and Porcher a half century earlier. To tell the truth Norton, apart from sheer bad luck and an unfavourable political situation, had gravely under-estimated the practical problems of digging on a site like Cyrene, and had also miscalculated the climatic conditions.

On the Acropolis hill there is an enormous accumulation of soil, and its removal by untrained workmen with baskets and donkeys was hopelessly un-economical. Wrapped in their unwieldly barracans, in protection against the cold, the raw labourers could hardly make much impression on this overlying deposit. What Hogarth had called "all that is most precious there, the soil of the true Hellenic age" remained elusive. If it exists at all, it is still there today on the Acropolis hill of Cyrene, because recent diggers have had more urgent tasks to occupy them.

As for the climate, one is bound to wonder what led Norton to choose the winter season for his campaign. For two and a half months from the end of November, rain held up the digging about half the time; and although it seems that the winter of 1910–11 was exceptionally severe, with some snowfall, Cyrene is always extremely wet between November and February, and sometimes even later. In his published report Norton admitted this climatic handicap, but claimed that this was the season when labour was most easy to obtain—an argument hardly valid since it is at the onset of the first rains, at the beginning of November that the local population go to plough their lands. In spring or autumn, before or after the summer harvest, they are only too anxious for employment.

One is tempted to conclude that Norton, like others before and even after him, had jumped to the conclusion that "winter sunshine" prevailed all round the shores of the Mediterranean, and that the best season for digging in Egypt would also be the best for mountain Libya. But, in fact, the summer season at Cyrene is quite mild, and it is the time of the year when the soil is most loose and easy to dig. The air is delicious and salutary for those from colder climes, whilst the Arab people are disposed to shed their barracans and work in more suitable clothing. On the coast of Cyrenaica winter digging is perfectly practicable, but up on the plateau of the Gebel el-Akhdar it should be avoided by anyone free to choose his season.

Thus it was that in May 1911, at the beginning of the most charming and healthy season in the Cyrenaican mountains, Norton and his colleagues struck their tents, locked up their bullet-ridden hut, and moved down to Apollonia to re-embark on Armour's yacht. They left behind not only their best finds, but also the body of De Cou, their friend and colleague. They were already in Europe, on their way back to their native land, when the Italian Government delivered its ultimatum to Turkey, and sent a fleet to Tripoli and Benghazi. The brief spell of American archaeological activity at Cyrene was concluded.

The Americans also left something else at Cyrene—a new word in the local dialect to describe the Antiquities. From this moment henceforward, any sort of ancient ruin in Cyrenaica was to be described as a "Melikan", corruption of "American". An Englishman, mindful of the fine survey work of the Beecheys, the literary achievement of Hamilton, and the epic treasure-hunting of Smith and Porcher, may feel rather humiliated by this fact. But there is an excellent reason for it.

The Norton expedition was the first one to engage local labour on a grand scale. The earlier explorers had made do with guides and domestics, Smith and Porcher had relied on their "good strong blacks", but it was Richard Norton who first convinced the local Arab population that antiquities meant money. The hundred Hasa tribesmen, wrapped in barracans, digging away on the Acropolis Hill had found, for Norton, remarkably little. But they had been very generously rewarded for their efforts. For the first time after many centuries of misery and near-starvation, all these remains of the *Jehalia*—the "period of ignorance", as assessed by pious Moslems, for whom culture began with the Prophet Mohammed—began to assume an economic importance. The quarter-of-a-century of Italian excavation that was to follow yielded even greater dividends to local labourers, but the name "Melikan" stuck, and still remains with the older people. The youngsters fresh from their schools and universities now use a better Arabic word, "Athar", but many years or even decades will pass before "Melikan" disappears from local currency.

BIBLIOGRAPHY

The American Fleet at Derna:
History of the War between the United States and Tripoli (Salem, U.S.A., 1806).

Expeditions mentioned between Smith and Porcher's in 1860/1 and Norton's in 1910/11:

G. Haimann, Cirenaica in *Bollettino della Società Geographica Italiana* vii (1882) 6 f., apparently referring back to journeys made in 1861 of which earlier accounts appeared in *L'Esploratore*, 1861.

G. Rohlfs, *Von Tripolis nach Alexandrien...im Jahren 1868 und 1869* (Bremen, 1871).

G. Dennis, *Transactions of the Royal Society of Literature*[2] ix (1870) 135 f.

G. Weld-Blundell, *ABSA* ii (1895) 113 f.

D. G. Hogarth, "Cyrenaica" in *Monthly Review*, January 1905 and *Accidents of an Antiquary's Life* (London, 1910) 131.

G. De Martino, *Cirene e Cartagine* (Bologna, 1908).

Report of the Commission of the Jewish Territorial Organisation for the Purpose of a Jewish Settlement in Cyrenaica (J.T.O. Office, London, 1909).

For F. Halbherr see S. Aurigemma, *Africa Italiana* iii (1930) 237 f. and G. Oliverio, *Africa Italiana* iv (1931) 229 f.

The American Expedition:

Richard Norton and others in *Bulletin of the Archaeological Institute of America* ii (1911) 57 f., 135 f. 141 f.

The Murder of De Cou:

Richard Norton, *ibid.*, 111 f.

R. G. Goodchild, in *Michigan Quarterly Review* viii (1969) 149 f. Goodchild there concluded, after further examination of the record, including unpublished papers in Michigan, that the shots were certainly intended for Norton and not De Cou, in the hope of driving the Americans out of the country. He stressed also that Norton did not accuse the Italian archaeologists nor the Italian government of complicity but noted that the Italian government paid an idemnity.

CHAPTER V

APHRODITE HAD LOST HER HEAD (1913–25)

Plate 92

If Norton had been able to visit Cyrene in the winter of 1913, he would have found the site profoundly changed. The bare hillsides now sprouted tented camps and wooden huts, and the lofty aerials of a wireless station crowned the Acropolis hill. Noisy lorries with solid rubber tyres chugged up and down roughly-paved roads, while mule-teams filled water-containers at the Fountain of Apollo. The terrace in front of the Fountain, where Senussi gardens had prevented the Americans from digging, now housed the Supply-Depot of General Tassoni's Fourth Special Division, which had landed at Tolmeita in April, 1913, and fought its way through the Gebel el-Akhdar to arrive at Cyrene on 20 May and establish there a major garrison centre.

Doubtless many of General Tassoni's young soldiers had envisaged a military life amidst burning sands and palm-trees, with the occasional consolations provided by dark-skinned ladies. "Tripoli bel suol d'amore" (Tripoli, beautiful land of love) was the popular song of the moment in their homeland. It must have been something of a shock to them to find themselves in a landscape reminiscent of Sicily or Calabria, and to encounter rain-clouds and chilly nights as the autumn advanced. But they settled in patiently in a country which was certainly beautiful, even if there was more hostility than love to be detected amongst the local population. What had happened to the promised "passeggiata militare"?

Their first Christmas at Cyrene was probably celebrated more cheerfully than Smith and Porcher's had been a half-century earlier. Chianti bottles and tomato-purée tins still form a distinct archaeological stratum over many parts of the classical site. On the second night after Christmas the Italian camps were shrouded in low-lying clouds while rain poured down with ever-increasing intensity. Those of the officers who remembered their Herodotus recalled the story of the "hole in the heavens", and came to the conclusion that the leak was getting worse.

The storm raged throughout the night, and was accompanied by heavy seas which lashed the hastily-improvised military port of Apollonia, washing ashore rowboats, lighters, tugs and even a small sailing vessel. Up at Cyrene a stream of rain-water flowed down from the heights of the Acropolis to augment the torrent already gushing from Apollo's Fountain. The troops huddled together in the most water-proof of their shelters and awaited the dawn.

In the morning light, grey and chilly, the Supply-Depot below the Fountain presented a dismal picture of water and mud. The company of Military Engineers commanded by Captain Fadda was given orders to set about digging drainage channels, and the sappers noticed that, on the very edge of the terrace where a motor-track had previously been laid out, the rains had exposed part of a curved block of white marble, over which the ration-lorries were bumping as they made their way through the mud. Cleaning this marble they saw immediately that it was the back of a nude statue, and very little digging was required to bring to light the headless Aphrodite ("La Venere di Cirene") which is now one of the most prized possessions of the National Museum of the Baths of Diocletian at Rome.

General Cavaciocchi, the Zone Commander, was immediately informed of the discovery and inspected the statue, which had been temporarily stored in a hen-house. Not unreasonably, he deemed this an inappropriate resting-place, and ordered that Venus be brought to the Officers' Mess of his Zone Headquarters. The news was also transmitted to Benghazi, and passed to Dr. Ettore Ghislanzoni, who had recently been appointed Superintendent of Antiquities for the newly-acquired territory of Cyrenaica. By arrangement with the Military Governor, General Ameglio, the statue was sent by sea to Benghazi, where a plaster-cast was prepared for display at the Colonial Exhibition at Genoa. But Ghislanzoni's hopes of keeping the Venus permanently in a projected new Museum at Benghazi were frustrated by Ministerial orders from Rome ordering her immediate trans-portation to the homeland. Here was something which, displayed in the capital, might serve to reinforce the myth of the "bel suol d'amore", and put heart into reluctant recruits!

Cyrene's Aphrodite was very beautiful indeed, but she had one grave defici-ency: she lacked a head. The Sappers, despite much impassioned digging, had failed to find it in the neighbourhood of the torso; and the only hope now lay in carrying out more extensive excavations. Thus the Ministry for the Colonies made available for this purpose 10,000 lire (a modest sum, though much more substantial in 1914 than it would be today): and with these slender resources began the long and fruitful period of Italian governmental excavations at Cyrene. These—continued over a period of thirty years—were to yield almost everything that a classical archaeologist might expect from a major site (and indeed more): but not, alas, the missing head.

These first excavations, made possible by the Ministerial subvention, were begun in the spring of 1914, and gradually laid bare the northern rooms of a large set of Roman public baths, situated in the eastern corner of the terrace below the Fountain. These baths had evidently been destroyed in an earthquake at the end of the fourth century A.D. and the collapsing vaults had sealed, beneath hundreds of tons of fallen stone, a rich haul of ancient statues. Some twenty important works of sculpture came to light, including the ever-popular group of the Three Graces, Alexander the Great, Eros with his bow, and Hermes. The wealth of the material lying hereabouts was so evident that the military Supply-Depot eventually received notice to quit, and by 1917 the greater part of the Sanctuary terrace—including the Temple of Apollo itself—was available for future excavation. But although the uncovering of this large area continued until 1938, the head of Aphrodite remained elusive.

The disappointment of the excavators can readily be imagined, for it seemed quite unfair that when so much of value was coming to light, the original object of their search should continue to elude them. Rumours began to spread to the effect that the head had been found at the outset by the soldier diggers, and had been spirited away. In 1920, for example, an incautious boast made by a cavalry sergeant-major in a restaurant near Lepcis Magna in Tripolitania, was overheard by antiquities employees and resulted in an official inquiry and much correspondence between Tripoli and Benghazi. In the end, after the sergeant-major had been severely grilled by the military police and civil authorities, it transpired that some sort of a head had been found while he was stationed at Cyrene, but that its present whereabouts were unknown and that it was, in any case, most unlikely to have belonged to the Aphrodite.

At Cyrene itself, hope of ever finding the head began to fade in the early 1920s, when the greater part of the Roman Baths had been cleared of soil. The very last chance seemed to come in 1922 when diggers began to clear away the deep deposit of soil that had accumulated outside and below the high retaining-wall forming the northern boundary of the Baths. "If the head exists at all", wrote Ghislanzoni to his superior authorities, "it can only be in the soil which is now being removed, having fallen there from the Baths above." But the soil did not yield the eagerly-awaited booty, and the last expectations died. There still remains, perhaps, some slight glimmer of hope; for the ground drops away steeply from the great retaining wall, and the head *might* have rolled downhill and been swept away in the winter torrent of the Wadi Bu Turkia to end up somewhere in the ravine below Cyrene. If it *is* there, perhaps we may let it rest in peace; for the corporal beauty of the "Venere di Cirene" is of universal acceptance, whilst the head itself might—who knows?—prove to be a disillusionment. Beauty above the neckline is so much more a matter of individual taste and temperament than in the case of what lies below.

There is only one other episode worth recalling in this affair of Cyrene's best-known Aphrodite (there are at Cyrene, of course, countless other representations of the goddess of love: Smith and Porcher found no less than seven in a temple near the Caesareum), and it occurred forty years after the goddess had emerged from the mud. In February, 1953 the Tribunal of Rome sat to hear rival contestants both claiming compensation from the Italian Government for their part in the discovery of the "Venere di Cirene". On one hand was the widow of Captain Fadda, whose part in the discovery we have already told; on the other was a General Frattini who claimed that it was his own pure passion of research and of curiosity, beyond the call of duty" that had been the real force behind the event. Frattini had failed to make good his claim in Fascist days, but had renewed it in 1943, after the eclipse of Mussolini.

The Rome Tribunal adjudged that neither claim was admissible, for although it was true that the law declaring archaeological finds as State property had not become formally valid in Libya before 1914, this principle had been admitted under previous Turkish legislation. Therefore the soldiers in question, whatever might have been their individual contributions in bringing Aphrodite to light, had merely carried out their duty in assuring the statue's consignment to the civil authorities, and they could claim no proprietary rights.

Who did, in fact, find the splendid, headless, Aphrodite? All tribute to the gallant and cultured soldiers who ensured her safe extrication from beneath the wheels of ration lorries; but surely, it matters little who was first on the spot, or who first encouraged his men to forget the discomforts of the previous night and to set to work to recover the fascinating marble figure. Basically it was the rain that discovered Aphrodite: the sea was too distant for her to emerge triumphantly from the waves, but the "hole in the heavens" played its part in a lesser apparition, just as in so many aspects of Cyrenean archaeology the rain still plays its part in assisting the archaeologist.

The discovery of the "Venere di Cirene" could not have occurred more opportunely, since it attracted public opinion in Italy to the archaeological wealth of Cyrenaica at a time when "military necessity" was beginning to constitute a serious threat to the monuments of the ancient Pentapolis. In 1911 the Italian forces had occupied the main coastal centres (Benghazi, Derna and Tobruk) without extending far beyond their strongly-defended perimeters. The Tolmeita landing of April, 1913 marked, however, the beginning of military operations in the very heart of the area of major Graeco-Roman occupation. Within a few months large garrisons were being installed at Tocra, Tolmeita, Apollonia, and Cyrene, all sites of ancient cities; and in all these places the industrious Italian soldier was becoming more and more occupied with collecting stone with which to build forts, defensive-walls, artillery platforms, barracks and officers' messes.

Constructional activity has always been a major characteristic of the Italian armed forces; and even before the beginning of the present century a famous British imperialist, Major (later Lord) Lugard, visiting Eritrea, had commented on the extraordinary capacity and inclination of Italian soldiers for solid field-works, comparing it favourably with the attitude of British forces in India and elsewhere. The modern military tactician may, perhaps, condemn this tendency as indicative of a "Maginot-mind"; but nobody who has had to deal with Italian military buildings (least of all those who—like the writer—have had to demolish some of them in order to excavate underlying ancient sites) can fail to admire the energy and skill that was put into their construction. The hills of Cyrenaica are still littered with picturesque "Crusader Castles" built by the occupying Italian forces between 1913 and 1918: although for some occult reason the majority of foreigners today call them "Turkish forts" even though the Turks built practically nothing outside Tripoli and Benghazi.

The Italian Government was well aware of the dangers inherent in the planting of military bases on ancient sites, and the creation of a Superintendency of Antiquities at the time of the Tolmeita landings was a direct result of this awareness. In addition a Royal Decree of 24 September, 1914 regulated the operation of the archaeological services in Libya, whilst a Governatorial Decree signed by General Ameglio on 28 October, 1915 later established a series of "monumental zones" in Cyrenaica, as called for by the Royal Decree.

But whilst the Ameglio Decree established, in principle, the inviolability of these monumental zones, it gave, in practice, broad powers of discretion to the military commanders whose garrisons sat astride them, and allowed for "unavoidable necessities of military defence".

Those who may think that this concession to military needs could easily have been avoided, would do well to study the recent International Convention for the Preservation of Cultural Property in the event of War, drafted by U.N.E.S.C.O. in 1957. There we find an equally well-intended attempt to preserve ancient sites from military damage equally rendered null and void by a similar concession to military necessity. When nations decide to kill one another they place their destinies in the hands of generals, and those generals are not going to allow any sort of restriction on the place and nature of their activities.

Montecassino is surely an adequate illustration of this basic fact; and whatever conclusions the individual may draw from the destruction of a great Monastery and cultural centre he will surely concede that at Cyrene, thirty years earlier, one could not reasonably expect a different attitude.

Thus Cyrene became a major military base, and remained such from 1914 until 1931; and the Superintendent of Antiquities, resident at Benghazi until 1921, could do no more than apply diplomatic pressure to restrict military activity potentially damaging to the ancient remains. The Superintendent himself, Ettore Ghislanzoni, could only visit the threatened sites by military convoys or by the postal steamers which plied between Benghazi and Tolmeita and Apollonia, and which in winter more often than not failed to disembark their passengers and goods owing to the high seas. But Cyrene was not entirely abandoned to the probable depredations of its military garrison. A small archaeological office was set up, and was put in charge of an "Assistente" named Senesio Catani.

An "Assistente" in the Italian antiquities service is both less and more than his title might seem to imply. In no sense a scholar, and sometimes of very modest education, he is usually adept in a wide variety of practical tasks. He knows how to direct a digging team, how to lift heavy weights (one of the most essential qualifications for a foreman working on a great classical site), and how to compile at the end of each day the routine "Giornale di Scavo", or Excavation Diary, listing briefly—and without truly scientific precision—what was found and where.

Modern archaeologists will doubtless condemn a system in which the titular director of excavations (the man responsible for drawing up the final report of work done) is not resident on the site, and leaves the day-by-day execution of the "dig" to an intelligent if unscholarly foreman. But there are occasions when no other system is possible, and at Cyrene in 1915–19 the presence of Catani (an exceptionally literate "Assistente") at a time when the soldiers of the garrison were digging out stones with which to build their defensive works, was an enormous advantage.

Catani died soon after the end of the First World War, and his manuscript Excavation Diary is, in fact, the only record of many important discoveries made in the Agora of Cyrene. This Agora, the main public square of the Greek and Hellenistic city, was brought to light more by accident than design. In consequence of the outbreak of the Great War it was necessary for Italy to reduce her overseas garrisons and to restrict her occupation of Libya to a small number of heavily-defended strongpoints. Cyrene, alas, was selected as one of these fortresses; and the military engineers therefore made elaborate plans for the construction of a perimeter-wall following very close to the line of the ancient defences of the city. Within this wall would be placed not only the hutments for the normal garrison troops, but also the encampments for the horsemen of the irregular Arab cavalry unit (the so-called "Banda Hasa") in Italian service and their families.

It would have been miraculous if the hard-pressed sappers had resisted the temptation to collect and use in their new wall-circuit the vast quantities of ancient building-stone that littered the site. Ghislanzoni, as a government official, was forced to recognise the "pressing needs of military defence" and to accept this stone-collecting, on condition that standing walls and fallen architectural elements were not touched. It was Catani who had the unenviable job of keeping the military labourers on the straight and narrow path of this compromise agreement; and, by and large, he succeeded reasonably well.

Just as Aphrodite's emergence in December, 1913 had marked the beginning of excavations in the Sanctuary of Apollo, so it was another statue, the colossal Jupiter-with-Aegis, the discovery of which inaugurated the uncovering of the Agora. This fine and complete statue was found on 25 August, 1914 by soldiers of the 52nd Infantry Regiment while they were digging for fallen stone on the north side of the Agora, and in the following January the whole Temple in which it had stood was laid bare by the Antiquities Service.

Once again, public opinion in Italy was stirred by this new confirmation that Smith and Porcher had not taken away *all* the works of art: a further sum of money was granted to the Antiquities service for the prosecution of excavations in the Agora. Thus during the years 1915–18 while the soldiers continued to dig out and take away the stone they needed for their ever-developing defence works, the government excavators worked close behind them—sometimes in front of them, so as to establish a prior claim.

An excavation carried out in these circumstances was inevitably rather messy; and it was not until 1924 that a serious attempt could be made to tidy up the Agora and remove the various pockets of soil and dumps of stone left untidily behind after the excavations. In the following year Ghislanzoni returned from Italy to complete the documentation of the Agora excavations for which he had been technically responsible; but in fact no report was published, and it is only in very recent years that the archaeological problems of the Agora have begun to be sorted out on a really scientific basis, by Prof. Sandro Stucchi.

The foreman Catani was not, however, left entirely on his own to control the destinies of ancient Cyrene during those difficult years 1914–18. Ghislanzoni obtained approval, in 1915, to add to his staff a young Inspector fresh from the Italian excavations under Halbherr in Crete. The new arrival on the Cyrenean archaeological scene was Dr. Gaspare Oliverio, a Calabrian from the village of S. Giovanni in Fiore: his specialised field was the study of Greek inscriptions. The figure of Oliverio was in later years to dominate the Cyrene excavations, and we shall have much more to say of him; but we may here only note that the earliest report from his hand surviving in the fragmentary Cyrene archives is dated 1 March, 1916, and describes a visit to the vast necropolis of Cyrene. This document is the original draft of a letter to Ghislanzoni, and it is interesting to observe how six lines of enthusiastic description have been cancelled and replaced by the bald statement "I beg you not to wonder if in this first letter I do not write down my impressions of the ruins of the city of statues which I have begun to visit with my fine escort of native soldiers. One is overwhelmed by it!"

Oliverio's first major undertaking at Cyrene was to enter the 200-yard long tunnel of the Fountain of Apollo to copy and photograph with flash-light the ancient inscriptions seen there by the Beecheys a century earlier. Most of these inscriptions were traced in liquid mud on the walls of the tunnel, despite which impermanent character they were still, for the most part, legible. With a small plate-camera suspended round his neck, and standing up to his thighs in frigid water, Oliverio made a number of excursions into the tunnel in October, 1916, and was able to document all the legible inscriptions, which he subsequently published. This arduous task he never forgot, and as late as January, 1937 he was reminding the photographer of the Cyrene excavations that some physical discomfort was inevitable in order to document underground archaeological features.

The situation of Oliverio at Cyrene was somewhat equivocal as long as his director resided at Benghazi and claimed full scientific responsibility for everything that was discovered at Cyrene. As an epigraphist Oliverio was allowed to study and publish some inscriptions, but it was always made clear to him that he was merely a junior executive officer. To a man already showing signs of distinct egotism, this was an intolerable situation, and gradually his relations with Ghislanzoni deteriorated until, in the early 1920s, the official correspondence between the Benghazi Superintendency and the Cyrene Archaeological Office had degenerated into a somewhat sterile polemic.

In June, 1920 Ghislanzoni began a long and bitter correspondence with Oliverio on the subject of the compilation of the "Excavation Diary", which the late Catani had always conscientiously submitted to his superior in Benghazi. Oliverio had different ideas. An excavation, he claimed, was "a living thing and must be lived by the person responsible for its publication". He was not prepared to accept the idea that a subordinate official resident on an ancient site could simply submit a daily diary to a distant superior who would then proceed to write up the official reports. No modern archaeologist will deny that Oliverio was completely right in taking this attitude; but it is symptomatic of human frailty that a decade and a half later Oliverio himself was pursuing a policy hardly distinguishable from Ghislanzoni's in 1920. In fact, far from trying to run the Cyrene excavations from Benghazi, he was trying to run them from ... Rome.

Oliverio's increasingly strained relations with his superior are illustrated particularly in the matter of the excavations begun in 1919 at Marsa Suza (ancient Apollonia). Here the Superintendent had decided to have excavated, with the help of the military engineers, the large Eastern Church; and had instructed the Cyrene Office to supervise the operations. The assistant Valentini, colleague of Catani, was sent down and given funds to undertake the task; but Oliverio refused to accept any responsibility for the operations. To these objections Ghislanzoni replied drily (14 June, 1920) "For the excavations at Marsa Suza no responsibility lies on the head of the Inspector Oliverio, nor indeed for any other excavation, since all these undertakings are carried out according to the directives of the Head of the Department."

Whether in science or in commerce, differences of opinion between heads of departments and their subordinates are as old as the hills; but such differences become acute problems when the departmental head is distant from the scene of operations. In many ways Ghislanzoni was wrong in thinking that he could, through official correspondence, initiate and supervise programmes which did not obtain the loyal collaboration of his subordinate on the spot. In commerce, he would either have abandoned the programme, or have sacked his subordinate; but bureaucracy, even in the field of archaeology, does not provide for the "hire and fire" principle.

As for Oliverio's misgivings, it must be confessed that they are far from convincing. The Eastern Church of Apollonia lay close to a large Italian military fort, and its fallen stone was constantly exposed to the ravages of the sappers. By having the building excavated and getting the sappers themselves to re-erect the marble columns, Ghislanzoni not only made attractive and intelligible a notable ancient monument, but helped to secure a greater respect from the military for the antiquities of that site.

In his curiously unobjective "Scavi di Cirene", published in 1931, Oliverio reiterated his opposition to the Apollonia undertaking. "Desiring, at a high level, a sensational excavation, part of the activities of the (Archaeological) Office had to be transferred to Apollonia; and sums of money, large in relation to the budget, were spent in uncovering and restoring the Christian Basilica which is commonly, and without conscious irony, called the Temple of Apollo. Unfortunately the real Temple of Apollo lies probably immediately below the Basilica and can no longer be excavated because it would be first necessary to dismount and remove from the site the heavy columns re-erected with so much effort."

However much one may admire Oliverio's long and unquestionable devotion to Cyrenean antiquities, this comment on the East Church of Apollonia can only be defined as bigoted and ridiculous. Whatever lies beneath the Church (and it is doubtless an ancient building of importance) can easily be investigated without demolishing the restored Christian columns. Indeed the re-erection of the Byzantine columns has made it more easy to undertake deeper soundings. The truth is that Oliverio was basically uninterested in Byzantine monuments, and in any case hostile to any initiative which came from Ghislanzoni, his superior. One also suspects that he may have been resentful of the fact that the Superintendent was residing comfortably down in the capital, whilst he had to put up with the not inconsiderable sacrifices of living in the mountains, surrounded by soldiers and barbed-wire. But this is not to suggest that Oliverio was one to hanker after the flesh-pots; for as the years passed he became more and more attached to the ruins of Cyrene, and was to pass twenty years there without ever proposing that the seat of Antiquities Administration should be anywhere else.

Despite, perhaps even because of, the increasing tension between Ghislanzoni and Oliverio, the Superintendent soon recruited another Inspector to assist in the work of protecting the antiquities of Cyrenaica. His choice, this time, fell on a man of very different stamp from Oliverio—Dr. Silvio Ferri, to-day a much-respected professor at Pisa University. Ferri spent the years 1919–22 at Cyrene and in its neighbourhood, and was also given the difficult task (in 1920) of conducting excavations at Zaviet el-Beida, where the suspected remains of the famous Sanctuary of Aesculapius had been shamefully quarried of stone to build a nearby military fort. These excavations, like those of Cyrene, Ghislanzoni strove to run, at long range, from his Benghazi office; and, in the outcome, Ferri narrowly missed finding the Temple of Aesculapius, which remained elusive for another thirty-five years.

Ferri was intensely interested in all the new light thrown on Greek history and religion by the Cyrenaican excavations, and was able to make a number of very useful and scholarly interpretations. Despite some initial frustrations, his great moment came in 1922 when excavations in the late Roman Baths in the Sanctuary of Apollo brought to light some inscribed stones of exceptional interest, including the Ptolemaic constitution of the Cyrenean state, and the equally famous "Stele of the Founders", recording the oaths taken by the first colonists before they left their island home of Thera. Owing to the difficulty of getting his account of these discoveries published promptly in Italy, Ferri sought the aid of German scholarship with the result that some of the most important discoveries ever to come out of Cyrenaica were first made public in German scientific publications. Needless to say this caused some heart-burnings in Italy, and was to have its part in the creation of the Italian "Archaeological Mission at Cyrene" in 1925.

Oliverio himself also had a document of primary importance to contribute to Graeco-Roman epigraphy—the famous "Decrees of Augustus" inscribed on a marble stele found in the Agora in 1921, and published six years later in the official "Notiziario Archeologico" of the Italian Colonial Ministry. The fact that Oliverio and Ferri were both allowed to study and publish these vital documents shows that Ghislanzoni had at last come to realise that subordinate Inspectors living at Cyrene and directing the work there were entitled to enjoy the fruits of their labours. Indeed it had long been apparent that with so much archaeological wealth emerging from the soil of Cyrene, the position of a Superindendent of Antiquities resident 150 miles away in Benghazi, was quite anomalous. The headquarters of archaeological research in Cyrenaica had to be moved to the ancient capital.

This movement took place in 1921, and the Superintendent at long last came to take up residence at Cyrene; but he was to remain there only another two years, before his transfer to Italy to take up another archaeological post in his homeland. It was on 28 August, 1923 that Ettore Ghislanzoni, with his family, left Cyrene for the port of Apollonia to take ship to Benghazi and thence to Italy. The best judgment on his conduct of archaeological affairs in Cyrenaica during the decade since the Superintendency of Antiquities was created has been written by a colleague, Carlo Anti:

"These were the circumstances and the difficulties which determined and hindered the excavations conducted by Ghislanzoni. His merits were of having defended the field of ruins from possible damage during the difficult moments of military operations, that is to say when military exigencies were logically predominant; of having revealed in definitive manner, especially by epigraphic discoveries of the first order, the enormous value of the ruins of Cyrene; and of having laid the basis of the Superintendency of Antiquities at Cyrene, the first essential for every future research."

This verdict may be endorsed by a modern excavator at Cyrene who has had access to the reports and correspondence of the period of Ghislanzoni's direction; with the proviso that it would have been far better if the Superintendency of Antiquities had been able to transfer its headquarters to Cyrene at least some five years earlier. But as we shall see in later pages of this narrative, the question of Benghazi versus Cyrene as the seat of archaeological direction did not end with the transfer of the office in 1921. The pendulum swung again to Benghazi in 1935, and swung again back to Cyrene after the Second World War.

BIBLIOGRAPHY

The Italian invasion and administration:
Martin Moore, *The Fourth Shore* (London, 1940).

Archaeological Reports:

For the Venus of Cyrene see G. Lippold, *Griechische Plastik* (München, 1940) p. 387, with bibliography.

For the Zeus Aegiochus see E. Paribeni, *Catalogo delle Sculture di Cirene* (Firenze, 1959) no. 185, with bibliography.

Reports of the Superintendency's work in the early days appeared in *Notiziario Archeologico del Ministero delle Colonie* (3 vols., 1915–27).

S. Ferri's German-assisted publications are in *Abh. Ak. Berlin* 1925.

CHAPTER VI

DON GASPARE (1925–38)

Plates 93, 94, 95

Ghislanzoni's transfer of his Antiquities headquarters from Benghazi to Cyrene, followed soon afterwards by his own departure from the scene, paved the way for a new phase in the archaeological exploration of the ancient city. In default of other better-qualified candidates, Gaspare Oliverio's seniority gave him a strong claim to the succession, even though his experience had been mainly confined to the study of inscriptions, rather than to the interpretation of complex groups of ancient monuments.

Perhaps in order to reinforce his own rather insecure position, certainly out of sincere conviction that Ghislanzoni's methods had just not been good enough, Oliverio hastened to make known his view that new policies were required at Cyrene. Indeed not content with insisting on an entire change of directive and organisation in the archaeological family, he even demanded an investigation of alleged (and doubtless non-existent) administrative irregularities under his predecessor's regime—not, perhaps, a very polite and endearing way of speeding the parting guest.

On the technical side, Oliverio recorded his opinions clearly in his booklet "Scavi di Cirene" published some years later:

"Certainly a great quantity of archaeological material had come to light (in 1914–23) but scientific research had not made a single step of progress in the study of the problem as a whole. Thus, in the summer of 1923, it became necessary to call a halt to the digging, in order to organise things and put oneself in a position to go ahead on a methodical basis. One cannot, in fact, in an excavation, ignore the stratigraphic study of the underlying soil; and one must try to re-integrate, reciprocally, the results from a number of areas, checked with great care during the work, so as to understand fully the various constructive phases. Every archaeological trace must be patiently examined, and no detail must escape such examination. There is no manifestation, however small and seemingly insignificant, of ancient life, that cannot contribute to the better understanding of an ancient monument, and thereby to the historical period to which that monument belongs. There must be no anxiety, either as to time or as to discoveries—that is the only guarantee of serious work. The ruin must, for its own sake, become a subject of vivisection ... it must be put together again as it was at the time of its creation, taking scrupulously into account the archaeological material brought to light, especially the inscriptions."

These are brave words, and ones which will be endorsed by most serious archaeologists; but the realist has to remember that by laying down rigid principles one does not only have the satisfaction of condemning one's predecessors, but is also providing a yard-stick by which one's own shortcomings may eventually be measured. It would be so much easier to forgive Oliverio's own failings—his selfish "reservation" of archaeological material found decades earlier, his failure to publish so many things, his increasing egotism during his long period of direction—had he not expressed so publicly a "holier-than-thou" attitude regarding those who had preceded him.

In pursuance of his plan for a "new deal" at Cyrene, Oliverio took advantage of a visit in 1924 by Luigi Federzoni, Minister of the Colonies, to set forth his views. There were two major problems to be solved: first, the removal of the modern settlement and the adjacent military installations which sat astride ancient Cyrene; second, the creation of a technical team competent to deal scientifically with a large-scale excavation on a classical site.

As regards the first aim, Federzoni did, at Oliverio's suggestion, nominate in 1924 a two-man commission to seek out an alternative site for modern Cyrene. The archaeologist Carlo Anti and the architect Marcello Piacentini examined the area around the ancient city, and decided in favour of the plateau above Ain Hofra, a couple of miles east of the old site. Of this area, relatively free from ancient remains, a detailed survey was made; but as Oliverio was to write despondently a few years later, "Alas, the funds necessary to begin the work were lacking, and soon afterwards nothing more was said of the project." Despite another and more determined effort, in 1931, to get rid of modern Cyrene, the problem is still with us today.

More effective was Federzoni's intervention to create an adequate archaeological team to direct the new programme of excavations. The Governor of Cyrenaica, General Mombelli, was instructed to invite an "Archaeological Mission" to come out from Italy each summer to collaborate with the resident Superintendent, Oliverio himself. The members of this "Mission" were to be: Professors Carlo Anti and Luigi Pernier, the former to study and publish the ancient works of art, the latter to analyse the ancient buildings; the architects Luigi Giammiti and Italo Gismondi, to make surveys of the individual buildings and of the whole site. Oliverio himself would study and publish the inscriptions.

Undoubtedly Luigi Pernier was to prove the mainspring of this new organisation. He was an extraordinarily able and patient archaeologist who had long worked in Crete under Halbherr. No better man could have been entrusted with the disentangling of the highly complicated stratigraphy of the Temple of Apollo; and his excellent volume on this subject, even if it now needs modification in the light of Professor Sandro Stucchi's recent acute observations, is still one of the most serious contributions to the bibliography of Cyrene.

Had Pernier lived longer, and been free to devote all of his time to Cyrene, there can be no doubt that the "Mission" of 1925–38 would have eventually produced a series of reports comparable with those of the Germans at Olympia and the French at Delphi; but after Halbherr's death in 1930, he took over direction of Italian archaeological work in Crete, and his time available for Cyrene was reduced. His last visit was in 1936, and his death soon afterwards robbed the Cyrene team of its most valuable component.

Carlo Anti lived until 1961, but his direct association with Cyrene was to be much briefer. In the earlier campaigns from 1925 onwards he came out fairly regularly, and began the documentation of the rich collection of ancient statues; but his last visit was in 1930, and after that date he was only a titular member of the "Mission". The promised catalogue and general analysis of Cyrene sculpture was never written by him, and it remained for Enrico Paribeni and Elisabeth Rosenbaum to do this essential work after the Second World War.

Apart from Oliverio himself, the only other member of the Mission who remained constantly associated with the actual work at Cyrene in pre-war days was Italo Gismondi. He prepared a splendid contoured map of the whole site of walled Cyrene (the extra-mural area of the vast Necropolis was much later to be planned by John Cassels, in 1956) and detailed plans of the Sanctuary and Agora areas. He completed the restorations of the Temple of Apollo and its Altar, of the Strategeion, the Greek Theatre and other minor monuments. His last visit with the old "Mission" was in 1936, though he returned briefly in 1957 to complete his documentation of the Theatre. One cannot speak too highly of the quality of his surveys and of the painstaking accuracy of the restorations he supervised.

Before describing the detailed programme of work of the "Mission", and discussing the extent to which it achieved its aims, reference must be made to a brief period in the winter of 1925 when Oliverio's place at Cyrene was temporarily taken by a young Inspector Dr. Giacomo Guidi, who was later to distinguish himself as Superintendent of Antiquities at Tripoli. Breaking away from Oliverio's deliberate policy of restricting all activity to the Sanctuary of Apollo, Guidi—in a very few weeks—made some interesting and novel discoveries. First, under instructions, he excavated the fine "Circular Tomb" that lies below the present Sculpture Museum, finding in the underlying tomb-chamber Greek pottery of the fourth century B.C. Then, on his own initiative, he cut some trial trenches in the so-called "Stadium", long visible in the north-eastern quarter of the city. Finding the foundations of the "spina", or central wall down the axis of the monument, he rightly concluded that it had been a *circus* for chariot-races, not a *stadium* or running-track; but it has still to be established whether it might not have started its life in the latter capacity, and have later been extended and modified.

Soon afterwards, Guidi dug a number of soundings under the stable-buildings of the "Batteria Libica", on the hill immediately behind the modern Cyrene Hotel, (The Gebel el-Akhdar Hotel), and was able to prove the existence of an archaic Doric temple of respectable dimensions. This was something which none of the nineteenth-century explorers of Cyrene had been able to recognise, presumably because the surface remains were too few or too mangled. Finally, in February, 1926, Guidi had great fortune in the course of cleaning out the interior of the large Temple of Zeus in the north-east quarter. Some deposits of soil left untouched by Smith and Porcher yielded not only important inscriptions, but also—broken (probably by early Christians) into more than a hundred fragments —the fine head of Zeus which is one of Cyrene's main treasures. Whether or not it is, as Guidi himself claimed, a first-hand copy of the famous Zeus of Pheidias at Olympia, it remains a splendid work of ancient art.

Guidi's brief stay at Cyrene had been liberally rewarded; but the resulting publicity was not entirely agreeable to Oliverio, the actual Superintendent. Nor was he to blame for being a trifle disgruntled, because in an account of "The excavations of Cyrenaica, in the past, present and future" published in a leading Italian literary review, Guidi made only a passing footnote reference to Oliverio, the real custodian of the site, and wrote as though he himself were the arbiter of excavation policy.

One of Guidi's proposals, in this same article, was that the three existing zones of excavation—the Sanctuary, the Agora, and the Hill of Zeus—should be joined together by extended excavations; and in his later guide-book, Oliverio drily commented that "some years must pass before the unification vaguely referred to by Guidi can take effect, because it would involve the excavation of two-thirds of the ancient city". Oliverio was doubtless right in throwing some cold water on the neophyte enthusiasm of Guidi; but, on the other hand, Guidi was equally right in emphasising that the topographical relationship of the Zeus temple to the rest of the site should be clarified.

At all events, Guidi soon disappeared from the Cyrenean scene, and Oliverio does not seem to have taken any steps to recruit another Inspector to assist him. For the remainder of his long period of office in Cyrene, he was content to engage a series of resident architects, who were expected to survey the ancient monuments rather than comment on them. Whether this was due to purely bureaucratic circumstances arising from the colonial establishment, and thus outside Oliverio's own control, or whether it was deliberate policy on his own part, must remain obscure.

Certainly Oliverio was already beginning to acquire a reputation of being egotistical and "difficult", and there were some who hinted that he was one of those unlucky possessors of the "evil eye", which still plays a large part in Mediterranean folklore.

The cold-blooded northerner may laugh at this widespread southern super-stition; but he would do well to read the amusing narrative written by Ardito Desio, the eminent Italian explorer, of what happened to a military column carrying an archaeologist and an Egyptian mummy from Giarabub to Cyrene in the autumn of 1926. The archaeologist was Gaspare Oliverio (although Desio discreetly does not reveal his identity), and he had been instructed to make an archaeological survey in the Giarabub area following the Italian occupation of that oasis in 1926. Giarabub had been a major centre of Senussi activity, and it was evidently felt that in the business of "showing the flag", culture should play some part.

Oliverio's journey was, scientifically, extremely valuable, because a large number of ancient monuments between Derna and Bardia, and in the desert to the south, were visited and photographed. But the military column taking him from Bardia to Giarabub met with a series of unaccountable mishaps. In the Mess at Giarabub Desio met the officer in charge of the column, who frankly told him "*That* man is a *iettatore* (possessor of the evil-eye). Never have I had a more disastrous convoy. Just imagine what will happen on the way back with an Egyptian mummy on my lorries!"

The mummy came under discussion, because Oliverio's aim was to recover, from the ancient tombs around Giarabub, one of the ancient mummies which were known to lie there, and to bring it back to Cyrene or Benghazi for the museum. At all events, Desio, not being superstitious, joined the archaeological column, and has left a vivid narrative of all that happened. It started with a man break-ing his leg while loading the mummy on to a lorry, which accident caused the gloomiest forebodings. The commander at Giarabub refused to allow the mummy to stay overnight in his fort, and the drivers in the convoy hastened to attach prophylactic devices—horseshoes, ram's horns, and the like—to their vehicles.

On the long journey back to the coast every conceivable disaster happened.

Vehicles dug themselves into the sand, loads fell out, the lorry with the mummy broke a spring, and when night fell the convoy was far short of its intended destination. During the night in an improvised camp, gusts of wind blew away some of the tents and were followed by torrential rainstorms.

So it went on; but the mummy *did* get back to the coast thanks to Oliverio's perseverance, and the Cyrene photographic archive includes a picture of it in all its wrappings on arrival. But oddly enough, what happened to it subsequently is completely unknown. It was not included in pre-war lists of the Museum's contents, nor in the lists of objects evacuated from Cyrenaica during the war. It would seem almost as though the mummy refused to sojourn so far away from its proper resting-place; and who can say whether the troubles described so vividly by Desio were in fact the fault of the "Jonah" archaeologist—or of the mummy itself?

To return to Cyrene; and to the programme of the Mission which began work there in the summer of 1925—it must be explained that although there was probably a vague long-term idea of excavating the *whole* of ancient Cyrene, both city and necropolis, the short-term aim was more modest and practicable.

It was proposed, according to Oliverio's own statement, "to excavate and systematise the following zones":

A. *The western hill:*
   1. Sanctuary of Apollo from its eastern margin westward to the Theatre.
   2. Agora, from the old Beida road to the Acropolis summit.
   3. The intermediate strip between the Agora and the Sanctuary, cut from east to north-west by the Sacred Way of Battus.
B. *The eastern hill:* the great Temple of Zeus.
C. *The central zone between the two hills:*
   1. The Christian Church,
   2. The "Great Gymnasium" (so-called).
D. *The northern necropolis:* area between the Governor's House (Villa Graziani) and the Apollonia gate on the Italian defensive circuit.

It was in the Sanctuary of Apollo that the effort began first and was to be most intensive. Quite apart from opening up new excavations, removing a street of post-occupation shops in the valley east of the Sanctuary, and arranging for the moving of the modern waterworks from the Fountain itself to a water-point outside, it was necessary to tidy up the somewhat messy area of the old excavations. In the Roman Baths, for example, the earlier excavators had left large quantities of fallen stones lying on top of the ancient walls, so as to avoid the fatigue of removing them. This undesirable practice, still sometimes encountered in more recent excavations, all round the Mediterranean, put later workers to a large amount of expensive and unprofitable labour.

The work in the Sanctuary continued each year from 1925 until 1938, and by the latter year it could be said that the greater part of the original programme had been achieved. One of the most interesting religious sites in the classical world had been cleared of soil, and its major monuments partially restored. So far as publication was concerned, annual reports [up to and including the "campagna di scavi" of 1928] appeared in the review "Africa Italiana" from 1927 to 1930; but for the subsequent years we have only manuscript reports, and occasional publications of individual works of art, monuments and inscriptions. This lack of documentation, unfortunate as it may appear at first sight, is by no means disastrous; the monuments are still there, and a lavish collection of photographs showing all stages of the work is in the archives. Indeed, far from the delay of publication impeding the attainment of scientific accuracy, there are many instances where time and weather have made things clearer than they were before. This is a factor which we must always bear in mind before making precipitate judgments.

The excavation of the upper area of Cyrene, centred around the Agora, had been suspended in 1923 and was only begun again in 1934. It continued until 1938, although we have no contemporary published reports but—as in the case of the Sanctuary—manuscript annual summaries and an excellent series of photographs. It is in this area that the work of the new Italian Mission has been concentrated since it began in 1956, and detailed reports should soon be forthcoming. It must be stressed, however, that in many parts of the upper area, the work of Oliverio consisted of what he termed "sterri", i.e. initial clearance of earth, without either re-erection of fallen elements or investigation of the subsoil. Such "sterri" are permissible enough provided too long a period does not intervene before the uncovered remains are given the full treatment. The blocks of soft Cyrene limestone when lying out of horizon (as in the case of fallen walls) are too easily cracked by the weather; and for this reason it is usually advisable to begin a programme of re-erection as soon as possible after (sometimes even *pari passu* with) the excavation itself.

The third item in the programme for the western hill, i.e. the excavation of the intermediate strip between Agora and Sanctuary, was never fully completed, mainly owing to the sharp descent of the ground and the consequent difficulty of creating effective light-railway lines for excavation purposes. From what was uncovered it has become clear (although the fact does not emerge in the contemporary reports) that the old idea of a major processional way from the Agora directly to the Sanctuary (an idea suggested by the poems of Pindar, and other literary sources) is no longer tenable. Because Pindar referred to a "paved street" created by the first King Battus, it was assumed that a narrow rock-cut track, rising beside the Fountain of Apollo, was this "Sacred Way". It seems today much more likely that Battus' original paved road was followed by the later broad and straight street that links Forum (Caesareum) and Agora, and that direct communication between Agora and Sanctuary could only have been used for public occasions in the earliest years of the city's life. Once the city had acquired a regular town-plan, the central valley must have been the principal route to and from the Sanctuary, even if it was not perhaps until Roman times that it was regularly paved and drained.

As regards the Eastern Hill and its Temple of Zeus, apart from Guidi's rapid exploration of the Temple *Cella* in 1926, nothing was done to execute this part of its programme, and it was only after the Mission's disbandment in 1938 that attention was seriously turned to this area of the ancient city. So, too, in the intermediate zone between the two hills, neither the (eastern) Christian church nor the alleged "Great Gymnasium" were excavated between 1925 and 1938, although Oliverio did make some soundings in the latter building, and re-erected a few columns of late Roman date.

In the Necropolis, the Mission could hardly excavate the sector of its Northern area provided for in the original plan, so long as many of the tombs were still occupied by Arab families. These latter were evicted after 1931, following Graziani's drastic intervention, but by that time both the Mission and the resident Superintendency were too fully committed in Sanctuary and Agora to be able to open up new areas.

Looking back objectively it must be said that if the Mission failed to achieve all its objectives between 1925 and 1938, it was mainly because the task of excavating Cyrene has always proved greater and slower than can be provided for in any logical estimate of time and resources. The heavy soil of Cyrene is not like the sand of Lepcis Magna in Tripolitania: it does not fall away from ancient buildings, and lend itself to being removed expeditiously. Moreover the complications of successive destructions and rebuildings, accompanied by hundreds of tons of fallen stone, are more onerous at Cyrene probably than on any other Mediterranean site.

In addition to these material handicaps, it must be frankly admitted that the Mission, which started so brilliantly in 1925, under Pernier's guiding hand, tended to lose impetus as the years passed. Pernier's Cretan commitments took up more and more of his time, and Gismondi's heavy duties at Rome and Ostia had the same effect. Although replacement members for the Mission were nominated and invited to come out to Cyrene, they too often had to decline owing to other engagements. By 1937 the Mission, far from being an effective team, as it had been for the first few years after 1925, had become a nominal organisation, and Oliverio was left alone and without the benefit of any interchange of ideas. Reading his annual reports in 1937 and 1938, one begins to suspect that this may have been how he wanted things. Repeatedly he asks for Gismondi's help, but towards the other nominal members of the Mission he seems to show indifference as to whether or not they can participate in the season's work.

This change of attitude on Oliverio's part resulted largely from a very important change in his own personal situation. In 1934 he had applied for, and obtained, a university chair in Italy; but, being reluctant to abandon his Cyrenean interests, he persuaded the Minister of the Colonies, De Bono, to allow him to retain direction of the Cyrene excavations. Thus it came about that whilst a new Superintendent of Antiquities in Cyrenaica, in the person of Dr. Giacomo Caputo, was appointed, in January, 1935, it was on condition that Cyrene itself was excluded from his own sphere of official activity.

This somewhat extraordinary situation was to last until 1938, and during the first of these three years Caputo had his Superintendency of Antiquities in Benghazi (a reversion to the Ghislanzoni situation) with ancient Ptolemais as his main centre of activity. At Cyrene the antiquities staff, although colonial employees, maintained their allegiance to their former director, Oliverio, who himself controlled their activities by means of voluminous correspondence from Rome.

The surviving remains of this correspondence are remarkable in many ways, and throw considerable light on Oliverio's character. No detail of what went on at Cyrene escaped his attention, whether it was furnished in the official weekly report from the architect-in-charge of the Office, or (more often than not) by confidential informants who were privileged to write to him direct. We find, for example, the architect being rapped on the knuckles because when he went to Derna to obtain necessary technical stores, he presumed to stay there the night. We find a minor employee warned that he is spending too much time in the local café. "Big Brother" was watching the Antiquities Staff all the time, and it was even considered necessary to consult him in Rome on subjects such as whether flowers from the Museum garden should be allowed to be cut for the Church or for the Hotel!

In May, 1936 a sad event occurred in Tripoli. Giacomo Guidi died unexpectedly, depriving the Superintendency of Antiquities there of a brilliant, if somewhat mystical, director. In his place was appointed Giacomo Caputo, and simultane-ously the direction of Antiquities in Libya was unified by the creation of a central office in Tripoli under a Superintendent for Monuments and Excavations in Libya (and, later, of a subordinate office in Benghazi serving as an Inspectorate for Eastern Libya). This change was a by-product of the more general reforms ordered by the new Governor-General of Libya, Italo Balbo, a dynamic character best remembered for his transatlantic flights, and for his building-up of Italian agricultural settlements in Libya.

Balbo, a remarkable man in every respect and the most human of the Fascist bosses, was a keen patron of archaeological research in his colony; and he probably saw clearly that what had once been a genuine collaborative team-effort at Cyrene had degenerated into a private empire directed by an absentee profes-sor. Hints were made that the tempo of the Cyrene excavations should be speeded up; and in July, 1937 Oliverio submitted a revised programme, which he claimed could be completed in three campaigns.

These three campaigns were duly carried out, one in the summer of 1937, and two in the spring of 1938; but it was more than apparent that little real progress was being made, and that new areas were being uncovered (probably mainly in the hope of finding inscriptions) without equivalent progress in the field of systematisation and restoration—except in the case of the Caesareum, where re-erection of some of the fallen walls and porticoes had begun. Balbo was evidently dissatisfied with these results, and on 4 July a letter was sent to Oliverio informing him that his Mission could be considered as terminated and that henceforward Cyrene would come under the technical administration of Caputo's Superintendency.

Oliverio's reply to this bombshell is a moving document. "I have received Your Excellency's letter", he wrote, "and would have thanked you sooner for your kind words regarding me, had I not been completely overwhelmed for several days by the news of the decision that has been made. Your Excellency knows well that for me Cyrene has been all my life—much more than the academic chair—in that from 1914 until today, apart from giving me the joy of new discoveries, Cyrene has provided me with the raw material for all my scientific work." He went on to say that he was quite prepared to accept admin-istrative control from the new colonial Superintendency over his work at Cyrene, but wanted only to "bring to completion" the current works, with which his name was associated. He was confident that the Governor who "has known how, in every field, to renew the life of Libya, would not want to cut short the life of a scholar who has drawn, from the ruins of Cyrene, his whole 'raison d'être'."

Caputo, invited by the Governor to comment on Oliverio's observations, pointed out that there was nothing to prevent an ex-Superintendent coming back to Libya from time to time to work, in collaboration with the resident Super-intendency. What was intolerable was that at Cyrene a large and well-equipped antiquities staff on the colonial pay-roll should be directed not by the titular Superintendent of Antiquities but by a private scholar living abroad. That Caputo's attitude was correct and logical, in the circumstances, is undeniable: moreover, the facilities which he had already accorded to other ex-Superintendents wishing to continue working in Libya, showed that there was no lack of goodwill towards their enterprises.

On the other hand, for all its rhetoric, Oliverio's letter to Balbo is not unmoving. There is no doubt that Cyrene did mean a lot to him: he had resided there continuously for nineteen years, and revisited annually for another four. A quarter of a century is a large piece out of a man's lifetime, and during it Oliverio had seen Cyrene change from the barbed-wire-encircled military camp of 1915 to the archaeological and touristic centre of the middle thirties. In these changes he himself had played a leading part; he had fought the military authorities and got them out of Cyrene, he had fought the civilian authorities into admitting that archaeological considerations should come first, he had got to know very intimately indeed the local Arab population, and had provided the labour that gave many of them their daily bread. If an intrinsic egotism had led him into believing that Cyrene was his, and his alone, at least the claim was not entirely groundless.

What is noteworthy, and cannot be ignored by any chronicler of Cyrene, ancient and modern, is that Oliverio is still vividly remembered there today, when most of his archaeological colleagues and the colonial officials under whom he worked (Graziani himself, of course, excepted!) are but dim spectres. The Arabs speak well of Oliverio. "He was a great worker" they say, and they recount with undisguised admiration his untiring efforts to get the most work out of them: these included the provision of distinctive uniforms for all labourers, so that they could instantly be spotted if they crept away from the excavation to drink tea in the local "suk".

He was not, however, just an exploiter of cheap labour, but went to pains to look after the people dependent on him. In a letter of November, 1937 addressed to one of his assistants at Cyrene, he wrote regarding the allocation of cultivable land to antiquities workers: "You, my dear fellow, are not as interested in the Arabs as you should be: remember that they are our working comrades, and deserve every consideration."

If we contrast such statements, and the deep impression of benevolence and activity which Oliverio left on the local population, with the often somewhat lukewarm attitude of his own co-nationalists and colleagues, we are forced to conclude that in terms of human relations he succeeded best with the Arabs. They never regarded him as a *iettatore* or as a "difficult" person: they loved and admired him. And it may well be that this creation of a local feeling of sympathy and respect for the archaeological work at Cyrene was a greater achievement even than his epigraphic studies.

BIBLIOGRAPHY

G. Oliverio, *Scavi di Cirene* (Bergamo, 1931) and in *Guida della Libia della C.T.I.* (Milano, 1937).
Reports of the work of the superintendency and publications of the Archaeological

Mission appeared in *Africa Italiana* (8 vols. 1927–40) cf. also L. Pernier, *Il Tempio e l'Altare di Apollo a Cirene* (Bergamo, 1935).

G. Oliverio, *Documenti Antichi dell'Africa Italiana* (Bergamo, 1932–6).

Post-war publication of discoveries made in this period is listed in the bibliography to the postscript.

A. Desio, *Risultati scientifici della Missione all'Oasi di Giarabùb* (Rome, Vol. I, 1928 and II, 1929)—I have not been able to consult this in order to discover if it contains the non-scientific "travelogue" referred to by Goodchild.

CHAPTER VII

THE NEW MANAGEMENT (1938–41)

Oliverio was never to return to Cyrene after the abrupt termination in 1938 of his long stewardship; and the "new management" (as it described itself even in official reports) was therefore completely free to pursue such policies as seemed expedient. Although under this arrangement the "Superintendent of Monuments and Excavations in Libya" (Giacomo Caputo, resident in Tripoli) was responsible for archaeological activity in both western and eastern Libya, the vast distance separating Tripoli and Benghazi made it essential to have a subordinate office in the eastern province. This office, calling itself an "Inspectorate of Monuments and Excavations in Eastern Libya", was placed in Benghazi, and to it were appointed as Inspectors, first Dr. Enrico Paribeni (1938–9) and subsequently Dr. Gennaro Pesce (1939–42).

The excavations at Cyrene were left to lie fallow for a year, while the essential work of reorganisation was in progress; but the pre-existing commitment of restoring the great "Caesareum" or "Forum of Proculus" continued unabated. This large "Quadriporticus", originally erected before the beginning of the Christian era, and subsequently repaired and modified several times, had ended its life in the Byzantine period as a military fortress, its once spacious interior now cluttered up with mean barrackrooms. Earthquake or natural decay had subsequently overturned its outer walls, so that the whole vast building, when excavated in 1934, resembled a collapsed and petrified card-castle. The re-erection of these fallen elements, begun under Oliverio and carried through to near completion by Caputo, was one of the finest achievements of the quarter-century of Italian colonial archaeology at Cyrene.

Apart from this splendid restoration, and the normal day-to-day business of cleaning and maintaining the excavated areas, the "new management" at Cyrene broke away from the digging policies of Oliverio and his former Mission. It was decided that the major effort would henceforward be in and around the Temple of Zeus, on the north-eastern hill. Here, as we have already seen, Guidi had made important discoveries in 1926, while engaged in a routine clean-up of the interior of the Temple cella. It still remained to excavate the outer sides of the building, study the fallen architectural elements, and make plans for their future restoration—if such were found practicable and desirable.

This task, a formidable one, was entrusted by Caputo to Pesce, the Inspector who had arrived in Cyrenaica early in 1939. The latter took steps to set up a new "Cantiere" or technical workshop in the group of huts that had once been the military "Polveriera" or ammunition-store, and stood conveniently close to the Temple. The old "Cantiere" had been on the Acropolis Hill in the Big Barracks (Casermone) which had been demolished in 1938, following King Victor Emmanuel III's visit to Cyrene, his then Majesty having decided (not without good reason) that it was an unbefitting encumbrance on the hilltop where the Palace of King Battus lay buried.

From the "Polveriera", Decauville light railway-lines were extended to, and around, the Temple of Zeus, and thence to a soil dump in low-lying marshy ground to the north-east. The distance to this dump was soon to prove a handicap, and later in the year a new Diesel locomotive was ordered from Germany. After arrival in March, 1940, and a trial run, it waited in its newly-built shed for the expansion of the excavations. But war-clouds were already gathering, and the poor little engine was itself to become a war-victim before it could ever prove its utility.

Meanwhile, on 1 June, 1939 the excavation of the Temple of Zeus began with a labour force of ten Arabs which rose to a maximum of thirty-seven in October, and later declined when casual labourers drifted to the great Gebel Aqueduct project, whose contractors offered the princely wage of 16 lire per day. By the Spring of 1940 the whole perimeter of the Temple had been cleared of soil, and the interior completely liberated except for the *opisthodomos*, or rear vestibule, and a small part of the *pronaos* (where subsequent work, in 1954, was to yield some important inscribed stones missed by the previous explorers). Pesce had hoped to find fallen remains of sculptured pediments on the two shorter sides of the building, and he later dug a series of trenches both to east and west in search of them; but this hope was not realised. Nor were any very notable discoveries of sculpture made during this exploration, except for additional fragments of the hands and feet of a gigantic statue of Zeus, at least eight times life-size, and probably modelled on the more famous work of Pheidias at Olympia. But the unearthing of the greatest Greek Temple in North Africa was worth doing for its own sake.

In Spring 1940, while the unearthing of the Zeus-Temple was still in progress, the course of the Second World War began to make an impact on the recently tranquil life of the Green Mountain. Hitherto, Italy had remained neutral; but it became increasingly improbable that this neutrality could be maintained. Early in April all Libyans between the ages of eighteen and forty-five were informed of their liability to serve in the Italian colonial armies, whilst most of the Italian technicians working at Cyrene were ordered to report to the Militia units in which they were registered. Fortunately, most of the key men were later released and returned to the antiquities service; but from this moment onwards the work at Cyrene came under the increasing shadow of the war-clouds, and man-power became scarcer and more expensive.

On 10 June, 1940, Italy entered the conflict, confident that Britain was already as good as knocked out of the war, and anxious to ensure her own claims to certain parts of an about-to-be-dismembered Empire. Eighteen days later Marshal Balbo, known to be lukewarm in his attitude towards the war, was shot down by his own anti-aircraft defences while landing at Tobruk airport. Marshal Rodolfo Graziani was immediately appointed to take his place both as Governor of Libya and as Commander-in-Chief of the Italian forces in North Africa. He arrived in Tripoli on 30 June, and a few days later reached Cyrene where the Governatorial Residence had served Balbo as a convenient command-post, even though his main General Headquarters had been sited in Derna.

Rodolfo Graziani remembered Cyrene well, from the days of his Vice-Governorship of Cyrenaica a decade earlier. It had been a haven of peace and repose at brief intervals during the stormy business of suppressing the Cyrenaican national movement, led by Omar Mukhtar. Moreover, marble inscriptions in Cyrene Museum extolled the Marshal's earlier intervention in declaring Cyrene an "Archaeological Zone", and removing its modern population both civil and military. Emotionally, therefore, Cyrene must have had an enormous appeal to the ageing colonial soldier, and this appeal may have played some part in bringing him to a decision which was to have fateful consequences both for his own military reputation, and for the continuance of Cyrene as a respected "archaeological zone".

Graziani, in fact, gave orders, within a few days of his arrival, that the whole General Headquarters under his command would be concentrated at Cyrene and in its immediate vicinity. And, in consequence, in a short time Cyrene once again became an armed camp, much as it had been in the years 1913–20. The large and commodious tourist Hotel, built in 1930, became the headquarters of the General Staff, under General Tellera. Every available building was requisitioned to house the staff officers, and already in July the top floor of the Epigraphic Museum was being emptied of its inscriptions for use by Air Force officers. Deep below Graziani's own villa, a group of ancient tombs was modified, extended, paved, lit by electricity, and embellished with ancient statues to serve as the Commander's own personal shelter and headquarters. From this remarkable "Aladdin's Cave", a "Tomb of Residence" certainly better equipped than had been Smith and Porcher's eighty years previously, Graziani launched his September offensive which brought Italian troops into Sidi Barrani. A month earlier Mussolini had told him that this offensive would be simultaneous with a German invasion of Britain, and would thereby ensure for Italy a strong position at the subsequent peace conference. But Hitler's "Operation Sea-Lion" was never to take place, and Graziani himself displayed a marked reluctance to advance east of Sidi Barrani before a new 100 km. road and an aqueduct had been completed by his sappers. Meanwhile Mussolini fumed with impatience, and Farinacci hinted maliciously that the Marshal was afraid to leave the protection of his Greek tomb far behind the lines.

The promised further advance to Mersah Matruh was on the eve of being launched when, on 9 December, Wavell nullified all Graziani's careful and judicious preparations by his own quite unexpected counter-offensive. The Italian camps in the Egyptian "Western Desert" were rapidly over-run, and one by one the coastal fortresses in Libya itself were captured until, at the end of January the British troops were on the outskirts of Derna.

A German eye-witness has attested to the "state of mind of panic and catastrophe" which prevailed among Tellera's staff at the Cyrene Hotel during the days of 10 and 11 December, when the first news began to come through from the front. Graziani himself is described as having displayed "an admirable calm", although this hardly appears in the longwinded and semi-hysterical "Man-to-man" telegram which he sent to Mussolini on 14 December, accusing the Duce of having misunderstood him and listened to hostile advisers ever since his return from Ethiopia. To this the Duce replied briefly and more relevantly: "Marshal Graziani, the past is the past. What matters is the future and the safety of Cyrenaica."

But Graziani could not save Cyrenaica, nor—even less—his own military reputation. That luxury bomb-proof residence in the Necropolis of ancient Cyrene had proved his own undoing, not only because of the facile criticisms to which it led, but also because of the air of unreality which it had given to the whole conduct of the Italian war in the Marmarica. Admittedly the British head-quarters staff officers in Egypt were equally open to an accusation of having tried to run a war from Shepherds Hotel and the Gezira Club; but, at least, Wavell knew it behoved him to be nearer the scene of the operations. Later Generals in Libya, on both Axis and Allied sides, took care to avoid the pitfalls displayed by past history: they lived in tents and caravans and kept pace with the movements of their own troops.

Meanwhile, at Cyrene in the middle of October, long before the possibility of a British invasion was seriously envisaged, certain precautions had been taken to protect the ancient works of art against air bombardment. A rock-cut chamber in the valley immediately east of the Sanctuary of Apollo had been selected as a safe "refuge" for these treasures, had been cleared of soil and consolidated. By the end of the first week of November Giuseppe Raganato, one of the most senior and competent technicians on the Cyrenaican Antiquities staff, had completed the removal to this cave of all the major works of art and the smaller objects from the showcases. There remained, however, in the Museum buildings the precious objects of gold and silver locked in a safe, and a large quantity of unexhibited material—from twenty years of excavation—laid out on a wooden platform forming a temporary upper storey to the west wing of the Epigraphic store-house.

Whilst the measures already taken insured against the dangers likely to arise from air attack (although, in fact, no air attack on Cyrene ever did take place during Wavell's campaign) there seems to have been no very clear policy as to what should be done with these same archaeological treasures in the event of enemy invasion. It had only been agreed, at the time of Italy's entry into the war, that the Inspectorate of Antiquities in Benghazi should have full autonomy of action in case of emergency.

Unfortunately the administrative links between the Inspectorate itself and the Cyrene excavation office became progressively weaker as military events reached their climax. The Antiquities lorry, the only vehicle permanently at the Inspector's disposal, had been withdrawn for military use back in June and was never seen again: thereafter he was dependent for transport on the good offices of the governmental motor-pool in Benghazi or the military authorities, and—as always in time of war—transport was becoming a very scarce commodity. An additional obstacle to the Inspector's effective control arose when, in December, his office was moved from Benghazi to Tocra. Although some 65 km. nearer Cyrene, this location in a small village only caused further complications in the arrangement of transportation.

Thus, in the middle of December, when the military crisis was more than apparent up at Cyrene, the acting head of the Antiquities office there, Signor A. Beccafichi, felt himself carrying an excessive responsibility without clear instructions as to policy. He wrote on the 13th to the Inspector pointing out that "the deterioration of the military situation and the extreme tension in military circles" necessitated a prompt directive as to what should be done to ensure the safety of the most valuable objects "such as the Head of Zeus and the gold and silver treasures". Having received no reply to this first anxious request for instructions, he wrote again on 4 January, saying that, prompted by the advice of Graziani's private secretary, he had, on his own initiative crated and sent down to Benghazi a number of precious antiquities. A copy of this letter was sent, for information, to Tripoli.

Meanwhile, on the Benghazi–Tocra front, something was at last stirring. On 6 January, Dr. Pesce was summoned to the office of the Prefect of Benghazi and informed that the Governor (still Graziani, who had moved down from Cyrene to the capital at this time) had ordered that the whole contents of Cyrene's Museums should be transferred immediately to Benghazi and thence, at some later date, by road to Tripolitania.

Pesce rightly pointed out the grave dangers inherent in such a transfer, not only arising from the hasty loading of delicate objects on to lorries, but—even more— because Benghazi itself was under constant bombardment and even a single night's sojourn there might have disastrous results. To these objections it was peremptorily replied that "at whatever cost, the antiquities of Cyrene must be removed from any danger, however remote, of becoming enemy booty". In consequence of these unequivocal orders Pesce hastened to Cyrene on 7 January and during the next few days the statues and other objects were removed from their safe refuge, and laid, as best they could be, on straw, mattresses and rags in the heavy military lorries. There was not even time to compile proper inventories.

When these lorry loads arrived at Benghazi, Pesce's attempts to have the vehicles continue to Tripolitania were frustrated. The most that was conceded, on 16 January, was that three lorry-loads of the most precious antiquities should continue westward to Lepcis Magna. The remaining, and greater part, of the archaeological material was offloaded at Benghazi and stored in requisitioned buildings in the centre of the city, where already, on 11 January, the offices of the Inspectorate had been hit by a bomb. Moreover, he had, in his official charge, all the gold and silver coins and other precious objects from Cyrene Museums, and the last lorry-load bound for Tripolitania had left before he could remove these things from the office safe. Fearing, with every justification, the activities of looters, he hid these objects in a recess in his house, walled up the door, and placed a large wardrobe in front of the blocking masonry. Although his house was in fact broken into, the "treasure" remained intact, was later sent to safety to Italy, and has since been restored to Libya by the generosity of the Italian Government. Meanwhile the contents of the minor museums at Apollonia, Tolmeita and Barce remained where they were.

While these energetic and determined efforts were being made at Cyrene to "save" its archaeological treasure from the predatory British, the "Army of the Nile" was advancing towards Cyrene, for the most part blissfully unaware that any such booty existed, and certainly quite unorganised to handle it. We must remember that there had been little direct British archaeological interest in Cyrenaica since the Italian occupation of 1911. Foreign expeditions were not allowed (or, at least, encouraged) to operate in the major archaeological centres of the Italian colonial Empire, and British tourists to Libya had been relatively few. A handful of scholars in Oxford and Cambridge knew that the Italian excavations at Cyrene were, every year, bringing to light an enormous wealth of ancient art, of which a large part still remained unpublished. But the majority of active British archaeologists had, by the time of Dunkirk, got themselves into uniform in armed forces which barely recognised the existence of cultural activities in time of war.

Since the invading British had not the slightest intention of carrying away the works of art found in a quarter-century of Italian archaeological activity at Cyrene (and the fact that these works of art are still in Libya is surely an adequate proof of this) why, then, was there all this anxiety, on the Italian side, to move these relics of the past out of grasp of the invading army?

As we have already seen, the Italian archaeological experts were not enthusiastic about this evacuation: they knew well the dangers involved. It was Graziani who ordered it, and we may suspect that he had been influenced by the attitude of Oliverio who, in all his writings on the subject of ancient Cyrene, had constantly laid emphasis on the wickedness of Smith and Porcher in taking away the treasures that belonged to the site. To give Oliverio his due, he was sincere about this, and himself had frequently and publicly urged that the "Venere di Cirene" should come back to Cyrene from Rome; moreover, apart from the "Venere" and a few objects loaned to exhibitions in Italy (and returned since the war), the Italians *did* leave in Libya what they found there. On the other hand it was somewhat futile to imagine, in 1941, that the British Museum had infiltrated a new team of Smiths and Porchers into the ranks of Wavell's army! Yet, as we shall soon see, even Pesce shared this odd suspicion.

Far from worrying about the possibilities of expatriating the Cyrenaican archaeological patrimony, the bulk of Wavell's army was content to enjoy—after long months in the arid desert—the pleasure of finding in the Gebel el-Akhdar green fields, running water, and an abundant stock of the strong red wine pressed from the grapes of the upper plateau. The Australians in particular, who led the advance through the Gebel region, profited from the latter amenity. Valiant and unrivalled followers of Mars, their devotion to Bacchus has always been equally fervid.

Derna fell to the Australians on 30 January, after some bitter fighting around its eastern outskirts. Four days later the invaders were in Cyrene itself, and here they were accompanied by the most literate of all the war-correspondents of the Second World War, Alan Moorehead, himself an Australian by birth though long accustomed to Italy and Italian ways, and therefore singularly qualified to comment on the impact of the Australian Army on an Italian colonial territory.

Moorehead arrived in Cyrene on the heels of the advancing troops, but several days after the Italian civil administration (including the antiquities staff) had withdrawn. During the interregnum some less responsible members of the local Arab community had profited from the vacuum to pay off the old scores and obtain possession of anything that was valuable and unattended. To restrain such activities a handful of Carabinieri left behind by the Italians had done their best. "In the barracks on the hill above the modern village", wrote Moorehead, "we came on two Italian gendarmes still armed. They had rounded up some twenty Arab looters and locked them in barracks without, so far as one could discover, food or water... The choice of action was not mine to take, but I did not agree when the British officer in charge took the rifles from the gendarmes and liberated the Arabs who ran delightedly across the compound shouting: 'Viva Inghilterra!' This treatment could have been interpreted by them as no other than licence to continue their looting, and I suspect they were already at it before we left the village."

Moorehead's gloomy forebodings were, in the outcome, completely justified. Indeed, the fact that so complete a breakdown of law and order had attended the advance of the British troops, and was to be rectified only after some delay, was later to give rise to Axis propaganda discreditable to the British forces, and to the Australians in particular. On the other hand, it is necessary to remember the very peculiar circumstances of this first advance into Libya—an advance of which the rapidity had never been anticipated in Cairo itself, and the provisions for which—in the sphere of civil administration—were somewhat rudimentary.

The machinery set up by the British military command to deal with adminis- tration of enemy territory was called "O.E.T.A." (Occupied Enemy Territory Administration) and was based on the supposition that an invading army would find, *in situ*, a functioning organisation which could be controlled adequately by a skeleton staff of British officers acting under general directives from the Civil Affairs branch of G.H.Q. The local representative of O.E.T.A., in rural areas, was to be the Civil Affairs Officer, a military equivalent of the District Officer of backward colonial territories. His main task was the unenviable one of keeping things quiet so that the armed forces would encounter the minimum disturbance in their basic task of prosecuting the defeat of the enemy.

In countries where the framework of civil administration had survived mili- tary occupation, and where the resident local population had ties of loyalty, or at least tolerance, towards this framework, such an improvised arrangement could, and often did, work. But in a colonial territory where only a small handful of Arabs had ever been given real administrative authority, and where many of these same administrators (usually on a village or tribal level) were already being branded as "collaborators", "traitors" and the like, the O.E.T.A. arrangement just did not work—or, if it did work from the immediate viewpoint of the military command, it did *not* work in the long-term interests of the territory itself.

So far as the antiquities of Cyrene were concerned—and this is the only aspect that concerns us here—the maintenance of the *status quo* was undermined by three separate factors: first, Graziani's previous selection of Cyrene as a military headquarters, which automatically stripped it of any claim to special protection; second, the withdrawal of all the Italian members of the antiquities staff; third, the failure of the occupying forces to make any speedy adequate provision for effective custody of the museums and ruins.

From statements after the Italian re-occupation by the Libyan personnel of the antiquities staff (none of them of higher rank than guards or office orderlies) it is quite clear that there was no effective custody of the antiquities assets until the second half of February, following a visit made to Cyrene on 15 February by Dr. Pesce and Captain Murray-West, whom the Military Governor, Brigadier Stephen Longrigg, had instructed to look into antiquities matters.

Considering the enormous political and economic problems with which O.E.T.A. was confronted in Cyrenaica, and the utter inadequacy of its own resources, it is probably fair to say that the fortnight's delay between the British occupation of Cyrene and the awakening of official interest in its antiquities was not excessive; but it was, on the other hand, quite long enough to provide opportunity for those same lawless local elements whom Moorehead had ob- served crying "Viva Inghilterra" at the moment of their liberation from Italian custody.

What happened at Cyrene in February, 1941 is, alas, too well documented to be a matter of conjecture. In the west wing of the Epigraphic (now Sculpture) Museum, the wooden staging erected in 1938 to hold all the minor finds which had previously been kept in the "Casermone" on the Acropolis Hill, was completely removed by Arabs, the archaeological material being thrown down to the floor, and where not irrevocably ruined, at least stripped of the context of its find-spot. In this scene of desolation, wandering soldiers doubtless found and removed "souvenirs", and it is just possible that there were some who had an eye open for objects of real artistic interest and value. The workshops and stores were equally looted of tools and materials. In the now empty rooms of the Museums and Offices (from which the statues had been removed the previous year) the soldiers of the Australian army established themselves, writing—as soldiers invariably do—their names and regimental numbers, sometimes accompanied by kangaroos and other emblems, on the walls.

On his return to Benghazi, after the inspection of the ancient sites, Pesce was invited by Brigadier Longrigg to submit proposals for the reorganisation of the archaeological service; but, once again, the ghosts of Smith and Porcher dominated the scene. "The deceit was easy to detect," wrote Pesce in a later report. "So much anxiety on the part of the English to reorganise the sites and begin again the excavations while the war was still in progress, undoubtedly disguised an intention to renew, with more perfect methods, what the English Smith and Porcher had done at Cyrene in 1861; i.e. to excavate and take away the most precious monuments found on the site." With these suspicions deeply rooted in his mind, the Inspector hastened to submit by 18 February a series of proposals so patently impracticable that (by his own confession) there could be no hope of their being put into effect. "I considered it my duty to prevent, at any cost, the actuation of such a plan, delaying the matter until the day of liberation (it being preferable that the reorganisation of the museums should be done by the Italian Government)." So, on this note of suspicion (probably mutual) ended any chances of the first British military government making good the damage that had already been done; and two months later the Axis forces, now led by Rommel, were back in Cyrenaica.

BIBLIOGRAPHY

Archaeological Reports:

Caesareum, E. Sjøquist, *Opuscula Romana* i (1954) 86 f.; J. B. Ward Perkins and M. Ballance, *PBSR* xxvi (1958) 137 f.; cf. S. Stucchi in *Quaderni dell' Istituto Italiano di Cultura di Tripoli* 3 (1967) 96 f.; L. Gasperini, *QAL* 6 (1971) 3 f.

Temple of Zeus, G. Guidi, *Africa Italiana* I (1927) 3 f.; G. Pesce, *BCH* lxxi–lxxii (1947–8) 307 f. and *Bull. Soc. Roy. Arch. d'Alexandrie* xxxix (1951) 83 f.; R. G. Goodchild, J. M. Reynolds and C. J. Herington, *PBSR* xxvi (1958) 30 f. Professor S. Stucchi is working there currently cf. *QAL* 6 (1971) 116 f.

The North African Campaigns:

Alan Moorehead, *The Desert War* (London, 1965).

CHAPTER VIII

THE DIFFICULT YEARS (1941–51)

In special bulletins issued on 5 May and 8 May, 1941, the Italian "Stefani" news agency informed the world that "the English and Australian troops, during their brief stay in Cyrenaica, have destroyed a large part of the precious archaeological and epigraphic collections of Cyrene." In default of any more precise information as to what had been destroyed, and in what circumstances, Roman press comment confined itself to generalities: "these collections were founded by Italian scholars in the course of 25 years of tiring research amidst the desert sands (sic!), and the vandalism of the English and Australians is an insult to civilisation".

It must be said at once that this charge of vandalism did not emanate from Italian official archaeological sources. Neither Pesce, nor his chief Caputo, had made any statement on which the "Stefani" report might have been based. Indeed, following a visit to Cyrenaica to investigate these charges soon after the Axis reoccupation, Caputo reported to the Governor's Office that "the assertions of the Press of the 8th of this month, alleging the destruction of large and numerous collections in Cyrene Museum, are excessive". (In the original draft of this letter, still extant, we can see how the last word has been substituted for the less diplomatic one, "unfounded"!) Moreover, when Caputo was asked to make comments on some propaganda photographs showing the "devastated" museums, he objectively replied. "The half statues on the ground are in their state of discovery." Careful checking did, however, show that five marble heads left behind during the feverish lorry-loading of the previous January, were now missing; in addition, two or three statues were damaged, and a large but unprecisable quantity of minor and more fragile objects had been destroyed or dispersed when the wooden staging that supported them was looted, as previously described.

Regrettable as it was, this sum total of archaeological losses at Cyrene was hardly sufficient to support the original charges of wholesale vandalism. The officials of the Italian propaganda section under the Ministry of Popular Culture (a delightful euphemism, akin to our wartime "Ministry of Information") were reluctantly obliged to abandon hopes of publishing detailed and signed affidavits attesting the wanton destruction of great works of art. They had to content themselves with publishing photographs of some of the more messy parts of the archaeological storehouse, with such captions as "Devastation of Roman masterpieces", "The state to which the Museum was reduced", "Australian soldiers' writing on the Museum walls".

Whilst, therefore, this particular propaganda device fizzled out rather ignominiously, it must be confessed that the Italians, returning to Cyrenaica, had adequate cause to be distressed by what they found. In place of the once neat and orderly colony, there was now a war-wracked territory with roads and public utilities demolished by withdrawing forces, and offices and houses looted of furniture. Their farmers in the Gebel had suffered much disturbance, to say the least, from the Libyan tribesmen who had seen a chance—during the British advance—of regaining their lost lands. In Benghazi where the few remaining Carabinieri, the Senussi gendarmes and the British Military Police had never really got the security situation under full control, shop-fronts, doors and windows had all been walled up, as much against the civil and military looter as against the danger of bomb-splinters. Benghazi was now "La città murata" (the walled-up city).

The Cyrene excavation office was re-opened in the last week of June, 1941 after a nucleus of its original staff had been reassembled. There were now only five Italians and twenty-five Libyans available to begin the task of cleaning up the mess, but they were not able to regain possession of the museum and office buildings in which first the Australians and now the returning Germans and Italians had installed themselves. Even the office typewriter had been stolen, and for the first fortnight all the office work had to be done in manuscript. The brand-new locomotive was found intact in its shed, less its set of tools; but the horse that pulled the water-cart had to be recovered from private possession at Beida, and was found to be "in pessima condizione". In the carpenter's and blacksmith's shops, all the more portable tools had disappeared. Nonetheless, teams were sent round to repair fences and scrub out the military graffiti on museum walls.

By the end of July the more urgent tasks had been completed, and it was now possible to resume the excavations on the Temple of Zeus. But the seven Arabs employed on this task had to push the trucks 500 m. by hand, as there was no fuel oil available to get the locomotive working. Work was therefore restricted to filling in deep soundings and levelling off the site.

The return of the Italo-German command to Cyrene may have brought with it a tranquillity that had been lacking during the brief Australian occupation, and a greater degree of law and order; but it raised its own special problems. On 11 August, for example, the technician Minardi in temporary charge of the Antiquities office was ordered by staff officers to hand over a Roman column, with base and capital, which General Cavallero wished to have in Rome. The object was not in itself of much importance, and in any case Minardi had no option but to comply; but he had good reason to be anxious when it came to light that two other large sealed boxes "of which the contents are unknown, but are certainly of archaeological material" were accompanying the column to Rome. On the other hand, only by obtaining the good-will of the highest authorities on the spot could the antiquities staff get the support necessary to protect the ancient monuments from civilians and military alike. Thus in September the Governor-General was persuaded to issue an order for the evacuation of all the Arabs who had installed themselves in the ancient tombs between the Sanctuary of Apollo and the "Apollonia Gate" of the old Italian military perimeter. It does not, however, appear that His Excellency handed back the "Tomb of Residence" which his predecessor Graziani had appropriated and adorned.

As winter approached, the patient and devoted work of the antiquities staff was beginning to show results in terms of a tidier and better protected site, and a technical organisation functioning with regularity, although necessarily on a very restricted scale. The soundings ordered by Dr. Pesce to be made on the west side of the Temple of Zeus, continued under a small digging team. But as the great tank battles raged in the deserts to the east, a growing tension became apparent in the Green Mountain. The Arabs employed by the antiquities office showed signs of restiveness: there was a tendency for labourers and custodians alike to absent themselves from duty. They had, after all, their families to consider; and previous experience earlier in the year had shown the danger of being accused of excessive loyalty to the Axis side.

In mid-December the British smashed through Rommel's defences at Ain el-Gazala, and the Italo-German forces beat a hasty retreat towards the Syrtic Gulf. It was no longer a question, as in Graziani's time, of "saving Cyrenaica", but rather of keeping the Axis armour intact for a later counter-offensive. Once again the Italian civilian officials in the Gebel prepared to move out, while the uncommitted (and major) part of the Arab population dug out from strange hiding-places the improvised Union Jacks they had stitched together the previous spring. No doubt the same hiding-places now received the Italian tricolour flags which, if temporarily in decline, might once again be useful.

The weekly reports conscientiously compiled by the new Assistente at Cyrene, Sig. Veneziano, give little indication of the increasing tension; but they show that in the last three days prior to 13 December, efforts were concentrated on preparing to evacuate the remaining antiquities from Cyrene's Museums. Meanwhile the military were erecting road-blocks in certain sectors of the Gebel Highway. A few days later the probability of an Allied advance right through Cyrenaica became a certainty; and most of the antiquities technicians found what transportation they could to get away. Only two remained, one of his own free will (he had relatives among the colonists nearby), the other because he left it too late to find a conveyance to safety.

From 18 to 23 December, 1941 Cyrene remained once again without any form of government, and much the same things happened as had happened on the previous occasion: corrugated-iron roofs and timbers disappeared mysteriously overnight. The incoming troops who arrived on the 20th were mainly Polish, and the wet cold season encouraged them to take firewood from any place where it could be found, not excluding the shelves on which the ancient inscriptions in the Museum had been laid out. The arrival of a Civil Affairs Officer on the 23rd brought some order into the prevailing chaos, but only at the cost of having a District Office (Mutasserrifiya, in local parlance) installed on the upper floor of the main Museum building. There it was to remain, with minor interruptions, until 1951.

This second British occupation of Cyrenaica was to be even briefer than the first. From his hide-outs in the marshes south of Agedabia, Rommel observed the thinness of the occupying forces, and on 21 January launched his counter-offensive which swept rapidly northward and eastwards. Benghazi fell to him on 28 January and by 4 February the British line was back at Ain el-Gazala. In June those defences were breached by the Axis and shortly afterwards Tobruk fell (20 June) to the consternation of the Allies and their sympathisers.

The affairs of Cyrene and its museums may seem trivial in the context of these gigantic events; but it is often the small things that bring into proportion the major stages in the march of events. Thus it is significant that although Cyrenaica suffered far more severely during the second British offensive than during the first, nobody bothered to make propaganda out of this fact. At Benghazi the impact of a high-spirited Australian army on to an Italian colonial city proved, retrospectively, to have been a mere picnic by comparison with what followed. In February Benghazi had been the "Walled City", by December it was the "Bombed City"—and there was still more to come.

Up in the Gebel, conditions were similar, although it had been looting rather than bombardment which had predominated. The war-correspondents Alan Moorehead and Alexander Clifford, passing through Cyrene, in the "Benghazi for Christmas" drive, found the Hotel an empty shell, containing nothing more useful than some typing paper and a recent copy of the *Popolo d'Italia*. They noted that in the surrounding areas of the plateau "Fewer of the colonists' houses remained occupied this time. The surface of the road had been worn rather more threadbare by a year's war-traffic. There were more derelict vehicles strewn along it than before, and some had the Afrika Korps emblem stencilled on them." The inquiries made after the Italian reoccupation showed that losses through civilian looting and military requisitions had been infinitely worse than at the time of Wavell's campaign. Soldiers had taken away large quantities of heavy timber and also the virgin locomotive. Civilians had removed literally tons of lighter stores, despite the gallant efforts of one loyal Arab antiquities custodian who had thrown hand-grenades at the attacking looters, his own compatriots.

Although the Italo-German forces had got back to Cyrene early in February, the antiquities office could not re-establish itself as quickly as it had done in the previous year. Most of its staff had to come back from Tripolitania, whereas on the previous occasion the key men had remained in Benghazi. Thus it was only on 7th May, 1942 that, in the words of the official "Weekly Report", the Assistente could report that "The martyred Excavation Office of Cyrene has been reconstituted for the second time, with such means as could be improvised". The report went on to describe "the wretched condition in which the Epigraphic Museum, the archaeological store, and the store of consumable materials have been found." The unfortunate technicians had now only one building at their disposal, all the others that had once belonged to the Antiquities Service having been requisitioned by the Axis High Command.

Not only Cyrene had suffered. At Barce, during the second British occupation, a large part of the contents of the archaeological museum—including some very valuable vases—had disappeared. At Apollonia, the same had happened to the Museum at the hands of the German troops stationed there before the Antiquities control had been re-established. At Tolmeita, where a number of marble heads had been lost in February, 1941, other depredations happened during the second Occupation.

There is no need to give more details in this narrative. The basic fact is already self-evident, namely that successive occupations and re-occupations had reduced the Antiquities Organisation at Cyrene to a mere shadow of its former state, and even this shadow was only kept in being by the extraordinary devotion of the Italian technicians and their senior officials. It is useless to try to apportion blame; for Arabs, British, Germans and Italians had all, at various moments, contributed, to greater or lesser extent, to the prevailing chaos.

We may, perhaps, ask why the contesting forces could not have kept out of Cyrene, which—after all—had no great strategic or tactical value. The answer is very simple: it has always been one of the most attractive places in Cyrenaica;

and tired soldiers could not be expected to renounce the charms of its wooded hills. If Graziani himself had kept out in the first place, and had issued orders that the place was "an open cultural zone", and if the Antiquities staff had remained behind in February, 1941 to present a front of organised control, things *might* have been different. But once the rot had set in, nothing but the return to peace-time conditions could prevent it becoming deeper and more malignant.

Meanwhile, following the third Italian reoccupation, Sig. Veneziani and his staff did what they could to restore the situation. The barbed-wire fence around the upper ruins, removed in February 1941, restored in the following May, and removed again in January, 1942, was gradually re-erected. Stolen stores were recovered from various rock-cut tombs where they had been hidden by looters. Attempts, not very successful, were made to remove Arab families from the tomb-chambers of the Necropolis into which they had moved again during the years of conflict.

What is quite extraordinary, and an eloquent testimonial to Italian tenacity, is that Pesce was even able to resume his archaeological soundings in and around the Temple of Zeus, and thus bring to a successful conclusion in September, 1942 his study of this notable Greek monument. It may also be noticed that as late as 23 October, when Montgomery's cannon were just beginning to pound the Axis positions at Alamein, the Italian Antiquities staff at Cyrene was calmly engaged in planting shrubs and making an artistic arrangement of ancient sculptures, at the entrance to the Sanctuary of Apollo. The last administrative report, dated 7 November, 1942 shows that five Italians and nine Arabs were still on the pay-roll of the "Scavi".

The third and final Italian evacuation of Cyrenaica was more complete than either of the two previous ones. The unfortunate peasants settled by Balbo in the Gebel farms in 1935 had already suffered abominably during what Moorehead termed "the biennial cross-country race across Cyrenaica". Most had remained in their homesteads during Wavell's occupation, and had enjoyed some slight if inadequate measure of protection from the occupying forces; almost half left on the eve of Auchinleck's advance, knowing too well what was in store for them when the local tribesmen saw the Italian forces once again withdraw. Of the remainder still in residence at the end of 1942, some would doubtless have preferred to stay on, facing the hardships and the hazards in the hope of, one day, having a piece of land of their own. But an Italian government decree, prompted by humanity, ordered their withdrawal.

A historian writing from the Arab viewpoint would doubtless point out, and with every justification, that the Italian settlers in 1941–2 had suffered considerably less than had the Bedouin tribes in 1930 when Graziani ordered the concentration of the whole Gebel population into camps in the desolate regions of the Syrtic Gulf. But two wrongs do not make a right, and in both cases it was the most poor and most innocent elements who suffered most. Such, alas, is usually the case in times of war.

In this narrative of the concluding phase of Italian colonial rule in Cyrenaica, and of the vicissitudes of ancient Cyrene during the long struggle, it remains only to refer once more to the evacuation of the antiquities of Cyrenaica. As we have seen already, three lorry-loads of selected objects had got away to Tripolitania in January 1941, on the eve of Wavell's invasion: the remainder of the objects remained in the vulnerable city of Benghazi, the larger statues stored in the offices of the "Tirrenia" shipping company, the smaller ones in the premises of the "Ganzini and Furia" company. Being walled-up, these deposits suffered no damage during the first British occupation; but on the night of 19 June, after the Italians had reoccupied Benghazi, two bombs hit the latter store-house destroying and damaging some of its contents. Pesce urgently advised the Italian authorities to provide transport for the complete evacuation of all these objects; and in mid-July this advice was finally accepted. Between that month and September a series of lorry convoys brought to Lepcis Magna and Sabratha not only the Cyrene statues, but also the contents of the archaeological library (some 10,000 books) and the irreplaceable photographic archive of some 9,000 glass negatives. There still remained a few minor objects, mainly from the Benghazi local museum, which only reached safety in Tripolitania the following year, after Rommel's second successful offensive into Cyrenaica.

Reading the fading documents in the official files, one can only admire the energy and devotion shown by Dr. Pesce and his technical staff in organising the evacuation of this mass of material, and carrying it through to a conclusion so successful that the bulk of the contents of the Cyrene Museum and their associated documentation could be re-established after the War. There is no doubt, given the status of Benghazi as a port, a centre of communications, and a garrison-town, that its bombardment and semi-destruction were inevitable; and therefore it is undeniable that the strenuous efforts made to protect the "archaeological patrimony" then stored in Benghazi did in fact save it from certain destruction.

What we may, perhaps, be allowed to doubt, is whether it had ever been necessary to remove all these things from Cyrene in the first place. As we have already seen, the initiative in the original evacuation came not from the Italian archaeological staff but from the High Command under Graziani; and certainly the archaeologists were in no position to resist this "Diktat". Given the circumstances they did what they could—and, in fact, far more than could be reasonably expected in the difficult circumstances prevailing. But if all these tons of marble statues, all these crate-loads of smaller objects, had remained in the "cave deposit" in the Sanctuary of Apollo, into which they had been—at the cost of such fatigue—brought in November, 1940, might they not have survived better?

On the occasion of the third British advance into Libya the British military authorities were considerably more conscious that an antiquities problem existed. Following the Italian propaganda charges made in 1941, there had been expressions of disquiet from American and neutral sources, and questions even asked in the House of Commons. General Headquarters, Middle East was now anxiously watching the situation, and the first document in the first Antiquities file of the third British Military Administration is a letter from G.H.Q. Cairo, dated 19 January, 1943, quoting a report that the main gates of the Cyrene ruins had been left open: this letter advised the Deputy Chief Political Officer (later Chief Administrator) that "It cannot be expected that very much time could be devoted to taking care of antiquities in the present phase of the occupation. Nevertheless I should be obliged if you could give some instructions to your Political Officer at Cyrene to do what he can to prevent anyone straying into the place enclosed for the purpose of preserving the ruins."

In fact the first Political Officer to be appointed to Cyrene after Montgomery's advance was a distinguished anthropologist, Capt. E. Evans Pritchard, who

arrived there on 23 November; and he had already appointed guards both on
what little remained of the Museum and on the outdoor sites. Unfortunately the
Royal Air Force soon arrived to set up a major headquarters (quoting the same
"operational necessity" with which Graziani had justified his own arrival in
1940), and once again most of the former antiquities buildings were taken over
by armed forces. Even the west end of the former Epigraphic Museum (scene of
the epic civilian looting of February, 1941) was seized by the new arrivals, who
began to set up within it a large operations-centre and plotting-room. They
partitioned off what once had been a vast museum hall, and after cracking a
marble sarcophagus while trying to move it, in the end walled it off and left it
where it was! The debris of former sackings and occupations was moved into
the east end of the building, where it still remained in 1946 when the writer first
visited Cyrene.

Meanwhile various staff officers both in Cyrenaica and in Cairo were showing
anxiety to bring in some professional British archaeologists, not to excavate or
remove works of art, as Pesce had feared in 1941, but to make recommendations
as to what was needed to ensure the safety of the remaining antiquities. As a
result of these well-intended if somewhat uncoordinated efforts, no less than
three unrelated archaeological advisers appeared on the Cyrenean scene in the
summer of 1943, each leaving a report of what seemed best to be done.

On 5 May arrived Mr. Alan Rowe, Director of the Graeco-Roman Museum
of Alexandria and honorary adviser to G.H.Q. on archaeological sites in the
Western Desert: he remained a fortnight. Rowe's terms of reference from G.H.Q.
included instructions to determine:

"(i) What, if any, damage has been done to Cyrenaican antiquities in the
     course of this war?
 (ii) How far the damage must be attributed to British troops?
 (iii) What steps ought to be taken to preserve the antiquities?"

His final report rightly pointed out that the Italian propaganda charges following
the Wavell occupation had been falsified; but through lack of access to the Italian
records and photographic archives then at Tripoli, he remained unaware of the
very real and grave losses that had been sustained both at Barce and at Apollonia
during and immediately after the brief Auchinleck campaign. He was thus able
to report, sincerely if inaccurately, "that practically no serious damage has
been done to the antiquities".

Professor Wace was in Cyrenaica from 12 to 26 August, invited by Brigadier
Cumming, the Deputy Chief Civil Affairs Officer; and his Report was concerned
less with inquiry into past events than with recommendations for the future
conservation of the site. While expressing general satisfaction with the situation
as he found it, he urged that a resident Archaeological Officer should be
appointed to re-organise the museums and sites.

Meanwhile, following representations made from Tripolitania by Sir Mortimer
Wheeler, then a Brigadier of the Royal Artillery, Major J. B. Ward Perkins
had been appointed Antiquities Adviser to the British Military Administrations,
and arrived in Cyrenaica on 5 July for a fortnight's visit. By this time a British
N.C.O. had already been appointed to Cyrene to look after the antiquities there;
and it was possible for Ward Perkins to leave detailed technical instructions

regarding the consolidation of ancient walls, mosaics, etc. His Report (dated September) also included a draft Antiquities Law; and the fact of his own residence at Tripoli made it possible to begin the listing and checking of all the Cyrenaican archaeological material that had been removed there.

In view of the obvious difficulty of obtaining *two* uniformed Antiquities Officers for Libya, while the war was still in progress, Ward Perkins suggested that—as a temporary expedient at least—the future Antiquities Officer appointed for Tripolitania should also supervise the custody of Cyrenaican antiquities. This proposal, despite the great distance separating the territories and the ensuing difficulties of transportation, had the advantage that the responsible officer would be in contact with the Italian archaeologists still in Tripoli, without whose collaboration and advice any attempt to restore the archaeological situation in Cyrene would be difficult and unrealistic. Thus the Ward Perkins Report marked a very notable step forward, and by the end of September, when its compiler was posted to A.M.G.O.T. in Italy, full inventories of the Cyrenean material in Tripolitania were already in the hands of the new Cyrenaican authorities.

In January, 1944 the War Office at last approved the establishment of an Antiquities Officer for the two Libyan territories under British control, but an appointment was only made in the following August, when Major C. G. C. Hyslop, a qualified architect, arrived in Tripoli to take up his duties. Meanwhile, at Cyrene, a new Non-commissioned-officer had been appointed, in the person of Sergeant S. Applebaum, a trained archaeologist who was soon to begin the compilation of numerous and detailed technical reports. The legal situation had been improved by the publication on 17 November, 1943 of the Military Administration's Proclamation No. 24, on the "Preservation of Antiquities".

Hyslop, with Applebaum's collaboration, quickly produced a finely-illustrated guide-book to the Cyrenaican sites, mainly for the use of troops and administrators. Despite the emergency conditions in which it was prepared, it is probably true to say that it was the best antiquities guide-book hitherto produced for Cyrenaica: Oliverio's "Scavi di Cirene" of 1931 had been a most curious and subjective publication, whilst his much-better description of the site prepared in 1937 was only a part of the more general Italian Touring Club "Guide to Libya", which is still the best published description of the whole country.

By October Hyslop was beginning the very delicate negotiations necessary for transferring from Tripoli to Cyrene three of the Italian technicians formerly employed on the latter site. By January 1945 this team, headed by Signor Salvatore Minniti, had arrived and taken up residence. With such technical skill and experience now available at Cyrene, the task of bringing back the statues evacuated to Tripolitania could be undertaken. By 10 May some 45 tons of sculpture had been despatched, and on arrival at Cyrene was offloaded and brought into the Baths Museum and ground-floor of the former Antiquarium, which the R.A.F. had at last evacuated.

Although this action to restore to Cyrene its legacy of ancient art had the blessing and approval of the more senior and enlightened officials of the Military Administration, there were still some lesser functionaries who could not see the point of it all. A finance officer, confronted with an unexpected transportation bill for £341, wrote in the file an indignant minute: "The Antiquities Officer must explain the necessity for moving this stuff about North Africa." Poor little creature, obsessed with his Estimates and Special Warrants! For him two centuries of passionate international inquiry into Cyrene's past meant no more than another ledger entry. At a time when the whole future of Cyrenaica was in the melting-pot, the country's artistic heritage was merely "this stuff"!

The "antiquities" files of the third British Administration of Cyrenaica grow thicker from 1945 onwards, and although bureaucratic activity is not in itself a desirable symptom, it sometimes means that something is being done. Hyslop's gargantuan efforts in implementing Ward Perkins' report, and Applebaum's activities at Cyrene itself had all contributed to the restoration of the situation. Minniti and his fellow-technicians brought back the know-how of a quarter-century of Italian activity. Things were looking up, even though the civil authorities of the B.M.A. still retained possession of the Antiquities Service buildings which they had inherited from war-time occupiers, whilst the allocated funds did not allow for any programmes of research and excavation.

By the end of 1945 Hyslop had left Libya on release from the Army, and had been replaced by Major D. E. L. Haynes (now head of the Greek and Roman Department at the British Museum). Applebaum had also left Cyrene and was not replaced, executive control of the antiquities being left to Sig. Minniti, under the guidance of the Civil Affairs Officer, then Capt. E. G. Butler, a dedicated officer whose term of duty at Cyrene is still remembered with affection by the local population. A new Antiquities Proclamation (No. 113) published in November, 1945 had reiterated the principal clauses of the previous one, whilst unfortunately omitting the essential recognition of the Antiquities Zones.

Haynes and his successor, (the present writer who arrived in Tripoli in September, 1946 and first visited Cyrene in October, 1946), could do little more than preserve the *status quo*. No effective Antiquities Department existed as yet, the visiting "Antiquities Officer" being merely a non-resident adviser who was obliged to work through the Civil Affairs Officers in the outstations and the Headquarters staff of the B.M.A. As an *ad hoc* arrangement of short duration this worked reasonably well, and in March, 1947 it was even possible to send a small Italian archaeological team (under Doctor Pesce) to complete the documentation of the important "Hellenistic Palace" at Tolmeita. This was the first post-war Italian archaeological mission in Cyrenaica.

In June the first appointment of a resident Antiquities Officer in Cyrenaica was made, in the person of Capt. T. Burton-Brown, previously in the Dodecanese Military Administration. He remained in Cyrenaica until February 1948 and was able, with the aid of the Italian technicians, to establish the first systematic post-war Museum of Antiquities at Cyrene. He also excavated some tombs at Cyrene and Tocra and drew attention to the necessity for an Antiquities Law which would not only ensure respect for the antiquities, but also define the constitution and responsibilities of a future Department of Antiquities. After his departure the responsibility returned again to the Antiquities Officer in Tripoli (R. G. Goodchild) until his own departure in November, 1948.

Before leaving Libya for an appointment at the British School in Rome, the writer submitted a proposal to the Civil Affairs Branch of G.H.Q. Middle East, (then still responsible for the former Italian colonies), that future Antiquities Officers in Libya should be resident at Cyrene, rather than at Tripoli. Since Professor Giacomo Caputo the former Italian Superintendent of Antiquities had returned to Tripoli in 1946, and was working in harmonious collaboration with the British occupying authorities, it seemed rather absurd to have two professional archaeologists resident in that city and none in Cyrenaica. The war was over, and whatever might be the final decision as regards the future of Libya, the time was past when nationalistic rather than professional considerations should influence the pattern of archaeological administration. Moreover the situation in Cyrenaica (and at Cyrene in particular) was far from satisfactory: the enormous damage and disturbance caused by the war still needed complete remedy. The Third British Military Administration had, in the main, shown an enlightened attitude towards the problem, but no amount of goodwill by local Civil Affairs Officers could be a substitute for resident archaeological direction. In Tripoli a "Department of Antiquities" had already been created on the solid basis already laid down by the former Italian administration. It was high time something similar was done in Cyrenaica.

The merit for putting this new programme into effect belongs to Mr. J. C. Morgan, a Cambridge graduate who resided at Cyrene from September, 1948–50 [when he was succeeded by Mr. C. N. Johns, who in turn was succeeded by Goodchild himself in 1953.

The manuscript breaks off in mid sentence.]

BIBLIOGRAPHY

Lord F. J. R. R. Rennell, *British Military Administration of Occupied Territories in Africa during the years 1941–7* (London, 1948).

CHAPTER IX

BEGINNING AGAIN (1951–THE PRESENT DAY)

Plate 96

In 1951, when Libya gained her independence, it became quite obvious that the future initiative for the conservation, and even the continued investigation, of Ancient Cyrene, would have to come from the Libyans themselves. Even if, as was hoped, foreign expeditions would come to work at Cyrene, their activities would always necessarily be extraneous, seasonal and confined mainly to the field of research. But research alone is not sufficient in a vast archaeological zone of the size and complication of Cyrene. The ruins do not stand in an uninhabited desert: there are people living in and among them. Graziani's plan to remove bodily the whole civil population was attainable only during the limited period of his repression of the national movement. It had begun to break down long before the Italians left Cyrenaica.

The idea that the indigenous Arabs might some day look after, and inquire into, the archaeological ruins scattered all over their own territory, had occurred in 1912 to the mind of a very brilliant, if somewhat unstable, Turk—Enver Pasha. In Turkish and western circles Enver's repute is clouded by his handling of affairs during the First World War, and during the Gallipoli campaigns. It was Mustapha Kemal rather than Enver who emerged as the Turkish hero in the immediate post-war period: the latter died ignominiously in exile from an assassin's hand.

Both these Turkish statesmen had fought in Cyrenaica while the Sultan's flag was still flying. But whilst Kemal is remembered there only through the rock-cut tomb in the harbour of Apollonia, where he spent summer afternoons drinking tea, his Commander-in-Chief Enver left a more durable imprint on Cyrenaican history. The name "Tarik Enver Bey" is still applied to the motor-track which he had constructed in the desert during the Turco-Arab campaigns against the Italian invaders. The "House of Enver Bey" from which he directed the siege of Italian-occupied Derna is still a topographical feature. A French war-correspondent who spent some months with the Turco-Arab armies in Tripolitania and Cyrenaica has left an impressive description of Enver's genius in handling a heterogeneous Army of disciplined Turkish conscripts and wild, brave Arab volunteers brandishing flintlocks. It was Enver, he says, who put his regular troops into solar topees, a form of headgear which had hitherto been the very symbol of Christian imperialism. The solar topee is, today, a discredited garment; but Enver's acceptance of it in 1912, in the face of prejudice, was as great a step forward as was its rejection, in the face of equal prejudice, by the armies fighting in Libya three decades later.

For Enver's interest in Cyrenaican antiquities, we have the testimony of Ulderico Tegani, an Italian historian of Benghazi writing in 1915, when the matter was still of recent knowledge. He says: "The ill-fated American enthusiasts (i.e. Norton's expedition) were succeeded, strange to say, by a Turkish enthusiast. It is even stranger that this was Enver Bey, and extremely odd that, in absolute contrast to the Koranic precept forbidding human figures in art, he should have meditated, during leisure-moments in the Italo-Turkish war, on the possibility of forming an archaeological school for Beduin. This fact, known by few people, and previously unsuspected, has a somewhat ridiculous aspect, has it not? But it remains true that Enver gathered together at Cyrene various statues with the idea of moving them into a *zawiya* which would thus be transformed into a sort of Greek-Turk-Senussi museum for educating the Beduin intellectuals in the study of artistic beauty."

Where Tegani got his information is not known, and his sarcastic attitude may seem to weaken his testimony, but there is something about this story that rings true, for when the Italians arrived in the Gebel in 1913 most of Norton's more transportable finds were no longer where he left them in the wooden expedition hut, but moved to the Turkish fort el-Ghegab. From what one knows of Enver it seems not improbable that he had something of this sort in mind; and if so, one can only say that he was being remarkably more clairvoyant than most of his contemporaries and many of his successors entrusted with Cyrenaican affairs.

Enver's project, if such it was, had to await the later years of the British caretaker administration of Libya for hesitant initiation, and the achievement of Libyan independence for effective fulfilment. The first task, after the final departure of the Italian Antiquities staff was not so much to create, immediately, Libyan archaeologists but rather to give added responsibility and technical capacity to the indigenous staff who, in Italian times, had been only guards and manual workers. It would probably be over-complimentary to suggest that this was a deliberate and long thought out policy of the British military administrators who came to Cyrenaica in 1943. Rather, it was a policy forced on them by lack of other, already-trained and therefore more efficient, personnel. The B.M.A. was a "shoe-string" government: its motto was "care and maintenance", although its funds were hopelessly inadequate to maintain the whole complicated administrative and economic structure of a former Italian colony. There were many experienced administrators who felt that the only future for Libya was a "camel economy". Little did they know that rich oil deposits, undetected by Italian geologists during the colonial period, were soon to make Libya a wealthy country.

The British military administrators had already, in the first years following their arrival, sought out and found Libyans to work under them in responsible posts; and this achievement, even if prompted mainly by necessity, more than compensates for their inability to re-create the tidy and efficient territory that Cyrenaica had undoubtedly been under the Italians. By 1948 there was already much talk of formal "Libyanisation" of the governmental services, and in February of that year the present writer felt obliged to state in an official report on the antiquities:

"Libyanisation" of direction can only be started at the bottom, by the training of young and sufficiently educated candidates. Any attempt to put a Libyan administrative official in control of a technical branch would be disastrous, without previous technical training. If a suitable Libyan candidate is available (and a young man of 19-25 years is desirable) he must receive instruction from a future British Antiquities Officer in Cyrenaica, or from myself in Tripoli. I should be delighted to accept the latter plan if you can approve and find a candidate willing to go to Tripoli for 4–6 months."

Although nothing then came of this proposal, the writer ventures to record it here as token of what he was then thinking, and of what he has subsequently tried to implement. The Cyrenaicans are, in general, a remarkably intelligent people, and there is nothing that they cannot learn to do if they receive adequate prolonged instruction in their youth.

Moreover, a foreigner employed in a newly-emergent country *must* consider his main responsibility to be that of creating something that will endure after his going. Indeed it may be said that the sooner he can make adequate preparations for his own departure, the better he is doing his job. This point of view is very different from the "après moi la deluge" attitude which one still sometimes encounters amongst some European administrators in African territories, a selfish and essentially destructive standpoint. There are moments, as any expatriate administrator can testify, when one *almost* begins to give up hope but in most cases there subsequently ensues, if one is looking out for it, some small episode which restores confidence and optimism. I remember vividly how Giacomo Caputo, in the difficult years of the British Administration in Tripoli, used to exhort his ill-paid Italian dependants with the words "Forza Pazienza! Corraggio!" These exhortations one may well apply to oneself, with particular emphasis on the "pazienza".

BIBLIOGRAPHY

Independent Libya:
Majid Khadduri, *Modern Libya* (Baltimore, 1963).

Enver Bey:
For a brief account in English see *Encyclopaedia of Islam* (2nd edition) s.v. Enwer Pasha; and for a full-scale biography, Aydemir, Sonket Surreya, *Makedonya'dan Orta Asyaya—Enver Pasa* (Ankara, 1971–2) in Turkish.

[POSTSCRIPT]

[In the concluding chapters Goodchild must have intended to give some outline of the administrative history and work of the new Libyan Department of Antiquities in its Cyrenaican section. Its administrative history is something which only he, in this country, was competent to write; but it can be said with confidence that he would have welcomed the decision which followed the Libyan Revolution of 1969 to place it under the responsibility of the Ministry of Education rather than that of Tourism as in the preceding few years. Of its work a brief appreciation is given in the Biographical note and much more emerges from the papers printed above. But it may be useful to add the following facts.

When he first took up the post of controller in 1953 the wartime chaos was not completely resolved and in addition there was a major backlog of unpublished pre-war excavation. He carried on the work of his immediate predecessors in restoring order on the site, in the museums and in the office and reorganised for consultation the Library, the magnificent photographic archive and what survived of the files of the Italian period (their papers spilt on to a floor by the military); and he initiated a policy of inviting European and American archaeologists and technicians to visit Cyrene and work on the unpublished material, or help in the conservation of fragile items in the museums and on the site. A list of the most important resulting publications not mentioned previously is attached. Above all he encouraged the undertaking of the Italian Archaeological Mission under Professor Sandro Stucchi which is now an established and outstanding feature of the site.

From about 1954 he felt able to embark on a series of excavations by the Department itself and planned a programme designed both to elucidate the town plan of Cyrene—above all the history of the main street which runs down the central valley and of the city's defences—and to anticipate modern "developers" by rescuing threatened buildings, simultaneously demonstrating that the archaeological zone was not arbitrarily defined but contained archaeological material even where it was not immediately obvious. He showed a remarkable ability to balance the need to conserve the monuments, both visible and buried, with the requirement for housing of a people in transition from the semi-nomadic to the settled—and his patent understanding of the latter point made his firmness in defence of the former all the more effective and acceptable.

Some of the results of the departmental excavation in these years were published in articles in the *Papers of the British School at Rome, Quaderni di Archeologia della Libia* and *Libya Antiqua,* and there is a survey of them in the book *Kyrene und Apollonia*; but the pressure of field work and administration was very heavy and much still inevitably remained unpublished at his death.

Teams sponsored jointly by the Department and the Society for Libyan Studies are preparing their publication.

Finally he certainly intended to discuss the special problems of excavation in Cyrene. He would no doubt have noted that, in the early days of the programme, excavation provided welcome work for an underemployed population but that after the development of the Libyan oilfields more highly paid employment was readily available and the Antiquities service found it increasingly difficult to recruit labour for digging. He would certainly have indicated how foreign archaeological missions and departmental digging programmes alike provided initial training for promising young Libyans who were then, if at all possible, enabled (often with financial aid from U.N.E.S.C.O.) to travel abroad and to follow archaeological courses in European universities or museums. Thus when he resigned in 1966 there existed a Libyan staff, keen and concerned to carry out their responsibilities in caring for the monuments; and he would have noted with pleasure that Mr. Awad Sadawiyah, the Director of Antiquities for Libya from 1969 until his tragic death in 1973, had worked with him in Cyrene. Two other indications of Libyan interest in the history and archaeology of the country have been the foundation in 1964 of the journal *Libya Antiqua* by the Department of Antiquities in Tripoli, but for Cyrenaican and Fezzanese as well as Tripolitanian material, and the organisation of a conference on Libya in History by the Faculty of Arts in the University of Libya at Benghazi in 1968 at which a number of Libyan speakers, including several members of the Department of Antiquities, read papers.

He would surely have pointed out the continuation since Libyanisation of the training schemes for Libyan members of the staff of the Antiquities Department and that of fruitful co-operation between the department and visiting archaeologists of other nations—observing perhaps in conclusion the emergence of extended interest in the Islamic monuments of the country.]

SELECTIVE BIBLIOGRAPHY

C. Anti (ed.), *Sculture Greche e Romane di Cirene* (Padova, 1959).

J. Cassels, *The Cemeteries of Cyrene* in *PBSR* xxiii (1955) 1 f.

F. Chamoux, *Cyrène sous les Battiades* (Paris, 1953).

P. M. Fraser, *Inscriptions from Cyrene* in *Berytus* xii (1958) 101 f. (a collection of Hellenistic inscriptions).

P. Mingazzini, *L'insula di Giasone Magno a Cirene* (Rome, 1966).

E. Paribeni, *Catalogo delle Sculture di Cirene* (Florence, 1959).

L. Polacco, *Il Volto di Tiberio* (Rome, 1955).

J. Reynolds, *The Christian Inscriptions of Cyrenaica* in *J.Th.S.* n.s.ix (1960) 284 f.

E. Rosenbaum, *Cyrenaican Portrait Sculpture* (London, 1960).

A. Rowe et al., *Cyrenaican Expedition of the University of Manchester, 1952* (Manchester, 1956).

——, *Cyrenaican Expeditions of the University of Manchester, 1955, 1956, 1957* (Manchester, 1959).

S. Stucchi, *L'Agorà di Cirene I, I Lati Nord ed Est della Platea Inferiore* (Rome, 1965).

——, *Cirene 1957–1966, un decennio di attività della Missione Archaeologica Italiana a Cirene* 3 (Tripoli, 1967).

G. Traversari, *L'Altorilievo di Afrodite a Cirene* (Rome, 1959).

——, *Statue Aniconiche Femminile Cirenaiche* (Rome, 1960).

A collection of Christian antiquities started jointly by Goodchild and J. B. Ward
Perkins is in preparation.

A collection of inscriptions of the Roman period started jointly by Goodchild and
J. M. Reynolds is in preparation.

Oliverio's papers published posthumously in *QAL* iv (1961) 3 f. and *ASAA* 39–40
(1961–2) 219 f.

The papers presented at the Historical Conference held from 16–23 March, 1968
in the University of Libya's Faculty of Arts at Benghazi were published in *Libya
in History*, ed. Fawzi F. Gadallah.

INDEX

Aesculapius 225, 228, 237, 241, 243, 250
Agabis (Ghegab) 151
Agedabia *see* Corniclanum
Ain Mara 152, 181, 186, 199f., 205, 251–2. *And see* Hydrax
Ain Scersciara 73–4, 84f.
Ain Wif *see* Thenadassa
Ammon, Ammonium 18f., 33, 72–3, 79f., 91–2, 147, 156–7, 162, 165, 167, 171
Anabucis *see* Automalax
Anastasius (emperor) 36, 116–17, 205, 220, 226–7, 248, 255
Andronikus (praeses) 248–9
Antipyrgus (Tobruk) 203
Apollonia (Sozusa, Marsa Susa) 143, 150, 205, 226, 228–9, 240–1, 255–6
Arab invasions 9, 153, 162, 195, 219, 226, 255–67, 272
Arae Philaenorum (Ras el Aali) 3, 17, 147, 149, 155–72, 188, 192, 196
Arcadius (emperor) 115, 226, 236–7, 248
Armatius (dux) 195
Arzuges (Arzugitani) 8, 35f., 92f.
Aspis 139, 156, 170
Astacures 37
Augustus (emperor) 91, 119
Aurelian (emperor) 45
Aurelius (Marcus) (emperor) 219
Austuriani 37, 92, 111f., 130, 153, 184, 195, 208, 216
Automalax (Anabucis, Bu Sceefa) 149, 155–72, 188, 192
Axomis 243

Balagrae, Balagritae (El-Beida) 225, 228–38, 241–3, 250
Banadedari 158, 170, 192
Barka (El-Merg) 136–7, 150, 154, 199, 204, 219, 226–7, 255, 257–8, 273
Beni Ulid (Wadi) 6, 9
Berenice (Benghazi) 150, 167, 187, 192, 196, 205, 247, 273, 278
Bir ed-Dreder 15–16, 37f., 59f.
Bir Scedeva 38, 70
Bir Tarsin 24, 29
Bir Umm el Garanigh 147, 162
Bomba (Gulf) *see* Paliurus

Boreum (Bu Grada) 135, 149, 155, 164, 166, 172, 181, 187–94, 196, 206, 247
Boreum (Ras Taiunes) 186
Bu Ngem 3, 20–1, 29, 32, 38, 44, 46f., 52, 57
Bureat (Gerrari) 200
Burgus 54
Bu Sceefa *see* Automalax

Caam (Wadi) *see* Cinyps
Canabae 48
Caracalla 19, 23–4, 33, 44, 56, 75, 91, 111, 127–9
Carthage, Carthaginian (Punic) 61f., 90–1, 101, 105, 133, 141, 147, 149, 155, 156, 163
Catabathmus (Sollum) 163
Centenarius, Centenarium 6, 19, 20–1, 28–30, 34, 70, 89, 100–1
Cephalae (Misurata) 47, 155
Cercar 76
Cerialis (dux) 241
Chaerecla 153
Chaminos (Ghemines) 150, 181f., 196
Charax 133f.
Christian monuments 22, 72, 92, 122, 124, 150–1, 186, 188, 199, 204, 209, 226, 233, 237, 243, 246, 248, 251, 254, 255
Cidamae (Gadames) 20–1, 46f., 55–6
Cinyps (Wadi Caam) 74
Claudiopolis (Cyrene) 225, 228, 234, 237, 246
Claudius Gothicus (emperor) 110, 225, 234, 246
Cohort 23
Coins 90–1, 105, 114f., 229–33, 237, 257
Comes et praeses 19
Commodus (emperor) 18, 216–19, 225
Constans (emperor) 37, 70, 115, 231–2
Constantine I (emperor) 57, 70, 115, 128–9, 222–4, 231
Constantine II (emperor) 231
Constantius I (emperor) 161
Constantius II (emperor) 37, 70, 115, 231–2
Corippus 9, 31, 34, 37, 44
Corniclanum (Agedabia) 136–7, 149–50, 155, 181, 192–3, 196, 208
Cyrenaica (province) 145, 147, 152–4, 163, 184

Cyrene, Cyrenaeans 150, 154–5, 163, 186, 195, 204f., 207, 209, 216–19, 225–9, 232–42, 244–6, 249–50, 252, 271–341

Darnis (Derna) 151–2, 200, 203, 206, 250–1
Digdiga 193–4
Diocletian (emperor) 57, 128–9, 132, 147, 153, 161–2, 168, 195, 216, 219–20, 225–7
Domitian (emperor) 18, 168
Driana see Hadrianopolis
Dux 19, 28, 41, 195, 208–9, 228, 253

El-Atrun see Erythrum
El-Avenia 33
El-Beida see Balagrae
El-Garib 103, 109f.
El-Merg see Barka
Eperos 135
Erythrum (El-Atrun) 152, 200, 250–1
Esh-Sceleidima 150, 197f.
Euphranta 134–5, 147, 163, 170

Farms (fortified) see Limitanei and Olive farms
Fezzan 46f.
Foederati 55–6, 70f., 185
Forts see Limes
Frontier markers 161f.

Gadames (Ghadames) see Cidamae
Galerius (emperor) 161, 222–4
Gallienus (emperor) 44, 108, 127, 130, 132, 234
Gallus Caesar 232
Garamantes 30, 46
Gasr Anessa (Hanesh) 33
Gasr el-Atallat 149, 191f., 196
Gasr el-Ataresh 183
Gasr Banat 30
Gasr Beni Gdem 152, 201, 205, 243, 253
Gasr Bir Scedeva 43
Gasr Bu Msceili 183
Gasr Bularkan 38f.
Gasr Carmusa see Mandis
Gasr Chanafes 33
Gasr el-Chel 183
Gasr Doga 24, 72–3, 76, 103
Gasr Duib see Tentheos
Gasr Faschia 30
Gasr Faschiet el-Habs 33, 45
Gasr el Geballa 199
Gasr Gheria (Geria), esh Scergia 30, 33, 50
Gasr Ghifa 43
Gasr Haddadia see Tugulus
Gasr el Heneia 154, 173f., 196, 200, 205
Gasr Migraua 43
Gasr el Mnechrat 205
Gasr Nagazza 70
Gasr er Remteiat 205
Gasr esh Shahden (Sciaden) 152, 154, 201f., 205, 243, 253
Gasr Shemek (Scemek) 30
Gasr Sidi el Chadri 205

Gasr es Suq el Oti 33
Gasr Tecasis 150
Gasr Tectana 204, 205
Gasr Uames 24, 28, 42
Gebel (Tripolitanian) 1–113 (el-Ala) 147f. (el-Akdar) 199f.
Gefara 5, 73
Gentiles 1, 111f.
Germa 47
Geta Caesar 23, 33
Ghegab see Agabis
Gheria (Geria) el Garbia 1, 20–1, 29, 38, 44, 47–8, 50f., 56
Ghirza 3, 8, 15, 30, 33
Giargiarrumah (Wadi) see Kuf
Gordian III (emperor) 19, 44–5, 52, 75–6, 91, 108, 110, 113, 225
Graces (Hill of) 74
Gratian (emperor) 115, 228, 248

Hadrian (emperor) 125, 130, 217–18, 226–7, 229
Hadrianopolis (Driana) 152, 219, 227
Hammama (Zaviet) see Phycus
Henscir Salamet 89f., 103
Henscir Suffit 43, 45
Henscir Taglissi 6
Henscir Uheda 92, 103
Heraclius (emperor) 255–7
Hexapolis 216–19, 225
Honorius (emperor) 33, 41, 115, 226, 248
Hydrax (?Ain Mara) 152, 200, 238, 250–2

Inscriptions (texts only) 5, 8, 17f., 23, 27, 54, 64f., 93f., 98f., 109–12, 158, 168–70, 207–8, 211–12, 218, 221–4, 248
Iscina 133f., 141–2, 147
Islamic (Arab) monuments 26, 31, 42, 133f., 137f., 150, 153, 162, 181, 186, 196, 199, 247, 257

Jewish revolt 135, 152, 195, 216, 219, 225–7, 236
Jewish settlements 135, 141–2, 147, 149, 188, 227
Julian (emperor) 115, 231–2, 235
Justin (emperor) 117
Justinian (emperor) 56, 70, 117, 129–30, 147, 149, 181, 185, 188–92, 196, 203, 205–6, 209, 226, 247, 249

Kilns (pottery) 85f., 96f.
Korax 135
Kozynthion 149
Krokodeilos 149
Kuf (Wadi) 151–2, 154, 199f., 208, 242–3, 253

Lamluda see Limnias
Legatus Augusti pro praetore 27–8, 47–8
Legio III Augusta 20–1, 23, 28, 48f., 91
Leo 116

Lepcis Magna 17, 19, 20, 31, 35, 36, 75–6, 91, 111, 114–32, 247, 249
Libya (province) see Pentapolis
Libyan monuments 30, 34, 37f., 59f., 101f., 173f., 186
Licinianus 222–4
Limes Cyrenaicus 36, 150, 173–93, 195–209
Limes Tripolitanus 1–71
Limitanei 1, 20–1, 28–31, 41–2, 55, 57, 70f., 107, 147, 152, 184f., 199, 204, 206, 252
Limnias (Lamluda) 151, 204

Macetae 185
Maci 196
Macomedes 135–6, 141, 147, 155, 170–2
Mandis (Gasr Carmusa) 151
Marmaric tribes 195, 225, 234
Masamones 168
Matropolis (Cyrene) 218–19, 225
Maximian 161
Maximinus 33, 44, 75, 91, 111
Maximinus Daia 222–4
Mazices 153, 195
Mechili 150, 203
Medina Doga (Mesphe) 5, 15, 24, 33, 72, 75f., 103
Medina Sultan 133–42
Merdum (Wadi) 33, 38
Mesphe see Medina Doga
Milestones 17f., 20, 24, 108f., 225
Misurata see Cephalae
Mizda 6, 24, 29
Moors 188
Mosaics 76, 84f., 91
Mselletin 15, 38f.
Msufin 5
Msus (Zaviet) 150, 154
Mtaugat 204

Naustathmus (Ras el Hilal) 250
Neapolis 153
Notitia Dignitatum 9, 19, 21, 28, 31, 55, 70
Numeri 21

Oea (Tripoli) 3, 17, 21, 76, 255, 276
Olive farms 5–6, 21, 43, 45, 72f., 76, 88f., 183

Palace (governor's) 122, 228, 255–6
Palaebisca 154, 251, 254
Paliurus (Bomba) 151
Pentapolis (Libya Pentapolis, Upper Libya) 36, 150, 153–4, 161, 170, 185, 187–8, 195–6, 203, 205–6, 216, 222–4, 226, 228, 239, 244–5
Pharax 135
Philip (emperor) 27–8, 44–5, 109, 225
Phycus (Zaviet Hammama) 152, 240–3, 247, 249–50, 254
Praepositus limitis 9, 19, 21, 28, 30, 41, 70f.

Praeses (Tripolitanae) 19, ?161
(Pentapoleos) ?161, 170, 224–5, 248–9
Proconsul (Africae) 17, 91, 168, 172
(Cretae et Cyrenarum) 218
Procurator Augusti 225
Ptolemais (Tolmeta) 150, 152, 162, 204f., 209–16, 219–28, 239, 244–9, 254
Punic see Carthage

Ras el Aali see Arae Philaenorum
Ras el Haddagia 72f., 79f., 91, 103
Ras el Hilal see Naustathmus
Ras Lanulf see Arae Philaenorum
Ras Taiunes see Boreum
Roads 17–18, 20–1, 24f., 32, 75–6, 107f., 150–2, 154, 168, 192, 249, 287

Sabratha 3, 17, 31, 34, 48, 113, 130–1, 255
Sacazama 171
Septimius Severus (emperor) 18, 21, 23–4, 44–7, 55–6, 130, 218, 225
Severus Alexander (emperor) 30, 44–5, 54–6
Sidi Ali ben Zaid 89, 92, 104
Sidi bu Laaba 92, 103
Sidi Sames 107f. 111f.
Soffeggiu (Wadi) see Limes Tripolitanus
Sollum see Catabathmus
Subventana, Subventani 35f., 45
Suellius Flaccus (procos) 168, 172
Synesius 36, 151–6, 185, 195, 200, 208, 210, 216, 226, 228, 233, 236, 238–54
Syrtica (Sirte, Sert, Sort, Syrte) 18, 29, 133f., 145–7, 153, 155, 184

Tabilba 188
Tailimun (Zaviet) 150, 184, 197f.
Tansoluch see Hadrianopolis
Tarhuna 18, 20, 24, 72f., 103, 107f.
Tariq Aziza 151, 154
Taucheira (Teucheira, Tocra) 150, 161, 186, 206, 209, 247, 257–8
Tazzoli 21, 72f., 103, 107f.
Tecapae 19
Temples 79f., 105, 151, 162, 167
Tenagino Probus 225, 234
Tentheos (Gasr Duib) 15, 19, 24f., 38, 42
Thenadassa (Ain Wif) 4, 20f., 75, 78–9, 91, 107
Theodosius I (emperor) 115–16, 220
Theodosius II (emperor) 33, 41
Tiberius (emperor) 17, 75, 91
Tibubuci 19
Tininai 33
Tobruk see Antipyrgus
Tocra see Taucheira
Tolmeta see Ptolemais
Trajan (emperor) 218, 227
Tripoli see Oea
Tripolitana 35f., 145, 147, 153, 161, 170, 184, 193, 195, 206, 208, 236

Troglila (John) 92–3
Tugulus (Tagulis, Gasr Haddadia) 147, 157–8,
    170, 192, 194
Turris Tamalleni 3, 17, 19, 75

Valentinian I (emperor) 115, 231–2
Valentinian II (emperor) 228, 234–6, 248
Valeus (emperor) 115, 234, 248
Vandals 19, 31, 42, 92, 114, 116–17, 120, 129,
    208

Veteraus 79, 91, 99
Vexillation 23, 48
Vezereos 18–19, 32

Zacusama 147, 166, 193
Zaguzaena 171
Zemzem (Wadi) *see* Limes Tripolitanus
Zeno (emperor) 116
Zintan 20, 28, 33
Zliten 30

1 Wadi Beni Ulid: pre-desert landscape with surviving vegetation

2 Msuñin, near Garian: Gebel landscape

Snemat, Wadi Merdum: Roman olive presses

4 Mselleten, Wadi Merdum: Romano–Libyan funerary monuments

5 Ghirza: relief of reapers

6 Lepcis Magna: ruins of a Roman coastal city

7 Ghirza: Romano–Libyan mausolea

8, 9, 10 (*above*) Ain Wif

11, 12 (*below*) Gasr Duib. The stones in 9 and 10
are in Triopli Museum

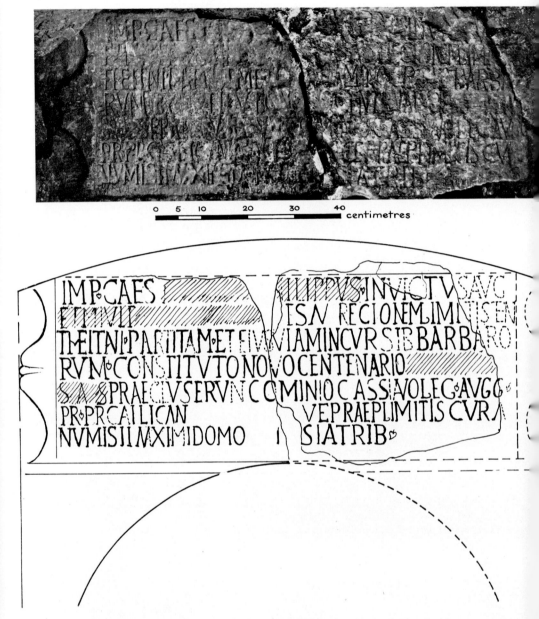

IMP·CAES /////////////// [PHI]LIPPVS·INVICTVS·AVG
ETIMP·[CAES] ///////// [FILIPP]ESN·REGIONEM·LIMITIS·EN
THEITNI·PARTTA·MET·FIV [?]VIAMINCVRSIB·BARBARO
RVM·CONSTITVTO·NOVO·CENTENARIO ////////
S·A·S·PRAECIVSERVNC·CMIN·IO·CASS·VOLEG·AVGG
PR·PR·CAILICAN [A]VE·PRAEPLIMITIS·CVRA
NVMISII·MXI·MIDOMO [?] SIATRIB·

13 Gasr Duib: inscription over doorway, left half *in situ*, right half walled into entrance
corridor

14 (*opposite above*) General view of oasis at Ain Wif

15 (*opposite*) Fortified building at Bir Scedeua (Wadi Sofeggin)

16 Fort at Mselletin (Gasr Bularkan): air view from the west

17 Fort at Mselletin (Gasr Bularkan): ground
view of west corner

18 Fort at Mselletin (Gasr Bularkan): detail of
masonry of north-east wall

wers and fortified farms: 19 Air view of Gasr Uames (12m. square) from south (Upper Sofeggin area)

Gasr El-Banat (Wadi Nfed), wall in masonry of Period I

21 Gasr "F" (near Bir Scedeua), corner in masonry of Period II

22 Bu Ngem

23 Gheria El-Garbia

24 Bu Ngem: east gate

25 (*top*)   Bu Ngem: north gate in 1819 (Drawing by G. F. Lyon)

26 (*above*)   Gheria El-Garbia: north-east gate

27 (*left*)   Gheria El-Garbia, north-east gate: interior of gate-tower

28 (*top*)   Gheria El-Garbia: north-east gate

29 (*left above*)   Gheria El-Garbia: north angle of fort with window of internal tower

30 (*left*)   Gheria Esh-Shergia: masonry of north-west corner

31 (*above*)   Medina Doga: baths, apse of frigidarium

32 (*top*) Ras El-Haddagia:
dedicatory inscription of
Ammonium

33 (*above*) Ras El-Haddagia:
remains of Ammonium, from the
north

34 (*right*) Ras El-Haddagia:
remains of Ammonium, from the
east

35   Ain Scersciara: the large kiln

36   Ain Scersciara: interior of the large kiln

37   El-Khadra: base of small mausoleum

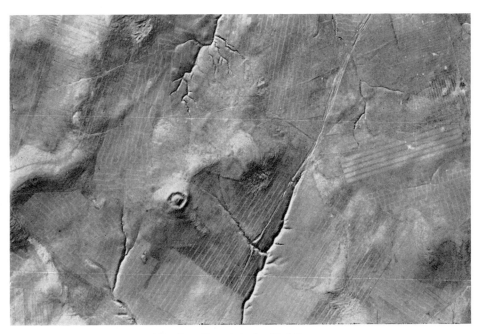

38   Ras Gassciut: fortified farm

42 (*top*)   El-Garib: milestone of Claudius Gothicus, Mile 57

43 (*above*)   Sidi Sames: ditched gasr where inscription was found

39 (*opposite top*)   Sidi Ali ben Zaid: inscription from fortified building

40 (*opposite centre*)   Breviglieri: inscription of Sebentius and Stiddin

41 (*opposite below*)   El-Garib: milestone of Philip, including base, Mile 56

44 (*above*)   Sidi Sames: inscription

45 (*below*) Lepcis Magna: south-east corner of "Hexagon", showing untrimmed blocks

46 (*bottom left*) Lepcis Magna: interior of "Hexagon", with remains of fallen dome

49 (*top left*) Lepcis Magna: late blocking walls on east side of "Hall" ("New Frigidarium")

50 (*top right*) Medina Sultan: Mosque   51 (*above*) Targunia: wheel ruts

(*opposite centre*) Lepcis Magna: interior of "Hexagon" after completion of avation

(*opposite bottom right*) Lepcis Magna: interior of "Hexagon" after excavation, king north; furnace archway, with blocked window above

52 (*below*) Mtaugat: fortified Christian church

53 Gasr El-Haddadia (Tugulus), from the north-east: Roman fort (right) and early Islamic fort (left)

54 Graret Gser Et-Trab (*Arae Philaenorum*), from the north, looking towards Gebel El-Ala: late enclosure of column-drums and (over car) corner of Building A

55 Graret Gser Et-Trab (*Arae Philaenorum*): inscribed column-drum (Inscription 2)

56 Graret Gser Et-Trab (*Arae Philaenorum*): capital, with recesses for feet of statue

57 Graret Gser Et-Trab (*Arae Philaenorum*): corner of Building A

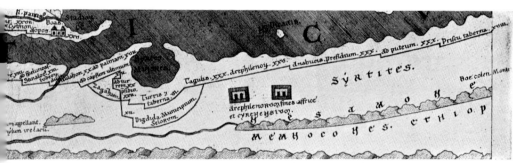

58 Extract from the Peutinger Map: road-stations on the Syrtic Gulf

59 Gasr El-Heneia: recesses for horizontal beams of bridge over south ditch, and for voussoirs of supporting arches

60   Gasr El-Heneia: staircase well looking south

61   Gasr El-Chel (Ghemines)

62   Gasr El-Atallat: detail of masonry
at south corner of fort

63   Bu Grada (Boreum): headland and
early citadel from fort on east wall

64   Gasr El-Atallat: vertical air photograph

65   Bu Grada (Boreum): oblique air
photograph from the east

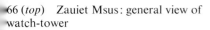

66 (*top*)   Zauiet Msus: general view of watch-tower

67 (*centre above*)   Gasr El-Geballa (Benia): north-east angle tower

68 (*above*)   Gsar Beni Gdem: general view

69 (*below*)   Zauiet Msus: detail of masonry of north wall

70 (*top right*)   Gasr Beni Gdem: interior of north tower

71 (*centre right*)   Gasr Beni Gdem: section of west wall, showing two periods

72 (*bottom right*)   Gasr Tectana: general view

73 (*top*)   Gasr Esh-Shahden: detail of masonry
of outer wall of keep

75 (*top*)   Tolmeta (Ptolemais): south wa
of fifth-century citadel

74 (*above*)   Gasr Ushish: general view

76 (*above*)   Tolmeta (Ptolemais): west wall of cita

77, 78, 79 (*below and opposite*)   Cyrene Museum: inscription from Temple B
80 (*opposite bottom*)   Balagrae (El-Beida): theatre of the Sanctuary of Aesculapius:
sounding, May 1917

BEDA 8-5-1917

81   Zaviet Hammama

82   Wadi Kuf

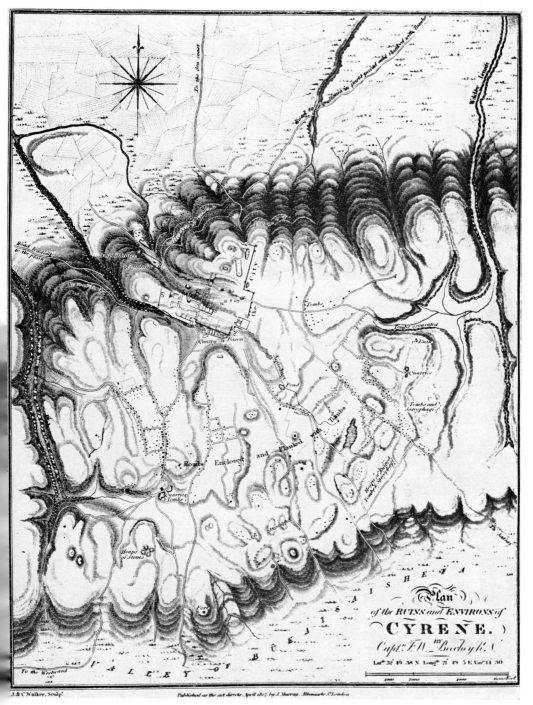

83　Cyrene: Beechey's plan of 1827

85 (*top*)   Cyrene: necropolis (Engraving after an original drawing by J. R. Pacho)

86 (*above*)   Cyrene: fountain of Apollo (Drawing by E. A. Porcher)

(*opposite*)   Cyrene : aerial view of Caesareum and Agera

87 (*top*) Cyrene: interior of tomb (Drawing
by E. A. Porcher)
88 Cyrene: tomb with soldiers (Drawing
by E. A. Porcher)

89 (*opposite top*) Ghegab: fort
90 (*opposite centre*) Cyrene: winter camp
91 (*opposite bottom*) H. F. de Cou,
epigraphist

92 Venus of Cyrene

93   Zeus of Cyrene

94   Gaspare Oliverio

95   Cyrene: inside water-channel of fountain

96   Kemal Ataturk in Libya